Business Studies

Dave Hall • Rob Jones • Carlo Raffo

Edited by
Ian Chambers and Dave Gray

Acknowledgements

Dedication

To Elaine, Holly, Caitlin, Amanda Jane, Mandy, Sandra, Georgina, Rebecca, Jan, Natalie and Holly Anne for all their love and support in the writing of this book.

Cover design by Caroline Waring-Collins, illustration provided by Getty Images.
Graphics by Caroline Waring-Collins, Tim Button, Anneli Jameson and Rob Gittins.
Photography by Andrew Allen and Dave Gray.
Typing by Ingrid Hamer.
Proof reading by Mike Kidson, Heather Doyle and Tony Barnes.

Acknowledgements

The publishers would like to thank the following for the use of photographs and copyright material. Other copyright material is acknowledged at source. Cafedirect p 276, Corel pp 70,274, Digital Stock p 156, DigitalVision pp 58,200(tl),255, Ian Sager pp 206,207, Photodisc pp 52,93,100,119,137,186,240, Rex Features pp 154,166,177,184, Stockbyte pp 8,32,76,77,79,81,107,127,130, 134,143,179,191(t),200 (tr,b),236,248,293, The Associated Press p 268, TopFoto pp 27,153.

British Library Cataloguing in Publication Data

A catalogue record for this book is available from the British Library.

ISBN 1-902796-85-3

Causeway Press Limited
PO Box 13, Ormskirk, Lancs, L39 5HP

1st impression, 2001
3rd impression, 2004

Typesetting by Caroline Waring-Collins, Waring Collins Ltd.
Printed and bound by Legoprint, Italy.

Contents

Preface

Business Studies does not provide a step-by-step guide to how to be 'good at business'. There is no simple set of rules that can be applied at all times which will always be successful. However, by being analytical, rigorous and critical it may be possible to develop skills and approaches which can be useful, at certain times and in certain situations, when making business decisions. It is possible that different approaches will be used by different people in business and there may be disagreement as to which approach to take.

Business Studies is integrated and different areas of business are interdependent. There are links, for example, between:

- what is being produced and the funds available to pay for it (production and finance);
- the selling of the product and ethical considerations (marketing and ethics);
- the type of business and many aspects of its operation.

Being aware of these aspects of business will help us to understand how and why business decisions are made, and how they affect a variety of people, both within and outside the business. The aim of **Business Studies A2 Level (Third Edition)** is to help those studying Business to understand business decisions and to be analytical, rigorous and critical in their business thinking. A number of features are included in the book which we believe will help this task.

Comprehensive course coverage The book contains material which should meet the demands of a wide range of courses. These include AS/A Level, Higher Grade, GCE in Applied Business, higher education and professional courses. The book is organised into 41 units across six sections:

- objectives, strategy and the business environment;
- marketing;
- accounting and finance;
- people in organisations;
- operations management;
- external influences.

In addition there are two units on study skills and assessment at the end. There is a development in the units contained in each section which reflects progress throughout a course and the requirements of different courses.

Guidance is given on exactly how the book can be used for specific courses in **Business Studies Teachers' Guide (Third Edition)**. To allow flexibility in course construction and teaching **Business Studies (Third Edition)** is available. It is a complete course book for A Level Business Studies and includes AS Level and A2 Level units. **Business Studies AS Level (Third Edition)** is also available. It contains the AS Level units from **Business Studies (Third Edition)** in a separate book.

Flexible unit structure The unit structure allows the lecturer or teacher greater freedom to devise the course. Business Studies teachers and lecturers often teach different aspects of the course in different orders. So, whilst there is a logical order to the book, it has been written on the assumption that teachers or lecturers and students will piece the units together to suit their own teaching and learning needs and the requirements of the course being taught.

Cross referencing has been used in many of the units. This helps the teacher, lecturer or student to follow the course as they want. It will also be useful for modular courses and courses where Business Studies is only one part of the total course. The units in the book which relate to specific aspects of business, such as marketing or accounting, can be used in specialist courses or provide a short course in that area. Cross referencing also helps to stress the integrated nature of Business Studies and the interdependence and possible conflict that may exist in many areas.

Accessibility The book has been written in a clear and logical style which should make it accessible to all readers. Each unit is divided into short, easily manageable sections.

A workbook The text is interspersed with a large number of questions. The questions which appear as part of the units mostly refer to preceding information. Answers in most cases are expected to be relatively short. Questions are based on a variety of case studies, data, articles, photographs, etc. They should allow the student and teacher/lecturer to assess whether the information has been understood. Shorter 'knowledge' questions provide a means of revising each unit. A longer case study appears at the end of each unit. It draws on information contained in the whole unit and answers are expected to reflect this. The questions asked reflect the type which are set in examinations. They help students to develop knowledge, application, analysis and evaluation - the criteria used in examinations to assess responses.

Business Studies Teachers' Guide (Third Edition) provides suggested answers and mark schemes for the activities and questions that appear in this book.

Use of business examples, case studies and data Modern technology has allowed much of the book to proceed from manuscript to book form in a very short period. This has meant that we have been able to use the latest statistics and business examples available. Materials used have been chosen to demonstrate appropriate arguments and theories. They should, therefore, allow students to answer questions which require knowledge of what has happened 'in recent years' or 'over the past decade', as well as questions which deal with current debates.

Study skills and assessment The last two units in the book provide guidance on how to study and the methods of assessment used in Business Studies. They are presented in the form of a manual and are designed to be used at various stages throughout the course.

Key terms Many units contain a key terms section. Each section defines new concepts, which appear in capitals in the text of the unit. Taken together, they provide a comprehensive dictionary of business terms.

Presentation Great care has been taken with how the book has been presented. It is hoped that the layout of the book, the use of colour and the use of diagrams will help learning.

We would like to thank the following for their efforts in the preparation of the three editions of this book: Richard Dunill, for keeping the debate sharp and yet accessible; Ingrid Hamer for her long hours of typing; Nigel Lewis; Michael J. Forshaw and Chris Sawyer for bringing a 'real' accountant's view to the book; all staff and students at Bolton Sixth Form College, King George V College, Loreto College, and Manchester University School of Education; Diane Wallace and Steve Robertson for working on the early development of the book; Alain Anderton for sharing his style ideas.

Dave Hall Rob Jones Carlo Raffo
Ian Chambers Dave Gray

1 Business Decision Making

Why do businesses make decisions?

Businesses are DECISION MAKING units. Making the 'right' decisions help a business to achieve its aims and objectives. Some of the decisions faced by a business might include:

- how much output to produce of different products in a week or a month;
- who should be promoted from the shop floor to a supervisory level;
- whether the price of a product should be raised;
- how the construction of a new warehouse should be financed;
- what should be the design a of a new company logo;
- which supplier should be used to provide components;
- whether a product should be withdrawn from the market;

and many others.

Businesses are forced to make decisions because choices nearly always exist. A business often has to decide which course of action to take from many different possible alternatives. For example, a company that needs to hire a van for a week might have to choose between 10-15 local companies, all of which are able to supply the van to the required specifications. The person responsible for vehicle hire in the company will need to make this decision. A more important decision may have to be made by a business that is rationalising production. The directors and management may need to choose which factory to close from all of those owned by the business.

Decision making is also necessary to solve problems in a business. For example, if the workforce goes on strike the management may have to decide on an appropriate course of action. A business may also have to take decisions to solve problems such as lengthy queues which develop when consumers are buying goods or possible delays which may take place in the construction of a new factory.

All decisions involve some risk. Decisions where the outcome is unpredictable, where many factors can affect success or which affect a large part of a firm's operations for a long period are most risky. A business may be able to minimise the risk by collecting accurate and comprehensive data and by using decision making models. These are dealt with later in this unit.

Types of decision

It is possible to classify the decisions made by businesses in different ways.

Programmed decisions This idea was put forward by H.A.Simon in his 1965 book *The New Science of Management Decisions*. These are repetitive decisions. A set routine for making the decisions will have been established. For example, a supermarket branch manager may have to prepare a rota every week. This will involve decisions about which staff should be on duty during various shifts. The decisions are repetitive (carried out weekly). Also, a procedure is likely to have been developed which specifies exactly how decisions should be made. There may be formal rules which control decisions, such as the minimum number of staff stacking shelves at any one time. The rules will have been developed and improved over time. The decisions may even be carried out on a computer. For these reasons the decisions have been programmed.

Non-programmed decisions Simon argued that these are novel or unstructured decisions. For example, a business may be forced to move its premises because its current location is subject to a compulsory purchase order by a local authority. This is an unusual problem and it is unlikely that a decision making procedure will have been developed to resolve the problem. A decision like this will also have a long lasting effect on the organisation.

In practice decisions will not fall neatly into the two categories above. Many decisions will be partly programmed and partly non-programmed. For example, managers may develop a decision making structure to apply to unforeseen events. Decisions in a business are also likely to be either strategic, tactical or operational.

Strategic decisions STRATEGIC DECISIONS concern the general direction and overall policy of a business. They are far reaching and can influence the performance of the organisation. They will also be **long term** decisions, which means that they will affect the business for a period of more than one year. Strategic decisions tend to have a high risk because the outcome of the decision is likely to be unknown.

Examples of strategic decisions might include:

- the planned sale by Northern Rock of its credit card business to the Cooperative Bank in 2003;
- the proposed £3 billion takeover of Safeway by Morrisons in 2003.

These decisions are all likely to have long term effects on the businesses concerned. They often involve moving into new areas which will require new resources, new procedures and retraining. Whether or not the decisions were the 'right' ones may not be known for several years because it will take time to evaluate their effects on the businesses involved.

Tactical decisions TACTICAL DECISIONS tend to be medium term decisions which are less far reaching than strategic decisions. They are tactical because they are calculated and because their outcome is more predictable.

In a business, tactical decisions may be used to implement strategic decisions. For example, as a result of Morrison's strategic decision to take over Safeway, some tactical decisions might have been:
- if any staff will be made redundant or if any staff need to be recruited;
- where duplication occurs, if stores should be closed;
- what should happen to any stores that are closed;
- what retraining of staff might be required and which staff would be retrained;
- what methods of promotion should be used for the new business.

Operational decisions OPERATIONAL DECISIONS are lower level decisions, sometimes called administrative decisions. They will be short term and carry little risk. Such decisions can normally be taken fairly quickly. They require much less thought and evaluation than strategic and tactical decisions. Every day a business makes a large number of operational decisions.

Examples might include:
- how many checkouts to have open in a retail outlet at a particular time of day;
- how much time should allocated to a task in a factory;
- how to stagger breaks for sales staff in a department store so that a minimum number are always on the shop floor;
- when to order new invoices for an office and what quantity to order.

Who makes decisions?

Decisions are made by all staff in a business. However, responsibility for the decision will vary according to the employee's position in the hierarchical structure. A senior manager can delegate decision making powers to a junior manager, but will retain ultimate responsibility for decision making. Also, the size of the company will influence who

Sony, the consumer electronics and entertainment group, has recently completed a four year restructuring programme. In light of the company's performance during that time critics suggest that it has lost its way. Sony responded to this criticism with a new restructuring plan and a preview of two products it hopes will convince sceptics it has a viable strategy for growth. Sony plans to spend a further ¥300 billion (£1.4 billion) mainly to restructure its electronic business in the next three years. It will allocate resources to strategic areas such as semi-conductors, while non-core assets and non-profitable activities will be sold off.

In its critical product strategy, Sony unveiled two prototypes it hopes will convince critics that its plan to integrate audio-video (AV) products and games can be effected and become profitable. One is the PSX, which incorporates the functions of a games machine, TV tuner, hard-disk and DVD recorder and will be released in Japan first later this year. A portable personal digital assistant, in the Clie series, will also be launched this year as a model for the integration of AV and mobile communications. Figures 1.1 and 1.2 and Table 1.1 show some financial information for Sony.

Source: adapted from *The Financial Times*, 29.5.2003.

Table 1.1 *Sales by business, 2003*

Year to Mar 31	¥bn	Year-on-year change(%)
Electronics		
Information & communications	959	-17.9
TV	846	0.4
Video	823	2.1
Audio	683	-8.7
Components	537	2.2
Semiconductors	205	12.3
Total	4,543	-4.8
Other businesses		
Games	936	-5.1
Pictures	803	26.3
Music	559	-5.0
Financial services	513	6.1
Total sales	7,474	-1.4

Source: adapted from Thomson Datastream, company information.

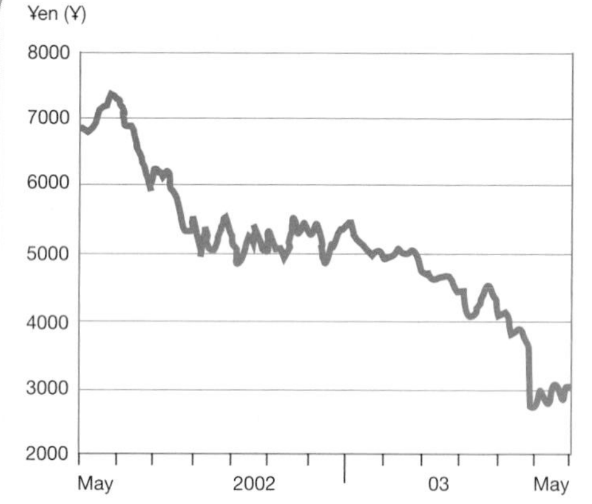

Figure 1.1 *Sony share price*

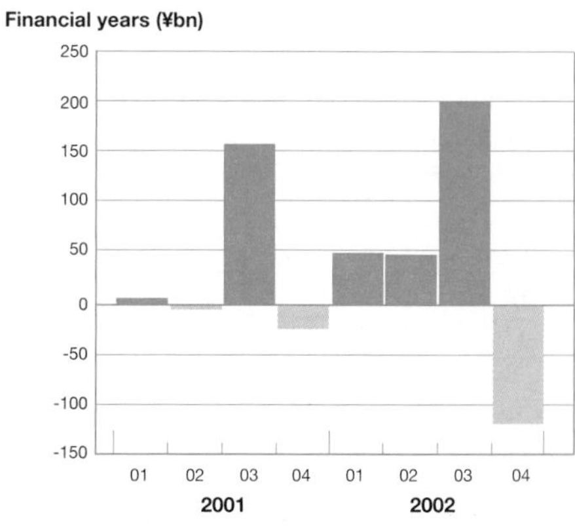

Figure 1.2 *Operating profit/loss*

(a) Describe the strategic decisions made by Sony and explain why you think they are strategic.
(b) What evidence is there to support the critics' view that Sony may have lost its way?

Question 1

makes decisions. For example, a sole trader with no employees will make all the decisions. As businesses grow and more staff are employed, decision making is likely to be delegated.

Strategic decisions These are likely to be made by the owners of the business. Such decisions are so important and far reaching that only the owners can be responsible for their outcome. However, in some public limited companies these decisions will be made by the board of directors. Directors are appointed to run plcs in the interests of the owners, the shareholders, who can number thousands. Some important strategic decisions may require the shareholder's consent. For example, shareholders at Hanson, the conglomerate business, were consulted before the group was demerged into four smaller companies in 1996.

Tactical decisions Business managers are likely to make tactical decisions. Such decisions are often required to implement the strategic decisions made by the owners or the senior management team. Important tactical decisions, such as the promotion campaign for a new product, tend to be made by those near the top of the business hierarchy. Less important tactical decisions will often be made by middle or junior managers.

Operational decisions Nearly all employees will be involved in operational decisions. Lower level decisions, such as what task should office staff at an NHS trust hospital perform, are constantly taken by all staff in the business. Sometimes managers may be consulted by their subordinates if they need guidance or approval for a decision.

It is argued that delegating decisions to those further down the hierarchy can help motivation. This **empowerment** of employees can also help to solve problems quickly without the need to consult managers. In the last decade a number of UK business have handed decision making to factory, team or group workers, giving them the authority to identify and solve problems before or as they occur. This has led to improvements in both efficiency and quality. The removal of layers of management has also improved decision making in some cases by reducing the number of levels in the chain of command, although this can lead to problems if not supported by retraining and changes in organisational culture (☞ unit 5).

The decision making process

A business makes decisions in order to achieve objectives. For example, it might decide to launch a new product in order to diversify. Decisions are made at all levels in a business and it is useful to have a flexible and logical process which can be followed by all involved. Figure 1.3 shows the stages in the decision making process.

Identifying objectives The first stage in the process is to identify the objective a business wants to achieve. The objective might be a corporate objective, such as growth or survival in a poor trading period. These decisions are likely to be complex and might be taken by the board of directors. For lower level objectives, such as filling a part time vacancy, decisions may be taken by junior managers. A business's objectives might be different at different stages in its growth. Business activities controlled by local government may have different objectives from public limited companies. The business also needs to develop criteria to measure whether it has achieved its objectives. Quite often the objective is to solve a problem. This might be planning for an uncertain future or dealing with a low level of profitability.

Collecting information and ideas People need information and ideas to make decisions. The amount and nature of the information needed will depend on the decision. For example, the decision whether or not to launch a new product might require some information about possible sales levels and consumer reactions, costs of production and reactions of competitors. It could take several months to collect all this

Conduit, the Dublin-based call centre business, is to cut 250 jobs at its new 11 88 88 directory inquiries service after only twelve days' operation. The new 118 directory service was launched in August 2003 after BT's 192 service was scrapped by phone regulator, Oftel. The measure was designed to end BT's monopoly over the directory enquiries market, worth over £280 million.

Conduit said the losses would be confined to temporary jobs only. The jobs were created to deal with the expected rush of calls in the immediate period after the withdrawal of the 192 service. Some of the jobs will be cut from Conduit's call centre in Cardiff, 110 from its Welwyn Garden City centre in Hertfordshire and 30 from its Gloucester call centre. Its Swansea centre will escape cuts.

Conduit, which also provides directory services in Ireland, Switzerland and Austria, said that the extra staff had been taken on in the knowledge that they may not be needed for very long. 'It was not possible to predict the level of calls made to various 118 services once 192 was switched off,' a spokesperson said. 'Conduit put in place the capacity to handle more calls than it expected to receive through a mixture of its own staff and short-term agency staff. It was a strategic decision to have over capacity which could be quickly scaled back, rather than face the criticism other 118 services have had, struggling with increased demand'.

Source: adapted from *The Guardian*, 5.9.2003.

(a) Using examples from the case distinguish between strategic and tactical decisions.
(b) Who might have made the decisions described in (a)? Explain your answer.

Question 2

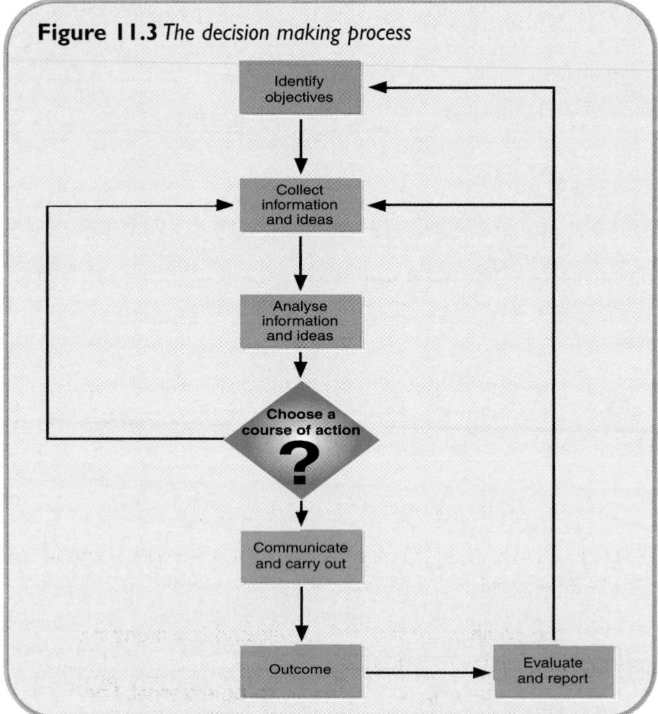

Figure 1.3 *The decision making process*

information. Other decisions could perhaps be made from information which the business already has. A decision whether or not to dismiss an employee might be made on the basis of information from the personnel department.

Where does the business get its ideas? It might set up a working party to collect information and ideas from within the firm. The working party would then produce a report or make a presentation to the decision makers. Alternatively, individuals or departments might submit ideas and information. Another way of obtaining information and ideas is to hold discussions amongst staff in the firm.

Analysing information and ideas The next stage in the process is to analyse information to look for alternative courses of action. Possible courses of action may be based on previous ideas or completely new ideas. The aim is to identify which course of action will best achieve the business's objective or solve the problem. It may be possible to test the alternatives before the one that is chosen is carried out.

Making a decision Next the decision has to be made. This is the most important stage in the process. Decision makers have to commit themselves to one course of action. It is difficult to change the decision, so getting it right is vital. For example, once production begins following the decision to launch a new product, it is difficult for the firm to change its mind. If the product does not sell, this can lead to a loss of money. Some decisions can be reversed. For example, if the owner of a shop decides to close on Tuesday afternoons, but then finds the loss of sales is intolerable, the owner can easily reopen again.

Sometimes the decision makers feel that they cannot reach a decision. They may have to obtain more information and complete the previous two stages in the process again.

Communication Once a decision has been made, personnel are informed and the decision is carried out. Quite often the people making the decisions are not those that carry them out. Instructions may be passed by the decision makers to someone else, probably a manager, explaining what action should be taken. For example, if the directors decide to begin selling their products in a new country, instructions must be sent to the marketing manager. In smaller firms decision makers are more likely to carry out their own decisions.

Outcome Once a decision has been carried out it will take time before the results are known. Sometimes this can be quite a long time. For example, the companies which decided to build the Channel Tunnel will not know for several decades whether or not it will be a commercial success.

Evaluate the results Finally, decision makers need to evaluate the outcome of their decisions. This is often presented as a report. It may be necessary to modify the course of action on the basis of the report. For example, it might be necessary to revise the objectives or collect some more information, as shown in Figure 1.3. There may be problems in following such an approach. Objectives may be difficult to identify or unrealistic. Information may be limited, incorrect or misleading. People making decisions in the process may have different views and this may lead to differences of opinion about what is the best course of action, for example.

Decision making models

The use of MODELS or SIMULATIONS is widespread in business. Models are replicas or copies of problem areas in business. They are theories, laws or equations, stating things about a problem and helping in our understanding of it. There is a number of common features to models.

- They reflect the key characteristics or behaviour of an area of concern.
- They tend to be simplified versions of areas of concern.
- They simulate the actions and processes that operate in the problem area.
- They provide an aid to problem solving or decision making.
- Models often make use of formulae to express concepts.

Some models can be carried out using computer software. This allows decisions to be made quickly and many variables affecting decisions to be included.

Management science and operations research are areas which often make use of decision making models. For example, linear programming (☞ unit 31) provides a model which allows decision makers to determine optimal solutions to a wide range of business problems. It has been used to make decisions such as:

- how to minimise waste in production;
- how to allocate resources between two competing tasks;

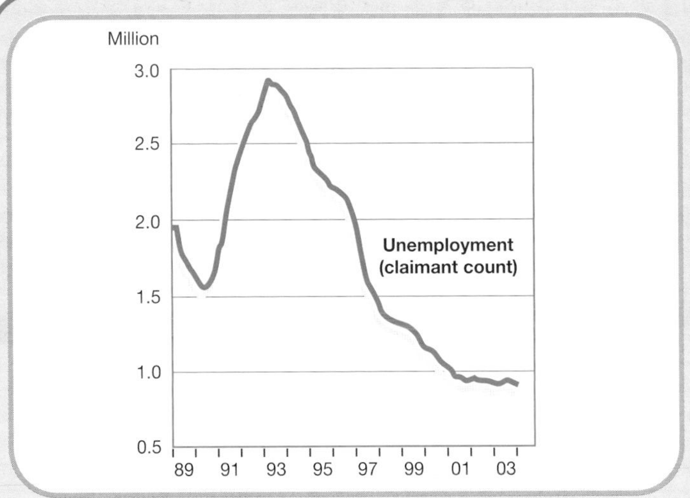

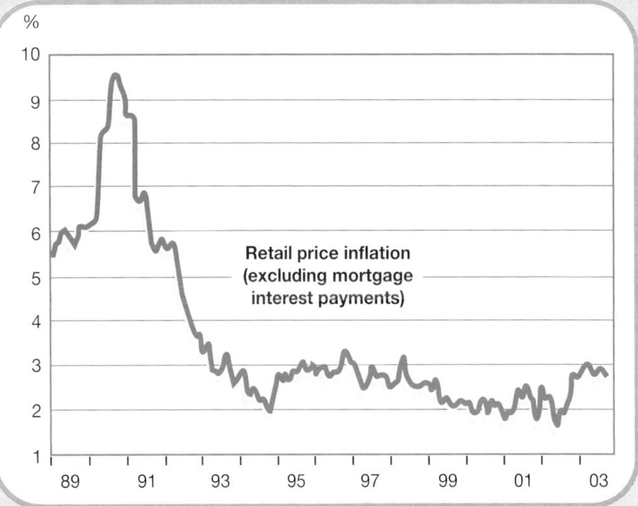

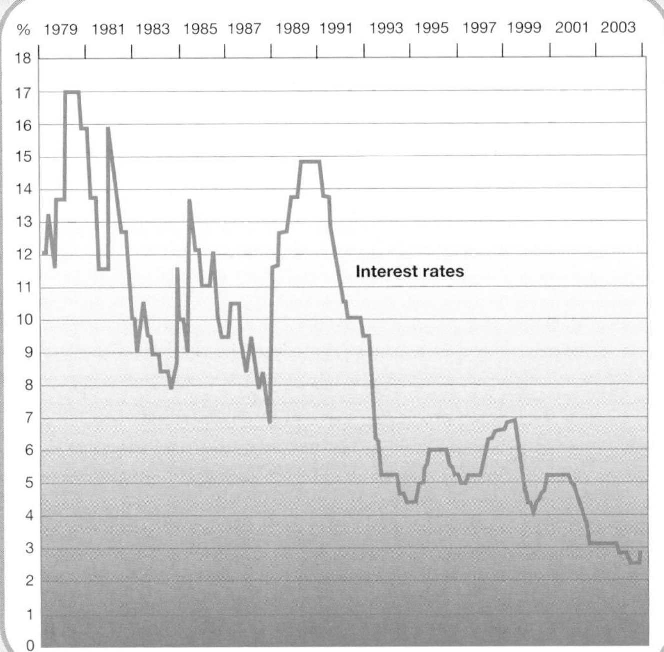

Figure 1.4 *Interest rates, inflation rates and unemployment in the UK*
Source: adapted from Thomson Datastream.

Wilson Hotels plc owns 18 country hotels in the UK. The company specialises in rural locations offering residents short breaks in peaceful surroundings with a strong emphasis on high quality cuisine. Wilson Hotels is profitable but wants to expand. It is considering raising £5 million to build 5 hotels in the Scottish Highlands. The company has already invested heavily in feasibility studies and seeking planning permission. It has got the go ahead to build 3 hotels and is waiting on permission for the other two.

Funding for the projects will have to be external. The company's reserves are modest because of its policy of paying shareholders relatively high dividends. It will also be necessary to recruit quite large numbers of staff. Each hotel will require up to 110 staff (a mixture of full-time and part-time).

The company is keen to go ahead with the investment programme but is worried about the size of the borrowing. A number of institutions have expressed an interest in providing funds and a decision must be made within the next month whether to go ahead with the investment or not. One or two people involved in the decision making process wonder whether the future economic conditions will suit such a large investment. Some economic data is shown in Figure 1.4.

(a) (i) Explain how the information in Figure 1.4 might help make the decision faced by Wilson Hotels?
(ii) What other information might be useful to the decision makers?

(b) Assuming that Wilson Hotels decides to go ahead with the investment project, how might it evaluate the outcome of the decision?

Question 3

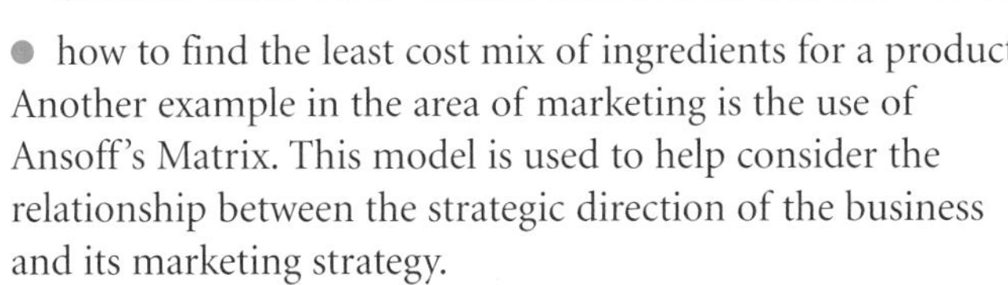

- how to find the least cost mix of ingredients for a product.

Another example in the area of marketing is the use of Ansoff's Matrix. This model is used to help consider the relationship between the strategic direction of the business and its marketing strategy.

A simulation involves trying to mimic what might happen in reality. It allows a business to test ideas and make decisions without bearing the consequences of 'real action' if things go wrong. Imagine a business has a problem. A simulation can be carried out several times, quickly and cheaply, in order to test alternative decisions. There is no risk and resources are not used up. Simulations are often used to deal with problems such as queues in business (☞ unit 32).

Constraints on decision making

Businesses cannot make decisions with complete freedom. In many situations there are factors which hinder, limit or restrict particular courses of action. These CONSTRAINTS may make the decision easier because they eliminate some courses of action. For example, a business may require an

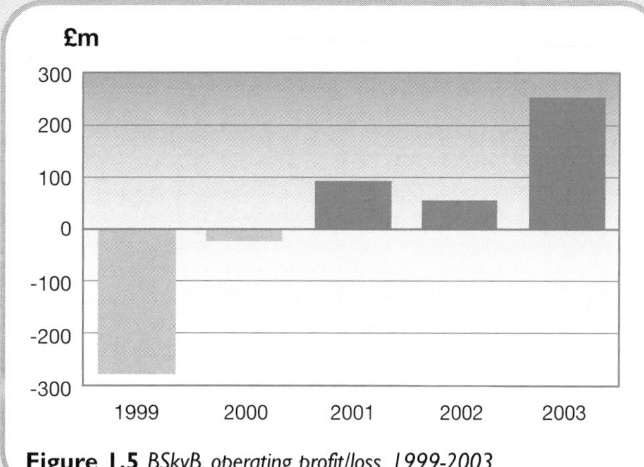

Figure 1.5 *BSkyB, operating profit/loss, 1999-2003*

BSkyB, the satellite broadcaster, made an operating profit of £254 million in 2003. It was felt that the company's strategy of investing heavily in football broadcasting and film rights and of converting its customer base to digital was starting to pay off.

Just before these trading results were announced, BSkyB decided to pay £1.024 billion to retain the rights to live Premier League football for a further three years from the beginning of the 2004-05 season. This deal represents a saving of around £100 million on the current arrangement. Many investors were hoping that a bigger saving would be made given the global collapse in the sports rights market and the lack of serious competition.

However, BSkyB's decision to pay over a billion pounds for these rights could turn out to be costly if the EU blocks the agreement and forces the Premier League to renegotiate. The commission is concerned that the deal brokered between the Premier League and BSkyB was completed fairly. A spokesperson for the commission said 'The commission is interested in both the fairness of the process and of the end result. We are interested in the bidding and whether it was open and unconditional. Each individual package (of broadcast rights) should have been subject to vigourous competition' he said. Brussels wants to know how many bids were made for each package and would only be satisfied if there had been 'several' bids for each rights package. The EU investigation is ongoing.

Source: adapted from *The Guardian*, 12.8.2003, BSkyB, *Annual Report and Accounts, 2003*.

(a) Describe (i) one internal constraint and (ii) two external constraints that may have affected BSkyB's decision to pay £1.024 billion for the broadcasting rights to televise live Premier League football for a further three years.
(b) Analyse the possible effects on BSkyB's financial performance if the external constraints mentioned above impact on the company.

Question 4

agency to carry out market research on its behalf. It may allocate a budget of £5,000 to pay for the research and invite tenders for the work. The tenders received could be:

- Sefton Research Associates - £4,700;
- Aston MR Ltd - £6,100;
- Salford Marketing - £4,900;
- Carlton Marketing - £5,400.

The business can only afford to pay the tenders offered by two of the agencies. Thus its choice is reduced and the decision simplified by its financial constraint. Note, however, that the best quality service may be provided by Aston MR Ltd and so the financial constraint has denied the business using a better quality service.

Internal constraints These may result from the policy of the business itself.

- Availability of finance. Decision makers are often prevented from choosing certain courses of action because the business cannot afford them.
- Existing company policy. For example, to control the wage bill, a firm's policy may be to restrict overtime to a maximum of 10 hours per week. The production manager may want to offer workers more overtime to reach a production target. However, she is not able to do so because of the firm's overtime policy.
- People's behaviour. Decisions may be limited by people's ability. For example, a manual worker is unlikely to be able to run a department if the manager is absent. People are also limited by their attitudes. For example, a company may wish to move three people into one office who work in separate offices at the moment, but this could meet with resistance.

External constraints These are limits from outside and are usually beyond the control the control of the business.

- Government and EU legislation. Businesses must operate within the law. For example, a manager may require a driver to deliver some goods urgently to a customer 600 miles away, which would require a 17 hour drive. The law restricts the amount of time a person can drive certain commercial vehicles to about 10 hours per day.
- Competitors' behaviour. Say a firm is deciding to introduce a new product. If Mars is enjoying some success with a new product Cadbury's might copy Mars and decide to launch its own version of the product. Because competition has become greater in recent years, this constraint has affected more firms.
- Lack of technology. There are many examples of operations in business that in the past were slow or physically demanding. Today tasks as varied as loading cargo onto ships to computer aided design can be carried on effectively with the use of modern technology.
- The economic environment. It is argued that business activity moves through booms, where demand rises, and

slumps. This can affect investment decisions. For example, if a company is deciding whether to build a larger plant, the decision makers may postpone the plan if the economy is in a slump and demand is low. During the recession of the early 1990s a large number of businesses cancelled investment projects.

The quality of decisions

If the right decisions are made the business will benefit. The quality of decisions depends on a number of factors.

Training If people are trained their performance is likely to be better. The people making important decisions in a business should receive training. Courses are offered by business schools and other educational institutions which concentrate on decision making.

Quantity and quality information Decision making will be improved if there is access to information. For example, if a firm is thinking of a price increase, the more information it has on the reactions of customers, the more likely it is to decide whether this is the right course of action. Information technology in business has helped decision makers a great deal. They are able to store more information, retrieve it instantly and change it into a form which is more useful to them.

Inadequate and inaccurate information can lead to the wrong decision being made and may cause serious problems. For example, when an insurance company is setting premiums for motor insurance, if the estimate of the cost of repairing cars is too low then premiums will be set too low. It is also argued that the use of quantitative information helps to improve the quality of the decision.

Ability to use decision making techniques The ability to use decision making techniques will help accurate decisions to be made. For example, one technique used to evaluate the likely returns from choosing a particular course of action is the use of decision trees (☞ unit 2).

Risk Some decisions involve considerable risk, such as the launching of a new product. It is argued that UK managers are too cautious in their approach to decision making. This is because they prefer to choose courses of action which carry the lowest risk, and avoid taking riskier courses of action which might result in higher profits.

Human element Most decisions are made by people. Different people are likely to make different decisions. How do people differ?

- The level of experience might be different. More experienced decision makers will often, but not always, make much more accurate decisions.
- The attitude to risk may differ. Cautious decision makers will choose different courses of action to 'risk takers'.
- People have different capabilities. Those who are skilled at decision making will enjoy better results than those whose judgements are poor.
- Self-interest may affect the course of action chosen. For example, management and trade unions are likely to reach different conclusions when setting wage levels for the workforce.
- People often have different perceptions. This may influence the decisions they make. For example, two people on an interview panel for a new recruit may have different views of an interviewee's performance.

Interdependence

Businesses are highly interdependent. Many businesses depend on others for supplies of materials and components. Other businesses supply ancillary services, such as cleaning, waste disposal, financial services and maintenance. When making decisions firms should consider how they affect these support services. In recent years some large businesses have put financial pressure on support businesses by delaying payments. This may lead to support services closing down.

Decision makers need to be aware of the interdependence between their own company and their competitors. In highly competitive industries one firm's decisions can affect the behaviour of other firms. For example, in the grocery trade if one supermarket decides to lower the prices of several hundred lines, other supermarkets may have to do the same or risk losing customers. This type of interdependence is particularly important in decisions concerning:

- price;
- launching new products;
- packaging;
- non-price competition;
- introducing new technology;
- exploiting new markets.

key terms

Constraints - factors which restrict decision making.
Decision making - choosing between alternative courses of action.
Models or simulations - simplified representations of a business situation or problem.
Operational decisions - lower level, often administrative decisions with little or no risk.
Strategic decisions - decisions concerning policy that have a long term impact on a business. Can be risky.
Tactical decisions - calculated, medium term decisions. May be used to implement strategic decisions.

Knowledge...Knowledge...Knowledge...Knowledge...Knowledge...Knowled

1. Why do businesses need to make decisions?
2. Why do decisions involve risk?
3 Explain the difference between programmed and non-programmed decisions.
4. Suggest 2 examples of a strategic decision.
5. Who makes decisions in business?
6. How might the size of a business affect who makes decisions?
7. Briefly describe the stages in an normative decision making process.
8. Explain the difference between a normative and a positive model of decision making.
9. What are the common features of scientific models?
10. List 3 internal and 3 external constraints on business decisions.
11. State 5 factors affecting the quality of business decisions.
12. 'Businesses can not make decisions without considering the effects on their suppliers.' Briefly explain this statement.

Case study Carparts

Carparts is a national parts distributor for motor cars. It has 112 distribution centres all over the UK. After a period of healthy sales growth in the mid and late 1990s, the company's sales have stagnated. It achieved much of its growth through acquisitions, however, the scope for further acquisitions in the UK has diminished. The company is considering its future and two strategies for further growth have been identified.

- **Set up an online sales service.** This would allow customers to buy spare parts using a computer. One of the main advantages of this is that payment would be received in advance so cash flow would improve. Most of Carparts' existing customers purchase parts on credit. The cost of processing orders would be reduced and new customers might also be attracted. However, there are some disadvantages. Carparts has no experience in computer sales and a lot of money would have to be spent on staff training and computer equipment. Money would also have to be invested in expanding the delivery service since all computer purchases will have to be delivered. This would involve purchasing more delivery vehicles and taking on more staff.
- **Buy AutoPlus, a French distributor of motor car parts.** This would allow Carparts to grow rapidly. AutoPlus is a medium-sized but established distributor in Northern France. Such an acquisition will bring economies of scale to Carparts and allow the company to develop its core activities. However, the company does not have any experience in overseas business development. It is also worried that the products demanded in France might be quite different to the ones bought in the UK due

to the differences in motor car models purchased in the two countries.

One of the problems faced by the company is that the board of directors is currently split over which course of action should be taken. Although the company Chairperson has a casting vote, on such an important issue he is reluctant to use it. One factor that will have to be taken into account is the cost of the two options. Setting up an online service will cost around £2.2 million while buying AutoPlus will cost at least £4.5 million. There is also the possibility that another bidder might enter the market for AutoPlus which would drive up the price. However, the purchase of AutoPlus will generate immediate returns whereas revenue from the online business is likely take a while to build up. The directors who favour the online services option have often been criticised for being too risk averse.

On the morning before the final board meeting when the decision will be made, the Chairperson, who is busy making final preparations for the meeting, delegates a number of tasks to his Personal Assistant.

- Book a table in a suitable restaurant for the Chairperson to entertain some important shareholders the next day.
- Choose four distribution centres for the Chairperson to visit at random the day after.
- Decide which branch manager should receive the monthly merit award.

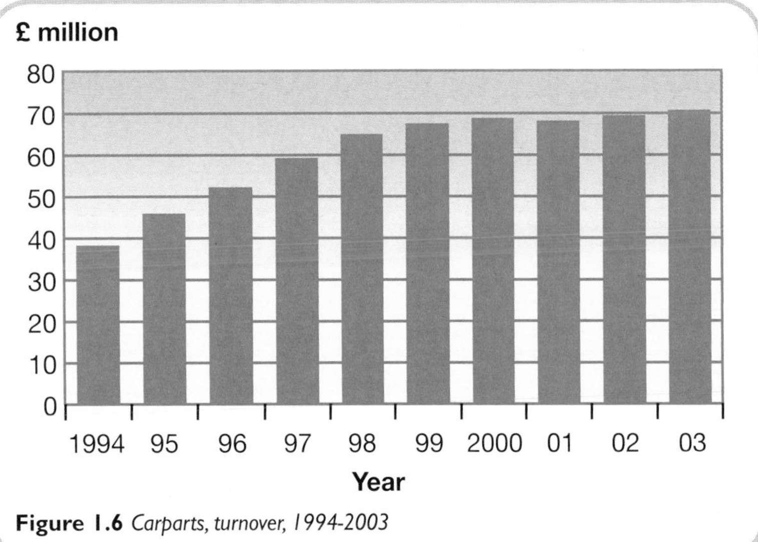

Figure 1.6 *Carparts, turnover, 1994-2003*

(a) What is the objective in the decision faced by Carparts? (4 marks)

(b) Using examples from the case, explain what is meant by an operational decision. (6 marks)

(c) Outline the possible (i) internal and (ii) external constraints that there might be on the decision facing Carparts. (12 marks)

(d) Discuss what other information might help the directors to reach a better decision. (12 marks)

(e) Evaluate the possible difficulties involved in this particular decision. (16 marks)

2 Decision Trees

Making decisions

Every day, businesses make decisions. Most, if not all, involve some risk. This could be because the business has limited information on which to base the decision. Furthermore, the outcome of the decision may be uncertain. Launching a new product in a market abroad can be risky because a firm may not have experience of selling in that market. It may also be unsure about how consumers will react.

When faced with a number of different decisions a business will want to choose the course of action which gives the most return. What if a printing company had to decide whether to invest £750,000 in a new printing press now or wait a few years? If it bought now and a more efficient machine became available next year then it might have been more profitable to wait. Alternatively, if it waits it may find the old machine has problems and costs increase.

When the outcome is uncertain, decision trees can be used to help a business reach a decision which could minimise risk and gain the greatest return.

What are decision trees?

A DECISION TREE is a method of tracing the alternative outcomes of any decision. The likely results can then be compared so that the business can find the most profitable alternative. For example, a business may be faced with two alternatives - to launch a new product in Europe or in the USA. A decision tree may show that launching a new product in Europe would give £5 million profit, whereas launching in the USA would only give a profit of £1 million.

It is argued by some that decision making is more effective if a **quantitative approach** is taken. This is where information on which decisions are based, and the outcomes of decisions, are expressed as numbers. In a decision tree, numerical values are given to such information. The decision tree also provides a pictorial approach to decision making because a diagram is used which resembles the branches of a tree. The diagram maps out different courses of action, possible outcomes of decisions and points where decisions have to be made. Calculations based on the decision tree can be used to determine the 'best' likely outcome for the business and hence the most suitable decision.

Features of decision trees

Decision trees have a number of features. These can be seen in Figure 2.1 which shows the decision tree for a business that has to decide whether to launch a new advertising campaign or retain an old one.

Decision points Points where decisions have to be made in a decision tree are represented by squares and are called decision points. The decision maker has to choose between certain courses of action. In this example, the decision is whether to launch a new campaign or retain the old one.

Outcomes Points where there are different possible outcomes in a decision tree are represented by circles and are called **chance nodes**. At these chance nodes it can be shown that a particular course of action might result in a number of outcomes. In this example, at 'B' there is a chance of failure or success of the new campaign.

Probability or chance The **likelihood** of possible outcomes happening is represented by probabilities in decision trees. The chance of a particular outcome occurring is given a value. If the outcome is certain then the probability is 1. Alternatively, if there is no chance at all of a particular outcome occurring, the probability will be 0. In practice the value will lie between 0 and 1. In Figure 2.1, at 'B' the chance of success for the new campaign is 0.2 and the chance of failure is 0.8.

It is possible to estimate the probability of events occurring provided information about these events can be found. There are two sources of information which can be used to help estimate probabilities. One source is **backdata**. For example, if a business has opened 10 new stores in recent years, and 9 of them have been successful, it might be reasonable to assume that the chances of another new store being successful are $^{9}/_{10}$ or 0.9. Another source is research data. For example, a business might carry out marketing research to find out how customers would react to a new product design. 80 per cent of people surveyed may like the product and 20 per cent may dislike it.

Expected values This is the financial outcome of a decision. It is based on the predicted profit or loss of an outcome and the probability of that outcome occurring. The profit or loss of any decision is shown on the right hand side of Figure 2.1. For

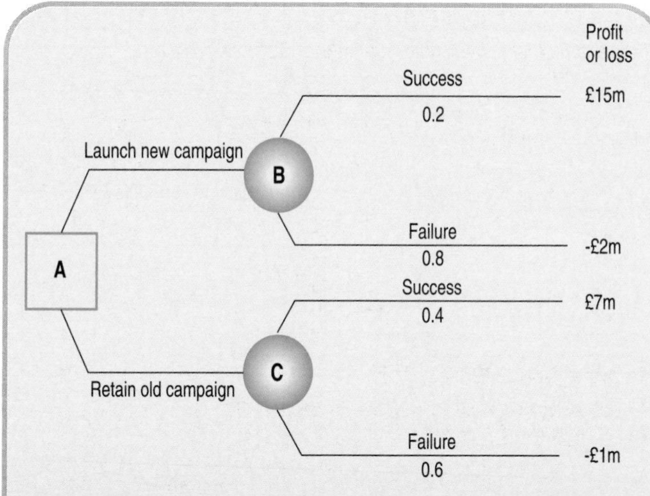

Figure 2.1 *A simple decision tree based on a decision whether to retain an existing advertising campaign or begin a new one*

example, if the launch of a new campaign is a success, a £15 million profit is expected. If it fails a loss of £2 million is expected.

Calculating expected values

What should the firm decide? It has to work out the expected values of each decision, taking into account the expected profit or loss and the probabilities. So, for example, the expected value of a new campaign is:

		Success		Failure
Expected value	=	0.2 x £15m (probability) (expected profit)	+	0.8 x (-£2m) (probability) (expected loss)
	=	£3m	-	£1.6m
	=	1.4m		

The expected value of retaining the current campaign is:

		Success		Failure
Expected value	=	0.4 x £7m	+	0.6 x (-£1m)
	=	£2.8m	-	£0.6m
	=	2.2m		

BGS Holdings owns a chain of 32 pubs and bars in the north of England. Due to intense competition, revenue has fallen in the last couple of years. As a means of boosting revenue it has been suggested that the chain, in line with many other competitors, should use 'happy hours' to attract more customers. Traditionally a 'happy hour' is a period of time (not always an hour) where drinks are sold at reduced prices. The problem though is choosing the right 'hour' when prices should be reduced. It is thought not to be a good idea to choose a period of time which is already popular. This is because sales of drinks would already be very high and to cut prices during this time would reduce margins significantly. In order to help make the decision an investigation was carried out in a sample of 4 pubs. The data gathered during the investigation is shown in Table 2.1.

Table 2.1 *Happy Hour data gathered by BGS Holdings*

Happy Hour period	Probability of success	Estimated effect on profit	Probability of failure	Estimated effect on profit	Expected value
3-4pm	0.5	+£1,300	?	-£200	?
4-5pm	0.5	+£1,700	?	-£400	?
5-6pm	0.7	+£400	?	-£1,200	?
6-7pm	0.6	+£1,000	?	-£800	?
7-8pm	0.6	+£1,100	?	-£400	?

(a) Complete Table 2.1.
(b) On financial grounds, when should the 'happy hour' be arranged?

From these figures the firm should continue with the existing campaign because the expected value is higher.

Numerous outcomes

It is possible to have more than two outcomes at a chance node. For example, at point 'B' in Figure 2.1 there might have been 3 outcomes:

- the probability of great success may be 0.2 with a profit of £15 million;
- the probability of average success may be 0.4 with a profit of £6 million;
- the probability of failure may be 0.4 with a loss of -£2 million.

The expected value is now:

= (0.2 x £15 m) + (0.4 x £6 m) + (0.4 x -£2 m)
= £3 m + £ 2.4 m - £0.8 m
= £4.6 m

Decisions, outcomes and costs

In practice businesses face many alternative decisions and possible outcomes. Take a farmer who has inherited some land, but does not wish to use it with his existing farming business. There are three possible decisions that the farmer could make.

- Sell the land. The market is depressed and this will earn £0.6 million.
- Wait for one year and hope that the market price improves. A land agent has told the farmer that the chance of an upturn in the market is 0.3, while the probabilities of it staying the same or worsening are 0.5 and 0.2 respectively. The likely proceeds from a sale in each of the circumstances are £1 million, £0.6 million and £0.5 million.
- Seek planning permission to develop the land. The legal and administration fees would be £0.5 million and the probability of being refused permission would be 0.8, which means the likelihood of obtaining permission is 0.2. If refused, the farmer would be left with the same set of circumstances described in the second option.

If planning permission is granted the farmer has to make a decision (at node E). If the farmer decides to sell, the probability of getting a good price, ie £10 million, is estimated to be 0.4, while the probability of getting a low price, ie £6 million, is 0.6. The farmer could also develop the land himself at a cost of £5 million. The probability of selling the developed land at a good price, ie £25 million, is estimated to be 0.3 while the likelihood of getting a low price, ie £10 million, is 0.7.

The information about probability and earnings is shown in Figure 2.2. What decision should the farmer make? The sale of the land immediately will earn £0.6 million.

The expected value of the second option, waiting a year, is:

Expected value = 0.3 x £1m + 0.5 x £0.6m + 0.2 x £0.5m
= £0.3m + £0.3m + £0.1m
= £0.7m

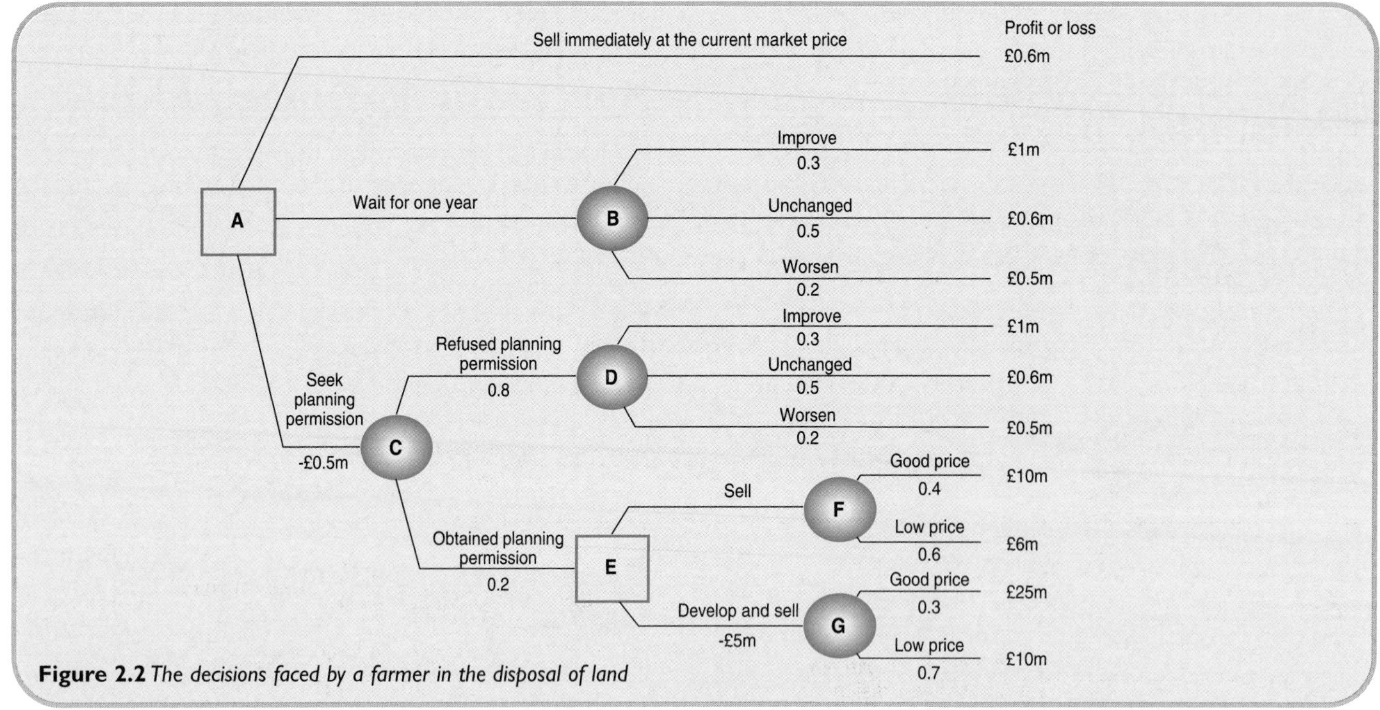

Figure 2.2 *The decisions faced by a farmer in the disposal of land*

Since this earns more than the first option, it would be a better choice. We could show this in Figure 2.4 (over the page) by crossing the 'selling immediately' path with a //, indicating that the first option will not be taken up. The expected value of the second option (£0.7 million) is shown in the diagram at node B.

A **rollback technique** can then be used to work out the expected value of the third option, seeking planning permission. This means working from right to left, calculating the expected values at each node in the diagram. The expected value at node D is:

Expected value = 0.3 x £1m + 0.5 x £0.6m + 0.2 x £0.5m
= £0.7m

The expected value at node F is:

Expected value = 0.4 x £10m + 0.6 x £6m
= £4m + £3.6m
= £7.6m

The expected value at node G is:

Expected value = 0.3 x £25m + 0.7 x £10m
= £7.5m + £7m
= £14.5m

Colin Andrews is the owner of Slade farm near Spalding. He specialises in vegetable crops and allocates about 400 acres of land each year to the production of potatoes and swedes. He decides what crops to plant in October each year.

If Colin plants potatoes he estimates that the probability of a good crop is 0.3, which will generate £50,000 profit. The probability of an average crop is 0.3, which would result in £30,000 profit. The probability of a poor crop is 0.4, which would result in only £10,000 profit.

If swedes are planted, either a good crop or a bad crop will result. He estimates that the probability in each case is 0.5. A good crop will generate a profit of £40,000 and a poor crop only £10,000. Figure 2.3 is a decision tree which shows this information.

Figure 2.3 *The alternative courses of action faced by Colin Andrews*

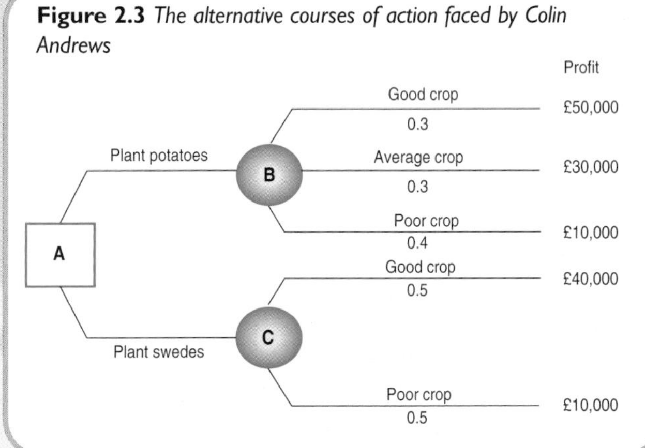

(a) What is happening at points B and C in the decision tree?
(b) Calculate the expected values of each course of action and decide, on financial grounds, which course Colin should take.

Question 2

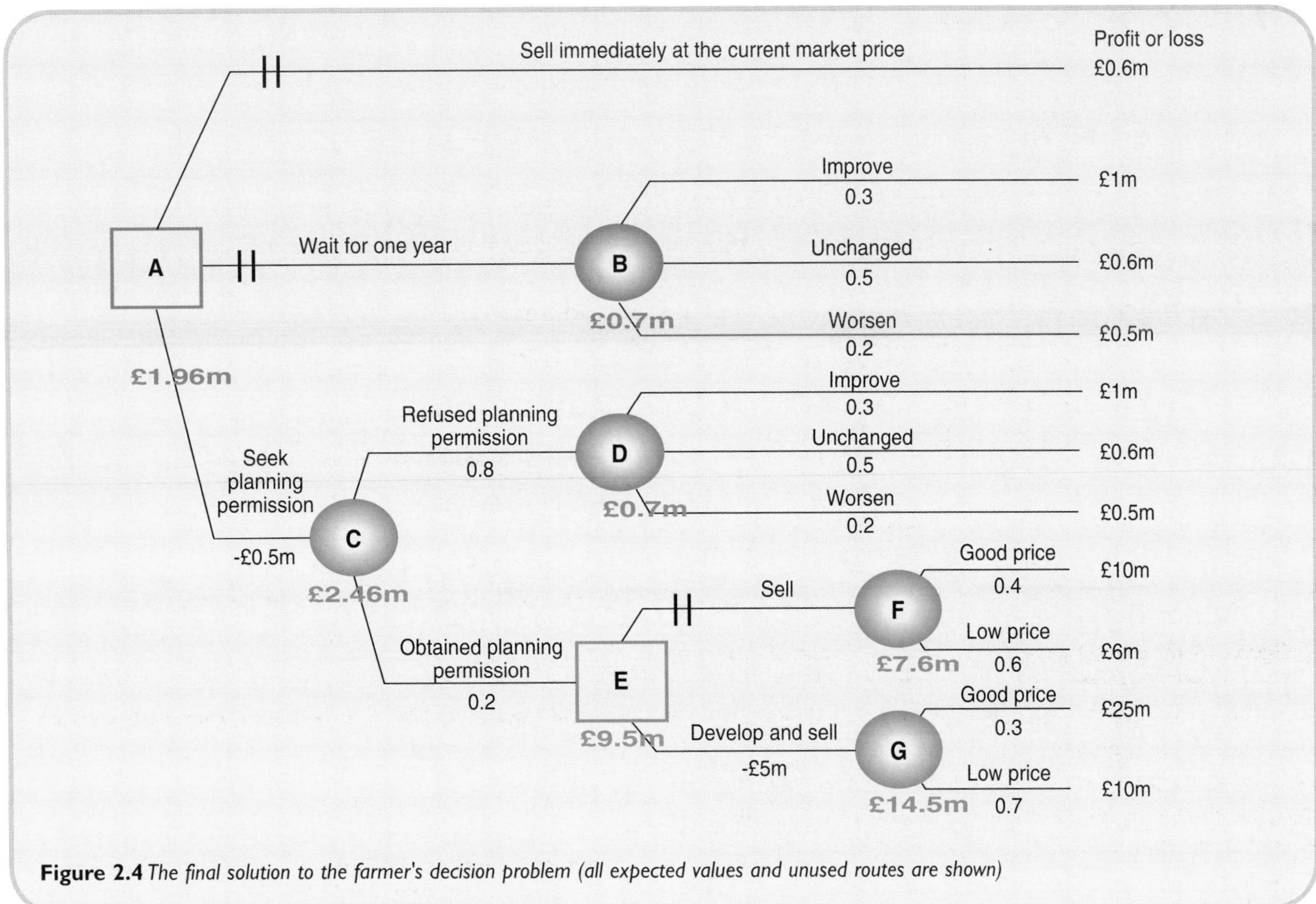

Figure 2.4 *The final solution to the farmer's decision problem (all expected values and unused routes are shown)*

At node E, a decision node, the farmer would choose to develop the land before selling it. This would yield an expected return of £9.5 million (£14.5 million - £5 million) which is higher than £7.6 million, ie the expected return from selling the land undeveloped. Thus, in Figure 2.4 the path representing this option can be crossed. The expected value at node C is now:

Expected value = 0.2 x £9.5m + 0.8 x £0.7m
= £1.9m + £0.56m
= £2.46m

Finally, by subtracting the extra cost of seeking planning permission (£0.5 million), the expected value of the final option can be found. It is £1.96 million. Since this is the highest value, this would be the best option for the farmer. This means a // can be placed on the line to node B as £0.7 million is lower than £1.96 million. All of the expected values are shown in Figure 2.4.

Figure 2.4 shows profit or loss (taking into account costs) and then the **extra** costs of planning permission are subtracted in the calculation. However, a decision tree may show revenue on the right side instead of profit and **all** costs indicated on the diagram must be subtracted. Whichever is shown, the method of calculation is the same.

Advantages and disadvantages of decision trees

Decision trees can be applied to much more complicated problems. They have some major advantages.

- Constructing the tree diagram may show possible courses of action not previously considered.
- They involve placing numerical values on decisions. This tends to improve results.
- They force management to take account of the risks involved in decisions and help to separate important from unimportant risks.

The technique also has some limitations.

- The information which the technique 'throws out' is not exact. Much of it is based on probabilities which are often estimated.
- Decisions are not always concerned with quantities and probabilities. They often involve people and are influenced by legal constraints or people's opinions, for example. These factors cannot always be shown by numerical values. Qualitatitive data may also be important.
- Time lags often occur in decision making. By the time a decision is finally made, some of the numerical information may be out of date.

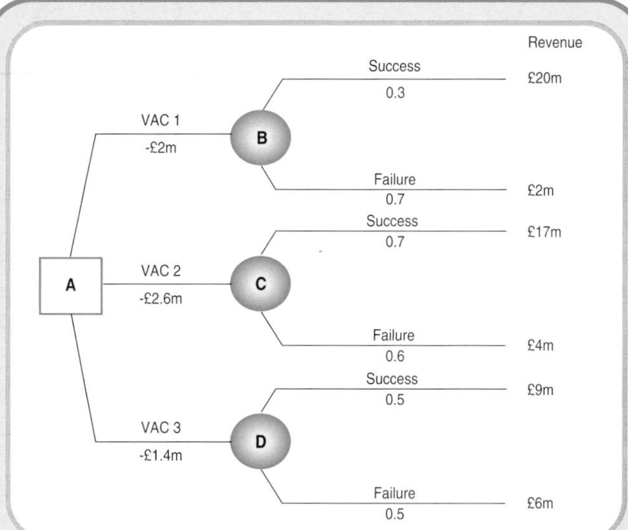

Figure 2.5 *The costs, revenues and probabilities of success and failure of each research programme for Trumed plc*

Trumed plc is a medical company that carries out research into new treatments for colds and influenza. It has won a contract from a large pharmaceuticals corporation to carry out research into new treatments. Trumed has identified three distinct research programmes to develop a vaccination to combat the strain. The code names for each programme are VAC1, VAC2 and VAC3. The cost of the programmes, the expected returns and the probabilities of success and failure are illustrated in the decision tree in Figure 2.5.

(a) Calculate the expected values of each research programme and advise Trumed which is the best option.

Question 3

- The process can be quite time consuming, using up valuable business resources. However, computerised decision making models can be used to analyse decision trees which can save some time.
- It is argued that decision makers, in an attempt encourage a particular course of action, may manipulate the data. For example, a manager might be 'biased' when attaching probabilities to certain outcomes. This will distort the final results.
- Decision trees are not able to take into account the dynamic nature of business. For example, a sudden change in the economic climate might render a decision based on a decision tree obsolete.

Knowledge

1. Why are decision trees useful when a business has to make important decisions?
2. What is meant by a quantitative approach to decision making?
3. What is meant by probability in a decision tree?
4. What is the difference between chance nodes and decision nodes?
5. How is the expected value of a course of action calculated?
6. What are the advantages and disadvantages of using decision trees?
7. State 3 possible situations where a business might make use of a decision tree.

key terms

Decision trees - a technique which shows all possible outcomes of a decision. The name comes from the similarity of the diagrams to the branches of trees.

Case study The DVD Shop

The DVD Shop is a small chain store that sells a very wide range of DVDs. It claims to be able to supply any listed DVD within 24 hours. It owns 23 branches, mainly in the West Midlands, and is under pressure from shareholders to expand quickly. The company was floated on the stock exchange seven years ago and has pursued a strategy of organic growth. This has been a little slow, but at the same time dividend payments to shareholders have been stable. A decision has to be made to take the company through its next phase of development. Three alternative strategies have been identified. The revenue from each option is expected to be generated over a three year period.

Continue to grow organically This has proved to be a reliable strategy in the past for The DVD Shop, opening about 3 new stores a year without having to raise large amounts of capital. If this strategy is continued the expected cost will be £20 million. If organic growth is successful an additional £80 million in revenue will be generated. However, if the strategy begins to fail only £20 million will be generated. The probability of success is estimated to be 0.9. Therefore the probability of failure will be 0.1.

Buy another small chain of DVD shops This is the most expensive strategy. Two chains have been identified – Sound&Vision in London with 12 branches and JustDVDs in Greater Manchester with 9 branches. Before any acquisition is made £4 million fees would have to be paid to consultants to check out the viability of an acquisition. Assuming that both options are acceptable Sound&Vision will cost £50 million to buy and JustDVDs £38 million.

If the purchase of Sound&Vision is successful £120 million in revenue is expected to be generated. If it fails £80 million will be generated. The chances of success are 0.6. If the purchase of JustDVDs is successful £100 million is expected to be earned. If it fails the revenue generated will fall to £70 million. The probability that the purchase of JustDVDs will be successful is estimated to be 0.7.

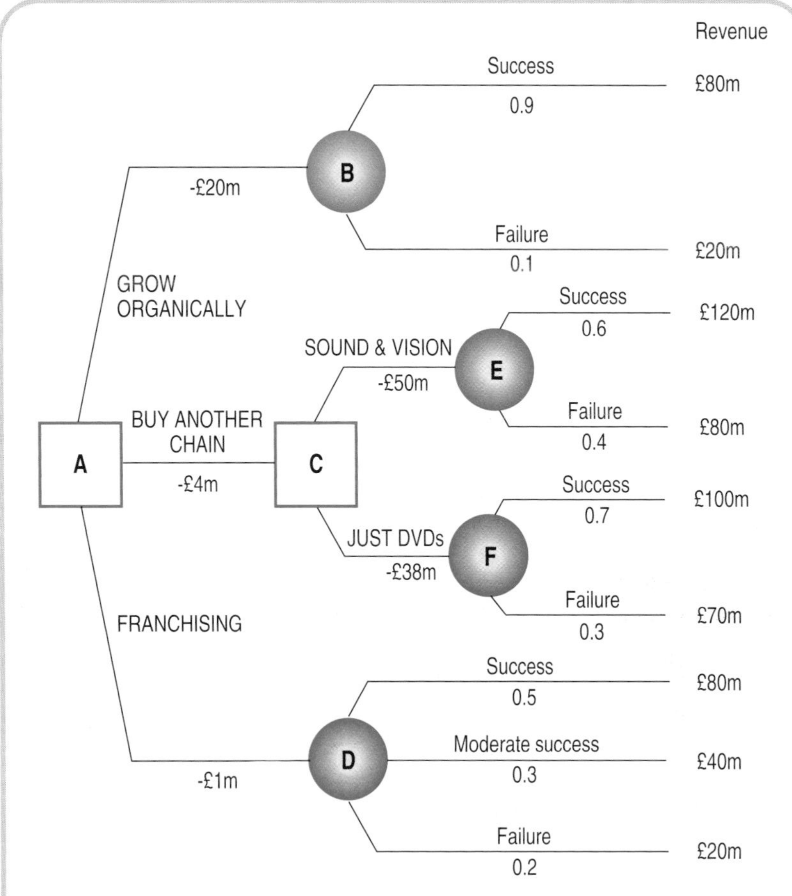

Figure 2.6 *The costs, revenues and probabilities of success and failure of the expansion strategies of The DVD Shop*

Set up a franchising operation It is thought that a franchising operation might speed up growth. Another advantage is that the setting up costs are very minimal, only £1 million. If this option were successful revenue would rise by £80 million. Even if the project was only moderately successful £40 million would be generated. If the franchising operation failed only £20 million would be generated. The chances of success were estimated to be 0.5, moderate success at 0.3 and the chances of failure are 0.2.

(a) If The DVD Shop decides to grow organically the probability of success is estimated to be 0.9. Explain what the probability of failure would be in this case. (4 marks)

(b) Calculate the expected values for each option and determine on financial grounds which option The DVD Shop should select. (14 marks)

(c) After the consultants had researched into the acquisition options it was found that Sound&Vision could be purchased for £45 million and that the expected revenue from a successful purchase would be £140 million. How might this affect your answer in (b)? (10 marks)

(d) Evaluate the disadvantages to The DVD Shop of using decision trees to make the decision about its strategy. (12 marks)

3 Analysing Data

Why analyse data?

A business can make great use of the data which it has collected about such things as costs, sales, markets and profits. Presenting the data will allow a firm to find out important information, such as the proportion of total costs accounted for by employees' wages. However, when looking at more complex problems, the data may need to be analysed in more detail. This can involve:

- finding out the most likely outcome, such as the most likely purchaser of a new product;
- forecasting what may happen in the future, such as the need for extra employees;
- finding out variations, such as by how much output changes at different times of the week, day or year;
- finding out whether the quality of a product is being maintained.

Sometimes businesses can use data which has been analysed for them. Government departments produce information on factors which might influence businesses, such as the rate of inflation. Industry bodies may provide data. For example, ABTA gives information on the market for tourism.

There is a variety of techniques which can be used to analyse data. This unit looks at measures of central tendency and dispersion, and the next looks at forecasting and predicting from data. While these methods can help a business to make better decisions, they must also take into account the nature of the data they are using. A certain amount of data is unreliable. It may be out of date, collected in less than a thorough way, or incomplete. Analysing this data, and making decisions based on incorrect figures, may cause problems. A firm that decides to increase its stocks because data show they are running low each week may have large quantities of unwanted goods if the data proves to be incorrect.

Central tendency

Much of the information that a business collects will be too detailed to be useful. It is necessary for this raw data to be organised into a form that decision makers can use more effectively. One method allows the business to discover the most **likely** or **common** outcome from the data. This involves calculating the CENTRAL TENDENCY from the data - usually known as the **average**.

Knowing the most likely outcome will be useful in a number of situations. A business may be interested in:

- the level of stock ordered most often;
- the production level a department achieves most often;
- the average sales each month;
- the average number of days lost through injury.

Table 3.1 shows the amount of stock ordered by a small business over a period of time. How can the business find the average quantity of stock ordered each week? There are three ways of doing this - finding the **mean, median** or **mode**.

Table 3.1 *Amount of stock ordered by a business over a 40 week period*

6	8	10	12	8	10	8	10	14	10
10	8	10	12	10	12	12	14	12	12
8	14	10	12	12	12	10	10	12	12
6	10	14	12	8	12	8	12	10	8

Arithmetic mean The arithmetic MEAN is the figure that most think of as an average. Simply, it can be calculated by adding the value of all items and dividing by the number of items. The formula for calculating the arithmetic mean ($\bar{x}$) is:

$$\bar{x} = \frac{\text{sum of items}}{\text{number of items}}$$

The mean for the first four orders in Table 13.1 would be:

$$\bar{x} = \frac{6 + 8 + 10 + 12}{4} = \frac{36}{4} = 9$$

Working out the mean in this way for all figures is time consuming. Imagine a multinational adding up the stock needed by every department for a year!

One method used to save time and improve accuracy is to work out the frequency (f) from the figures. The frequency is the number of times an item occurs. The **frequency distribution** for the figures in Table 3.1 is shown in Table 3.2.

Table 3.2 *Frequency distribution for stock ordered by a business over a 40 week period*

Quantity of stock ordered (x)	Frequency (f)	Quantity (x) x frequency (f)
6	2	12
8	8	64
10	12	120
12	14	168
14	4	56
	$\sum f = 40$	$\sum fx = 420$

where $\sum$ = the sum of (adding up all the values).

The mean can be calculated by:

- multiplying the quantity of stocks ordered (x) by the frequency (f);
- then adding up all these values and dividing by the total frequency.

The formula for calculating the mean of a frequency distribution is:

$$x = \frac{\Sigma fx}{\Sigma} = \frac{420}{40} = 10.5$$

Therefore, when the business orders stock, on average it orders 10.5 units. The company might use 10.5 as its average order quantity for stock control.

The advantage of using the mean as a measure of average value is that it takes into account all data. It is also a figure which is generally accepted as representing the average. However, it can be distorted by extreme values, resulting in a figure which is untypical and which may be misleading. For example, if the order in the ninth week had been 94 instead of 14 as in Table 3.1, the Σfx in Table 3.2 would have been 500 and the mean would have been 500 ÷ 40 = 12.5

The median The MEDIAN is the **middle** number in a set of data. When figures are placed in order, the median would be half way. For example, the median of the figures 3, 6, 8, 10 and 12 would be 8. The median for 1, 2, 3, 4, 5, 6 would be 3.5, the half way point. If a business had production figures of 200, 220, 240 and 260 units, the median would be half way between 220 and 240. In this case the median is found by an average of 220 and 240:

$$\frac{240 + 220}{2} = \frac{460}{2} = 230$$

Again, these are simple figures. Businesses, however, have large amounts of data and finding the median may require the use of a formula:

$$\frac{n + 1}{2} \text{ (for odd numbers) or } \frac{n}{2} \text{ (for even numbers)}$$

where n is the number of values or total frequency. In practice, with large numbers of figures, the latter formula is used.

In Table 3.1 there are 40 values. The median value would be 40 ÷ 2 = the 20th item if they were placed in order from smallest to largest, ie 6, 6, 8, 8, 8 etc. This is orders of 10 units. You can see from the cumulative frequency in Table 3.3. The 20th item in the cumulative frequency column must have been for an order of 10 units.

Table 3.3 *Cumulative frequency of stock ordered by a business over a 40 week period*

Quantity of stock ordered (x)	Frequency (f)	Cumulative frequency
6	2	2
8	8	10
10	12	22
12	14	36
14	4	40

The median is a useful measure of the average because, unlike the mean, it is not distorted by extreme values. However, the problem with the median is that it ignores all data other than the middle value.

The mode This is the value that occurs most frequently. From the figures in Table 3.1, the MODE would be 12 units, as this is the order quantity which occurs most often (14 times). As with the median, the mode is unaffected by mean values and has the added attraction of being easy to calculate. The main problem with the mode value is that it does not take account of all values and might, therefore, prove misleading when taken as a measure of the average. There might also be several modes within a set of data, which will make the measure less useful.

Ashwear is a company that manufactures a variety of clothing. Table 3.4 shows information about the cost of its various products.

Table 3.4

Cost of production	Number of products
£2	4
£4	10
£6	18
£8	8
	40

(a) Calculate:
   (i) the arithmetic mean;
   (ii) the median;
   (iii) the modal;
   cost of production.

(b) The firm is considering launching 10 new products and has estimated that they will all have a production cost of £10. Calculate the likely effect that this will have on your answers to question (a).

Question 1

Grouped data

Data is often put into convenient groups, called **classes.** Table 3.5 shows the results of marketing research into the ages of people buying a particular firm's products. The quantity purchased by each age group (the frequency) is shown in the second column.

How does a business find the average? It is not possible to find the mode, but it is possible to find the **modal group**. This is the group with the highest frequency, in this case consumers between the ages of 30-39 (25).

To find the mean, take points at the centre of each age group, such as 24.5, which is the central point between the ages of 20 and 29. This is shown in column 3. Multiplying the frequency (f) by the central point (x) allows column 4 to be calculated. The **mean** can be found using the formula:

$$x = \frac{\sum fx}{\sum f} = \frac{3{,}600}{100} = 36$$

where $\sum$ is the sum of all values.

Table 3.5 *Marketing research results showing the ages of people buying a firm's products*

Ages of consumers	Quantity purchased (f)	Centre of interval (x)	fx
0 - 9	3	4.5	13.5
10 - 19	10	14.5	145.0
20 - 29	21	24.5	514.5
30 - 39	25	34.5	862.5
40 - 49	22	44.5	979.0
50 - 59	14	54.5	763.0
60 - 69	5	64.5	322.5
	$\sum f = 100$		$\sum fx = 3{,}600.0$

The figure of 36 is an estimate because it has been assumed that the average age of the 10 people in the age group 10-19 is 14.5. In fact, it could have been more or less. This is true of all age groups.

The **median** can also only be estimated. To find the median a business would need to calculate a cumulative frequency table. The information in Table 3.5 has been used to do this in Table 3.6. Part (a) shows the original table. Part (b) shows how a cumulative frequency table can be calculated. 3 goods were bought by consumers under the age of 9. 10 goods were bought by consumers aged 10-19, so 13 goods in all were bought by consumers under the age of 20. The last point is 100, showing the 100 goods bought altogether by all consumers. It is possible to draw this as a cumulative frequency polygon or **ogive** as in Figure 3.1.

What is the median age of consumers buying the products? If there are 100 goods, the median value can be found by drawing a line at 50 to the cumulative frequency curve. This gives a median of 35.

Table 3.6 *Frequency and cumulative frequency tables*

(a)		(b)	
Ages of consumers	Quantity purchased	Ages of consumers	Cumulative frequency
0 - 9	3	10 or less	3
10 - 19	10	20 or less	13
20 - 29	21	30 or less	34
30 - 39	25	40 or less	59
40 - 49	22	50 or less	81
50 - 59	14	60 or less	95
60 - 69	5	70 or less	100
	= 100		

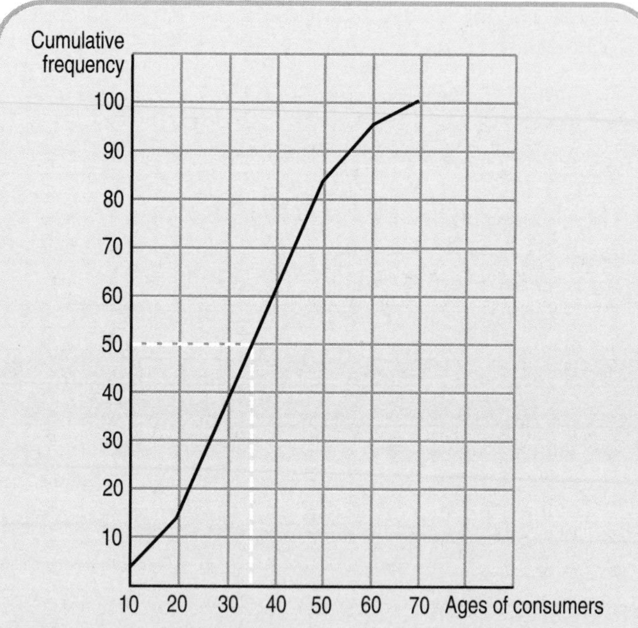

Figure 3.1 *A cumulative frequency polygon showing the ages of consumers purchasing a firm's product.*

Table 3.7 shows the salary ranges of employees in a business.

Table 3.7

Salary range (£)	Number of employees
8,001 - 9,000	6
9,001 - 10,000	15
10,001 - 11,000	40
11,001 - 12,000	25
12,001 - 13,000	10
13,001 - 14,000	4
	100

(a) What is the modal salary group?
(b) Estimate the mean salary. Use approximate mid class values of 8,500, 9,500 etc.
(c) Estimate the median by drawing a cumulative frequency graph on graph paper.

Dispersion

The previous section explained how a business can calculate an average. The business may also be interested in how wide the data are spread - the DISPERSION. It may be that information is widely spread or there is a narrow dispersion. If the data are widely spread, the average is likely to be distant from the rest of the data. If, however, there is a narrow spread, the average will be close to the rest of the data and more typical.

Table 3.8 *Monthly production figures*

Units

Month	Jan	Feb	Mar	Apr	May	Jun	Jul	Aug	Sep	Oct	Nov	Dec
Sales	40	46	52	54	54	52	58	56	54	56	42	36

Table 3.8 shows the monthly output figures for a production plant. In order, the figures will be:

36 40 42 46 52 52 54 54 54 56 56 58

It is possible to calculate the spread in a number of ways.

Range The RANGE is the most simple method. It is the difference between the highest and lowest value. In Table 3.8 this would be 58 - 36 = 22. The main problem with the range is that it can be distorted by extreme values. Just one rogue figure can vastly increase the value of the range out of all proportion to its size.

Interquartile range The INTERQUARTILE RANGE considers the range within the central 50 per cent of a set of data. It therefore ignores the bottom and top 25 per cent (quarter). This gives it the advantage of being far less prone to distortion by extreme values than the range.

In order to calculate the interquartile range it is necessary to arrange data with the lowest item first and the highest item last. The first quartile, which is a quarter of the way along, must then be found, followed by the third quartile, which is three-quarters of the way along. The difference between the first and the third quartiles provides the interquartile range.

Using the data in Table 3.8 it is possible to calculate the first quartile using the formula:

$$\text{First quartile (Q1)} = \frac{n}{4}$$

where n equals the number of values. The first quartile shows the value below which 25 per cent of all figures fall.

So:

$$\text{Q1} = \frac{12}{4} = 3$$

The third quartile can be calculated using the formula:

$$\text{Third quartile (Q3)} = \frac{3(n)}{4} = \frac{3 \times 12}{4} = \frac{36}{4} = 9$$

In the data the third item is 42 and the ninth is 54. So the interquartile range is 54 - 42=12. The interquartile range for these production figures is therefore narrower than the range. When dealing with large amounts of data **deciles** or **percentiles** may have to be used as they give more exact figures. Deciles are the 10, 20 etc. per cent values. In the production figures, the 50th per cent of the values will be 50 per cent of 12 (6), or the sixth value of 52 units of production.

Mean deviation The range and the interquartile range only take into account the spread between two figures in a set of data. However, there are many figures and each will **deviate** from the mean. In business this could be for reasons such as:

- the results from market surveys varying between regions;
- sales varying on a monthly or weekly basis;
- the output from a machine varying in quality as parts begin to wear out;
- the quality of products received from different suppliers varying according to the specifications they have used.

In Table 3.8 the arithmetic mean of the production figure is:

$$\frac{600}{12} = \frac{\text{(total production over the period)}}{\text{(the number of months)}} = 50 \text{ units}$$

The deviation of each production total from the mean is shown in Table 3.9.

Table 3.9

units

Months	Production (x)	Deviation $(x-\bar{x})$
Jan	40	-10
Feb	46	- 4
Mar	52	+2
Apr	54	+4
May	54	+4
Jun	52	+2
Jul	58	+8
Aug	56	+6
Sep	54	+4
Oct	56	+6
Nov	42	- 8
Dec	36	-14
	$\Sigma(x) = 600$	$\Sigma(x-\bar{x}) = 72$ (ignoring signs)

The MEAN DEVIATION provides one figure, by averaging the differences of all values from the mean. It is usual to ignore the plus and minus signs and use the formula:

$$\text{Mean deviation} = \frac{\Sigma(x-\bar{x})}{n}$$

where Σ = the total of all values
$(x-\bar{x})$ = the difference between the mean and the value ignoring the sign
n = the number of values.

The mean deviation for the monthly production figures in Table 3.9 would be:

$$\frac{72}{12} = 6$$

This is the average deviation of all values from the mean. The larger the mean deviation, the wider the spread or dispersion. As a method of calculating dispersion, mean deviation has problems, notably the removal of the plus and minus signs. The next section shows two other measures of dispersion, the **variance** and the **standard deviation**, which attempt to deal with this.

Table 3.10 shows the petrol consumption per annum for area sales representatives working for Quantex plc, a producer of office equipment.

Table 3.10 *Monthly figures*

Gallons per annum

Region	North West	North East	South West	South East	West Midlands	East Midlands	Wales	Scotland
Number of gallons used	1,200	1,360	1,140	1,000	1,150	1,300	1,250	2,000

(a) Calculate the mean deviation from the figures.
(b) Calculate the;
(i) range;
(ii) interquartile range;
from the figures.
(c) Which of your answers to (b) do you think is of more use to the business?

The variance and the standard deviation

Both the range and the interquartile range are basic measures of dispersion. They only take into account the spread between two figures in a set of data. The mean deviation is also of limited use because of cancelling out of positive and negative deviations. A more sophisticated measure of dispersion is needed if businesses are going to be able to gain accurate and useful conclusions from a set of raw data.

By using the VARIANCE a business can look at the average of the spread of all data from the mean. Table 3.11 shows the figures for production from Table 3.9. To remove the plus and minus figures the deviations have to be squared, rather than ignoring the signs as in the mean deviation calculation. This is shown in the fourth column of Table 3.11.

Table 3.11

Months	Production figures	Deviations from mean $(x-\bar{x})$	Deviations squared $(x-\bar{x})^2$
Jan	40	-10	100
Feb	46	- 4	16
Mar	52	+2	4
Apr	54	+4	16
May	54	+4	16
Jun	52	+2	4
Jul	58	+8	64
Aug	56	+6	36
Sep	54	+4	16
Oct	56	+6	36
Nov	42	- 8	64
Dec	36	-14	196
			$\Sigma (x-\bar{x})^2 = 568$

The variance can be calculated by:

$$\frac{\Sigma (x-\bar{x})^2}{n} = \frac{568}{12} = 47.333$$

The original figures were expressed in units of production, but the variance figures are expressed in units 'squared'. To return to the original units it is necessary to find the **square root** of the variance. This is known as the STANDARD DEVIATION, ie:

$$\sqrt{\frac{\Sigma (x-\bar{x})^2}{n}} = \sqrt{47.333} = 6.88$$

Using the variance and the standard deviation

It is possible to use the variance and standard deviation with far more detailed data. Say that a local council is interested in the age profile of its employees because it is considering the introduction of an early retirement policy, and it wants to calculate the likely costs of such a policy over the next few years. Table 3.12 shows how it might use the mean and the standard deviation.

- As group data are shown in the table, the total frequency is found by multiplying the mid-point of each age class (column 2) by the frequency (column 3) and then adding these values (bottom of column 4). The mean age is then found by:

$$\frac{\Sigma f(x)}{\Sigma f} = \frac{8,365}{230} = 36.4 \text{ years}$$

- The variance is found first by calculating how much each mid-point deviates from the mean (column 5). Next each of these values must be squared to cancel out the plus and minus signs (column 6). Finally, the frequency of these squared values can be found by multiplying column 6 by column 3 to give column 7.

- The variance is the sum of column 7 divided by the total frequency so:

$$\frac{\Sigma f(x-\bar{x})^2}{\Sigma f} = \frac{37,673}{230} = 164$$

- The standard deviation is:

$$\sqrt{\frac{\Sigma f(x-\bar{x})^2}{\Sigma f}} = \sqrt{164} = 12.8$$

The standard deviation is a measure of the average deviation from the arithmetic mean of a set of values. It is calculated by using the formula:

$$\text{1 standard deviation equals} \quad \sqrt{\frac{\Sigma f(x-\bar{x})^2}{\Sigma f}}$$

Table 3.12

1 Age class	2 Age class mid-point (x)	3 Frequency (f)	4 Mid-point x frequency (fx)	5 Deviation from mean $(x-\bar{x})^2$ mean = 36.4	6 Deviations squared $(x-\bar{x})^2$	7 Frequency of deviations squared $f(x-\bar{x})^2$
16-20	18	25	450	-18.4	338.6	8,456
21-25	23	29	667	-13.4	179.6	5,208
26-30	28	32	896	-8.4	70.6	2,259
31-35	33	36	1,188	-3.4	11.6	418
36-40	38	27	1,026	1.6	2.6	70
41-45	43	23	989	6.6	43.6	1,003
46-50	48	18	864	11.6	134.6	2,423
51-55	53	17	901	16.6	275.6	4,685
56-60	58	13	754	21.6	466.6	6,066
61-65	63	10	630	26.6	707.6	7,076
		$\Sigma f = 230$	$\Sigma fx = 8,365$			$\Sigma f(x-\bar{x})^2 = 37,673$

Unlike the interquartile range it takes into account all items in a set of data. It is thus much less likely to be distorted by a 'rogue' piece of data within a range. In the example above of the local council, the data had a mean of 36.4 years with a standard deviation of 12.8 years. This would tell the organisation information about both the average age of its employees and the spread of ages.

The standard deviation can be used in a number of ways by a business.

- To establish whether the results of a market research survey are significant and show variations from what was expected (☞ unit 11).
- To find out the quality of batches of products being bought (eg grain being bought by a flour mill) where it would be impossible to check all the batches.
- To check on the standards of output of a production line.
- To identify the likely range of productivity in a workforce where it would be impossible to carry out a work study of all those employed.

Index numbers

When faced with large amounts of data, it may be difficult for firms to see exactly what is happening. Also figures are often for very large amounts and are measured in different values. This makes interpretation and comparison a problem.

One method to help a business analyse and interpret data is the use of INDEX NUMBERS. Table 3.13 shows the production figures and unit costs for a company manufacturing small components. It is not easy to immediately see the changes in production or costs from the data. Changing these figures into index numbers will make them easier to interpret.

The first stage in working out an index is to decide on a BASE YEAR. This is given a value of 100 and acts as the base from which all other figures in the index can be compared. In the example, 2000 is taken as the base year and has a value of 100 in the index. Next, all other figures must be changed into index figures based upon the base year.

Table 3.13 *Production levels and unit costs of a small component manufacturer*

Year	2000	2001	2002	2003	2004	2005
Production levels (units)	25,000	24,350	25,500	26,300	26,950	25,950
Unit Costs (£)	1.23	1.25	1.24	1.27	1.30	1.31

For production levels in 2001, this is:

$$\frac{\text{Number produced in 2001}}{\text{Number produced in 2000}} \times 100 = \frac{24,350}{25,000} \times 100 = 97.4$$

In 2002, it would be:

$$\frac{\text{Number produced in 2002}}{\text{Number produced in 2000}} \times 100 = \frac{25,500}{25,000} \times 100 = 102$$

A similar process would be carried out for the material costs. The results are shown in Table 3.14 and Figure 3.2.

Table 3.14 *Index numbers for production levels and unit costs of a small component manufacturer*

Year	2000	2001	2002	2003	2004	2005
Production levels	100	97.4	102.0	105.2	107.8	103.8
Unit costs	100	101.6	100.8	103.3	105.7	106.5

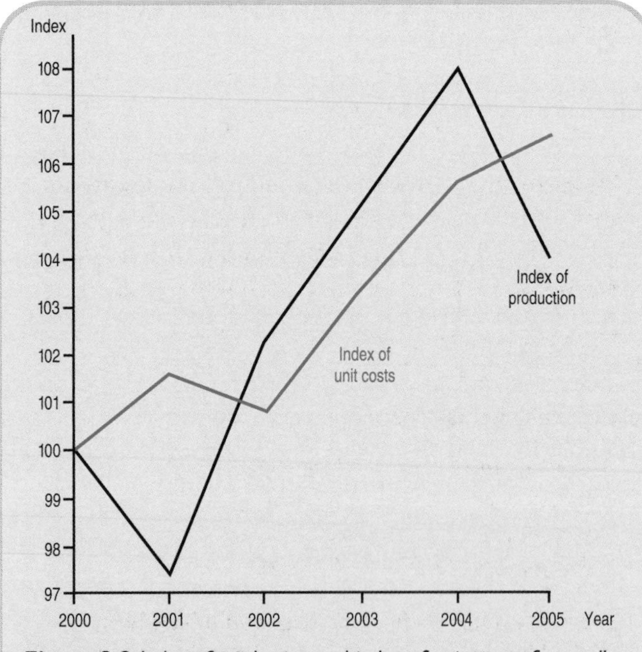

Figure 3.2 *Index of production and index of unit costs of a small component manufacturer*

It is now easier for the business to analyse this data. It could use the results in a number of ways.

- To identify trends and forecasts.
- The percentage increase in production or costs can be calculated. For example, between 2000 and 2005, the index of unit costs rose from 100 to 106.5 or 6.5 per cent.
- To compare figures that are measured in different values. The production levels of the business are measured in units and costs are expressed in money values. It is possible to compare the trends in both on the same graph. This is particularly useful for the business. Between 2004 and 2005, for example, production had started to fall whereas material costs were continuing to rise, although not at as great a rate.
- Presenting the data in a clear and easy way for shareholders or managers.

Problems of index numbers

A business will need to take care when producing its index.

- Updating the base year. From time to time a business will need to change its base year which will affect index figures in the years that follow. After a number of years the firm will no longer be interested in comparing this year's figures with those of, say, 10 years ago (the base year). It will want to compare this year's figures with a more recent base year. So for example, in Table 3.13 if the base year was 2003 instead of 2000, the index of production in 2004 and 2005 would be:

2004 $\frac{26,950}{26,300} \times 100 = 102.5$

A manufacturing company in the South East employs 100 workers. It has become concerned at the level of pay increases over recent years. Table 3.15 shows the average level of wages for some groups in the business.

Table 3.15

£

	2000	2001	2002	2003
Managers	25,000	30,000	32,000	35,000
Administration	10,000	10,500	11,000	12,000
Production	12,000	15,000	16,800	18,000

(a) Using 2000 as a base year, calculate the index for each category.
(b) If 5 per cent of workers are employed as managers, 25 per cent in administration, 55 per cent in production (the other 5 per cent being cleaners etc.), calculate the total cost in 2003 of each category.
(c) How could the business use the index in future pay bargaining?

and 2005 $\frac{25,950}{26,300} \times 100 = 98.7$

- Choice of base year. A firm must be careful to choose a base year which is representative. If a year is chosen where costs, prices or output are high, then index figures in later years will be lower than if a more appropriate year was picked. A base year where figures were low will inflate index numbers in following years.
- Nothing has been said so far about the importance of different items that make up an index. A firm's unit costs would be made up of many different items. This is dealt with in the next section.

A weighted index

A more accurate index would take into account that changes in some items are more important than others. The costs of a business may be made up of labour, capital, electricity, etc. The firm might be able to construct an index showing how costs change over a period. However, if it spends more on, say, machinery than labour, then the figures for spending on capital must be WEIGHTED.

Table 3.16 shows a business which spends different amounts on various costs of production over a period. Using year X as the base year, the index of the total cost is calculated by:

$$\frac{\text{Year Y index}}{\text{n items}} = \frac{424}{4} = 106 \text{ or } 6 \text{ per cent}$$

where n = total amount.

Table 3.16

£ per annum

	Year X	Year Y	Year X index	Year Y index ([Costs in year X ÷ costs in year Y] x 100)
Wage costs	100,000	103,000	100	103
Rent/rates	50,000	55,000	100	110
Materials	250,000	260,000	100	104
Production costs	100,000	107,000	100	107
Total costs	500,000	525,000	400 ÷ 4 =100	424 ÷ 4 =106

This says nothing, however, about the weightings of the different costs. Looking at Table 3.16, it is possible to work out the proportion of spending on each item in year X.

Total wage cost = 20 per cent (100,000 ÷ 500,000) x 100
Rent/Rates = 10 per cent
Materials = 50 per cent
Production costs = 20 per cent

A business can now calculate a weighted index using these figures. This is shown in Table 3.17. The index in year Y is multiplied by the weighting, so the weighted index of, say, total wage costs is 103 x 20 per cent = 20.6

Table 3.17

	Weighting	Year Y index	Weighted Year Y index (weighting x Year Y index)
Total wage costs	20%	103	20.6
Rates/rents	10%	110	11.0
Materials	50%	104	52.0
Production costs	20%	107	21.4
			105.0

The weighted index is now 105. When the percentage spent on each item is taken into account the increase in prices is 5 per cent rather than 6 per cent, as shown in Table 3.16.

A weighted index over time

The example so far has only dealt with an index over two years. Table 3.18 shows calculations for another 2 years based on changes in the index numbers. The proportion spent on each item is assumed to remain the same. This is known as the **base year** or **Laspeyre** method of calculation.

It is also possible to recalculate the index each year based on the weightings in the current year. This is known as the **Paasche** method and can be useful if weightings change frequently. In Table 3.18 the weighting in year A (the most recent year) may have been:

Table 3.18

	Year X Index	Year Y Index	Year Z Index	Year A Index
Total wage costs	100	103x20% = 20.6	105x20% = 21	106x20% = 21.2
Rent/rates	100	110x10% = 11	110x10% = 11	108x10% = 10.8
Materials	100	104x50% = 52	106x50% = 53	110x50% = 55
Production costs	100	107x20% = 21.4	110x20% = 22	115x20% = 23
Weighted index	100	105.0	107.0	110.0

Total wage cost = 15 per cent
Rents/rates = 10 per cent
Materials = 45 per cent
Production costs = 30 per cent

The index numbers for each year would have been multiplied by current percentages and not the weightings for the base year. So in year A the weighted index using the Paasche method would be:

Total wage cost	106	x	15%	=	15.9
Rents/rates	108	x	10%	=	10.8
Materials	110	x	45%	=	49.5
Production costs	115	x	30%	=	34.5
					110.7

Businesses can use weighted indexes in a number of ways, especially where there is a number of items which they wish to include in an index. For example, a business which sells five products and wishes to construct a single index to show its changes in sales over the last ten years may consider using one. Products with high sales levels could be given a higher weighting than those with low sales levels. In this way, a weighted index would more accurately reflect overall changes in sales.

A well known index in the UK is the Retail Price Index (RPI). This measures the rate of inflation by finding out how the average household spends its money and monitoring any falls or rises in the prices of those goods and services. The RPI is an example of a **weighted index** as it gives greater importance to some items than to others. For example, a rise in the price of petrol might be given a higher weighting than a rise in the price of soap. A change in the price of a product with a high weighting will consequently have a relatively greater impact upon the index than a similar change in the price of a product with a low weighting.

In 2004 the government announced that inflation would now be measured by the Consumer Price Index (CPI). This is calculated using a similar method to the RPI, but with different features.

key terms

Base year - a period, such as a year, a month or a quarter, which other figures are compared to, It is given a value of 100 in the index.

Central tendency - a measure of the most likely or common result from a set of data (the average).

Dispersion - a measure of the spread of data.

Index number - an indicator of a change in a series of figures where one figure is given a value of 100 and others are adjusted in proportion to it. It is often used as an average of a number of figures.

Interquartile range - the range between the central 50 per cent of a set of data.

Mean - the value in a set of data around which all other values cluster; commonly used in business as the average of a set of data.

Mean deviation - the average deviation of all figures from the mean, which ignores plus and minus signs in its calculation.

Median - the value which occurs in the middle of a set of data when the data is placed in rank order.

Mode - the most commonly occurring item in a set of data.

Range - the difference between the highest and the lowest values in a set of data.

Standard deviation - the average deviation from the arithmetic mean of a set of data (accounting for plus and minus signs in the calculation) found by the square root of the variance.

Variance - the average deviation of all figures from the mean, which removes plus and minus signs by 'squaring' the deviation figures.

Weighting - a process which adjusts an index number to take into account the relative importance of a variable.

Knowledge

1. Why might businesses need to analyse data?
2. What are the differences between the mean, median and mode as measures of central tendency?
3. How is the mean of grouped data calculated?
4. List 5 measures of dispersion that might be used in analysing data.
5. Explain 2 possible uses in business of the standard deviation.
6. Why might a business use index numbers rather than actual figures?
7. State 3 uses that a business might have for index numbers.
8. Why might weighted index numbers be more useful than a simple index?
9. Explain the difference between the Laspeyre and Paasche methods of calculating a weighted index.

Case study EcoFibre Ltd

EcoFibre Ltd is a manufacturer of cereal products. Four years ago it launched a range of cereal bars after research indicated a growing trend towards more healthy 'snack eating' amongst its potential customers. One of its products, Nutrafibre, is a low sugar grain bar. The product was well received in tests. But it has not been selling as well as the business would like. So EcoFibre has developed a marketing campaign to inform customers of the possible benefits of reduced sugar intake.

Table 3.19 *Market research results*

Quantity of Nutrafibre purchased in a year	Before the campaign	After the campaign
1-10	16	36
11-20	44	44
21-30	84	112
31-40	142	162
41-50	204	182
51-60	160	184
61-70	138	136
71-80	114	92
81-90	62	30
91-100	36	22
	1,000	1,000

Table 3.19 shows the results of a market research survey of 1,000 customers into the amount of this product they would buy in a period of time, before and after the promotion campaign.

The business will now analyse the information. It is particularly interested in the average or mean quantity purchased per year and the standard deviation before and after the campaign.

The business is also concerned generally about customer spending on the range of cereal bars. It has collected the information in Table 3.20. It aims to calculate a weighted index of expenditure to examine how overall spending on the range has changed. It will use the Year 1 as the base year.

Table 3.20 *Expenditure on products in the cereal bar range*

£000

Product	Year 1	Year 2	Year 3	Year 4
A	30	45	45	60
B	10	22	24	22
C	60	60	45	42
D	10	12	14	16
E	50	55	50	40
F	40	48	50	44
	200			

(a) What is meant by:

(i) the mean quantity purchased; (2 marks)

(ii) the standard deviation; (2 marks)

(iii) a weighted index of expenditure? (2 marks)

(b) Using the information in Table 3.19, calculate:

(i) the modal group before and after the promotion campaign; (2 marks)

(ii) the mean quantity of Nutrafibre purchased before and after the promotion campaign (use the central points as 5, 15, 25, 35, etc.) (8 marks)

(c) (i) Calculate the standard deviation of Nutrafibre purchased before and after the promotion campaign. (8 marks)

(ii) Using your calculation of the mean and standard deviation values, evaluate the success of the promotion campaign. (8 marks)

(d) (i) Calculate a weighted index of expenditure for years 1-4 using the information in Table 3.20. (8 marks).

(ii) Using your calculations discuss whether the business has cause for concern. (10 marks)

4 Business Expansion

Expanding the business

Many businesses start up each year in the UK and many fail. Table 4.1 shows that in 2002, 175,800 businesses started up based on VAT registrations. Those that do survive will expect to grow, expand production and increase sales and profits.

Table 4.1 *Business start-ups and failures (based on VAT registrations and de-registrations), UK*

	Registrations	De-registrations
1997	187,700	151,900
1998	187,500	153,500
1999	181,400	160,400
2000	184,000	165,500
2001	174,600	167,200
2002	175,800	176,000

Source: adapted from Small Business Service.

Growth can take place by producing and selling larger numbers of existing products or services, launching new products or services or by finding new markets. For example, a taxi firm setting up in a town area may gain more customers and increase sales as a result of its prompt timekeeping and helpful drivers. It may then decide to offer a limousine service, to drive people to theatre shows or functions, which charges a higher price and raises more revenue.

Growth can also take place when businesses join together. A business may decide to buy another. The turnover of the combined businesses will be higher. For example, in December 2000 GlaxoSmithKline plc was created from the merger of two London based pharmaceutical companies, Glaxo Wellcome and SmithKline Beecham. In 2001 the combined company had a turnover of 33.4 billion euros.

Some businesses grow by franchising their operations or licensing. For example, a large car manufacturer might give businesses the franchise to sell its products or a multinational manufacturer of drinks may give a foreign business a licence to use the company name abroad for a fee.

As a business grows it is likely to face issues and challenges that may not exist in a smaller organisation. Even if they do, they are likely to be less complex and relatively less important.

Raising finance

Different methods of finance are available for a business that is starting up. Some of these methods will also be suited to a business seeking to expand. The method that a business chooses is likely to depend on how much is required, the position of the business and the use of the funds.

Private funds Small business entrepreneurs may be willing to put their savings into a business to expand. Unless they have built up a large amount of savings, have had a windfall gain or have been given a large sum of money, this is only likely to provide limited funds. There are some examples, such as multi millionaires ploughing large amounts of their own money into football clubs in order to finance transfers which they hope will bring success and benefit the club in future.

Partners'/shareholders' funds The owner of a small business may decide to bring in a partner to finance expansion. However, the partner is likely to want some control of the business and some reward for the investment. Private limited companies can raise funds by selling shares to existing or new shareholders. They also have the option of 'going public' and becoming a public limited company (plc). The shares of plcs may be traded 'second hand' on stock exchanges, such as the London Stock Exchange. The Alternative Investment Market (AIM) and OFEX were set up in the 1990s to give smaller, young growing companies the opportunity to raise capital by selling their shares. All of these methods reduce the control and ownership of existing shareholders.

Bank loans A business can apply to a bank for a loan, for example to buy more equipment or new technology. The bank may want some **collateral** against the loan in case of failure to pay. It would also consider the current position of the business, perhaps by examining its accounts. The business may also need to write a business plan to explain its strategy to the bank.

Asset leasing and hire purchase These provide useful sources of finance for the funding of new investment when a business lacks sufficient funds, for example to purchase new technology.

Venture capital/business angels These are organisations or individuals that are prepared to invest in growing businesses, hoping to see rewards in future. They often provide funds for businesses that are considered too risky by other investors. The problem is that they often take a certain share in the business as reward for their investment.

Government and EU funds Examples of funds available for expansion include Regional Selective Assistance for projects that would create or safeguard jobs in EU countries or loans from the European Investment Bank for capital projects (☞ unit 28).

Merger capital A merger or joint venture with another business may provide capital for growth. For example, one company may have a potentially profitable area into which it can expand, but not have the liquid funds to do so. Another business may have stockpiled money over a period. A merger or joint venture would give the combined business the funds to take advantage of the opportunity for growth.

Retained profit As a business grows, it would hope eventually to make a profit. It will be able to use retained profit to fund further expansion. The amount of money available for expansion will depend on the amount of profit from previous years. Large plcs often have huge retained profits in any year.

The **cash flow** of a business is affected by growth. A growing business is likely to have increased production and sales, which it hopes will lead to greater profits. However, often the business will have to pay out for raw materials, wages and perhaps machinery before it produces and sells its products. This can lead to cash flow problems if the business does not have enough money to pay for its inputs. Possible solutions to a lack of cash might be delaying payments or taking out a short term loan, although these are likely to be temporary measures. Improving credit control might be a better option. A situation where a business has grown so rapidly that it has put a strain on its financial resources is known as **overtrading**.

Jayney de Nordwall started life as a producer of television commercials. But she left to make her own films. Her plan was to make three short films and build up relationships with film makers. Initially, everything went smoothly. She found out about Techinvest, an organisation that would put her in touch with business angels to raise the finance needed. Her first two films were a success. 'Jump' starred Cold Feet's John Thompson and 'About a Girl' was entered for the Sundance Film Festival. She then moved on to feature films. But her first film had to be scrapped after seven months of work when a similar film appeared. She is now looking to produce a new film, but realises that bills still need to be paid so she does a lot of freelancing. Alice Morrison, chief executive of North West Vision which offers grants and loans to budding directors and producers says 'It's important to keep your day job'.

North Star productions was set up by Neil Fitzmaurice, co-writer of Phoenix Nights, and his brother Tony. Their first film was low budget, with money raised from family and friends. Their second film will cost around £1.7 million, but this time the company is trying to attract 17 private investors.

Red Productions in Manchester creates drama for television, including 'Clocking Off' on BBC and 'The Second Coming ' drama on ITV. A ten series project can cost around £3 million. But one issue is payment. Different broadcasters pay in different ways. Channel 4, for example, pays in tranches, with some upfront for development. ITV pays on delivery.

Source: adapted from *en*, December, January 2004.

(a) Identify the sources of finance used by the businesses in the article to fund expansion.
(b) Explain why these sources of finance may have been chosen.
(c) Suggest why the businesses might experience cash flow difficulties.

Question 1

Accounting

Keeping records As a business expands, the records it keeps become larger and more complicated. A supplier of pine furniture may increase its sales from 20 to 100 retailers over a period of time. The amount of materials it buys from suppliers will also increase. Records of these transactions must be kept. Invoices must be sent out with the products sold. The business may decide that it needs to buy or improve its computers or computer software in order to keep efficient records of these transactions.

Keeping accounts The accounts of a small business may be fairly straightforward. Sole traders can produce their own accounts and provide information to the Inland Revenue on a self assessment form. As a business grows it may employ an accounting firm to produce its accounts to comply with legal requirements. The annual accounts of sole traders and limited companies have slightly different categories, although all transactions are recorded. Very large companies employ their own accountants, not only to produce the accounts, but to provide help and guidance to the company when making decisions.

Payments As the number of customers increases, so do problems in getting payments from them. Credit control becomes more complex the larger a business becomes. Computer software may be used to maintain lists of age debtors, people who have been owing money for certain periods. Credit controllers may be employed by the business. Alternatively, a factor may be employed to chase outstanding debt.

Changing legal status

As a business grows it is possible that it will change its legal organisation.

A **sole trader** wishing to expand by bringing in others who will invest and help to run the business may be forced to change to a **partnership**. Partners may want some say in the business. Partnership legislation or a partnership deed of agreement will set out the responsibilities and the rewards to each partner.

Some people willing to put money into a business would not be prepared to accept the unlimited liability of certain types of partnership. This is because they would be personally responsible for the debts of the business. Changing to a limited company would give them the security of limited liability.

Setting up a **private limited company** has certain implications for a business. For example, the owners of the business, the shareholders, must sign a Memorandum of Association and Articles of Association. These provide details about the company, such as its name, objectives and capital, as well as the rights of shareholders and the role of directors.

A private limited company may decide to become a **public limited company.** This also has implications for the business. The company name must change, from Ltd to plc. Shares in a public limited company are available to outside investors and traded second hand on stock exchanges. This means that plcs have larger numbers of investors and can raise large amounts of finance. Controlling a plc may require owners to buy larger numbers of shares. Investors are willing to buy shares hoping to receive a dividend or to sell them for a higher price than they paid and make a profit.

Planning

Planning is vital to all businesses, no matter what size. Even a small retailer must plan what to buy, what to sell, how large the business will be in the next few years and when to employ more staff. The larger a business, however, the more complicated planning becomes. Larger businesses have more resources. They have more sales, more stocks, more employees etc. This makes accurate marketing, human resource and production plans essential.

- Without careful and co-ordinated planning, individual departments may make decisions which conflict with each other. Poor communication can raise the costs of the business. This is an example of a **diseconomy of scale.**
- Inaccurate forecasts and predictions will lead to greater problems in larger businesses and could increase costs.
- Without planning, the most efficient method of working may not be used. For example, too many workers may be working on a project or workers without suitable skills may be doing a job.
- The plans must be appropriate. Sometimes managers are accused of **short-termism.** This is where they set plans which they know can be achieved in the short term. Setting short term, achievable plans allows managers to achieve the results required by shareholders or lenders of money. However, taking a short term view is not always

The Carphone Warehouse is a well known success story. It provides a one stop shop for mobile phones and accessories. It was started in 1989 by Charles Dunstone with just £6,000. By 2002 it had 470 stores in the UK and 647 in the rest of Europe, and had appeared in fast track 100 league tables as one of the UK's fastest growing companies. The business initially expanded rapidly by targeting smaller customers, including small businesses and private individuals, when existing mobile phone companies were ignoring these groups.

The business was floated in July 2000 on the London Stock Exchange. Shares were sold at 200p and the business raised £185 million, mainly for expansion in Europe. 11,500 people applied to buy shares. By 2003 it had become one of only a handful of dotcom companies to pay dividends on its shares to shareholders. Its founder and major shareholder Mr Dunstone, with over third of shares, would receive just over £3 million in dividends.

The company has been branching out into related telecom product areas. In February 2003 it launched a cheap rate fixed line telephone service called Talk Talk, for example.

Figure 4.1 shows the results of a survey by City lawyers Eversheds into the reasons why businesses float. It shows, for example, that very few (3 per cent) said that they would float to start up a new company.

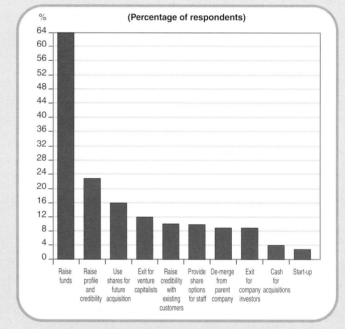

Source: adapted from www.fastrack.co.uk, news.zdnet.co.uk, www.guardian.co.uk.

Figure 4.1 *Reasons for seeking a stock market flotation*

(a) Explain the implications of the flotation of the company on the business.

(b) Discuss whether the flotation was necessary for further growth of the business.

the best strategy. For example, a business might decide that it does not want to invest in machinery that uses new technology now because of the cost. Although this might leads to short term profit, in the long run it could be a disaster if the machine is needed to produce new products. The business might fail because it has not planned for long term changes.

Some companies make use of theories or models to help understand the markets in which they operate (☞ unit 1). A business may even try to develop a corporate culture (☞ unit 5) so that everyone in the organisation works towards the same business goals.

Marketing

An expanding market, increasing output and an increase in sales can have a number of implications for the marketing of a business.

Marketing research A small business such as a window cleaner is likely to know his market. The revenue of the business may be determined by the buildings in the area, how often people want their windows cleaning and the competition faced. A UK retailer selling imported American comics may know most of his customers personally. As businesses get larger it becomes more difficult to keep and find out information about the consumers of the product. The importer of a new comic may know that 100 people will buy it each month. Estimating the sales of a new car is more difficult. This is why large businesses spend great sums on researching the market. They also look for new ways to find out about customers, such as finding out the products bought by holders of loyalty cards in supermarkets. Larger businesses also make use of databases to collect information about the buying patterns of customers.

Distribution As a business and its markets grow, the difficulties of getting the product to consumers increase. The producer of a local newspaper perhaps needs to send its current issue to an area such as Yorkshire or an even smaller local region such as Stafford. A multinational company, such as Coca Cola, has to get its products to customers in many countries around the world. As a business grows the total costs of distribution will increase. The total costs of distributing newspapers nationally will be larger than the costs of circulating a local newspaper. However, the cost for a textile manufacturer transporting 1,000 products to a retailer in a large van instead of a fleet of smaller vans is likely, on average, to be less. This is an example of an economy of scale. Some businesses continue to own and distribute their own products as they grow. Others employ specialist businesses to deliver their products.

Marketing methods A small business may be able to advertise its products by a leaflet or an advert in the local paper. As a business grows it may have to consider other methods of advertising and promotion. Large businesses make use of relatively expensive television and cinema advertisements. They also make use of other forms of promotion such as free products, display material and exhibitions. As a business grows its name itself may become a marketing tactic. Well known company names become a corporate brand. People will buy products and services of the business because of the reputation. In some cases, certain specialist small firms also have a company brand.

Target markets Business that start may sell into local markets or niche markets. One of Richard Branson's earliest business ventures was selling second hand records. As a business expands it may either sell into wider markets or produce other products to sell. It is then said to have a product portfolio. Large businesses have many different products selling into a variety of markets.

Production

As a business grows, this is likely to affect the way in which it produces goods or provides services.

Changing production methods As a company grows so might its production methods. A small company making hand made furniture may employ a worker to produce the goods from start to finish. This is likely to be time consuming and costly for a business expecting to produce 1,000 kitchen units a day. It may therefore be necessary to buy new machinery, retrain employees and change methods of production as a business grows. Many large companies use large scale machinery and assembly lines to mass produce products. This large scale production of similar products reduces the average costs of each product. Some large businesses are recognising the benefits of combining the advantages of large scale output with producing a product from start to finish. They are organising production into teamwork, known as cell production.

Relocation and land As a business grows it may become 'too big' for its premises. It then has a decision to make. Should it expand in its current location or should it relocate? This decision is likely to be based on a number of factors, including available land and employees, the need for related businesses, the market and government and EU aid (☞ unit 28).

Reorganisation As output increases and production methods change, it may be necessary to reorganise production. For example, some businesses have found that time can be saved and efficiency improved if related operations are carried out in a cell, with machines near to each other.

Purchasing A larger business will tend to order more supplies than a smaller business. This will increase total costs, although buying in bulk may be able to reduce the average costs. It is vital for all orders to be on time, but perhaps even more so for a larger business. Large amounts of supply will require storage space, as will stocks of finished goods for distribution. Some businesses have reduced this cost by asking for supplies just before production begins.

Human resources

Business growth can have a major impact on human resource management.

Reorganisation The organisation of the business may need to change as it grows. A sole trader making candle holders may be the manager of the business, might make the products and may even deliver them to the retailer. As a business grows the owners may delegate some work to other employees and give them responsibilities. The larger the business grows, the greater may be the need to delegate. A limited company will have a hierarchy. The overall responsibility for company-wide policy will be taken by the directors. Departmental managers may be responsible for employees in their area. Some large business have recognised the problems caused by too many layers in the hierarchy, such as poor communication or task duplication. This has led to delayering (☞ unit 30), for example removing one layer of managers. Businesses that grow by means of a merger sometimes find that jobs are duplicated. This may lead to reduction in the workforce or redundancies in certain types of jobs and expansion in other areas.

Recruitment As a business grows it will need to recruit more workers. It must make sure that the workers it recruits have the appropriate skills required. It may employ staff from outside the business or from within.

Industrial relations A larger business may find that more conflicts of interest develop between different stake holders. Workers in smaller businesses may feel that they and the owners all have the same interests. In large organisations disagreements can take place over many things. Workers may push for higher wages just at the time that the company needs to control costs. Workers may feel aggrieved at large dividends paid to shareholders. Individual workers may disagree with the decisions of managers.

Motivation It has been suggested that one problem with larger businesses is the motivation of workers. Some workers feel isolated in large operations. They may feel that they are just a 'cog in the machine' and their work is not valued. Workers on assembly lines have often complained of monotonous and boring operations. Businesses use a variety of motivational techniques to deal with this problem. These range from:

- financial incentives such as bonuses;
- reorganising work so that the employee does not carry out the same task all the time;
- other non financial incentives, such as company health schemes or company cars;
- ideas to develop company loyalty, such as group activities.

New Heights is a furniture retailer in London. The business started in 1999 with £740,000 from family and friends and in 2001 it had a turnover of £5.5 million. It offers an alternative to the humdrum world of flatpack and veneer. The business idea is that people will pay more for well crafted solid wood furniture. Wood such as cherry and maple is imported form suppliers in the USA, where supplies are abundant and the price is right.

The first store was set up in Cricklewood, away from the furniture mecca of central London but on a good high street position and in a good catchment area. This strategy paid off and the business now has five stores in London. Continued growth is the aim, with two new stores planned for Nottingham and West London.

Staff are vital. Each new member receives 2-3 weeks' training in product knowledge and IT. They are trained to be socially confident and not just sit behind a till. The aim is for staff to be multi-tasking and the business argues that this is 80-90 per cent complete.

New Heights has loftier ambitions for the future. Chief executive Gareth Williams argues 'We are totally driven by the idea of building a natural furniture brand.' The company has its eye on taking this wider part of the furnishings market, although this aim is limited by its cash flow as the founders are loathe to give anything away to new investors.

Source: adapted from *Growing Business*, September 2002.

(a) Examine the effects on:
(i) marketing;
(ii) production;
(iii) human resources;
of the growth plans of New Heights.

Is business growth desirable?

One argument put forward for the growth of businesses is that they can reduce average costs. A small business may buy a computer for £1,200. If it is used by a part time worker for 15 hours a week, the average cost per hour each week is £80. If a larger business makes use of the computer for a full working week of 40 hours, the average cost falls to £40.

There are other benefits of large size. A large business is more likely to obtain sizeable finance than a small firm. A large business may also have a stronger marketing image than a smaller business and be able to buy in bulk.

In some cases a business might decide to reduce the size of its operations. This is known as RETRENCHMENT. There is a number of reasons why a business might do this.

- If a business grows too large it may experience rising average costs or diseconomies of scale. For example, a large factory might find that it has to spend large amounts on pollution control. A smaller factory may not generate as much pollution, and may not have to spend as much.

- The business might decide that a smaller operation might be more efficient and better able to compete with other businesses in the market. For example, a printing business might decide that it is better able to meet the needs of its customers with smaller presses that can be changed quickly than with large presses that require long print runs.
- Companies realise the mistakes they have made in the past. For example, they might have expanded into markets which were not profitable or produced products which did not make a profit.
- Changes in the market may have taken place. For example, many businesses that grew rapidly as a result of the Internet boom found that they later had to operate as smaller organisations as the nature of the market changed.
- Economic and social changes. Recessions in the economy often lead to organisations going out of business. Some attempt to survive by reducing the size of their operations, hoping that demand will increase at a later time.
- Business strategy. Examples might be the sale of unprofitable parts of a business not related to its core activities or a reduction in the number of branches in order to concentrate on increasing sales in those that are retained.

Retrenchment has a number of implications for business. Investment is likely to be put back and objectives could be changed. There may be a high turnover of staff, particularly senior staff. New managers may be needed who are more suited to cost control, for example.

1. How might a business be able to grow?
2. State 5 ways in which a business might obtain funds for expansion.
3. Why might obtaining funds from partners or shareholders be a problem?
4. Why might a investor in a business wish a partnership to become a limited company?
5. Suggest 2 reasons why planning in a larger company is important.
6. Explain 3 effects that the expansion of a business might have on its marketing.
7. Explain 3 effects that the expansion of a business might have on its production.
8. Explain 3 effects that the expansion of a business might have on its human resource planning.
9. Explain 3 reasons why retrenchment might take place.

key terms

Retrenchment - a decision by a business to reduce its size of its operations in an attempt to improve them.

BT is now in better shape than at any time since the telecommunications bubble burst in 2001. Debt has been cut from £30 billion to £9 billion. BT's finances were in a terrible state after it overpaid for third generation mobile licences and over-expanded abroad. One of the consequences of support by investors for the business was that Cellnet, BT's mobile phone arm, was demerged and separately listed on the stock exchange.

The business has increased profits as a result of effective cost cutting. The management system has been streamlined and old bureaucratic methods of working have been done away with. Thousands of jobs have been axed and call centre work has been shifted to low cost countries such as India.

Some City analysts are worried that even a slimmed down, leaner and fitter BT might find it difficult to compete. They suggest its massive fixed line system is in long term decline. But the company argues that 'BT owns the only fixed network' which is a 'cash cow that minimises downsize risk'. The company plans to enter other markets in future. These include the pay-per-view TV market with the launch of a new BT branded digital TV and Internet service.

Source: adapted from *The Observer*, 26.10.2003.

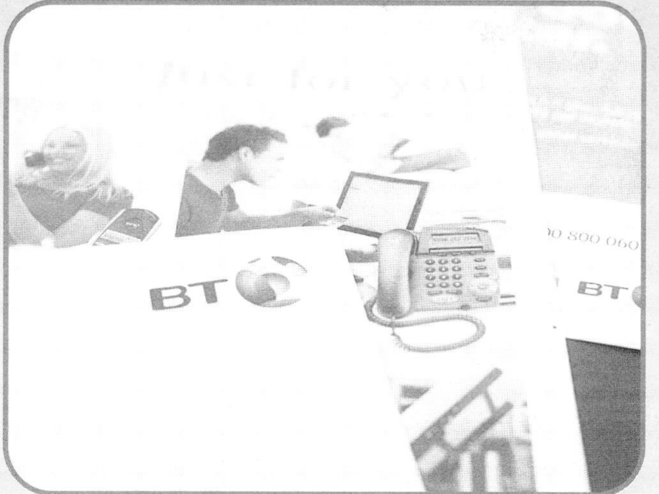

(a) Using examples from the article, explain why the strategy of BT after 2001 might be an example of retrenchment.

(b) To what extent might the 'leaner and fitter BT' be able to compete in new markets?

Case study Kidstuff

Kidstuff is a business run by James and Judith Johnson in the North West, Merseyside and the Wirral. The business provides specialised, originally designed and unusual children's clothing. Fabrics are bought in bulk from wholesalers, the clothes are made up and then sold in local markets in the area. The average price of a stall per day was £15. The business operated 4 out of 7 days a week. James and Judith charged between £7 and £18 for the clothes although the average price was around £12. They felt that they could charge a slightly higher price than other clothing stalls because of the uniqueness of their service. Sometimes customers will suggest their own designs and these can be made up at an extra cost.

The business was set up as a partnership. It was started with the £11,000 that Judith and James received when they were made redundant. They were keen not to borrow from a bank. Judith's mother also put in £5,000 of her own savings. Part time machine operators were employed to make the clothes in their own homes. When they were finished, they would be stored at Judith's and James' house, ready to be taken to markets in the area.

Figure 4.2 shows the change in revenue, profit and costs of the business in the first three years. Costs include the materials, the wages of the operators, the hiring of stalls and some leaflets to advertise the business. The market for their product was likely to be limited in the areas in which the business operated and they decided that they had to expand. They have had a meeting with an independent adviser. A number of alternatives were suggested.

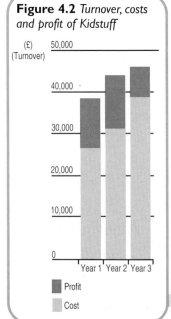

Figure 4.2 *Turnover, costs and profit of Kidstuff*

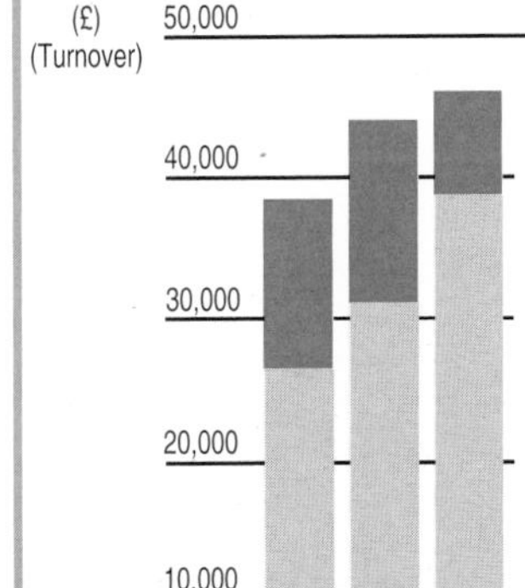

If the method chosen was a success and resulted in expansion, this would have a number of implications for the business.

(a) Describe the main changes in:
(i) turnover;
(ii) costs;
(iii) profit;
of the business in the first three years. (12 marks)

(b) Identify the effects that the changes in sales in the last three years might have had on the business. (10 marks)

(c) Examine the possible effects of each of the five alternative strategies on the business in future. (14 marks)

(d) Discuss the most suitable alternative strategy for the business. (14 marks)

Markets further afield Markets in Salford and North Wales had not been considered initially because of the distance and greater costs. This might involve leaving earlier in the morning and arriving home later. Costs might include vehicle maintenance, petrol, other costs such as staying overnight at a hotel if they worked late. One problem was that the markets would have to take place on days that they did not work already. It would also mean an increase in the number of days a week they worked. James and Judith had considered employing someone from another area to sell their products in these markets.

Other markets Craft fairs, village fairs and other related sales opportunities could be one way of expanding. Again this would mean working extra days, with increased costs, but nor further afield. The size of these markets was likely to be fairly limited and people were not likely to spend a great deal. It was suggested that they would only provide a small increase in turnover.

Changing production The success of the business so far had been based on the uniqueness of the product and the chance to charge a relatively high price. Now that it was successful, the business could perhaps offer more standardised clothing at a slightly cheaper price. It may also offer related products, such as hand made table mats or chair backs. They could be sold at existing markets on the same days they were operating. James and Judith were concerned that the new products would appear the same as those of others and the price reduction would not make them as profitable.

Opening a shop The business had considered opening its own shop. Premises in Formby, an area of relatively high income earners, had recently become available to rent at £6,000 a year. The shop would then give them an established base from which to build up regular clients. They could also use the shop to store stock. The shop could be opened 6 days a week, or even 7 perhaps, by employing a part time sales assistant.

Remain the same size The business could operate exactly as it is at present, without any major changes in markets, production or premises.

5 Corporate Culture

What is corporate culture?

Corporate or organisation culture is a set of values and beliefs that are shared by people and groups in an organisation. A simple way of explaining corporate culture might be to say that it is the 'way that things are done in a business', eg the McDonald's way. For example, at Microsoft, the computer company staff work long hours, dress casually and communicate by e-mail. These are the **norms** of behaviour.

The corporate culture of a business will often be reflected in its **mission statement**. So, for example, if the mission statement of a business includes that it aims to protect the environment, then parts of its culture could involve recycling where possible, using renewable resources and buying the most efficient energy saving equipment. Staff might be expected to be vigilant about turning off lights and reusing paper.

The corporate culture of a business can influence decision making. For example, General Electric in the USA stresses that employees should feel ownership for the company. It also encourages low level managers to behave like entrepreneurs. This means that managers tend to make their own decisions and often take risks. Insurance companies may encourage caution and conservative attitudes in employees as they do not want risky decisions to be made.

Business leaders are able to create a corporate culture as part of the **strategy** of the company (☞ units 6 and 7). Computer companies often encourage employees to perform tasks in a creative way. This is because they believe that it will lead to innovation, which is the source of their **competitive advantage**.

It is important that the corporate culture of a business is understood by all the people that work in the organisation. It is usually transmitted to new members and reinforced informally, by stories, symbols and socialisation, and more formally through training.

The growth of corporate culture

The idea of corporate culture became popular in the 1980s. Tom Peters and Robert Waterman (1982), in their book *In Search of Excellence*, highlighted the potential impact that company values could have on the success of a business. Terrence Deal and Allan Kennedy's (1982) book, *Corporate Cultures*, suggested that the culture of any organisation could be managed to improve the effectiveness of the business. There was a certain amount of evidence to support these ideas.

- The success of Japanese organisations. Japanese businesses appeared able to establish and maintain cooperative, team-based organisational cultures.
- A growing awareness that successful leadership was not only concerned with profits, costs and sales, but also with the ability to motivate and to gain the commitment of employees.
- The belief that there was a relationship between a strong corporate culture and improved business performance. It was suggested that a company's corporate culture could be made stronger by the actions of managers.

Management theorists have therefore stressed the importance of developing a strong corporate culture. To help with this, the idea of a '**culture gap**' has been used. This is the difference between the culture that a company possesses and the kind that senior management would like to have. Businesses can fill this gap by techniques that change the corporate culture.

Developing a strong corporate culture

All organisations have cultures to some extent. However, only a minority have a 'strong' culture that is highly visible and which affects the behaviour of employees and other stakeholders. It has been suggested that firms with a strong culture and little or no 'culture gap' are the ones that are likely to perform effectively. How might a business develop a strong corporate culture? Buchanan and Huczyenski (1991) argued that four areas can be examined.

Core elements of corporate culture The corporate culture of a business is its shared values, beliefs and norms. For a corporate culture to form, a stable collection of people needs to have shared a significant history, involving dealing with problems. This allows a social learning process to take place. Top managers are often viewed as 'culture carriers'. They are the people that set the firm's standards and its values and beliefs. The way that a culture develops is often influenced by the founders of the business. For example, Anita Roddick, the founder of The Body Shop, created a strong corporate culture of fair trade, fair employment practices and ethical standards for products.

Packaging corporate culture The values, beliefs and norms must be effectively 'packaged'. The corporate culture must be embedded into the everyday 'fabric' of the business. It must inform individuals how things are done. Packaging can come in different forms. Each helps to strengthen the company values, beliefs and norms.

- Stories. They are based on original events, but can include a mix of truth and fiction. Stories help to explain current practices. For example, an employee at Procter & Gamble noticed that the labels on a product at his local supermarket were mounted off centre. He bought the whole stock, assuming that P&G would reimburse him, which it did. This story helps to communicate the importance of quality in the business.

- Heroes. These may be living or dead people. Through their deeds and words they represent the culture of the organisation and can be role models for others to follow. They might be company founders, leaders or successful employees. For example, the thoughts of Ray Kroc, who bought the hamburger restaurants from the McDonald brothers, are played to staff who attend the company's training courses.
- Sagas and Legends. These are historical accounts of actual events, which may have become embellished over time. An example is the 3M worker who tried to find a use for rejected sandpaper minerals. He was fired for spending time on this. However, he kept coming back and eventually succeeded. He went on to become vice-president of the company's Roofing Granules Division, which he helped to create.
- Symbols, slogans and mottoes. Examples of symbols include the Coca-Cola, Nike and IBM logos. Slogans such as Caterpillar's 'Forty-eight hours part service anywhere in the world' are well known. The Hard Rock Café's staff motto has been 'Love All, Serve All'.

Communicating corporate culture The corporate culture of the business must be communicated to employees and other stakeholders. Formal and informal methods can be used to do this. Formal methods are highly visible, consciously designed, regular events and activities. They provide opportunities for employees to acquire the company values and beliefs. Examples include:

- rites and occasions - planned, often dramatic, activities that show different aspects of culture. Examples may be the unveiling of a product, the honouring of employees' work and a lecture from an inspirational leader about future company prospects;
- rituals - a sequence of activities which express and reinforce the ideas, values, beliefs and norms of the company. Many American companies arrange regular Friday afternoon 'beer busts' at which employees can get together and relax.
- courses - induction, orientation and training courses which have the values, beliefs and norms of the organisation communicated within them.

Informal cultural transmission refers to the informal way in which culture is passed on. For example, the ways in which employees typically communicate and express themselves represent their company's culture.

Cultural networks The strength of a business's corporate culture depends on the homogeneity (similar beliefs and ideas) of group members. It also depends on the length and intensity of shared experiences by members of cultural networks. Cultural networks are groups of individuals that are socialised into the values, norms and beliefs of the business through working together over time.

Virgin is a brand that is familiar to millions of people. It was founded by Richard Branson and the Virgin Group has operated in many areas including music, holidays and airlines, cola, radio, rail travel and financial services. It is suggested that Branson looks for business opportunities where large organisations have become 'lazy'. He prefers to build his own corporate culture and embody learning and fun into his aggressive plans. Staff of the Virgin Atlantic Airways, for example, reflect the ideals of Branson. It is argued that 'Mr.Branson's presence is felt through the enthusiasm evident in his employees, most of whom seem to be having a better time at their jobs than their counterparts on other airlines.'

Richard Branson's best selling books and his autobiography contain stories of his early business ventures. He began entrepreneurial life growing Christmas trees as a youngster. At 16 Branson started the youth magazine, *Student*. At 21 he set up Virgin Records, signing the Rolling Stones, Peter Gabriel, and Janet Jackson. In 1991 Virgin was sold for close to $1 billion.

New projects are launched with extensive media coverage. The Virgin train's launch party also marked the opening of ticket sales via the Virgin website in February 1999. In November 2003, over 1,000 gold members of Virgin Atlantic's Flying Club attended a party in central London to celebrate the launch of Virgin's Upper Class Suite.

The Management Centre of Europe says 'Virgin is one of many companies that fits the prototype of a business which can benefit from empowerment strategies. Employees work closely with customers, innovation is critical, the environment and processes are changing rapidly, and employees need motivation'. It also argues 'Giving employees more input, personal accountability and responsibility can directly turn into reduced labour costs. Many companies have found enlightened work practices result in less safety problems, less turnover, and better efficiency through improved interdepartmental coordinate. A good example here is the low-fare airline Virgin Express which has a fun and flashy public relations image, but also tries to be equally cutting edge in its approach to employees.'

Source: adapted from www.ltbn.com, www.vnunet.com, www.crash.net, www.mce.be.

(a) Using examples, explain the methods used at Virgin to establish a corporate culture.
(b) Explain how the corporate culture at Virgin might affect:
(i) the business;
(ii) employees;
(iii) customers.

Question 1

Types of corporate culture

Studies have shown that there are different ways of categorising corporate cultures. John Kotter and James Heskett (1992) suggested that there are two types of culture.

Adaptive cultures In businesses with adaptive cultures, managers are able to introduce a culture that allows a business to adapt to changes in its external environment. Such businesses are more likely to survive in a changing environment. Features of businesses with an adaptive culture include:

- a bias for action - employees are encouraged to be entrepreneurial and take risks and managers have a 'hands on' approach;
- the company sticks to 'what it knows best'. It also emphasises close relations with customers;
- the organisation should be lean and decision making should be decentralised.

Inert cultures These are businesses where managers all accept the values and norms of the business, which never change. Such cultures promote inertia. Decision making is often centralised. The problems with such structures is that managers can not see problems if the environment changes.

Another way of describing cultures is to look at the solidarity and sociability in businesses. This was proposed by Gareth Jones and Rob Goffee (1998) in *The Character of a Corporation*. **Sociability** is the relations between individuals who see each other as friends. **Solidarity** describes cooperation between individuals which takes place when the need arises or when there is a shared interest.

Networked organisations These have high sociability and low solidarity. Examples might be Heineken and Phillips. Such a culture encourages teamwork, creativity and openness. Workers enjoy working. However, discipline may be difficult because of friendships and productivity may suffer. There may also be too much concern with compromise, rather than the best solution.

Mercenary organisations These have low sociability and high solidarity. Examples may be PepsiCo and Mars. The culture is about getting things done, now. Targets are set. Roles are clearly defined. People consider: 'What's in it for me' when working. The advantages of this are that a business has a focus. It can respond to threats and does not tolerate poor performance. However, workers only work together if they have to. Also, because roles are clearly defined, there may be conflict over 'grey' areas of work.

Fragmented organisation These have low sociability and low solidarity. Examples might be law firms, consultancies or newspapers. This form of culture is best suited to businesses where individuals do not need to work with each other.

Communal organisations These have high solidarity and high sociability. Examples might be Hewlett Packard and Johnson & Johnson. They are like networked businesses, but more cohesive and goal orientated, and less mercenary than mercenary organisations. They are concerned with shared values and seek to find ways to support and maintain such values. They are careful to recruit, induct and train employees that have similar values to the business. Leaders are important as they guide the business. One problem despite the advantages of shared goals is that they may stifle individual creativity. There is also a need to recruit those who fit in with the culture of the business.

In 2002 BP, the oil giant, had to cut production targets for the third time in a year. Year on year net income had also fallen 13 per cent. It was suggested that at the heart of the problem was BP's corporate culture. The company was accused of entrenched arrogance and of ignoring internal warnings that its goals were unrealisable, and that the businesses had a 'culture of fear'.

Mike Phillips, oil analyst at Datamonitor said 'BP has long been considered the cream of oil stocks, with a decade-long reputation for hitting ambitious growth targets, but a third cut to production targets in eight weeks has injured its reputation'. He suggested that pressure may have been put on business managers at BP and 'some of them seem to have thought it would be a good idea to promise targets that were difficult to achieve'. The company argued that a number of factors had led to it not meeting its production targets, such as project delays and hurricanes in Mexico. It did have contingency plans in place to deal with such occurrences, but did not envisage so many problems. A further criticism was that the company felt that it could 'buck the trend' of declining gas production, whereas others had cut back.

There was a suggestion that targets could be replaced as a measure of performance in future by profitability. This could affect middle managers. They were likely to be the first to feel any wide-ranging shake-up in an attempt to trim costs out of a business that had grown through the acquisitions of Burmah Castrol, Arco and Amoco in the 1990s. There might also be sales of non-core assets, chiefly in Europe.

Source: adapted from *The Observer*, 3.11.2002.

(a) Identify the type of culture (networked, mercenary, fragmented or communal) that might have existed at BP using examples from the article.

(b) Discuss the (i) benefits and (ii) problems to the

Resistance to change

At times senior management may decide that the corporate culture of a business is not appropriate for the new corporate strategies (☞ units 6 and 7) that it is trying to introduce. One indication of this might be a CULTURE GAP - a difference between the current culture and the culture that managers want.

To what extent can a business change its culture? Some argue that if the culture of a business can be sustained by the strength of management, company stories and socialisation, it should be possible for these to be changed. A new culture can then be introduced. On the other hand, the longer a culture is allowed to develop, the stronger it will become. Beliefs and practices become more widely shared and deeply held. This makes them harder to change. A corporate culture learned over many years can not be altered overnight.

There might be certain **constraints** on a business's ability to change corporate culture.

- Structural and technological issues. A company's culture is affected by factors such as businesses procedures, the way buildings and plant are organised, the type of technology used, and the responsibilities of employees in the organisational hierarchy. It may be possible to change these over time. In the short term, changing technology, for example, may be difficult and costly.
- Cultural change brought about by managers is often resisted by employees. There is often a limit to the amount of change to values and norms that they will accept. Mergers are a particularly difficult time for staff. Familiar symbols, beliefs, values and shared meanings are often disrupted.
- Managers may be an obstacle to change. They may have an interest in keeping things the same. A change in corporate culture may threaten these interests.
- The effects of external factors. The operation of pressure groups or competitors may constrain how a business can change its culture. For example, it might be difficult for the police force to develop a culture which promotes norms of casual dress, rewards risk takers and encourages radical ideas, such as the legalisation of soft drugs.
- Corporate culture and national cultures. Attempts to establish a corporate culture in a multinational firm can be undermined by the strength of national cultures. Geert Hofstede (1984) examined the attitudes of 116,000 employees in the same multinational company located in 40 different countries. He found, for example, that in countries such as Argentina and Spain, inequality was accepted. Managers were expected to make decisions. There was a lack of trust between superiors and subordinates.Workers wanted to be directed by the boss. In Australia and Canada, however, the relationships between individuals at different levels in the organisation were close and there was mutual trust. Employees expected to be involved in decision making.

Corus was created from the merger of British Steel and Dutch business Koninkliike Hoogvens in 1999.After the merger it became the fourth biggest steel company in the world, with market value of £4.1 billion. In 2003 it was worth only 3 per cent of that.The problem was the differences in the two companies, particularly the way that business was done in the Netherlands and in the UK. Under Dutch law, large companies are required to have works councils and supervisory boards. Supervisory boards are independent and oversee the activities of management boards.These are made up of executives who are forbidden to be employees or hold stocks.The un-elected nature of the supervisory board may seem strange to UK businesses. UK management is largely ignorant about the strength of works councils and supervisory boards which can make or break mergers and deals.

The Netherlands also works on consensus.There is continuous consultation and cooperation between government, employers associations and trade unions. It was suggested that it was naive to think that this would sit easily with the UK style of 'Anglo Saxon' decision making from management at the top.A criticism of Corus by UK trade unions was that decisions were not put forward to a supervisory board, as they are in Holland. Instead they were just announced by management. However, the company argued that it is a very decentralised organisation.Allan Johnson, the executive director for HR said 'We don't beam down too much from the head office to out there.' He argued that external factors such as the exchange rate and a loss of customers abroad led to problems, not the internal organisation culture of the business.

Source: adapted from *People Management*, 3.4.2003.

(a) Identify the different corporate cultures mentioned in the article.
(b) Explain why corporate culture at Corus became a problem.

Question 3

Advantages of a strong corporate culture

It is argued that there are certain advantages to a business of establishing a strong corporate culture.

- It provides a sense of identity for employees. They feel part of the business. This may allow workers to be flexible when the company needs to change or is having difficulties.
- Workers identify with other employees. This may help with aspects of the business such as team work.
- It increases the commitment of employees to the company. This may prevent problems such as high labour turnover or industrial relations problems.
- It motivates workers in their jobs. This may lead to increased productivity.

- It allows employees to understand what is going on around them. This can prevent misunderstanding in operations or instructions passed to them.
- It helps to reinforce the values of the organisation and senior management.
- It acts as a control device for management. This can help when setting company strategy.

Criticisms of corporate culture

It has been suggested that a business will benefit if management ensures that:

- there is a strong corporate culture:
- the 'culture gap' is kept to a minimum and there is a single corporate culture that all people in the business work towards.

Certain criticisms of this view have been put forward.

Corporate culture and economic performance John Kotter and James Heskett (1992) researched the relationship between corporate culture and economic performance. They tested the idea that a strong culture improves performance by measuring the strength of the culture of 207 large firms from a variety of industries. A questionnaire was used to calculate a 'culture index' for each firm. They then looked for any correlation between a strong culture and the firm's economic performance over an eleven year period. The research did show a positive correlation, but weaker than most management theorists would have expected. Strong culture firms seemed almost as likely to perform poorly as their weak-culture rivals.

Different perspectives on corporate culture There are other views on the nature of corporate culture.

- A business is made up of sub-cultures which coexist. Sometimes these are in harmony, but sometimes in conflict. There may be differences of interests and opinions among different groups. As a result, cultural practices in companies are interpreted in different ways by employees. These may not always be those intended by management. For example, a profit-sharing scheme may be seen as a sign of equality by one group. Everyone gets a share in the profits, not just management and shareholders. Another group, however, may see it as a bribe for employees to conform with the company.
- The main feature of business life is ambiguity. Companies lack clear centres due to decentralisation, delegation and the employment of temporary and part-time workers. Also, new working practices often leave employees physically separated and socially distant. As a result, employees share some viewpoints, disagree on others and are indifferent to yet others.

These approaches are seen as positive, to meet the requirements of the complexity of business life. The way businesses do things can be interpreted in a variety of ways. Values, beliefs, and norms may not be shared between individual employees or between employees and management. The reason why someone does something in the way they do may not be just because management has created a culture that everyone follows. It may be because of other factors, such as outside influences, internal politics, self- interest, the sub-culture of a group, or different individual personalities.

Royal Dutch/Shell group, the oil group, believes that managing talent is a matter of 'tugging at the heartstrings' of employees. It argues that young recruits choose companies because of the values, beliefs and the culture of the organisation. As a result, Shell has developed a set of business principles which places honesty, integrity and respect for people at the core of its corporate culture. Shell organises a worldwide survey of all employees to find out how they feel about the company. Michael Osbaldeston, head of Shell Global Learning, says 'The result gives us a clearer picture of how attractive a company Shell is to work for and how we could do better in the future'.

Retaining innovative workers is crucial for the Pentland Group, which designs and produces sportswear such as Speedo and Ellesse. It changed the working environment by incorporating lots of natural light, communal space, coffee bars and a gym into its new building. But it found that this, in itself, was not enough without good management practice. It has just completed a company-wide assessment of its management behaviour. It found that the immediate supervisor is massively influential in terms of people's productivity. 'Good management is fundamental to releasing talented workers to do what they do best and when you do that you retain them' says Chris Matcham, group human resources director.

Source: adapted from Guardian Unlimited.

(a) Explain the features of successful corporate cultures of the businesses in the article.
(b) Suggest possible benefits to these businesses of the corporate cultures they have adopted.

key terms

Culture gap - a difference between the culture that a business has and what it would like it to be.

Knowledge

1. How can corporate culture affect decision making?
2. Suggest 3 reasons for the growth in corporate culture.
3. State 4 ways in which a business might develop a strong culture.
4. Suggest 4 different types of culture.
5. How might corporate culture be packaged?
6. How might corporate culture be communicated?
7. What are the constraints on the ability of a business to change culture?
8. How might national culture affect the introduction of a corporate culture?
9. State 5 advantages of a strong corporate culture.
10. Explain 2 criticisms of the idea of a corporate culture.

Case study AXA

How does a global insurance company create an effective corporate culture? Deciding on a name might not seem vital. AXA's original suggestion 'Elan' meaning 'leap forward' in French seemed well suited. However, it was then suggested that it referred to a moose in Canada and was dropped.

Cultural and linguistic barriers were just some issues facing the French company Mutuelle Unis (now AXA) when creating a global culture. Today AXA employs 140,000 people across 50 countries after a series of acquisitions of other business, including Guardian Royal Exchange in the UK and Nippon Nantai in Japan. The culture needs to cross language, social, cultural and ethnic barriers. Senior executive vice president Francoise Colloc'h said 'It has been more about taking the best part of each company to try to make that part of the AXA culture, rather than destroying the past of those companies and saying there is only one way - the Unis way'.

The company originally set about putting in place values representing how to treat clients, shareholders and employees. Seven values were identified, as shown in Table 5.1. However, the business found that, because they were devised by the French company, they reflected French rather than global culture. For example, the word loyalty in Japan could be interpreted as committing ritualistic suicide - hari-kiri. So in 2001 employees from seven countries reworked the values. Five new values were identified.

Was this enough to create a global culture? To make it work, staff had to 'live' the values. So staff were recruited against behaviour linked to values. These values were explained at interviews and induction. Appraisal is also based on behaviour of staff and whether they fit in with the values. Staff that do not meet the values are helped with a development plan and performance is reviewed regularly. Those that can not adapt are asked to leave. Its a slightly 'big brother' approach, underlined by the fact that people have been let go over behaviour and replaced by others with the same values as the company.

Table 5.1 *AXA's old and new values*

Old	New
loyalty	professionalism
courage	integrity
pride	team spirit
ambition	innovation
realism	pragmatism
imagination	
integrity	

Some analysts believe that AXA has done a great job in creating a uniform culture across all businesses. However, others point out that there may still be problems if businesses are acquired in non-western countries. For example, China has largely removed the idea of professionalism after its cultural revolution. So AXA has tried to let individual countries interpret the values. It has also tried to use graphic representations rather than words to show values, such as pictograms.

Source: adapted from *People Management*, 6.2.2003.

(a) Why might the business have needed to change its corporate culture? (6 marks)

(b) What type of culture now exists at AXA? Explain your answer. (8 marks)

(c) Examine the barriers that may have prevented the new corporate culture being introduced. (12 marks)

(d) Explain the benefits of the approach to corporate culture used at AXA for the business. (12 marks)

(e) As the business grows in future, discuss the extent to which it will be able to keep its corporate culture in the same form or whether and how it might need to be changed. (12 marks)

6 Strategy and Planning 1

What is strategy

In 2004 the UK's largest car dealer Pendragon announced a £230 million takeover of smaller rival CD Bramall. Pendragon would double its nationwide chain of franchises to 250 as a result. In the same year Greeting Card Group Ltd, the UK's largest 'value' greeting card retailer, bought a warehouse, office building and 2.7 acres of expansion land in Peterborough to set up a new head office with 100 staff.

These are examples of strategies used by businesses. A business's strategy is the pattern of decisions and actions that are taken by the business to achieve its objectives. A business is likely to have a variety of objectives. For many businesses, the major goal is to improve performance so that profits increase. For example, in 2003 *The Times* followed *The Independent* to launch a tabloid version of the newspaper. Official circulation figures reported that this boosted sales of *The Times* by 14,000 copies a day, although others reported it as closer to 35,000. It was the only broadsheet, apart from *The Financial Times*, to increase its readers in December, usually a poor month because of a lack of interest in news over Christmas. The increase in sales was so encouraging that the paper doubled its print run to 150,000.

Changes in the external environment of the business have led many businesses to rethink their strategy. The success of businesses from Japan and other Asian countries in global markets has led Western companies to rethink their approach to quality, delivery, price and satisfying employees' and consumers' needs. Changes such as the opening up of markets in eastern Europe, the introduction of the euro in 1999 and growing EU regulations are all likely to affect the strategy of UK businesses.

In 2003 it was announced that British Airways (BA) would install 190 IBM self service kiosks at Heathrow Airport and all British Airways destination airports across Europe. The kiosks are designed to make check in faster and more convenient, whilst optimising space at airports. Customers can use the touch sensitive screens to check in, select seats and ask for upgrades without having to queue at desks. The new system was expected to reduce check in queues, providing a major boost to the volume of passengers that BA could handle at peak times.

The move was part of BA's ceBA business transformation strategy, which will change how customers do business with the airline. BA expected to achieve 50 per cent self service check in by 2005. BA's CIO, Paul Coby, said 'Effective use of IT is fundamental in simplifying the way in which British Airways does business' and that the new machines would improve customer service and achieve greater levels of efficiency. He also argued that it takes less than a minute to check in 'so the benefits for both passengers and British Airways are significant in an industry being driven to increase lead factors while reducing costs.'

Source: adapted from www.ibm.com/news/uk.

(a) Explain the objectives that BA may have had in its transformation strategy.

Planning and strategy

It is likely that the strategy of a business will, to some extent, be a planned strategy. Business planning involves deciding what is to be done, setting objectives and developing policies to achieve them. The planning process that a business might carry out is shown in Figure 6.1. It could be argued that businesses go through a number of stages when planning their strategies.

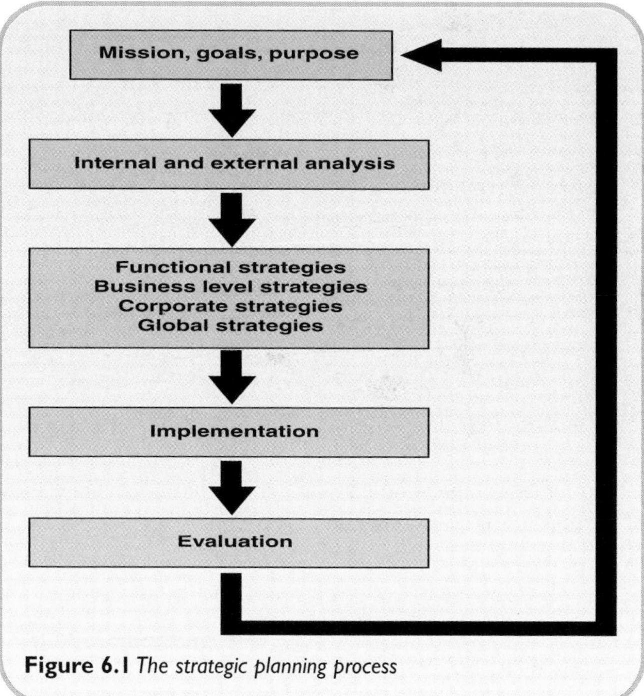

Figure 6.1 *The strategic planning process*

Identifying missions and goals Businesses have many objectives and goals, the things they want to achieve. A company may want to increase its market share over a period of time or have more specific goals such as achieving a 10 per cent market share over the next 5 years. Companies also have missions. These are the reasons why the company exists and what it is trying to do. They are often found in **mission** or **corporate statements**. For example, the mission of EasyJet, the low cost airline service in 2004 was:

> 'To provide our customers with safe, good value, point to point air services. To effect and to offer a consistent and

reliable product and fares appealing to leisure and business markets on a range of European routes. To achieve this we will develop our people and establish lasting relationships with our suppliers.'

The mission statement of EasyInternetcafe was:

'To be the world's leading Internet café chain that is the cheapest way to get online.'

Analysis of the position of the business A business will analyse the aspects within and outside the organisation. External factors might be the opportunities that exist, such as new markets, and threats, such as increased competition. Internal analysis might examine the strengths of the business which give it a **competitive advantage** over rivals, such as the skills of its workforce. It would also consider the company's weaknesses, such as a poor supplier network.

Developing strategies A business may have a number of different strategies and plans that it might use. These might be operational strategies designed to improve the efficiency of marketing, production or human resources. Examples might be building up brand loyalty, introducing Total Quality Management techniques or training the workforce. Business strategies might be differentiating products from those of others. Corporate strategies might involve merging with others. Global strategies may involve setting up production in another country.

Implementing strategies Once a business has identified the strategies it wishes to use it must then carry them out. The business needs to put into place the organisational and management system needed to carry out the strategies. This might involve adapting existing systems or designing new ones. Businesses must also be able to control the way new strategies are implemented. For example, they may need to make sure that a strategy remains within a budget.

Evaluation A business must have some way to decide if its strategies have been effective. To do this it must measure its performance against the targets that it has set. It must also use the outcomes to decide if the strategy needs to be changed.

Not all strategies are planned. Some emerge from the day to day operation of the business. However, strategies are vital, especially for large, complex organisations. The rest of this unit will cover the internal and external analysis of the position of the business. Unit 7 will deal with different strategies, the factors affecting how they are implemented and their evaluation.

The elements of effective planning and strategy

Purpose A business must be clear about its purpose. This may be defined in terms of the type of products or services it wants to produce or whether it is a profit or a non-profit making organisation. If the purpose of the business is unclear, its plans, operations and practices that are devised in the strategy will lack focus and direction.

Vision Without a strategic vision, a business might struggle to succeed. The vision is the creative idea, image or imagination about the business. It is often the idea of the founder of the business or those responsible for particular projects or initiatives. A vision that is communicated effectively to others is likely to be shared by all and to be successful. The visions of businesses such as Virgin are well publicised. Virgin Atlantic, for example, was created by Richard Branson in the 1980s as a top quality niche airline to fly between London, the USA and the Far East. To promote this Branson created a distinctive image based on quality and the ability to identity with the passenger. He reinforced the image by keeping himself and the company in the public eye. The result has been the creation of a profitable business with strong image and identity.

Commitment Effective strategies have a 'commitment to achieve'. This can be done in a variety of ways, including financial gains and profits, effectiveness and quality of service. Commitment is also reflected in the volume, quality and nature of resources used, the ways of working, management styles and the ethical stance of the company. Table 6.1 shows the corporate purpose of Unilever, reproduced in its past Annual Report and Accounts.

Customers and clients Effective strategies are geared towards customers and clients. They must take into account:

- the nature, locations, and numbers of customers;
- their needs and wants in relation to the products offered by the business;

Table 6.1 *Unilever's Corporate Purpose*

Our purpose in Unilever is to meet the everyday needs of people everywhere - to anticipate the aspirations of our consumers and customers and to respond creatively and competitively with branded products and services which raise the quality of life.

Our deep roots in local cultures and markets around the world are our unparalleled inheritance and the foundation for our future growth. We will bring our wealth of knowledge and international expertise to the service of local consumers - a truly multi-local multinational.

Our long-term success requires a total commitment to exceptional standards of performance and productivity, to working together effectively and to a willingness to embrace new ideas and learn continuously.

We believe that to succeed requires the highest standards of corporate behaviour towards our employees, consumers and the societies and world in which we live.

This is Unilever's road to sustainable, profitable growth for our business and long-term value creation for our shareholders and employees.

Source: Unilever, *Annual Report and Accounts*.

- the importance of these products to customers;
- the advantages of products in relation to those of competitors;
- the confidence in and loyalty to the firm by its customers;
- financial viability.

Strategies must be designed to satisfy the needs of customers over the long term. If not, they will go elsewhere.

Timescale A business must make sure that its objectives are achievable in the time it has set for its plans (its **planning horizon**). It is likely that there will be different timescales for different plans and strategies. For example, a business may have a short term objective to train the accounting department to use a software programme. This sort of **operational planning** is likely to be achieved in a relatively short space of time, perhaps a few weeks or months. However, a **corporate strategy** to enter into a joint venture with an Eastern European country to set up a printing works make take years to research and set up.

Sainsbury's has a commitment to organic products in a number of ways.

- In 2000 it opened the first organic restaurant certified by organic farmers and growers in its supermarket in Sevenoaks. The restaurant sports a sign 'Go organic every day'.
- The Sainsbury's organic website is a joint initiative between Sainsbury's and Greenvale AP, a UK potato supplier. It allows consumers to trace information about the source of over 120 different types of organic fresh produce. It also gives information on organic recipes and growing practices.

The Sainsbury's website contains the following information.

We've won more organic product quality awards than any other UK supermarket. Generally, there is insufficient supply of organic food from British producers to satisfy current demand and we are committed to encouraging an increase in the proportion of organic farming in this country. We support The Organic Targets campaign to increase the supply of organic food and in January 2002 announced that we will be working to ensure that key organic areas in the dairy and meat sectors are 100% British sourced by January 2004. Sainsbury's currently imports 60% of its organic food range, compared with an industry average of 70%.

- By the end of 2003 all our own-label organic range will be accredited by the International Federation of Organic Agricultural Movements [IFOAM] global guarantee system.
- We have already achieved 100% British sourcing for fresh organic milk, eggs, beef, pork and poultry and are exploring how best to increase UK sourcing of processed foods. The Organic Partnership (TOP) suppliers are making significant contributions to this. Sainsbury's currently sources 40% of its organic food range from the UK and has pledged to increase this figure to 55% by 2004.
- Customers should be aware of the true cost of organic foods and our prices reflect that. We do not believe in subsidising the retail price of organic foods nor do we make additional profit on organic products in comparison to a conventional alternative of similar quality and value. We aim to work together with suppliers and producers to reduce costs within the organic supply chain. The Organic Partnership (TOP), a forum for Sainsbury's and 20 of our key organic suppliers, is one way in which this can be achieved.

Source: adapted from www.j-sainsbury.co.uk.

(a) Examine the factors which have led Sainsbury's to have an effective strategy.

Flexibility and dynamism Strategy is a continuous and dynamic process, not a single event. A business needs to allow its staff to seek out commercial opportunities. However, they must not deflected from the standards and direction set out in the plan. Tom Peters, the management 'guru', calls this the 'simultaneous loose-tight properties'. A business must be 'loose' enough to give employees some responsibility for finding opportunities. But it must be 'tight' enough not to allow employees to take the business into areas not outlined in plans.

Suitability The plans and strategies of the business must be suitable for the goals it is trying to achieve. Business often have a variety of plans for different situations. For example, as well as the overall strategic plan of the business, there will be functional plans, such as **marketing plans** and **human resource plans**. There may also be plans for unexpected situations. A company may plan to launch a new product in six months, but have a **contingency plan** that it could be introduced the following year if there are production problems. This is explained in the next section.

Bridging a strategic planning gap A strategic planning gap is the difference between where a business is forecast to be and where it wants or needs to be. Assessing the extent of any gap and planning how to fill it is an important part of corporate business planning. For example, a multinational business (☞ unit 38) may have the objective of achieving a target level of profit abroad. It may assess that it is not likely to achieve this target with its current strategy. An internal and external audit may show that this is due to increasing competition. The business may decide that the most effective strategy is to form an alliance with a foreign business to achieve its goals and bridge the gap.

Crisis planning

At times businesses may face CRISES. These are situations where unstable conditions exist. As a result problems can occur for businesses. Crisies are usually unexpected. Effective planning should reduce the impact of a crisis on a business. Firms often have contingency plans to cope with unforeseen or changing conditions. Why might a crisis arise?

Financial crises An example of a financial crisis might be a lack of working capital to pay immediate bills. The business could be said to have a liquidity problem. This might arise because the business has too many assets that are not easily converted into cash. Another reason might be because it has built up a large number of long term debts or is unable to recover money owed. Smaller firms may go out of business because they have been unable to collect large amounts of money owed to them.

Production crises An example might be the breakdown of a crucial piece of machinery. This would lead to a loss of production for the manufacturer and perhaps a failure to deliver products on time. Delays in the deliveries of components can cause major problems for businesses that use just-in-time production. Other possible crises might include fire or water damage to machinery, premises and stock. Natural disasters such as crop failures may affect the supply of agricultural products. The provision of services may also be affected. For example, a problem with the computer system at an airport may lead to delayed flights or customers might miss flights because they have been given incorrect information.

Human resources problems At times of industrial action businesses may face problems. Production may be halted. Sales may suffer because of a lack of supply or because the image of the business is affected. Strikes (☞ unit 23), called suddenly, can cause damage and may lead to conflict. Other human resources problems might be very high levels of staff turnover or poor motivation amongst the workforce which lead to a loss of productivity. This may develop over time without the knowledge of management.

Environmental problems A business may find that its operations are leading to environmental damage. This might result in opposition from pressure groups and perhaps the halting of the activity. For example, a road may be re-routed around an area of natural beauty, or a business may be prevented from building a waste incinerator in an area because of opposition from local residents.

Corporate problems Certain crises may affect the whole organisation. An example might be an attempted hostile takeover by a larger company. Another might the loss of confidence in a public limited company. This might lead to its share price falling greatly on the stock exchange as shareholders sell their shares.

Product and legal problems At times crises take place when faulty or dangerous products are produced which break the law. A child's toy that was found to be causing harm could be banned. Products that have been found to cause health problems have led to difficulties for food manufacturers.

Image problems Many of the problems above will affect the image of the business. Consumers may lose faith in its products or change their opinions about a firm being a 'good employer' for example. This is likely to affect the sales and profitability of the business.

Contingency planning

Effective planning will allow a business to cope with the crises mentioned above. The CONTINGENCY PLANS of the business should be designed to cope with the problems that arise from crises. How might a business do this?

Finance Large firms may have contingency funds set aside to deal with liquidity problems. Other solutions include finding alternative funds to deal with a short term lack of finance.

Production One solution to interruptions in production is to find alternative sources. A business may be able to **outsource** some of the work to other producers. It may also be able to switch production from one machine or one factory to another. It might even rearrange the time of production. If productions stops in the day, the product may be manufactured overnight. This is easier if production systems and the workforce are flexible (☞ unit 24). Having a pool of suppliers may prevent problems if components are not delivered on time by one firm. The same method may be used for crises that result in the supply of services. Services may be sub-contracted or an alternative may be offered.

Human resources management Effective consultation and grievance procedures will help minimise difficulties and may speed up the solution to industrial relations problems. Motivational rewards may be used to deal with poor staff motivation. Establishing a corporate culture (☞ unit 5) may prevent some of these problems occuring in the first place. A business might make use of the flexible workforce (☞ unit 24) to deal with a lack of employees as a result of high labour turnover.

Image Faulty products or damage to the environment can have an enormous effect on the image of a business. A business must act quickly and effectively when faced with an image problem. Faulty products must be withdrawn immediately. The business should attempt to alleviate any public concern for its products. For example, it might promote the fact that it has found the problem and how it has solved in in the media. Other forms of promotion may be used to support the company's image. Businesses with operations that affect the environment often spend money on recycling and improving their environmental performance and promote this in their Annual Reports.

Management and communication Management has a vital part to play at time of crisis. There must be strong leadership from the top of the company hierarchy. Others in the business must be clear about their roles and responsibilities. A business also needs clear communication channels to ensure that messages are being passed on effectively. Use should be made of information and communication technology.

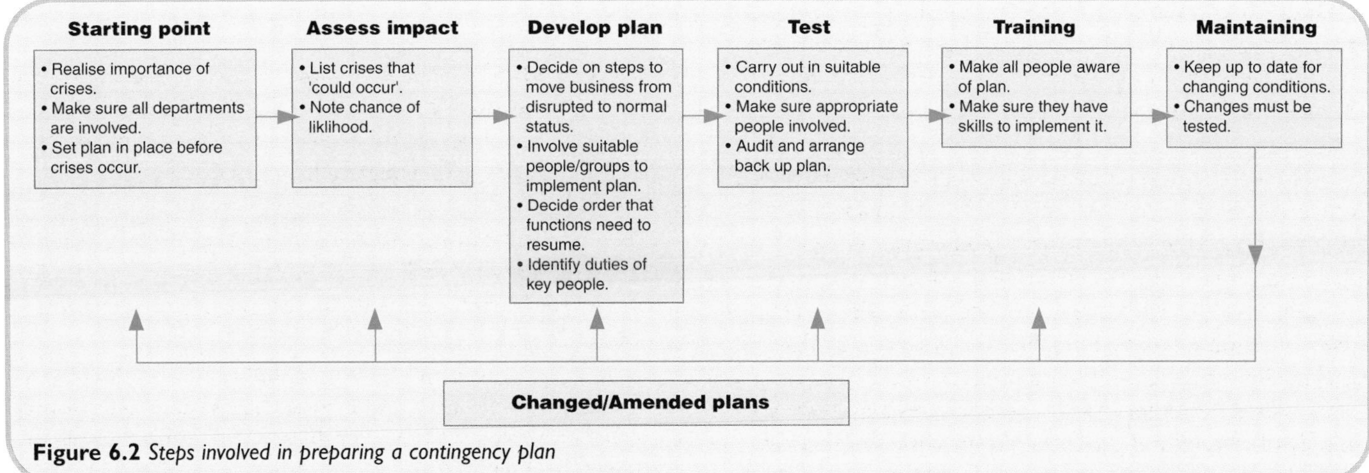

Figure 6.2 *Steps involved in preparing a contingency plan*

While contingency plans are important, a business must not give them too much emphasis. They must not affect the corporate plans of the firm. Keeping a large amount in a contingency fund, for example, may reduce the funds that the business has available for expansion or investment. Figure 6.2 shows the steps that businesses can take when preparing contingency plans.

Business analysis

Business analysis is the examination of the 'how, what, why' of business activity. It may involve analysing the possible **internal** problems and advantages that a business has by means of an **internal audit**. It might also determine the factors **external** to the business that could affect its stategy, by means of an **external audit**. The outcome of analysis should be to find the organisations's strengths and capabilities, its commercial and operational advantages and wider general pressures and constraints on the business. Businesses have a number of methods to carry out analysis. These are dealt with in the following sections.

Compuquest is a design and printing business. It has recently faced a major problem. It prepared an advertising campaign for a large London plc. Part of this involved producing big posters for billboards and a large number of small leaflets. Just as it was about to save the work to disk and send it to printing its computer network broke down and it lost a lot of the designs. It must now produce the designs again and still get the posters and leaflets printed on time. But it has recently had another large job come in. The printer of the smaller leaflets says that they can only print the job next month, far too late for the client. The business has contingency plans for such situations. It can call on outside workers, part time or use teleworkers. It can get jobs printed abroad, at cheap rates or in the UK. It also has the option of asking a specialist business to recover the disks, although it is not guaranteed that all information will be recovered. It can ask workers to work extra hours to meet the deadline or use shift work.

(a) Identify the reasons why the business faces problems.
(b) Suggest and justify the most appropriate contingency plan that the business should use in this case.

SWOT analysis

The purpose of SWOT analysis is to conduct a general and quick examination of a business's current position so that it can identify preferred and likely directions in future. SWOT analysis involves looking at the internal strengths and weaknesses of a business and the external opportunities and threats.

Strengths These are things that the business and its staff do which:
- they are effective at;
- they are well known for;
- make money;
- generate business and reputation;
- lead to confidence in the market;
- cause customers to come back for repeat business;
- cause other businesses to try to learn from them.

Weaknesses These are the things that the business does badly, that it is ineffective at or that it has a poor reputation for. It also includes the factors that cause losses, hardships, disputes, grievances and complaints for a business.

Opportunities These are the directions that the business could profitably take in future because of its strengths or because of the elimination of its weaknesses. This involves a consideration of the business environment from the widest and most creative possible standpoints.

Threats Threats to as business arise from the activities of competitors and from failing to take opportunities or to build on successes. Threats also come from complacency, a lack of rigour, and from falling profits, perhaps due to rising costs.

Rob Wilkinson set up Live Publishing in November 1999. He had previously worked for magazines publishers Emap, and IDG which was bought by Paragon. But Paragon didn't take any of the IDG staff and he thought they would take time to get to grips with IDG publications. So he set up Live Publishing to compete. The new company had two directors who knew the market and had experience of launching new products. It also negotiated a deal with former distributor Comag and leased office space easily. This all happened within 10 days, which was essential as time was of the essence. One of his main issues was capital. Rob had £80,000 from his own assets. So he had some working capital. But he needed to raise the rest in eight weeks. He obtained £130,000 from the Small Firms Loan Guarantee Scheme, loaned by the Royal Bank of Scotland.

By 2002 the business had thrived. It had 35 employees, 5 titles and a £2.6 million turnover. The cyclical video games market was entering a period of growth and Live was keen to capitalise. Wilkinson felt Live's turnover could treble in the following 2-3 years. More than 50 per cent of Live's turnover came from premium priced PC mags. They are hugely profitable. But sales were predicted to tail off soon. The real money lies in magazines for the games console market aimed at users of Sony's PS2 and Microsoft's XBox. One in four console buyers regularly buy a gaming magazine. The business has opportunities in the UK and overseas. Live is also looking to diversify. It bought business related titles, for example. And it has produced magazines licensed to a third party, such as the Lord of the Rings Poster magazine.

Reactions to the business situation by analysts are varied. A venture capitalist commented that, although the market is

growing, if Live is to thrive it must maintain a strong pool of writers and keep its cost in check. It also needs to focus more on selling ad space in its mags. And it must plan its acquisitions carefully. It's easy to buy to grow, but the growth must be profitable and there must be synergy between the companies. A former publisher of computer magazines, however, thought that the business may face problems because it does not have a unique selling point. He suggested that the products offered are not different enough to attract investment in a very competitive market, with limited funds available from investors.

Source: adapted from *en*, February 2003.

(a) Carry out a SWOT analysis of the business using information from the article.

The analysis is often carried out as a brainstorming discussion. It is an effective way of gathering and categorising information, illustrating particular matters and generating interest in the business and its activities quickly. The result of such an exercise may provide a basis on which a more detailed analysis can be conducted. SWOT analysis is often used as a method by which marketing departments can plan their marketing strategy.

PEST-G analysis

PEST-G analysis examines the external environment and the global factors that may affect a business. It can provide a quick and visual representation of the external pressures facing a business, and their possible constraints on strategy. It is usually divided into five external influences on a business - political, economic, social,technological, and green.

Political This is concerned with how political developments, regionally, nationally and internationally, might affect a business's strategy. It might include a consideration of legislation, such as consumer laws, regulation, such as control of water companies, political pressures and the government's view of certain activities.

Economic This might involve the analysis of a wide variety of economic factors and their effects on a business. They might include:

- consumer activity - confidence, spending patterns, willingness to spend;
- economic variables - inflation, unemployment, trade, growth;
- government policy - fiscal, monetary, supply side, exchange rate;
- fixed and variable costs of the business;
- the effect of changes in product and labour markets.

For example, in a recession demand for many products and services tends to fall. Businesses may also need to analyse the possible effects on their plans of government policy designed to lift the economy out of the recession.

Social What competitive advantage might a business gain by social changes taking place outside of the business? For example, after the year 2000 the UK had a falling birth rate, an increase in life expectancy and an ageing population. This has led to the development of products, particularly private pensions, private medical schemes, sheltered housing developments and 'third age' holidays, aimed at the older age group. Pressure groups can also affect businesses. The anti-smoking lobby, for example, has led to smoke free areas in restaurants, in hotels, and on aircraft.

Technological Businesses operate in a world of rapid technological change. Organisations need to regularly review the impact of new technologies upon their activities. Products can become obsolescent quickly and production methods can become out of date. Communication may become inefficient as ICT develops. New markets may open. For example, some music companies have considered sales via the internet. The strategy towards R&D (☞ unit 27) is vital in industries where technological change is rapid.

Green Environmental factors that might affect a business could include issues concerning pollution, methods of production which might lead to destruction such as deforestation, or how the image and landscape of an area is affected by a new factory.

The five forces model

Michael Porter developed a model that allows business to analyse competitive forces in an industry in order to identify opportunities and threats. These include:

- the risk of entry of new competitors;
- the degree of rivalry amongst established firms;
- the bargaining power of buyers;
- the bargaining power of suppliers;
- the threat of substitute products.

Porter argued that the stronger each of these forces is, the less able a business is to raise prices and profits. For example, when cheap airlines such as Ryanair and EasyJet entered the market in the 1990s, established companies such as BA arguably had to offer lower priced services.

Industry structure analysis

A similar method of business analysis may involve an examination of the structure of the industry in which a business operates. There are four components to this.

Competitors This examines the nature and extent of the rivalry among organisations operating in a market and the implications of this for the future. A business may consider the extent of product differentiation, the prospects of price wars and profit margins. It may also include questions about the current and future productive capacity of the industry.

Suppliers This focuses on the bargaining power of suppliers, including their ability to withdraw or flood the market. Either will affect a business buying supplies. Scarcity of components, for example, may lead to delays in production, increased costs or loss of business. Flooding the market may lead to falls in supply prices and possible new entrants to the market.

Substitution This looks at the ability of customers to change to the products of a competitor. It is dealt with under 'competitor analysis' below.

Potential entrants This examines the nature of potential entrants and any advantages they would have.

Competitor analysis

This involves assessing rivals. It may examine initiatives that they may take to promote their own strategic advantage. It could also evaluate the likely response to such initiatives by other businesses and consumers. The purpose of competitor analysis is to highlight the strengths and opportunities present in the 'rest of the field' and to learn from other businesses in the industry. Competitor analysis looks at a number of areas.

- The strategy of the competitor.
- The driving forces and constraints upon it.
- Its current business operations, capacities and strengths.
- Its current marketing operations and activities.
- Assumptions about the competitor.
- Assumptions about the industry itself.
- Detailed profiles of each competitor. This might include an assessment of their satisfaction with their current position, their likely responses to competitors' strategies, their positions in the market and the extent to which they are operating at under or over capacity.

Product life cycle and product portfolio analysis

The **product life cycle** shows how the sales and profits from a product change over a period of its 'life', from its launch to its withdrawal. **Product portfolio analysis** looks at the relationships between the performance of different products sold by a business, each which is likely to be at different stages in its cycle. These are essential components of a business's analysis. They provide a detailed understanding of what stage of the life cycle each product of a business is at, what is the present mix of products and how that portfolio might be developed in future. It is difficult for a business to develop a strategy for the future if it does not know the performance and mix of its current products.

Cost and value analysis

Cost analysis is essential to business strategy. A detailed knowledge of the costs of machinery, workers and materials will be needed before a strategy can be chosen. It provides the exact costs incurred in manufacturing a product or providing a service. It helps a business to calculate margins of profit for each product or service and what each product or service might contribute to fixed costs. A variety of costing methods can be used to do this (☞ unit 13).

Value analysis (☞ unit 27) is used to identify activities and areas of a business that add value, and to find out where value is lost. A business can concentrate on solving problems in areas were value is lost and attempt to reproduce or improve activities that add value. Value analysis is a likely indicator of the points in operation where profits and losses are likely to be made.

key terms

Contingency plans - plans designed to enable a business to recover from a disaster or crisis.

Crises - unstable situations which arise, often in unforseen circumstances.

Knowledge

1. 'Strategy is designed to achieve business goals.' Explain this statement.
2. Outline the stages of planning strategies, placing them in order.
3. Identify 5 important elements of planning and strategy.
4. Identify the 4 areas of SWOT analysis, stating which are external and which are internal.
5. Identify the 5 areas of PEST-G analysis, giving an example of each.
6. What are the 5 forces that affect a business's ability to compete?
7. How might a supplier's actions to flood the market with materials affect businesses?
8. State 6 factors about a competitor that a business may be interested in.
9. What does:
   (a) the product mix;
   (b) value analysis;
   tell a business about its operations?

Case study Supermarket strategy

The drive by supermarkets such as Asda and Tesco into non-food products is causing serious problems for some of the UK's biggest retail chains, from chemists, to fashion stores to electrical retailers to bookshops. A few years ago supermarkets were criticised for deserting high streets to set up in edge of town shopping areas. Now they are back, snapping up local shops and rebranding them as 'Local' or 'Express'. Boots blamed 900 job losses on tough supermarket competition. Toiletries have been pinpointed as a growth area for supermarkets. They have squeezed the prices of big brands to persuade shoppers to switch from their regular loyal Boots visits to wait till they go to the supermarket.

The appeal for the supermarkets is that non-food items, from fashion to photolabs, have much larger profit margins. This is especially true when they are sold by supermarket giants running highly efficient large scale operations from low rent out of town locations. And they also have the power to force down the purchase price by buying in enormous quantities.

Tesco accounts for £1 of every £8 spent in the UK on everything. It had 7.5 per cent growth in like for like sales this Christmas compared to last. Tesco announced that it wants more and was aiming to raise £1.6 billion to fund further expansion. But it stated that it only had 5 per cent of the non-food market in the UK, 6 per cent of the convenience store market and 2-3 per cent of the banking market, and that in all these areas it could get much bigger. Its Cherokee and Florence and Fred clothing lines are the fastest growing in the UK, with sales growing at six times the market rate. Asda's George Label has annual sales of £1 billion a year, making it the fifth largest clothing retailer.

The pressure on retailers from supermarkets is intense. Matalan is one business that has suffered as Asda and Tesco have targeted the same value conscious shoppers. So has Mark & Spencer, which admitted that it does not have enough low cost options on its rails. In particular, its sales of children's clothing have suffered.

Part of the success of the supermakets it is suggested is the fact that shoppers are busy. They want to buy everything in one place. Tesco is considering launching its own up market clothing bearing its 'Finest' label.

To compete with this retailers now need to offer something special to pull people out of the supermarkets. Even Argos, with its respected chain of catalogue shops, has suffered. Christmas sales were up

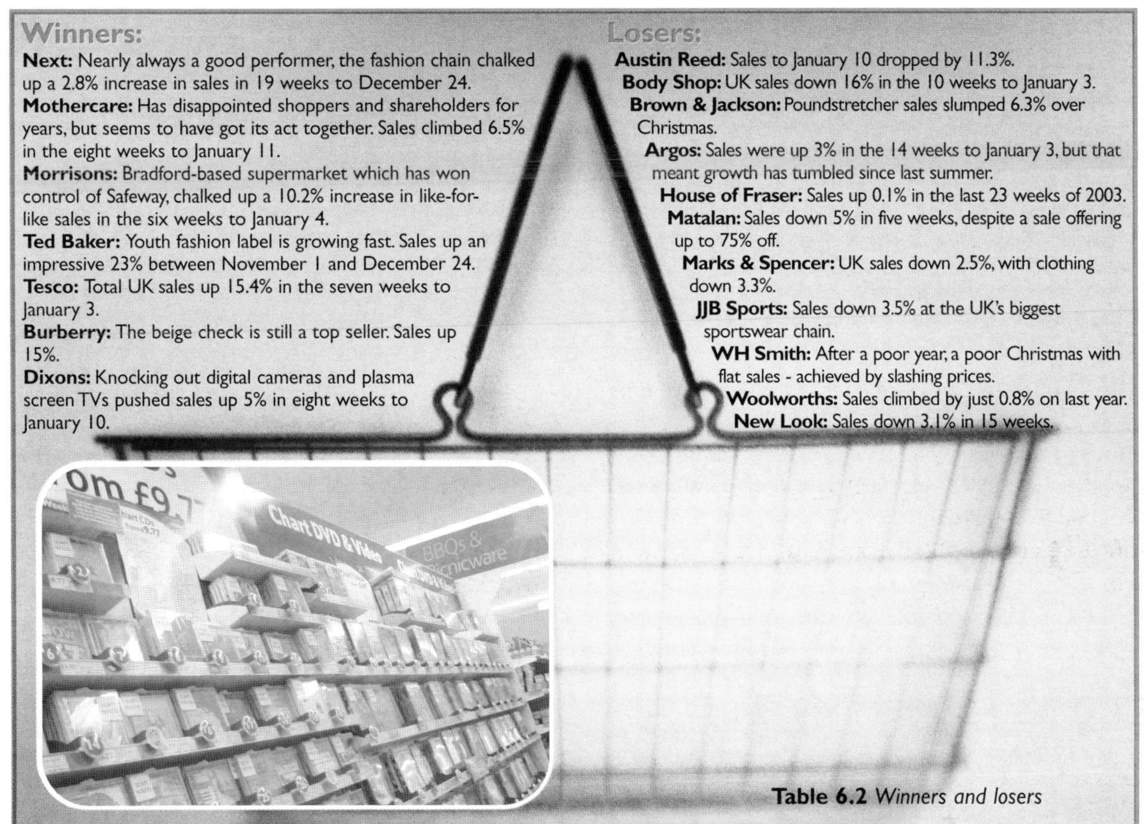

Winners:

Next: Nearly always a good performer, the fashion chain chalked up a 2.8% increase in sales in 19 weeks to December 24.
Mothercare: Has disappointed shoppers and shareholders for years, but seems to have got its act together. Sales climbed 6.5% in the eight weeks to January 11.
Morrisons: Bradford-based supermarket which has won control of Safeway, chalked up a 10.2% increase in like-for-like sales in the six weeks to January 4.
Ted Baker: Youth fashion label is growing fast. Sales up an impressive 23% between November 1 and December 24.
Tesco: Total UK sales up 15.4% in the seven weeks to January 3.
Burberry: The beige check is still a top seller. Sales up 15%.
Dixons: Knocking out digital cameras and plasma screen TVs pushed sales up 5% in eight weeks to January 10.

Losers:

Austin Reed: Sales to January 10 dropped by 11.3%.
Body Shop: UK sales down 16% in the 10 weeks to January 3.
Brown & Jackson: Poundstretcher sales slumped 6.3% over Christmas.
Argos: Sales were up 3% in the 14 weeks to January 3, but that meant growth has tumbled since last summer.
House of Fraser: Sales up 0.1% in the last 23 weeks of 2003.
Matalan: Sales down 5% in five weeks, despite a sale offering up to 75% off.
Marks & Spencer: UK sales down 2.5%, with clothing down 3.3%.
JJB Sports: Sales down 3.5% at the UK's biggest sportswear chain.
WH Smith: After a poor year, a poor Christmas with flat sales - achieved by slashing prices.
Woolworths: Sales climbed by just 0.8% on last year.
New Look: Sales down 3.1% in 15 weeks.

Table 6.2 *Winners and losers*

only 3 per cent compared to 7 per cent last year. But HMV has perhaps bucked the trend. It was suggested that the reason for this was that it operates in a different market to the supermarkets selling CDs and DVDs. Sixty per cent of its sales are from 'off-chart' items. Supermarkets tend to concentrate on the top 20. Tesco now sells more chart CDs and DVDs than HMV and WH Smith together. Asda reported that at Christmas it was selling DVD players at a rate of one every minute.

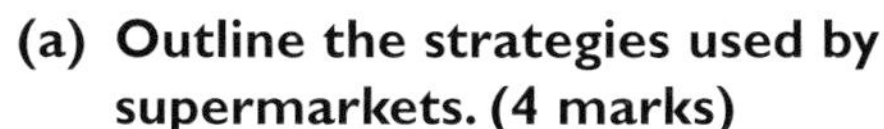

Source: adapted from *The Guardian*, January 2004 and www.guardian.co.uk/supermarkets.

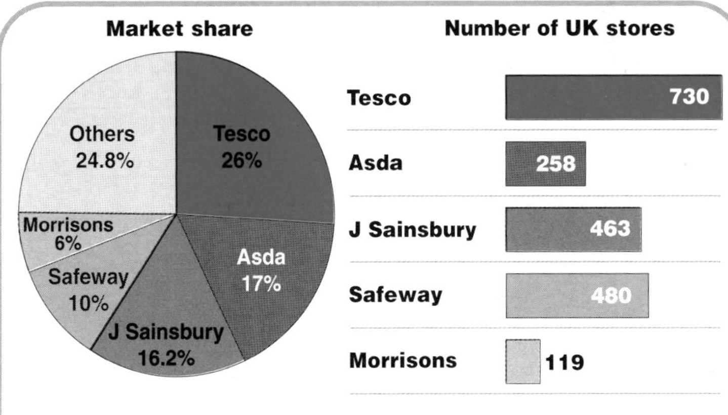

Figure 6.3 *UK supermarkets, market share and number of stores, 2004*

(a) Outline the strategies used by supermarkets. (4 marks)

(b) Explain the reasons for the supermarket strategies. (6 marks)

(c) (i) Why might retailers have needed contingency plans at Christmas? (4 marks)

(ii) Explain the type of contingency plans that retailers might use. (8 marks)

(d) Analyse the position of Tesco from the information using a suitable method. (14 marks)

(e) Discuss how successful the strategies of the supermarkets have been. (14 marks)

7 Strategy and Planning 2

Developing, implementing and evaluating strategy

Unit 6 explained that there are steps a business can take when planning its strategies. The first two stages of the process involve identifying the goals to be achieved, and analysing the business's position and the effects on it of internal and external factors. This unit looks at the next stages - developing and implementing strategies, and their evaluation.

A business has to decide on the types of strategy it will use. Some of these are strategies at the functional level, to improve the efficiency of business operations. Generic strategies are designed to improve the ways that a business can compete against its rivals in an industry. A business may also consider strategies designed to compete in global markets (☞ unit 37) and corporate strategy aimed at the long term development of the organisation. Once a business has implemented a strategy it must have some way of assessing how successful the strategy has been.

Functional/operational strategies

FUNCTIONAL or OPERATIONAL STRATEGIES are designed to improve the efficiency of a business's operations. They often focus on one area, such as production methods, marketing, human resources or research and development. However, to be effective they involve cooperation between departments. Examples of different methods for improving efficiency include:

- achieving economies of scale. For example, a business will reduce its costs if it delivers products in one large van, making one journey, rather than in three small vans making three trips;
- lean production methods. For example, just in time manufacturing means that a business does not receive materials until they are needed, to save on storage costs and speed up the production process;
- total quality management (TQM). For example, giving work groups responsibility for solving quality problems during the process reduces the quantity of wasted finished products;
- matching consumers' needs better, through marketing research for example;
- improving customers' response, through better distribution;
- improving staff motivation with rewards;
- accurately forecasting the need for staff and the loss of staff;
- improving staff skills by training;
- encouraging research, development, and innovation;
- improving waste management.

Business level strategies

Business level strategies are plans a company uses to gain a competitive advantage over rivals in a market. They are sometimes called GENERIC STRATEGIES because all firms can use them, whether manufacturing or service businesses. It is unlikely that a business can serve an entire market all of the time. Competition exists. Consumers have a choice whether to buy a rival's products or not to buy at all. Firms, therefore, have to decide which parts of the market to aim at and how to be distinctive from competitors. Michael Porter, in his book *Competitive Strategy* (1980), suggested that there are three generic strategies that could be used to gain competitive advantage - cost leadership, differentiation and focus.

Cost leadership This is where a business attempts to produce goods or services at a lower cost than its competitors. It will

Robbins Ltd is a bottling plant in Glasgow. It has decided to introduce TQM in order to achieve the ISO 9000 quality standard. A problem facing management is the need to inform all workers that they are now responsible for the quality of their own work. Before a foreman had always checked work that was proceeding to the next stage of the operation.

It was likely that staff would need to be retrained to deal with their new responsibilities. In the short term management expected some staff loss and morale may fall with teething problems. It was considering some way of motivating employees in the changeover stage. Part of the new process involved a requirement of suppliers to provide materials just in time. It was likely that some suppliers would not be able to fulfil this and so there would be a rationalising of business suppliers.

The new system would be geared towards quality assurance. Focus groups of consumers would be asked for their views before changes were made. They would also be allowed to inspect production as it took place. Some changes were also likely to be needed in the product itself, to make it more suitable to the new working methods.

(a) How might changes in the strategy of Robbins Ltd affect the following functions?
  (i) Management.
  (ii) Human resources.
  (iii) Marketing.
  (iv) Materials control.
  (v) Production.
  (vi) Research and development.
(b) Explain two reasons why coordination between different areas would be needed.

do this to charge lower prices than rivals and to compete in price wars that may take place. Organisation, production, marketing and distribution will all be geared at reducing costs. These firms are likely to offer standard, adequate, medium quality products. For example, supermarkets Netto and Aldi's strategy may be classified as cost leadership. Their approach to retailing is low cost and price, 'no frills', and cheap packaging and distribution. So might low cost airlines such as Ryanair and EasyJet.

Differentiation This is where a business tries to make a product that is seen as unique by customers. A business may carry out promotion to give the goods or services a distinctive identity. A business can charge a PREMIUM PRICE, higher than other prices, and so gain a competitive advantage. Examples of such products might be BMW cars or Rolex watches.

Focus This is where a business concentrates on a particular segment or consumer group. It tries to identify, anticipate and meet the needs of this group. The segment could be a geographical area or a certain income group. Once it has chosen a segment, it might then try to take either a low cost or a differentiation approach.

According to Johnson and Scholes (1993), organisations have a variety of strategies. All of these can be cost based, differentiated or focused.

Consolidation This is where a business tries to preserve its position in the market, niche or sector, range of activities and operations, and customer base. This could be achieved by increasing marketing and promotional activities, improvements in productivity, quality or delivery and reductions in costs. Consolidation may take place in declining markets. As a product starts to decline, a firm will try to gain every possible benefit from the product before sales make it unprofitable. Strategies might be the sale of the brand, licences, franchises, technology or distribution rights for a product.

Withdrawal, retrenchment and contraction These strategies are used when a business decides to move out of a particular market or reduce its portfolio of products or services. This may not be a negative thing. SWOT or PEST-G analysis may suggest that certain products are not performing as well as others. For example, in 2002 Sega, the manufacturer of the Dreamcast video gaming console, stopped production of video game hardware faced with intensive competition from Sony's PlayStation 2, Microsoft's; XBox and Nintendo's GameCube. The business aimed to concentrate on producing software games for other consoles.

Market entry and penetration This is where a business can see an opening in a market. It will use strategies to gain entry to these markets. Market entry is more likely to occur when certain conditions exist.

- Where the market is growing, can be made to grow or has growth potential. There is likely to be sales potential that existing businesses are unable or unwilling to fill.
- Where organisations leave the market, leaving unfilled demand for products.
- Where the new entrant has a real or perceived advantage. These are likely to be cost, price, value or quality advantages over the existing operators. For example, in the soft drinks market, the perceived or real advantage of Pepsi and Coca-Cola is 'image and lifestyle'. New entrants must be able to compete with this.
- Where existing operators are complacent or where there has been a fall in the level of quality or service.
- Where a business is able to bring its reputation from one area to another, to gain a foothold. Stagecoach, for example, has taken its reputation as a successful bus operator into other transport services, such as railways.

Market development and domination Businesses may try to develop their share of the market, in order to dominate it. Domination of a market can lead to economies of scale. These include the ability to negotiate discounts with suppliers, attract the best staff and find the best sites for the business.

New product development Marketing research may indicate the need for a product that has not yet been developed. For example, Saga holidays recognised that there was a growing market for foreign holidays for over 50s which had not been fully exploited by other holiday companies. Technological advances may also result in new products being developed that create a new market. 'New' products may also be created based on existing products.

Diversification Diversification strategies occur where a business seeks to extend its current range of products or services. This may be by integration with other businesses or through new product or market development. Related diversification is where a business develops products which are similar to those that it is currently offering. Similarities may be in:

- existing provision, for example, an industrial building company seeking to diversify in the house building sector;
- existing technology or expertise, for example, an electrical goods company adapting its technology in order to produce digital wrist watches;
- related markets, for example, a confectionery company producing dog and cat biscuits because of the advantages of having the same product outlets;
- complementarity of products or services, for example, moves by dairy companies into the sale of bread (to complement butter);
- extensions of production, for example the output of

Today you can't go into a shop without being offered the chance to drive a Ferrari or take an exclusive health spa break. The woman to thank for this £120 million plus market is Rachel Elnaugh. Back in 1989 she was looking to give a present that would never be forgotten, not just another pair of socks. She came up with the idea of Red Letter Days - a business offering experiences people would never forget. By 2002 the company expected to turn over £26 million. The business also offers bespoke packages. These include multi-choice experiences and gold and silver packages which cater for wedding lists, at £500 a time.

The business has faced competition from a number of operators that have set up. WH Smith launched Amazing Adventures in 600 stores. Virgin has the Virgin Experience and there is also lastminute.com. Red Letter Days has not lost business to many of these companies because they have such a diverse product range. In fact the business plans to expand in future, with a number of franchise deals in the offing.

Source: adapted from *Growing Business*, February 2003.

(a) Identify the types of generic, business level strategies used by Red Letter Days.
(b) Examine the advantages of using these strategies for the business.

components for one industry may easily be changed into production of components for others;
- 'New' products may also be created by adapting existing products slightly.

Unrelated diversification is where the organisation moves into completely new areas. For example, the Virgin Group expanded from music retailing into airlines, soft drinks, financial services and rail travel. This was arguably a complete change in direction.

Corporate strategy

CORPORATE STRATEGY is aimed at the long term position of the business. A company, for example, may consider where it will be in 10 years time and how it will get there. Should it expand? If so, how and in what direction? These are all likely to be long term decisions that will affect the entire organisation. There is a variety of methods by which corporate strategic development can be achieved.

Internal development This is where the business grows by increasing sales, output and profit over a period of time. In some ways the internal development can be seen as the least risky corporate strategy that an organisation may pursue. Corporate culture and structure will evolve 'organically' to meet the new requirements of the business. However, one of the disadvantages is that the business may not have all the necessary technology or personnel to implement the new strategy quickly. It may also take time for business to grow internally. This may not fit in with the overall objectives of the organisation.

Takeovers, mergers and acquisitions This involves companies joining together to form one single organisation (☞ unit 29). A merger is often when two companies of relatively equal size join to become one company. Takeovers or acquisitions usually, though not always, involve a larger company 'buying' a smaller organisation.

This corporate strategy has a number of benefits. An organisation may be able to introduce new products and services quickly by buying a business that is already set up to deliver such a product. Business expansion can lead to reduced costs and other economies of scale. A business may get access to new customers and product portfolios, new markets, specialised technology and expertise, high profile brands and prime retail or manufacturing sites.

Takeovers and mergers are not without problems. They may be resisted. Employees of companies that are taken over may be hostile to the new organisation. This could result in a demotivated and unproductive new workforce. There are also likely to be organisational difficulties, such as duplication of roles and assets and the need for retraining.

Some larger companies have attempted to demerge or divest themselves of unprofitable arms of the business. This allows them to focus on their core products. It may be that two separate companies may operate more efficiently than one large one.

Collaborative strategies and alliances Collaborative strategies and alliances are when organisations work together to the mutual benefit of both. They may remain as separate legal businesses. Sometimes they may have an arrangement where a new separate business is formed. They can come in a number of forms.
- Joint ventures and consortia. Joint ventures and consortia are when two or more organisations pool their resources for projects, research, offensive strategies or initiatives. The principle behind joint ventures is SYNERGY. This explains how the coming together of organisations ends in a greater result than would have been the case if the businesses had done things separately. So, for example,

certain car manufacturers may share similar components. Working together, cost reductions can be achieved in the production of each of their new cars.

- Hook-ups, associations and networks. This occurs where, for example, one organisation agrees to give prominence to or provide an exclusive outlet for the products of another. For example, Starbucks has many alliances. It has an alliance with Dreyer's ice cream to market coffee ice cream. It has an alliance with Barnes and Noble the bookstore to operate bookstore cafes. And it has an alliance with Microsoft to add wireless network capabilities to Starbucks coffee shops.

On 1 August 2002 EasyJet and Go completed a merger to create Europe's number one low cost airline under the EasyJet name. The transaction cost £374 million and made EasyJet the leading low cost airline in Europe. In June 2002 the new combined airline carried 14 million people, more than all but a few of Europe's largest airlines. In December 2002 all bookings in Go's system were redirected into easyJet.com. The new company is committed to taking the best practices of both airlines. Over time there will be changes in the way the company interacts with customers. For example, there will be a common call centre and one website. EasyJet will also take advantage of the Go routes into Europe, including those into Rome and Milan.

(a) Assess whether this type of corporate strategy used by EasyJet would be the most beneficial to gain expansion.

Global strategy

Businesses often expand to operate outside their national markets. It is argued that expanding outside national markets can benefit businesses for a number of reasons.

- A business that is successful in one country may have a unique strength or 'distinctive competence'. This may also be the case in other countries. So, for example, McDonald's has been successful in taking its unique skills and products from the USA to countries that did not have fast food chains, such as China and Brazil. This has allowed it to make even greater profit.
- It can reduce its costs. For example, it may be that production is more suited to a location abroad. Manufacturing in a country with lower wage costs may also reduce the production costs of a business. Selling a standard product in a variety of countries is also likely to gain economies of scale for a business.

What strategies might a business use to enter and compete in international markets?

International strategy This is where a business transfers skills or products to a foreign country because competitors in those countries lack these. An example might be a business setting up a computer software business in an eastern European country. This approach is useful if products are not available from competitors in foreign countries.

Multidomestic strategy This approach involves **customising** the product to suit the needs of different foreign markets. It may also mean setting up factories in each particular country. The advantage of this is that products can be targeted to the needs of particular markets. A problem may be the costs of duplicating production facilities in different countries.

Global strategy This approach means that production is concentrated in a few, favourable locations. Organisations are pursuing a low cost strategy. Companies tend to produce a standard product to reduce production costs. They do this to charge low prices for products in markets where there is pressure for prices to be kept low.

Transnational strategy It has been suggested that markets today are so competitive that a business must gain economies of scale, transfer competences and also pay attention to the needs of different markets. It is also argued that companies can benefit from a flow of skills and products from foreign subsidiaries back to home countries. This is likely to be a very difficult strategy for a business to follow.

Implementing strategy

Once a business has decided and planned its strategy it has to implement it. This may involve a number of features of the business.

Organisational structure A business must organise itself into the structure that best suits its strategies. It may have to decide:

- on the type of hierarchy or organisational hierarchy of the company. For example, some businesses prefer to delayer, so that there are fewer layers of management in the hierarchy. They give employees lower down the organisation the power to make decisions;
- whether to organise by function, region, product, process or customer, or some combination of these. For example, some businesses prefer to organise by area and have different marketing departments, each with knowledge of the markets in particular parts of the world.

Control systems A business must have some way of controlling its activities. This involves setting targets, measuring and feedback. Controls may be in the form of:

- financial controls, such as the return on investment to be achieved by the new strategy;
- output controls, where managers forecasts targets to be met. An example might be management by objectives, which is a way of evaluating the performance of managers;
- organisational culture (☞ unit 5) which determines the

norms of behaviour in the business;
- the leadership and management style adopted by the business;
- reward systems, both financial and non-financial.

The implementation of change A business must decide how change is to take place. Strategic change involves a move away from the present method of operation to another method. There is a variety of methods a business might use. Some of these include:
- reengineering, which involves redesigning processes of operation (☞ unit 30);
- Kaizen, or continuous improvement;
- restructuring, possibly involving delayering or downsizing (☞ unit 30);
- total quality management.

Evaluating strategy

A business must have some way of telling if its strategies have been successful. This will provide important **feedback** which may influence future decisions taken by the business. First a business needs to set strategic performance targets and indicators. No real understanding of the success, failure, viability or otherwise of any strategy can be achieved unless accurate, measurable and achievable performance targets are drawn up. Targets and indicators need to be specific, measurable, achievable, realistic and time based, known as SMART targets. They must be easily understood by all concerned. These may be drawn up in the following ways.

Earnings A number of different measures of earnings could be used to evaluate strategy.
- Earnings per employee, including all the employees of the business, not just the sales force or production line workers.
- Earnings per customer. The total income over a period is measured against the number of customers.
- Earnings per outlet. The outlet could be an office, a sales person, a department store, an airliner or a restaurant.
- Earnings per square foot, for example of individual premises or total premises.

Profit Each of the items above may be represented as profit (per employee, per customer, per outlet, per square foot). Again, this would be calculated over given periods of time.

Returns on capital These are explained in unit 17. Examples might be:
- earnings per share in organisations where share capital has been issued or per partner where this form of organisation exists;
- returns on total capital employed.

Volume The volumes of business conducted and the quantities of products and goods moved may be measured. These may include:
- sales, production or throughput per employee, either overall or by occupation, department or function;
- volume of goods sold per customer or per outlet;
- rate of volume turnover per outlet.

Caring For You is a chain of 10 salons in the Newcastle area which specialises in all aspects of hair, nail and beauty care. The business was originally set up as a fast and cheap service aimed largely at younger people. It had been relatively successful, but sales had started to decline in recent years. The owner of the business consulted staff and customers about what they wanted and found that the market had moved on.

Customers wanted a slower, more stylish experience and were prepared to pay for it. So the salons were redesigned at great expense. A London consultant was brought in to retrain staff. A customer care training programme was introduced and salaries were increased. These were all aspects of what is known as an 'inclusive' approach to business. Successful companies, it was suggested, focused on all those who contributed to the business including staff, shareholders, customers, suppliers and the community rather than just profit per share.

The redesigned salons were taking 10 per cent more than the old ones, turnover was expected to rise from £1 million to £2.5 million within 5 years and pre-tax profits increased from £80,000 to £500,000.

(a) Explain the aspects of implementing change at Caring For You.
(b) Using information in the article, evaluate the new strategy of the business and discuss how such a business might use other methods of evaluation.

Costs Cost targets may be appropriate in relation to earnings, profits and volumes. They may also be used where a business is seeking constant improvement. A business may take into account premises and equipment costs, capital charges, administrative and bureaucratic charges, and purchasing, lease and rental costs. Target costs per employee, per department, per square metre and per premises may be calculated.

Comparisons It is useful for many businesses to analyse their operations in relation to other companies, particularly competitors in their industry. This benchmarking may help to find out whether there is any scope for improvement, overall or in certain activities similar to those of competitors. On the other hand, a business may find that competitive advantage can only be gained by adopting strategies that are different from those of competitors. Comparisons are vital in the area of pricing and customer satisfaction. In certain markets, for instance, a business may find that customers will only buy a quality product and are prepared to pay a premium price, rather than receive a poorer product or service at a lower price.

Comparisons of output, volume, profit margins and turnover are also useful. However, care must be taken to compare like with like. For example, care must be taken when comparing the figures of a large car manufacturer such as Ford with those of a kit car manufacturer such as The Chesil Motor Company which hand builds kit cars. Although they are both car manufacturers, they may not operate in the same markets, they may have different customers, their prices may differ and their production techniques may vary.

Percentages and annual comparisons Organisations may set themselves targets of 'increasing sales or output by a particular percentage'. Usually the performance is based on performance in previous years. Care needs to be taken when making this type of comparison. A business may make a 2 per cent increase in sales in one year and not regard that as successful. However, in a year when it is facing a difficult market a sales increase of 2 per cent may be very good.

Qualitative aspects Achieving qualitative targets can be as important as meeting quantitative targets such as sales targets. Being seen as 'the top quality operator in the field' by customers is likely to be a route to success.

key terms

Corporate strategies - strategies aimed at the long term position of a company.
Functional or operational strategies - strategies designed to improve the efficiency of the operations of a business.
Generic strategies - strategies that can be used by any type of business organisation.
Premium price - a price above the average charged by businesses in the market.
Synergy - where the activities of two or more businesses when brought together create more value than they do separately.

Knowledge

1. What is meant by functional level strategies of a business?
2. State 5 functional level strategies a business might use.
3. State 3 generic strategies a business might use.
4. In what type of market situation might a consolidation strategy be used?
5. Suggest 3 conditions under which market entry might be a suitable strategy.
6. State 4 circumstances where diversification might be a suitable business strategy.
7. Explain when internal growth may not be a suitable strategy.
8. State 4 approaches to operating in global markets.
9. Why might feedback on the effectiveness of strategy be important to a business?
10. Suggest 5 ways in which a business might evaluate strategy.

Case study Latina Brands

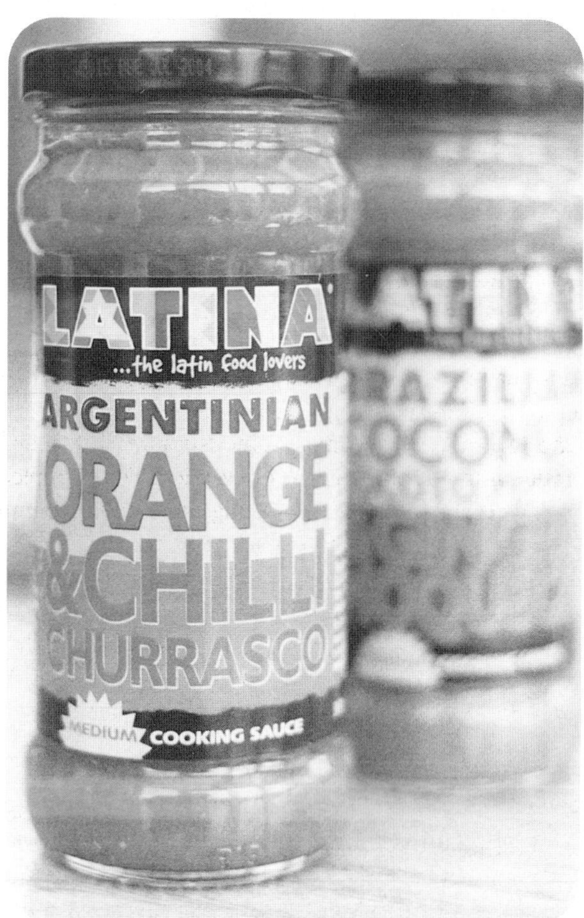

The Old Bothy, a workers' lodge just outside Guildford, is the last place you might expect to find an Ecuadorian feast. It is the home of South American foods company Latina Brands. Chief Executive Officer Elaine Underwood started the company in 2001. She aimed to bring South American food to the UK market. The company now has its products in Waitrose, Sainsbury's and Safeway. It not tex-mex, but authentic Brazilian, Chilean and Argentinean products.

The ethnic food market grew by 13 per cent in 2001 to an estimated £908 million. Whilst the business accepts that South American food will never be as big as Indian, the target is a £10 million turnover in two years, with even £120 million possible eventually.

The business ran research groups to find out whether people were open to the idea of Latin American food - particularly the key ingredients of Chili, corn, lime, chocolate and coffee. But they are also an attempt to educate people in these tastes. The company develops and owns recipes which it then uses other manufacturers to make.

Latina is still a niche range of products. The product is being positioned as a premium brand, although the business recognises that customers still demand value for money.

At the moment the business is concentrating on its new product programme and the education and marketing process. It has outsourced its PR. It has attended food shows and bought advertising in food magazines. When Asda started stocking its products it hired salsa dancers for an instore launch event. The company has also invested heavily in direct mail and a newsletter to help collect names for its database. This all helps to establish the brand image, which is vital.

There is the possibility of investing in manufacturing in future. If one of the products become big enough then the company recognises that it would be sensible to look at producing it itself. Another possibility in future is expanding into mainland Europe. It has had a trial run with a request from the middle east, although Holland and France are more likely long term targets. But there is still room for expansion in the UK. Latina products are currently not in Tesco stores, as its process of taking new products has slowed down.

Source: adapted from *Growing Business*, February 2003.

(a) Outline the (i) functional and (ii) generic strategies used by the business. (6 marks)

(b) Explain why the business may have chosen these strategies (8 marks).

(c) (i) Suggest possible strategies that the business may use in future. (10 marks)

(ii) Examine the reasons for these strategies. (12 marks)

(iii) Evaluate the likely success of these strategies. (14 marks)

8 Marketing Budgeting

The MARKETING BUDGET specifies and sets out clearly the financial elements of the marketing plan. Like budgets for other aspects of business activity (☞ unit 15), the marketing budget is a **plan** of what the business hopes to achieve in the forthcoming period. So, for example, a business may plan to achieve an increase in sales or profits next year. The marketing plan will then outline the spending the business intends to make on marketing next year in order to achieve this increase. It will show the planned sales and the planned costs of marketing to generate these sales.

When setting marketing budgets a balance must be maintained. On the one hand businesses must set precise financial plans associated with marketing activities. It is important that plans are precise if managers are to use the budget to control spending and to set **targets** for sales. However, changes in the internal and external marketing environment mean that some flexibility may be built into the budget.

Businesses that have planned well are more likely to remain within their budget and achieve the sales levels targeted. However, sometimes the actual marketing spending and sales are different from the budget. A business must identify why these **variances** (☞ unit 15) have taken place. If sales are lower than planned or marketing expenditure higher, a business can identify the reasons and make sure that any problems are corrected in future budgets.

Marketing budgets are often planned for a year and may be broken down into monthly amounts. They may also be broken down into more detailed categories. For example, a business might plan how much it is spending on different forms of promotion and advertising.

Types of marketing budget

There is a number of ways in which a business might construct a budget.

The affordable budget This is where the budget for marketing expenditure is based upon what is expected to be left over after more important expenses have been met. So a business might decide, for example, that once it has paid for its raw materials, labour costs and overheads, it has £10,000 left over to spend on marketing. The problem with this method is that it takes no account of market requirements and conditions. It could be that the business actually needs to spend £30,000 for its marketing to be effective.

Historical budgeting This is where the budget for marketing expenditure is based upon what has been spent on marketing activities in previous years. Sometimes an extra amount is added to allow for the effects of inflation. As with affordable budgets, it takes no account of market factors. It is also based upon the sometimes mistaken assumption that previous years' expenditures have been appropriate.

As a percentage of past sales This is where the budget for marketing expenditure is based upon previous sales of a product. Products are allocated a marketing budget in line with their sales records. So, for example, a product that has sold particularly well in the past may have a higher amount spent on its advertising than a product with poor sales.

The benefit of this method is that successful products are rewarded with high promotional budgets. This should help their future success. Businesses using this method sometimes refer to their **advertising: sales ratio**. This is the means by which businesses decide on the proportion of sales revenue to allocate to future advertising. Businesses in the cosmetics industry, for example, generally have a ratio of 20 per cent or more. Businesses operating in industrial markets may have ratios as low as one per cent or even less. For example, scrap metal dealers may have advertising expenses per annum of less than 0.1 per cent of their sales revenue.

The problem with this budgeting method is that it can lead to particular products being sent on a downward spiral. Falling sales lead to lower marketing expenditure, which leads to lower sales and so on. Sometimes, however, it may be in the strategic interest of a business to increase marketing expenditure on a product with falling sales.

Competitor based budgeting This involves setting marketing budgets in relation to competitors' spending. It may mean spending amounts similar to that of competitors, matching competitors' spending exactly, or exceeding competitors' spending. The problem with this method is that marketing expenditure may not be set in relation to the marketing objectives of a business itself. Instead such expenditure may be set in relation to the marketing objectives of the competitor.

Objective and task budgeting This method involves setting marketing expenditure in relation to marketing objectives and the tasks or actions which must be completed to achieve these objectives. To do this a business must cost all of the marketing activities in which it expects to be engaged over a particular period of time. Many regard this as the most desirable method of marketing budgeting. This is because it is based upon the needs of particular businesses and products operating in particular market conditions.

Factors influencing the marketing budget

A number of factors might influence the marketing budget set by a business.

Business aims and objectives The marketing budget must be planned with the corporate aims of the business in mind and its business objectives. For example, if the business aims to grow in future, it is likely that the marketing budget will plan for an increase in sales, perhaps brought about by an increase in promotion expenditure. The marketing budget is also constrained by other budgets. A business might want to spend an extra £50,000 on promotion. However, if there is a need to employ more specialist workers, then funds might be diverted to the budget of the human resources department.

Rewards The level of reward is likely to affect the marketing budget. For example, a business might be faced with a choice when expanding. It might have the alternative of spending more on marketing or alternatively on reorganisation of production. If the rewards gained by the reorganisation are likely to be greater then the business might decide not to increase promotion. Similarly, if a business might decide to spend more on marketing a new product because it predicts that it will be very profitable.

Behaviour of competitors The actions of rival businesses can affect marketing. Large increases in spending on marketing by competitors might have to be matched if a business wants to remain competitive. Some businesses could not compete with others if they did not have enormous marketing budgets, such as in the motor car industry.

Nature of the market and customers Some markets do not require large amounts of promotion. For example, a wholesale business selling imported cycle parts to cycle shops might simply need to send out regular price lists and product descriptions or use a website. Businesses selling to customers around the world, such as Coca-Cola or McDonald's, are likely to spend vast amounts on marketing. Businesses also sometimes spend large amounts to launch new products on the market. They might reduce marketing spending later in the product life cycle as sales decline to gain greater profit.

Benefits and problems of marketing budgeting

There are certain benefits of marketing budgets for a business.

- They provide a business with a means of controlling marketing costs.
- They can be used to identify where costs have been too high or where marketing has been ineffective in raising sales.
- They can be used to plan the future of the business with some certainty, so other decisions can be made.
- They can be used by other departments to coordinate strategies to make the business more efficient.
- They set targets for the marketing department, which can be used to motivate employees and identify improvements in productivity.

However, there may also be problems.

- They might be too much of a straightjacket on decision making. This is particularly important if there are sudden and unexpected changes in the market.
- They might be seen by employees as a means by which a business can judge them if targets are not met, and so could be demotivating.
- They might lead to poor decision making if they are inaccurate.
- They might conflict with other objectives of the business. Different stakeholders often have different objectives. Managers, for example, might attempt to 'empire build' by trying to obtain large budgets.
- They can be constraining on other business decisions. For example, managers might over or understate budget requirements, fearing they will lose their budget or may be given too great a target next year.

Holland & Knight is a large law firm. It has more than 1,200 attorneys in 333 offices and over 100 practice areas. The marketing budget is derived from the annual strategic plans drawn up by business. Each year there is a clean plan and a new budget. Expenditure is evaluated on the return on investment (ROI). A high ROI signals a good marketing investment. Marketing expenditures are constantly evaluated by both the attorney and marketing staff during the year.

Holland & Knight is a very client-orientated business. It relies heavily on relationship marketing, including client events, sponsorship, newsletters and seminars. It also spends on web development but not a great deal on advertising. During the past several years around 2.5-3 per cent of turnover has been allocated to marketing budgets.

There is an emphasis on 'cross marketing' within the business. Clients are 'owned' by the whole business rather than one member of the business. So the whole business is accountable for each client. This helps it to identify other services which might be useful for the client.

Source: adapted from www.firmmarketingcentre.com.

(a) Explain reasons why marketing budgeting is likely to be important for this business.
(b) Examine the factors that are likely to affect the marketing budget of the business.

Trends in marketing expenditure

What trends are taking place in marketing expenditure in the UK? Figure 8.1 shows that the UK experienced a slowdown between 2002-03, but expected to see an increase between 2003-04. However, the overall picture between 2001 and 2004 was an increase in expenditure. Some reasons given for increases in expenditure by businesses included:

- to drive forward the growth of the company;
- to help with the launch of new products;
- in response to competition - either to match others'

increases or to take advantage when others cut their budgets;

- in response to external factors, ie fears by US holidaymakers about flights, agricultural disease such as foot and mouth or economic slowdown.

A breakdown of the types of marketing spending shows some interesting trends. Figure 8.2 shows that advertising in

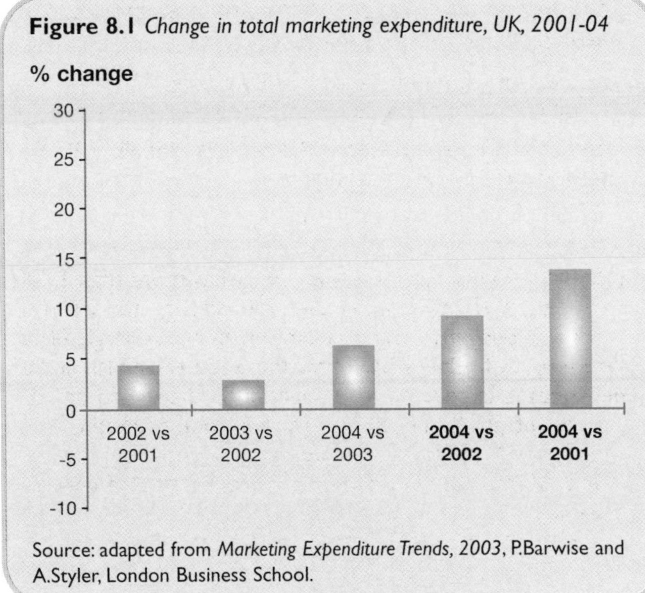

Figure 8.1 *Change in total marketing expenditure, UK, 2001-04*

Source: adapted from *Marketing Expenditure Trends, 2003*, P.Barwise and A.Styler, London Business School.

the media accounted for by far the largest proportion of marketing expenditure in 2003. But of greater interest to businesses for the future might be the trends taking place in Figure 8.3. They show that the greatest changes in expenditure over the period 2001-04 have been on 'interactive marketing' or the use of the Internet for marketing purposes.

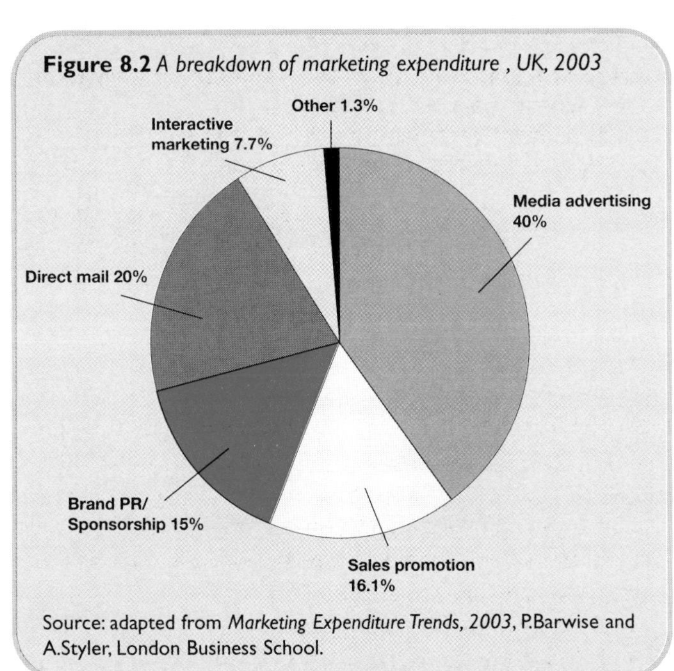

Figure 8.2 *A breakdown of marketing expenditure , UK, 2003*

Source: adapted from *Marketing Expenditure Trends, 2003*, P.Barwise and A.Styler, London Business School.

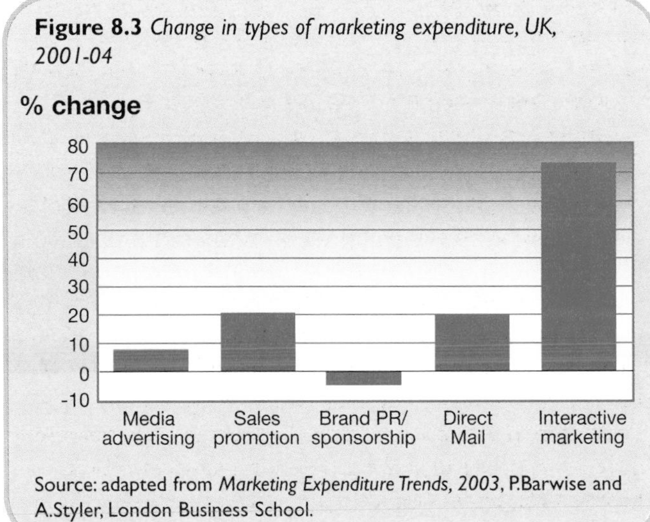

Figure 8.3 *Change in types of marketing expenditure, UK, 2001-04*

Source: adapted from *Marketing Expenditure Trends, 2003*, P.Barwise and A.Styler, London Business School.

these include a number of marketing methods, such as:

- online promotions and incentives;
- advertising on other websites;
- the use of password protected websites;
- online sales;
- the use of permission based emails.

Another feature has been the long term growth of direct marketing and the use on inhouse marketing rather than advertising agencies. Businesses were increasingly carrying out their own marketing rather than employing specialist outside organisations. The growth in the use of the Internet would have helped businesses to do this.

key terms

Marketing budget - a plan, agreed in advance, showing the funds to be used for marketing and how they will be allocated. The budget shows expected sales and marketing expenditure.

1. What does a marketing budget show?
2. What will a variance in a marketing budget show?
3. What is the difference between historical budgeting and task based budgeting?
4. State 4 factors that might influence a marketing budget.
5. State 4 benefits of marketing budgets.
6. State 4 problems of marketing budgets.
7. 'There has been a growth in emphasis on interactive marketing.' Explain what this means.

Case study Jenson Ltd

Increasingly manufacturing businesses are making use of computer aided technology. Computer aided design (CAD) is the use of computers and computer software in the design of products. Computer aided manufacture (CAM) is the use of the use of computers to aid the manufacture of products, such as in computer numerically controlled (CNC) milling machines and lathes. Many computer aided products and services are sold to other businesses by manufacturers and software providers.

In 2002 a survey was carried out on the marketing expenditure of businesses in the computer aided technology industry. Figures 8.4 - 8.7 show some of the results of the survey.

Jenson Ltd is a designer of computer software for the industry. It is setting its marketing budget for next year. It is concerned that budgets in recent years have been inaccurate. In particular marketing expenditure seems to have been planned poorly and costs have often been higher than expected. One of the reasons is that they were always based on figures in previous years, but circumstances changed. It also tended to budget carefully, without any real consideration of what might be happening to marketing in the industry generally.

The business wants to expand rapidly next year. So it is looking to market its products more aggressively. It has decided to launch a number of new software products and feels that they will be well received by users of computer software in the industry. But it must make sure that it is targeting its market correctly, with the right type of promotion. It has decided to use some of the information in the survey to set the components of its marketing budget. It plans to spend around 5 per cent of its turnover on marketing this year. It has targeted direct mail to businesses as its main expenditure. However, it is also considering spending a lot more of its marketing budget on media advertising, such as trade magazines, as it feels this could reach an untapped market.

Figure 8.4 *Survey results on marketing budgets - What proportion of your turnover is spent on marketing?*

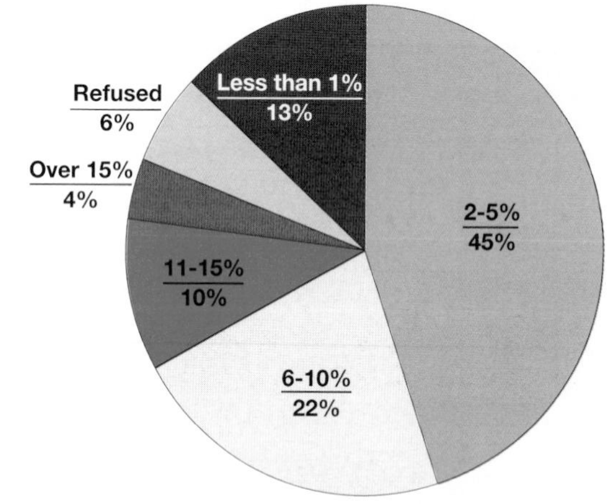

Figure 8.5 *Survey results on marketing budgets - Has the proportion of the marketing budget spent on the following activities increased, decreased or stayed the same?*

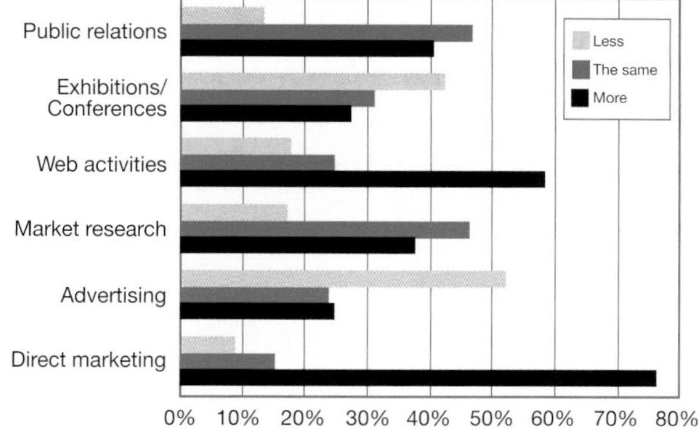

Source: adapted from www.business advantage.co.uk/Spaghetti/cam.htm.

Figure 8.6 *Survey results on marketing budgets - What proportion of your turnover is allocated to direct marketing?*

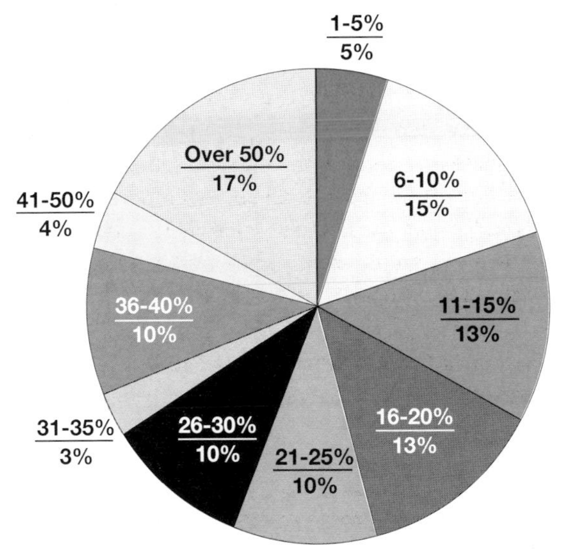

Figure 8.7 *Survey results on marketing budgets - What proportion of your turnover is allocated to advertising?*

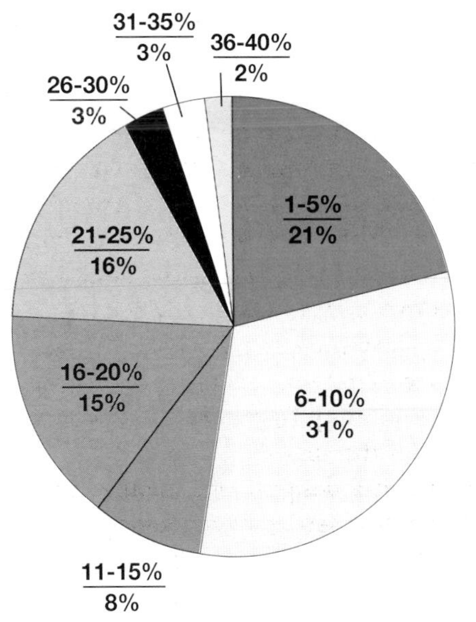

Source: adapted from www.business advantage.co.uk/Spaghetti/cam.htm.

(a) (i) What is meant by a variance in a marketing budget? (4 marks)

(ii) Identify why a variance took place in the budget of Jenson Ltd in previous years. (4 marks)

(b) Explain the types of budget setting that Jenson Ltd has used. (10 marks)

(c) Examine the factors that might influence the setting of Jenson Ltd's budget next year. (10 marks)

(d) Evaluate the choices that Jenson intends to make about the allocation of its marketing budget. (12 marks)

9 International Marketing

The importance of international marketing

At one time businesses may have thought that marketing products overseas was an adventurous act. It was generally undertaken by large businesses which had grown too big for domestic markets. Today, however, the world has 'shrunk' due to, amongst other things, rapid changes in international transport and telecommunications. One effect of this is that a business now needs to consider the threat from foreign competition and the opportunities which might be gained from marketing internationally.

For many firms international marketing is no longer an option. It is necessary if a business is to survive in a competitive business environment. For British firms this was the case after trade barriers between European Union nations were lifted in 1992 and perhaps with the expansion of the EU in 2004. The increase in the size and number of multinationals has contributed to the increase in international trading. The globalisation of business activity has also affected business marketing strategy.

Why might businesses market their products internationally?

- Profits. By selling in overseas markets, a business might have the potential to increase its profits through an increase in sales. Overseas markets may be more lucrative than domestic ones. Manufacturing and distribution costs may be lower abroad. The product might also sell at a higher price on foreign markets than in the home market.
- Spreading the risk. If a business only produces in one country then it may face problems caused by downturns in demand due to recession. The more countries a firm operates in, the less vulnerable it is to changes in the business climate of any single country.
- Unfavourable trading conditions in the domestic market. Businesses often find that the market for a product is saturated or in decline. One option for a firm is to try and breathe new life into the product by introducing it into an overseas market. This is an example of an **extension strategy**. British American Tobacco industries, for example, have started to sell in developing countries as domestic market sales have declined.
- Legal differences. Legal restrictions on the sale of products vary from one country to another. For example, developing countries have fewer restrictions on which drugs can be offered for sale. Some pharmaceutical companies (in what many regard as unethical practice) have sold drugs banned on health grounds in the UK to these nations.

Why the overseas market is different

There can be many rewards for a business entering an overseas market.

One problem that it will face, however, is that market conditions will be different to those in the domestic market. This makes selling abroad very risky. What are the differences that are likely to affect the success of foreign sales?

Political differences A firm must take into account the political stability of the country in which it plans to sell. Political instability can make trading almost impossible. Also, a change of government can bring about a change in attitude towards foreign companies. A firm thinking of investing a large sum in its operations abroad will need to weigh up the political situation carefully. A number of businesses, for example, were affected by the change in government in Hong Kong in 1997 as ownership of the area was transferred from the UK to China.

Cultural differences One difference which often causes problems for British businesses is that English is not the main or even the second language in many countries. In Eastern

Philips is a manufacturer of a wide range of television, video, audio, computer and communications products. Its website contained the following information in 2003.

Achievements per region
Global market share growth 2002, 10.5% to 2003. Year to date 10.8%.

Europe
- Continued prominence in Western and Central Europe.
- Making inroads in developing and emerging markets.

North America
- Repositioned brand and established credibility with leading retailers.
- Expanded placements significantly.
- Major progress with Wal Mart, DirecTV and other key channel partners.

Asia Pacific/Middle East/Africa
- Regained growth momentum in Monitors, GSM and TV.

Latin America
- Derisked business model implemented.
- Continued leadership in Brazil.

Source: adapted from www.philips.com.

(a) Using examples from the data, explain why the business might want to operate in different markets.

Europe for example, German and Russian may be more widely spoken than English.

Other cultural differences may influence the way a product is marketed. For example, a product name suitable in one country may have a totally different meaning in another - the French lemonade Pssschit would require a new name were it to be sold in the UK. Colours have different meanings throughout the world. In the Far East, white rather than black is associated with mourning. In India fashion models of the sort used to promote products in the West are considered too thin. In some countries, what may be regarded as a 'bribe' in the UK is common business practice. Payments to government or industry officials may be required to get things done, from electricity connection to securing contracts.

Differences in legislation Such differences can affect the way in which a business produces and markets its products.

- Product labelling. US laws are far more stringent than UK laws about the amount of information which should be included on food labels.
- Product safety. Some countries have very strict legislation governing safety standards on childrens' toys. Others are less strict.
- Environmental impact. All cars sold in California, for example, must be fitted with a catalytic convertor.
- Advertising. Cigarette advertising on television is outlawed within EU countries.

Economic and social differences Some of the economic factors which businesses must consider include levels of income, levels of sales and corporation tax, how income is distributed, the use of tariffs or other import barriers and the level and growth of population. For example, many foreign businesses took advantage of investment opportunities in China in 2004 after the country 'opened up' its economy and its trading arrangements.

Social factors which firms may need to consider include literacy levels, the role of women, religious attitudes, readiness to accept new ideas, and the habits and attitudes of social groups.

Differences in business practice The usual amount of time it takes to receive payment may vary in different countries. Other differences include accounting techniques, company ownership (most British companies are relatively independent whereas those in other EU nations are often controlled by families or banks) and distribution (in many EU

Whirlpool, a US based company, is one of the world's biggest manufacturers of 'white goods', household appliances such as fridges, dishwashers and cookers. In 2002 it had a turnover of more than $11 billion.

In the case of dishwashers, the products for the main markets in North America and Europe are quite different. Because in many US homes the machines double as garbage disposers, US-style dishwashers have mechanisms for chopping up bits of food. They also use more energy and water and tend to be noisier.

Consumers' tastes for fridges vary even more. US consumers prefer 'larder-size' cabinets which nearly all contain air-blowing systems to make them frost-free. The Germans want lots of space for meat, while the Italians are keen on special vegetable compartments. To cater for the large number of vegetarians in India, often within families that contain meat eaters, the fridges often require internal sealing systems to stop smells of different foods intermingling.

The company also received a bronze award for the Supermatic Tapa Lava-Lava scrubber lid, a scrubbing and drying attachment to manual washing machines used by customers in Mexico.

The Whirlpool *Annual Report and Accounts, 2002* contained the following statements.

Figure 9.1 *Whirlpool, turnover by region, $ million*

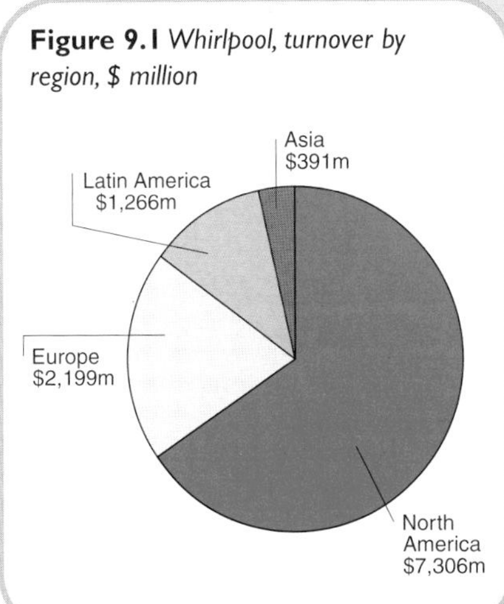

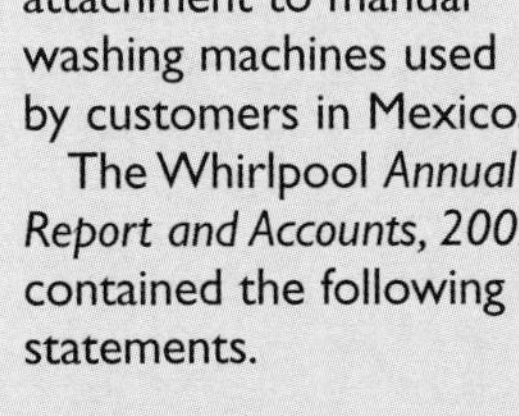

Europe

'With the 2002 acquisition of Polar S.A., Whirlpool Europe gained a strategic, low cost manufacturing position in Poland that will help serve the entire region. The company expects its ... strategy ... to result in improved contributions and productivity... .'

Latin America

'Whirlpool's Brazil-based compressor business, Embraco, remained a strong performer for the company. In 2002 exports from the regional operations, which include compressors and major appliances, reached a record high, rising more than 50 per cent. The company expects exports in the region will be an increasingly positive factor in the operation's ongoing performance.'

Asia

'Among the significant introductions in Whirlpool China was the launch of a new Whirlpool sixth sense clothes washer with sensor washing technology suited to the Chinese market. We also acquired the remaining 20 per cent of the shares from our former partner in a washing machine joint venture in Shanghai.'

Source: adapted from *The Financial Times* and Whirlpool, *Annual Report and Accounts, 2002.*

(a) Identify the ways in which the business enters foreign markets.

(b) Examine the potential implications for the business of using these methods.

countries greater use is made of rail transport than in the UK).

Adapting products to fit in with local, national and regional needs can be costly. It is cheaper to have one product with one brand name and a promotional package which fits all markets. Businesses must attempt to cater for national consumer tastes, whilst trying to gain economies of scale from operating in international markets.

Methods of entering overseas markets

Once a business has made the decision to enter an overseas market, it must decide the best way to do this.

Exporting This is often the first step for a business wishing to enter an overseas market. It involves manufacturing products at home but selling them abroad. The great advantage of exporting is that it minimises the risk of operating abroad. It can also be used as a means of testing out the ground.

Sometimes, the business may have little or no control over how the product is actually marketed in the countries to which it is sent. For this reason many firms exporting abroad make use of overseas agents. These agents are able to play an active role in the marketing of the product.

Franchising This involves one business selling a licence to others. The licence allows one firm to use another's name, product or service in return for an initial payment and further commission or royalties.

This is a quick and relatively easy way into foreign markets and it allows the franchiser a high degree of control over the marketing of its product. However, a share of the profit does go to the franchisee. Firms such as PizzaExpress, Budget Rent-a-Car and Kentucky Fried Chicken have used this as a way of entering overseas markets.

Licensing This is similar to franchising. Franchising is used in service industries, such as fast foods and car hire. Licensing, however, involves one firm producing another's product and using its brand name, designs, patents and expertise under licence. This means that goods do not have to be physically moved abroad. Instead they are produced abroad by the foreign licensee. Also, it means that firms can avoid operating overseas. The main disadvantage is that the success or failure of the venture is largely in the hands of the licensee.

Joint ventures This involves two companies from separate countries combining their resources. One new enlarged company is formed to launch a product onto one market. An example of this is the Royal Bank of Scotland's alliance with Banco Santander of Spain to provide banking and financial services throughout Europe. Joint ventures are increasingly being used by businesses wishing to enter Eastern European markets.

One advantage of this form of venture is that the risks are shared between two firms. Also, each business can draw on the strengths of the other. One business may have research and development strengths, for example, while others may have strengths in manufacturing. However, many joint ventures have broken down due to conflicts which occur.

Direct investment Direct investment requires the setting up of production and distribution facilities abroad. They can be obtained by merger or takeover, or they may be built for this specific purpose. It is an increasingly common way for firms to reach overseas markets. For example, many Japanese manufacturers such as Nissan and Toyota set up plants in the UK in the 1990s. It was argued that there were a number of advantages to these businesses of direct investment.

- They could avoid paying import duties that were placed on foreign products entering the EU.
- They could take advantage of the relatively low costs and availability of relatively cheap labour in the UK.
- They could take advantage of government and EU incentives to invest in the area.
- There would be lower distribution costs.
- They could take advantage of local knowledge.

Mergers or takeovers Buying a business in another country may allow a company to produce and sell its products more easily. This method of entering foreign markets has similar advantages to direct investment and is most often used by **multinationals** (☞ unit 38).

The ethics of international marketing

The behaviour of some businesses in their international marketing activities has been questioned. Concerns have been raised about businesses from wealthier countries operating in areas such as Africa, Asia and South America. For example, some tobacco companies have focussed their marketing efforts on countries with lower incomes. With health concerns about smoking and laws being passed to reduce smoking there has been a decline in the number of cigarettes purchased in western Europe and North America. One response of tobacco companies has been to focus their efforts upon poorer countries where attitudes to smoking are less negative. Also, some food companies have engaged in selling what many regard as unnecessary products to poorer consumers. Examples include sales of baby milk to mothers when breast feeding babies would be a cheaper and healthier option.

Knowledge

1. Give 5 reasons why international marketing can be so important to firms.
2. How does entering an overseas market allow a firm to spread its risks?
3. State 3 differences between overseas and domestic markets.
4. How can an agent help a business to export its products?
5. In what ways can a business enter an overseas market?
6. What is meant by licensing?
7. What is the difference between direct investment and joint ventures?
8. List 2 concerns about businesses marketing their products overseas.

Case study McDonald's

McDonald's is the world's leading food service retailer with more than 300,000 local McDonald's restaurants serving 47 million customers each day in more than 100 countries. More than 70 per cent of McDonald's restaurants around the world are owned and operated by independent, local businessmen and women.

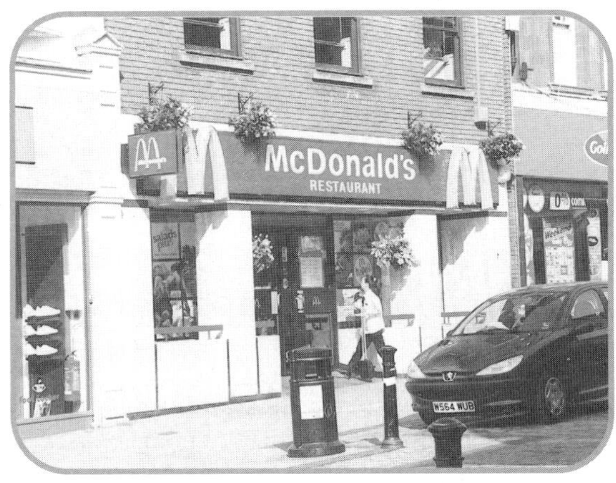

Table 9.1 *McDonald's total revenues, nine months ended 30 September, $ million*

Country	2003	2002
US	4,460.6	4,076.3
Europe	4,291.2	3,789.1
APMEA*	1,811.8	1,788.0
Latin America	620.4	619.4
Canada	561.6	473.7
Partner brands	839.5	760.0
Total	**12,585.1**	**11,506.5**

* Asia Pacific/Middle East/Africa.
Source: adapted from www.mcdonalds.com/corp/news.

In 2002 McDonald's warned that it was on track to post its first ever loss. It suggested that it might make a loss in the final three months of the year. Intense competition from rivals offering alternative fast food, such as pizzas, sandwiches and tacos, had put the business under pressure. In a retrenchment exercise, the business pulled out of three countries in Latin America and the Middle East.

Source: adapted from news.bbc.co.uk.

In 2004 McDonald's Japan, which is 50 per cent owned by US giant McDonald's, said sales increased 2 per cent in November 2003 compared with a year earlier. This broke a two year slump in the country which had been affected by mad cow disease, competition from local rivals, such as beef bowl restaurant chain Yoshinoya D&C, and weak consumer spending. McDonald's was likely to benefit from the remodelling of its stores and menu changes. To revive fortunes, McDonald's aimed to offer promotional products such as 'Gratin Croquette Burgers' which appealed to local tastes.

Source: adapted from www.ccfa.org.cn.

In December 2003 McDonald's announced another step in its revitalisation plan. Part of this included:

- discontinuing its development of non-McDonald's brands outside the US, including Donatos Pizzeria in Germany and Boston Market in Canada and Australia;
- retaining a minority investment in Pret a Manger in the UK, but closing its Pret operations in Japan.

Source: adapted from www.mcdonalds.com/corp/news.

Figure 9.2 *McDonald's operating margins, company operated and franchised restaurants, nine months ended 30 September, $ million, 2003*

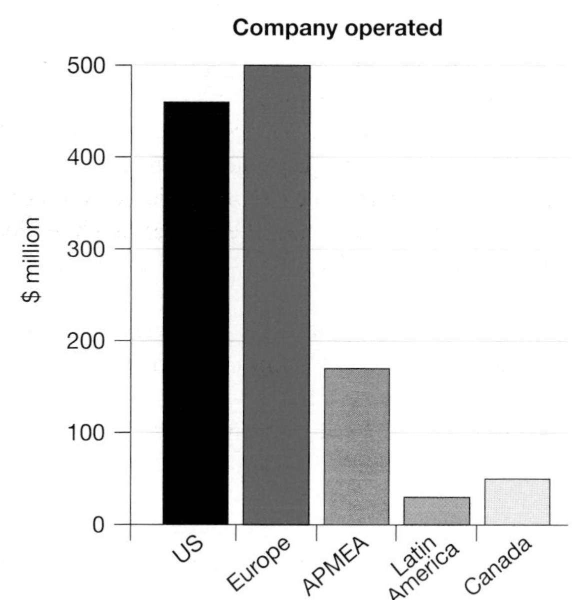

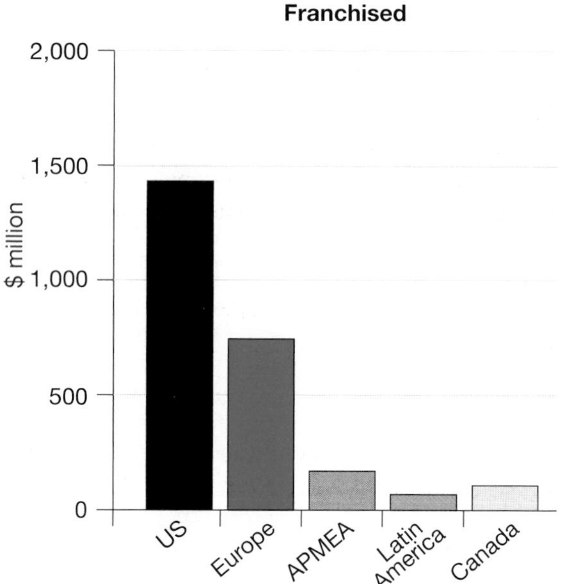

Source: adapted from www.mcdonalds.com/corp/news.

In 2003 McDonald's announced positive results for the nine months to end September 2003. It reported 'Europe delivered its highest quarterly sales increase this year. We've had solid performance in many European markets ...' and 'To strengthen the business we are working to increase relevance ... by enhancing our value positioning and adding more menu choice.' It also added that around the world it recently launched its first ever global marketing initiative, 'I'm lovin' it'. This initiative was designed to reaffirm McDonald's marketing leadership.

(a) Describe how McDonald's has differentiated its marketing in different countries. (6 marks)

(b) Explain how McDonald's has entered overseas markets. (10 marks)

(c) Examine the factors that are likely to affect McDonald's marketing success in overseas markets.(12 marks)

(d) Assess the extent to which McDonald's international marketing marketing (i) has been a success in the past and (ii) might be a success in future. (12 marks)

10 Sampling

Sample results

Businesses carry out market research to find out what their customers want. It is highly unlikely that a business will be able to carry out market research on everyone in the population. So businesses tend to choose a **sample** of people to survey. There is a variety of sampling techniques that can be used. These vary from completely random samples, where everyone has an equal chance of being chosen, to quota sampling, where the population is segmented into groups with similar characteristics and a certain number of people are selected out of each segment.

Market research will provide a wide variety of information about the people in the sample. Businesses then analyse this data to find out the significance of the sample results. For example, a business may be interested to know the likely proportion of the population that would pay between £10 and £20 for its product or whether a new promotional campaign has increased the sales of its product.

To analyse sample market research data, businesses make use of probability, average and standard deviation calculations and the normal distribution (☞ unit 3).

Probability and sampling

The reason why businesses carry out surveys and take samples is to try to reduce the risk and uncertainty that exists in every business decision. PROBABILITY is a technique that helps a business to quantify risk and it forms a basis for the analysis of sampling data.

A probability is a simple ratio between the event the business is interested in and the total number of events that could occur, ie:

$$\text{Probability (P)} = \frac{\text{Required event}}{\text{Total events}}$$

Take an example of a card drawn from a pack of 52 playing cards. The probability of drawing a 'Heart' would be:

$$\text{P(a Heart)} = \frac{13}{52} = \frac{1}{4} = 0.25$$

Similarly, for drawing a card that is from one of the other suits:

$$\text{P(a Club)} = \frac{13}{52} = \frac{1}{4} = 0.25$$

$$\text{P(a Diamond)} = \frac{13}{52} = \frac{1}{4} = 0.25$$

$$\text{P(a Spade)} = \frac{13}{52} = \frac{1}{4} = 0.25$$

There are three important laws of probability:

- The sum of the probabilities of all the possible events will equal 1. Thus the probability of drawing a Heart, a Club, a Diamond or a Spade will equal 1 (0.25 + 0.25 + 0.25 + 0.25 = 1).
- To obtain the probability of one event or another event occurring, **add** the probabilities (the addition rule). Thus the probability of drawing a Diamond or a Spade = 0.25 + 0.25 = 0.5.
- To obtain the probability of one event and another occurring, **multiply** the probabilities (the multiplication rule). Thus the probability of drawing a Diamond and a Spade on two successive draws = 0.25 x 0.25 = 0.0625.

Two examples can be used to illustrate how probability might affect a business. The first example considers its use in marketing. However, it is possible to use probability in other areas of the business, such as production or stock control. The second example shows how the business might evaluate problems arising in its administration department.

To quantify the risk associated with making a decision Say that a business has the following information about the launch of a new product.

- Probability of gaining a high demand = 0.6, expected return £6 million.
- Probability of gaining a medium demand = 0.2, expected return £3million.
- Probability of gaining a low demand = 0.2, expected return £1 million.

This information about the likelihood of high, medium or low demand would have been derived from market research. The likely outcome from the decision to launch the new product will be:

- 0.6 probability of a return of £6m = 0.6 x £6m = £3.6m;
- 0.2 probability of a return of £3m = 0.2 x £3m = £0.6m;
- 0.2 probability of a return of £1m = 0.2 x £1m = £0.2m.

Given that these are the only three outcomes possible (the sum of the three probabilities = 1), then the average return the company can expect from the launch of such a product = £3.6m + £0.6m + £0.2m = £4.4m. If, for example, the cost to the business of launching such a product is £3m, then by the laws of probability, such a launch would be worth the risk. This use of probability is found in decision trees (☞ unit 2).

To establish the possible range of events that might occur in business situations Say an estate agency has three photocopiers in operation. The photocopiers are known to break down one day in every ten. What is the chance that all three are out of operation at once? There is a number of alternative combinations to consider.

- All 3 copiers are working.
- 2 copiers are working and 1 is faulty.

- 1 copier is working and 2 are faulty.
- All 3 copiers are faulty.

If a working copier is (w) and a faulty copier is (f), the possible combinations amongst the three machines are:

Machine	1	2	3	
	w	w	w	All 3 machines are working
	w	w	f	2 are working and 1 is faulty
	w	f	w	
	f	w	w	
	w	f	f	1 is working and 2 are faulty
	f	w	f	
	f	f	w	
	f	f	f	All 3 machines are faulty

If the probability of a working machine (p) is 0.9 then the probability of a faulty machine (q) is 0.1. It is possible to work out the probability of all these combinations.

- All 3 machines working = 1 x 0.9 x 0.9 x 0.9 = 0.73 (or 73%).
- 2 machines working and 1 faulty = 3 x 0.9 x 0.9 x 0.1 = 0.24 (or 24%).
- 1 machine working and 2 faulty = 3 x 0.9 x 0.1 x 0.1 = 0.027 (or 2.7%).
- All 3 machines are faulty = 1 x 0.1 x 0.1 x 0.1 = 0.001 (or 0.1%).

In algebraic terms the probabilities are worked out using the binomial expansion:

$$p^3 + 3p^2q + 3pq^2 + q^3 = 1$$

Thus for this business there is only a 0.001 chance (0.1 per cent) of all three machines being out of action at once. But there is a 0.24 (24 per cent) chance of at least one machine being out of action, which might be a problem for the company. Although 3 machines have been used in this example, a business might need to look at combinations involving 2, 4 or more machines. Probabilities would then be worked out using, for example:

$$p^2 + 2pq + q^2 = 1 \text{ (for 2 machines)}$$

$$p^4 + 4p^3q + 6p^2q^2 + 4pq^3 + q^4 = 1 \text{ (for 4 machines)}$$

The normal distribution

The NORMAL DISTRIBUTION is a statistical model that will tell a business what the expected range of outcomes from a particular population will be. It is used where businesses have been carrying out large scale sampling, for example in market research or in quality control, where they want to find out what range of results to expect.

The normal distribution occurs in many different contexts. For example, if a large group of sixth form students, representing the full ability range, took a Business Studies examination, then the frequency distribution of their marks may resemble a normal distribution, as shown in Figure 10.1.

Littlehurst is a manufaturer of electronic sensor equipment. Its most popular product is a sensor device that is used to test corrosion in metal on equipment. It has tested two new hand held sensor devices with a sample of its customers and has found the following information.

Test product A	Probability of success - 0.3 Expected revenue - £200,000
	Probability of failure - 0.7 Expected revenue - £50,000
	Cost of launch - £90,000
Test product B	Probability of success - 0.5 Expected revenue - £120,000
	Probability of failure - 0.5 Expected revenue - £30,000
	Cost of launch - £80,000

(a) Calculate:
  (i) the returns that the company can expect from each product;
  (ii) the profit or loss that the company can expect from each product.

(b) Suggest which product the company the company should launch based on the above information alone.

(c) If the cost of the launch of product B fell to £65,000, how might this affect your answer to (a)?

Some students will do very well, some students will do very badly, but the majority of students will fall close to and either side of the average (mean) score.

The resulting NORMAL DISTRIBUTION CURVE shows all the possible outcomes (range of marks) and the frequency at which they occurred (number of students at each mark). It is 'bell-shaped' and symmetrical about the mean value.

Normal distributions will differ in their shallowness or steepness. The weights of people in a population are likely to be quite evenly spread as in Figure 10.2(a), whilst IQ scores in a population are likely to be more closely bunched around the average, with few high or low scores as in Figure 10.2(b). It is the spread of the data that determines the curves' steepness or shallowness. This spread can be measured by the use of **standard deviations** (☞ unit 3).

Whatever the spread of the normal distribution curves,

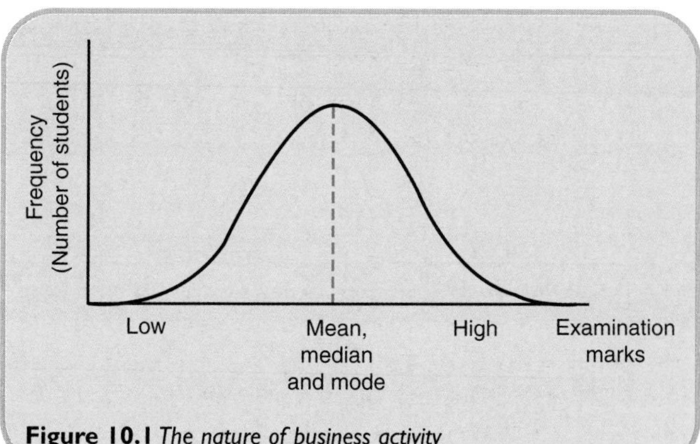

Figure 10.1 *The nature of business activity*

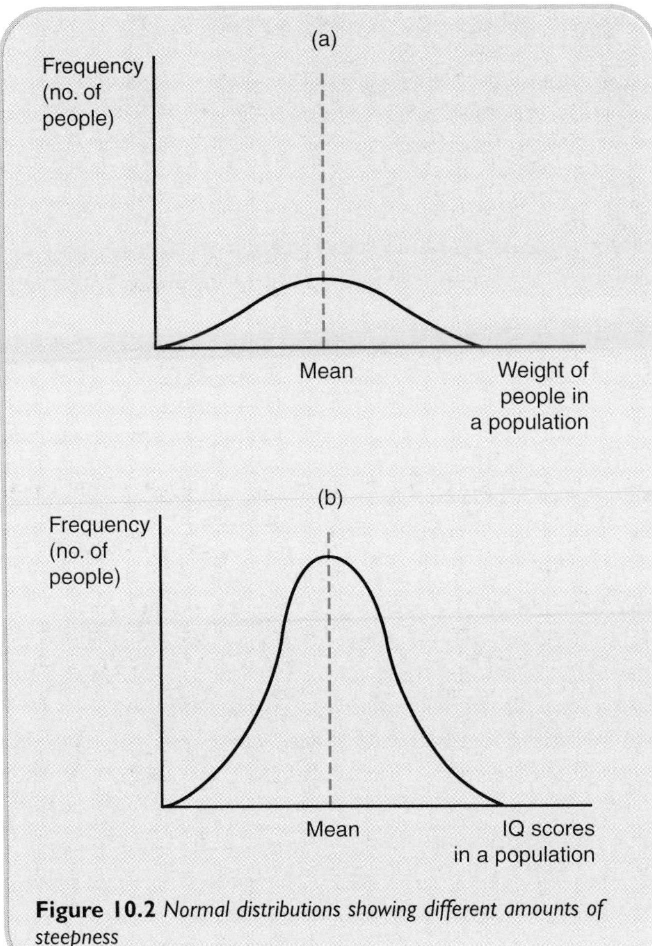

Figure 10.2 *Normal distributions showing different amounts of steepness*

they have particular features in common.

- The curve is symmetrical about the mean.
- The mean, mode and median of the distribution is equal.
- 50 per cent of all values lie either side of the mean value.
- The curve can be divided into 3 standard deviations (SDs) either side of the mean.
  68 per cent of the population will lie between + or - 1 SD.
  96 per cent of the population will lie between + or - 2 SDs.
  99.8 per cent of the population will lie between + or - 3 SDs.

Thus nearly all results will lie within + or - 3 SDs of the mean. A small proportion (0.2 per cent) will lie outside this range, but this is so small businesses are not concerned about it in practice. The exact distribution of the range of results possible is shown in Figure 10.3. The normal distribution has a certain predictability. Therefore any results that lie outside the expected range become significant and unexpected.

Using the normal distribution

One business context where the normal distribution can be used is in the analysis of market research data. A business might ask, 'was the result of a survey possible purely by chance or was there a significant difference between the actual result and the expected one?'

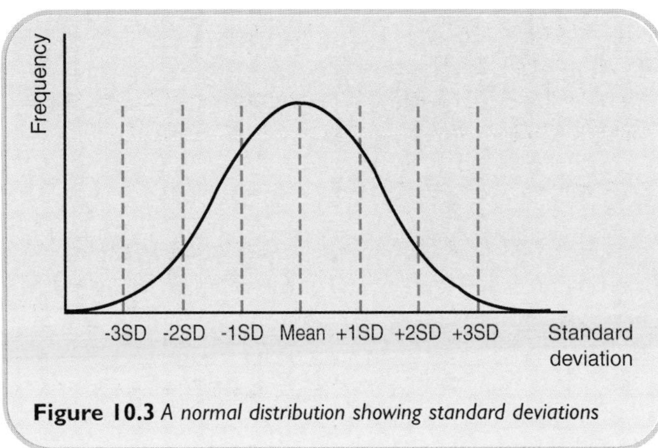

Figure 10.3 *A normal distribution showing standard deviations*

Say that a company which manufactures potato crisps has used a market research company to discover whether their new 'Sweet and Sour' flavour, which has been heavily promoted since its launch, is well known by the public. On average, the company would expect 50 per cent of those asked to recognise a flavour, but following the promotion they would expect a higher recognition. If the market research company asks 900 consumers, what results might the company expect to get to measure whether the promotion was successful?

The first stage in the use of normal distribution to answer this question involves the calculation of the expected RANGE OF RESULTS from such surveys. To do this it is necessary to calculate the mean and the standard deviation for this particular distribution.

The mean for a normal distribution can be calculated using the formula:

$$\text{mean} = n \times p$$

where n = the sample size
and p = the probability of an event occurring.

The standard deviation for a normal distribution can be calculated using the formula:

$$1 \text{ standard deviation } (1SD) = \sqrt{npq}$$

where n = the sample size;
p = the probability of an event occurring;
and q = the probability of an event not occurring.

For the market research on the 'Sweet and Sour' crisps:

$n = 900$
$p = 0.5$
$q = 0.5$

Therefore, for such surveys as this:

$$\text{mean} = 900 \times 0.5 = 450$$

$$1SD = \sqrt{900 \times 0.5 \times 0.5} = \sqrt{225} = 15$$

The full range of results can be + or - 3SD from the mean where:

2SD = 30
3SD = 45

Therefore, the range for this normal curve will be:

450 + or - 45 = 405 to 495.

The normal curve can now be drawn based on this information as in Figure 35.4. For the company, this normal curve provides a tool to help it analyse any market research results.

- 68 per cent of all results will show that between 435 and 465 people recognise the flavour (given a mean of 450).
- 96 per cent of all results will show that between 420 and 480 people recognise the flavour.
- 99.8 per cent of all results will show that between 405 and 495 people recognise the flavour.

These percentages are usually referred to as **confidence levels.**

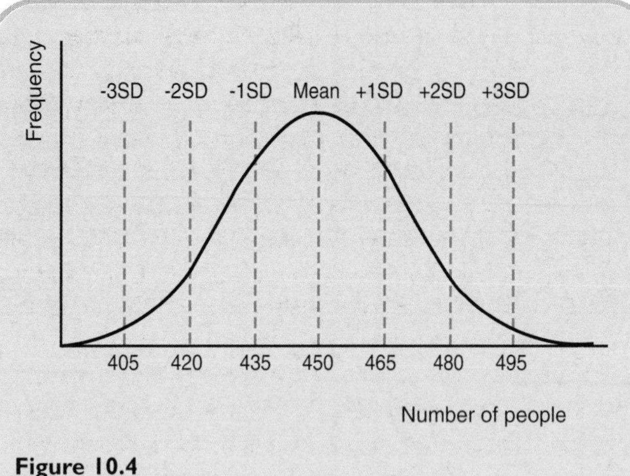

Figure 10.4

A manufacturer of dental products is particularly interested in the hygiene habits of its customers. The business expects that the average length of time people take before changing their toothbrush is 90 days and the standard deviation is 20 days.

(a) Draw a normal distribution. Assuming that the information is normally distributed, calculate and plot onto the graph:
  (i) the expected average length of time people take to change their toothbrush;
  (ii) the range of results between minus 3 and plus 3 standard deviations (in days).

(b) What percentage of its customers might the business expect to change their toothbrush:
  (i) after 70 days;
  (ii) after 130 days?

Confidence levels

Look again at the previous example about sweet and sour flavoured crisps. Only if marketing research results showed more than 495 people recognised the flavour could the company be totally confident that its promotion has been effective in increasing recognition above the 50 per cent level. Suppose the actual result was 486 people recognising the product? How significant would this be? We can find this in terms of standard deviations (z) by using the formula:

$$z = \frac{x - m}{s}$$

where x = the value
m = the mean
s = the standard deviation

so:

$$z = \frac{486 - 450}{15} = \frac{36}{15} = 2.4 \text{ SDs from the mean}$$

To find out what percentage of the population lies between the mean and +2.4SDs, a normal distribution table, as in Table 10.1, can be used. This shows the areas under the standard normal distribution from the mean. Because this is a frequency distribution, the area represents the number in the population between each value.

Reading from the left hand column of the table, 49.18 per cent (or 0.4918) of the population will lie between the mean and +2.4SDs. To include all values up to and including 486 it is necessary to add this to the 0.5 or 50 per cent on the other side of the mean. This gives a total of:

0.5 + 0.4918 = 0.9918 or 99 per cent

This is shown as a shaded area on Figure 10.5. The company can therefore be 99 per cent certain that a result of 486 represents an improvement over the 50 per cent average. If it wanted to be even more certain, it would need to take 3 standard deviations (rather than 2.4) into account.

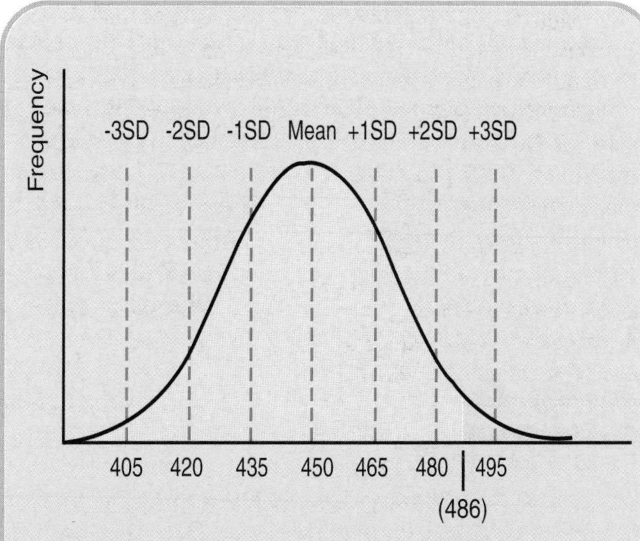

Figure 10.5 *A normal distribution showing standard deviations*

Table 10.1 *Table of standard normal curve areas*

(z)	.00	.01	.02	.03	.04	.05	.06	.07	.08	.09
0.0	.0000	.0040	.0080	.0120	.0160	.0199	.0239	.0279	.0319	.0359
0.1	.0398	.0438	.0478	.0517	.0557	.0596	.0636	.0675	.0714	.0753
0.2	.0793	.0832	.0871	.0910	.0948	.0987	.1026	.1064	.1103	.1141
0.3	.1179	.1217	.1255	.1293	.1331	.1368	.1406	.1443	.1480	.1517
0.4	.1554	.1591	.1628	.1664	.1700	.1736	.1772	.1808	.1844	.1879
0.5	.1915	.1950	.1985	.2019	.2054	.2088	.2123	.2157	.2190	.2224
0.6	.2257	.2291	.2324	.2357	.2389	.2422	.2454	.2486	.2517	.2549
0.7	.2580	.2611	.2642	.2673	.2704	.2734	.2764	.2794	.2823	.2852
0.8	.2881	.2910	.2939	.2967	.2995	.3023	.3051	.3078	.3106	.3133
0.9	.3159	.3186	.3212	.3238	.3264	.3289	.3315	.3340	.3365	.3389
1.0	.3413	.3438	.3461	.3485	.3508	.3531	.3554	.3577	.3599	.3621
1.1	.3643	.3665	.3686	.3708	.3729	.3749	.3770	.3790	.3810	.3830
1.2	.3849	.3869	.3888	.3907	.3925	.3944	.3962	.3980	.3997	.4015
1.3	.4032	.4049	.4066	.4082	.4099	.4115	.4131	.4147	.4162	.4177
1.4	.4192	.4207	.4222	.4236	.4251	.4265	.4279	.4292	.4306	.4319
1.5	.4332	.4345	.4357	.4370	.4382	.4394	.4406	.4418	.4429	.4441
1.6	.4452	.4463	.4474	.4484	.4495	.4505	.4515	.4525	.4535	.4545
1.7	.4554	.4564	.4573	.4582	.4591	.4599	.4608	.4616	.4625	.4633
1.8	.4641	.4649	.4656	.4664	.4671	.4678	.4686	.4693	.4699	.4706
1.9	.4713	.4719	.4726	.4732	.4738	.4744	.4750	.4756	.4761	.4767
2.0	.4772	.4778	.4783	.4788	.4793	.4798	.4803	.4808	.4812	.4817
2.1	.4821	.4826	.4830	.4834	.4838	.4842	.4846	.4850	.4854	.4857
2.2	.4861	.4864	.4868	.4871	.4875	.4878	.4881	.4884	.4887	.4890
2.3	.4893	.4896	.4898	.4901	.4904	.4906	.4909	.4911	.4913	.4916
2.4	.4918	.4920	.4922	.4925	.4927	.4929	.4931	.4932	.4934	.4936
2.5	.4938	.4940	.4941	.4943	.4945	.4946	.4948	.4949	.4951	.4952
2.6	.4953	.4955	.4956	.4957	.4959	.4960	.4961	.4962	.4963	.4964
2.7	.4965	.4966	.4967	.4968	.4969	.4970	.4971	.4972	.4973	.4974
2.8	.4974	.4975	.4976	.4977	.4977	.4978	.4979	.4979	.4980	.4981
2.9	.4981	.4982	.4982	.4983	.4984	.4984	.4985	.4985	.4986	.4986
3.0	.4987	.4987	.4987	.4988	.4988	.4989	.4989	.4989	.4990	.4990

High Style is a manufacturer of clothing for tall people. It provides a bespoke leg length service. It will turn up trousers to suit the leg length specified on an order. On average, it expects the people buying its trousers to have an inside leg length of 35 inches with a standard deviation of 0.5 inches.

(a) Assuming the leg lengths of its customers are normally distributed, what range of lengths would the business expect its customers to have? Plot these figures onto a normal distribution.
(b) If the business tested a sample of 100 people, what percentage would expect it to be:
(i) above 36.5 inches;
(ii) between 35 inches and 36 inches;
(iii) between 35 inches and 35.8 inches;
(iv) below 34.2 inches?
Use Table 35.1 to answer this question.

Limitations of the normal distribution

As with all models used in business decision making, there are possible problems with its use.

- The sample size has to be large otherwise it is unlikely that the distribution will be normally distributed. A large sample size helps to smooth out the peaks and troughs in smaller frequency distributions.
- The calculation of the mean and the standard deviation are based on probability figures that themselves might be based upon estimates rather than exact figures. In the example of market research, the 0.5 probability used to calculate the likely response to the market research on crisps was an estimate based upon previous experience.
- Especially in the area of quality control, a 'one-off' reading which is a long way from the expected mean may not be sufficient to reject a batch or shut down a machine. Further sampling would be important to confirm the evidence of the first sample before costs are incurred by the business.
- Not all large distributions will resemble the normal distribution. The distribution might be skewed and therefore not symmetrical about the mean. Figure 10.6(a) shows a positively skewed frequency distribution, which might represent the distribution of teachers' salaries in a school or college. In a positively skewed distribution, the mode will have a lower value than the median, which will have a lower value than the mean. Figure 10.6(b) shows a negatively skewed frequency distribution, which might represent the number of people per day attending a successful cinema over a period of time. In a negatively skewed distribution, the mode will have a higher value than the median, which will have a higher value than the mean. Normal distribution analysis could not be used with such skewed distributions.

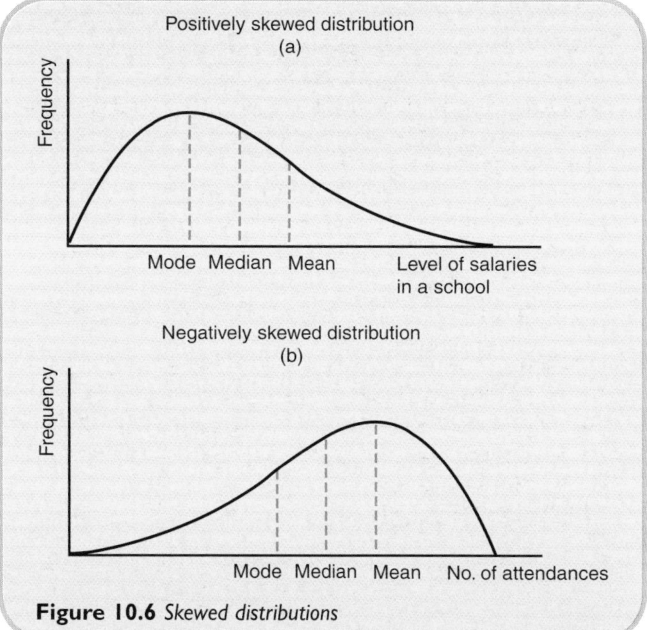

Figure 10.6 *Skewed distributions*

key terms

Normal distribution curve - a graphical representation of the normal distribution.
Normal distribution - a naturally occurring frequency distribution where many of the values cluster around the mean, but where there are a few high and low values away from the mean.
Probability - a quantification of the likelihood of an event occurring.
Range of survey results - the highest and lowest results from market research surveys.

Knowledge

1. What statistical concepts are used to analyse market research data?
2. What does probability measure?
3. Why is the normal distribution a useful tool for businesses to use in analysing data?
4. What are the distinguishing features of a normal curve?
5. What is the difference between a normal distribution and a skewed distribution?

Case study Heritage Cottages Ltd

Heritage Cottages Ltd is a company which hires out cottages and bungalows in various areas of England. Most customers book directly with the business via the telephone and view properties in the company brochure which shows the cottages that are available. The brochure is produced each November and Heritage has traditionally advertised the availability of the brochure in a range of weekly magazines between December and April. The management was always careful to analyse the responses that resulted from these advertisements each week. Over a five year period it calculated that the mean number of responses was 1,500 each week with a standard deviation of 125.

For the 1998-99 season Heritage decided to shift its advertising over the December to April period to the Sunday papers, such as *The Sunday Times* and *The Observer*. It wanted to see if this resulted in a significant increase in the number of customer enquiries. It carried out a survey of the responses over the twenty week period that it ran the advertisements. Heritage found that the mean level of response had risen to 1,800 for the 1989-99 season. The company was pleased with the outcome and decided, on the basis of these figures, to continue advertising in the Sunday papers for the following season.

(a) What is meant by the terms (i) mean number of responses and (ii) significant increase in customer enquiries? Use examples from Heritage Cottages in your explanation. (6 marks)

(b) Explain why the results from the 5 year analysis by Heritage Cottages of responses to a magazine advertisement might be normally distributed. (8 marks)

(c) (i) Draw a normal distribution curve which shows the full range of responses that the company achieved. (6 marks)

(ii) How many standard deviations from the mean did the 1,800 responses from the Sunday newspaper advertisements represent? (6 marks)

(d) Was the business right to be pleased with the outcome from the switch to newspaper advertisements? Consider the normal distribution diagram from your answer to (c) and other factors that Heritage Cottages might need to take into account in evaluating the move from magazine to newspaper advertising. (14 marks)

11 Forecasting

Forecasting

Businesses are keen to know about what might happen in the future. Anything they can predict accurately will reduce their uncertainty and will allow them to plan. Predictions may be based on a variety of data. They could be based on current information provided by managers. Most forecasts are based on **backdata** gathered from a variety of marketing research techniques. The accuracy of forecasts will depend on the reliability of the data.

What might a business like to predict with accuracy? Some examples might include:

- future sales of products;
- the effect of promotion on sales;
- possible changes in the size of the market in future;
- the way sales fluctuate at different times of the year.

A variety of techniques can be used to predict future trends. One of the most popular is **time series analysis**, which is discussed in the next section.

Dairy Crest is the UK's leading chilled food company. It operates in six major areas - spreads, cheeses, liquid products, fresh dairy products, household products and ingredients. Its consumer foods division sells to retailers and its food services division includes the household milk business and dairy ingredients operation. Figure 11.1 shows the annual turnover over the last five years.

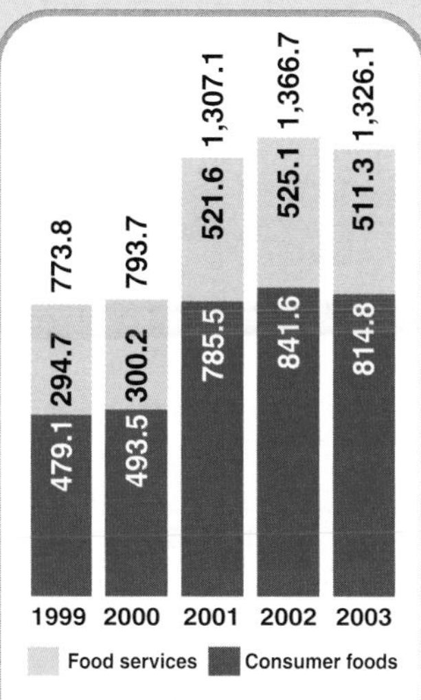

Figure 11.1 *Turnover, £m*
Source: adapted from Dairy Crest, *Annual Report and Accounts*, 2003.

(a) Identify the trends shown in the data.
(b) Explain the factors that might lead to a rising trend of sales in future.

Question 1

Time series analysis

TIME SERIES ANALYSIS involves predicting future levels from past data. The data used are known as **time series data** - a set of figures arranged in order, based on the time they occurred. So, for example, a business may predict future sales by analysing sales data over the last 10 years. The business, of course, is assuming that past figures are a useful indicator of what will happen in the future. This is likely to be the case if trading conditions are **stable** or if the business needs to forecast trends in the short term. Time series analysis does not try to explain data, only to describe what is happening to it or predict what will happen to it.

There are likely to be four components that a business wants to identify in time series data.

- **The trend**. 'Raw' data can have many different figures. It may not be easy to see exactly what is happening from these figures and so a business often tries to identify a trend. The trend shows the pattern that is indicated from the figures. For example, there may be a trend for sales of a new product to rise sharply in a short period as it becomes very popular.
- **Cyclical fluctuations**. For many businesses there may be a cycle of 'highs and lows' in their sales figures, which rise over a number of years and then fall again. It is argued that these are a result of the recession-boom-recession of the trade cycle in the economy. In a recession, for example, people have less money to spend and so the turnover of a business may fall in that period.
- **Seasonal fluctuations**. Over a year a business is unlikely to have a constant level of sales. The seasonal variations are very important to a business such as a travel agent or a 'greetings card' producer, where there may be large sales at some times but not at others.
- **Random fluctuations**. At times there will be 'freak' figures which stand out from any trend that is taking place. An example may be the sudden boost in sales of umbrellas in unusually wet summer months or the impact on consumers' spending of a one-off event such as a summer music festival.

Identifying the trend

An analysis of figures will tell a business whether there is an upward, downward or constant trend. Identifying the trend allows the business to predict what is likely to happen in future. The first step is to smooth out the raw data. Take an example of a toy manufacturer, whose yearly sales over 10 years are shown in Table 11.1.

Table 11.1 *Yearly sales of a toy manufacturer (£000)*

1995	1996	1997	1998	1999	2000	2001	2002	2003	2004
300	500	600	550	600	750	850	1,100	800	1,100

It is possible to calculate a trend by using a MOVING AVERAGE. The average can be taken for any period the business wants, such as a year, a month or a quarter. For now we will assume the toy manufacturer uses a 3 year average.

The average of sales in the first 3 years was:

$$\frac{300 + 500 + 600}{3} = \frac{1,400}{3} = 466.7$$

The first year's sales 'drop out' and the next year's sales are added to give a moving average. The average for the next three years was:

$$\frac{500 + 600 + 550}{3} = \frac{1,650}{3} = 550$$

If the business continues to do this, the results will be as shown in Table 11.2. Notice that the moving average is placed at the centre of the 3 years (ie the average for 1995-97 is plotted next to 1996).

Table 11.2 *3 year moving average for sales of a toy manufacturer (£000)*

1995	1996	1997	1998	1999	2000	2001	2002	2003	2004
300	500	600	550	600	750	850	1,100	800	1,100
	466.7	550	583.3	633.3	733.3	900	916.7	1,000	

What if the firm had used a 4 year period instead of 3 years? No one year is the centre point and simply placing the figure in between two years may result in misleading predictions in future. The solution is to use CENTRING. This uses a 4 and 8 year moving **total** to find a mid point. So, for example, in Table 11.2:

Year	1995	1996	1997	1998	1999
(£000)	300	500	600	550	600

1,950 + 2,250 (4 year moving totals) = 4,200 (8 year moving total)

This can then be used to find the mid-point, which is 1997. The **trend** or **four period centred moving average** can be found by dividing the 8 year moving total by 8, the number of years, as shown in Table 11.3.

Plotting the four period centred moving average figures onto a graph (as shown in Figure 11.2) shows the trends in the figures. It is clear to see that sales appear to be rising over the period. The trend line is 'smoother' than the line showing the actual sales figures. It eliminates any fluctuations in sales each year and gives a more obvious picture of the trend that has been taking place.

Predicting from the trend

Having identified a trend that is taking place the business can now predict what may happen in future. Figure 11.3 shows the trend data from Figure 11.2, but with a line drawn to

Table 11.3 *Calculating a 4 year moving average for a toy manufacturer*

£000

Year	Sales	4 year moving total	8 year moving total	Trend (4 year centred moving average = 8 year moving total ÷ 8)
1995	300			
1996	500	1,950		
1997	600	2,250	4,200	525.00
1998	550	2,500	4,750	593.75
1999	600	2,750	5,250	656.25
2000	750	3,300	6,050	756.25
2001	850	3,500	6,800	850.00
2002	1,100	3,850	7,350	918.75
2003	800			
2004	1,100			

Figure 11.2 *Annual sales of a toy manufacturer*

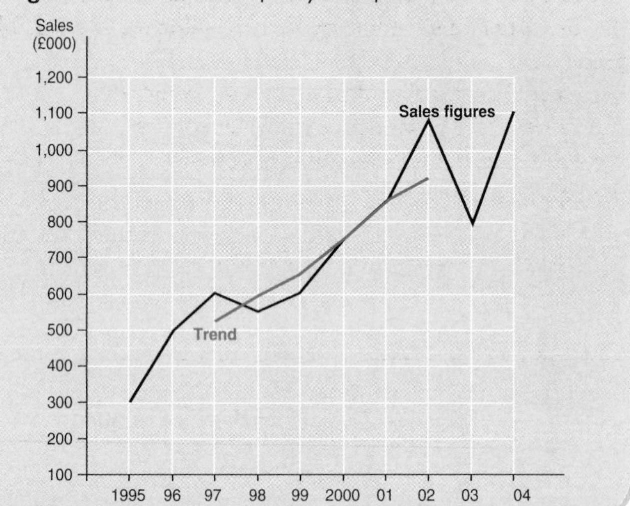

A business has recently gathered data on its sales revenue as shown in Table 11.4, and wants to calculate a 3 and 4 period moving average.

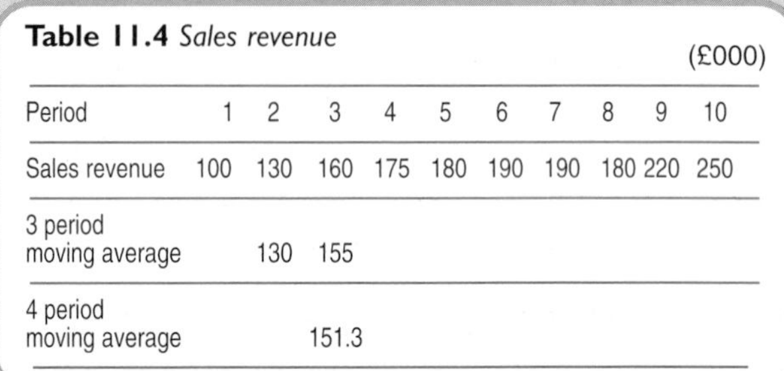

Table 11.4 *Sales revenue*

(£000)

Period	1	2	3	4	5	6	7	8	9	10
Sales revenue	100	130	160	175	180	190	190	180	220	250
3 period moving average		130	155							
4 period moving average			151.3							

(a) Calculate the 3 and 4 period moving averages for as many years as you can to complete the table.
(b) Plot the sales figures and both trend lines onto a graph on graph paper and explain the relationship between the trend and the actual sales revenue figures.

Question 2

predict the likely sales in 2005. The graph shows that sales of the toy manufacturer's goods may reach about £1,160,000.

The business has made certain assumptions when predicting this figure. First, no other factors were likely to have changed to affect the trend. If other factors changed, resulting in different sales figures, then the prediction is likely to be inaccurate.

Second, the sales figures are predicted by drawing a line through the trend figures and extending it to the year 2001. The broken line through the trend in Figure 11.3 is called the LINE OF BEST FIT. It is the best line that can be drawn which matches the general slope of all points in the trend. The line is an average, where points in the trend on one side of the line are balanced with those on the other. In other words, it is a line which 'best fits' **all** points in the trend.

It is possible to draw the line of best fit by plotting the trend figures on graph paper accurately and then adding the line of best fit 'by eye', so that points fit equally either side of the line. Extending the line carefully should give a reasonable prediction.

To help draw the line, it should pass through the coordinates ($\bar{X}$,$\bar{Y}$) where $\bar{X}$ is the average of the years and $\bar{Y}$ is the average sales. These coordinates can be calculated using the figures in Table 11.3.

$$\bar{X} = \frac{\sum X \text{ (the total years)}}{\text{N (the number of years)}} = \frac{1997+1998+1999+2000+2001+2002}{6} = \frac{11,997}{6} = 1999.5$$

$$\bar{Y} = \frac{\sum Y \text{ (the total sales in the trend)}}{\text{N (the number of years)}}$$

$$= \frac{£525,000 + £593,750 + £656,250 + £756,250 + £850,000 + £918,750}{6} = \frac{£4,300,000}{6}$$

$$= £716,667$$

This point is shown on Figure 11.3. The actual predicted figure for the year 2005 is £1,162,550. This can be found by a method known as 'the sum of least squares'. Computer software can be used by businesses to calculate the line of best fit and to predict from the trend.

Variations from the trend

How accurate is the prediction of **around** £1,160,000 sales of toys by the year 2005? Even allowing for the assumptions above, the prediction may not be accurate because it is taken from the trend, and the trend 'smoothed out' variations in sales figures. To make an accurate prediction, the business will have to find the average variation over the period and take this into account.

We can find how much **variation** there is from the trend by calculating:

Actual sales - trend.

Figure 11.3 *Annual sales of a toy manufacturer*

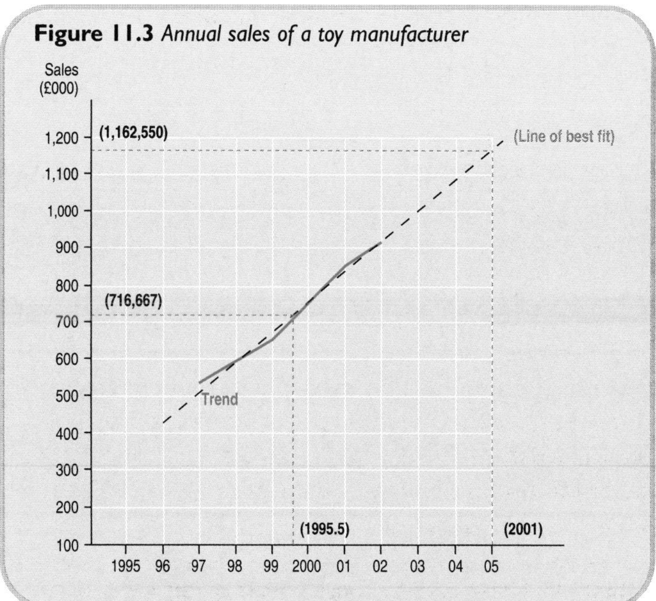

Table 11.5

(£000)

Year	Sales	Trend (4 year centred moving average)	Variation in each year
1995	300		
1996	500		
1997	600	525.00	+75.00
1998	550	593.75	-43.75
1999	600	656.25	-56.25
2000	750	756.25	- 6.25
2001	850	850.00	+/- 0
2002	1,100	918.75	+181.25
2003	800		
2004	1,100		

So, for example, the **cyclical** variation in Table 11.3 would be as shown in Table 11.5. The average of the variations over the period 1995-2004 is (in £000):

$$\frac{+75 - 43.75 - 56.25 - 6.25 +/-0 +181.25}{6} = \frac{+150}{6} = +25 \text{ (or } +£25,000)$$

If the predicted value based on the trend was £1,160,000, then adding £25,000 may give a more accurate predicted figure of £1,185,000.

Seasonal variations

Earlier it was stated that a business may be interested in variations in any one year. It is possible to predict from a trend and use **seasonal** variations to make a more accurate prediction. Table 11.7 shows sales of a business over a 3 year period, including sales in each quarter. A 4 quarter moving

Question 3

Table 11.6 shows the yearly sales figures of a furniture manufacturer over a period of 10 years.

Table 11.6

units

Period	1	2	3	4	5	6	7	8	9	10
Sales	5,000	5,200	5,800	6,000	5,800	7,000	8,200	7,400	7,600	8,400

(a) Calculate a four yearly moving average from the figures to show the trend taking place.
(b) Plot the trend onto a graph on graph paper and predict the likely output in year 11.
(c) Calculate:
(i) the cyclical variation for each year;
(ii) the average cyclical variation over the period.

average has been calculated and also the variation in each quarter.

Carrying on the trend to predict the sales for the fourth quarter of the year 2003 might give a figure of £470,000. (It would be possible to find this by drawing and extending a line of best fit through the trend.) As we know, this is a 'smoothed out' figure. A more accurate prediction might be to calculate the **average seasonal variation** in the fourth quarter, for example (in £000):

$$\frac{-97.125 - 117.5}{2} = \frac{-214.625}{2} = -107.313$$

By subtracting £107,313 from the total of £470,000, this gives a more accurate prediction of £362,687.

Table 11.7

(£000)

Year	Quarter	Sales	4 quarter moving average	Variation
2000	3	460		
	4	218		
2001	1	205	328.5	-123.5
	2	388	346.0	+42.0
	3	546	358.25	+187.75
	4	272	369.125	- 97.125
2002	1	249	383.625	-134.625
	2	431	396.625	+34.375
	3	619	404.0	+215.0
	4	303	420.5	-117.5
2003	1	277		
	2	535		

Causal modelling

Time series analysis only describes what is happening to information. Causal modelling tries to explain data, usually by finding a link between one set of data and another. For example, a business may want to find whether there is a link between the amount that it spends on advertising and its sales.

Table 11.8 shows data that have been collected about advertising and sales by a business at different times. The data in the table are plotted onto a SCATTER GRAPH in Figure 11.4. Advertising (the **independent** variable) is shown on the horizontal (X) axis. Sales (the **dependent** variable) are shown on the vertical (Y) axis. The figure shows, for example, that in one period (E) the business had advertising spending of £1,500 and sales of 1,800 units. In another period (G) the business had advertising spending of £3,500 and sales of 5,800 units.

Table 11.8

Period	Advertising expenditure (£000)	Sales (000)	(£million)	(million)	(£million)
	X	Y	X^2	Y^2	XY
A	1.0	3.2	1.0	10.24	3.2
B	2.0	4.5	4.0	20.25	9.0
C	3.0	1.8	9.0	3.24	5.4
D	4.0	3.0	16	9.0	12.0
E	1.5	1.8	2.25	3.24	2.7
F	2.5	1.6	6.25	2.56	4.0
G	3.5	5.8	12.25	33.64	20.3
H	1.2	4.7	1.44	22.09	5.64
I	2.7	5.9	7.29	34.81	15.93
J	3.0	3.5	9.0	12.25	10.5
K	3.6	3.1	12.96	9.61	11.16
L	7.0	3.5	0.49	12.25	2.45
			ΣX^2 =81.93	ΣY^2=173.18	ΣXY=102.28

Figure 11.4

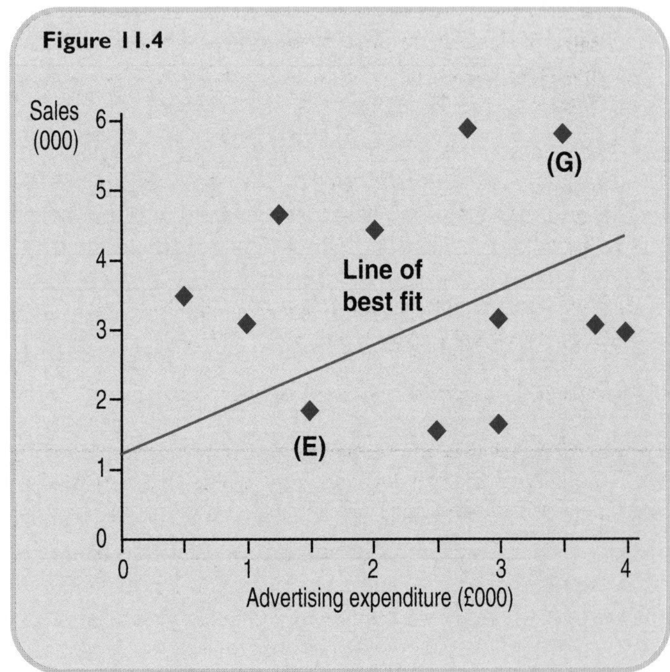

Looking at the graph, there appears to be a positive CORRELATION between the two variables. The more that is spent on advertising, the higher the level of sales. The line of best fit is drawn through the data to show this relationship better. It is also possible to calculate the extent of the relationship by means of a CORRELATION COEFFICIENT, using the formula:

$$r = \frac{\Sigma XY}{\sqrt{(\Sigma X^2)\ (\Sigma Y^2)}}$$

Using the data in Table 36.8, the correlation coefficient for advertising and sales can be calculated as follows.

$$r = \frac{£102.28m}{\sqrt{£81.93m \times 173.18m}}$$

$$r = \frac{£102.28m}{£119.117m}$$

$$r = +0.86$$

- A correlation coefficient of +1 means that there is an absolute positive relationship between the two variables. All points in the scatter graph fall on the line of best fit and the line slopes upwards from left to right. As the values of the independent variable increase, so do the dependent variable values.
- A correlation coefficient of 0 means that there is no relationship between the variables.
- A correlation coefficient of -1 means that there is an absolute negative relationship between the two variables. All points in the scatter graph fall on the line of best fit and the line slopes downwards from left to right. As the values of the independent variable increase, the values of the dependent variable fall.

The formula itself does not show **positive** and **negative** values. However, it is easy to see whether the relationship is positive or negative from the graph. A positive coefficient of 0.86 suggests a strong correlation between the spending on advertising and the level of sales. As advertising increases, so do sales. This information could help a business in future when making decisions about its marketing. It is suggested that if the figure falls below 0.7 it becomes difficult to see any correlation from the scatter graph. An example of a negative correlation might be the relationship between prices and customers' demand. As prices rise, demand falls.

Businesses must be careful when basing decisions on such calculations.

- A large quantity of sales in any period may be due to factors other than advertising, such as other forms of promotion.
- There are sometimes examples of 'nonsense correlations'. These are correlation coefficients that appear to show a strong relationship between two variables, when in fact the relationship between the figures is pure coincidence.

Denten Limited is a manufacturer of bins and other storage equipment. It exports a large amount of its products abroad. It makes use of direct sales to customers and also employs some overseas agents. The managing director has asked the marketing department to examine the relationship between the number of agents it employs and sales of three of its most popular products and make recommendations. The research found the following information.

Product 1	ΣY^2 = 5,360	ΣXY = 2,720
Product 2	ΣY^2 = 17,360	ΣXY = 3,200
Product 3	ΣY^2 = 25,080	ΣXY = 3,240
Agents	ΣX^2 = 1,400	

(a) Calculate the correlation coefficients to show the relationship between spending on overseas agents and products 1, 2 and 3.
(b) Explain the relationship between the variables in each case.
(c) What advice do you think the marketing department should give the managing director concerning agents from this information?

Qualitative forecasting

Qualitative forecasting uses people's opinions or judgments rather than numerical data. A business could base its predictions on the views of so-called experts, or on the opinions of experienced managers in the marketing or production department. Such methods are usually used by businesses:

- where there is insufficient numerical data;
- where figures date quickly because the market is changing rapidly.

1. Why might a business want to predict the future?
2. What are the four components of time series data that a business might be interested in?
3. What does a trend show?
4. How might a business use the calculation of a trend?
5. What is meant by causal modelling?

key terms

Centring - a method used in the calculation of a moving average where the average is plotted or calculated in relation to the central figure.
Correlation - the relationship between two sets of variables.
Correlation coefficient - a measure of the extent of the relationship between two sets of variables.
Line of best fit - a line plotted through a series of points which balances those on one side with those on the other, and best represents the slope of the points.
Moving average - a method used to find trends in data by smoothing out fluctuations. It involves calculating an average for a number of periods, then dropping the first figure and adding the next to calculate the average that follows.
Scatter graph - a graph showing the performance of one variable against another independent variable on a variety of occasions. It is used to show whether a correlation exists between the variables.
Time series analysis - a method which allows a business to predict future levels from past figures.

Case study Jamesons

Jamesons is a retail outlet which specialises in selling outdoor clothing and equipment. This includes walking boots, shoes and weatherproof clothes and also skiing and mountain equipment. Its sales have been increasing over the past two years as increasing numbers of people are becoming interested in outdoor activities and are taking holidays involving sports and exercise. Sales tend to be best in winter months, although recently it has introduced a range of lightweight clothing that seems to have sold well in summer. Table 11.9 shows its sales revenues over a period from 2001 to 2004.

Table 11.9 *Jamesons sales revenue, 3rd quarter 2001 to 2nd quarter 2004, (£000)*

(£000)

Year	Quarter	Sales revenue
2001	3	100
	4	180
2002	1	140
	2	60
	3	180
	4	220
2003	1	180
	2	100
	3	220
	4	260
2004	1	220
	2	180

(a) What is meant by:
   (i) a trend in sales figures; (2 marks)
   (ii) a four period centred moving average? (2 marks)

(b) (i) Using a four quarter centred moving average, calculate the trend from the sales figures in Table 11.9 that the business might have found. (10 marks)
   (ii) Explain why centring might be used by the business when calculating a trend. (4 marks)

(c) Calculate:
   (i) the seasonal variation for as many quarters as you can; (6 marks)
   (ii) the average seasonal variation for the fourth quarter. (4 marks)

(d) Plot the trend line onto a graph. Using the trend line and the average seasonal variation for the fourth quarter, predict the sales in the fourth quarter of 2004. State the assumptions that you have made in your prediction. (12 marks)

12 Business Transaction and Accounting Concepts

Business transactions

Business activity involves purchasing resources, such as raw materials, labour and machinery, and selling goods or services that have been produced using these resources. The purchase of resources from suppliers and the sale of products to customers are examples of BUSINESS TRANSACTIONS. Other examples include borrowing money from a bank and the payment of taxes. For a small business, such as Robinson's fish and chip shop, examples of business transactions might include:

- the purchase of potatoes from a wholesaler for £250;
- the sale of fish and chips to a customer for £4.30;
- the payment of £140 interest to a bank;
- the sale of a portion of chips and curry sauce to a customer for £2.90;
- a payment of £120 to an employee.

It is important for a business to keep accurate records of these transactions. Every single transaction should be recorded. In this example the sales made by the fish and chip shop are likely to be recorded on a till roll. The value of purchases may be written in a book. During the year such a business may be involved in possibly thousands of individual transactions.

In contrast, for a very large business such as BT, the number of transactions that take place in a year is immense. Every telephone call made using the BT network is recorded as a separate transaction. Such transactions are recorded electronically and their value is calculated by computer. BT's customers receive quarterly statements summarising these transactions. BT must also record details of its expenditure, such as payments to its employees and purchases of telecommunications equipment.

Recording business transactions and the accounting process

Bookkeepers are responsible for recording business transactions. They play an important role in the **accounting process**. This involves recording, classifying and summarising business transactions. The aim of the process is to generate useful financial information that can be communicated to a range of business stakeholders, such as shareholders, managers and the media, for example. Many sole traders keep their own records because they cannot afford bookkeepers. As a firm grows, it may become cost effective to take on a bookkeeper, part-time perhaps. In large businesses, with their own finance departments, bookkeepers will work under the supervision of accountants. It is also likely that most of their work will be done on a computer.

Jules Germaine runs a music business and is also a professional musician. He makes part of his income from hiring his services to touring bands who want a musician to play on a few songs, but not to be a permanent band member. Sometimes he is paid in a lump sum after a gig. Other times he is paid regularly over a period of time.

Another part of his business involves, selling instruments to collectors. He is a regular visitor the USA and he has a number of contacts there who can find him old instruments from people's houses. They try to hunt down 'finds' in attics or garages that might be worth something. Jules can fix these up and then sell them to shops or to specialist collectors.

A final part of his services is the teaching of music. He will often buy in music notation paper for this students, reeds for instruments and DVDs and videos to show playing techniques.

(a) Identify the business transactions that take place in the Jules Germaine's music business.
(b) Explain why the business might find it difficult to keep accurate records of transactions.

Question 1

Figure 12.1 illustrates the stages in the accounting process. When a transaction takes place, it should be verified by a **document** - an invoice, receipt or cheque stub perhaps. From these documents entries are made in the company's books. The first entries are likely to be made in the books of **prime entry**, where details of all transactions may be recorded almost as they happen. The **day books** will contain records of purchases and sales, while the **cash book** lists the flows of money into and out of the business. At the end of the month, entries in these books will be totalled and recorded in **ledgers**. The main purpose of these subsidiary books is to avoid overloading the ledgers.

Ledgers form the basis of any book-keeping system. A ledger contains details of individual business accounts. The **sales ledger** records transactions with customers and the **purchase ledger** records those with suppliers. The accounts of customers and suppliers are called personal accounts. All others are impersonal and are recorded in the nominal ledger. The headings in the nominal ledger might include:

- the wages account, which records the wages paid to

employees;

- the purchase account, which records all business purchases from suppliers;
- the sales account, which records all business sales.

From time to time a company may wish to check that all previous entries were made correctly. This can be done by producing a TRIAL BALANCE. Finally, various accounts can be produced using the information gathered from book-keeping. They include the profit and loss account, the balance sheet and cash flow statements.

Figure 12.1 *Stages in the accounting process*

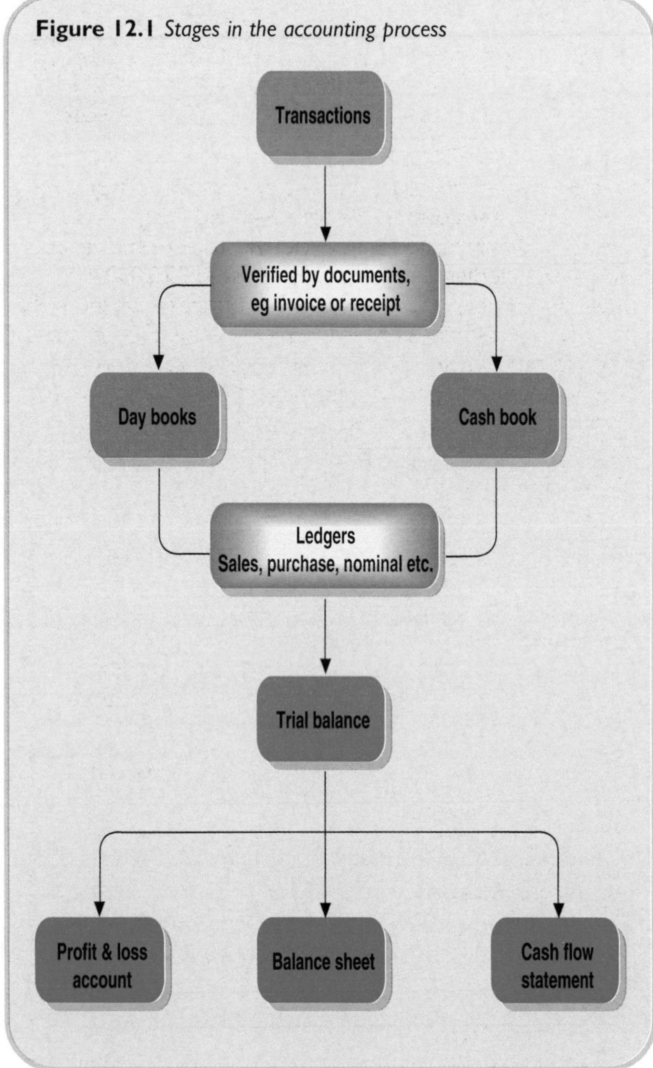

The need for accounting concepts

The accounts of a business should reflect a 'true and fair' view of its financial position. To achieve this accountants apply a series of 'rules' or ACCOUNTING CONCEPTS. These are also known as **conventions** or **principles**. In the USA, and increasingly in the UK, the expression GAAP is used to refer to 'generally accepted accounting principles'.

By using agreed concepts when analysing and presenting financial information, accountants can avoid confusion and inconsistency. There is also less scope for presenting misleading financial information and the accounts of different businesses can be compared more easily.

The concepts or principles have developed over time as a framework within which accountants operate. In the UK, the Accounting Standards Committee (ASC) was established in the 1970s. This committee issued a number of **Statements of Standard Accounting Practice (SSAPs)**. The ASC described four 'fundamental accounting concepts' in its Statements of Standard Accounting Practice (SSAP 2). These are the:

- going concern concept;
- consistency concept;
- prudence concept;
- accruals or matching concept.

Since 1990, the regulation of accounting in the UK has passed over to the Accounting Standards Board (ASB). SSAPs still exist, but any new standards are now called **Financial Reporting Standards (FRSs)**. During 2001, the Financial Reporting Standard *Accounting Policies (FRS 18)* was introduced to replace SSAP 2. These are:

- relevance;
- reliability;
- compatibility;
- understandability.

FRS 18 states that a business should regularly review its accounting policies to ensure they remain the most appropriate to the business's circumstances. Specific disclosure about the policies used, and any changes to the policies, must be made.

In addition to the fundamental concepts listed above, a number of others are generally accepted. These include objectivity, business entity, money measurement, historical cost, dual aspect, realisation and materiality.

Accounting concepts

Objectivity As far as possible accounts should be based on verifiable evidence rather than on personal opinion. In other words they should be objective rather than subjective. So, for example, an accountant should value a transaction on the basis of an invoice rather than his or her own personal opinion. This avoids bias. Consider what might happen if two accountants were asked their opinion on the value of a particular transaction, for example the purchase of new premises. They might disagree because value can be measured in many different ways. However, if they were asked to value the transaction according to the invoice, they would likely record exactly the same value.

Going concern Accountants assume that the business will continue for an indefinite period of time. Assets are valued as if they will continue in their present use, rather than at NET REALISABLE VALUE - the value the asset would raise if it were sold. Assets are therefore valued at the cost when they are bought, known as HISTORICAL COST. This holds even if the asset is bought at a bargain, eg half the manufacturer's recommended price. If things change, and it is necessary for the business to cease trading, assets may be valued according to what they 'might realise'. In some cases this might be less than their cost. Special accounting techniques will then be used to deal with the situation.

Accruals or matching This means that costs and revenue should be matched with the period in which they occur. For example, at the end of the trading year a company may have an outstanding electricity bill for power used in that trading period. According to this principle, the cost should be included even though the bill is unpaid. Related to this is the **realisation** concept. This states that profit occurs when goods or services change hands and not when payment is made.

Consistency Once a decision has been made about the allocation of costs or the valuation of assets it should not be changed. This will make comparisons more meaningful and reduce the chance of figures being distorted.

Prudence and caution If an asset is bought at a bargain price, rather than the recommended price, the lower value is always recorded. This conforms with the concept of **prudence** and **caution**. Accountants undervalue future revenue or profit until it is realised. In contrast, they make provision for costs or losses immediately they occur, even if they are only forecast.

Materiality Accountants should avoid wasting time trying to accurately record items of expenditure which are trivial. For example, a business might purchase a waste paper bin for the office for £1.50. This bin might last for 15 years or more, however, the bin is not a 'material' item. Even though it is expected to be used for many years the purchase should be recorded once and treated as an expense in the year it was bought. No attempt should be made to 'write off' the expenditure over the period of time the bin is in use. There is no law which governs materiality. Different firms may use a variety of arbitrary methods to determine which items of expenditure are material and which are not. For example, a business may decide that all items of expenditure under £50 should be treated as expenses in the period for which they were bought, even if some items are actually used for many years. The method of assessing materiality will be selected by accountants using their judgment.

Separate entity A business is a 'legal' person in its own right and has a separate identity from that of the owners. Where a sole trader, for example, uses a van for personal reasons and business, it is important to divide the running costs between the owner and the business.

Money terms When recording business transactions, it has long been common practice to record them in money terms.

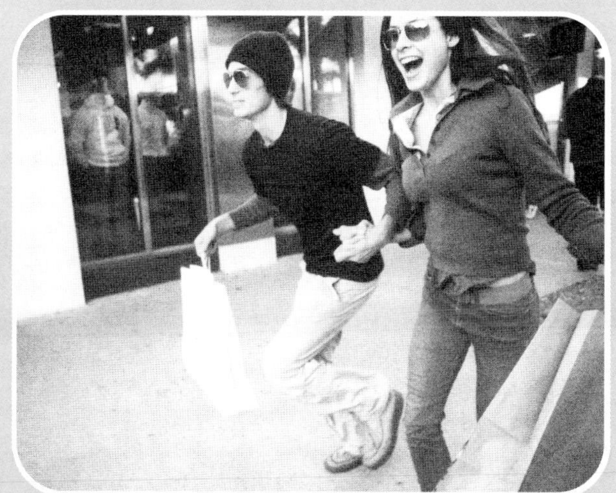

Chris and Amy Phillips opened up a modern boutique in a fashionable part of London in September 2003. They took out a lease, transformed the premises with very stylish fittings and purchased some exclusive stock from French and Italian clothes suppliers. They invested £25,000 of their own money in the venture. The business started well, but after Christmas trade fell away. In March 2004 it was running out of cash. Chris and Amy were overdrawn at the bank and losing heart very rapidly. They felt that the business might have to close down and wondered how much money they would be left with. The balance sheet for the boutique is shown in Table 12.1.

Table 12.1 *Balance sheet for Chris and Amy's business*

	£	£
Assets		
Fixtures and fittings		9,800
Stock		12,200
Debtors		2,400
		24,400
Less Liabilities		
Trade creditors	7,500	
Lease	2,000	
Bank overdraft	1,300	
		10,800
		13,600
Financed by:		
Capital		13,600
		13,600

(a) Explain how an accountant might have valued Chris and Amy's fixed assets if the business was a going concern.

(b) If Chris and Amy did close down the business, what factors might have affected the value of the assets?

Money acts as a unit of account. This allows the values of goods and services to be expressed accurately and makes comparison easier. Financial statements only include those matters which can be easily expressed in money terms. For example, the skills of the workforce would not be included.

Historical cost All assets are valued according to their original cost rather than what they are currently worth. Accountants prefer to deal with values which have, in the past, been confirmed with evidence. They do not like to rely on estimates, even if the historical entries are dated. This convention has been subject to change, particularly when, due to inflation, the historical cost values become inaccurate and do not provide a true and fair view of the company's financial position.

Dual aspect The DUAL ASPECT concept states that every transaction has two effects on the business's accounts. Suppose, for example, that a business buys some goods on credit. Assets, increase, because stocks increase, and liabilities also increase because money is owed to a creditor. Similarly, if the business repays a loan of £1,000 to a bank, there is a dual aspect. Liabilities decrease, because the loan is repaid, and assets decrease because the business has less money. In accordance with the dual aspect concept, each transaction is recorded twice by bookkeepers.

key terms

Accounting concepts, principles or conventions – rules or guidelines that accountants follow when drawing up accounts.
Business transactions – an event that affects the finances of the business, for example, the purchase of resources from suppliers and the sale of products to customers.
Dual aspect – the idea that every transaction has two effects on the accounts.
Historical cost - the value of an asset when purchased, ie the amount paid.
Net realisable value - the value of an asset when sold, ie the amount received.
Trial balance - a statement that lists all the balances on all accounts in the accounting system.

Knowledge

1. Describe the stages in the accounting process.
2. What is the role of the bookkeeper in the accounting process?
3. What is the difference between day books and ledgers?
4. What is the function of the trial balance?
5. State 3 final accounts of a business that are produced from the accounting process.
6. What is the role of the Accounting Standards Board?
7. What is an FRS?
8. What are the fundamental concepts which aim to make the accounts a 'true and fair' view of the firm's financial position?
9. What is meant by the concept prudence and caution?
10. Explain the difference between objectivity and subjectivity in accounting.

Case study Healthcare Staffing Services

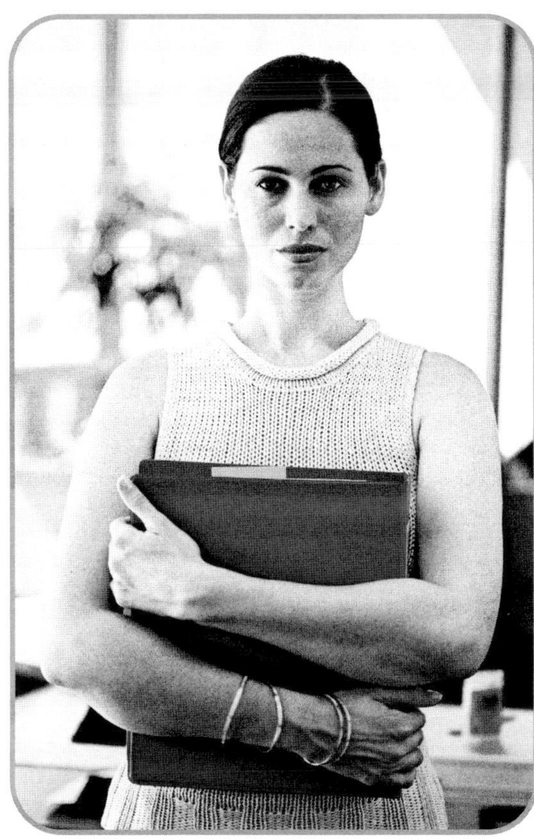

Christine Thompson runs Healthcare Staffing Services, an employment agency in Ealing, London. The business specialises in the provision of staff for local hospitals, nursing homes and retirement homes. She has a total of 450 staff registered with her agency and is developing a very profitable business at a time when there are staff shortages in the industry and the rates paid for supply staff are very high.

She enjoys most aspects of the business, particularly interviewing prospective recruits and dealing with health care managers. However, she is not so keen on recording the business's transactions. Like many sole traders she records business transactions herself. In one respect she is quite diligent. Christine keeps all receipts and invoices. However, the only written records that she makes are the payments and receipts in a cash book. She does this on the last Sunday in every month. At the end of the financial year Christine pays a local accountant to produce her accounts. At the end of 2003 five transactions were giving Christine some concern.

- One month before the end of the trading year Christine paid her annual office rent of £12,000. However, Christine decided not to include the payment in her records because nearly all of the amount related to next year.
- During the year Christine purchased the following items - a calculator for £12, an office kettle for £9 and a painting for £8.50. These items are expected to be used by the business for many years to come and Christine wonders whether the expenditure should be 'written off' over their life, just like the office computer.
- Christine uses her car for business purposes throughout the week. However, at weekends she uses it for personal travel. Total motor expenses for the whole year are £6,700. She is not sure how to divide the motor expenses between business and personal use.
- During the year Christine purchased a new printer for her computer which cost £400. However, she noticed that the supplier had reduced the price of the printer three months later to £199. She is not sure which value to record.
- Christine has been supplying relief nursing staff to a small private hospital in West London for 3 months, but has not yet received payment for their wages from the hospital, a total of £24,000.

(a) Describe three possible business transactions that might be undertaken by Healthcare Staffing Services. (6 marks)

(b) Explain why Christine keeps all the receipts and invoices for the business. (6 marks)

(c) Christine keeps records in a cash book. Explain what this means. (6 marks)

(d) Explain why accounting concepts are necessary when producing the accounts of Healthcare Staffing Services. (8 marks)

(e) Explain how Christine should treat each of the above transactions according to the appropriate accounting concepts. (14 marks)

13 Costing Methods

What is costing?

The process of measuring the likely consequences of a business activity is called COSTING. Costing systems benefit a business in a number of ways. They provide managers with financial information on which to base decisions. They help to identify the profitable activities, avoid waste and provide information for cost cutting strategies. Costing can also assist the marketing department in setting the price of products. Examples of costing exercises include:

- measuring the cost of manufacturing individual products;
- calculating whether or not it would be more economical to contract out a particular business operation, eg security;
- determining the cost of moving to a new business location;
- estimating the cost of decorating the office.

What costing methods might be used by firms? Methods include absorption, standard and marginal costing.

Absorption costing

ABSORPTION COSTING is also known as FULL COSTING or TOTAL COSTING. The main principle of absorption costing is that all the overheads or indirect costs are 'absorbed' by cost centres. In other words, all overheads are included when calculating the cost of producing particular items. The main problem is how to allocate a firm's overheads between different cost centres. One simple approach is to use an arbitrary method. For example, a manufacturer which makes two metal components code named ZX 1 and ZX 2 may have the direct costs of producing 100,000 of each component shown in Table 13.1.

Assume that total indirect costs are £300,000. We need to calculate the percentage each component contributes to total direct cost.

$$\text{For ZX 1} = \frac{200}{500} \times 100 = 40\%$$

$$\text{For ZX 2} = \frac{300}{500} \times 100 = 60\%$$

The £300,000 indirect costs can now be allocated to each component.

For ZX 1 indirect costs = 40% x £300,000 = £120,000
For ZX 2 indirect costs = 60% x £300,000 = £180,000

Table 13.1 *Direct costs of two components*

			£000
Component	ZX 1	ZX 2	Total
Direct cost	200	300	500

Bantom Ltd manufactures motorbikes in its Bristol factory. It makes three models:

- the Fury - a racing bike with a 1000 cc engine;
- the Trialmaster - a popular trials bike;
- the XL10 - a standard 500 cc road bike.

Details of the direct production costs are shown in Table 13.2. Bantom also incurs indirect costs of £600,000 per month. The company manufactures 100 of each bike per month.

Table 13.2 *Direct costs for Bantom Ltd*

(£ per bike)

	Fury	Trialmaster	XL10
Direct labour	250	150	200
Raw materials	150	120	100
Components	400	300	340
Other direct costs	200	130	160

(a) Calculate the direct costs of producing 100 of each motorcycle.
(b) Allocate the indirect costs of production to each product as a percentage of direct costs.
(c) Calculate the full cost of producing 100 of each bike.

The total cost or full cost of producing 100,000 of each component can now be calculated. This is done by adding the allocated indirect costs to the direct costs.

For ZX 1 full cost = £120,000 + £200,000 = £320,000
For ZX 2 full cost = £180,000 + £300,000 = £480,000

This approach is often criticised for the arbitrary way it allocates indirect costs. It could result in misleading costings because the allocation of indirect costs is not based on any

Table 13.3 *Bases for apportioning overheads*

Indirect costs	Basis
Rent and rates	Floor area of cost centres
Heating and lighting	Floor area, the volume or size of cost centres
Personnel costs (ie health & welfare)	Number of staff employed by each centre
Buildings insurance	Floor area or book value of buildings in each centre
Machinery & equipment insurance	Book value of machinery used by each centre
Depreciation (plant, machinery & tools)	Book value of assets used by each centre
Maintenance	Book value of assets used by each centre
Supervisory costs	Number of staff, or hours worked by supervisor in each centre
Staff canteen	Number of staff employed by each centre
Administration	Number of staff employed by each centre

actual indirect costs incurred.

To improve the accuracy of absorption costing a business may prefer to **apportion** overheads or indirect costs. This involves allocating a certain percentage or proportion of indirect costs to each cost centre. A business must decide on what basis to apportion indirect costs. The basis depends on the nature of the indirect cost. Table 13.3 shows how a selection of overheads might be apportioned.

To illustrate absorption costing take the example of Dudley Car Exhausts which manufactures three types of exhaust systems, the E1, E2, and E3. Factory time and direct cost details (per system) are shown in Table 13.4. Annual indirect costs include rent, selling costs, overheads and administration. These are £12,000, £18,000, £24,000 and £4,000 respectively. Rent is apportioned according to the factory time used by each system. Selling costs and overheads are apportioned equally between all systems. Administration is apportioned according to the labour input of each system (most administration costs in this case are labour related, eg wages). Dudley Car Exhausts produces 1,000 of each system every year.

Table 13.4 *Factory time and direct costs for Dudley Car Exhausts*

System	Labour (£)	Materials (£)	Fuel (£)	Factory time(hrs)
E1	2	3	1	1
E2	2	4	2	3
E3	4	4	2	2
Total	8	11	5	6

Using the absorption costing method it is necessary to allocate every single business cost to the production of the three systems. For E1 the total direct cost is calculated by adding labour, materials and fuel, ie (2 + 3 + 1 = £6). To apportion rent to the production of one E1 system it is necessary to take into account the amount of factory time one E1 system uses, ie $^1/_6$ of the total time and also the number of E1 systems produced, ie 1,000 during the year. The following calculation must now be performed:

$$\text{Rent apportioned to one E1 system} = £12{,}000 \times \frac{1}{6} \times \frac{1}{1{,}000} = \frac{£12{,}000}{6{,}000} = £2$$

Selling costs and overheads are split equally between each system, so that selling costs are £6 and overheads £8 for each system. Administration costs are apportioned according to the amount of labour used to make each system. For the E1 system the allocation can be calculated as follows.

Administration costs apportioned to one E1 system

$$= £4{,}000 \times \frac{£2}{£8} \times \frac{1}{1{,}000} = £4{,}000 \times \frac{1}{4} \times \frac{1}{1{,}000} = \frac{£4{,}000}{4{,}000} = £1$$

The complete cost schedule for all three systems is shown in Table 13.5.

Table 13.5 *The cost of producing the three exhaust systems using the absorption method of costing*

(£)

System	Direct	Rent	Selling	Overheads	Admin.	Total
E1	6	2	6	8	1	23
E2	8	6	6	8	1	29
E3	10	4	6	8	2	30
Total	24	12	18	24	4	82

Some businesses use the absorption method to set the price of their products. Once the cost of each unit has been calculated a profit percentage is added to determine the selling price.

Advantages and disadvantages of absorption costing

There are certain advantages to a business in using the absorption cost method of apportioning indirect costs.

- It ensures that all costs are fully recovered. This means that that businesses will cover their costs as long as the actual costs and level of activity are similar to the budgeted figures. Therefore if a business uses a cost-plus pricing policy, it knows that the prices charged will generate a profit.
- It is fair provided overheads are not allocated in an arbitrary way. This is because costs are apportioned to those activities that actually incur them.
- The method conforms to the accounting standard SSAP 9 *Stocks and work-in-progress.* This states that absorption costing should be used when valuing stocks in the final accounts. This is because absorption costing includes a share of the fixed costs. It therefore recognises these fixed costs in the same period as revenues, and so conforms to the 'matching' principle.

However, the method does have some limitations.

- Cost information used might be inaccurate. This is because the figures are generally based on historical data which may not reflect future costs or activity levels. As a result, businesses might **underabsorb** or **overabsorb** their overheads and could set prices that are too low or too high.

- In practice, absorption costing can be complex, time consuming and expensive to gather detailed information from different cost centres. This is particularly the case for small firms that do not employ specialist cost accountants.
- Some costs are difficult to apportion exactly to a particular cost centre. For example, how can a business apportion electricity costs to different cost centres accurately if there is only one meter?

Renfrews is a small department store in Leeds. It has five departments and each one is operated as a cost centre. This helps to monitor the costs of running the business. A newly appointed cost accountant has suggested that the current method of apportioning overheads is inappropriate and should be reviewed. Table 13.6 shows the direct costs and some other details relating to the various cost centres. An analysis of overheads is also given. The value of overheads in 2003 was £500,000.

Table 13.6 *Information for each cost centre operated by Renfrews, 2003*

	Food Hall	Women's wear	Men's wear	Electrical goods	Toys	Total
Direct costs	£400,000	£200,000	£100,000	£200,000	£100,000	£1,000,000
Staff employed	12	8	4	6	6	36
Floor space	800m^2	600m^2	600m^2	400m^2	200m^2	2,600m^2

Overheads

Rent & electricity	= £300,000
Administration	= £200,000
Total	**= £500,000**

(a) Suggest suitable bases for apportionment for the overheads. Explain your answer.

(b) Using the bases of apportionment shown in (a), calculate the full or total cost of operating each department at Renfrews in 2003.

Standard costing

Some businesses focus on standard costs. A standard cost is a planned or 'target' cost. It is normally associated with a specific activity or a particular unit of production. For example, a business manufacturing cans of fizzy drink may say that the standard cost per can is 17p. This means that the **usual** cost per can is 17p. STANDARD COSTING involves calculating the usual or planned costs of an activity and then comparing these with the actual costs incurred. The difference between the standard cost and the actual cost is called a **variance** (☞ unit 15). Standard costing helps businesses to monitor and control costs. For example, the standard cost and actual cost of making a circuit board for an electronics company is shown in Table 13.7. In this example the actual cost is 50p more than the standard cost.

Table 13.7 *The standard cost and actual cost of producing a circuit board*

Description	Standard cost	Actual cost
Materials	90p	90p
Components	120p	120p
Labour	350p	400p
Indirect costs	140p	140p
Total	700p	750p

This means that there is a variance of 50p. Such a variance is likely to result in the business carrying out an investigation to determine why the actual cost of manufacturing the circuit board was higher than expected, ie higher than the standard cost. In this case the actual cost is higher because the labour cost was £4 compared with an expected labour cost of £3.50. This may have been caused by, say, a new recruit working a little more slowly than a fully experienced operative.

Advantages and disadvantages of standard costing

There are certain advantages to a business in using standard costing.

- By comparing standard costs with actual costs a business can identify areas of weakness and inefficient practice. For example, large adverse variances on materials costs might suggest that materials are being wasted in production.
- Staff can be motivated if they achieve cost targets which they are involved in setting. In some cases staff might be rewarded financially if they reach or exceed targets.
- Standard costs may represent the best estimate of what a product should cost to make. So, by using standard costs, estimates of costs for products and price quotations for orders are likely to be more reliable.

However, there may also be disadvantages.

- Like absorption costing, standard costing requires a business to gather a large amount of information. This process can be time consuming and expensive. Also, since standard costs are updated regularly, this cost is ongoing.
- The method may be inappropriate if certain management methods are used. For example, if kaizen is adopted, where workers are expected to strive for continuous improvement, standards might become a barrier to innovation. Employees might regard standards as 'ceilings' and therefore the incentive to improve further is removed.

- Standard costing may encourage staff to strive for favourable variances, even if this harms the firm's overall objectives. For example, staff may take short cuts to reduce costs. This might reduce the quality of the product and lead to a fall in sales.

Contribution or marginal costing

CONTRIBUTION or MARGINAL COSTING ignores fixed costs and focuses on variable costs. The method involves looking at the amount of **contribution** a product or order makes. Contribution can be calculated as selling price minus variable cost for a unit. Total contribution is the revenue from units sold (price x quantity) minus the total variable costs. Generally, if the revenue from products or orders exceeds the variable costs, ie the contribution is positive, then managers are likely to consider them for production.

A situation where contribution costing might be helpful is when choosing which orders to accept from customers. For example, Thompson Engineering has received two late orders and only has the resources to accept one. One is for 1,000 metal panels and the other for 800 metal brackets. Details of the revenue, variable costs and contribution are shown in Table 13.8.

Table 13.8 *Sales revenue, variable costs and contribution for two orders received by Thompson Engineering*

(£)

	Metal panels	Metal brackets
Revenue	**12,000**	**17,000**
Variable costs		
Materials	3,000	5,500
Direct labour	4,200	6,900
Other variable costs	1,700	3,000
Total variable costs	**8,900**	**15,400**
Contribution	**3,100**	**1,600**

In this example, where only one order can be accepted, Thompson Engineering is likely to accept the order for the metal panels. This is because the panels make the largest contribution out of the two orders. Even though the metal brackets generates more revenue, the panels' contribution is £1,500 higher (£3,100 - £1,600). Note that the marginal costs of the orders are £8,900 for the panels and £15,400 for the brackets. In each case they are the same as the total variable costs.

In this case fixed costs have been ignored. This is because accepting either of the orders had no effect on Thompson Engineering's fixed costs. However, in circumstances where accepting orders results in additional fixed costs, they must be taken into account.

Coates manufactures biscuits in its Derby factory. The company has a reputation for innovative product development. It generally introduces at least one new product each year. Sometimes the new products are added to the product range, other times they replace existing products. A new product, 'Coates Krunchie', is ready for launch which the company plans to use as a replacement for one of its existing products. Two products are being considered for withdrawal, both nearing the end of their life cycle. Table 13.9 shows the 2003 revenue and variable costs for the two products facing withdrawal.

Table 13.9 *Sales revenue and variable costs for the two products that Coates is considering for withdrawal*

(£)

	Dairy Krunchie	Coates Shortcake
Revenue	**129,000**	**112,000**
Variable costs		
Materials	67,500	56,400
Direct labour	36,400	32,100
Other variable costs	16,900	19,200

(a) Calculate the contribution made by each of the existing products in 2003.
(b) Which of the two products should be withdrawn to make way for 'Coates Krunchie'? Explain your answer.

Special order decisions

Sometimes businesses receive orders which are unexpected, from a new customer or for a new product perhaps. On these occasions a business has to decide whether or not to accept the order. The business will consider whether or not the order is profitable. However, even if the order is not profitable it may still be accepted. This may be because the business is considering the size of the **contribution** when making the decision to accept the order.

For example, Powerfire Ltd makes high speed powerboats for the luxury boat market.

- Its **fixed costs** are £500,000 per annum and **variable costs** £18,000 per boat.
- The **price** of the boats is £23,000 each and last year the business **produced and sold** 120 boats.
- The **total costs** of the business are £500,000 + (£18,000 x 120) = £2,660,000.
- The **total revenue** of the business is £23,000 x 120 = £2,760,000.
- This generated a **profit** of £2,760,000 - £2,660,000 = £100,000.

What if, unexpectedly, the business received an order from a new customer for 10 boats, for which the customer was only willing to pay £19,000 each? The contribution that this order would make is:

revenue of 10 x £19,000 (£190,000) *minus*
variable costs only of 10 x £18,000 (£180,000)
= £10,000.

Note that only the variable costs are taken into account for the order of 10 extra boats because the fixed costs have been covered by production of the original 120 boats. Sale of the extra 10 boats at £19,000 would help to raise profit to £110,000 assuming last year's figures (£100,000 plus £10,000). If Powerfire sold all 130 boats for £19,000 it would make a **loss** of £370,000. This is found by revenue of £2,470,000 (£19,000 x 130) minus costs of £2,840,000 (£500,000 + [130 x £18,000]).

The single unexpected order is worth accepting on financial grounds because the contribution is positive and annual profit rises. However, it would only be accepted if the price of all other boats is unchanged. A number of non-financial factors might also be considered before accepting the order:

- Capacity. A business must ensure that it has enough resources to complete the order. For example, are workers prepared to work extra hours? Is there enough space in the factory? Will it replace other, more profitable, production?
- Customer response. If existing customers find out that products have been sold to others for lower prices this might cause resentment. It might damage the image of the company and lead to lost sales in the future.
- Future orders. Sometimes unprofitable orders are accepted in anticipation of future, more profitable orders, from the new customer.
- Current utilisation. An unprofitable order may be accepted to keep staff occupied. It may be better to have permanent staff employed completing orders with small contributions rather than doing nothing.
- Retaining customer loyalty. A business may accept an unprofitable order from a regular customer as a favour in order to retain their loyalty.

Phillip Partington manufactures golfing umbrellas. He sells them to a wide range of wholesalers and golfing organisations for a price of £4. He is not operating at full capacity and has just been approached by a Swedish company to see if he could supply 20,000 umbrellas for £3.50. Phillip's cost structure is shown in Table 13.10. He currently produces 100,000 umbrellas a year, but has the capacity to produce 130,000.

Table 13.10 *Phillip Partington's cost structure*

Materials and components	per unit	£0.70
Direct labour	per unit	£1.60
Other variable costs	per unit	£0.50
Fixed costs		£80,000

If the Swedish order was accepted, a further £13,000 in fixed costs would be incurred to cover exporting expenses.

(a) Calculate (i) the annual contribution and (ii) the amount of profit made; without the Swedish order.
(b) On financial grounds alone, advise Phillip whether or not to accept the Swedish order. Show all calculations.
(c) Discuss two non-financial considerations which might influence the final decision.

Advantages and disadvantages of contribution costing

There are advantages to a business in using the contribution costing method.

- It is simple to operate. Unlike absorption costing, the difficulty in sharing fixed costs between different products or cost centres is avoided. There is the advantage that under or overabsorption of overheads does not occur.
- It is a useful decision making tool. It can be used when ranking products or choosing between orders. It is also useful when deciding whether to make or buy-in a particular product or component.

However, there are some disadvantages.

- In some industries contribution costing is inappropriate, particularly when fixed costs represent the majority of a firm's costs. For example, the cost to a train or bus operator of carrying one more passenger is almost zero. Most of the operator's costs are fixed and the variable cost of transporting one more passenger is perhaps just the cost of issuing the ticket. If most customers only pay fares that cover the low variable costs, a business will make a loss because it will not cover the huge fixed costs. However, this does explain the benefit of filling empty seats at discount fares, as long as fixed costs are already covered. The money earned from these passengers adds a lot more to revenue than it does costs.
- When valuing stocks in final accounts, SSAP 9 *Stocks and work-in-progress*, states that the absorption method should be used and not the marginal costing method.
- It can lead to bias in costing calculations. For example, a cost centre that uses a high proportion of overheads may be making a positive contribution. However, when the amount of overheads are taken into account that same centre may be making a loss for the business.

The relationship between marginal and average cost

Average total cost and marginal cost curves are shown in Figure 13.1. Notice that the marginal cost curve cuts the average cost curve at its lowest point. Why? Consider a business building houses with an average cost of £50,000.

- If another house is built (the marginal house) with a higher than average cost, the average cost will rise;
- if the marginal house cost less than the average cost, the average cost would fall;
- if the marginal house cost £50,000 (the same as average cost) then the average cost would remain the same.

So the marginal and average costs are equal when average costs are constant. On a U-shaped average cost curve this is only at the one point, the lowest point. At all other points the average cost curve in Figure 13.1 is either rising or falling.

Figure 13.1 *Average total cost and marginal cost*

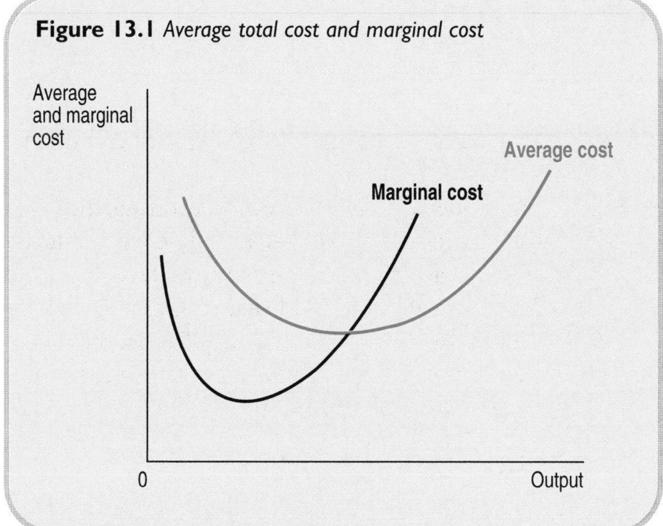

The closing-down point

In the short run it may be worth continuing production of a product even when a loss is being made. This can be shown for a whole company as well. Consider the case of a shop whose present cost and revenue conditions are shown in Table 13.11. If the shop remains open it incurs total costs of £1,500 and generates £700 in sales revenue. This results in a loss of £800. However, if the shop closes this loss is increased to £1,000. Although total costs fall to £1,000 because there are no variable costs to pay, total revenue falls to zero because there are no sales. Thus, in the short run it pays the shop to remain open because losses are lower. However, when revenue is incapable of covering variable costs the firm should close down.

Diagrammatically, the CLOSING-DOWN POINT can be shown by combining the average total cost, average variable cost and marginal cost curves, as in Figure 13.2. The closing-down point is where marginal cost is equal to average variable cost. When the price falls below P_1 on the diagram, the firm can no longer cover its variable costs. At this point the firm may decide to close down.

Table 13.11 *Cost and revenue information for a shop*

£	Open	Closed
Fixed cost	1,000	1,000
Variable cost	500	-
Total cost	1,500	1,000
Total revenue	700	-
Loss	800	1,000

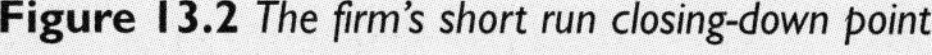

Figure 13.2 *The firm's short run closing-down point*

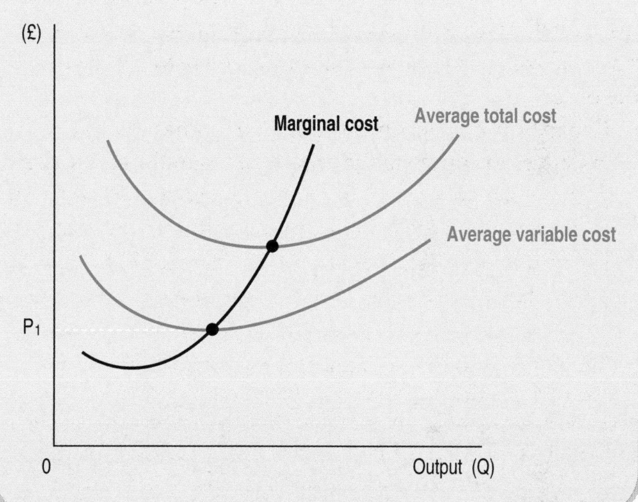

key terms

Absorption costing or full costing or total costing - a method of costing which involves charging all the costs of a particular operation to a unit of output.
Closing-down point - the level of output in the short run where a firm should cease its operations, ie where marginal cost is equal to average variable cost.
Costing - the process of measuring the likely economic consequences of a particular business activity or operation.
Contribution or marginal costing - the process of costing the production of one more unit of output.
Standard costing - the process of calculating the costs of a specific activity and then comparing them with the actual costs incurred.

1. Describe the benefits of costing.
2. How might the following indirect costs be apportioned: (a) office wages; (b) corporate advertising; (c) factory insurance?
3. What is the main advantage of the absorption costing?
4. In what way is the absorption method limited?
5. How are fixed costs treated in contribution costing?
6. What is meant by standard costing?
7. What are the advantages and disadvantages of contribution costing?
8. When might a loss making contract be accepted?
9. Explain when a firm should close down in the short run.

Case study AK Instruments

AK Instruments makes machines for the food processing industry. The company leases a factory and employs 228 staff. To deal with the wide variety of designs and customers the business uses a system called 'cell production'. There are four cells and each is responsible for its own design, purchasing, production and maintenance of a specific 'family' of products. Each 'family' of products has its own similarities and features. Two hundred of the staff are split between the various cells and most of the remainder are employed in the office, dealing with administrative work.

The business has been under pressure recently from foreign competition. As a result profits have been modest. It has also been suggested that cells 2 and 3 are 'holding the company back' because in some years they make a loss. However, the team leader of cell 3 says that the way overheads are currently allocated favours cells 1 and 4. At the moment the overheads are divided equally between the four cells. This is an arbitrary method of allocation.

Following a formal request from the leaders of cells 2 and 3 the financial director is to investigate the claim that the allocation of overheads is currently unfair.

(a) Calculate the contribution that each cell makes. (4 marks)

(b) Calculate the profit each cell makes, allocating the overheads equally between each cell. (6 marks)

(c) What do your results in (a) and (b) tell you about the performance of cells 2 and 3? Explain your answer. (6 marks)

(d) Using an appropriate basis for apportioning overheads, recalculate the profit made by each cell. (12 marks)

(e) To what extent is the claim made by the leader of cell 3, that the current method of allocating overheads (dividing them equally between each cell) is unfair, true? (12 marks)

Table 13.13 *Overheads*

	£000s
Leasing charges	1,200
Factory canteen	2,000
Administration	2,000
Depreciation	3,000
Total	**8,200**

Table 13.12 *Financial and other information relating to AK Instruments*

(£000)

	Cell 1	Cell 2	Cell 3	Cell 4	Total
Revenue	**9,900**	**5,100**	**6,200**	**10,400**	31,600
Variable costs					
Materials & components	1,900	1,200	1,300	2,000	6,400
Direct labour	2,800	1,500	2,100	2,400	8,800
Other variable costs	1,800	900	800	2,800	6,300
	Cell 1	Cell 2	Cell 3	Cell 4	Total
Staff employed	75	25	50	50	200
Floor space	1,000m^2	1,000m^2	1,000m^2	3,000m^2	6,000m^2
Book value of machinery	£8m	£4m	£4m	£8m	£24m

Applications of Break-Even Analysis

Constructing break-even charts

Break-even charts provide a visual means of analysing the effect of changes in output on total cost, total revenue, profit and the margin of safety. The effects of changes in fixed costs, variable cost and price on profit and the margin of safety can also be shown. A break-even chart can be constructed by plotting the total cost and total revenue equations on a graph. The graph should measure output on the horizontal axis and costs, revenue and profit on the vertical axis.

Consider Reidle Bros, a small canoe manufacturer. It incurs fixed costs of £20,000 per annum and variable costs of £75 per canoe. The canoes are sold for £125 to agents and wholesalers. The following steps can be used to construct a break-even chart.

Calculating the break-even point It is helpful to calculate the break-even point before constructing the graph. For Reidle Bros the total costs (TC) and total revenue (TR) equations are:

TC =£20,000 + £75Q (fixed costs + variable costs)

TR = £125Q (price x quantity)

Reidle Bros will break-even when total revenue equals total costs. This is where:

$$\begin{aligned} £20{,}000 + £75Q &= £125Q \\ £20{,}000 &= £125Q - £75Q \\ £20{,}000 &= £50Q \\ \frac{£20{,}000}{£50} &= Q \\ 400 &= Q \end{aligned}$$

Therefore, Reidle Bros will break-even when it manufactures 400 canoes.

Calculating points on the total revenue and total cost functions Both the total cost and total revenue functions are **linear** or straight. Therefore the lines can be drawn by joining two points which lie on each function. To plot the total revenue function we need to choose two levels of output and calculate the total revenue at each level. Any two levels of output could be chosen. However, construction will be simpler if 0 is chosen as one of the points. It is also helpful to choose a second value which is twice that of the break-even point. This would be 800 (2 x 400) in the case of the canoe manufacturers. This will ensure that the break-even point is in the centre of the chart. This improves presentation. The value of total revenue at each of these output levels is shown in Table 14.1.

Table 14.1 *Values of TR and TC at two levels of output for Reidle Bros*

Q	TR	TC
0	0	£20,000
800	£100,000 (125 x 800)	£80,000 (20,000 + [75 x 800])

Plotting the total revenue (TR) function The TR function can now be plotted on the graph. The output axis should run from 0 to 800 canoes and the other axis from 0 to £100,000. Using the information in Table 14.1, the two points, or coordinates, on the TR function are (0, 0) and (800, £100,000). If these are plotted on the graph and joined up the TR function will appear as shown in Figure 14.1.

Plotting the total costs (TC) function To plot the TC function we need to calculate the total cost at two levels of output. It is useful to use the same values as those used for the TR function, ie 0 and 800. The TC function can now be plotted on the graph. From Table 14.1 the two points which lie on the TC function are (0, £20,000) and (800, £80,000). If these are plotted on the graph and joined up the TC function will appear as shown in Figure 14.1. Note that the total cost function does not start at coordinates 0,0. At an output of zero, the business still has fixed costs of £20,000.

Analysis from the diagram The break-even chart is now complete. An analysis of certain points on the diagram can be made.

- The break even point can be identified and plotted. It is usual to draw lines to show the number of canoes Reidle Bros must sell to break-even (400), and the value of TR and TC at this level of output (£50,000). The break-even point should coincide with the calculation made in the first step, ie 400 canoes.

Figure 14.1 *Break-even chart for Reidle Bros*

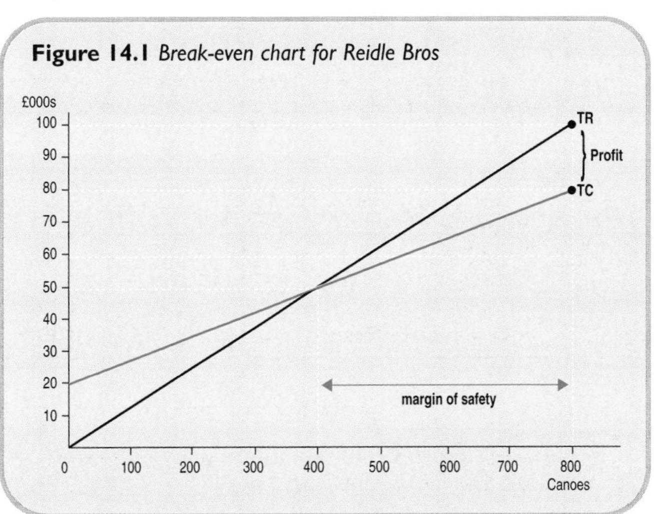

- The profit at certain levels of output may be indicated. For example, at an output of 800 canoes, the profit is £100,000 - £80,000 = £20,000.
- The margin of safety can be indicated. This is the difference between the output of the business and the break-even point. At an output of 800 canoes it is 800 -400 = 400 canoes.

Joanne Williams, a student, believed she could make some money during the summer holidays by operating as a mobile ice-cream vendor. She hired a purpose built van from one of the national ice-cream producers. This cost £200 per week. The variable costs per ice-cream cone were 30p. Joanne was under contract to sell ice-cream cones for 80p each. In order to analyse the profit potential at different sales levels she drew up a break-even chart.

(a) Draw a break-even chart for Joanne Williams.
(b) Using your chart state: (i) the number of cones needed to break-even; (ii) the profit she would make if she sold 700 cones.
(c) On your chart show the margin of safety if 700 cones were sold.

Question 1

Target rate of profit

Break-even analysis can be used to calculate the amount of output needed to generate a certain level of profit. For example, if Reidle Bros wanted to make £15,000 profit, the level of output required to do this would be:

$$\frac{\text{Fixed cost + profit target}}{\text{Contribution}}$$

$$= \frac{£20{,}000 + £15{,}000}{£50\ (£125 - £75)}$$

$$= \frac{£35{,}000}{£50}$$

$$= 700 \text{ canoes}$$

Thus, when Reidle Bros produces and sells 700 canoes profit is:

$$\text{Profit} = \text{total revenue - total costs}$$

$$= £125 \times 700 - (£20{,}000 + [£75 \times 700])$$

$$= £87{,}500 - (£20{,}000 + £52{,}500)$$

$$= £87{,}500 - £72{,}500$$

$$= £15{,}000$$

Palmer and Minton manufacture lawn tractors in their Hereford factory. They are sold through mail order for £900 each. Their fixed costs are £50,000 p.a. and variable costs £700 per tractor. Palmer and Minton established their partnership in 1998 and for the first two trading years they broke-even. In the next financial year they set a profit target of £150,000.

(a) Calculate how many lawn tractors Palmer and Minton need to produce and sell to reach their profit target.
(b) Calculate the margin of safety if the profit target is reached.

Question 2

Break-even price

Sometimes a business may want to know how much to charge for its product to break-even. In these circumstances a business must know how much it is going to produce and sell. For example, assume Reidle Bros aimed to sell 500 canoes and its objective was to break-even at that level of output. The price it should charge to break even would be:

$$\text{Break-even price} = \frac{\text{Total cost}}{\text{Output}}$$

$$= \frac{£20{,}000 + (500 \times £75)}{500}$$

$$= \frac{£20{,}000 + £37{,}500}{500}$$

$$= \frac{£57{,}500}{500}$$

$$= £115$$

Thus, if output was 500, Reidle Bros must charge £115 per canoe to break-even.

Price needed to reach a target rate of profit

A business may want to determine the price it needs to charge in order to reach a target rate of profit. For example, if Reidle Bros wanted to make a profit of £40,000, and its production capacity was 1,000 canoes, the price it would need to charge to reach this target rate of profit would be:

$$\text{Price} = \frac{\text{Profit target + total cost}}{\text{Output}}$$

$$= \frac{£40{,}000 + (£20{,}000 + 1{,}000 \times £75)}{1{,}000}$$

$$= \frac{£40{,}000 + £95{,}000}{1{,}000}$$

$$= \frac{£135{,}000}{1{,}000}$$

$$= £135$$

Thus, Reidle Bros would have to charge £135 for each canoe in order to make £40,000 profit if it produced and sold 1,000.

Accounting for changes in costs and revenues

One of the weaknesses of break-even analysis discussed in unit 41, is the assumption that the total cost and total revenue functions are **linear.** This indicates that as output increases, total cost and total revenue rise by the same proportion. What actually happens to total costs and total revenue as output increases can affect the decisions a business makes based on its break-even analysis, given a fixed amount of capital.

Total cost Assume a factory is built for 1,000 workers. As more workers are employed they can specialise in different tasks. 500 workers are likely to be more productive than one, for example. At some point, however, the opportunity to take advantage of specialisation may be used up and although total output will continue to rise, each extra worker will be less productive. For example, if 2,000 workers were employed in the above factory, there would not be enough machinery available for all workers to be usefully employed.

This is called the law of DIMINISHING RETURNS. It states that as more of a variable factor (labour here) is added to a fixed factor (say capital) the output of the extra workers will rise and then fall. In other words output will rise but at a diminishing rate. In extreme cases output may even fall. This is called negative returns.

How does this affect the costs of a business? Table 14.2 shows the effect on output and total cost of hiring labour at £200 per week with fixed capital costs of £100 per machine. The output per worker always rises, but eventually at a diminishing rate. For example, when the fourth worker is employed output rises by 47 units, but the fifth worker adds only 28 units. Total costs rise as the firm employs more labour. The effect of diminishing returns on the firm's total cost function is shown in Figure 14.2. Notice that it is non-linear.

Table 14.2 *The effect on output and total cost as a firm employs more workers given a fixed amount of capital*

Capital (machines) costing £100 each	Labour (workers) costing £200 per week	£ Fixed costs (machinery)	£ Variable costs (labour)	Total cost (£)	Output (units)
10	0	1,000	0	1,000	0
10	1	1,000	200	1,200	20
10	2	1,000	400	1,400	54
10	3	1,000	600	1,600	105
10	4	1,000	800	1,800	152
10	5	1,000	1,000	2,000	180
10	6	1,000	1,200	2,200	192

Total revenue The total revenue function drawn earlier in this unit assumed that each unit would be sold for the same price. In reality, it is unlikely that a firm can continually sell

Julia Robinson owns a large farm and supplies apples to cider producers. Apple production is only part of the farm's output. Most of the profit is generated from milk production. Julia is happy if apple production breaks even each year. The orchard was inherited from her grandfather and Julia does not wish to cease apple production for sentimental reasons, even though it is generally unprofitable. Whether she achieves her aim depends on how many apples she harvests and the going market price. At the end of the season Julia had picked 60,000 kilos. The fixed costs associated with apple production were £6,000 for the year. Variable costs were 40p per kilo.

(a) Calculate the price per kilo Julia would need to receive in order for apple production to break-even.
(b) Calculate the profit Julia would make from apple production if the market price was: (i) 48p per kilo; (ii) 51p per kilo.

Figure 14.2 *A total cost function subject to the law of diminishing returns*

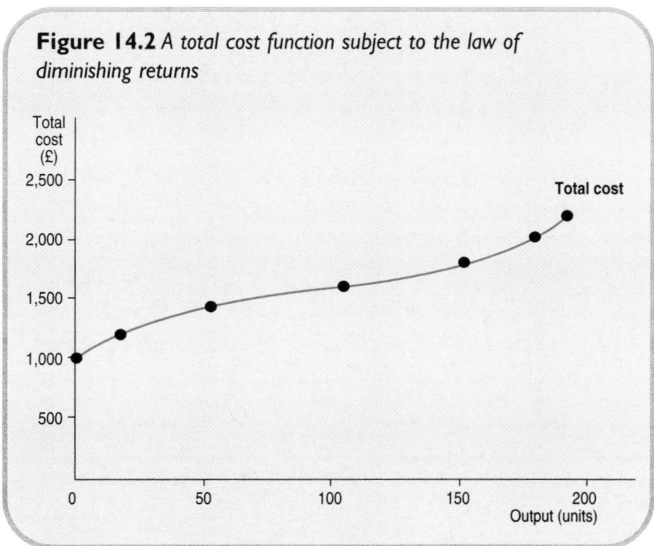

its output for the same price. There comes a point where additional sales can only be made if the price is lowered, for example a business may offer lower prices to customers who buy larger quantities. Figure 14.3 shows that as the price is lowered to encourage more sales the total revenue earned by the business falls.

Aimsley House is a private nursing home located in Bournemouth. It is well established and has served the local council for many years. Aimsley House generally operates at full capacity. It can accommodate up to 25 patients. Up until 1998 Aimsley House and the local council had negotiated financial terms upon which patients would be accepted. However, in 1999 the council informed the management of Aimsley House that, in the future, terms would not be negotiable. The council would state how much they are prepared to pay per patient and local homes would have to tender for the business at the 'going price'. This announcement was a cause of concern for the management of Aimsley House. They wondered whether the business would continue to make a healthy profit. The fixed costs at Aimsley House are £150,000 per annum and variable costs are £5,000 per resident.

(a) Assuming that Aimsley House continues to operate at full capacity, calculate the price that would enable the management to make £50,000 profit per annum.
(b) Assume that the council offers a price of £12,500 per patient every year.
  (i) Calculate the amount of profit Aimsley House would make.
  (ii) Discuss whether the management of Aimsley House should accept this offer.

Question 4

The graph also shows a total cost function subject to diminishing returns. Notice that there are now two break-even points, Q_1 and Q_2. When linear functions are used on a break-even chart, as output is increased beyond the break-even level of output, profit continues to increase indefinitely. When non-linear functions are used profit can only be made over a particular range of output, ie between Q_1 and Q_2. If production is pushed beyond Q_2 losses are made.

Figure 14.3 *A break-even chart with non-linear total cost and total revenue functions*

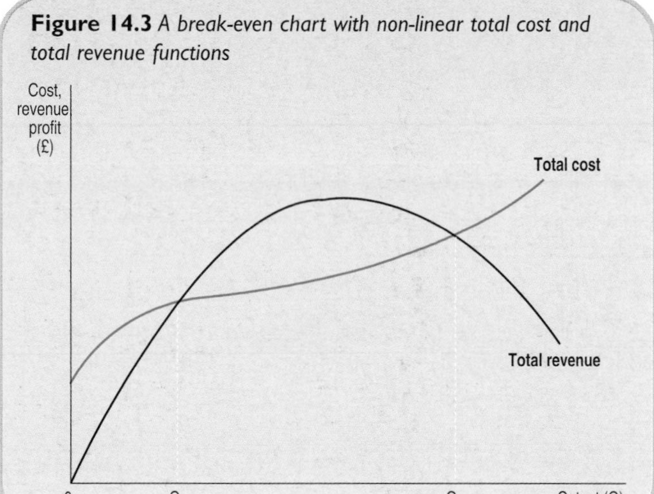

key terms

Diminishing returns - the eventual decline in output each extra worker adds to total output when the opportunity to specialise is used up.

Case study Falcon Ltd

Falcon Ltd, set up by Eric Hobson in 2002, supplies and puts up greenhouses and outhouses. In the first year of trading the business lost £23,600. The main reason for this was that the product range offered by the company was too big.

Eric's original idea was to supply tailor-made greenhouses to customers. This meant that a customer could buy a greenhouse to any specification. This caused two main problems for the business. First, it took too much time to design, manufacture and supply different styles and sizes of greenhouse to different customers. Second, there was a lot of waste material. For example, panes of glass left over from one construction were not reused in the next because the design was different. Eric also had staffing problems. He only employs two staff but during the first year he recruited and lost 11 employees. It seemed that the problem was low pay. All 11 workers left for higher paid jobs. The disruption caused by the high labour turnover compounded what turned out to be a very frustrating year for Eric.

During the winter Eric attended a seminar for new business people organised by his local Chamber of Commerce. This was a valuable experience. He learnt a lot and decided to rethink his business strategy for the next year. One key decision was to supply standard greenhouses only which he would sell for £800. He also

Figure 14.4 *Fixed costs for Falcon Ltd*

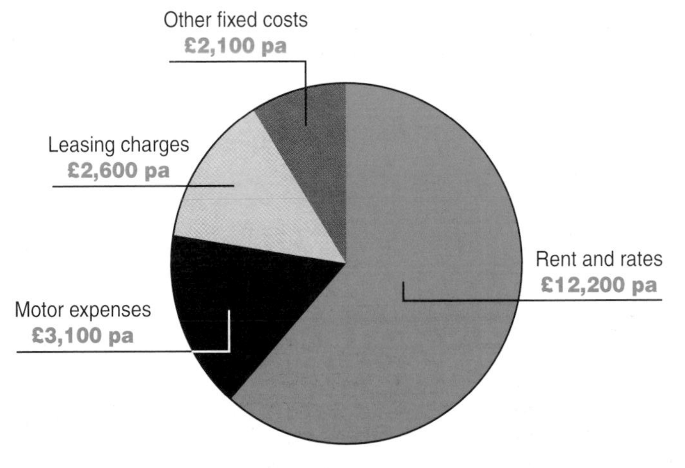

Figure 14.5 *Variable costs for Falcon Ltd*

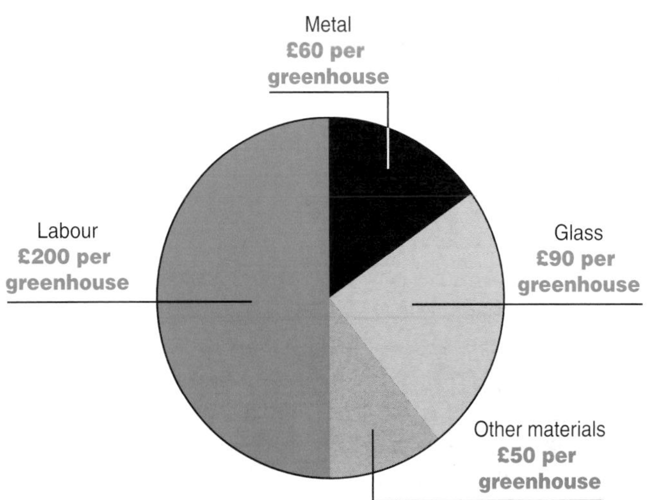

set a financial target. He wanted the business to break-even next year. However, in order to do this Eric had to gather some information on costs. This information is shown in Figures 14.4 and 14.5.

(a) Show the equations for total cost and total revenue and calculate the number of greenhouses that Falcon Ltd needs to sell to break-even in 2003. (6 marks)

(b) (i) By the end of the year Eric had sold 60 greenhouses. Construct the break-even chart and show the profit made by Falcon Ltd at this level of output. (12 marks)

(ii) Label the margin of safety on the graph and explain what it means for Falcon Ltd. (8 marks)

(c) In 2004, Eric decided to outsource the production of the greenhouse frames to reduce construction time. It would also reduce fixed costs since he can now operate from much smaller premises. Assuming that fixed costs fell by £4,000, make the necessary adjustments to the break-even chart and show the new level of break-even output. (8 marks)

(d) In 2004, Eric decided to set a profit target of £26,000 for the business. Calculate how many greenhouses Falcon Ltd would need to sell to meet this target. (6 marks)

(e) To what extent might Falcon Ltd be affected by the law of diminishing returns in the future? (10 marks)

15 Budgetary Control

What is budgetary control?

BUDGETARY CONTROL involves a business looking into the future, stating what it wants to happen, and then deciding how to achieve these aims. The control process is shown in Figure 15.1.

- Preparation of plans. All businesses have objectives. If the sales department increases sales by ten per cent, how does it know whether or not this is satisfactory? Targets are usually set which allow a business to determine if its objectives have been met. The results it achieves can then be compared with the targets it sets.
- Comparisons of plans with actual results. Control will be effective if information is available as quickly as possible. Managers need budgetary data as soon as it is available. Recent developments in information technology have helped to speed up the supply of data. For budgeting purposes the financial year has been divided up into smaller control periods - usually four weeks or one calendar month. It is common to prepare a budget for each control period. At the end of the period the actual results can then be compared with targets set in the budget.
- Analysis of variances. This is the most important stage in the control process. VARIANCE ANALYSIS involves trying to find reasons for the differences between actual and expected results. An unfavourable variance, when planned sales are 1,000 units and actual sales are 800 units, for example, might be due to inefficiency. It is then up to the management to take some action. A variance might be the result of some external factor influencing the business. In this case the business may need to change its business plans and adjust the next budget.

Figure 15.1 *Stages in budgetary control*

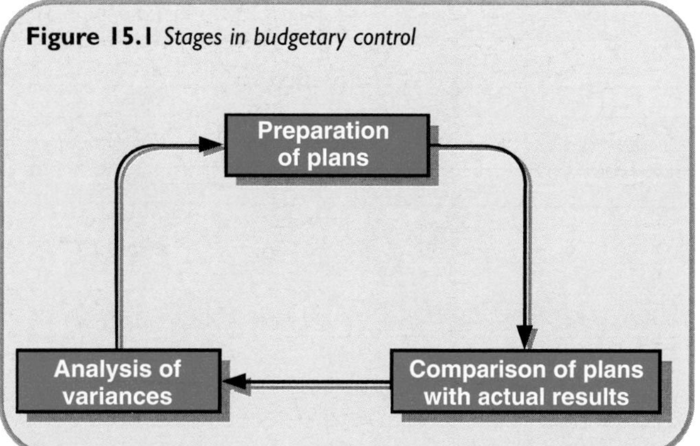

Types of variance

A **variance** is the difference between the actual and the planned figure that the business had budgeted for. It can be calculated by:

Variance = actual value - planned value

A favourable variance is where, for example, actual sales revenues are greater than planned revenues or actual costs are

Figure 15.2 *A summary of the key variances*

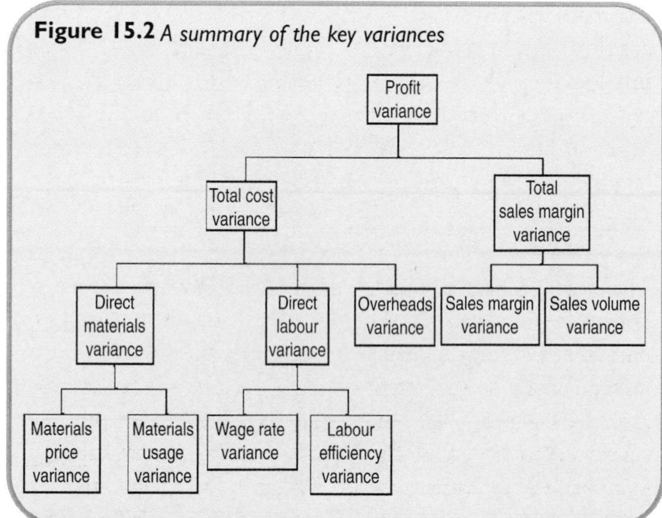

Llantrisant Holdings design and manufacture dials, instruments and sensor equipment for the electronics industry. The company relocated when it won a substantial contract to supply a large South Korean electronics company. The South Korean company set up a factory in Cardiff and was keen for its suppliers to be located in close proximity. Llantrisant Holdings delivers just-in-time to its Korean customer. Llantrisant has begun to enjoy substantial efficiency gains in the last 18 months. Representatives from its South Korean customer visited the Llantrisant factory before awarding the contract. During their visit they made helpful recommendations about alternative working practices.

Table 15.1 *Budgeted profit and loss account and actual figures for Llantrisant Holdings (2004)*

	Budgeted	Actual	Variances
Sales revenue	7,435	7,546	
Cost of sales	4,950	4,100	
Gross profit	2,485	3,446	
Overheads	1,250	1,280	
Operating profit	1,235	2,166	

(a) (i) Complete Table 15.1 by calculating the variances.
(ii) Explain whether the operating profit variance is adverse or favourable.

(b) Analyse the variance which has had the most influence on the operating profit variance.

lower than planned. An adverse variance may be where actual sales revenues are less than planned or actual costs are higher than planned.

Figure 15.2 shows examples of variances that a business might decide to calculate and analyse. The profit variance is influenced by all other variances. A change in any one of the variances will affect profit. Most variances are linked to the costs incurred by a business. This suggests that variance analysis provides a very good way of monitoring business costs. There may be other variances which are not shown in the diagram. The number of possible variances is equal to the number of factors which can influence business costs and revenue.

Profit variances

The most important of all variances is the **profit variance**. Differences between actual profit and planned profit will be of particular interest to business owners, managers and other stakeholders. The performance of most businesses is often measured by profit. All other variances will affect the profit variance, though not by the same magnitude. For example, if planned sales in January are £45,000 and actual sales are £48,500, there is a favourable sales variance of £3,500 (£48,500 - £45,000). This does not necessarily mean that the profit variance will improve by £3,500. This is because the extra sales are likely to generate a cost variance. This will offset some of the benefit.

Direct materials variance

Figure 15.2 shows that the **total cost variance** can be influenced by several cost variances. One of these is the **direct materials variance**.This is the difference between budgeted direct materials costs and actual direct materials costs. Direct materials include raw materials, components and any other resources used directly in production. For example, a biscuit manufacturer may use flour as one of its raw materials. Table 15.2 shows the budgeted and actual price of flour and the budgeted and actual usage of flour in a particular budget period. According to the table, the budgeted direct materials cost of the flour is £3,000. However, the actual direct materials cost is £2,860. This gives a favourable direct materials variance of £140 in this budget period.

Table 15.2 *Cost and usage of flour for a biscuit manufacturer*

	Price (per kilo)	Usage (kilos)	Direct materials cost
Budgeted	£1.50	2,000	£3,000
Actual	£1.30	2,200	£2,860
Direct materials variance			£140 (F)

The favourable variance in Table 15.2 is influenced by two other variances.

Materials price variance This will result when the actual price of direct materials is different from the budgeted or standard price. In Table 15.2 this is calculated by:

Materials price variance = (budgeted price - actual price) x actual usage
= (£1.50 - £1.30) x 2,200
= £0.20 x 2,200
= £440 (F)

The materials price variance is favourable because the actual cost is lower than the budgeted cost. This variance may be the responsibility of the purchasing department. Materials price variances could arise for a number of reasons, for example:

- materials may be obtained at a special discount;
- a new supplier might have been found;
- unexpected inflation may raise prices;
- a price war may have broken out in the market.

Materials usage variance A materials usage variance is found by comparing the actual usage of materials and the budgeted usage. The difference is valued at the budgeted price. For the biscuit manufacturer above the variance is:

Materials usage variance = (budgeted usage - actual usage) x budgeted price
= (2,000 - 2,200) x £1.50
= -200 x £1.50
= £300 (A)

The materials usage variance is adverse because the actual usage is greater than the budgeted usage. The effect will lead to lower profit. This variance might be the responsibility of the production manager. Materials usage variances might arise

Simpson's potato chips are produced by Simpson Ltd. It supplies the retail trade in Yorkshire and a few other outlets in the north. Its factory is located in Dewsbury and it employs 24 staff. The most important raw material is potatoes which it purchases from a large potato farmer in Lincolnshire. Table 15.3 shows the budgeted and actual prices paid for potatoes and the budgeted and actual usage of potatoes in a particular budget period.

Table 15.3 *Budgeted and actual prices and usage of potatoes for Simpson Ltd*

	Price (per kilo)	Usage (kilos)	Direct material cost
Budgeted	10p	20,000	£2,000
Actual	12p	24,000	£2,880

(a) For the budget period calculate:
  (i) the materials price variance;
  (ii) the materials usage variance;
  (iii) the direct materials variance.
(b) Explain how the results in (a) might affect the business.

because materials are:

- wasted in production due to sloppy or careless work;
- wasted because they are inferior;
- used more efficiently because staff take more care in their work;
- wasted due to a machine malfunction.

The direct materials variance for the biscuit manufacturer is £140 (F). It is influenced by both the materials price variance which is favourable, £440, and the materials usage variance which is adverse, £300. Notice that the adverse usage variance is outweighed by the favourable price variance.

Direct labour variances

The direct wage bill is the amount of money paid to workers involved in production. A direct labour variance will occur when the budgeted direct wage bill is different to the actual direct wage bill. In the case of the biscuit manufacturer, the budgeted wage rates and actual wage rates, and the budgeted number of labour hours and the actual number of labour hours used in a particular budget period, are shown in Table 15.4. The planned direct wage bill is £7,500. However, the actual wage bill is £8,320. This results in a £820 adverse variance. The direct labour variance is influenced by two other variances.

Table 15.4 *Budgeted and actual wage rates and labour hours for the biscuit manufacturer*

	Wage rate	No. of labour hours	Direct wage bill
Budgeted	£5.00	1,500	£7,500
Actual	£5.20	1,600	£8,320
Direct labour variance			£820 (A)

Wage rate variances A wage rate variance will result if there is difference between the budgeted wage rate paid to workers and the actual wage rate paid. In the case of the biscuit manufacturer the wage rate variance is :

Wage rate variance = (budgeted wage rate - actual wage rate) x actual hours
= (£5.00 - £5.20) x 1,600
= - £0.20 x 1,600
= £320 (A)

The wage rate variance is adverse because the actual wage rate is higher than the budgeted wage rate. The personnel manager may be responsible for this variance. The factors which might influence wage rates could include:

- trade union pressure;
- shortages of skilled labour;
- using a different type of labour;
- government legislation, such as raising the minimum wage.

Labour efficiency variances There will be a labour efficiency variance if there is a difference between the budgeted number of labour hours required in a budget period and the actual number of labour hours used. In the case of the biscuit manufacturer, the labour efficiency variance is:

Labour efficiency variance = (budgeted hours - actual hours) x budgeted wage
= (1,500 - 1,600) x £5.00
= - 100 x £5.00
= £500 (A)

The labour efficiency variance is adverse because the actual number of hours worked is greater than the budgeted number. The production manager may be responsible for this variance. The factors which might influence the number of labour hours used might include:

- the productivity of workers;
- the reliability of machinery used by workers;
- how well trained workers are.

Wallace & Co. makes a range of swimwear which it sells to retailers in the UK. It operates six monthly budget periods. The direct labour budget is shown in Table 15.5. The actual figures for 2004 are also shown. Although swimwear is subject to seasonal demand, Wallace & Co. prefers to keep production fairly constant and build up stocks during the winter. This has helped to maintain good industrial relations in the past.

(a) For the six month budget period calculate:
(i) the wage rate variance;
(ii) the labour efficiency variance;
(iii) the direct labour variance.

(b) Explain what is likely to have caused the direct labour variance.

Table 15.5 *Direct labour budget and actual figures for Wallace & Co, 2004*

	Jan		Feb		Mar		Apr		May		Jun	
	Btd.	Act.	Btd.	Act.	Btd.	Act.	Btd.	Act.	Btd.	Act.	Btd.	Act.
Labour (hrs)	800	810	800	820	800	810	800	200	800	800	800	810
Wage rate	£5	£5	£5	£5	£5	£5	£5	£5	£5	£5	£5	£5
Direct lab. costs (£)	4,000	4,050	4,000	4,100	4,000	4,050	4,000	1,000	4,000	4,000	4,000	4,050

Btd. = budgeted Act. = actual

The direct labour variance for the biscuit manufacturer is £820 (A). It is influenced by the wage rate variance, £320(A), and the labour efficiency variance, £500 (A).

Overheads variances

Overheads variances arise when planned overhead costs are different from the actual overhead costs. Overheads are the general expenses incurred by a business. Table 15.6 shows the annual budgeted and actual overheads for the biscuit manufacturer. The overhead variances are also shown. The total overheads variance is adverse (£4,200). The main reason for this is the adverse distribution variance of £7,000. Some of the overheads in Table 15.6 do not have any variances. This is because the budgeted figures are exactly the same as the actual figures. This may happen when a business pays some of its bills in advance. For example, a business will normally know what rent is going to be charged in the next twelve months. This helps businesses to produce more accurate budgets.

Sometimes a business might separate overheads into fixed and variable costs. A business could then calculate the fixed overhead variance and the variable overhead variance. Overhead variances might be caused by:

- excessive or under utilisation of a service, such as wasteful or uneconomic use of a service;
- price changes for a service, such as an increase in accountancy fees;
- a change in the nature of a service, such as using oil for heating instead of electricity.

Table 15.6 *Annual budgeted and actual overheads for the biscuit manufacturer*

Description	Budgeted	Actual	Variance
Rent	£60,000	£60,000	0
Rates	£5,500	£5,500	0
Insurance	£1,200	£1,300	£100 (A)
Maintenance	£16,000	£15,000	£1,000 (F)
Distribution	£78,000	£85,000	£7,000 (A)
Telephone	£1,700	£1,600	£100 (F)
Administration	£64,000	£62,000	£2,000 (F)
Accountancy fees	£4,500	£4,700	£200 (A)
Depreciation	£20,000	£20,000	0
Total	£250,900	£255,100	£4,200 (A)

Sales margin variances

A sales margin variance will arise if there is either a change in the price charged by the business or a change from the budgeted volume of sales. Table 15.7 shows budgeted and actual prices and budgeted and actual sales volumes for cases of biscuits in a particular budget period. The budgeted value of sales is £20,000. However, the actual sales value is £21,320. This generates a favourable sales margin variance of £1,320 in this budget period.

Table 15.7 *Budgeted and actual prices and sales volumes for cases of biscuits*

	Price (per case)	Sales (cases)	Sales value
Budgeted	£2.50	8,000	£20,000
Actual	£2.60	8,200	£21,320
Sales margin variance			£1,320 (F)

The favourable variance shown in Table 15.7 is influenced by two other variances.

Sales margin price variance This will occur if the actual price charged by a business is different from the budgeted price. For the example above this is:

Sales margin price variance = (actual price - budgeted price) x actual sales
= (£2.60 - £2.50) x 8,200
= £0.10 x 8,200
= £820 (F)

The sales margin price variance is favourable because the actual price charged is higher than the budgeted price. This variance may be the responsibility of the sales or marketing department. Such variances might arise due to:

- the chance to charge premium prices;
- sales in non-planned markets with different prices;
- changes in market conditions, such as a rival leaving the market.

Sales volume variance This will occur if the actual level of sales is different from the budgeted sales. For the biscuit manufacturer this is:

Sales volume variance = (actual sales - budgeted sales) x budgeted price
= (8,200 - 8,000) x £2.50
= 200 x £2.50
= £500 (F)

The sales volume variance is favourable because the actual number of sales is greater than the budgeted number. This variance is likely to be the responsibility of the marketing department or the sales manager. Sales volume variances may arise due to:

- changes in the state of the economy;
- competitors' actions;
- changes in consumer tastes;
- government action, such as a cut in income tax;
- changes in the quality of the product;
- changes in marketing techniques.

The sales margin variance for the biscuit manufacturer is £1,320 (F). It is influenced by both the sales price margin variance, £820 (F), and sales volume variance, £500 (F).

Bromford Motors is a large car dealership based in Wimbledon, London. It sells cars for a Japanese car manufacturer. The company operates a very strict budget regime. The five sales staff have a fraction of their pay linked to budget performance. Table 15.8 shows the budgeted and actual prices and volume of cars sold for a particular budget period.

Table 15.8 *Budgeted and actual prices and sales of cars for Bromford Motors*

	Average price	Volume	Sales value
Budgeted	£9,500	250	£2,375,000
Actual	£9,325	269	£2,508,425

(a) For the budget period calculate the:
   (i) the sales margin price variance;
   (ii) the sales volume variance;
   (iii) sales margin variance.

(b) Explain the possible causes of the variances in (a).

Cash variances

One variance not shown in Figure 15.2 is the cash variance. This is because cash and profit are not the same. Cash budgets are concerned with liquidity, not profitability. A cash variance will show the difference between budgeted cash flows and actual cash flows. Table 15.9 shows the budgeted and actual cash flows for a carpet retailer in a three month budget period. The cash variances are also shown. A favourable cash variance arises when more cash flows in than was planned and if cash outflows are lower than planned. An adverse cash variance is caused by more cash flowing out than budgeted or less cash flowing in. In Table 15.9 all the closing balance cash variances are adverse. This means that the amount of cash actually left at the end of each month was lower than budgeted. For example, in January it was planned to have £5,500 at the end of the month. However, the actual closing balance was £3,900 giving an adverse variance of £1,600. Cash variances can be caused by many factors. Some examples include:

- lower or higher than expected cash sales;
- customers not settling their accounts on time;
- unexpected costs;
- unexpected inflation.

Benefits of variance analysis

- It allows senior managers to monitor the performance of the organisation as a whole, as well as different sections of the organisation. For example, analysing departmental cost variances may allow a business to find out why certain costs are too high. Alternatively, it allows businesses to identify good practice and discover why some costs are lower.
- Prompt variance analysis allows managers to assess whether variances are caused by internal or external factors. Once causes have been traced, they can be corrected.
- By identifying variances and their causes managers may be able to produce more accurate budgets in future. This will aid planning and perhaps improve the performance of the business.
- Budgetary control in general helps to improve accountability in businesses. It can also be linked to performance related pay. For example, budget holders may receive a bonus payment at the end of the budget period if they can show favourable variances.

key terms

Budgetary control - a business system which involves making future plans, comparing the actual results with the planned results and then investigating causes of any differences.

Variance analysis - the process of calculating variances and attempting to identify their causes.

Table 15.9 *Budgeted and actual cash flows for a carpet retailer*

(£)

	JANUARY			FEBRUARY			MARCH		
	Budgeted	Actual	Variance	Budgeted	Actual	Variance	Budgeted	Actual	Variance
Cash receipts	25,000	25,600	600F	26,000	27,100	1,100F	30,000	29,800	200A
Cash inflow	25,000	25,600	600F	26,000	27,100	1,100F	30,000	29,800	200A
Purchases	15,000	17,000	2,000A	15,000	16,000	1,000A	20,000	22,000	2,000A
Wages	6,500	6,600	100A	6,500	6,700	200A	8,000	7,600	400F
Overheads	2,000	2,100	100A	2,000	1,800	200F	2,500	2,000	500F
Cash outflow	23,500	25,700	2,200A	23,500	24,500	1,000A	30,500	31,600	1,100A
Net cash flow	1,500	(100)	1,600A	2,500	2,600	100F	(500)	(1,800)	1,300A
Opening balance	4,000	4,000	0	5,500	3,900	1,600A	8,000	6,500	1,500A
Closing balance	5,500	3,900	1,600A	8,000	6,500	1,500A	7,500	4,700	2,800A

1. Describe the 3 steps in budgetary control.
2. Why is the profit variance probably the most important of all?
3. What is the difference between the materials price variance and the materials usage variance?
4. What might cause a direct materials variance?
5. What is the difference between the wage rate variance and the labour efficiency variance?
6. What might cause a direct labour variance?
7. Why might some overhead variances be 0?
8. Explain the difference between the sales margin price variance and the sales volume variance.
9. What is a cash variance?
10. State 4 benefits of variance analysis.

Case study Windrush Training Services

Windrush Training Services is a small company quoted on AIM. When it was floated in 1994 it offered a range of training services to businesses in London. However, it got into difficulties and its shares were suspended in 2000. A new management team was appointed and the company became more focused by specialising in training courses for the financial services sector. The new managing director identified a market niche. There was a need for employees in the financial services sector to be kept in touch with a growing body of regulatory guidelines. Windrush used direct marketing to sell its short update courses to financial analysts, stockbrokers, equity houses and financial advisers.

The company raised some fresh capital through a rights issue and trading in its shares began again in January 2002. The new management team recognised a greater need for financial direction. It produced a twelve month cash budget for 2003 and used variance analysis to aid cash control.

Table 15.10 *Cash budget for Windrush Training Services, 2003*

(£000)

	JAN	FEB	MAR	APR	MAY	JUN	JUL	AUG	SEP	OCT	NOV	DEC
Fresh capital	800											
Course fees	200	200	220	220	250	250	300	300	350	350	300	300
Total inflow	1,000	200	220	220	250	250	300	300	350	350	300	300
Wages	100	100	100	100	100	110	110	110	110	110	110	220
Rent	10	10	10	10	10	10	10	10	10	10	10	10
Marketing	20	20	15	15	10	10	10	5	5	5	5	5
Heat & light			5			5			5			5
VAT			92			108			142			142
Other expenses	25	25	25	25	25	25	25	25	25	25	25	25
Total outflow	155	155	247	150	145	268	155	150	297	150	150	407
Net cash flow	845	45	(27)	70	105	(18)	145	150	53	200	150	(107)
Opening balance	(990)	(145)	(100)	(127)	(57)	48	30	175	325	378	578	728
Closing balance	(145)	(100)	(127)	(57)	48	30	175	325	378	578	728	621

Table 15.11 *Actual cash movements for Windrush Training Services, 2003*

(£000)

	JAN	FEB	MAR	APR	MAY	JUN	JUL	AUG	SEP	OCT	NOV	DEC
Fresh capital	800											
Course fees	160	180	170	160	190	240	300	310	390	590	530	200
Total inflow	960	180	170	160	190	240	300	310	390	590	530	200
Wages	100	100	100	100	100	110	110	110	110	110	110	300
Rent	10	10	10	10	10	10	10	10	10	10	10	10
Marketing	20	20	15	15	20	20	25	25	25	30	30	30
Heat & light			5			5			5			5
VAT			76			88			150			196
Other expenses	20	19	21	10	23	19	15	5	21	17	19	32
Total outflow	150	149	227	135	153	252	160	150	321	167	169	573
Net cash flow	810	31	(57)	25	37	(12)	140	160	69	423	361	(373)
Opening balance	(990)	(180)	(149)	(206)	(181)	(144)	(156)	(16)	144	213	636	997
Closing balance	(180)	(149)	(206)	(181)	(144)	(156)	(16)	144	213	636	997	624

(a) Explain, using an example from the case, what is meant by a cash variance. (6 marks)

(b) Calculate the annual variances for each item of receipts and expenditure and show whether they are favourable or adverse. (10 marks)

(c) Explain a possible link between the course fee variance and the marketing expenditure variance. (6 marks)

(d) What might account for the 'other expenses' variances? (8 marks)

(e) Discuss the possible benefits of budgetary control to Windrush Training Services. (10 marks)

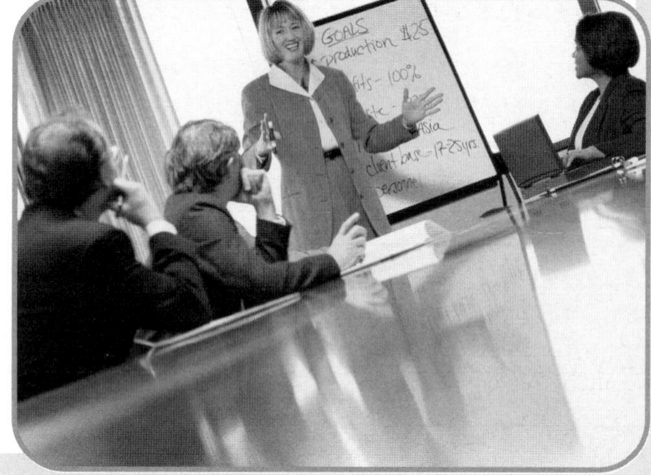

16 The Compilation of Accounts

When are accounts compiled?

The compilation of accounts involves using the information generated by recording business transactions to produce a balance sheet, profit and loss account and cash flow statement. Some businesses use computer software to compile accounts on a regular basis.

Final accounts are compiled at the end of the trading year. Small businesses such as sole traders, partnerships and small limited companies may employ chartered or certified accountants to compile their accounts. Business owners provide records of transactions and supporting documents. Most large companies and many medium-sized companies employ their own accountants who compile accounts for the business. However, companies which produce their own accounts must get them audited by an independent firm of accountants.

Once the accounts have been compiled they can be used by the various stakeholders. Public limited companies distribute their annual reports and accounts to all their shareholders.

Compiling the balance sheet

Figure 16.1 shows a summary of the balance sheet structure. Accountants produce balance sheets according to accounting convention set out by the Accounting Standards Board (ASB) and the **Companies Act, 1985**.

A balance sheet can be compiled by inserting the appropriate information in the correct positions in the structure. Consider the financial information in Table 16.1 for Corporate Signs Ltd, a business which makes neon signs for companies. All the information relates to the assets, liabilities and capital of the company on 31.1.2004.

Figure 16.1 *Balance sheet summary diagram*

	£	
Fixed assets	A	
Current assets	B	
Current liabilities	C	
Net current assets (working capital)	D	B-C
Total assets less current liabilities	E	(A+B)-C *or* A+D
Creditors: amounts due after one year(Long term liabilities)	F	
Net assets	G	E-F *or* (A+D)-F
Capital and reserves (Capital employed or shareholders' funds)	H	G=H

Table 16.1 *Financial information for Corporate Signs Ltd, 31.1.04 (£)*

Mortgage	100,000
Share capital	100,000
Other reserves	71,000
Premises	231,000
Debtors	75,000
Vehicles	87,000
Stocks and work in progress	98,000
Plant and equipment	199,000
Current liabilities	201,000
Retained profit	290,000
Cash at bank	112,000
Unsecured bank loan	60,000
Intangible assets	20,000

To compile the balance sheet for Corporate Signs Ltd, the following step-by-step approach might be used.

- Identify which of the items are assets, which are liabilities and which are capital and reserves.
- Write the title and date at the top of the account.
- List the fixed assets and add them up. Fixed assets are premises (£231,000), plant and equipment (£199,000) and vehicles (£87,000). All these are tangible assets (a total of £517,000). Intangible assets are £20,000. Fixed assets are therefore tangible plus intangible assets, a total of £537,000.
- List the current assets and add them up. Current assets are stocks and work in progress (£98,000), debtors (£75,000) and cash at bank (£112,000) which total £285,000.
- List the current liabilities and add them up. Current liabilities are stated as £201,000. These are the amounts falling due within one year.
- Enter the value for net current assets by subtracting current liabilities from current assets (£285,000 - £201,000 = £84,000).
- Enter the value for total assets less current liabilities by adding fixed assets to net current assets (£537,000 + £84,000 = £621,000).
- List the creditors: amounts falling due after one year and add them up. These are the mortgage (£100,000) and the unsecured bank loan (£60,000) which total £160,000.
- Enter the value for net assets by subtracting creditors: amounts falling due after one year from total assets less current liabilities (£621,000 - £160,000 = £461,000).
- List the capital and reserves and add them up. Capital and reserves are share capital (£100,000), other reserves (£71,000) and retained profit (£290,000) which total £461,000.
- Check that the value of capital and reserves (also shown as shareholders' funds or capital employed on some balance

sheets) are the same as net assets. If the balance sheet has been compiled accurately, the value of net assets should be exactly the same as capital employed.

If the above steps are followed the result should be the same as the balance sheet shown in Table 16.2. Remember that normally both the current trading figures, and the previous year's figures, are shown in the accounts.

Table 16.2 *Balance sheet for Corporate Signs Ltd, 31.1.2004*

CORPORATE SIGNS LTD - BALANCE SHEET AS AT 31 JANUARY 2004	£
Fixed assets	
Tangible assets	
Premises	231,000
Plant and equipment	199,000
Vehicles	87,000
	517,000
Intangible assets	20,000
	537,000
Current assets	
Stocks and work in progress	98,000
Debtors	75,000
Cash at bank	112,000
	285,000
Current liabilities	201,000
Net current assets	84,000
Total assets less current liabilities	621,000
Creditors: amounts falling due after one year	
Mortgage	(100,000)
Unsecured bank loan	(60,000)
Net assets	461,000
Capital and reserves	
Share capital	100,000
Other reserves	71,000
Retained profit	290,000
Capital employed	461,000

Superscape Group plc develops 3D technology and applications for mobile devices. The company's Swerve technology has been developed specifically for wireless environments. Swerve is being used by many of the mobile industry's leading businesses. Table 16.3 shows some financial information about the assets, liabilities and capital of the company in 2002 and 2003.

Table 16.3 *Financial information for Superscape plc, 2002-03*

(£000)	2003	2002
Retained profit	-46,673	-37,993
Intangible assets	110	324
Share premium	47,679	46,172
Tangible assets	359	636
Share capital	8,954	3,775
Current liabilities	957	1,257
Other fixed assets*	0	90
Debtors	1,105	868
Cash at bank	9,343	11,293

* Long term investments.

Source: adapted from Superscape Group plc, *Annual Report and Accounts, 2003.*

(a) Compile the balance sheet for Superscape plc using the information in Table 16.3.
(b) What might account for the change in the value of tangible assets over the two years?

Transactions and the balance sheet

How might a transaction affect the balance sheet? There are two sides to every transaction and transactions can affect both assets and liabilities. For example, when a business makes a sale it will receive cash (an increase in assets) but reduce its stock of finished goods (a decrease in assets). Table 16.4 shows the balance sheet of Gregory Issacs plc, a construction company, as at 31 August 2004. How might four transactions affect the balance sheet?

- **Transaction 1.** The company buys a range of new equipment for one division of the business for £1 million. It arranges to pay by credit. This will increase fixed assets (equipment) by £1 million and current liabilities (trade creditors) by £1 million.
- **Transaction 2.** A consignment of stocks is ordered costing £500,000 on credit. This will increase current assets (stocks) by £500,000 and current liabilities (trade creditors) by £500,000.
- **Transaction 3.** The company makes an interim dividend payment to shareholders of £1.8 million. This will decrease current assets (cash at bank) by £1.8 million and creditors: amounts due within one year (dividend) by £1.8 million.
- **Transaction 4.** A debtor repays £200,000 to the company. This will only affect current assets. Debtors will fall by £200,000 and cash at bank will increase by £200,000.

It is assumed here that all these transactions are carried out on 1 September 2004. The effects of these transactions are shown in Table 16.4.

Table 16.4

GREGORY ISSACS PLC BALANCE SHEET AS AT 31 AUGUST 2004	£m	GREGORY ISSACS PLC BALANCE SHEET AS AT 1 SEPTEMBER 2004	£m
Fixed assets		**Fixed assets**	
Tangible assets	84.8	Tangible assets	85.8
Investments	0.8	Investments	0.8
	85.6		86.6
Current assets		**Current assets**	
Work in progress and stocks	802.4	Work in progress and stocks	802.9
Debtors	84.4	Debtors	84.2
Cash at bank	10.8	Cash at bank	9.2
	897.6		896.3
Creditors: amounts falling due within one year (current liabilities)		**Creditors: amounts falling due within one year** (current liabilities)	
Trade creditors	246.6	Trade creditors	248.1
Taxation	12.8	Taxation	12.8
Dividend	20.8	Dividend	19.0
	280.2		279.9
Net current assets (working capital)	617.4	**Net current assets** (working capital)	616.4
Total assets less current liabilities	703.0	**Total assets less current liabilities**	703.0
Creditors: amounts falling due after one year	(199.8)	**Creditors: amounts falling due after one year**	(199.8)
Net assets	**503.2**	**Net assets**	**503.2**
Capital and reserves		**Capital and reserves**	
Called up share capital	91.2	Called up share capital	91.2
Revaluation reserve	91.5	Revaluation reserve	91.5
Profit and loss account	320.5	Profit and loss account	320.5
	503.2		**503.2**

Equipment is a tangible asset. The value of tangible assets rises by £1m, from £84.8m to £85.8m

The value of fixed assets has also increased by £1m from £85.6m to £86.6m

The value of stocks has increased by £500,000, from £802.4m to £802.9m

The value of debtors has fallen by £200,000, from £84.4m to £84.2m

The value of cash at bank has fallen by £1.8m and then risen by £200,000, an overall fall of £1.6m from £10.8m to £9.2m

The value of current assets has fallen by £1.3m, from £897.6m to £896.3m

The value of trade creditors has increased by £1m and £500,000 (£1.5m) from £246.6m to £248.1m

The value of dividends has fallen by £1.8m, from £20.8m to £19m

The value of current liabilities has fallen by £300,000 from £280.2m to £279.9m

The value of net current assets has fallen by £1m from £617.4m to £616.4m

The value of total assets less current liabilities, creditors due after one year, net assets and capital and reserves have not changed. This is because transactions on that particular day have not affected either long term liabilities or capital and reserves

Compiling the profit and loss account

Accountants produce profit and loss accounts according to accounting convention set out by the ASB and the Companies Act. There is, however, some variation when looking at the profit and loss accounts of limited companies.

The profit and loss account will contain three key sections.

- The trading account, where gross profit is calculated.
- The profit and loss account, where net profit is calculated.
- The profit and loss appropriation account, which shows how the net profit is distributed.

Consider the financial information in Table 16.6, which shows the revenue and expenses incurred by a supermarket chain. The following steps could be used when compiling a profit and loss account from a set of figures:

For the trading account

- Write the title and date at the top of the account.
- Enter the value for turnover (£3,000m).
- Enter the value for cost of sales (remember that the cost of sales must be adjusted for stock. The value of cost of sales

Look at Table 16.5 showing information that may be contained in the balance sheet of Barden Ltd. On 1.5.2004 the following transactions were undertaken by Barden.

- Debtors repaid £1,000,000, deposited into the bank.
- £2,500,000 of materials were bought on trade credit.
- A machine was sold off for £500,000 and money paid into the bank.

(a) Produce a new balance sheet for Barden Ltd which takes these transactions into account.

(b) A year later the balance sheet for Barden Ltd showed the following values:

- fixed assets of £20,000,000;
- current assets of £12,000,000;
- current liabilities of £8,000,000;
- long term liabilities of £4,000,000.

Calculate the value of:

(i) net current assets;

(ii) total assets less current liabilities;

(iii) capital and reserves.

Table 16.5 *Information from a balance sheet for Barden Ltd, as at 30.4.2004*

	£000	£000
Fixed assets		
Factory	11,000	
Plant and machinery	5,000	
Equipment	2,500	
Financial assets	1,000	
		19,500
Current assets		
Stocks	3,000	
Work-in-progress	2,500	
Debtors	3,500	
	9,000	
Current liabilities		
Trade creditors	3,500	
Other liabilities	2,500	
	6,000	
Net current assets		**3,000**
Total assets less current liabilities		**22,500**
Creditors falling due after more than one year	6,000	
Net assets		**16,500**
Capital and reserves		
Share capital	9,000	
Other reserves	2,000	
Retained profit	5,500	
		16,500

Table 16.6 *Financial information for a supermarket chain 2004*

	£m
Turnover	3,000
Administrative expenses and distribution costs	400
Taxation	45
Cost of sales	2,500
Interest paid (net)	5
Dividends	30
Non-operating income	30

has already been adjusted in Table 16.6 and is £2,500m.

- Enter the value for gross profit by subtracting cost of sales from turnover (£3,000m - £2,500m = £500m).

For the profit and loss account

- Enter the administrative/operating expenses underneath the gross profit (£400m).
- Enter the value for operating profit by subtracting operating expenses from gross profit (£500m - £400m = £100m).
- Enter the value of other income below operating profit (£30m).
- Enter the value for profit before interest and tax by adding non-operating income to operating profit (£100m + £30m = £130m).
- Enter the value for (net) interest payable underneath the value of profit before interest and tax (£5m).
- Enter the profit on ordinary activities before tax by

Table 16.7 *Profit and loss account for a supermarket chain*

PROFIT AND LOSS ACCOUNT
YEAR ENDED 31.1.2004

	£m
Turnover	3,000
Cost of sales	2,500
Gross profit	500
Administrative expenses and distribution costs	400
Operating profit	100
Non-operating income	30
Profit before interest and tax	130
Interest paid (net)	5
Profit on ordinary activities before tax	125
Taxation	45
Profit on ordinary activities after tax	80
Dividends	30
Retained profit	50

subtracting (net) interest paid from profit before interest and tax (£130m - £5m). This gives a total of £125m.

For the profit and loss appropriation account

- Enter taxation underneath profit on ordinary activities before tax (£45m).
- Enter the value for profit on ordinary activities after tax by subtracting taxation from profit on ordinary activities before tax (£125m - £45m) which gives £80m.
- Enter dividends underneath profit on ordinary activities after tax (£30m).
- Enter the value for retained profit (or loss) for the financial year by subtracting dividends from profit on ordinary activities after tax (£80m - £30m = £50m).

The retained profit for the financial year figure is the last entry in the accounts (although the earnings per share is usually listed in public limited company accounts underneath retained profit). If the above steps are followed then the result should be the same as the profit and loss account shown in Table 16.7.

Additional entries for inclusion in the profit and loss account

The profit and loss account shown here is fairly simple. Profit and loss accounts for other businesses may appear slightly different. This is because they contain additional information. Whether they do or not depends on the nature of their business and what has happened during the trading year. Some possible differences are described below.

- Exceptional items, if they occur, should be included after operating profit in the account. If the exceptional item is a cost, such as a bad debt, then it should be subtracted from operating profit. If it is revenue, it should be added.
- Sometimes the operating expenses are split into specific expenses. For example, they might be divided between distribution costs and administration expenses. It is quite normal to show these items separately and then subtract them from gross profit.
- The figure for interest paid shown here is a net figure (net interest = interest paid - interest received). The actual breakdown of interest paid and received would be shown in the notes to the accounts. Net interest can be positive or negative. Some businesses receive no interest, so the figure would simply be for interest paid. In other accounts both the figures for interest paid and received will be shown.
- Some businesses do not calculate gross profit in the account. This might be because they provide services rather than make goods. If this is the case all costs and expenses are added together and subtracted from turnover to calculate operating profit.

The list above is not definitive. In reality it is rare to find two companies with identical entries in their profit and loss accounts.

The trial balance

In practice accountants use the **trial balance** (☞ unit 12) to compile final accounts. The trial balance is an account which lists all the debit balances and all the credit balances in the entire book-keeping system. In the trial balance:

- **debit entries** represent assets and expenses. They show where money has gone, for example, expenditure on assets such as plant, equipment and vehicles or expenses such as wages, advertising and materials.
- **credit balances** represent liabilities and revenue. They show inflows of money from sales, loans, capital and other sources.

In the trial balance the debit total should equal the credit total. This is because all transactions have been entered twice using the double entry system of recording. This helps to check that transactions have been entered accurately. However, it is still possible for the trial balance to balance even if errors have been made. This is because some errors will not be traced, for example, if a transaction is not recorded at all.

Table 16.8 shows the trial balance for Kingsmead Leisure Park. The debit side shows all balances relating to expenses, such as marketing expenses, and assets such as cash. The credit side shows all balances relating to revenue, such as turnover, and liabilities, such as creditors. Note that the total value of debits £4,901,000 is equal to the total value of credits £4,901,000.

Table 16.8 *Trial balance for Kingsmead Leisure Park as at 31.7.04*

	(£000)	
	Debit	Credit
Turnover		2,413
Purchases	380	
Marketing expenses	920	
Operating expenses	712	
Non-operating income		100
Interest paid	200	
Taxation	80	
Debtors	71	
Stock as at 31.7.03 (opening stock)	34	
Bank account	804	
Tangible assets	1,700	
Creditors		901
Long term loan		1,000
Share capital		200
Profit and loss account		287
	4,901	4,901

MSB International is a business that offers recruitment services. It has tended to specialise in the recruitment of IT and telecommunications staff for businesses. However, in August 2003, to reduce its dependency on these sectors, MSB Finance was launched to recruit qualified accountants across a range of sectors. Table 16.9 shows some financial information for MSB International.

Table 16.9 *Financial information for MSB International, 2002-03*

		(£000)
	2003	**2002**
Turnover	84,062	145,987
Cost of sales	71,252	121,698
Administration expenses	12,667	21,866
Exceptional item	-422	0
Net interest paid	142	534
Taxation	32	646
Dividends	410	546

Source: adapted from MSB International, *Annual Report and Accounts, 2003.*

(a) Using the information in Table 16.9, compile a profit and loss account for MSB International by calculating (i) gross profit, (ii) operating profit, (ii) profit before interest and tax, (iv) profit on ordinary activities before tax, (v) profit on ordinary activities after tax and (vi) retained profit.
(b) Describe the main changes over the two years.

Question 3

Compiling the profit and loss account from the trial balance

By following the steps described earlier it is possible to compile a profit and loss account for Kingsmead Leisure Park, from the information in the trial balance. However, there are some additional factors which need to be taken into account.

- Only the revenue and expense entries in the trial balance are needed to compile the profit and loss account.
- The cost of sales figure needs to be adjusted for stock. In the case of Kingsmead Leisure Park the opening stock is given in the trial balance (£34,000). If the closing stock is £40,000, cost of sales can be calculated by:

Opening stock	£34,000
Add purchases	£380,000
	£414,000
Less closing stock	£40,000
Cost of sales	£374,000

- In the case of Kingsmead Leisure Park there is no dividend payment for the year. As a result retained profit will be the same as profit after tax.

The completed profit and loss account for Kingsmead is shown in Table 16.10.

Table 16.10 *Profit and loss account for Kingsmead Leisure Park*

KINGSMEAD LEISURE PARK - PROFIT AND LOSS ACCOUNT YEAR ENDED 31.7.04

	(£000)
Turnover	2,413
Cost of sales	374
Gross profit	2,039
Marketing expenses	920
Operating expenses	712
Operating profit	407
Non-operating income	100
	507
Interest paid	200
Profit on ordinary activities before tax	307
Taxation	80
Profit on ordinary activities after tax	227
Dividends	-
Retained profit	227

Compiling the balance sheet from the trial balance

By following the steps listed earlier it is possible to compile a balance sheet from the trial balance. The asset and liability entries in the trial balance are transferred into the normal balance sheet structure. However, when preparing a balance sheet in this way a number of factors must be taken into account.

- The stock figure in the current assets section of the balance sheet will be the closing stock figure (£40,000) not the opening stock figure in the trial balance.
- The retained profit in the profit and loss account (£227,000) is added to the profit and loss account entry in the trial balance (£287,000). This gives a new profit and loss account balance of £514,000.

The completed balance sheet for Kingsmead Leisure Park is shown in Table 16.11.

Compiling accounts for sole traders

The examples used so far in the unit have involved the accounts of limited companies. When compiling the accounts of sole traders the same principles for account construction still apply. However, there are some important differences to be recognised.

- The bottom of the balance sheet for a limited company shows capital and reserves. For a sole trader the bottom of the balance sheet shows the capital owed to the owner. It is made up of the opening balance plus the net profit for the year.
- Drawings will usually appear on the trial balance for a sole trader. Drawings are usually transferred to the capital account in the balance sheet. They are subtracted at the end of the capital account to determine the closing capital balance. For example, the closing capital for G.M. Smith, a market trader, is:

Opening capital	£56,811
Add net profit	£21,006
	£77,817
Less drawings	£15,000
Closing capital	£62,817

Table 16.11 *Balance sheet for Kingsmead Leisure Park*

KINGSMEAD LEISURE PARK - BALANCE SHEET AS AT 31.7.04

	(£000)
Fixed assets	
Tangible assets	1,700
Current assets	
Stock	40
Debtors	71
Cash at bank	804
	915
Current liabilities	901
Net current assets	14
Total assets less current liabilities	1,714
Long term liabilities	(1,000)
NET ASSETS	714
Capital and reserves	
Share capital	200
Profit and loss account	514
CAPITAL EMPLOYED	714

Table 16.12 *Trial balance for Paulo Campolucci*

PAULO CAMPOLUCCI - TRIAL BALANCE AS AT 31.1.2004

	Debit £	Credit £
Turnover		121,001
Purchases	52,009	
Stock at 31.1.03	5,991	
Operating expenses	36,002	
Non-operating income		567
Interest paid	21,000	
Tools and equipment	13,532	
Vehicle	12,500	
Debtors	4,399	
Cash at bank	10,000	
Current liabilities		16,001
Long term bank loan		14,000
Drawings	12,000	
Capital account		15,864
	167,433	167,433

Paulo Campolucci runs a small shoe manufacturing business in Bath. At the end of each trading year his daughter, Ellen, compiles his business accounts. Ellen handles her father's tax affairs and the first task before completing his self-assessment tax form is to compile the business accounts. The trial balance for the business is shown in Table 16.12.

(a) What is the advantage to Paulo Campolucci of producing a trial balance?

(b) Compile the profit and loss account for Paulo Campolucci from the trial balance and show that net profit is equal to £12,897. Note that the closing stock is £6,331.

(c) Compile the balance sheet for Paulo Campolucci from the trial balance and show that the value of closing capital is £16,761.

Knowledge...Knowledge...Knowledge...Knowledge...Knowledge

1. When do businesses normally compile their accounts?
2. Which assets are listed first in the balance sheet?
3. How is net current assets calculated in the balance sheet?
4. How is the net assets figure calculated in the balance sheet?
5. How is gross profit calculated in the trading account?
6. What entries will appear in the profit and loss appropriation account?
7. How are exceptional items dealt with in the profit and loss account?
8. Under what circumstances might gross profit not appear in a profit and loss account?
9. What do: (a) debit entries; (b) credit entries; represent in the trial balance?
10. Why should the value of debit entries equal the value of credit entries?
11. Does the trial balance include closing stock or opening stock for a business?
12. State 2 differences between a sole trader balance sheet and a limited company balance sheet.

Case study Somerfield

Somerfield, a UK supermarket chain, operates 589 stores under the Somerfield brand and 680 under the Kwik Save brand. Somerfield merged with Kwik Save in 1998 after concerns that, on their own, the two companies might find it difficult to survive in the market. The company employs 54,000 staff and has over 6,000 own label products.

During the year 2002-03 Somerfield continued the development of a new format for the Kwik Save stores. This involved a new concept with brighter, fresher and more colourful stores. Layouts are more logical and easier to shop, with new shelving and refrigerator units. Somerfield also invested in new business ideas.

- **Somerfield forecourts.** This was a joint venture with Elf to open Somerfield convenience stores on petrol forecourts. A sharpening-up exercise was undertaken on its existing 18 sites during the year and sales grew by 9 per cent.
- **Somerfield franchises.** A number of partnerships were being developed. For example, under a pilot scheme six stores were being converted into convenience outlets trading under a joint Somerfield/Martin's name.

Table 16.13 shows some financial information for Somerfield.

(a) Compile the 2003 profit and loss account for Somerfield (include the 2002 figures). (12 marks)

(b) Compile the 2003 balance sheet for Somerfield (include the 2002 figures). (14 marks)

(c) To what extent has the performance of the business improved over the two years? (14 marks)

Table 16.13 *Financial information for Somerfield, 2002-03*

		£ million
	2003	2002
Turnover	4,668.3	4,640.5
Cost of sales	4,544.3	4,514.5
Administration expenses	101.9	96.6
Non-operating income*	17.0	6.1
Net interest paid	4.3	13.3
Taxation**	5.0	6.0
Dividends	8.0	4.9
Tangible assets	1,013.9	941.7
Other fixed assets***	7.6	7.0
Stocks	290.4	324.8
Debtors	117.8	115.2
Cash at bank and in hand	127.7	86.2
Other current assets****	0.5	2.6
Current liabilities	766.8	669.7
Long term liabilities	25.2	74.7
Share capital	49.6	49.4
Share premium	34.2	33.4
Revaluation	69.6	76.2
Other reserves	335.3	335.3
Retained profit	277.2	238.8

* Profit on disposal of fixed assets.
** In both years Somerfield received tax credits from the Inland Revenue. These amounts should be added to profit.
*** Investments.
**** Short term investments.

Source: adapted from Somerfield plc, *Annual Report and Accounts, 2003.*

17 Ratio Analysis

The investigation process

Stakeholders are likely to be interested in a company's accounts. Different users are interested for different reasons. For example, shareholders may want information to assess the rewards for holding shares. Managers may try to gauge performance. This unit explains how the information in the final accounts can be interpreted. It is possible to base investigation on some of these figures alone. Also, information can be obtained by combining some of these figures and carrying out a RATIO ANALYSIS. The chairperson's report, the directors' report and the notes to the accounts provide extra material as well.

Figure 17.1 *Steps in the investigation process*

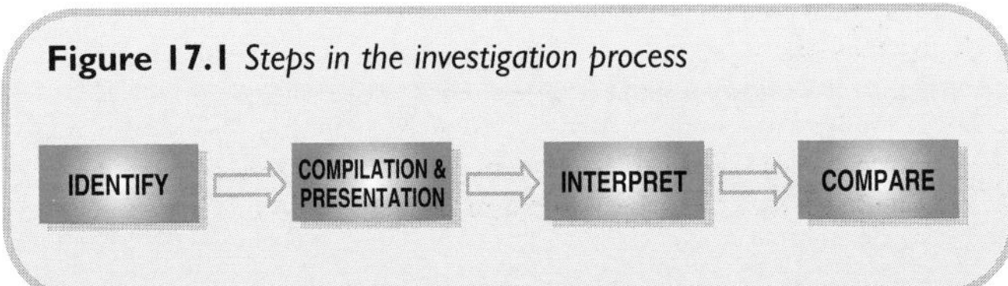

The investigation process is shown in Figure 17.1. The first step is to **identify** the figures that are relevant from the final amounts. Suitable data must be used. For example, an accountant might need information on current assets and current liabilities, rather than total assets and total liabilities, in order to assess the solvency of the business.

Once the correct figures have been chosen they can be **compiled** and **presented** into a useful form, such as percentages.

To **interpret** ratios an understanding of their significance is needed. Ratios can be used to find out the firm's financial position, assess performance, analyse capital structure and help shareholders when deciding whether to invest.

Finally, ratios may be used to make a variety of **comparisons**. For example, it is common to compare this year's figures with those of last year.

What are ratios?

Financial ratios can be calculated by comparing two figures in the accounts which are related in some way. It may be one number expressed as a percentage of another or simply one number divided by another. For an accounting ratio to be useful the two figures must be connected, eg profit is arguably related to the amount of capital a firm uses.

Ratios on their own are not particularly useful. They need to be compared with other ratios. For example, knowing that a firm has a net profit to sales ratio of 11 per cent may not be helpful. However, if it was 9 per cent the year before, this can be compared with the present figure. There is a number of ways in which ratios can be compared.

Over time The same ratio can be compared in two time periods, eg the current financial year and the previous one. Comparisons over time also show trends. This allows a business to decide whether or not certain aspects are improving.

Interfirm comparisons It is possible for a business to compare its results with others in the same industry. This could highlight particular strengths or weaknesses. For example, a handbag manufacturer with a turnover of £120,000 might think its £30,000 profit satisfactory. Another manufacturer may have a profit of £50,000 on a turnover of £130,000. Assuming that the two firms are very similar, the relative profit of the first business is not as good. It is important that firms compare 'like with like'.

Interfirm comparisons over time Using the two standards above we can make interfirm comparisons over time. This shows trends that may exist. Such comparisons are quite popular and could help analyse the behaviour of a whole industry, over a lengthy time period.

Results and forecasts Management, for example, may want to compare actual results with predicted results. Management prepare budgets and make forecasts about the future. Decision makers will also try to account for differences which exist between the actual results and their estimates. This is called variance analysis (☞ unit 15).

Types of ratio and their users

Ratios fall into one of four general categories.

Performance ratios or profitability ratios Performance ratios help to show how well a business is doing. They tend to focus on profit, capital employed and turnover. Stakeholders such as owners, managers, employees and potential investors are all likely to be interested in the profitability and efficiency of a business. However, when measuring performance a business must take into account its objectives. For example, a performance ratio using profit may not be appropriate if the business is pursuing another objective, such as survival. Competitors might also use performance ratios to make comparisons of performance. Activity ratios are likely to be used internally by managers. This is because they focus on how well a business uses its resources. For example, the performance of the credit control department could be assessed by looking at how quickly debts are collected.

Liquidity ratios Liquidity ratios illustrate the solvency of a business - whether it is in a position to repay its debts. They focus on short term assets and liabilities. Creditors are likely to be interested in liquidity ratios to assess whether they will receive money that they are owed. Money lenders and suppliers, for example, will be interested in how easily a business can repay its debts. Potential investors might also have an interest in liquidity ratios for the same reason. In addition, managers might use them to aid financial control, ie to ensure that they have enough liquid resources to meet debts.

Gearing ratios Gearing ratios show the long term financial position of the business. They can be used to show the relationship between loans, on which interest is paid, and shareholders' funds, on which dividends might be paid. Creditors are likely to be concerned about a firm's gearing. Loans, for example, have interest charges which must be paid. Dividends do not have to be paid to ordinary shareholders. As a business becomes more highly geared (loans are high relative to share capital) it is considered more risky by creditors. The owners of a business might prefer to raise extra funds by borrowing rather than from shareholders, so they retain control of the business. Gearing ratios can also show the relationship between fixed interest bearing debt and the long term capital of a business. This is discussed later in this unit.

Shareholders' ratios The owners of limited companies will take an interest in ratios which help measure the return on their shareholding. Such ratios focus on factors such as the earnings and dividends from shares in relation to their price. Potential investors will also show an interest in shareholders' ratios.

There may be other bodies or institutions which might use the above ratios. The media produce reports about businesses which they publish. They might use a range of ratios when reporting on particular businesses. In some newspapers the dividend yield and price/earnings ratio are actually published every day for a range of public limited companies. The Inland Revenue might also use ratio analysis when investigating the performance of a business. Some businesses collect business

Table 17.1 *Profit and loss account, Hudsons plc*

HUDSONS PLC PROFIT AND LOSS ACCOUNT
Y/E 31.7.04

	2004 £000	2003 £000
Turnover	70,000	63,000
Cost of sales	55,000	50,000
Gross profit	15,000	13,000
Operating expenses	9,500	9,000
Operating profit	5,500	4,000
Income from investments	100	80
Profit on ordinary activities before tax and interest	5,600	4,080
Net interest paid	1,100	600
Profit on ordinary activities before tax (net profit)	4,500	3,480
Taxation	1,100	680
Profit on ordinary activities after tax	3,400	2,800
Dividends	900	700
Retained profit	2,500	2,100

Table 17.2 *Additional financial information, Hudsons plc*

	2004	2003
Number of ordinary shares	40,000,000	40,000,000
Share price 31st July	135p	94p

Table 17.3 *Balance sheet, Hudsons plc*

HUDSONS PLC BALANCE SHEET
AS AT 31.7.04

	2004 £000s	2003 £000s
Fixed assets		
Tangible assets	21,000	19,800
Investments	500	400
	21,500	20,200
Current assets		
Stocks	8,500	7,100
Debtors	500	400
Cash at bank and in hand	3,000	2,100
	12,000	9,600
Creditors:		
amounts falling due within one year *(current liabilities)*	8,100	7,000
Net current assets *(working capital)*	3,900	2,600
Total assets less current liabilities	25,400	22,800
Creditors:		
amounts falling due after one year *(long term liabilities)*	(8,000)	(6,500)
Net assets	17,400	16,300
Capital and reserves		
Called up share capital	2,000	2,000
Other reserves	1,400	2,800
Profit and loss account	14,000	11,500
Shareholders' funds	17,400	16,300

data and sell it to other users. For example, an agency might write a financial report on a business and part of it might consist of comments about particular ratios.

Ratio Analysis

Tables 17.1-17.3 show the profit and loss account and balance sheet for Hudsons plc, and some additional information from the notes to the accounts. Hudsons sells electrical goods such as TVs, videos, DVD players, music systems and computers. The figures shown in the accounts will be used in this unit to illustrate how ratios can be calculated and interpreted.

Performance ratios or profitability ratios

Assuming that a company's aim is to make a profit, performance ratios will focus on the year's profit. The profit figure alone is not a useful performance indicator. It is necessary to look at the value of profit in relation to the value of turnover, for example, or the amount of money that has been invested in the business.

Return on capital employed (ROCE) One of the most important ratios which is used to measure the performance of a business is the RETURN ON CAPITAL EMPLOYED (ROCE). This is sometimes referred to as the **primary ratio.** It compares the profit, ie return, made by the business with the amount of money invested, ie its capital. The advantage of this ratio is that it relates profit to the size of the business. When calculating ROCE, it is standard practice to define profit as net profit (or operating profit) before tax and interest. This is sometimes described as **earnings before interest and tax** (EBIT). Tax is ignored because it is determined by the government and is therefore outside the control of the company. Interest is excluded because it does not relate to the business's ordinary trading activities. ROCE can be calculated using the formula:

$$\text{ROCE} = \frac{\text{Profit before tax and interest}}{\text{Long term capital employed}} \times 100$$

For Hudsons the profit before tax and interest in 2004 was £5,600,000. Long term capital employed was £25,400,000. Long term capital employed is shareholders' funds plus any long term loans, ie £17,400,000 + £8,000,000.

$$\text{For 2004 ROCE} = \frac{£5,600,000}{£25,400,000} \times 100 = 22.0\%$$

$$\text{For 2003 ROCE} = \frac{£4,080,000}{£22,800,000} \times 100 = 17.9\%$$

The return on capital employed will vary between industries, however, the higher the ratio, the better. Over the two years Hudsons has seen its ROCE increase from 17.9 per cent to 22.0 per cent. To decide whether Hudsons has performed well, this would have to be compared with another business in the same industry. An investor might also compare the ROCE with the possible return if the capital was invested elsewhere. For example, if £25,400,000 was placed in a bank account in 2004 it might have earned a 4 per cent return. So the 22 per cent ROCE in 2004 seems impressive. However, an investor in the company will also want to be rewarded for the risk involved. The £25,400,000 invested by shareholders in Hudsons is at risk if the business fails. So, for the investment to be worthwhile, the ROCE must be far greater than the return that could be earned in a 'safe' investment. Increasing profit with the existing capital employed will improve the ROCE ratio for a business.

It is possible to use other measures of capital when calculating the ROCE. These are explained in Table 17.4.

Table 17.4 *Calculating ROCE using other measures of capital*

ROCE (Total capital employed) Total capital may be used to calculate the ROCE. Total capital employed can be found by:

- adding together the fixed assets and the current assets. For Hudsons in 2004, fixed assets were £21,500,000 and current assets were £12,000,000, so total capital employed was £33,500,000;
- adding capital and reserves (£17,400,000), long term liabilities (£8,000,000) and current liabilities (£8,100,000) together to give £33,500,000.

For Hudsons, the profit before tax and interest in 2004 was £5,600,000. The ROCE for 2004 can be calculated as:

$$\text{ROCE} = \frac{\text{Profit before tax and interest}}{\text{Total capital employed}} \times 100 = \frac{£5,600,000}{£33,500,000} \times 100 = 16.7\%$$

This measure of ROCE gives a lower percentage than ROCE using long term capital because the figure for capital is higher.

ROCE (Shareholders' capital or net assets) This looks at the return on the shareholders' capital, which is total share capital plus reserves. However, it is conventional to use the term net assets rather than shareholders' capital. Hudsons' balance sheet shows that shareholders' capital/funds is £17,400,000 in 2004. This is the same as net assets. The RETURN ON NET ASSETS for Hudsons in 2004 can be calculated using the formula:

$$\text{Return on net assets} = \frac{\text{Profit before tax and interest}}{\text{Net assets}} \times 100 = \frac{£5,600,000}{£17,400,000} \times 100 = 32.2\%$$

The return on net assets gives a higher percentage than other measures of ROCE because the figure for capital is lower.

Gross profit margin The GROSS PROFIT MARGIN is also known as the **mark-up**. This shows the gross profit made on sales turnover. It is calculated using the formula:.

$$\text{Gross profit margin} = \frac{\text{Gross profit}}{\text{Turnover}} \times 100$$

For Hudsons in 2004 gross profit was £15,000,000 and turnover was £70,000,000.

$$\text{For 2004 Gross profit margin} = \frac{£15{,}000{,}000}{£70{,}000{,}000} \times 100 = 21.4\%$$

$$\text{For 2003 Gross profit margin} = \frac{£13{,}000{,}000}{£63{,}000{,}000} \times 100 = 20.6\%$$

Higher gross margins are usually preferable to lower ones. It may be possible to increase the gross profit margin by raising turnover relative to cost of sales, for example by increasing price. Or cost of sales could be reduced relative to turnover. However, the gross profit margin required will tend to be different for different industries. As a rule, the quicker the turnover of stock, the lower the gross margin that is needed. So, for example, a supermarket with a fast stock turnover is likely to have a lower gross margin than a car retailer with a much slower stock turnover. Some supermarkets are therefore very successful with relatively low gross profit margins because of the regular and fast turnover of stock.

The gross margin for Hudsons has improved slightly over the two years. Interfirm comparisons would help to confirm whether this was a satisfactory performance.

Net profit margin The NET PROFIT MARGIN helps to measure how well a business controls its overheads. If the difference between the gross margin and the net margin is small, this suggests that overheads are low. This is because net profit equals gross profit less overheads. The net profit margin can be calculated by:

$$\text{Net profit margin} = \frac{\text{Net profit before tax and interest}}{\text{Turnover}} \times 100$$

For Hudsons in 2004 net profit before tax and interest was £5,600,000 and turnover was £70,000,000.

$$\text{For 2004 Net profit margin} = \frac{£5{,}600{,}000}{£70{,}000{,}000} \times 100 = 8.0\%$$

$$\text{For 2003 Net profit margin} = \frac{£4{,}080{,}000}{£63{,}000{,}000} \times 100 = 6.5\%$$

Again, higher margins are usually better than lower ones. The net profit margin for Hudsons has improved over the two years. This suggests that the business was able to restrict overhead spending as a proportion of turnover more effectively in 2004 than in 2003.

Tony Parker owns two thriving businesses in London. The first, managed by his eldest daughter, is a fish and chip shop in Greenford. It is located just round the corner from Greenford tube station. The second, managed by his son, is a gift and souvenir shop located by the Tower of London. He monitors the performance of both businesses very carefully and likes to compare the two at the end of the year. Tony uses the gross and net profit margins to make comparisons. Table 17.5 shows some financial information for both businesses.

Table 17.5 *Turnover, gross profit and net profit for Tony Parker's businesses*

(£)

	Fish & chip shop	Gift & souvenir shop
Turnover	252,600	365,900
Gross profit	75,400	154,900
Net profit	32,000	38,700

(a) (i) Calculate the gross and net profit margins for the two businesses.
(ii) Based on the results in (i), which business has the best performance? Explain your answer.
(b) To what extent are the comparisons useful?

Activity ratios

Activity ratios or 'asset usage ratios' are used to measure how effectively a business employs its resources.

Asset turnover The ASSET TURNOVER ratio measures the productivity of assets. It looks at how much turnover is generated by the assets employed in the business. The formula is:

$$\text{Asset turnover} = \frac{\text{Turnover}}{\text{Net assets}}$$

The turnover for Hudsons in 2004 was £70,000,000 and the net assets were £17,400,000.

$$\text{For 2004 Asset turnover} = \frac{£70{,}000{,}000}{£17{,}400{,}000} = 4.02$$

$$\text{For 2003 Asset turnover} = \frac{£63{,}000{,}000}{£16{,}300{,}000} = 3.87$$

The ratio shows that, in 2004, for every £1 invested in net

assets by Hudsons, £4.02 of turnover was generated. Over the two years the asset turnover improved by a few pence. The asset turnover varies in different industries. In retailing, where turnover is high and the value of fixed assets is relatively low, like Hudsons, the asset turnover can be 3 or more. In contrast, in manufacturing, where there is often heavier investment in fixed assets, the ratio is generally lower. For example, it can be 1 or less. Increasing turnover using the same assets, so that assets work more effectively, is a method of improving the ratio.

Stock turnover The STOCK TURNOVER ratio measures how quickly a business uses or sells its stock. It is generally considered desirable to sell, or 'shift', stock as quickly as possible. One approach to stock turnover is to calculate how many times during the year a business sells its stock. The formula is:

$$\text{Stock turnover} = \frac{\text{Cost of sales}}{\text{Stocks}}$$

The cost of sales for Hudsons in 2004 was £55,000,000. The value of closing stocks as shown in the balance sheet was £8,500,000.

$$\text{For 2004 Stock turnover} = \frac{£55{,}000{,}000}{£8{,}500{,}000} = 6.5 \text{ times}$$

$$\text{For 2003 Stock turnover} = \frac{£50{,}000{,}000}{£7{,}100{,}000} = 7.0 \text{ times}$$

Another approach to stock turnover is to calculate the number of days it takes to sell the stock. This is found by:

$$\text{Stock turnover} = \frac{\text{Stocks}}{\text{Cost of sales}} \times 365$$

$$\text{For 2004 Stock turnover} = \frac{£8{,}500{,}000}{£55{,}000{,}000} \times 365 = 56 \text{ days}$$

$$\text{For 2003 Stock turnover} = \frac{£7{,}100{,}000}{£50{,}000{,}000} \times 365 = 52 \text{ days}$$

High stock turnovers are preferred (or lower figures in days). A higher stock turnover means that profit on the sale of stock is earned more quickly. Thus, businesses with high stock turnovers can operate on lower profit margins. A declining stock turnover ratio might indicate:

- higher stock levels;
- a large amount of slow moving or obsolete stock ;
- a wider range of products being stocked;
- a lack of control over purchasing.

So improvements to purchasing methods or better control of stock levels, for example, should improve the stock turnover ratio of a business.

Stock turnover differs considerably between different industries. Supermarkets often have a relatively quick stock turnover of around 14 to 28 days. This means that they sell the value of their average stock every two to four weeks. Manufacturers generally have much slower stock turnover because of the time spent processing raw materials. However, in recent years, many manufacturers have adopted **just-in-time production** techniques. This involves ordering stocks only when they are required in the production process and, therefore, stock levels tend to be lower. As a result stock turnover is faster. Businesses which supply services, such as banks, travel agents and transport operators, are not likely to hold very much stock. Therefore this ratio is not likely to be used by service industry analysts.

Over the two years, Hudsons' stock turnover has worsened very slightly. However, to determine whether a stock turnover of 56 days is good, comparisons with other electrical goods retailers would have to be made.

Debt collection period This ratio measures the efficiency of a business's credit control system. The DEBT COLLECTION PERIOD is the average number of days it takes to collect debts from customers. It can be calculated using the formula:

$$\text{Debt collection period} = \frac{\text{Debtors}}{\text{Turnover}} \times 365$$

According to the balance sheet the value of debtors for Hudsons in 2004 was £500,000. Turnover was £70,000,000.

$$\text{For 2004 Debt collection period} = \frac{£500{,}000}{£70{,}000{,}000} \times 365 = 2.6 \text{ days}$$

$$\text{For 2003 Debt collection period} = \frac{£400{,}000}{£63{,}000{,}000} \times 365 = 2.3 \text{ days}$$

Businesses often vary the amount of time they give customers to pay for products they have bought on credit. Credit periods may be 30, 60, 90 or even 120 days. Businesses prefer a short debt collection period because their cash flow will be improved. Retailers will have a very low debt collection period, perhaps just a few days. This is because most of their sales are for cash. This appears to be the case for Hudsons. Although the debt collection period has risen from 2.3 days to 2.6 days over the two years, there is unlikely to be a problem. Hudsons' sales will be for cash and the debtors value on the balance sheet is likely to be for prepayments not customer debts. Improving turnover relative to debtors will improve the ratio. However, businesses often try to improve this ratio by reducing debtors relative to turnover using credit control.

Liquidity ratios

A business must make sure that it has enough liquid assets to pay any immediate bills that arise. Liquid assets include cash and assets that can be quickly switched into cash such as stocks, debtors and short-term investments. Two widely used ratios to monitor liquid assets are the current ratio and the acid test ratio.

Current ratio The CURRENT RATIO focuses on current assets and current liabilities. It is also known as the **working capital ratio** and is calculated using the formula:

$$\text{Current ratio} = \frac{\text{Current assets}}{\text{Current liabilities}}$$

For Hudsons, current assets were £12,000,000 in 2004 and current liabilities were £8,100,000. Both of these figures are shown in the balance sheet.

$$\text{For 2004 Current ratio} = \frac{£12{,}000{,}000}{£8{,}100{,}000} = 1.48 \text{ or } 1.48{:}1$$

$$\text{For 2003 Current ratio} = \frac{£9{,}600{,}000}{£7{,}000{,}000} = 1.37 \text{ or } 1.37{:}1$$

It is suggested that a business will have sufficient liquid resources if the current ratio is between 1.5:1 and 2:1. If the ratio is below 1.5 it might be argued that a business does not have enough working capital. This might mean that a business is **overborrowing** or **overtrading**. Operating above a ratio of 2:1 may suggest that too much money is tied up unproductively. Money tied up in stocks does not earn any return.

The current ratio for Hudsons has hardly changed over the two years, rising slightly from 1.37:1 to 1.48:1. As with other ratios, judgement on what is satisfactory depends to a large extent on comparisons within the industry. For example, retailers often have very low current ratios, perhaps 1:1 or below. This is because they hold fast selling stocks and generate cash from sales. Since Hudsons is a retailer, it might be well satisfied with a current ratio of 1.48:1 in 2004.

Hudsons may be able to improve its current ratio by increasing its current assets relative to current liabilities, or reducing its current liabilities relative to its current assets. For example, current assets might be improved by better stock or credit control. Current liabilities might be reduced by reducing short term creditors.

Acid test ratio The ACID TEST RATIO or QUICK RATIO is a more severe test of liquidity. This is because stocks are not treated as liquid resources. Stocks are not guaranteed to be sold and they may become obsolete or deteriorate. They are therefore excluded from current assets when calculating the ratio.

$$\text{Acid test ratio} = \frac{\text{Current assets} - \text{stocks}}{\text{Current liabilities}}$$

The information required to calculate the acid test ratio are found in Hudsons' balance sheet.

$$\text{For 2004 Acid test ratio} = \frac{£12{,}000{,}000 - £8{,}500{,}000}{£8{,}100{,}000} = 0.43 \text{ or } 0.43{:}1$$

$$\text{For 2003 Acid test ratio} = \frac{£9{,}600{,}000 - £7{,}100{,}000}{£7{,}000{,}000} = 0.36 \text{ or } 0.36{:}1$$

If a business has an acid test ratio of less than 1:1 it means that its current assets less stocks do not cover its current

Baxter & Son supplies local shops, hotels, restaurants and pubs in the Lincolnshire area with poultry and game. The business has been in the family for 132 years and makes good returns on the capital employed. However, it had started to suffer from liquidity problems. Baxter & Son paid its suppliers cash, but gave its customers 30 day credit terms. In 2004 Phil Baxter, the managing director, decided to offer customers a 5 per cent discount if they paid cash on delivery. Some financial information is shown in Table 17.6.

Table 17.6 *Turnover, current assets and current liabilities for Baxter & Son, 2001–2004*

(£)

	2004	2003	2002	2001
Turnover	138,100	141,800	136,200	121,000
Current assets				
Stocks	2,500	2,600	2,300	2,200
Debtors	6,400	12,100	11,200	9,800
Cash & bank	1,800	0	0	700
Current liabilities				
Bank loan	7,000	7,000	8,000	8,000
Other creditors	3,100	4,600	4,300	5,100
Bank overdraft	0	4,600	2,200	0

(a) (i) Calculate the current ratios for Baxter & Son between 2001 and 2004.
(ii) What evidence is there to suggest that the business was beginning to experience liquidity problems?
(b) (i) Calculate the debt collection period for Baxter & Son between 2001 and 2004.
(ii) Discuss whether the 5 per cent cash discount offered to customers has worked.

liabilities. This could indicate a potential problem. However, as with the current ratio, there is considerable variation between the typical acid test ratios of businesses in different industries. Again, retailers with their strong cash flows, may operate comfortably with acid test ratios of less than 1. Since Hudsons is a retailer and its stock is likely to be sold quite quickly, an acid test ratio of 0.43:1 may be acceptable to the business. The methods of improving the current ratio can all be used here, although changing stock levels are not an option as stocks are excluded from the calculation.

Gearing ratios

Gearing ratios can be used to analyse the **capital structure** of a business. They compare the amount of capital raised from ordinary shareholders with that raised in loans and, in some cases, from preference shareholders and debentures. This is important because the interest on loans and dividends for preference shareholders are fixed commitments, whereas the dividends for ordinary shareholders are not. Gearing ratios can assess whether or not a business is burdened by its loans. This is because highly geared companies must still pay their interest even when trading becomes difficult.

Gearing ratio There are several different versions of the GEARING RATIO. One widely used relates the total long term loans and other fixed cost capital to long term capital employed. The formula is:

$$\text{Gearing ratio} = \frac{\text{Fixed cost capital}}{\text{Long term capital}} \times 100$$

Fixed cost capital includes long term loans from banks, certain preference shares and debentures. Long term capital includes shareholders' funds, any reserves and long term loans. For Hudsons in 2004 the fixed cost or interest/dividend bearing debt, according to the balance sheet, is loans of £8,000,000 (creditors: amounts falling due after one year). The value of shareholders' funds, including reserves, was £17,400,000.

$$\text{For 2004 Gearing ratio} = \frac{£8{,}000{,}000}{£17{,}400{,}000 + £8{,}000{,}000} \times 100 = 31.5\%$$

$$\text{For 2003 Gearing ratio} = \frac{£6{,}500{,}000}{£16{,}300{,}000 + £6{,}500{,}000} \times 100 = 28.5\%$$

If the gearing ratio is less than 50 per cent the company is said to be low geared. This means that the majority of the capital is provided by the owners. If the ratio is greater than 50 per cent the company is high geared. This means that a much higher proportion of total capital is borrowed. With a gearing ratio of around 30 per cent in both years, Hudsons is low geared. Although gearing rose slightly over the two years, the increase is not significant.

Another version of the gearing ratio looks at the relationship between borrowing and equity. In this context borrowing is defined as long term loans. For Hudsons in 2004 it was the creditors: amounts falling due after one year of £8,000,000. Equity is defined as ordinary share capital plus reserves which for Hudsons in 2004 was £17,400,000. The ratio is calculated using the formula:

$$\text{Gearing ratio} = \frac{\text{Borrowing}}{\text{Equity}} \times 100$$

$$\text{For 2004 Gearing ratio} = \frac{£8{,}000{,}000}{£17{,}400{,}000} \times 100 = 46.0\%$$

When this definition of gearing is used, a ratio that is greater than 100 per cent means that debt is greater than equity. In most industries, this would be regarded as high geared and could prove to be an unacceptable risk for potential lenders. This is because, if there was a downturn in trading, a company might struggle to meet interest payments. However, this is not the case for Hudsons since the ratio is below 100 per cent. A business can improve its gearing ratio by reducing its long term borrowing relative to its capital.

Interest cover The gearing ratio is a balance sheet measure of financial risk. INTEREST COVER is a profit and loss account measure. The ratio assesses the burden of interest payments by comparing profit and interest payments. It is calculated using the formula:

$$\text{Interest cover} = \frac{\text{Profit before interest and tax}}{\text{Interest}}$$

The profit before tax and interest for Hudsons in 2004 was £5,600,000 as shown in the profit and loss account. The amount of interest paid during the year was £1,100,000.

$$\text{For 2004 Interest cover} = \frac{£5{,}600{,}000}{£1{,}100{,}000} = 5.1 \text{ times}$$

$$\text{For 2003 Interest cover} = \frac{£4{,}080{,}000}{£600{,}000} = 6.8 \text{ times}$$

If interest cover is 1, this means that all of the firm's profit would be used to pay interest. This is obviously not sustainable in the long term. In the case of Hudsons, the cover has fallen over the two years. However, for a low geared company like Hudsons, this is still likely to be satisfactory. A figure of between 1 and 2 is likely to cause problems for a business, suggesting that it is becoming difficult for a company to meet its debt payments.

AmSong plc manufactures electronic equipment for the music and media industries, including mixing desks, digital recording equipment and monitor speakers. Its factory is in Leicester and it employs 143 staff. The company has done very well in recent years and is beginning to receive orders from Europe. However, AmSong is running short of capacity and needs to extend its premises and buy more plant and machinery. To do this it must raise some fresh capital, about £500,000. The directors are hoping that a bank loan might be granted. In 2003, AmSong made a profit before tax and interest of £750,000. The net interest paid during the year was £90,000. Some financial information is shown in Figure 17.2.

Figure 17.2 *Financial information for AmSong in 2003*

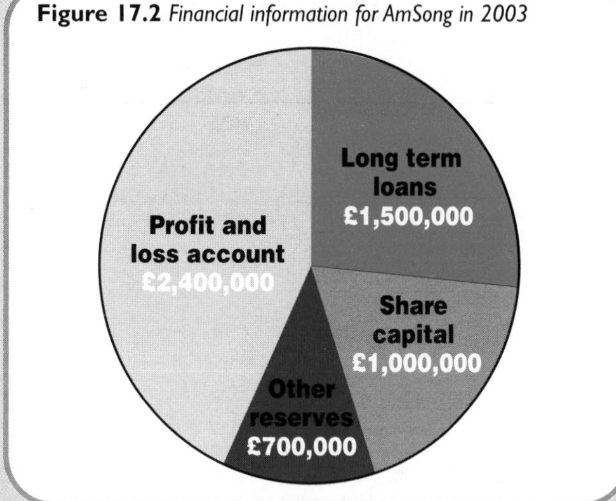

(a) Calculate (i) the gearing ratio and (ii) the interest cover for AmSong.
(b) Based on the results in (a), do you think a bank is likely to grant AmSong a £500,000 loan?

Shareholders' ratios

Shareholders' ratios provide information to help investors to make decisions about buying or selling shares. They are often used to analyse the performance of public limited companies. However, they can also be helpful to the owners of private limited companies.

Earnings per share The EARNINGS PER SHARE (EPS) is a measure of how much profit each ordinary share earns after tax. It does not, however, show how much money is actually paid to ordinary shareholders. This is because companies usually retain some profit in reserve. The EPS is generally shown at the bottom of the profit and loss account in the published accounts of plcs. EPS can be calculated by:

$$\text{Earnings per share} = \frac{\text{Profit after tax}}{\text{Number of ordinary shares}}$$

For Hudsons in 2004 the net profit after tax was £3,400,000 as shown in the profit and loss account. Note that if the company had any preference shareholders, any dividends paid to these would have to be subtracted from profit. According to the additional information shown in Table 56.2, the number of ordinary shares issued in 2004 was 40,000,000.

$$\text{For 2004 Earnings per share} = \frac{£3{,}400{,}000}{40{,}000{,}000} = 8.5\text{p}$$

$$\text{For 2003 Earnings per share} = \frac{£2{,}800{,}000}{40{,}000{,}000} = 7.0\text{p}$$

Over the two years the EPS for Hudsons has improved. However, on its own, this does not necessarily indicate a satisfactory performance. Only when the EPS is compared with the company's share price and with the EPS of comparable companies is it possible to make a judgment. Improvements in profits relative to the number of shares will improve this ratio.

Price/earnings ratio The PRICE/EARNINGS (P/E) RATIO is one of the main indicators used by investors in deciding whether to buy or sell particular shares. The P/E ratio relates the current share price to the EPS. It is calculated using the formula below. The ratio is often expressed as the number of times by which the share price can be divided by the EPS.

$$\text{Price/earnings ratio} = \frac{\text{Share price}}{\text{EPS}}$$

In the case of plcs which are listed on the Stock Market, their share price is published daily in *The Financial Times*, other newspapers and on the Internet. The share prices for Hudsons on 31st July are shown as additional information in Table 17.2. In 2004 the share price was 135p. The EPS was 8.5p as calculated above.

$$\text{For 2004 Price/earnings ratio} = \frac{135\text{p}}{8.5} = 15.9 \text{ times}$$

$$\text{For 2003 Price/earnings ratio} = \frac{94\text{p}}{7.0\text{p}} = 13.4 \text{ times}$$

The P/E ratio of 15.9 means that the market price of the share is 15.9 times higher than its current level of earnings. Assuming that nothing changes, it would take 15.9 years for these shares to earn their current market value. The P/E ratio for Hudsons rose over the two years from 13.4 to 15.9, indicating that investors had increased confidence in the future profitability of the company. As a result, demand for the shares rose, causing the price to jump from 94p to 135p. Rising investor confidence in this case may have been justified since Hudson's EPS rose from 7.0p to 8.5p.

Price/earnings ratios provide a useful guide to market confidence and can be helpful in comparing companies. However, a general rise or fall in share prices will affect P/E ratios, so care must be taken when interpreting changes.

Dividend per share The DIVIDEND PER SHARE is the ratio that shows how much money ordinary shareholders receive per share.

$$\text{Dividend per share} = \frac{\text{Dividend (ordinary shares)}}{\text{Number of shares}}$$

For Hudsons the dividend paid to shareholders in 2004 was £900,000. This is shown in the profit and loss account. The number of shares issued by Hudsons in 2004 is shown as additional information and was 40,000,000.

$$\text{For 2004 Dividend per share} = \frac{\pounds 900{,}000}{40{,}000{,}000} = 2.25\text{p per share}$$

$$\text{For 2003 Dividend per share} = \frac{\pounds 700{,}000}{40{,}000{,}000} = 1.75\text{p per share}$$

The dividend per share paid to Hudsons' shareholders increased from 1.75p per share to 2.25p over the two years. This is quite a significant improvement. However, to determine whether or not it is satisfactory the dividend per share must be compared with the share price. This involves calculating the dividend yield.

Dividend yield The DIVIDEND YIELD is the dividend per ordinary share expressed as a percentage of the current share price.

$$\text{Dividend yield} = \frac{\text{Dividend per share}}{\text{Share price}} \times 100$$

For Hudsons the share price is shown in Table 17.2 under additional information. On 31.7.04 it was 135p. The dividend per share was calculated above and was 2.25p in 2004.

$$\text{For 2004 Dividend yield} = \frac{2.25\text{p}}{135\text{p}} \times 100 = 1.7\%$$

$$\text{For 2003 Dividend yield} = \frac{1.75\text{p}}{94\text{p}} \times 100 = 1.9\%$$

Over the two years the dividend yield has fallen for Hudsons, even though the dividend per share rose significantly. The reason for this is that the share price also rose sharply. Whether a dividend yield of 1.7 per cent is adequate depends on what might be earned in other companies and other forms of investment. However, when making this judgment, it must be remembered that dividends are not the only reward for holding shares. Investors may make a capital gain if the shares are sold for a higher price than when they were bought.

Return on equity The RETURN ON EQUITY looks at the return on the money contributed by, and belonging to, ordinary shareholders. It defines equity as the ordinary shareholders' capital plus reserves. Profit after tax is used in this calculation. Note also that any payments made to preference shareholders should also be subtracted from this profit. The formula to calculate return on equity is:

$$\text{Return on equity} = \frac{\text{Profit after tax}}{\text{Equity}} \times 100$$

For Hudsons the net profit after tax in 2004 was £3,400,000. The value of ordinary share capital and reserves or shareholders' equity was £17,400,000.

$$\text{For 2004 Return on equity} = \frac{\pounds 3{,}400{,}000}{\pounds 17{,}400{,}000} \times 100 = 19.5\%$$

$$\text{For 2003 Return on equity} = \frac{\pounds 2{,}800{,}000}{\pounds 16{,}300{,}000} \times 100 = 17.2\%$$

Hudsons' return on equity improved slightly over the two years from 17.2 per cent to 19.5 per cent. As with all ratio analysis, judgment on whether this was satisfactory depends to a large extent on comparisons with similar companies in the same industry.

Dividend cover The DIVIDEND COVER measures how many times a company's dividends to ordinary shareholders could be paid from net profit.

$$\text{Dividend cover} = \frac{\text{Profit after tax}}{\text{Dividends (ordinary shares)}}$$

For Hudsons the profit after tax in 2004 was £3,400,000. The dividend paid to ordinary shareholders is shown in the profit and loss account and was £900,000 in 2004.

$$\text{For 2004 Dividend cover} = \frac{\pounds 3{,}400{,}000}{\pounds 900{,}000} = 3.8\text{ times}$$

$$\text{For 2003 Dividend cover} = \frac{£2,800,000}{£700,000} = 4.0 \text{ times}$$

For Hudsons the dividend cover has fallen slightly over the two years. A cover of 3.8 means that the dividends could have been paid 3.8 times over in 2004. If the cover is too high, shareholders might argue that higher dividends should be paid. If it is too low, it may mean that profits are low or that the company is not retaining enough profit for new investment.

It is possible for a business to pay dividends even when there is not sufficient profit in the current year to cover the payment. A company might do this to help retain the loyalty of shareholders. The money to cover the payment would have to come from reserves.

Lorraine Day has around £50,000 of her savings invested in QuantiFact, an online business information provider. She has seen reports in the media suggesting that the company is struggling, due to growing competition in the market. Lorraine gathered some up to date financial information about the company which is shown in Table 17.7.

Table 17.7 *Financial information for QuantiFact*

	2004	2003
Earnings per share	41p	39p
End of year share price	480p	515p
Dividends	£10.5m	£12m
Number of shares issued	105m	100m

(a) Calculate (i) the price earnings ratio, (ii) the dividend per share and (iii) the dividend yield for QuantiFact for 2004 and 2003.
(b) On the basis of the results in (a), explain whether you would advise Lorraine to sell the shares or not.

Limitations to ratio analysis

Although ratios offer a useful method of analysing business performance, they do have several limitations. The following factors all affect their usefulness.

The basis for comparison It is important when analysing differences between businesses to compare 'like with like'. This means that valid comparisons can often only be made between businesses in the same industry. Even then, differences in the size of the business, in their accounting policies, product ranges and in their financial year-ends can make comparisons difficult.

The quality of final accounts Ratios are usually based on published financial statements and therefore depend on the quality of these statements. One factor that can affect the quality of accounting information is the change in monetary values caused by inflation. Rising prices distort comparisons made between different time periods. For example, in times of high inflation, asset values and turnover might rise rapidly in monetary terms. However, when the figures are adjusted for inflation, there might be no increase in **real terms.** There is also the possibility that accounts have been **window dressed** (☞ unit 18). This would result in distorted ratios.

Limitations of the balance sheet Because the balance sheet is a 'snapshot' of a business at the end of the financial year, it might not be representative of the business's circumstances throughout the year. If, for example, a business experiences its peak trading activity in the summer, and has its year end at a time when trade is slow, in the New Year, balance sheet figures for stock and debtors will be unrepresentative.

Qualitative information is ignored Ratios only use quantitative information. Some important qualitative information may affect the performance of a business. For example, in the service industry the quality of customer service may be an important indicator. Ratio analysis cannot take this into account very easily.

Knowledge

1. Briefly describe the steps involved in the investigation process when analysing a set of accounts.
2. Why might interfirm comparisons be useful?
3. What is the difference between performance and activity ratios?
4. What is the difference between liquidity ratios and gearing ratios?
5. How do gross and net profit margins differ?
6. What do stock turnover and debt collection period measure?
7. Describe the difference between the current ratio and the acid test ratio.
8. What is meant by a high geared company?
9. Why is interest cover a profit and loss account measure of financial risk?
10. Which of the shareholders' ratios measures the actual financial return shareholders receive ?
11. Which ratio reflects the prospect of capital growth?
12. Describe the limitations of ratio analysis.

key terms

Acid test ratio - similar to the current ratio but excludes stocks from current assets. Sometimes called the quick ratio.
Asset turnover - a measure of the productivity of assets.
Current ratio - assesses the firm's liquidity by dividing current liabilities into current assets.
Debt collection period - the number of days it takes to collect the average debt.
Dividend cover - how many times the dividend could have been paid from the year's earnings.
Dividend per share - the amount of money a shareholder will actually receive for each share owned.
Dividend yield - the amount received by the shareholder as a percentage of the share price.
Earnings per share - the amount each ordinary share earns.
Gearing ratios - explore the capital structure of a business by comparing the proportions of capital raised by debt and equity.
Gross profit margin - expresses operating profit before tax and interest, ie gross profit, as a percentage of turnover.
Interest cover - assesses a firm's ability to meet interest payments by comparing profit and interest payable .
Net profit margin - shows the firm's ability to control overheads and expresses net profit before tax as a percentage of turnover.
Price/earnings ratio - relates the earnings per share to its market price and reflects the return from buying shares.
Ratio analysis - a numerical approach to investigating accounts by comparing two related figures.
Return on equity - measures the return on shareholders' investment by expressing the profit earned by ordinary shareholders as a percentage of total equity.
Return on net assets - expresses profit as a percentage of long term assets only.
Return on capital employed - the profit of a business as a percentage of the total amount of money used to generate it.
Stock turnover - the number of times in a trading year a firm sells the value of its stocks.

Case study Glyme Valley Farm and Cold Aston Farm

Patrick and Gillian O'Rourke have always wanted to own a farm. Patrick has worked on farms all his life and has a great deal of experience in mixed farming. Gillian, on the other hand, has been in publishing and recently sold her Gloucester-based publishing business for £350,000. They are now in a position to buy a small farm, although they expect to have to borrow some money to help fund the purchase. After several months of searching they have identified two possible targets. Both farms are private limited companies and both owners are keen for a quick sale.

Glyme Valley Farm - Price £400,000

Glyme Valley Farm is located in Glympton, Oxfordshire. It consists of 1,200 acres of arable land owned by a local educational establishment, farm buildings, agricultural machinery and a flock of 400 sheep. The current owner, 72 year old Reginald Enser, has recently been taken into care and the farm is up for sale so that the sale proceeds can be used to meet the cost of caring. The profit and loss account and balance sheet are shown in Tables 17.8 and 17.9.

Table 17.8 *Glyme Valley Farm profit and loss account, 2004*

GLYME VALLEY FARM -
PROFIT AND LOSS ACCOUNT Y/E 31.1.04

	£
Turnover	1,532,000
Cost of sales	451,000
Gross profit	1,081,000
Overheads	900,000
Operating profit	181,000
Non-operating income	2,000
Profit before interest	183,000
Interest (net)	152,000
Profit on ordinary activities before tax	31,000
Taxation	11,000
Profit for the year after tax	20,000
Dividends	8,000
Retained profit for the period	12,000

Table 17.9 *Glyme Valley Farm Balance sheet, 2004*

GLYME VALLEY FARM - BALANCE SHEET
AS AT 31.1.04

	£
Fixed assets	
Buildings	610,000
Machinery	567,000
	1,177,000
Current assets	
Stocks	13,000
Debtors	15,000
Cash at bank	1,500
	29,500
Creditors: amounts falling due in one year	28,000
Net current assets	1,500
Total assets less current liabilities	1,178,500
Creditors: amounts falling due after one year	(800,000)
Net assets	378,500
Capital and reserves	
Share capital	200,000
Retained profit	178,500
	378,500

Table 17.10 *Cold Aston Farm profit and loss account, 2004*

COLD ASTON FARM -
PROFIT AND LOSS ACCOUNT Y/E 31.3.04

	£
Turnover	1,141,000
Cost of sales	322,000
Gross profit	819,000
Overheads	761,000
Operating profit	58,000
Non-operating income	2,000
Profit before interest	60,000
Interest (net)	15,000
Profit on ordinary activities before tax	45,000
Taxation	18,000
Profit for the year after tax	27,000
Dividends	9,000
Retained profit for the period	18,000

Table 17.11 *Cold Aston Farm Balance sheet, 2004*

COLD ASTON FARM -
BALANCE SHEET AS AT 31.3.04

	£
Fixed assets	
Buildings	210,000
Machinery	167,000
	377,000
Current assets	
Stocks	36,000
Debtors	27,000
Cash at bank	5,000
	68,000
Creditors: amounts falling due in one year	36,000
Net current assets	32,000
Total assets less current liabilities	409,000
Creditors: amounts falling due after one year	(56,000)
Net assets	353,000
Capital and reserves	
Share capital	100,000
Retained profit	218,000
Other reserves	35,000
	353,000

Cold Aston Farm - Price £450,000

Cold Aston Farm is situated in Cold Aston, Gloucestershire, near to where Patrick and Gillian currently live. The farm has more land, 1,700 acres, but some of it is prone to flooding. As a result, yields from the land can be quite variable. The land is owned by a wealthy landowner. The farm is also quite run down. For example, the cattle sheds are derelict and the barn roof has been blown off. The agricultural machinery is also old and much of it needs replacing. The farm is owned by Roger and Davina Bartlett who inherited it from their father two years ago. Roger and Davina have lost interest in farming and want to sell up. The profit and loss account and balance sheets are shown in Tables 17.10 and 17.11.

(a) Calculate the (i) gross profit margin; (ii) net profit margin; (iii) ROCE for both farms. (6 marks)

(b) Using the answers from (a), analyse the profitability of both farms. (8 marks)

(c) Use ratio analysis to assess the liquidity and gearing of both farms. (16 marks)

(d) Based on your calculations and information in the case, which farm would you advise Gillian and Patrick to buy. (10 marks)

(e) What other factors might be taken into account before a final decision about the purchase is made? (10 marks)

18 Valuation and the Manipulation of Accounts

The valuation of a business

Unit 17 showed that financial ratios can be used to investigate a company's accounts. A relatively high net profit margin might show that one business has performed better than another. It might also show that its own performance has improved over time. A relatively low gearing ratio might indicate that a business has raised most of its finance from its shareholders, rather than through loans.

To some extent, calculating financial ratios can help place a VALUE on a business. For example, businesses which have adequate working capital and high profit margins and returns on capital employed will tend to have more value than those which do not. The value of a business is how much it is worth to a **stakeholder** or any other interested party, such as a potential buyer. For example, in May 2003, a management team bought Holmes Place, the health group. The purchase price was £25.4 million. This was the agreed value of the business at the time of the sale.

Different people might place different values on the same business. A seller is likely to place a higher value on a company than a buyer. This is sometimes called the **expectation gap**. Differences in value might also occur because a business might be worth more to one particular buyer. For example, Asda might place a higher value on an independent supermarket located in a town where it was not represented than Tesco might if they already had a store in that town. The difference in value occurs due to strategic considerations.

Reasons for valuation

There may be times when it is necessary to have some idea how much a business is worth.

Planning a sale If the owners are considering the sale of a business, it will be necessary to know its value before putting it 'on the market'. Homeowners will normally ask an estate agent to value their house before putting it up for sale. Similarly, business owners might consult an accountant to help place a value on their business. Such valuations normally provide a starting point for negotiations between buyers and sellers. In many cases the agreed sale price will be different from the original valuation.

A takeover One company may be thinking about taking over another. In this case it will need to know the value of the company it is buying in order to decide whether it has enough funds to go through with the acquisition. Sometimes a takeover can work out more expensive than anticipated. This is often the case in a hostile takeover (☞ unit 29). The current owners might resist the takeover by refusing to sell their shares. This could drive up the price. Also, another company might want to take over the same firm. This could result in a bidding war, where the price is inflated until the business is eventually sold to the highest bidder.

Merging When two companies merge, they need to know the value of each business. This is because the conditions of the merger have to be determined so that both companies can agree. For example, if one firm is twice the value of the other, it might mean that the new board of directors is made up of

---

In May 2003, Chiron, the US biotechnology company, agreed to buy PowderJect, the UK vaccines group. The agreed cash price for PowderJect was £542 million, the equivalent of 550p per share. This was at the higher end of analysts' expectations and about 30 per cent higher than the share price three months before, when the approach by Chiron was first made.

Analysts were concerned about PowderJect's dependence on sales of Fluvirin, its influenza vaccine, which was about to be subjected to competition from the US. Paul Drayson, chief executive, suggested that the sale of the company to Chiron was a better alternative than trying to broaden the base of the business through acquisitions. Last year PowderJect became only the second biotech company in the UK to report a profit. Chiron had been stalking PowderJect for sometime. They even made an informal offer of 450p per share about 12 months ago. Figure 18.1 shows the PowderJect share price and the global market shares of vaccines.

Source: adapted from *The Financial Times*, 20.5.2003.

Figure 18.1 *PowderJect Pharmaceuticals' share price and global vaccines market share 2001*

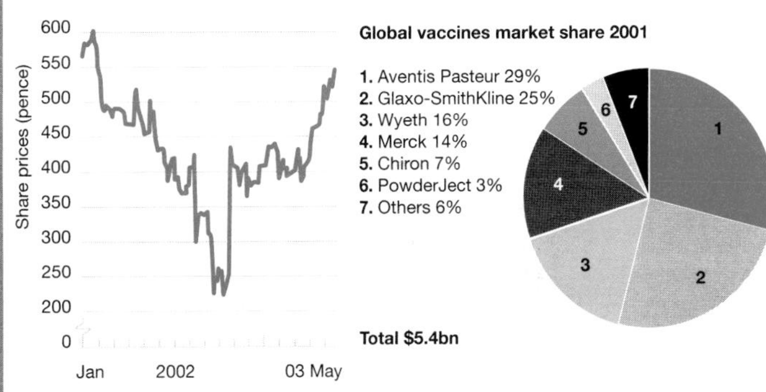

Source: adapted from Thomson Datastream, Merrill Lynch.

(a) What was the value of PowderJect in May 2003?
(b) Why was it necessary to value the company at that time?
(c) Who will benefit from the sale of PowderJect?

Question 1

six representatives from the highest valued company and three from the other. It is also necessary to know the value of the merging companies so that accountants can merge their financial affairs.

Demerger or management buy-out This is very similar to the sale of a business. In the case of a demerger it is necessary to calculate the value of the company before it is divided into smaller units. This then helps to calculate the value of the new, smaller companies when demerger takes place. Valuation of the new companies is required so that the number of new shares being issued, and their price, can be determined. In the case of a management buy-out or buy-in, valuation of the business or part of the business being sold is necessary to help set the sale price.

Flotation If a business, or part of a business, is being floated on the stock exchange it is necessary to know the value. Again, this is required so that the number of shares being issued and their price can be determined. During the privatisation era of the 1980s it was suggested that many companies, such as BT and Powergen, were sold off by the government way below their true value. The government argued that it was necessary to price the share issues attractively in order for the flotation to be a success.

Securing loans When a business wants a loan the bank may require some collateral for security. If this is the case, the business, or part of the business, may be used. The bank may need to know the value of the business in order to clarify the value of the collateral.

Other reasons It may be necessary to calculate the value of the business if:

- the owner is involved in a divorce settlement, where the business is being shared out between husband and wife;
- a business has been inherited and inheritance tax is being calculated by the Inland Revenue;
- business owners or shareholders are curious about how much their business would be worth if sold;
- a business person is considering the sale of the business to retire;
- to make financial comparisons between businesses in an industry, for example, in an industrial survey.

Methods of valuation

There is a number of techniques which could be used to value a business.

Market capitalisation This can be calculated using the formula:

MARKET CAPITALISATION
= the current share price x the number of shares issued

For example, on 14 February 2004, the share price for British Airways was 311p and the number of shares issued in the company was 1,082,636,656. The value of the company could have been £3.367 billion using this measure. This method of valuation may be distorted because external factors can cause the share price to change, such as interest rates and the actions of speculators. If the share price falls by 10 per cent due to one of these factors, this does not necessarily mean that the value of the company has fallen by 10 per cent.

Capitalised earnings This method is often used to value the holdings of the majority shareholders in a business. When shareholders buy shares, they buy the right to a future stream of profits that the business will make, known as **maintainable earnings**. Multiplying these maintainable earnings by the price/earnings ratio of a company gives the capitalised earnings. So:

CAPITALISED EARNINGS
= price/earnings ratio (P/E) x maintainable earnings

Unit 17 explained that the price earnings ratio shows the relationship between the amount each share earns for the investor and the current market price of the share. The P/E ratios of plcs are published each day in newspapers such as *The Financial Times*. A discount is often applied to the P/E ratios of private limited companies as their shares are not sold openly.

Maintainable earnings are the sustainable profits, after tax, that a business is capable of generating on a recurring basis. How can a value for maintainable earnings be estimated? It is necessary to consider all factors affecting a company's ability to maintain its current level of profit. This usually means starting with profits after tax for the current financial year. Then the figure is adjusted for one-off items of income or expenditure and directors' payments in excess of the market rate. So the estimate of maintainable earnings requires some human judgment. A subjective decision needs to be made about what non-recurring income and spending to take into account.

Discounted cash flow (DCF) This method may be used to value an entire company. It may also be used as a benchmark to compare the capitalised earnings value. To calculate the DCF a business needs to forecast annual cash flows and a discount factor. The discount factor will be the purchaser's cost of capital, such as the interest rate. It is possible, using the DCF method, to calculate the net present value of a future stream of income. This will tell a business what the value of any future income streams is worth now.

Financial institutions, such as banks and venture capitalists, tend to prefer this method. It focuses on future cash flows rather than historic profit. They argue that valuations based on forecasts of future cash flows provide a better guide to the firm's ability to repay capital than a valuation based on past profits.

Net assets This method is most suitable when assets make up a major part of the value of the business. This might be the case with property or investment companies, for example. It might also be used if the company is a loss maker and the buyer of the business intends to sell the assets and then reinvest the cash. It might be used if a business has had difficulties and is being purchased from a receiver (☞ unit 35) for example. In this case the business may be bought at a discount to the value of net assets. The net assets of a business are:

Net assets = (fixed assets + current assets)
- (current and long term liabilities)

This is quite a simple method of valuation because the value of net assets is shown clearly on all business balance sheets.

Return on investment (ROI) This method might be used, for example, when a choice has to be made about which business to buy from two alternatives. This method uses similar techniques to the calculation of capitalised earnings. However, rather than maintainable earnings after tax it uses **maintainable operating profits** (profit before interest and tax). ROI can be found by:

$$\text{ROI} = \frac{\text{Maintainable operating profit}}{\text{Purchase price}}$$

When using this method to choose between different businesses for acquisition, the business with the highest ROI will be selected. Again, a subjective judgment is required regarding non-recurring income and spending when estimating maintainable operating profits.

The pricing curve Accountants have developed a rule-of-thumb measure to determine the value of a business. The pricing curve shown in Figure 18.2 can be used to give some idea of a company's value. The curve is based on aggregate sales values of private companies. To use the curve it is necessary to determine the operating profits of the company before tax and interest. However, the profit figure must be adjusted to take into account factors specific to the company. For example, if the current owners are paying themselves too much money, the profit figure should be raised accordingly. Once profits have been adjusted the curve can be used to obtain a value. For example, if earnings (profits) before interest and tax were £3 million, reading from the curve, the business would be worth £35 million.

Figure 18.2 *The PCPI Pricing Curve*

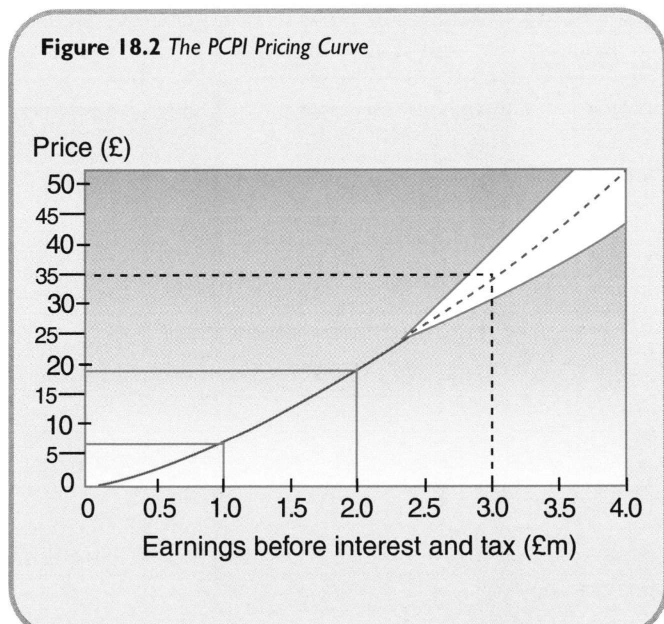

Oasis Healthcare plc, through its wholly owned subsidiary, Oasis Dental Care Ltd, is the leading owner/operator of dental practices in England and Wales. The company has over 120 dental practices, predominantly under the 'Oasis' brand.

The UK dental market is worth about £3.5 billion and is currently growing at 10 per cent a year. However, the market is highly fragmented and underdeveloped. Individual practice partnerships, of which there are over 3,000 with three or more surgeries, represent the typical business unit. Oasis Healthcare's strategy is growth through acquisition. The company believes there are significant cost savings to be made through volume buying and centralisation of administration. Since flotation on AIM in July 2000, Oasis has raised £50 million to fund its acquisitions. It has purchased 67 practices and is becoming a national provider of dental care services.

Table 18.1 shows some financial information for Oasis Healthcare. Note that the fixed assets value includes £44.155 million of intangible assets. Most of this is accounted for by goodwill resulting from the acquisition of dental practices.

Table 18.1 *Financial information for Oasis Healthcare as at 31.3.2003*

Fixed assets	£56,285,000
Current assets	£8,003,000
Creditors: amounts falling due within one year	£13,048,000
Long term liabilities	£36,101,000
Share price	16.5p
Number of issued shares	63,939,466

Source: adapted from Oasis Healthcare, *Annual Report and Accounts, 2003.*

(a) Calculate the value of Oasis Healthcare plc using the (i) market capitalisation method and the (ii) net assets method.
(b) Explain how this case illustrates some of the problems of valuation.

Problems of valuation

The valuation of a business is often difficult. A company's value may not be known until it is placed on the market and sold. Certain problems exist when calculating the value of the business using the methods in the last section.

- When calculating the market capitalisation of a business the current share price is used. Sometimes the share price does not reflect accurately the performance of the business. Share prices can be influenced by external factors, such as interest rates and the actions of speculators. Also, the share price of a particular company may be a lot lower than one would expect because the company is 'out of favour' with the City. If share prices do not reflect the performance of the business the valuation will be inaccurate.
- The determination of maintainable earnings and maintainable operating profit require some human judgment. They are both concerned with the sustainable profits that a business is capable of generating on a **recurring** basis. The profit figures in the current accounts therefore need to be adjusted for non-recurring income and spending. This decision about what is non-recurring is likely to vary depending on who is making it.
- The DCF method also requires some human judgment. It is necessary to predict future cash inflows. This is difficult to do because a wide range of external factors, such as competitor's actions and the state of the economy, might influence future cash inflows.
- When using net assets to value a company, the true value of some assets may not appear on the balance sheet. These are intangible assets such as goodwill, brand names and copyrights. Therefore, if excluded, the value of the company would be understated. Many accountants choose not to include the value of intangible of assets because they are difficult to value. Also, the value of intangible assets can change quite sharply and suddenly.

To overcome some of the problems, businesses might use more than one method of valuation.

The regulation and manipulation of accounts

The preparation of financial accounts in the UK is subject to a regulation. This is necessary to establish some uniformity in accounting. Before the regulatory framework existed it was difficult to make comparisons between company accounts. There were serious differences in the way accountants calculated profits due to the different methods they used. To overcome this problem the Accounting Standards Committee (ASC) was formed. Over a period of about 20 years this committee issued 25 statements of standard accounting practice (SSAPs). The statements provided uniform methods for practice, such as dealing with VAT (SSAP 5) and accounting for depreciation (SSAP 12). These SSAPs did help to reduce the variations in profit reporting. However, during the 1980s the ASC was subject to criticism because it had no legal power to enforce its standards, the standards were often too general and they were slow.

The regulatory framework is now the responsibility of the **Accounting Standards Board**. The board took over SSAPs. Any new standards are now called Financial Reporting Standards (FRSs). By 1998 the ASB had issued 8 FRSs. For example, FRS1 deals with the preparation of cash flow statements. In addition, Company Acts have certain requirements regarding accounting procedures. For example, businesses should adopt the accounting conventions discussed in unit 51, such as prudence, caution and going concern. Company accounts should also be presented in certain formats. Generally, the law requires that accounts should give a 'true and fair view' of a company's financial position.

Despite the existence of a regulatory framework, it is still possible to disguise the true financial position of a business. Information may be presented so that the financial position appears to be different than it really is. This is called MANIPULATING or WINDOW DRESSING the accounts.

Why might accounts be manipulated?

There is a number of reasons why accounts might be manipulated.

To appease shareholders Stakeholders may not be satisfied with the performance of the business. Shareholders might also be concerned that poor performance might affect the size of the dividend. The accounts might exaggerate the performance of the company to pacify these groups.

To attract investment A business might be trying to raise funds externally. Overstating the financial position of the company might persuade lenders to provide funds. They might be attracted by the potentially large future returns.

To fend off a takeover bid By making a company look stronger than it really is, a predator might decide against a bid for a business. If a company looks as though it is financially sound and performing well, it will appear to be more expensive to buy.

To show a stronger market position A company might want to suggest to outsiders, such as competitors, that it is financially sound. It might hope to show that it is in a stronger position to compete in the market. It might also try to show that it is the market leader and hope that this may influence customers when buying its products.

To affect share sales If the accounts show that the business is performing poorly, this might panic shareholders into selling their shares. They may be prepared to sell shares at lower prices to avoid holding unprofitable assets. Current directors might then be able to buy up shares at these lower prices, knowing

Caldy plc is a company which operates a chain of 'themed' public houses. The company, which is listed on AIM, has seen its market capitalisation fall recently since it published its annual accounts. This is illustrated by movements in the share price shown in Figure 18.3. However, this has not discouraged the three executive directors in the company from purchasing substantial blocks of shares.

Figure 18.3 *Share price of Caldy plc, 2002-03*

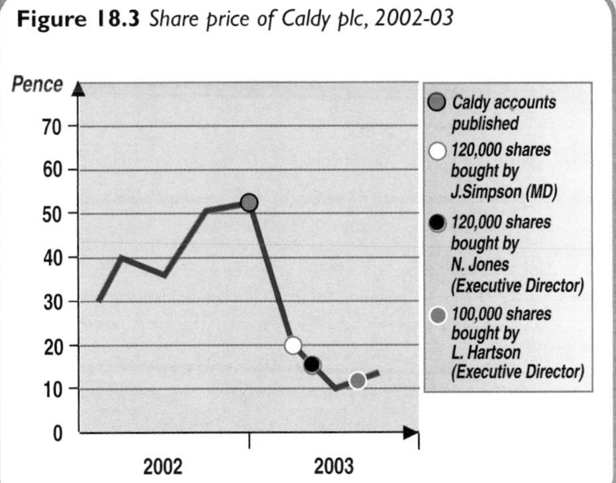

(a) What evidence is there to suggest that the accounts of Caldy plc may have been window dressed?
(b) State two reasons, apart from window dressing, why share prices may not reflect the value of the business.
(c) (i) What stakeholders may be interested in the information in the accounts suggested by Figure 18.3 and the article?
(ii) Evaluate how they may react to this information.

that the business is actually in a stronger position than is indicated. On the other hand, this may have the adverse effect of allowing outsiders to buy shares in a plc.

To reduce taxation The accounts may disguise the true financial strength of the business to reduce tax liability. Reducing the profit of a business should reduce the amount of corporation tax paid.

Methods of manipulation

There is a number of ways in which accounts can be manipulated.

Depreciation It is possible for assets to be depreciated at a slower or faster rate. This will affect both the balance sheet and the profit and loss account. A change in the depreciation charge can be achieved by changing the method of calculating depreciation. For example, if a company buys a new machine for £100,000 (with a 6 year estimated life and residual value of £10,000), the depreciation allowance in the first year could be £15,000 using the straight line method (SLM) or £40,000 using the reducing balance method (RBM). If the RBM is used rather than the SLM, the higher depreciation charge would reduce the company's profit by £25,000 (£40,000 - £15,000). The choice of method would also mean that the book value of the machine would be lower in the balance sheet. Therefore the value of tangible assets and net assets would be lower.

Creditors and debtors By changing the value of creditors or debtors the solvency of a company can be manipulated. For example, if a business makes a serious effort to collect outstanding debts before the end of the trading year then the value of liquid assets will increase. The company will therefore appear to be in a healthier position. Similarly, if the value of creditors can be reduced on the balance sheet by repaying outstanding debts, the company will appear to be financially stronger.

Stock valuation By changing the method of stock valuation the book value of stock might be increased or decreased. This will affect the profit and loss account and the balance sheet. For example, by using the FIFO method of stock valuation, a firm's closing stock might be £2,400,000. By using the AVCO method it might be reduced to £1,900,000 (if stock prices have risen during the year). By switching from FIFO to AVCO the value of cost of sales will be increased by £500,000 and therefore the value of profit will fall by £500,000. In the balance sheet, if the value of stocks is £500,000 lower the value of current assets will also be lower by the same amount. This will also reduce working capital and net assets.

Writing off A business can reduce its profits by 'writing off' investments or debt. This means, for example, if a debt of £40,000 is 'written off', it is called a bad debt and included as an expense in the profit and loss account. It is subtracted from gross profit and as a result net profit would fall by £40,000. The same would happen if an investment was written off.

Profits By suppressing costs, accountants can show greater profits. For example, a business might decide to pay month 12 salaries to staff in month 1 of the next trading year. This will reduce the salary bill in the current year, which is part of the operating expenses on the profit and loss account.
Reducing the value of perating expenses will increase the value of net profit. The amount of retained profit can be manipulated by raising or lowering the dividend payment for the current trading year. If the dividend payment is reduced than retained profit for the year will be higher.

Asset manipulation A company can improve its gearing (☞ unit 17) by selling fixed assets and leasing them back. By selling fixed assets the business can use the proceeds to repay debt, such as loans. Reducing the amount of money raised from loans relative to the amount raised from shareholders will improve the gearing of the business. For example, a company's gearing may be:

$$\text{Gearing} = \frac{\text{Debt}}{\text{Equity}} \times 100 = \frac{£12m}{£24m} \times 100 = 50\%$$

If fixed assets of £4 million are sold and then leased back, with the money being used to repay loans, gearing is now:

$$\text{Gearing} = \frac{£8m}{£24m} \times 100 = 33.3\%$$

As a result of this the company has become more low geared. However, it will have to meet the cost of leasing assets in the future. This will reduce profit.

Any manipulation made to the accounts in the current trading year will usually show up in the next trading year. For example, an effort to suppress costs this year by postponing certain payments will mean that profit this year will be higher. However, assuming that the payments are made in the next trading year, the profit for that year will be lower.

Earnings management In some industries it is possible for a business to choose when to 'recognise' business income. For example, a TV production company can choose to recognise the income from a new programme when the programme contract is signed, when the programme is delivered, or when the invoice is issued. By choosing to recognise income in the next financial year, the current year's profit will be reduced. This reduces the tax liability for the year.

key terms

Capitalised earnings - the value of a company determined by multiplying the P/E ratio by maintainable earnings.

Manipulating or window dressing - where accounts are presented in such a way that the financial position of a business appears to be different than it really is.

Market capitalisation - the value of a company determined by multiplying the share price by the number of shares issued.

Value (of a business) - the amount a business is worth to a stakeholder or any other interested party.

Knowledge

1. What is meant by the expectation gap in relation to the value of a business?
2. Explain 2 reasons why a hostile takeover might lead to a rise in the value of a business.
3. State 5 reasons for valuing a business, other than for a takeover.
4. What information is needed to calculate (i) market capitalisation and (ii) maintainable earnings?
5. How does DCF allow a business to be valued?
6. State 4 problems which might occur when valuing a business.
7. Why is it necessary to regulate the presentation of accounts?
8. State 4 reasons why the accounts might be manipulated.
9. Briefly explain 2 ways in which accounts could be manipulated to exaggerate the value of a company.
10. Briefly explain 2 ways in which accounts could be manipulated to show a company in a poorer light.
11. How can the gearing of a company be affected by window dressing?

Case study JMC

JMC is a quoted construction company that undertakes large scale construction work such as roads, bridges and other infrastructure projects. Jane Marsh owns 51 per cent of the company and is the chief executive. The company has doubled in size in the last three years due to a programme of acquisitions. This growth has pleased shareholders since both profits and dividends have grown as well. The company's share price has also risen from 162p in 2002 to 325p in 2004. JMC is currently looking at another acquisition. It wants to break into the Scottish market and two companies have emerged as possible targets, although only one will eventually be bought. The two companies, Thistle Holdings and Glasgow Construction, have both heard on the 'grapevine' that they may be subject to takeover bids. However, no official announcement has yet been made.

Thistle Holdings This appears to be a soundly run company. It has a lot of road maintenance contracts with various Scottish councils. It will not take kindly to a takeover bid, but if the price is right the shareholders may be happy to sell. Jane thinks this would be a good company to buy, but the price could be high.

Glasgow Construction Much less is known about this company. Its main area of business is the construction of hydroelectric power stations in the Scottish Highlands. It is felt that a bid by JMC would be regarded as entirely hostile and unwelcome. However, the company could be bought cheaply and there is a suspicion that the accounts have been boosted artificially. For example, JMC's accountant thinks that some assets may have been sold and leased back. It is also thought that the year's profit may have been inflated by the management of earnings. It is thought that some of the income (about £2 million) for a project due to start next year, has been included in this year's profit and loss account. The contracts for the project were signed this year.

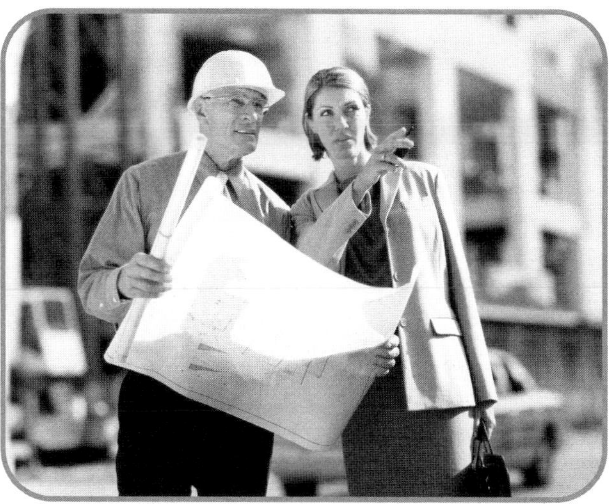

(a) Why will it be necessary to value Thistle Holdings and Glasgow Construction? (6 marks)

(b) Use two methods of valuation to determine the value of Thistle Holdings and Glasgow Construction. (12 marks)

(c) Explain the effects on the accounts of Glasgow Construction if the alleged manipulations have taken place. (10 marks)

(d) Explain why Glasgow Construction might have manipulated its accounts. (10 marks)

(e) Assuming that the alleged manipulations have taken place, evaluate which company would be best for JMC to take over. (12 marks)

Table 18.2 *Financial information for Thistle Holdings and Glasgow Construction*

	Thistle Holdings	Glasgow Construction
Fixed assets	£104m	£71m
Current assets	£32m	£20m
Creditors: amounts falling due within one year	£28m	£12m
Long term liabilities	£50m	£25m
Share price	£3.25	£1.10
No. of shares issued	20m	50m
Profit after tax	£4.6m	£4.9m

19 Individuals in Organisations

Individuals, groups and organisations

A business is made up of individuals. Individual production workers, office workers or managers etc. belong to groups within the firm (☞ unit 20). Many tasks in modern business are technically complex, such as the production of a vehicle, and can only be carried out in groups using the combined skills of individuals. Other tasks, such as market research, may require people to work together as a co-ordinated 'team'. As well as these formal groups, individuals will also belong to informal groups, for example a group of workers who become friends after joining a company at the same time. Individuals and the groups they belong to make up the business **organisation**.

No two individuals are the same. They have different characteristics, attitudes, needs and personalities. Why does a business need to know something about these differences? It will help a business to:

- make sure it has chosen the most suitable person for a job from a number of applicants;
- make certain employees' skills are used effectively;
- ensure workers are satisfied and motivated;
- tell how individuals in the workforce will react when faced with a decision or a situation at work.

Physical differences

It is very rare indeed for two individuals physically to be the same in all respects. It is possible, however, to group people based on their shape, size, hair colour etc. Sometimes certain groups are more suitable for a job than others and this may be part of the job description. For example, people wanting to join the police force must be over a minimum height and an applicant to the fire service must have a certain chest expansion. A business, however, must be careful not to restrict physically demanding jobs to men as this type of discrimination is unlawful.

Personality differences

An individual could be described by the way they behave, such as 'happy-go-lucky' or 'quiet'. These give an indication of that person's personality. Psychologists call these words TRAITS. They form the basis of important theories of personality, some of which are used by businesses to make decisions about individuals at work.

Cattell In 1965 Raymond Cattell suggested that people have 16 main traits. To measure these traits he developed a test known as 16 Personality Factor (16PF). Figure 19.1 shows the 16 traits or factors that are measured in the test. Each one has a scale of 1-10. For example, factor 'A' could be reserved (1), outgoing (10) or somewhere in between. People taking the test choose a point on each scale which reflects their personality. Linking together the 'scores' will give a personality profile.

The 16PF is widely used in the selection of business managers. Kellogg's the cereal manufacturer has used it successfully in the past. By looking at the profiles of successful managers a firm is able to build up a 'suitable' personality profile. When interviewing candidates in future, the business could ask them to fill in a 16PF test and compare their results with the 'ideal profile' to see if the candidate is suitable. Figure 19.1 shows the results of a study by Makin, Cooper and Cox. The line linking the scores shows the average personality profile of managing directors.

Figure 19.1 *Cattell's 16 Personality Factor questionnaire showing managing directors' average personality profile*

	LOW SCORE DESCRIPTION		HIGH SCORE DESCRIPTION
A	Reserved, detached, critical, aloof	1 2 3 4 5 6 7 8 9 10	Outgoing, warm-hearted, easygoing
B	Less intelligent, concrete thinking	1 2 3 4 5 6 7 8 9 10	More intelligent, abstract thinking
C	Affected by feelings, easily upset	1 2 3 4 5 6 7 8 9 10	Emotionally stable, calm, mature
E	Humble, mild, conforming	1 2 3 4 5 6 7 8 9 10	Assertive, competitive
F	Sober, prudent, taciturn	1 2 3 4 5 6 7 8 9 10	Happy-go-lucky, enthusiastic
G	Expedient, disregards rules	1 2 3 4 5 6 7 8 9 10	Conscientious, moralistic
H	Shy, timid	1 2 3 4 5 6 7 8 9 10	Socially bold
I	Tough-minded, realistic	1 2 3 4 5 6 7 8 9 10	Tender-minded, sensitive
L	Trusting, adaptable	1 2 3 4 5 6 7 8 9 10	Suspicious, hard to fool
M	Practical, careful	1 2 3 4 5 6 7 8 9 10	Imaginative, careless
N	Forthright, natural	1 2 3 4 5 6 7 8 9 10	Shrewd, calculating
O	Self-assured, confident	1 2 3 4 5 6 7 8 9 10	Apprehensive, troubled
Q1	Conservative, respects established ideas	1 2 3 4 5 6 7 8 9 10	Experimenting, radical
Q2	Group dependent, good 'follower'	1 2 3 4 5 6 7 8 9 10	Self-sufficient, resourceful
Q3	Undisciplined, self-conflict	1 2 3 4 5 6 7 8 9 10	Controlled, socially precise
Q4	Relaxed, tranquil	1 2 3 4 5 6 7 8 9 10	Tense, frustrated

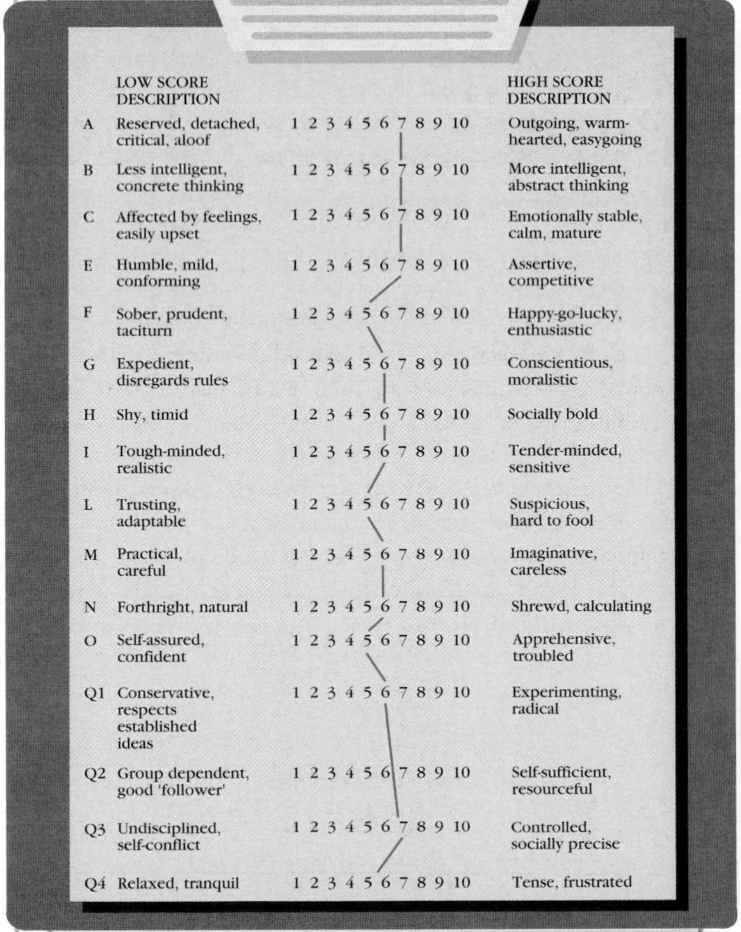

Ingvar Kamprad is self-made. He decided that working on a farm was not for him and started selling door to door. At 20 he was selling furniture. He called his company IKEA, from his initials, Elmtaryd, the family farm and Agunnaryd, the village where he grew up. Today Kamprad is said to be worth £32 billion. But he is also said to be careful with his money. He drives an 11 year old Volvo and still searches the Internet for cheap air fares. His idea of luxury is Swedish fish roe rather than a yacht. Although disputed, a study has suggested that he controls almost the whole of the private company he founded.

Kamprad is also a ruthless and inventive businessman. In 1956 he invented the flat pack concept of furniture. After starting IKEA he quickly undercut his competitors to gain market share. When he became too busy to operate the shop himself, he invented the retail system where, instead of the business taking goods to the customer, the customer picked up the goods. Today this is one of IKEA's hallmarks. When Kamprad wanted to see how well his sons could perform in business, he gave them each a separate part to run and compete with each other to see who would do best.

Some have argued the working for Kamprad is not easy. He dresses informally and tells his staff to call him by his first name. But it is suggested that he keeps a tight reign on his workforce.

Source: adapted from *The Daily Mail*, 7.4.2004.

(a) Using the 16PF, examine some of the possible traits of Ingvar Kamprad.
(b) Suggest why these traits may be important for establishing a successful business such as IKEA.

Eysenck In 1975 Hans Eysenck reduced the number of scales upon which personality traits could be measured to two:

- stable-unstable;
- extroverted-introverted.

The stable-unstable scale showed emotional stability. Stable people tended to be calm and reliable, whilst those with low stability tended to be anxious or reserved. The extroverted-introverted scale described people who were either passive, quiet and withdrawn (introverted) or changeable, outgoing and impulsive (extroverted).

Using these traits, Eysenck built a matrix of an individual's personality. This is shown in Figure 19.2. Individuals can be placed in one of the four quarters. A stable-introverted person may be calm and reliable, and perhaps suited to a job such as librarian. However, if the library needed an injection of new ideas a 'stable-extrovert' may be more suitable.

The matrix can have a number of uses for a business. For example, it could help judge how an employee might deal with a new situation or indicate how well a candidate might suit a particular job. A business may also use the information to build up a team of workers whose personalities complement each other to carry out a task.

Costa and McRae In the early 1990s Eysenck's work was developed by a number of theorists, such as Paul Costa and Robert McRae (1992). They outlined what have come to be known as the '**big five**'. The big five are broad personality types or trait clusters. In research studies they have been found consistently to capture the traits that we use to describe ourselves and other people. They are shown in Table 19.1. Research seems to have reproduced these dimensions, in many different settings, with different people, with different forms of data collection and in different languages.

Figure 19.2 *Vertical and lateral communication*

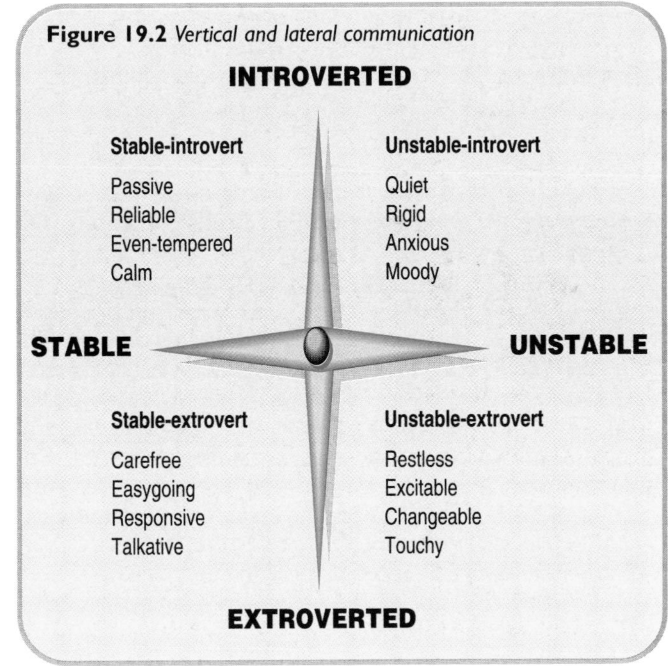

Table 19.1

Definitions			
extroversion	gregarious, warm, positive	versus	quiet, reserved, shy
agreeableness	straightforward, compliant, sympathetic	versus	quarrelsome, oppositional, unfeeling
conscientiousness	achievement-orientated, dutiful, self-disciplined	versus	frivolous, irresponsible, disorganised
neuroticism	anxious, depressed, self-conscious	versus	calm, contented, self-assured
openness	creative, open-minded, intellectual	versus	unimaginative, disinterested, narrow-minded

Padraig Cruikshank started as a builder from school, working with his father repairing and laying roofs. At 20 he had set up his own business, employing three workers. Two of these workers were friends and the other a friend of his father. Padraig tended to rely on his father's friend for advice on tricky jobs and tried to make sure that all workers had a say if there were problems. As the business expanded and later became a company, Padraig wanted to retain this organisational culture. He offered share options to workers and was keen on the idea of works councils, which he introduced into the business in 2002.

Padraig also felt that it was important to realise that there are sometimes other things in life than work. He knew that some of his father's friends had suffered greatly during the decline of the housing market in the late 1980s. So he tended to take the view that you should 'live for the day'. In 2003 there had been some problems in one of his operations in the Norwich area. There was a rising demand for housing and the local manager had asked workers to work longer hours. They complained that these contravened the European Work Time Directive. Padraig was sure that this did not apply to UK businesses at that time, although it was likely to in future. However, he did have the feeling that any attempt to force longer hours on workers would affect the goodwill he had built up in the company. Padraig visited the local depot where the manager tended to be very anxious about meeting deadlines all the time. Padraig thought that perhaps the answer was to discuss other ways in which deadlines could be met, such as outsourcing, job sharing or flexible hours.

Source: adapted from research information.

(a) Using examples from the data, identify Padraig's personality on Eysenck's two dimensional matrix.
(b) Suggest how such a personality might help the business given the issues that it faces.

There are, however, limits to how useful these theories can be. They do not precisely predict what a person will do in any situation, only indicate what a person is likely to do given their personality. Behaviour might, for example, change when faced with stress. Also, people with different personalities may still be able to do a 'good' job when faced with the same situation. Another problem is that they assume an individual will give an honest response. But often it is easy to pick out the acceptable answer or the one that is best in terms of the job. For these reasons, the theories are usually used only for selection and internal promotion.

Personality and stress

Personality and health may be linked in a way that is relevant to business. In 1974, M. Friedman and R. Rosenman claimed to have identified two extreme personality patterns or 'behaviour syndromes', Type A and Type B, as shown in Table 19.2. These help to explain differences in stress levels at work and allow a 'stress-prone' personality to be identified.

Type A people are more impatient, competitive and aggressive than Type B people, and are more likely to suffer stress-related problems. For example, Friedman and Rosenman found that Type A personalities were three times more likely to suffer heart disease than Type B personalities. Type As thrive on long hours, large amounts of work and tight deadlines. These may be useful social and business characteristics. However, Type As may not be able to stand back from a complex business problem to make an effective decision. They tend to lack the patience and relaxed style required for many management positions. Their impatience can also increase the stress levels of those they work with.

Table 19.2

Type A personality characteristics	Type B personality characteristics
Competitive	Able to take time out to enjoy leisure
High need for achievement	Not preoccupied with achievement
Aggressive	Easygoing
Works fast	Works at a steady pace
Impatient	Seldom impatient
Restless	Not easily frustrated
Extremely alert	Relaxed
Tense facial muscles	Moves and speaks slowly
Constant feeling of time pressure	Seldom lacks enough time

Assessing personality in practice

The work of Cattell and Eysenck tries to 'measure' personality. In business, however, people judge the personality of others in less formal ways, and often fairly quickly. The decision may be based on what they themselves think is important. It could also be influenced by a

Portsmouth County Council's 'Future Leaders' policy asks every head of service to look out for 'high flyers' in their areas. Such employees often constantly challenge the status quo of the organisation and at times may appear confrontational. The council argues that future leaders often want things to be changed. This can be the case even if they are still working adequately. Such workers tend to be learn quickly and can often seem impatient. However, it argues that successful future leaders will experiment and are more likely to be willing to take risks.

Candidates who are selected for interview for the programme are interviewed on leadership and management qualities, intelligence, professional relationships, attitudes and skills and understanding the needs of the community.

Source: adapted from *People Management*, 24.7.2003.

(a) Would you categorise the potential leaders that the council is looking for as Type A or Type B? Explain your answer.

(b) How might employing this type of employee as a leader:
(i) benefit;
(ii) cause problems for the organisation?

'stereotype', where personality is linked to race, sex or age. For example, it may be claimed that female managers are more emotional than male.

It is argued that people get an impression of someone from the first piece of information they receive about that person's characteristics. In an interview, for example, recruiters often make up their minds in the first four minutes and rarely change them. A candidate that did not seem prepared, looked untidy or was abrupt may well have lost the job straight away. People make these decisions because they do not like being uncertain about others. A decision based on first impressions may make the interviewer feel more secure, even if it is wrong. It may take time and further contact before people are seen 'as they really are'. Employers and employees must be prepared to change their minds about people they meet and work with. Only then will they be able to make an 'accurate' assessment of someone's personality.

Differences in intelligence

As well as differing in personality, people differ in intelligence or IQ. There is considerable debate about what intelligence is. One definition, by American psychologist Arthur Jensen, is that it is the ability to discover rules, patterns and principles, and apply these to problems.

Intelligence is usually measured by using **IQ tests.** They test an individual's ability to reason. A simple IQ test question may ask for the next number in the sequence 1,3,6,10. This tests the ability to find a sequence and to apply it. An IQ 'score' is usually given at the end of the test. A high score is supposed to indicate a higher level of intelligence. Such tests are often criticised, particularly when comparing the intelligence of people in different social groups.

There is a number of factors which are thought to influence an individual's IQ although there is little agreement on exactly how they affect the IQ.

- Culture and class. Many researchers argue that IQ tests are biased in favour of the middle classes, since tests are largely constructed by members of this group. Working class people tend to do less well on tests, so comparisons of intelligence between people in these groups are not really valid. It has also been shown that 'Western' IQ tests are not suitable for non-Western people. Cultural differences can mean they often approach and carry out the tests in an inappropriate way.
- Genes. There is general agreement that intelligence can be inherited. Some psychologists, such as Hans Eysenck in Britain, suggest that some 80 per cent of intelligence is inherited from parents. The rest is influenced by environmental factors such as the environment where we live and grow up, diet, quality of housing and family size.
- Environment. Some argue that differences in IQ are largely due to environmental factors. Research has shown that IQ test results can be affected by the education, motivation and physical health of the person taking the test. They can also be influenced by the person's rapport with whoever is carrying out the test and the language the test is set in.

Businesses today are now less likely to use IQ tests as a means of assessing an individual. Evidence suggests there is little connection between a person's IQ and how well he might do a job. It may be more important for a business to find out about an individual's knowledge and skills (which may include elements of IQ) as this could give a greater understanding of how a person might contribute to the organisation.

Differences in knowledge and skills

A business needs to know what knowledge and skills an employee has so that she can be given a position in the business where she will be of most use.

Knowledge can be technical, job specific, vocational or general. To be a plumber, a worker would need the technical knowledge of the trade, eg what types of materials and techniques are used for certain jobs. Also, the plumber would need to have knowledge about the way tasks should be carried out and a thorough knowledge of what is involved in the trade - the vocational aspects of being a plumber. In addition, the plumber may need to have more general knowledge, such as the ability to do simple mathematics.

As well as having knowledge, an employee will also need skills. These are the abilities needed to complete a task. The skills required at work can be job specific, communication skills, IT skills, numeracy and literacy skills or problem solving skills. A plumber would not only need to

Today's candidate for most famous knowledge worker might be Bill Gates, the founder of Microsoft. The information revolution has made the management of knowledge vitally important for businesses. Some companies believe that the answer to creating knowledge workers is to recruit the brightest people. This may make sense. A 1995 study in 3,100 US workplaces looked at the relationship between education and productivity. The research showed that, on average, a 10 per cent increase in the workforce's education level led to an 8.6 per cent gain in productivity. This could be compared with a 10 per cent rise in plant and equipment values, which increased productivity by 3.4 per cent.

Another example showing the financial value of people who might be called knowledge workers was the move by institutional investors to have Maurice Saatchi dismissed from Cordiant, the advertising agency (formerly Saatchi & Saatchi). When he left, several directors left in protest and customers such as Mars and BA also defected, leading to a halving of the company's share price. This answers the question often asked by Charles Handy, a management specialist: 'What happens when your assets walk out of the door?' In effect the institutional shareholders thought they owned Saatchi & Saatchi. In fact, they owned less than half of it. Most of the value could be attributed to the human capital of the knowledge workers.

But employing bright people is not a guarantee of success. You might have the best brains, but they must be working for you. Some 150,000 of what might be called 'the brightest workers in the world' left IBM. The problem had been, as IBM later admitted, that many of them were working to their own agenda. Another problem is that some companies believe you can be too intelligent for the job. The most brilliant people are not always easy to manage. However, if the job demands a brilliant mind, then it seems logical to seek out the best.

Source: adapted from *The Financial Times*.

(a) What are the potential problems of knowledge workers for a business?
(b) Why might it make sense to recruit the 'brightest' people to be knowledge workers?
(c) Using evidence from the article, discuss the importance of knowledge workers as assets to a business.

know how to complete a task, but have the appropriate skills to carry it out. The ability to communicate with customers may also be a useful skill.

Businesses want a more qualified and more skilled workforce. They expect workers to update their skills through training, and to develop new and different skills. This makes employees more adaptable and flexible.
It has been suggested that **knowledge work** and **knowledge workers** are critical to business success in a changing business environment. Knowledge work requires employees who can:

- use their own existing knowledge;
- acquire new information;
- combine and process information to produce and communicate new information;
- learn continuously from their experiences.

Management theorists such as Peter Drucker and Michael Porter have suggested that knowledge is an important resource for businesses and a source of competitive advantage. They argue that work increasingly involves the processing and production of ideas, images, thoughts, concepts and symbols rather than physical materials. Knowledge workers are most suitable to carry out this sort of work. Knowledge workers are sometimes combined to make knowledge teams (☞ unit 20).

Problem solving and decision making

Businesses are not only interested in the abilities of their employees, but in the way they use them to solve problems. The way in which an employee prefers to work may cause problems if it differs from the way colleagues work or from what the business expects.

In 1984, Michael Kirton studied the way management initiatives in a business might succeed or fail. He suggested that success may depend on how **problem solving** was tackled and identified two approaches. ADAPTORS tend to solve problems by using existing or slightly modified approaches. They do not make rapid changes in the way problems are solved. INNOVATORS, however, try to find exciting and possibly unexpected ways of solving problems. Take the example of a small business having problems finding information quickly and easily when it is stored in files. The adaptor might suggest a better method of organising the files. An innovator, however, may feel that replacing the paper filing system with a computer system will be a better solution. These are two extremes. It is likely in business that people will have a combination of the two approaches.

Both these approaches have their strengths and weaknesses. The adaptor can effectively work within the present system, but does not find it easy to seek new solutions. For example, an 'adaptor' working in marketing might look for new product developments using existing products. The innovator, on the other hand, may produce ideas for new products.
This approach often means that the innovator finds it difficult to get ideas accepted. Innovators may be seen as extroverts, generating lists of new ideas, but ignoring the needs of the business. Their attitude can often mean that an adaptor feels uncomfortable working with them. The adaptor, however, may appear conservative and always willing to agree with a superior.

What can managers do to minimise clashes? A study in 1991 by Makin, Cooper and Cox argued that the solution lies in understanding, together with an acceptance of the other person's position. Knowing someone else's style allows a manager to predict what they are likely to do in any situation.

Differences in emotional intelligence

In 1995 Goleman, an American Harvard Management specialist, coined the term **emotional intelligence**. It is the ability of a person to sense and understand their own and others' emotions and to apply that understanding to achieve an outcome, for example in a business situation. Successful businesses are able to harness emotional intelligence. Goleman argues that the 'business intelligence' of employees is affected by emotions rather than technical expertise, because emotions drive thinking.

Different individuals will have different emotional intelligence. A study of four year old children found that those who controlled their emotions, and resisted the temptation to eat a marshmallow, performed better on college entry tests fourteen years later. The theory may explain why some employees have problems after early career success. Problems arise because of their inability to understand their impact on others rather than to a lack of expertise. A study by the US company 3M found 90 per cent of the problems which affected its employees' performance were unmeasured. This was because they related to a lack of interpersonal skills, stress, emotional conflicts and personal health, rather than technical failure, absenteeism or poor training.

key terms

Adaptors - individuals who tend to solve problems by using existing or slightly modified approaches already used by the business.
Innovators - individuals who tend to solve problems by finding new, exciting and unexpected solutions to problems in a business.
Traits - a distinguishing feature in character, appearance or habit used in identifying an individual's personality.

Knowledge

1. State 3 reasons why businesses need to know about the different characteristics of individuals.
2. What is meant by the 16 Personality Factor?
3. Explain the terms:
   (a) stable;
   (b) unstable;
   (c) extrovert;
   (d) introvert;
   in relation to the work of Eysenck.
4. What characteristics might an unstable-extrovert have?
5. How might Eysenck's analysis of personality traits be used by business?
6. State 3 factors which are thought to influence an individual's intelligence.
7. What are the problems a business might face in using IQ tests?
8. State 5 differences in skills and knowledge that one employee might have from another.
9. What is meant by the term knowledge worker?
10. Explain the difference between an innovator's and adaptor's approach to problem solving.
11. What might cause a clash between an innovator and an adaptor in the work setting?
12. Why might understanding emotional intelligence be important for a business?

Case study A woman with ideas

Emma Rickson is a personnel officer in a large advertising agency. She has achieved rapid promotion in the company from her role as a secretary in the sales department to personnel officer with responsibility for recruitment. She did this by completing the Institute of Personnel Management qualifications through evening and weekend courses over a four year period. She was determined to do it and had the intelligence and perseverance finally to achieve her goal.

She has been in personnel for 2 years and has developed skills and knowledge in many different areas of the profession - in employee legislation, industrial relations issues and in her main interest of recruitment. Emma is outgoing (she had been tested and categorised as stable and extrovert using Eysenck's typology of personality) and popular with her peers. She has always believed in finding new ways to solve particular problems.

The latest problem she faced was the shortage of well qualified administrative staff who were competent in using the newly-installed computer system. The training given by the company was extremely comprehensive and it was difficult to replace lost employees with the same level of expertise.

Emma recognised that the problem consisted of two main elements. Firsty, not enough men were attracted to this area of work and, second, some of the women who had been trained were leaving to start a family. Due to poor local nursery provision, these women tended to stay at home rather than return to work after having children.

Her plan of action encompassed both aspects of the problem. She devised an educational campaign for the company aimed at men, in order that they might review their own ideas about the suitability of administrative work for males. In it she wanted to emphasise the promotion opportunities in administration work and how it was possible to achieve management status through the administrative route. She showed how administrative work had changed from traditionally repetitive office tasks to ones where high technology and problem solving skills were vital. She targeted the male sector by demonstrating that administrative work required types of skills that were often associated with men. At the same time, she planned to introduce creche facilities for the female employees of the company that would cost them far less than a private nursery and would also be cost effective for the organisation.

Emma drew up her plans and costed them out. The campaign materials and accompanying workshop sessions would be £5,000 for the year. The creche facilities would need capital expenditure of approximately £15,000. The ongoing costs would be met by the employees willing to make use of the service. At present it was costing them £35,000 to recruit and train the staff required for the administration vacancies in the company. She presented her findings to the executive board in a confident and assertive way.

The plan was rejected by senior management as too expensive in the short term and too far fetched. She was told to improve her selection procedures so that she recruited people that would stay. She was also told not to involve herself in other aspects of personnel work that were not her responsibility.

Emma felt saddened and disillusioned by this experience.

(a) Identify the characteristics that have gained Emma promotion. (6 marks)

(b) Classify Emma's personality using a suitable method. Explain your answer. (6 marks)

(c) What potential problems might her personality and approach have for the business? (8 marks)

(d) Examine the reasons why Emmas ideas were rejected by management. (10 marks)

(e) Suggest and justify an alternative approach that Emma might have used when putting forward her plan. (10 marks)

20 Groups and Teams in Business

Working in groups

Working with other people in groups is something that many employees do in business. An employee in a marketing consultancy business may be part of a team developing TV adverts for a client, part of a group set up to think of ideas to improve working methods and may meet with friends for lunch. Only in a small number of cases will individual employees work on their own, as in the case of a freelance journalist. Even an employee delivering goods on his own from a van will interact with staff and management when he returns to the office or factory.

Individuals may behave differently when working in a group than if they were working on their own. For example, an employee on a building site might want to work at a leisurely pace or find ways to avoid carrying out a task immediately. Group pressure could persuade or embarrass the employee into working harder than he would have wished. The group may want to finish the job early or earn any bonus that is available. In this case the employee's behaviour has changed as a result of being a group member. He is behaving in a way that conforms to the GROUP NORM. In other words, he is behaving in a way that is 'normal' for that group.

There is a certain amount of evidence to support the idea that individual behaviour is influenced by the group. The Hawthorne Studies showed that group behaviour can influence workers' motivation. It is possible to identify certain common features of groups that exist in businesses.

- The behaviour of the group influences all members, eg if a decision is made to take industrial action (☞ unit 23).
- Members of the group have some common interests and objectives, eg a production team may want to increase its level of overtime payments.
- Members meet and discuss common interests, eg assembly line workers might discuss the latest changes to working conditions.
- There are rules or norms influencing members' behaviour, eg members of the finance committee of a business are expected to report back to the managing director after each meeting.

It could be argued that, given the emphasis on team work in many modern organisations, it is essential for businesses to understand how people work in groups. If employees in a group do not work 'well' together, this may reduce productivity and make decision making more difficult.

Types of group

It is possible to distinguish different groups that exist in business. One common method is to divide them into FORMAL and INFORMAL groups.

Formal groups These are groups which are set up by a business specifically to carry out tasks. Formal groups are an actual part of the organisation, with arranged meetings and rules determining their behaviour and actions. Examples of formal groups might be management teams that control one aspect of a business, such as the finance department.

Other examples of formal groups might be groups which are set up to deal with certain problems. For example, a unit might be set up by a business to monitor the introduction of new machinery. The group may include the production manager, an engineer, a supervisor and a number of operators. Its task may be to make sure the changeover is as efficient as possible and it would meet to discuss ways in which this could be achieved.

Formal groups can be **temporary** or **permanent**. A temporary group might be a working party to investigate a computerised information system. Permanent groups include standing committees, such as health and safety committees or a trade union, which is a formal group, but not one created by management. The type of group depends on whether the task involved is recurrent or a 'one-off'.

Informal groups Informal groups are made up of employees with similar interests. They are not a formal part of the

(a) Identify the possible:
(i) formal;
(ii) informal;
groups that the successful candidates might belong to using information in the advertisement.
(b) Explain how belonging to informal groups might help:
(i) the new employees when settling into their job;
(ii) the business in its relations with the new employees.

Exciting Opportunities

The First vacancy is for a person who is dynamic, hardworking, approachable, organised and capable of dealing with the public and their children. They will join the management team and help to develop the future of this growing business, knowledge of the food and beverage industry would also be an advantage. (Hours of business 10am-6pm)

The Second vacancy is for people who like animals and willing to work within their environment. The right person must be outgoing, reliable, friendly and will be expected to work with the public.

business itself. They do not have any formal 'rules', although there are often unofficial norms which influence members' behaviour. An example of an informal group might be a casual meeting over lunch between managers in the production, marketing and finance departments to discuss a new product launch. It could also be a group of hospital workers discussing possible job cuts in their rest room.

There are certain reasons why informal groups exist. It is argued that these groups meet the psychological needs of employees. These might be some of the following.

- The need to be with other people.
- Status is determined by membership of various groups. This will also influence the view people have of their personal value and self-esteem.
- Groups offer a feeling of security and mutual support. By doing so, they reduce uncertainty and anxiety.
- The group may act as a problem solver for its members.

The informal groups that develop will be determined, to a large extent, by the physical layout required for work. Distance has a powerful influence on who will interact with whom. In general, the more frequent the interactions, the more likely informal groups are to be formed. Informal groups can have considerable influence on group members and the norms and values that a group develops may or may not support those of the organisation.

It may appear that formal and informal groups are separate. This is not the case. Groups that start off as formal often develop powerful informal relations. 'Part' of a company, as well as being a department, may be a department of friends. Japanese organisations, such as Sony, deliberately encourage this. Informal groupings, such as friendships outside work, can provide useful channels of communication for the organisation. The **grapevine** is a term used for such channels.

It is also possible to divide groups into primary and secondary groups.

- Primary groups are small groups where people can have regular contact, eg a small department or office.
- Secondary groups are large groups where people have less regular contact, eg a large open-plan office or a large meeting.

A **team** is a particular type of group. Teams are usually put together for a purpose. For example, a business may have team meetings of workers to discuss production problems or have a team of designers developing a new product. Teams are dealt with later in this unit.

Group decision making

The aims of businesses are to try and create groups that are effective and efficient. If the business can motivate the group to work harder in order to achieve goals, the sense of pride in the group's own competence might create job satisfaction. There is a number of factors that can help group decision making.

Group members The characteristics and goals of the individual members of the group will help to determine the group's characteristics and goals. An individual is likely to be influenced more strongly by a small group than by a large group. In a large group the person may feel overwhelmed and, therefore, unable to participate effectively in team decisions.

It has been suggested that the effectiveness of a group depends on the blend of the individual skills and abilities of its members. A group might be most effective if it contains:

- a person of originality and ideas;
- a 'get-up-and-go' person with considerable energy, enthusiasm and drive;
- a quiet, logical thinker, who ponders carefully and criticises the ideas of others.

This is why groups set up to consider new products often draw members from a number of different departments in the business. This means the group will have a wide range of skills and abilities.

Figure 20.1 *The roles of individuals in groups*

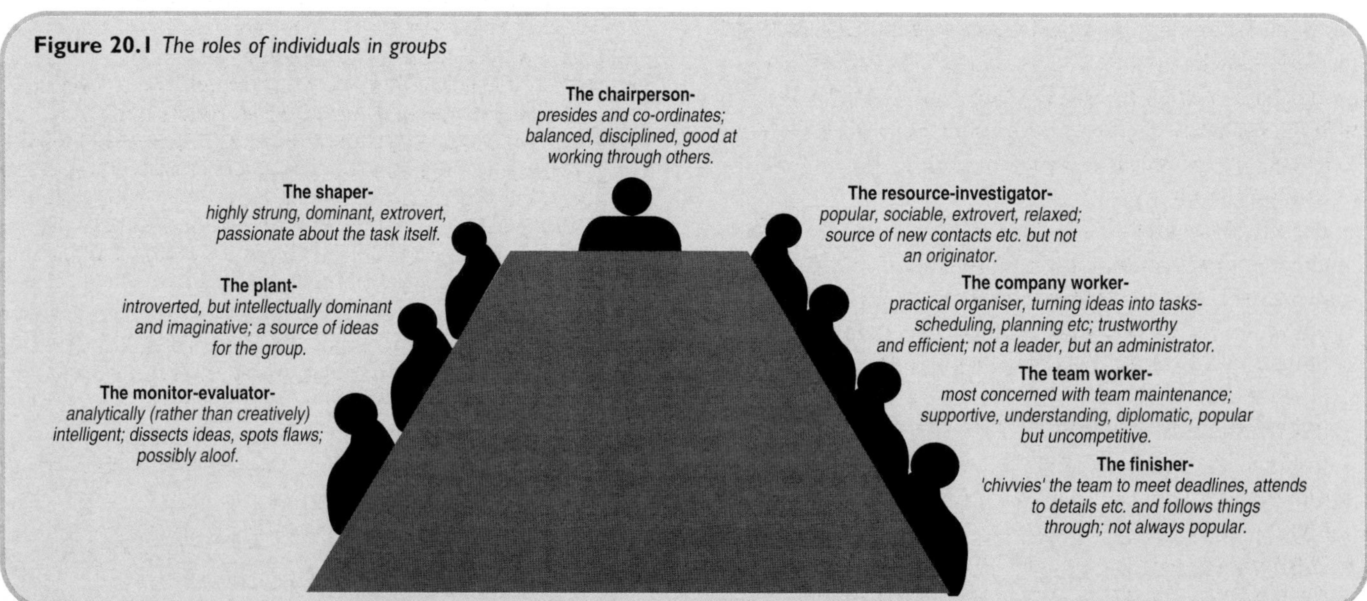

The chairperson-
presides and co-ordinates; balanced, disciplined, good at working through others.
The shaper-
highly strung, dominant, extrovert, passionate about the task itself.
The plant-
introverted, but intellectually dominant and imaginative; a source of ideas for the group.
The monitor-evaluator-
analytically (rather than creatively) intelligent; dissects ideas, spots flaws; possibly aloof.
The resource-investigator-
popular, sociable, extrovert, relaxed; source of new contacts etc. but not an originator.
The company worker-
practical organiser, turning ideas into tasks- scheduling, planning etc; trustworthy and efficient; not a leader, but an administrator.
The team worker-
most concerned with team maintenance; supportive, understanding, diplomatic, popular but uncompetitive.
The finisher-
'chivvies' the team to meet deadlines, attends to details etc. and follows things through; not always popular.

Group roles The most comprehensive study of group roles within a work setting is most probably that of **Meredith Belbin** (1981). He found that successful teams consisted of a mix of individuals, each of whom performed a different role. A summary of these roles is shown in Figure 20.1.

According to Belbin each person has a preferred role and for a group to be effective all the roles need to be filled. So a business might select people to ensure that they fill one or more of the roles which a group lacks. This is not always possible. Most formal groups within business are predetermined by who has the technical expertise to carry out the task.

How then can a knowledge of these roles help?

- For a group to work efficiently the business must be aware of the roles people prefer. These may become apparent through observation. People should be given tasks which allow them to operate in their preferred roles, whether in a sporting team or in a team of medical staff in a casualty department.
- There should be an understanding of which roles are missing that may cause inefficiency. For example, some researchers conducted a study into why some quality circles continued to meet, while others ceased to. They found that all the groups that failed lacked someone who preferred the 'finisher' role. Apparently these groups were good at problem solving and finding solutions but never carried their ideas through.

The group's task The nature of the task may affect how a group is managed. If a job must be done urgently, it is often necessary to dictate how things should be done, rather than to encourage participation in decision making. Jobs which are routine and undemanding are unlikely to motivate individuals or the group as a whole. If individuals want authoritarian leadership, they are also likely to want clearly defined targets.

Group development Groups do not come into existence fully formed. B.Tuckman and N. Jensen (1977) suggested that groups pass through five stages of development. Progress through all stages may be slow, but is necessary for the group to be effective. Some groups get stuck in the middle and remain inefficient.

- **Forming** is when individuals in the group start to find out about each other and are keen to impress other group members. They usually require guidance from a leader about the nature of the group's task.
- **Storming** is a conflict stage. Members bargain with each other and try to sort out what each of them wants individually and as a group. Individuals reveal their personal goals. Hostility may develop if people's goals are different. Individuals may resist the control of other members.
- **Norming** is where group members develop ways of working together. The question of who will do what and

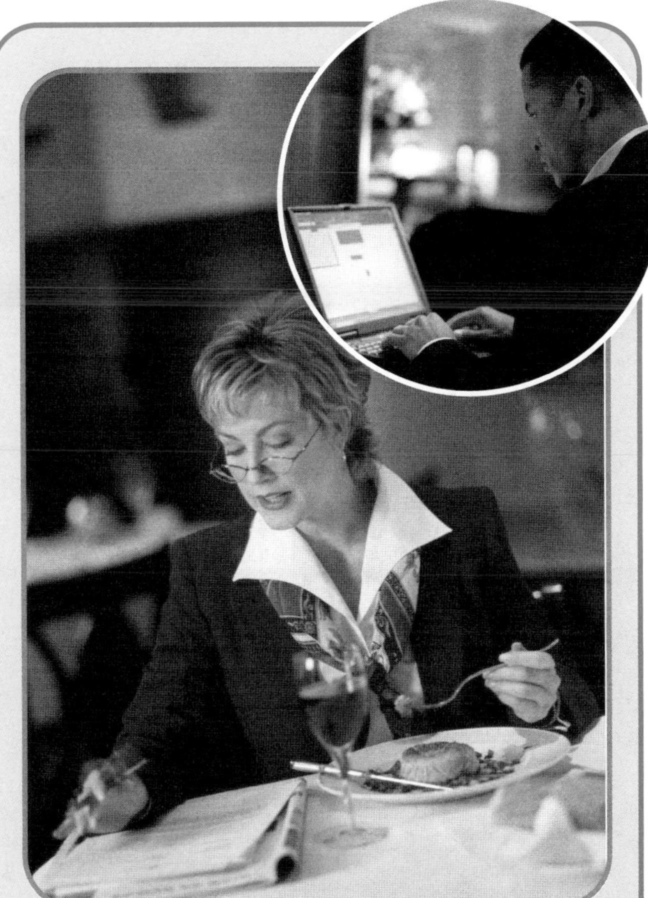

The Waterfront is a hotel in Bournemouth. It considers that its staff are effective because they operate as a team. It has recently been awarded Investors in People status because of its commitment to its employees. Employees are flexible. Staff absences are covered by other staff, so that shortages do not lead to a reduced quality of service. Employees have made a number of suggestions that have solved problems in the hotel. For example, in busy periods some bookings were not taken up. This left empty rooms which could have been filled. One member of staff suggested a reminder be sent in busy periods and this reduced unfilled rooms by 50 per cent.

The hotel had recently promoted its services as a 'wedding centre'. It offered accommodation and a room for the wedding, and provided food for guests. At one reception, however, the owners were on holiday. Staff were unsure who was responsible for ordering flowers. Two sets of flowers were ordered as a result, which raised the costs of the wedding to the hotel. Two of the more senior members of staff also disagreed on the time at which the food would be served.

(a) What might have been the characteristics that made the group at the hotel operate effectively?
(b) Explain the problems that were faced by the group when the new service was introduced.
(c) Examine ways in which the group operation might be improved in future.

Question 2

how it will be done is addressed. Rules are established. There is greater cohesion and information is passed between group members.

- **Performing** is where the group has developed cohesion. It is concerned with getting the job done and accomplishing its objectives. There is a feeling of interdependence and a commitment to problem solving.
- **Adjourning** is where the group disbands because the task has been achieved or because the members have left.

A group may be ineffective if it has failed to sort out certain issues at earlier stages. For example, problems may result if the issue of leadership has not been decided. Another problem is that people may pull in different directions if the purpose of the group has not been clarified or its objectives agreed.

The characteristics of an effective work group

If a business is to try and improve the effectiveness of groups it must be able to identify the characteristics of an effective work group. These may include some of the following.

- There is a high commitment to the achievement of targets and organisational goals.
- There is a clear understanding of the group's work.
- There is a clear understanding of the role of each person within the group.
- There is a free and open communication between members of the group and trust between members.
- There is idea sharing.
- The group is good at generating new ideas.
- Group members try to help each other out by offering constructive criticisms and suggestions.
- There is group problem solving which gets to the root causes of the work problem.
- Group members seek a united consensus of opinion.
- The group is motivated to be able to carry on working in the absence of its leader.

Factors influencing group decision making

There is a number of factors which determine how effective groups are when making decisions.

Size of the group Research has been carried out into the effects of group size on decision making. It has been argued that groups become ineffective once they have 21 members. Other researchers have tried to measure an optimum size for groups. It is felt, in many cases, that the best size is between 3-7 members, with 5 often being quoted as an ideal number.

Why might groups containing these numbers be effective? Larger groups often have communication problems, as more and more people wish to contribute to group discussions. In a small group, the chairperson's role may be fairly informal. When groups get large, however, more formal management may be needed. To address all remarks through the chair in a meeting of 4 people is perhaps being over-formal. To do so in a meeting of 20 may be a necessity.

The size of the task can determine group size. A group designing and building a motor racing car may require many people, with a variety of skills. Each member is likely to make some contribution to the task of the group. But a group which decides who is to drive the car in a Grand Prix may be small in order to reach a clear decision.

Communication Communication in groups can influence how group decisions are made. A distinction is often made between two types of group.

- Centralised groups are groups where individuals can only communicate with other group members via a central member.
- Decentralised groups are groups where every member can communicate directly with every other member.

Communication in groups can take place in a number of ways.

- The wheel. This is where a person at the centre of the group can communicate with all the other members. They, on the other hand, can only communicate with him or her. If they wish to communicate to other members they can only do so through the same central person. This might be the case in a formal meeting.
- The chain. Information is passed from one individual to the next before it reaches the last person in the group. Any individual only ever communicates with one other person. This might be the case in a police operation, for example.
- The circle. Communication is circular, in other words, messages pass between certain people, who pass it on to others, such as in a large office.
- The all-channel. Every member of the group can communicate directly with every other member, as in an open discussion on where an 'awards' evening should be held.

The degree of centrality is highest in the wheel and is less in the chain and circle. The all-channel has no centre; decisions are made by reaching an agreement. The degree of centralisation can affect the group's efficiency, but this also depends on the complexity of the task. When the task is simple, eg deciding on the recruitment policy for a particular job, centralised groups like the wheel are faster and make fewer errors. When the task is more complicated, eg organising and putting into practice a recruitment policy for a particular job, decentralised groups may be more suitable.

Leadership It is likely that a group will have a 'leader' to control or guide it. Leadership may be informal, in the sense that one person 'dominates' a group because of their personality, position or access to information. Leaders can also be elected or nominated by the group, such as the chairperson.

There is a number of different leadership styles.

- Autocratic. This involves one-way communication between the leader and others in the group. The leader makes all the decisions and gives out instructions, expecting them to be obeyed by other group members without question. An example might be a powerful head of a large business like Rupert Murdoch.
- Persuasive. The leader makes all the decisions, but believes that other group members need to be motivated to accept them before they will do what she wants them to. She therefore tries to explain her decisions in order to convince them of her point of view, as a teacher or lecturer in a class might.
- Consultative. This involves discussion between the leader and the other group members involved in making a decision, but the leader retains the right to make the decision herself. By consulting with her group members before making any decision, the leader will take into account their advice and feelings. A council leader might have to operate in this way.
- Democratic. This is an approach where the leader makes a decision based on consensus and agreement within the group. Group members with the greatest knowledge of a problem will have greater influence over the decision. A trade union representative is likely to adopt this style.
- Paternalistic. This is similar to autocratic, where a leader makes the decisions. But leaders are also concerned about the welfare of subordinates.

Skills used in groups For individuals to work well in groups, they need to have a variety of skills. These skills can be categorised into three general areas.

- Contribution. Individuals need to communicate their ideas effectively, informing group members of their thoughts, views and motives. They also need to be able to initiate ideas and evaluate both their own contribution and those of others.
- Co-operation. Individuals need to support other group members so that everyone is involved. This is more likely if individuals share their ideas and listen to others. They should also be able to negotiate and consult, so that everyone feels part of the group's activities.
- Production. Group members need to gather information, materials and ideas, and share them with other group members. They need to show the skills of perseverance and reliability especially if the group is struggling with a problem.

Advantages and problems of group decisions

To what extent are groups more effective in making decisions than individuals? There is a number of advantages in allowing groups to make decisions for a business.

- Groups can pool ideas and draw on a variety of expertise. This makes them particularly good at finding errors. For example, in the design and construction of nuclear reactors, a whole variety of groups working on safety aspects are more likely to ensure that all safety measures are thought of and solutions found to safety problems.
- Groups can handle a great deal of information and involved tasks in a shorter period of time than an individual would take. An example might be the design and writing of a computerised information program.
- Group members may support, motivate and help other members when making decisions.
- Groups provide a basis for accountability within a firm. They can also be used as the basis for a bonus system to increase productivity.

Despite these advantages, there are sometimes problems in group decision making.

- Group decisions may take time. When a decision needs to be made quickly, such as a decision to re-order stock, an individual may be more effective from a business point of view. There will be no debate, which will delay any decision that is made.
- Where one person is an obvious expert in the field, that person may make a more accurate and effective decision, for example, a personnel manager in deciding how best to train certain employees.
- There could be conflicting views and personalities within groups. This can lead to a lack of cohesion, with no shared aims or objectives. The result is that the group becomes inefficient in carrying out a task.
- There may be a possibility of 'risky-shift' decisions. Groups may make riskier decisions than individuals would, due to too much group cohesion. For example, a board of directors might decide as a group to take over a potentially profitable, but inefficient, firm. An individual entrepreneur might have considered this decision too risky to take.

Inter-group relations and conflict

One problem that may result for the business from group activity is a conflict between groups. Many managers would agree that some inter-group competition is inevitable and perhaps useful. If there was no competition the business may become stagnant, with few pressures to make changes. This could lead to inefficiency. The other extreme, of very high levels of competition and conflict, may also cause problems. It could lead to anxiety and tension in the workforce which are counter-productive.

Why might conflict result between groups?

- Groups are often in competition with each other over resources. One example might be where the sports and leisure department in a local council needs funds for a swimming pool, but this may result in another group such as the social services department having less. Another example would be where an employee who is an integral part of a production team may have to leave the team at a vital time to attend a health and safety meeting. Conflict

IceCool, a major ice cream manufacturer, is concerned with two major business problems - reduced profitability due to rising costs and a lack of appeal among the youth market. It has asked the production and marketing departments for their diagnosis of the problem. Both departments are keen to impress, as it could mean greater resources being dedicated to them if they won the argument.

The marketing department managed to have funds allocated to it so that it could carry out market research on the development of a new ice-cream snack. The results of its work suggest that a market segment of 16-19 year olds would particularly like a dynamic, sports and fitness orientated ice-cream snack - a 'Lucozade Sports' ice cream. The price for this product would have to be in the 80p-90p bracket and the packaging would have to be bright, young and dynamic. The advertising approach would be a nationwide television campaign backed up by national billboard displays. It forecast that the payback period will be 2 years, but that high profit margins will then be generated for a further 2 years before going into decline. It has presented its plans to the board of directors.

The production department was far more concerned with the lack of productivity caused by poor capital investment over the last two years. Without any extra allocation of funds, it presented a paper to the board of directors that suggested attacking the problem of poor productivity first so that it might compete more effectively using the product range that was already tried, tested and successful. It was particularly scathing about introducing a new product without solving the underlying problems. Likewise the marketing department was amazed at the lack of vision from the production department.

(a) Why did conflict arise between the production and marketing departments at IceCool?
(b) What benefits might there be for the company in this conflict?
(c) How can IceCool ensure that the two departments work together when a final decision is made?

Question 3

results from the groups' competition for the employee's time.

- There may be conflict between groups at different levels in the business organisation. For example, non-graduate entrants to a bank may be restricted because of the promotion or higher pay of graduate entrants.
- Conflict can result when groups have different goals. For example, that when there is a divorce of **ownership and control** managers may attempt to satisfy their own aims, such as market leadership by a series of price cuts. At the same time they would attempt to make a satisfactory profit for shareholders, who may have wanted the business to maximise profits.
- There are certain psychological factors which can often lead to conflict between groups. When groups are in competition, each will tend to underplay its weaknesses, overestimate its strengths and degrade the other group. The other group may also be seen as hostile or aggressive. As a result it becomes the enemy - 'them' against 'us'. Because of these two factors, interactions between the two groups become strained and decline.

How can conflict either be avoided or, if it already exists, defused? One method that involves low levels of risk is by getting members of one group to work with the other group. This can be achieved by organising joint projects or by some form of exchange. The leaders of the group could initially either work together or exchange roles for this approach to be effective. It can be further developed by communication and swapping of group members. This technique is often used when one organisation takes over another (☞ unit 29) and there is a need to avoid conflict at all levels within the 'new' business. Another possibility is for a business to rotate membership of groups to prevent divisions taking place.

Team building

Businesses often try to improve the productivity and motivation of people working in groups. The 'planned, systematic process designed to improve the efforts of people who work together to achieve goals' is known as TEAM BUILDING.

Team building is based on the idea that before organisations can improve performance, group members must be able to work together effectively. It was first introduced in UK business in the 1970s. Exercises were used to help group members develop trust, open up communication channels, make sure everyone understood the goals of the group, help individuals make decisions with the commitment of all members, prevent the leader from dominating the group, openly examine and resolve conflicts, and to review work activities. Team building exercises often involve taking groups to outdoor locations and setting them problems to solve. Examples include the pension department at Siemens training in outdoor exercises in Finland and operators at DuPont carrying out charity work such as constructing a play group for disabled children.

A study by W. Dyer (1994) found that many companies said they believed in team building. However, only 22 per cent actually carried out any team building activities. The main reasons suggested for this were that:

- managers did not know how to do team building;
- managers did not understand the benefits of spending time on team building and thought it would take too much time;
- team building efforts were not really rewarded in the company;
- people felt their teams were all right;
- people felt it was not supported by their superiors.

Decision teams and work teams

A distinction can be made between **decision teams** and **work teams** in business. A decision team might be a management executive committee, a university academic department or a collection of doctors or lawyers in a clinic. The main function of the team is to make decisions. The team members do not rely on each other to carry out individual tasks. However, they do make decisions about the operation of a department or a business.

In contrast a work team must work together to accomplish a goal. It must coordinate its efforts constantly. Examples might be a hospital operating unit or a police SWAT team. Some businesses today organise workers into autonomous work groups. These are groups of employees with a variety of skills who carry out whole tasks, such as manufacturing a complete product. The group exercises a high level of control and makes its own decisions over the work that it carries out.

Knowledge teams

Knowledge teams can be both work teams and decision teams. They are teams of **knowledge workers** (☞ unit 19) who are collectively responsible for a product or service. Knowledge work requires employees who can:

- use their own knowledge;
- acquire new information;
- combine and process information to produce and communicate new information;
- learn continuously from their experiences.

Knowledge teams can be made up of specialist workers from a variety of areas or disciplines. The team integrates the work of the specialists. Specialists may only have a small amount of common values, information and skills, so it is important that they communicate and work together. On the other hand, teams are sometimes made up totally of specialists with skills in a particular area. These can be contacted by anyone in the organisation for information that may help to solve problems.

Examples of knowledge teams may be a team responsible for new product development, a management team made up from managers across the business that develop strategic directions (☞ unit 6) or a process improvement team that examines and makes changes to a business's work methods. The advantage of a knowledge team is that a problem can be examined from a variety of perspectives. For example, a business that is trying to cut production costs can have suggestions from finance, marketing and administration staff as well as technical staff.

It's hard enough to work as a team when you are in the same building. But what about when you are a 'virtual' team of IT developers? The task of creating an effective team was one that faced pharmaceuticals manufacturer Eli Lilly. The 15 strong team was split between a main site in Germany and two smaller sites in Berlin and London. The team had a shared professional background. But there were still problems when e-mail was used to send messages between members of the group. Task co-ordination also became a problem as new members arrived. As role boundaries were not clearly defined, and with the added problem of distance, people were often uncertain about what they should be doing. Some tasks fell into the 'cracks' because someone thought that someone else was doing them.

So what was the solution? The team responded by clarifying roles. Team building events also helped to cement working relationships between team members. Communication was often a bit impersonal, especially between countries. The team building events were held three times a year. They included workshops and team meetings as well as fun activities such as go-karting. Afterwards, telephone conversations included a social chat as well as information and people felt that they belonged to a team.

External communications proved a little harder to solve. Eventually the company sent two German software developers to the UK to learn how things were done there. The software was also upgraded to solve technical problems.

Source: adapted from *People Management*, 8.4.2004.

(a) Explain the problems of team operation at Eli Lilly.
(b) Discuss appropriate solutions to these problems.

Effects of team working

The Workers Employment Relations survey of the late 1990s found that up to 65 per cent of workplaces in the UK operate team working at some level, although autonomous work groups are only found in 3 per cent of organisations. Why do businesses introduce team work?

- Team working motivates employees. Edwards and Wright (1998) and Wilkinson (1997), for example, suggest that employees in team situations tend to be more satisfied and motivated than those who are working under more traditional regimes.
- Businesses can use team work as a method to gain a competitive advantage over rivals.
- Team working appears to have a positive influence on employee commitment and identification with the business. Cotton (1993) suggested that self-directed teams have a strong effect on employee attitudes.

Teamworking is not always possible and may not work effectively, however. This may be because work cannot be redesigned for a team. Managers may also fail to implement teamwork properly. Also, certain employees may see team working as simply giving them management responsibilities without the pay or power.

Thames Water leads the water business for global utilities group RWE. It serves more than 50 million customers in more than 46 countries. The company has moved from a UK centred structure to a regional one in four geographical areas - Asia Pacific, the Americas, UK, Ireland and Europe, and the Middle East and Africa. It aims to make knowledge visible by creating knowledge sharing communities. The communities include, for example, a group of bidding professionals or a community with experts in physical and commercial losses of water, who share ideas to avoid water loss.

Members of the team agree the scope and mission of the group. Electronic 'tea rooms' then allow them to share information with others across the world. The communities are self-organising and responsible for how often they should meet and what business issues to focus on. This collaborative way of working has led to some significant benefits, with solutions being developed in one area of the world being used in other areas.

Source: adapted from *People Management*, 6.2.2003.

(a) Explain why the communities at RWE might be examples of knowledge teams.
(b) Examine the effects on the business of these teams.

Question 5

key terms

Formal groups - groups specifically set up by a business to carry out tasks. They have certain formal rules of behaviour.
Group norm - the usual characteristics of behaviour of a group.
Informal groups - groups made up of individuals in business with similar interests. They are not part of the formal business organisation.
Team building - the process designed to improve the effectiveness and motivation of people working together in groups.

Knowledge

1. 'Group behaviour is different from individual behaviour.' To what extent is this statement likely to be true in business?
2. State 4 common features that groups in business organisations have.
3. Why might a business set up a temporary formal group rather than making it permanent?
4. Give 4 advantages for employees of informal group membership.
5. Give 6 characteristics of effective groups.
6. Briefly explain why optimal group size may be between 3-7 members.
7. What is likely to influence the size of a group?
8. Explain the difference between centralised and decentralised group decision making.
9. What are the advantages to the business of group decision making?
10. In what circumstances might individual decision making be more beneficial to a business?
11. What factors within a business might lead to inter-group conflict?
12. What are knowledge teams?

Case study Tyler Farndon

Sunita Shah is head of human resources at Tyler Farndon, a manufacturer of mobility products for older people and the disabled. When she says 'the future of the business is too important to be left to management alone' both Nick Gregson, the union official, and Gail Anne Knight, the executive director, agree. The business aims to take the thoughts of its mission statement to provide 'excellent products, ethically produced' into the workplace in as many ways as possible.

Sunita, Nick and Gail meet on the works council set up in 2000. Part of their discussions involve the progress of the 'Working together, working better' strategy that the business implemented in an attempt to make sure the employee voice at the organisation was being heard. It is an ambitious project, combining flexible work patterns with elements of a single status organisation, where all employees have the same terms and conditions whether they are union members or not. Staff also receive the same annual wage rises, and a bonus if the business is doing well.

The works council has 20 members. It discusses a number of areas, including production, changes in organisation and the development of the business in future. Decisions made by the council are often accepted by employees in the business as they feel that they have been represented in discussions.

Recently the business has been approached by another company and the possibility of a merger has arisen with a business which specialises in artificial limbs. However, employees feel that the business is doing well and should carry on growing organically. A further option is to transfer some production to an outsourced business and expand into this area itself. Whichever route is taken, the business feels that it would have to be agreed by employees and employers for it to work effectively.

Sunita regularly meets with other departmental managers of the business to review the human resources needs of their departments. The finance manager tends to take the lead in most of these meetings. He argues that the bottom line of the business must be 'to be profitable'. He will often put pressure on the other department heads to 'remain within budget'. Sunita has noticed that the head of R&D often seems to get more than other departments. She wonders whether this is because both the finance and R&D heads joined the company together. They have been with the business a long time and often attend

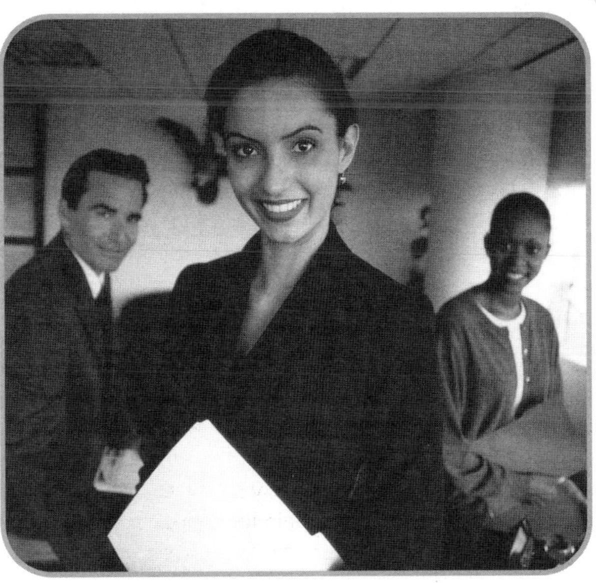

conferences where they discuss trends in the industry.

Gail will have to get any decision approved by the other shareholders in the business. Nick will also have to report any decisions back to his union members at meetings. He feels that some expansion is important. But what type? What if his members disagree and feel that some form of industrial action is necessary? He would then need to consult the head office of the union about procedures. Nick has been approached by some employees who say they have heard that any merger is likely to involve redundancy because of the duplication of skills. They thought that everyone was the same at the business, but now managers seemed to be fighting for a strategy which would benefit them.

(a) Identify examples of (i) formal and (ii) informal groups suggested in the article. (6 marks)

(b) Explain how formal and informal groups have influenced communication at the business. (10 marks)

(c) Suggest benefits of team operation and group decision making at the business. (10 marks)

(d) Examine potential areas of conflict between members of groups in the business. (12 marks)

(e) To what extent do you think that the operation of groups and teams is effective at the business? (12 marks)

21 Representation at Work

How are groups represented?

There are many different organisations which represent employees and employers in business. Although they are not part of actual businesses themselves, they influence how firms operate.

Trade unions These are perhaps the best known of the representative bodies. A TRADE UNION is an organisation of workers who join together to further their own interests. Trade unions have existed in the UK for over 200 years. Early unions were made up of workers with similar skills and interests, for example the General Union of Operative Spinners set up in 1829.

What features are trade unions likely to have? It is likely that a trade union would:

- register itself as a union;
- become affiliated to the Trades Union Congress (although not all do);
- be independent of employers in negotiations;
- regard collective bargaining (☞ unit 22) and the protection of its members' interests as its main functions;
- be prepared to use industrial action (☞ unit 23) to further its members' interests if agreement cannot be reached with employers or through bodies such as ACAS (☞ unit 22).

There are different unions affiliated to the TUC in the UK.

- Large trade unions representing many workers. For example, UNISON the UK's largest union with over 1.3 million members represents public sector workers. AMICUS has over 1 million members in industries such as energy, construction, IT, chemicals and pharmaceuticals, shipbuilding, electronics and telecommunications, food and drink, textiles and paper.
- Unions which have members belonging to a particular business, such as the Nationwide Group Staff Union with over 11,000 members.
- Unions with members mainly from one industry, such as the National Union of Rail, Maritime and Transport Workers (RMT) with around 60,000 members and the Ceramic and Allied Trades Union (CATU).
- Organisations which represent particular occupations and skills. Examples include the Bakers, Food and Allied Workers Union (BFAWU) with around 29,000 members and the General Union of Loom Overlookers with less than 300 members.

Staff associations Staff associations represent workers, but tend to perform only some of those functions carried out by trade unions. These might include consultation and bargaining with management. Their members are often made up of workers in a particular business. Examples of staff associations are the Retail Book, Stationery and Allied Trades Employees Association (RBA) or the Balfour Beatty Group Staff Association. In some cases staff associations develop into trade unions. For example, Unifi, the finance sector union, is made up from members of the Banking, Insurance and Finance Union (BIFU) and the NatWest Staff Association (NWSA). Some associations are affiliated to the TUC, such as the Guinness Staff Association.

Professional associations Professional associations perform similar functions to trade unions and are sometimes become TUC members. They represent 'professional' occupations. Examples include the British Dental Association with its 20,000 members, the Prison Officers (POA) Association with around 39,000 members, the Scottish Police Federation with around 15,000 members, and the Professional Footballers' Association with over 3,000 members. Some associations, such as the British Medical Association (BMA), represent their members in collective bargaining with employers. They are also responsible for the setting and maintaining of standards. For example, the BMA insists on certain qualifications before admitting employees to its membership. For this reason professional associations tend to be associated with 'white collar' workers and higher paid groups of employees.

Employers' organisations Just as certain bodies represent workers, there are organisations which help and support employers. They are often useful for small firms that may be negotiating with a large union. These organisations give advice to employers about collective bargaining and help with technical problems and overseas trade. They may also provide research and training facilities and act as a pressure group for industries. Examples include the Newspaper Society (NS) and the Engineering Employers' Federation (EEF).

All of the groups mentioned above will aim to protect or further their members' interests. The rest of this unit will concentrate mainly on the role of trade unions, although many of the points dealt with apply to other representative bodies.

The functions of trade unions

What is the role of a union in a business situation? Unions are an example of a representative body that aims to further its members' interests. It could be argued that this includes some of the following.

- Obtaining satisfactory rates of pay.
- Securing adequate work facilities.
- Ensuring satisfactory work conditions, such as the number of hours worked or the number of breaks in any period of work.

- Negotiating bonuses for achieving targets.
- Obtaining job security for members.
- Negotiating employment conditions, such as contracts of employment or rights relating to redundancy and dismissal.
- Negotiating grievance procedures.
- Negotiating job descriptions and job specifications.

Trade unions are responsible for **collective bargaining** in the workplace. They bargain on behalf of their total membership with employers and attempt to obtain the best possible conditions. It is argued that unions are in a far better position to negotiate with management than an individual employee, who will have little bargaining 'power'.

Trade unions are also responsible, along with management, for **industrial relations**. They communicate their members' wishes to employers and try to negotiate the most favourable conditions. However, successful industrial relations means that each party must take into account the wishes of the other when bargaining. It may not be in members' interests for a union to push for a longer work break if this reduces the efficiency of the business, perhaps resulting in job losses in future. However, it may not be in employers' interests to reduce breaks, even if this cuts costs, if it results in worker dissatisfaction.

The ability of trade unions to carry out these functions may depend on the union membership and UNION DENSITY. A small union, with few members, is unlikely to have as much influence as AMICUS with its 1 million plus members. Union density is expressed as:

$$\frac{\text{actual union membership}}{\text{potential union membership}} \times 100$$

If unions only represent a small percentage of all workers in an industry, they might be less likely to have influence. Figure 21.1 shows union densities in various industries in the UK. It shows that in industries such as public administration union density is high, at over 60 per cent. In the hotel trade it is only 6 per cent. This might suggest that union influence is weak in this industry.

Figure 21.1 *Union density by industry*

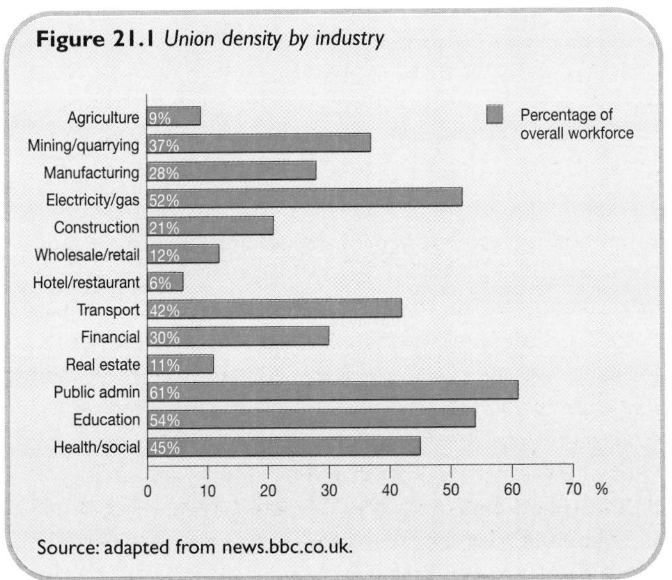

Source: adapted from news.bbc.co.uk.

USP is a parcel delivery firm. When it first entered the UK market in 1992 by taking over Carryfast, the UK's largest private parcel delivery business, it only negotiated with T&G union reps at depots, not at national level. In 1997 the company agreed to bargain nationally with representatives of its 2,100 drivers and loaders and to give the union the right to appoint shop stewards who would then negotiate on local issues. The human resources director of USP said that the business wanted to adopt a national set of terms and conditions, which was agreed with the T&G in 1996. The 1997 agreement merely formalised the arrangement.

In 2000 USP signed a three year agreement on pay and conditions. This would help employees to know where they were in the longer term and USP to budget for improvements in terms and conditions, including a union request for a reduction in the working week.

Source: adapted from *People Management*, 13.9.2001.

(a) Identify the functions of the T&G at USP mentioned in the article.
(b) Discuss to what extent changes in the negotiating process at USP might affect the ability of the T&G to carry out its functions.

Question 1

Types of union

There is a number of ways in which unions can be classified. The most common method is to place unions into one of three categories.

- Craft unions are the oldest type of union, developed directly from traditional crafts. Workers with common skills often joined together to form unions. Examples today might be the Musicians Union (MU) or the Bakers, Food and Allied Workers Union (BFAWU).
- Industrial unions. In the past a number of unions have been formed by employees of particular industries, such as coalminers, railway or gas workers. An example of an industrial union is the National Union of Mineworkers (NUM). It is made up of employees with different skills in the mining industry.
- General unions. These unions are made up of workers with a wide range of skills in many different industries. Examples today might be AMICUS, the Union of Shop, Distributive and Allied Workers (USDAW) and the Transport and General Workers Union (T&G).

Although this division appears straightforward, it does have problems.

- It forces unions into one category, whereas many unions

often have features common to all classes.

- Very few unions actually fall into the 'craft' category.
- Mergers of unions in recent years have blurred many of these distinctions. This is dealt with later in this unit.

Another way of dividing unions might be into those with more **open** and those with **restricted** recruitment policies. Those with restricted recruitment policies may recruit their membership from employees with certain skills. For example, only musicians tend to join the Musician's Union. Some unions recruit mainly from specific industries, occupations or businesses. Examples might be the National Union of Lock and Metal Workers (NULMW) and the Community and Youth Workers Union (CYWU). This can mean that their membership expands and contracts according to the changing levels of human resource needs in the industry.

More open membership policies tend to be associated with the larger unions. They often seek membership regardless of their members' jobs or industries, such as the T&G, or recruit from a wide variety of related or unrelated industries, such as UNISON, which recruits from public services industries. Such unions organise themselves to deal with different membership needs. This can sometimes lead to conflict, as unions are accused of 'poaching' members from other areas. Many of the larger unions have been formed by the merger of smaller unions with more restricted membership.

Unions and pay

One criticism often made of unions is that if they negotiate very high wage increases, this can lead to redundancies. Unions can force up wages by:

- negotiating a minimum wage;
- restricting the supply of workers.

In a free market for labour, it is argued that a business can only pay for these higher wages and maintain profits by making workers unemployed.

Against this it could be argued that:

- if there is an increase in productivity by employees, this should pay for higher wages, without the need for job losses;
- other countries have similar unit costs of production to the UK, and pay skilled workers relatively high wages, and yet have not had such high unemployment rates;
- there is evidence in the UK that unemployment still exists even if wages are held down or cut.

Trade unions and legislation

Much of the legislation that existed in the UK in the 1980s and the early 1990s was the result of the then Conservative government's view of unions. It believed that:

- trade union power was becoming excessive, particularly in wage negotiations;
- unions were often disruptive in preventing changing work practices or the introduction of new machinery;
- unions were increasingly creating industrial stoppages;
- unofficial picketing was disrupting business;
- SHOP STEWARDS were disrupting industry by calling unofficial strikes - strikes not supported by the unions (sometimes called 'wildcat strikes');
- there was undemocratic decision making within unions, especially about industrial action;
- closed shops restricted the rights of employees not to belong to a union;

and that these factors were harming the efficiency of British industry and its ability to compete. Others have argued that it is not trade union power that has made British business uncompetitive, but a lack of good management and poor levels of education and training within the workforce. They suggest that union legislation does not address the long standing issues of UK businesses - the lack of capital investment and the 'laissez-faire' approach of management.

The Labour government, elected in 1997, signed the **European Social Chapter**. This meant that employees were to be given new rights in the workplace. Businesses would also have to take into account new regulations and legislation on working practices and union activities. The government believed that a greater 'partnership' with more cooperation between business and unions would develop. This would involve more union consultation and unity in the workplace.

The effects of legislation

Trade union activities in the UK are regulated by legislation. This is COLLECTIVE LABOUR LAW as opposed to the **individual labour law** relating to individual employees' work conditions.

Legislation between 1980-96 was designed to restrict union power, give employees choice and protect employers. After 1997 some of the legislation remained. But new legislation was introduced to comply with EU regulations. This legislation aimed to give employees greater workplace protection and encourage participation between unions and business. Legislation has focused on a number of areas.

Legal immunity Certain Acts have dealt with whether unions can be sued by a business or individuals as a result of damages caused by their actions. The **1982 Employment Act** made unions liable for any action that was not in 'furtherance' of an industrial dispute. Employers were also able to obtain injunctions. Injunctions are court orders which prevent unions taking action whilst a hearing is taking place. The injunction might be granted if a judge felt a business would suffer if the action continued. The **1990 Employment Act** made unions liable for action induced by any union official, unless written repudiation (a refusal to acknowledge or a disowning) is sent to all members.

Picketing PICKETING involves the rights of workers on strike to assemble and persuade others to help or join them. **Official pickets** (those nominated by unions) can stand outside a workplace to inform the public, employees, suppliers and managers that a strike is taking place. SECONDARY PICKETING involves the picketing of a business by strikers or union members who may be involved in a dispute, but not employed at the location being picketed. The **1990 Employment Act** made all secondary action unlawful.

The closed shop A CLOSED SHOP (or union membership agreement) is an agreement between an employer and a trade union that makes it a condition of employment for each employee to be a member of that trade union. It could be argued that such a union membership agreement is useful as it allows a union to represent all employees. This removes the possibility of conflict or bad feeling between members of the union and non-members. However, a closed shop may make employees join a union against their will. Although earlier Acts allowed closed shops to exist under certain conditions, the **1990 Employment Act** made it unlawful to refuse to employ a non-union member. This effectively prevented closed shops being operated.

Members', businesses' and consumers' rights Certain legislation has been passed to make the unions more democratic and to protect the rights of workers belonging to unions. The **1984 Trade Union Act**, for example, forced unions to conduct secret ballots before industrial action took place if action was to be legal. The **1988 Employment Act** gave union members the right not to strike if they wished.

The **1993 Trade Union Reform and Employment Rights Act** further attempted to support employees' and consumers' rights and protect business from union action with the following measures.

- The right for workers to have a postal ballot on union action and the right not to have union subscriptions deducted without consent.
- The right for workers not to be expelled or excluded from a union other than for certain reasons, such as not belonging to a certain trade as stated in union rules.
- The right for employers to have 7 days' notice of industrial action.
- The right for people deprived of goods or services by industrial action to take action to prevent it happening.

The **Employment Act 2002** introduced a new right for trade union representatives to have paid time off for training to carry out their duties.

Trade union recognition The **Employment Relations Act, 1999** set out a process to enable employees to have a trade union recognised by their employer. The government wanted to encourage voluntary agreement between employers and employees. However, a legal process was set in place in case of disagreement. In some cases trade unions would be automatically recognised. In others, a ballot would take place. In these cases, for a union to be recognised it must win a majority of the ballot and get a 'yes' vote from at least 40 per cent of those eligible to vote. The Act also made it unlawful for dismissal on grounds of trade union membership or union action and gave a right of complaint if dismissal took place.

In 2003 workers at The Telegraph Group, one of Britain's most conservative newspaper publishers, voted for union recognition. In a ballot, 91 per cent of those who voted, 55.5 per cent of all journalists on *The Daily Telegraph*, *The Sunday Telegraph* and *The Spectator* gave their backing to the NUJ. It took *Telegraph* journalists more than a year to gain union recognition, for which they first applied in December 2001.

In 2004, in a ballot of staff, 83 per cent of NUJ members said they would support strike action 'if necessary'. Journalists were also asked whether they were in favour of other industrial action, such as a work to rule. 85 per cent said they were. The result is extraordinary for The Telegraph Group, given that it did not even have union representation a year before.

Source: adapted from *The Guardian*, 9.5.2003 and 11.2.2004.

(a) Examine how legislation might affect:
   (i) unions voting for recognition;
   (ii) unions voting on industrial action;
   (iii) the industrial action taken by the NUJ;
   (iv) the response of the business to the industrial action.

Question 2

The changing face of trade unions

Over the last two decades a number of important changes which have taken place have affected trade unions.

Membership and union density The numbers of members a union has and union density can influence the ability of a union to perform its functions. In 1980 there were around 12 million union members in the UK. By 1997 this had fallen to around 7.1 million, the lowest total since 1954. However, since then there has been a levelling off and even a slight increase in the number of members. In 2002 there were 7.3

Figure 21.2 *Trade union membership, 1991-2002*

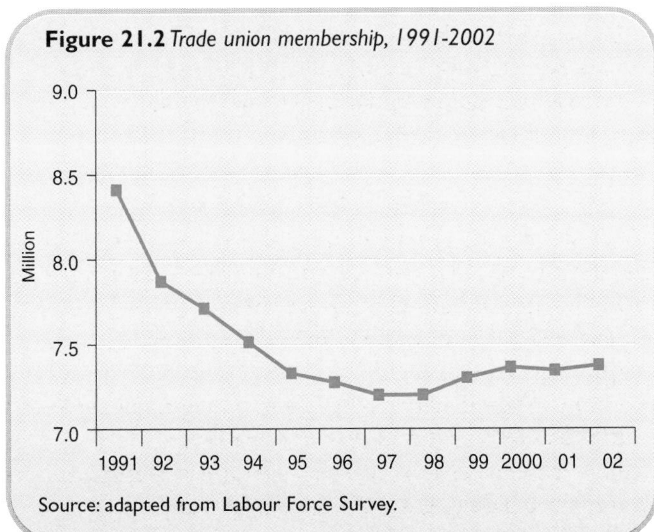

Source: adapted from Labour Force Survey.

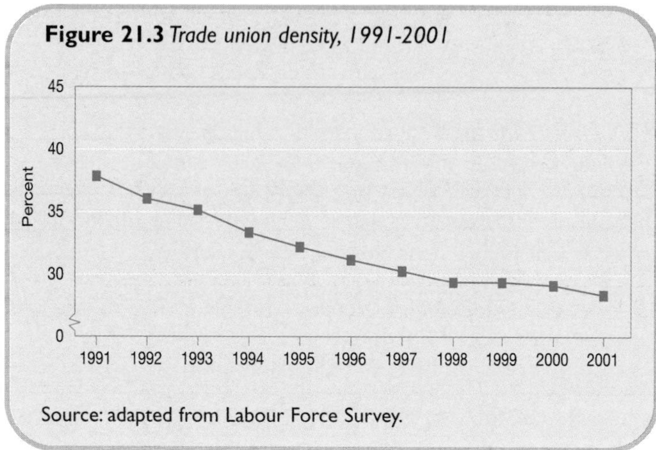

Figure 21.3 *Trade union density, 1991-2001*

Source: adapted from Labour Force Survey.

million, as shown in Figure 21.2. Union density has fallen constantly over a ten year period, from over 35 per cent in 1991 to below 30 per cent in 2001, as shown in Figure 21.3.

What factors are likely to influence union membership?

- Legislation. Acts passed in the 1980s and 1990s made it easier for employees to 'opt out' of union membership. Restrictions on union activity and influence may also have affected workers' willingness to join a union. After the year 2000, the encouragement of union participation in business and the growth of legislation to protect workers' rights, such as the minimum wage or the length of the working week, may have persuaded workers to join unions. European Union legislation to protect workers' rights, with which the UK has to comply as a member, may also have encouraged workers to join unions.
- The economy. It is argued that in periods of recession and high unemployment union membership falls, as people become unemployed and allow their membership to lapse. The opposite should be true in periods of growth. The recession in the early 1990s may have contributed to the fall in membership. It has been suggested that when the economy grew in the mid-1990s unemployment was slow to fall, so membership may not have risen as a result. In periods of inflation, people may join unions to protect their living standards. They hope that unions can negotiate higher wages to keep pace with inflation. The relatively low rates of inflation in the UK in the 1990s perhaps made it less important for employees to join a union.
- Economic, technological and labour market changes. Certain industries in the UK, such as shipbuilding and steel, have declined over a number of years. Workers in these and other manufacturing industries have tended to belong to unions. Their decline may have led to a fall in membership. Other industries, particularly in the service sector, have grown relatively. This may mean that individual unions may have seen their membership grow.
- Union amalgamation. When unions join together, the new union has the combined membership of the smaller unions that existed previously. Sometimes new, larger unions may gain membership because of the greater benefits offered to workers.
- It could be argued that the growth of smaller independent businesses has affected union membership. Many employ less than 10 workers and are not affected by some employee protection legislation. Such employees are less likely to belong to unions.
- The growing use of flexible workers (☞ unit 24). Businesses have tended in recent years to develop a flexible workforce made up of part time workers, temporary staff or teleworkers. These workers have been less likely to be covered by employee legislation. They may also feel that the costs and time involved in joining a union are of little benefit, so fewer tend to be union members.
- Participation. The growth of business/union partnerships may encourage workers to join unions to be more involved in business decisions.
- There has been a fall in **collective bargaining agreements** (☞ unit 22), where unions agree deals for numbers of workers in an industry. More deals have been agreed between the individual employee and management based on the contract of employment. This may have discouraged membership. However, any rise in collective agreements may lead to increasing membership.
- Privatisation. The privatisation of the transport and power industries (eg rail and gas) may have affected membership. These unions tended to have large numbers of union members and strong union representation. Splitting them after privatisation is likely to have reduced union influence and may have led to a fall in membership.
- It has been suggested that non-TUC affiliated unions, such as The Royal College of Nursing and the National Association of Head Teachers, have seen their membership grow. One reason for this may have been fear of redundancy in health and education sectors.
- Leadership. Dynamic leaders that are seen by potential members as furthering their interests may encourage them to join a union.
- Demographic trends. The UK faces a 'demographic timebomb' with falling numbers of school leavers and an ageing population. This may mean that fewer new recruits will be available as union members. However, this might be offset to some extent by women returning to work in greater numbers.

Trade union influence There is a number of factors that might affect the ability of a union to influence businesses for the benefit of their members.

- Membership. As discussed above, union membership and union density can affect a union's power.
- Government legislation. Government legislation between 1980-96 limited the ability of unions to take industrial action (☞ unit 23). Since the **Employment Relations Act, 1999**, union influence may have been greater in a number of areas. Employees were entitled to union representation at disciplinary or grievance cases. The government proposed that employers had to consult with unions on

redundancies or pay penalties, and on training. Many businesses as a result of signing the Social Chapter of the EU were setting up European works councils to negotiate with workers (☞ unit 22).

- Public opinion. Union action is likely to be more effective if there is support from the public. If unions are shown as disruptive in the media or if they affect customers, for example by transport strikes, they may lose support. An example of public support between 1995-98 was for dockers locked out of the Liverpool docks for refusing to cross a picket line. Sports people wore T-shirts on television and fundraising took place in theatres and from concerts.
- Managers', employers', unions employees' attitude. The views of the different stakeholders in the business might affect union influence. Managers and employers who are hostile to unions might isolate them them from decision making, apart from those decisions which are required by law. Unions that regard management as hostile might take action, which may or may not be successful. However, some businesses have owners and unions which work together to benefit both employers and employees. In this case, unions may be regarded as important to the future of the business and be consulted over key decisions.
- Organisation. When unions are well organised and have a clear objective they can still be effective in influencing businesses.
- Competition and the need for investment can affect the influence of unions. Businesses that need to attract investment from abroad or face stiff competition may be more prepared to work with unions to become more efficient. On the other hand, they may be hostile to unions and their wage demands in an attempt to reduce costs.
- The economic and political climate. In periods of low inflation unions are less likely to be able to argue that wages need to increase to keep pace with rising prices. Low inflation since 2000 has perhaps been reflected in low wage settlements.

Non-union businesses, union recognition and derecognition In the UK **non-union** firms may be small, private sector businesses. Exceptions in the 1990s were Marks & Spencer and the John Lewis Partnership. There was a trend in that period for union **derecognition**. This is where a businesses refuses to negotiate with certain unions over workers' conditions. If only one union is recognised, it avoids problems of many different pay negotiations for a business. It means that restrictions placed on a business by many different unions are reduced. If a business does not recognise any union, this allows negotiations with individuals, which may be more flexible. The proportion of UK businesses recognising unions fell from 66 per cent to 44 per cent in the period 1984-97.

In 2001 the TUC reported that over 500 union recognition deals were signed.One of the reasons for greater recognition was in response to the **Employment Relations Act, 1999,**

Figure 21.4 *Number of trade unions, 1981-1999*

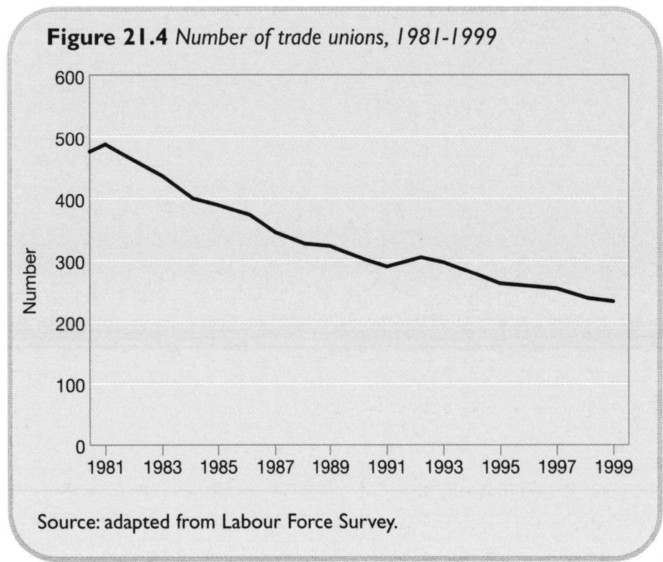

Source: adapted from Labour Force Survey.

which encouraged union recognition and partnership with business, and increased workers' rights. The Central Arbitration Committee (CAC) (☞ unit 22) was given a key role in union recognition. Where workers have voted for union recognition, but the employer or union has not followed the correct procedure, either party could go to the CAC to enforce the recognition agreement.

Mergers Figure 21.4 shows that the number of trade unions in the UK has fallen since 1981. There were nearly 500 unions in the 1980s. By the year 2000 there were below 250. In 1993 the public services unions NALGO, NUPE and COHSE merged to form today's largest union UNISON, with around 1.3 million members. In 1999 the finance sector union Unifi was created from a merger of three unions, BIFU, Unifi and the NatWest Staff Association.

Why do unions merge? The fall in membership in some unions may have led to mergers. However, some unions have joined to become larger bodies which represent more workers in an industry. This would then place them in a far stronger bargaining position with employers. These larger unions will also have more finance to offer the range of services that today's members demand. This is dealt with in the next section.

The changing role of trade unions

It could be argued that the 'traditional' role of unions has changed. A number of new practices have become part of union activities.

Single union and no strike agreements Some businesses have negotiated single union and no strike (or strike free) agreements with unions. Single union agreements enable a business to recognise and negotiate with one union over pay and conditions. A union may agree not to strike in return for wage increases, improved conditions or limited redundancies.

Michael Leahy,
General Secretary of ISTC-The Community Union

'... Steel communities and knitwear and footwear communities have faced similar problems as a result of the industries on which they were founded reducing employment opportunities, and, in some cases, closing completely, in consequence of technological changes and competition from developing countries. The ISTC has responded by investing in our communities, building learning centres to help people re-skill and gain education in order to help them cope with industrial change, and by offering the benefits of trade unionism to those who work in non-unionised workplaces. I know that KFAT share that same commitment and our vision to provide a new style of trade unionism for the 21st Century. I believe that this merger is in the interest of both unions' current members and also of those potential members in the community.'

Paul Gates, General Secretary of KFAT

'Like the ISTC, KFAT is committed to revitalising the communities in which its members live and I believe that we will be better able to do this as part of a union that remains close to its members, but yet has greater resources to be able to develop this wider policy. The new union will have the financial and organisational strength to play a positive role in supporting the members of the ISTC and KFAT in their industrial base, but also to provide the benefits of a newly focused trade union philosophy which will give greater access to training and education and lifelong development beyond the workplace. During our discussions with the ISTC it has been clear that both unions share the same ideas and values such as the development of partnership where possible, but not being afraid of supporting our members in the face of adversarial employers, and the need for trade unions to be supportive of their members in developing a community philosophy. I am truly excited by the prospect of a new union which will be able to punch above its weight and play a constructive role both in the workplace and society at large.'

In January 2004 ISTC -The Community Union and the National Union of Knitwear, Footwear and Apparel Trades (KFAT) voted in favour of a merger between the unions subject to members' approval. The new union would have a membership of approximately 45,000. ISTC represents a variety of workers in current and former steel and metal communities. KFAT represents members in the textiles, footwear, lace, leather and other apparel goods industries. The new union aimed to have a new philosophy - 'supporting people throughout their working lives, not just in the workplace, but whilst seeking work and through education, training and career development programmes, in order to play its part in revitalising these communities'.

Source: adapted from www.istc-tu.org.

(a) Examine the reasons for the possible merger of the unions.

The first such agreement was by Toshiba in 1981. There are certain features of these agreements that benefit employers.

- Single union recognition. This reduces the time, complexity, conflict and administration costs of negotiation.
- Single job status for 'white' (non-manual) and 'blue' (manual) collar workers. This removes differentials in salaries, conditions, uniforms, car parking etc.
- Job flexibility. For example, this may mean workers agreeing to annualised hours rather than a fixed number of hours a week. Job flexibility is dealt with in detail in unit 24.
- Union acceptance of training or retraining of employees. This improves the flexibility and the quality of the workforce.
- The use of negotiation or arbitration rather than industrial action. This prevents damaging strikes, for example, taking place.

There may be problems with such deals. In 1998 the AEEU signed a single union agreement with British Airways' budget airline at the time Go! This created tension as the main air transport union, the T&G, had also been recruiting among the 180 staff and would be excluded from negotiations by the deal.

Business and union partnerships There has been growing evidence of businesses and unions working together in **partnership**. Although employers and unions have different interests at times, they work together to achieve common goals. The main attraction is that unions have a 'stake' in the business. Businesses benefit because unions help support improvements and improve competitiveness. Unions benefit because they are able to influence the business in areas such as job security and training. It is suggested that partnership companies have a competitive edge in terms of profit, sales, productivity and employment relations.

Examples of partnerships have included:

- an agreement between Tesco and USDAW, the shop workers union, which allows consultation through workplace, regional and national forums and improved facilities for recruitment;
- an agreement between cement manufacturer Blue Circle and three unions including the T&G in which job security was agreed in return for steps towards harmonisation of conditions;
- an agreement between unions and management on new working practices at Rover kept the firm in business;
- the learning centre developed by the GMB and BICC cable company, where workers got up to three hours extra pay a week for brushing up on communication or IT skills.

An agreement between the MSF (which became part of AMICUS) and Legal and General identified a number of features which they felt were important for the success of any partnership.

- A tradition of stable industrial relations.
- A campaigning and socially aware union.
- Well trained and committed union representatives.

- A union with regular 'people friendly communications' in the workplace and recruitment that is supported by management.
- Management and unions taking time and effort to make it work.
- A desire on both sides to listen to each other.
- Recognising that both sides win by the partnership's success.

However, some have criticised partnerships in business and suggest a number of factors could lead to the end of the partnership. Faced with difficulties, unions and business may not be as committed to the partnership as they were at the start. They may also 'see' the partnership differently, so that there is conflict over decisions. The gains from the partnership may also be too one sided. Unions may also be cut out from key decisions and managers may prefer to communicate directly with employees.

Negotiations The nature of negotiated agreements between unions and employers has changed in recent years. Unions are far more likely to negotiate on aspects other than pay. These may include facilities for women members or for older or disabled workers, reflecting the changing nature of the workforce.

The 1990s saw a number of agreements:

- at plant or local level rather than national level to take into account the needs of a particular business activity (mainly in the private manufacturing sector);
- over a larger fixed period, so that a business has knowledge of its future costs and can build these into its budgets.

The number workers covered by collective bargaining agreements, where unions agree deals for workers in an industry, fell from 71 per cent in 1984 to just 35 per cent in 2002 (☞ unit 22). This has meant that more agreements have taken place without unions being involved.

Services Unions increasingly offer a wide range of services to employees. These may include:

- insurance schemes;
- pension schemes;
- financial and legal advice;
- discounts on travel and goods;
- education courses;
- mortgage discounts;
- welfare and sickness benefits.

The TUC

The Trades Union Congress (TUC) is an organisation which represents all major trade unions in the UK. In 2003, its 71 affiliated unions had nearly 7 million members. There were also around 180 unions outside the TUC.

Each year a conference is held and TUC policy is decided. Member unions send delegates to the conference, the number sent depending on the size of the union. The conference also elects the General Council of the TUC. This is responsible for carrying out policy and running TUC affairs in between conferences. A General Secretary is elected, who is often seen as the mouthpiece of the TUC and is directly involved in TUC negotiations with member unions and government. The TUC has a permanent staff which deals with the day to day issues in between the annual Congress.

In the 1980s and early 1990s the TUC was excluded from consultation by government. Since the mid-1990s, however, it has been involved in a number of new initiatives. For example, it has worked with government and the CBI to encourage **partnerships** in business.

In 2004 the main functions of the TUC were to:

- bring Britain's unions together to draw up common policies and avoid clashes with each other;
- lobby government to implement policies that will benefit people at work;
- campaign on economic and social issues;
- represent working people on public bodies and British workers in international bodies in the European Union and the International Labour Organisation;
- carry out research on employment related issues;
- run training and education programmes for union representatives;
- help unions develop new services for their members;
- build links with other trade union bodies worldwide.

In 2002 Amicus, the manufacturing union, refused to sign a draft no-strike agreement with Honda in an attempt to take a tougher industrial relations approach. The union was concerned that the agreement specified binding arbitration to solve disputes and that this would rule out strike action. Derek Simpson, joint general secretary of Amicus, said 'The Honda agreement as it stands is an offspring of agreements done in the 1980s and 1990s' and had 'no place modern industrial relations.' 'Most companies recognise that productive partnerships are based on mutual respect and the right, if necessary, to take industrial action when procedures are exhausted.' Mr Simpson said that under him the union would not seek single union agreements behind the backs of other unions. Supporters of Mr Simpson say that Honda refused to recognise a union until workers used employment legislation to win a legally binding agreement. However, critics argue that workers are worried about the implications of threatening strike action, claiming it will alienate workers and undermine the union's position to represent workers.

Source: adapted from *The Guardian*, 21.9.2002.

(a) Identify the different union practices mentioned in the article.
(b) Examine the reasons for the changing industrial relations approach of Amicus.
(c) Discuss the extent to which Amicus is likely to be successful in its new approach.

The CBI

The Confederation of British Industry (CBI) was formed in 1965. It has a similar role to the TUC, but voices the opinions of employers rather than union members. CBI membership is drawn from private sector industry, service and commercial enterprises, major public sector employers, and some employers' associations, trade associations and Chambers of Commerce.

The internal organisation of the CBI is complex, but it has a ruling council which decides on policy. It also employs permanent staff, headed by the Director General. Detailed policy proposals are examined by standing committees. The CBI is organised to deal with local and area issues through its regional councils. These aim to keep in touch with the needs of small firms and local employers and help them solve their day to day business problems. The membership services of the CBI are wide ranging, both nationally and locally, and are backed up by skilled professional advice from lawyers, accountants and tax specialists.

What role does the CBI have? It attempts to represent its members' interests in a number of ways.

- Government policy. Just like the TUC, it attempts to influence government policy.
- Services. It provides legal, financial and economic advice to its members.
- Local businesses. It provides support and advice to local businesses through its regional offices.
- Through its office in Brussels, the CBI acts in the interests of British industry in the European Union.
- Trade unions. The CBI works with the TUC on consultative bodies such as ACAS (☞ unit 22).
- Other groups. The CBI provides information for a variety of other organisations and the public in general.

key terms

Closed shop - a practice which prevents workers from being employed in a business unless they belong to a trade union.
Collective labour law - legislation which affects the rights and conditions workers operating together, ie in pay negotiations, with outcomes which affect all workers involved in the same way.
Picketing - involves the rights of workers on strike to assemble and persuade others to help or join them.
Secondary picketing - where union members from one place of work picket an unrelated place of work.
Shop steward - an elected union official who represents workers' interests in the place in which the shop steward works.
Trade union - an organisation of workers that join together to further their own interests.
Union density - the actual membership of a trade union as a percentage of the total possible membership.

Knowledge

1. Explain the difference between a trade union and an employers' organisation.
2. State 6 functions of trade unions.
3. Why are good industrial relations important to a business?
4. What is meant by an 'open' union recruitment policy?
5. Explain 3 reasons why union legislation has taken place.
6. Briefly discuss 3 effects that legislation has had on union activity in business.
7. State 4 factors that have contributed to changes in the organisation and role of trade unions in the UK.
8. What is meant by:
   (a) single union agreements;
   (b) no strike deals;
   (c) union recognition?
9. What are the main functions of:
   (a) the TUC;
   (b) the CBI?

Case study Eurotunnel

Eurotunnel is the operator of the high speed shuttle service which links the UK to France. It has a 99 year lease to operate the Channel Tunnel link, running freight trains and maintaining the infrastructure. It employs 3,400 people, of which about 1,400 are based in the UK on British contracts. To harmonise the workforce, management set up a company council in 1992.

Until June 2000 the company only recognised the council for consultation. But after the Employment Relations Act, 1999, it signed a recognition agreement with the T&G (Transport and General Workers Union) and a single partnership deal to cover all non-managerial employees and a joint management-union negotiating forum. The company suggested that the threat of industrial action and having to negotiate with many different unions swayed its decision, and the fact that the costs involved of action and negotiations would affect a company already £6.5 billion in debt. There were now two negotiating bodies - the council, representing all employees, and the TU forum, representing union members with sole negotiating rights over pay and conditions.

Two surveys were carried out, one just before recognition and the other 18 months after. Certain results were found.

- About 35 per cent of employees said they were union members in the second survey, but only 12 per cent in the first.
- Over 50 per cent of employees said there was an active union presence in the second survey compared to 6 per cent in the first.
- In the first survey there had been strong support for unions in all sections at Eurotunnel. Most said that unions would improve their pay and benefits (over 70 per cent), work conditions (75 per cent), health and safety, and grievances. In the second survey fewer than a third agreed that the T&G had been effective in representing employee interests and only 10 per cent said that the union had improved pay and benefits.
- Most employees wanted the council to be retained. But this was not a vote to replace the TU forum, as employees agreed the council had largely been ineffective as well.

In 2003 proposals for the EU Information and Consultation of Employees Regulations, 2005, were being discussed. They encouraged a more formal approach to information and consultation. The draft regulations would force employers to establish a framework so that requests by employees for information and consultation must be granted under certain circumstances. The regulations say that existing arrangements must cover all employees in a company. This threatens the use of single union agreements, which do not cover all employees. A further issue is that the arrangements give no automatic participation rights to union representatives, who must stand for election alongside non-union representatives. This might affect the traditional role of unions in collective bargaining.

Source: adapted from *People Management*, 11.9.2003.

(a) What is meant by the terms:
(i) the traditional role of unions in collective bargaining;
(ii) shop steward? (6 marks)

(b) Explain how the role of trade unions changed at Eurotunnel. (8 marks)

(c) Examine the reasons for these changes (12 marks).

(d) Discuss to what extent employee representation has been affected as a result of the changes at Eurotunnel. (12 marks)

(e) Assess the possible implications for employee representation at Eurotunnel in future. (12 marks)

22 Industrial Democracy, Bargaining, Consultation and Participation

Employer and employee conflict

Conflict can exist between different groups and individuals working in business. One type of conflict which may lead to major problems is between the objectives of employers and employees. Conflict between these two groups may result from a number of factors.

- Rates of pay. Employers could attempt to keep wage costs down to remain competitive, whereas unions could try to maximise employees' rewards.

In July 2003, 250 British Airways staff took part in an unofficial strike. The action was reported as costing BA £40 million. It was in reaction to the introduction of an electronic swipe-card, clocking-in system. Although some colleagues argued it was a small matter, and the public felt largely indifferent, experts suggested that the fact employees were willing to take unofficial action showed the severity of the breakdown in relations. BA staff were concerned that the system, designed to identify busy working periods, would mean the introduction of annualised hours. This could affect the flexibility of working, which staff find useful, especially to retain a balance between home and work life.

A further concern was the increasing monitoring of staff and the distrust that this suggests. Management argued that this was simply a means of turning a paper based system into an electronic one, but workers did not believe them.

It was argued that this was just the straw that broke the camel's back and unrest had been developing for some time. Unions had made concessions in the past to keep airlines in business and were less inclined to do so now. There had been a rise in disputes in other airline industries. Workers at Australian airline Quantas went on strike claiming the business failed to honour agreements to reward workers for improved productivity. Albanian Airlines' workers took strike action in support of improved working conditions. In France, Corsair employees took part in a 24 hour strike over pay.

Source: adapted from *People Management*, 7.8.2003.

(a) Examine the reasons for the sources of conflict between airlines and their employees.

Question 1

- The introduction of machinery. For example, a business may want to introduce machinery which requires workers to learn new production techniques. Employees, however, may feel that this extra responsibility is an unwanted burden.
- Flexible working (☞ unit 24). Businesses often require a more flexible workforce. A printing works might decide to operate a 24 hour shift, for example, to cope with extra work. Employees may be unwilling to work at night.
- Work conditions. Workers may feel that better canteen facilities are needed, but employers could see this as an unnecessary increase in costs.

The aim of **industrial relations** procedures (☞ unit 21) is to make sure that each party finds an acceptable solution to any conflict that may exist. Successful industrial relations should prevent the need for industrial action (☞ unit 23) by employers' or employees' groups.

Collective bargaining

COLLECTIVE BARGAINING is one way of minimising conflict in the workplace. It involves determining conditions of work and terms of employment through **negotiations** between employers and employee representatives, such as trade unions. These bodies represent the views of all their members and try to negotiate in their interests. One individual employee working for a large company would have little or no influence in setting their wages or conditions. The representative body has more strength and influence and can negotiate for its membership. Without such a bargaining process, employers and managers would be able to set wages and conditions without taking into account employees' interests.

For collective bargaining to take place:

- employees must be free to join representative bodies, such as trade unions;
- employers must recognise such bodies as representative of workers and agree to negotiate with them;
- such bodies must be independent of employers and the state;
- bodies should negotiate in good faith, in their members' interests;
- employers and employees should agree to be bound by agreements without having to use the law to enforce them.

The result of collective bargaining is a COLLECTIVE AGREEMENT. These agreements are usually written and are signed by the parties and will be binding. Collective agreements can either be **substantive agreements** or **procedural agreements**. Substantive agreements are concerned with terms and conditions of employment. They include pay, work conditions and fringe benefits. Procedural agreements set out how the parties in the bargaining should relate to each other on certain issues. They include negotiating, redundancy, dismissal, recruitment and promotion procedures.

The number of workers covered by collective agreements fell from 71 per cent in 1984 to 35 per cent in 2002. There were many reasons for this including legislation, union membership, union organisation and the type and nature of employment (☞ unit 21).

Collective bargaining is one method by which a business can achieve greater INDUSTRIAL DEMOCRACY. This is a term which is used in different contexts, but, by analogy with political democracy, generally refers to a situation where workers are entitled to a significant voice in the decisions affecting the business in which they work. This is dealt with again later in this unit.

Levels of negotiation

Negotiations can take place at a number of different levels.

International bargaining Large multinational companies (☞ unit 38) operate in many different countries. Some have considered the possibility of negotiating the same conditions for all employees in the business, no matter what country or factory they work in. This has the advantages that conditions can be standardised and workers in one country will not feel envious of those in another. The major problem of this approach is the inflexibility it causes.

National level Employers and employees may agree a deal which applies to all employees. Negotiations may take place to set wage or salary scales, or to discuss national conditions of work. For example, an agreement could be reached on the number of hours that teachers or lecturers should work a year, or their length of holidays, between teachers' unions and the government. A private sector example might be negotiations between the train union RMT and Virgin Trains over health and safety conditions.

Local level Discussions may take place at a local level, so that any settlement can reflect local conditions. An example of local negotiations might be wages or salaries based on the area of operation. From time to time the weightings given to local authority workers for working in the London or surrounding areas are revised. These weightings are added to workers' salaries to take into account the higher cost of living in the area. A locally based engineering company may negotiate with regional union representatives about the need to reduce the workforce because of falling sales. Again, this is likely to take place at local level.

Factory or plant-wide level Negotiations at factory or plant-wide level can take place over a variety of aspects of work. They may involve the personnel department, departmental managers, shop stewards and employee representatives.

Examples of matters that might be agreed upon could be:

- productivity targets;
- the introduction of new machinery;
- hours of work and flexibility within the plant;
- health and safety conditions.

Individualised bargaining Individualised bargaining is where the result of negotiations is the agreement between the employee and the employer in the contract of employment. Union representatives are not involved in negotiations. This means that the employee does not receive advice and does not have the backing of an influential group when discussing terms and conditions. However, it may mean that both sides in the negotiations have greater flexibility.

A report published by train drivers union ASLEF in 2003 argued that there was a need for a far more integrated approach to collective bargaining on the railways. The report, by Keith Ewing of the union-backed Institute of Employment Rights, suggested that such an approach would be far more in the public interest. The current system of negotiations were 'a non-cohesive and incoherent' local bargaining system, where different train operators each negotiated with employees and their representatives at local level. This had led to unacceptable pay differentials, skills shortages and poor staff morale. This in turn had led to a growing number of pay disputes. There was also a lack of procedures for dispute resolution in the current set-up. Ewing said 'It is no more sensible to run an integrated national railway system on the back of a fragmented industrial relations system than it is to run an integrated national railway on the back of a fragmented track and signalling system'.

Source: adapted from *Labour Research*, July 2003.

(a) Identify and describe the types of pay negotiations mentioned in the article.
(b) Discuss whether a change in negotiation methods would be an improvement.

The negotiation process

For negotiation to be successful in collective bargaining, an agreement must be reached which satisfies all parties. This is far more likely to be achieved if a pattern is followed during negotiation.

The agenda A meeting between all parties involved in negotiation needs an agenda. This will outline what is to be discussed and all parties must agree to it. The order of items on the agenda may influence the outcome of negotiations. If, for instance, all the employees' claims come first and all the management's points come later, then anything that is agreed at the beginning of the meeting cannot be accepted until the management side is given. An agenda that places management and employee items in alternate and logical order can make negotiations easier.

Information Both parties need 'facts' to support their arguments. Negotiators have to collect the information they need, analyse it and make sure that each member of the negotiating team has a say in its interpretation. Often managers make information about a company's financial position available to representatives before meetings. This ensures that both parties have the correct information on which to base discussions.

Strategy It is important for each side in the negotiations to prepare a strategy. This will help them to achieve their objectives. Developing a strategy could include the following stages.

- Agreeing objectives. What do negotiators seek to achieve? The objectives set by employers or unions should, if achieved, lead to improvements. For example, a change in employment rules might improve efficiency or motivation. Negative objectives that emphasise not 'losing ground' are not usually helpful.
- Allocating roles. Who will do what in the negotiations? Negotiators need specific roles. For example, there may be a chairperson to lead the discussion, someone to put the case and a specialist to provide advice. The roles of group members are discussed in unit 20.
- Predict what the other side might do. Strategies are unlikely to remain the same during negotiations. Their chances of success are improved if the negotiators have tried to predict what they will hear from the opposition. Negotiators must be prepared not only to put forward their own arguments, but also to respond to arguments put to them.

Unity Because negotiation involves different sets of interests, each team must work out a united position before negotiations begin. If the group's position changes, all members must agree. It is important that a group shows unity at all times during negotiations or its position may become weaker.

Size of the group The number of people representing each side will influence the negotiations. The larger the group the greater the problem of managing communications between group members. When asked to suggest a number, most experienced negotiators opt for three or four in each group. Meetings of fewer people may be accused of 'fixing' an outcome.

Stages of the negotiation Negotiators begin by making it clear that they are representing the interests of others. They often emphasise the strength of their case and start by saying they are unwilling to move from that position. The displays of strength are necessary to convince themselves and the 'opposition' that they are willing to fight for their position. By the time this part of the negotiations starts, both sides should be very clear on the matters that divide them. After the differences have been explored, the next stage is for negotiators to look for solutions that might be more acceptable to each party. Each party will sound out possibilities, float ideas, ask questions and make suggestions. No firm commitments are made at this stage. Negotiations are likely to be more successful if each group is willing to change its position.

Decision making The next stage is to come to some agreement. The management may make an offer.The decision about what to offer is the most difficult and important task in the whole process. The offer may be revised, but eventually it will be accepted or rejected. Agreement is usual in all but a small minority of situations. Employees do not really wish to disrupt an organisation. Even if they take strike action, they will eventually return to the firm. The management need the

Question 3

Korvac and James is a manufacturer of chemicals. It operates from a factory in Newcastle. Despite a number of years of falling sales in the 1990s, it has recently had 2 good years of orders.

This year's pay negotiations are due to take place, and the management has offered a 2 per cent pay increase, which it feels is a good offer given the need to grow in future and the current rate of inflation. The union representative at the factory thinks this is poor given the work by employees to pull the business around. He has suggested to two local union officials who will be involved in negotiations that a 6 per cent increase should be bargained for or strike action should be considered. He feels certain that the company can afford this, although no figures are yet available on this year's profits. The local officials are not so sure. They suggest that other options are available before calling for a vote on strike action. In particular, they are concerned that higher wages will result in redundancies, although they feel in a strong position to argue that increased productivity by workers will pay for any wage increases.

Another unknown factor is the likely installation of new machinery for the next year, which could lead to new grades for certain workers, but also redundancies in some areas.

(a) Write a letter from one of the union officials to the factory representative outlining the steps that should be taken and the strategy that should be adopted before they enter negotiations with management.

employees to work for them. They have to reach an agreement no matter how long it takes.

Written statement Producing a brief written statement before the negotiation has ended will make it clear what both parties have decided, if agreement has been reached.

Commitment of the parties So far, agreement has been reached between negotiators only. This is of no value unless the groups represented by the negotiators accept it and make it work.

Employee representatives have to report back to their members and persuade them to accept the agreement. Management representatives may also have to do the same thing. Once the terms have been agreed by both employees and employers, the negotiating process is complete. It is the joint responsibility of both parties to carry out and monitor the agreement.

Consultation

Negotiation, as we have seen, is an activity by which the two parties make agreements which may cover pay and conditions at work and relations between management and employees. JOINT CONSULTATION, by contrast, is the process where management representatives discuss matters of common interest with employee representatives before negotiating or making a decision. There are three types of consultation.

Pseudo-consultation Pseudo-consultation is where management makes a decision and informs employees of that decision through their representatives. Employees have no power to influence these decisions. Some have suggested that it would be more accurately described as information-giving.

Classical consultation Classical consultation is a way of involving employees, through their representatives, in discussions on matters which affect them. This allows employees to have an influence on management decisions. Unions may be involved, for example, in restructuring (☞ unit 30).

Integrative consultation Pseudo and classical consultation do not directly involve employees in decisions which affect them. Integrative consultation is a more democratic method of decision making. Arguably it is neither consultation nor negotiation. Management and unions discuss and explore matters which are of common concern, such as ways of increasing productivity or methods of changing work practices. The two groups come to a joint decision having used, in many cases, problem solving techniques. An example of an integrative approach to consultation might be the use of quality circles in a number of UK businesses and in foreign firms setting up in the UK.

The Advisory, Conciliation and Arbitration Service (ACAS)

Sometimes parties fail to reach agreements after consultation and negotiation. In these situations the Advisory, Conciliation and Arbitration Service (ACAS) can be of great value to both sides.

During the period of industrial action in the 1970s, groups of employers and employees called for the setting up of a conciliation and arbitration service, independent of government control and of civil service influence. The result was ACAS, which took up its formal duties in September 1974. ACAS is a public body funded by tax, with over 900 staff employed in 11 regional centres and a head office in London. It has a chief executive and a council made up of 12 members ranging from union members to academics. Its main role is to prevent and resolve problems in the workplace. It provides a wide range of services to employers and employees in business.

Industrial disputes ACAS has conciliation duties. It can intervene in industrial disputes (☞ unit 23) at the request of either management or unions. Its role is to try and encourage a settlement that all parties may agree to, using procedures that both parties accept. In 2003 ACAS was called in to 1,353 cases.

Arbitration and mediation Arbitration is where both parties in a dispute put forward their case to ACAS. ACAS then independently assesses each case and recommends a final decision. Mediation is where ACAS makes recommendations about a possible solution and leaves the parties to find a settlement.

Advisory work ACAS carries out advisory work with employers, trade unions and employers' associations. This can be short visits to answer specific questions or long term, in-depth, projects and surveys. The questions ACAS deal with are wide ranging and can include issues such as contracts of employment, industrial relations legislation, payment systems and personnel policies.

Codes of practice ACAS issues codes of practice. These contain practical guidance on how to improve industrial relations between employers and employees.

Enquiries ACAS has carried out enquiries into the flexible use of labour, appraisal systems, labour turnover, employee involvement, handling redundancy and the use of quality circles. Much of this research is published by ACAS as advisory booklets. Employers use them to help improve industrial relations and personnel management practices.

Individual cases ACAS investigates individual cases of unfair discrimination and unfair dismissal. The number of cases dealt with has increased from around 4,100 in 1987 to over 95,000 in 2003.

Tribunals Employment tribunals hear a wide range of employment disputes, including unfair dismissal and discrimination. ACAS operates independently from the tribunals. Its role is to offer conciliation on disputes, with the aim of settling the matter without a tribunal hearing. This is known as alternative dispute resolution (ADR). The **Employment Rights (Dispute Resolution) Act, 1998** set up an ACAS arbitration scheme designed to find other methods than the courts for solving disputes. In 2003, 77 per cent of the 96,000 complaints to tribunals went no further than the ACAS conciliation stage.

ACAS has developed its services to meet the needs of a changing industrial relations climate. While the bulk of its work continues to be conciliation, mediation and arbitration, it has steadily developed advisory and training services. ACAS has also become more involved in helping business to improve personnel and management practices. These include:

- effective recruitment and selection of employees;
- setting up and operating equal opportunities policies;
- improving communications and joint consultation;
- developing the skills of managers to help them introduce changes in work organisation.

Merseyrail had a poor history of industrial relations in the 1990s. This resulted in some well publicised stoppages and industrial action when the franchise was operated by MTL. ACAS helped set up a Committee of Enquiry into industrial relations at the company. As a result of its findings, an ACAS-led joint working group was set up. It comprised managers from the company and representatives of train worker unions such as RMT, ASLEF and TSSA. The group's task was to develop proposals that would improve industrial relations. These included awareness policies, and procedures, roles and responsibilities of industrial relations. ACAS also advised the company to bid for a Department of Trade and Industry grant to help improve employer-employee relations, including joint training. The bid was successful.

Logics Resource Services (LRS) had experienced a number of employment tribunal cases at which ACAS had provided conciliation services. The company approached ACAS to develop preventative action. This included a new handbook with discipline and grievance procedures. Once the procedures were agreed, they had to be accepted by staff who were then trained in the new procedures. Problems had occurred in the business as a result of the rapid growth of the company through mergers, which led to a variety of disciplinary systems being in place. The involvement of ACAS led to a legitimising of the new system for employer and employee. The new system resulted in a fall in enquiries regarding disciplinary matters and industrial claims, and also an improvement in employer-employee relations.

Source: adapted from ACAS report, April 2002-March 2003.

(a) Identify the services offered to companies by ACAS using examples from the article.
(b) Examine the benefits to the companies of involving ACAS in discussions.

Question 4

The Central Arbitration Committee

The **Employment Relations Act, 1998** set out a process for unions to be recognised automatically or where a majority of workers voted for it (☞ unit 21). The **Central Arbitration Committee** (CAC) is a permanent independent body responsible for union recognition. It has a number of functions.

- It judges applications relating to the statutory recognition and derecognition of trade unions when recognition or derecognition cannot be agreed voluntarily.
- It helps to determine disputes between trade unions and employers over the disclosure of information for collective bargaining.
- It handles claims and complaints regarding the establishment and operation of European works councils in Great Britain.
- It provides voluntary arbitration in industrial disputes.

Within its first two years the CAC investigated 127 cases. Union success rate in ballots is high. In 37 ballots ordered by the CAC, employees voted for union recognition in 62 per cent of cases. In the case of union recognition, the CAC would first encourage parties to settle the matter themselves. If this failed it could award recognition or the union could hold a ballot. The CAC has the power to instruct the employer to co-operate with the ballot or risk a fine.

Employee participation and industrial democracy

Employees are increasingly participating in the operation of businesses and decision making. Decision making is often more accurate and effective when those involved in carrying out instructions have a say in the decision. Many businesses today recognise the value of their employees' views and contributions when deciding on objectives and strategies. The participation of employees in business decision making can take many forms.

Autonomous work groups Autonomous working groups and cells are increasingly being used by businesses to improve performance. They are groups of employees who operate without direct supervision from superiors, making their own decisions about the allocation of tasks, selection and training of new group leaders and methods of working, for example.

Teamworking Team working is where employees work together on tasks rather than individually (☞ unit 20). Teams can take a variety of forms. There may be permanent teams that meet from time to time, such as a management team or a quality circle. They might be permanent teams that are set up and work together constantly each day, such as an autonomous production work group or cell. They might be teams set up for a specific purpose over a particular time period, such as a team to investigate a production problem or whether market research supports a new product.

It is argued that working in teams motivates workers, especially if they are empowered to make decisions. Decisions might benefit from the input of a number of people with different skills. Responsibility for tasks might be shared and productivity improved. However, there can be conflict, differences of ideas, time consuming meetings and slow decisions, which may lead to problems for a business.

Employee shareholders Employees are stakeholders of businesses. In some cases they might also be shareholders. They might own shares in the company they work for as part of an incentive scheme or they might buy shares in other companies on a stock market. Shareholders in limited companies may be able to influence the decisions that are made depending on the percentage of shares that they have. For example, in some limited companies, employee groups may own a percentage of shares and have some influence at annual general meetings.

It could be argued that greater industrial democracy, where employees have a significant say, may exist in a number of situations.

European works councils Works councils are bodies set up by businesses which allow employees and employers to consult, discuss and pass information about decisions which concern the business. In September 1996, the European Works Council Directive came into force, which was adopted in the UK in 2000. It obliges multinational companies operating across the EU to set up groups and forums to inform and consult with employees, known as EUROPEAN WORKS COUNCILS (EWC).

Any company can set up a works council. But EWCs must be set up in companies that employ at least 1,000 workers in Europe and have at least 150 employees in each of at least two member states. Even before 2000, many multinationals in the UK had to set up EWCs because the number of their employees elsewhere in Europe took them over the threshold. Most of these companies included their UK employees as a matter of good business.

Special negotiating bodies are set up to determine the scope, functions and make-up of the EWC. Typically EWCs negotiate in areas of the business such as business structure, the economic and financial position, development, production and sales, employment, organisational change, mergers, cutbacks, closure and collective redundancies.

Research has indicated that councils have a number of benefits for businesses including:
- increased trust between managers and employees;
- greater employee involvement;
- a better understanding by employees of the factors affecting management decisions;
- helping to build a positive corporate culture;
- showing a company's concern for its employees.

It was argued in 2003 that EWCs should be reformed. It was likely that any future reform could change the thresholds for qualification and improve the procedures for their setting up and operation. For example, a greater emphasis might be given to the need to train members of the councils.

Employee owned businesses Some businesses are owned by their employees. These include worker co-operatives and democratic employee owned organisations. The employees of the business will be involved in all its main decisions. An example is Arthurlie Taxis in Barrhead. It was created by private hire taxi drivers who formed a company to act as a marketing co-operative and operates the back-up controller and radio service. The individual drivers are all self employed and pay a levy from their earnings to operate the co-operative.

It is argued that employee owned businesses improve motivation and company performance. However, some studies have shown that this is not guaranteed. Those that are successful must have a corporate culture and organisation that is suited to democratic decision making.

Factors affecting participation and industrial democracy

The extent to which participation and industrial democracy takes place in business may depend on a number of factors.

Legislation UK government legislation and European laws are likely to have an effect. For example, **the Employment Act, 2002** set in place regulations for fixed conciliation to allow quicker and more amicable settlements to disputes. The EU **Information and Consultation of Employees Regulations, 2005** suggested that in certain cases the workforce could make a written request to businesses asking for information and consultation procedures on decision likely to affect work arrangements, future business developments and restructuring.

Consultative bodies It was suggested that the introduction of **European works councils,** as a result of the UK signing the Social Chapter of the EU, was likely to increase industrial democracy after the year 2000.

Corporate culture Some businesses have developed a culture that recognises the importance of participation and industrial democracy when decisions are made. They value the contribution that employees can make to effective decision making. Businesses that make use of knowledge teams (☞ unit 20) are likely to see participation and industrial democracy as important.

Representation and power In certain parts of the private sector, where unions are weak, or collective bargaining does not take place, industrial democracy may be limited. An example might be where the owner of a small, non-unionised business decides to move premises and simply informs the workers that this will take place.

Communication and information technology The introduction of company intranets and other communication technologies has helped to speed up and extend the process of industrial democracy.

Quality standards Organisations may seek a quality award, such as **Investors in People**, for the way in which they work with employees. Consultation, the passing of information and involvement in decision making are standards that businesses have to maintain to keep this award. Such an award may attract customers and good quality candidates.

The advantages of participation and industrial democracy

Greater participation and industrial democracy is likely to have a number of advantages for a business.

- It may avoid damaging industrial action.
- It may motivate employees more as they feel part of the decision making process.
- It may lead to an input of new or different ideas which could, for example, make any changes easier to carry out.
- It may help to develop a more open organisational culture in the business (☞ unit 5) and allow a firm to achieve its objectives. Workers in the business might feel their opinions are valued and be prepared to put forward ideas, for example in suggestion boxes.
- It may encourage worker representatives to take a long term view and adopt similar strategies to management, by making them better informed about the reasons behind decisions.
- It might make management more sympathetic to workers' needs. This might put them in a better position to decide if changes in work organisation will be accepted or not by employees.

The drawbacks of participation and industrial democracy

There may be certain drawbacks of greater participation and industrial democracy for a business.

- The structure of the business must be suitable. There may be need to change the organisational structure of the business. Many businesses are organised in a hierarchy. Although some industrial democracy may be possible within the existing structure, over time it may have to change. This can lead to disruption.
- It can be expensive and time consuming, increasing business costs. Studies have suggested that in 2003 the cost to businesses of setting up European works councils, was between £150,000 and £250,000 a year.
- It may lead to conflict. Management may not be prepared to accept the greater involvement of employees. It may try to marginalise the input of employees, so the business will not gain the benefits of greater employee involvement.

key terms

ACAS - a body which mediates where conflict exists in business.
CAC - the government body responsible for union recognition.
Collective agreement - an agreement reached through the process of collective bargaining.
Collective bargaining - a method of determining conditions of work and terms of employment through negotiations between employers and employee representatives.
European works councils (EWC) - bodies set up to allow consultation with employees by employers and the passing of information to employees.
Industrial democracy - the different situations in business where employees have a significant say in decisions.
Joint consultation - discussion between management and employee representatives before a decision is taken.

Knowledge...Knowledge...Knowle

1. What factors may lead to conflict between employers and employees?
2. Why is collective bargaining important to employees?
3. What are likely to be the results of collective bargaining?
4. Explain the difference between:
   (a) collective bargaining at national and plant level;
   (b) collective bargaining and individualised bargaining.
5. Briefly explain the stages in negotiation that may help to lead to a satisfactory outcome.
6. Explain the different types of consultation.
7. Briefly explain the main areas of activity that ACAS is involved in.
8. What is the role of a European works council?
9. Suggest 3 benefits of greater industrial democracy.
10. Suggest 3 problems of greater industrial democracy.

Case study Industrial democracy

Heineken

Heineken, the beer company, works closely with trade unions and works councils. It concluded a series of agreements under the title 'People make Heineken', between 1992-1997 and 1998-2002. They provided for a number of measures:

- changes in work organisation and skill levels;
- payment for voluntary redundancy;
- testing of workers' skill levels and suitability for teamwork.

1,777 employees were tested and 80 per cent were deemed suitable for teamwork and trainable. Of the remaining 20 per cent unsuitable for training, about half were then redeployed throughout the company in jobs outside teams. Others were offered early retirement or a financial reward to leave the company. Though the rewards have been debatable, unions, works councils and management are generally positive about the results of the project.

The Heineken European Works Council publishes a monthly newspaper which is distributed to all the representatives. There is a provision for two meetings per year during May and November. There may also be another meeting per year for educational reasons in the form of a seminar.

Source: adapted from various website articles.

Wave

Hastings-based graphics designers Wave specialises in design work for charities and voluntary organisations. It employs eight full-time staff who run the business as a workers' co-operative. Each has an equal say in management decisions and draws the same wages (about £22,000 a year). To remind people of its democratic credentials, Wave's website address uses the new .coop tag, launched in January 2002.

Felix Lozano has worked at Wave since 1989. He talks of the liberating effect of not having a boss. But finding capital is a problem. Unlike most small businesses, Wave does not use individuals' own private capital. Mr Lozano says 'it is co-op policy that members' homes are not offered as security', a principle that was eventually accepted by its bank. The logic is that, as a co-op, the rewards of the business should be shared on the basis of the work undertaken. Wave's development has been funded partly from retained profits, partly from an overdraft and also from loans provided by Industrial Common Ownership Finance, a specialist source of loan funding for co-ops and social enterprises.

Source: adapted from *Financial Times*, 2002.

Greater Manchester Weekly Newspapers

In 2002 Greater Manchester Weekly Newspapers agreed to recognise the National Union of Journalists (NUJ) in an attempt to prevent strike action. Mark Dodson, the chief executive of GMWN, said 'GMWN and its parent company, Guardian Media Group, recognise the NUJ for the purpose of collective bargaining and intend to continue doing so.'

The union was also negotiating on low pay. Dodson said 'With recognition off the table, we can concentrate on the issue of pay'. 'We want an agreement and, if our negotiations run into problems, we are prepared to go to ACAS for independent binding arbitration.' An offer of a 2.5 per cent increase for staff across the board, with an 8.3 per cent increase for the lowest pay band and 5 per cent for the second lowest pay band, was on the table. The NUJ had so far rejected the offer.

Source: adapted from *The Guardian*, 26.4.2002.

(a) Describe the different ways in which employee participation and industrial democracy has taken place in these businesses. (8 marks)

(b) Examine the possible role of ACAS in the GMWN-NUJ dispute. (8 marks)

(c) Assess the factors that may have influenced the extent of participation and industrial democracy in the businesses. (12 marks)

(d) To what extent is industrial democracy likely to benefit the businesses? (12 marks)

23 Industrial Action

Industrial action in the UK

Conflict between employees and employers can lead to **industrial action**. Industrial action can be taken by both employers against employees (such as close supervision of work, or a lock out) and by employees against employers (ranging from an overtime ban to strike action). It is in the interests of both groups to reconcile differences through negotiation and consultation (☞ unit 22) before taking action, although this is not always possible.

The number of stoppages and the number of working days lost through stoppages fell over the period 1982-2002. In part, this was due to legislation restricting union action (☞ unit 21). It was also partly due to a change in the attitudes of management and unions towards industrial democracy (☞ unit 22), which helped to reduce conflict and the number of disputes that arise in business.

Employers' industrial action

Action by management against employees can take a number of forms. Sometimes sanctions can be imposed by individual managers. Some may include, for example, close supervision of employees' work, tight work discipline, discrimination against certain groups, lay offs, demoting workers or speeding up work practices. These actions are usually taken by one member of the management team and will not be repeated in other departments in the company. They might lead to individuals or groups of workers starting grievance proceedings against the manager concerned.

Sanctions can also be organised and carried out throughout the business. Management may use some of the following actions when dealing with trade unions.

The withdrawal of overtime and benefits A business could withdraw all overtime that it offers to workers. This is likely to reduce workers' earnings. The business might also withdraw other benefits it offers to employees, including flexitime, vouchers or other benefits such as leisure club membership.

Lock-outs A LOCK-OUT by employers involves closing the factory for a period of time. Employees' wages may not be paid during this period. This action might adversely affect the image that the public have of the company. In 2004 the government proposed to change legislation so that if employees were locked out by their employer, the lock-out will not be counted as part of the eight-week period after which an employer can lawfully dismiss a striking workforce.

Changing standards and piecework rates Management may change work standards or alter piecework rates when in dispute with employees. This can have the effect of making the employees' task more difficult or reducing the earnings of employees unless they work a lot harder.

Sometimes a management tactic may be to use a strategy of increasing work standards so that unions will call a strike. This might happen when order books are low and stocks are high. By causing a strike, management does not need to lay anyone off or pay redundancy money. At the same time further stockpiling is reduced.

Closure Management may close down factories and offices or remove plant and machinery from their premises. Some people might not view such activities as industrial action. They may see them as the normal rights of management to shut down uneconomic enterprises or force uncooperative workers to comply with employers' needs in the workplace.

Dismissal In some cases, employers might threaten employees with dismissal. The **Employment Relations Act 1999** set out criteria where it was unfair to dismiss employees for taking industrial action. Employees that are dismissed can take their case to a tribunal, which will judge against the criteria.

Hiring workers If unions take action to withdraw their

Figure 23.1 *Working days lost in the UK due to stoppages, 1982-2002*

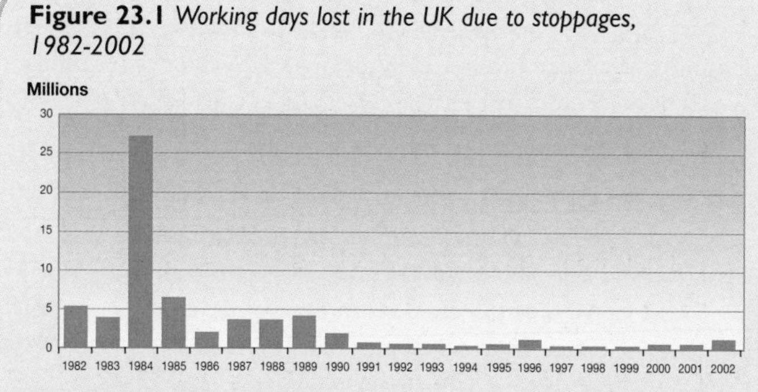

Source: adapted from *Labour Market Trends*, Office for National Statistics.

Figure 23.2 *Stoppages in progress, UK, 1982-2002*

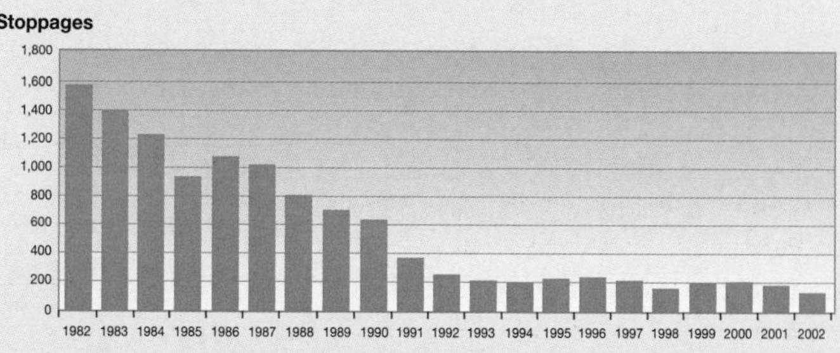

Source: adapted from *Labour Market Trends*, Office for National Statistics.

Social security managers offered civil servants bonuses and put staff up in hotels to break strikes in job centres and benefit offices in 2001. Staff who agreed to move to sites hit by industrial action were paid an extra £14.22 a day subsistence allowance (around £71.10 a week) to defy the strikes. An overnight allowance of £35 a night was also paid in addition to travelling time, an hour's reduction in the working week and a weekend overtime rate of time-and-a-half plus a day off in lieu. The Secretary of State for Work and Pensions, said 'It is absolutely essential that we do all we can. Millions of vulnerable people depend on us. Hundreds of thousands would be left without money if we don't do all we can because of the strike action. No responsible minister or government could tolerate that.'

Source: adapted from *The Guardian*, 30.10.2001.

In 2003 workers at the Trellebourg chemical company in Leicester took strike action. This was in response to management action which introduced tags which had to be worn in break time by staff.

Source: adapted from *Labour Research*, November 2003.

Culina Logistics launched an anti-union recognition campaign using the slogan 'vote no way to the TSSA'. According to the union staff were also 'threatened with derisory pay deals, reductions in breaks, loss of bonus schemes' and job losses if TSSA won recognition.

Source: adapted from *Labour Research*, January 2004.

(a) Identify the methods of industrial action being used by employers.
(b) Explain why employers might justify taking such action.

labour, employers sometimes recruit outside workers or contractors to do their jobs. It has also been suggested that some employers hire 'union busters' to intimidate workers to stop unions winning strike ballots.

The use of courts Businesses might challenge the right of unions and their members to take action through the courts. This might prevent the action taking place. They might also claim damages.

Employees' industrial action

Industrial action used by employees can be wide ranging. It is possible to distinguish between **unorganised** action and **organised** action. R Hyman, in his book *Strikes*, wrote that: '... in unorganised conflict the worker typically responds to the oppressive situation in the only way open to him as an individual ... Such reaction rarely derives from any calculative strategy ... Organised conflict, on the other hand, is far more likely to form part of a conscious strategy to change the situation which is identified as the source of discontent.'

Unorganised (or unofficial) action by employees can come in a number of forms.

- High labour turnover.
- Poor time keeping.
- High levels of absenteeism.
- Low levels of effort.
- Inefficient work.
- Deliberate time wasting.
- Unofficial strikes not backed by the employees' union.

These are often taken when workers 'down tools' immediately in reaction to employers' actions.

Such action can be disruptive for a business if it continues for a long period of time. The business, however, can use disciplinary procedures against employees and may even be able to terminate contracts in some cases. However, unofficial action may lead to organised action backed by the union. Organised action can take a number of different forms.

Work to rule or go slow Organised and group industrial action by trade unions against management can take the form of a WORK TO RULE or GO SLOW. A work to rule means employees do not carry out duties which are not in their employment contract. They may also carry out management orders to the letter. This can result in workers strictly observing the safety and work rules which are normally disregarded. Working to rule does not mean that employees are in breach of contract, simply that they carry out tasks exactly according to their contract. This means that tasks are not carried out efficiently. The impact of train drivers working to rule, for example, could mean that trains are late arriving or are cancelled. Drivers may delay taking trains out until rigorous checks are carried out. A go slow is where employees deliberately attempt to slow down production, whilst still working within the terms of their contract.

Overtime ban An overtime ban limits workers' hours to the agreed contract of employment for normal hours. Overtime bans are usually used by trade unions to demonstrate to management that the workforce is determined to take further collective action if their demands are not met. An overtime ban does have a disadvantage for workers as it results in lost earnings. It can lead to a reduction in costs for the business, but may also lead to lost production. It can be especially effective where production takes place overnight, for example on large production lines.

Sit-ins and work-ins A SIT-IN or WORK-IN involves a mass occupation of premises by workers. A work-in is where employees continue production with the aim of demonstrating that the factory is a viable concern. It is sometimes used when there is a threat of closure. In a sit-in, production does not continue. The aim is to protest against management decisions and, in the case of factory closure, prevent the transfer of machinery to other factories. A

Figure 23.3 *Working days lost by principle cause of dispute, UK, 1993-2002*

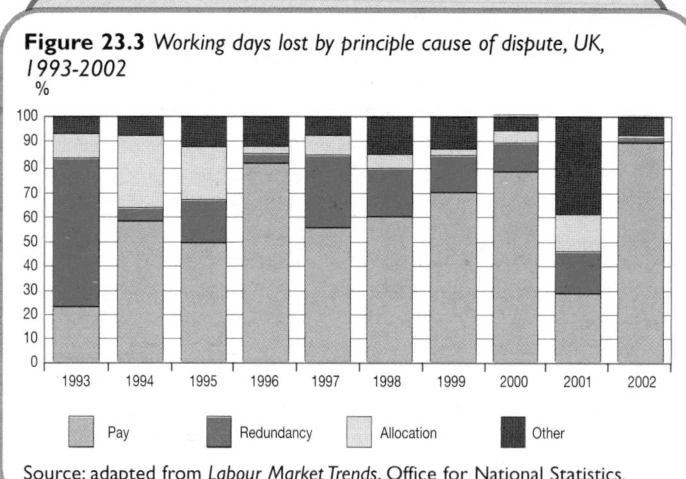

Source: adapted from *Labour Market Trends*, Office for National Statistics.

Figure 23.4 *Proportions of stoppages in progress by duration, UK, 2002*

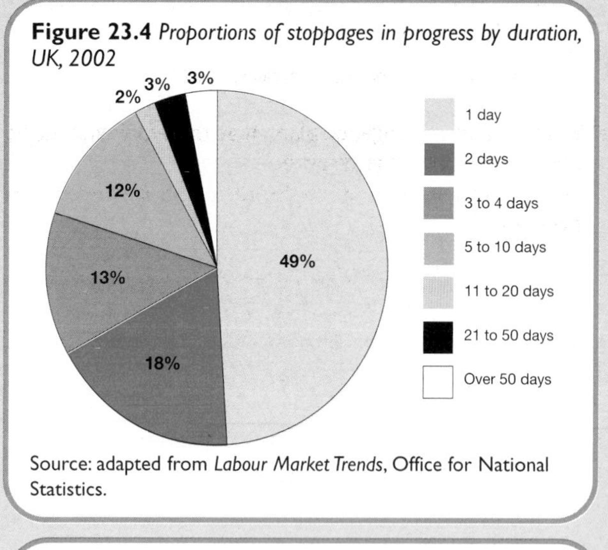

Source: adapted from *Labour Market Trends*, Office for National Statistics.

Figure 23.5 *Working days lost by principal cause of dispute, UK, 2002*

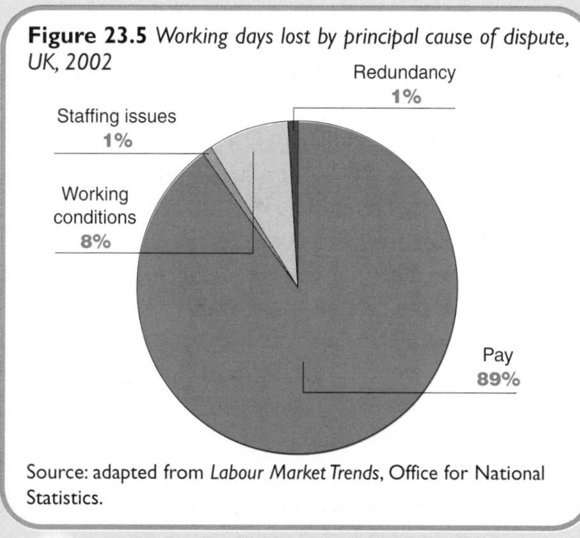

Source: adapted from *Labour Market Trends*, Office for National Statistics.

(a) Explain the trends and characteristics of industrial action in the UK over the period 1993-2002.
(b) Analyse why these trends may have taken place.

Question 2

redundancy sit-in or work-in is a protest against the closure of a plant or company. A **collective bargaining sit-in** may be used instead of other forms of industrial action such as working to rule, overtime bans and all out strikes, to give employees a position of strength in negotiations.

Sit-ins and work-ins mean the illegal occupation of premises by workers. They also allow workers to gain control over the factory. Why are these tactics used? First, they offer some degree of control over the factory or plant being occupied, which is obviously important in redundancy situations where the removal of plant and machinery to other locations is being threatened. Also by working-in or sitting-in, employees are better able to maintain their group solidarity.

Strikes The ultimate sanction used by trade unions against employers is the strike or industrial stoppage. Stoppages at work are normally connected with terms and conditions of employment. Strikes can be **official** or **unofficial**. Official strikes are where a union officially supports its members in accordance with union rules during a dispute after a ballot for action has been carried out and agreed by union members. Unofficial strikes have no union backing or support. They have, in the past, been called by shop stewards in particular factories, often in response to a particular incident. Such strikes are likely to be short term, local, unpredictable and disruptive for a business.

There is no single reason that explains the trend in stoppages in the UK. A study of strikes in Britain over an extensive time period was carried out by researchers for the government. They discovered that:

- strikes appear to be over major issues;
- strikes are concentrated in a very small proportion of plants - often the larger ones in certain industries and in certain areas of the country;
- industries and regions that have large factories, on average, tend to experience relatively high numbers of strikes. These strikes occur fairly often.

Factors influencing the success of employees' industrial action

Whether industrial action by workers and unions is successful in helping them achieve their aims depends on a number of factors.

Nature and strength of the union A large union negotiating with a small business is more likely to be able to influence the employer. Where large unions are negotiating with large multinational companies or with the government, action may not always be successful.

It has also been argued that unions are less influential if representation in the industry is split. This was perhaps the case when some mine workers left the NUM to form the Union of Democratic Mineworkers. It may also have been a reason for the merger of NALGO, NUPE and COHSE to form the UK's largest union, Unison.

Smaller unions tend to have less influence. The Musicians Union, for example, whilst having rates per hour for performers, is unlikely to be able to force club owners to pay the 'going rate' for performances.

Location and organisation of the workforce It has been suggested that unions are in a stronger bargaining position if a number of their members are employed in the same 'place'. Farm workers, for example, have traditionally been in a weak bargaining position with employers, as few are employed on any one farm. Also, their places of employment are geographically dispersed. This makes meetings and support difficult.

Public support and union views Public support for a dispute may strengthen a union's position. This may be particularly true of public sector workers such as nurses, where the public often 'feel' workers deserve higher wages or not to be made redundant. However, public opinion may change once industrial action begins. This may also be the case in industrial action by railway workers, for example, especially in commuter belts around London. Health unions have, in the past, refused to strike because of the damaging effects on patients.

Management tactics Union action is likely to be less effective if management action can reduce the problems for business. In the car industry, a strike by employees may not affect a producer if there are stocks of cars and orders can still be met.

Management may encourage non-union workers or even union members to cross the picket line, or even be prepared to 'bus in' workers from other areas. The government has, in the past, been prepared to use army vehicles and members of the armed forces when fire service workers have taken industrial action.

Legislation Laws restrict the actions of employers and employee groups such as trade unions (☞ unit 21). For example, trade unions are liable in certain circumstances for damages during industrial action. Similarly, under certain circumstances, employers cannot make employees involved in industrial action redundant.

Economic climate The state of the economy might affect the relative bargaining strength of employers and employees. For example, take a situation where growth is low in the economy, spending is falling and unemployment is high. There may be excess supply of labour willing to work at cheap wages. So employers may feel that they are in a stronger position. If growth and spending is low in the economy, employers might also feel that they are not in a position to pay high wages. On the other hand, employers may not be able to afford the damaging effects of industrial action during periods of recession.

In December 2003 around 800 staff at Sainsbury's distribution centre in Haydock staged a 24 hour strike after rejecting a pay offer. The centre distributes goods to stores in the north of England. Nearly all workers at the site are members of the union USDAW. A union spokesperson said that the pay offer was significantly behind other warehouse workers in the north west and other Sainsbury's depots. The current offer increased pay from £5.75 to £7.55 an hour, but not to the regional average of £8 an hour, which was initially promised by the company. It was suggested that the company accepted it was paying below the average in 2002. Workers had recently agreed to new working practices at the depot.

Sainsburys said that it did not expect the walkout to affect customers in supermarkets. The company had contingency plans in place to deal with the action. It argued that the overall package offered to employees was one of the best in the area and that pay offers had been above inflation in the last three years.

Source: adapted from news.bbc.co.uk, breaking.tcm.ie.

(a) Examine the contingency plans that the employer might have to deal with the dispute.
(b) Assess the strengths of employers and employees in the dispute.

Question 3

Problems of industrial action

There are certain problems which result from industrial action, both for employers and employees.

Employers' problems

- Industrial action can lead to lost production for the business. A go slow or work to rule may reduce output. Strike action could mean that orders are unfulfilled and revenue and profits could fall.
- If industrial action results in production being stopped, then machinery and other resources will be lying idle. A business will have many fixed costs which have to be covered, even if production is not taking place. If output ceases, revenue will not be earned to pay for these costs.
- Industrial action may lead to poor future relationships in a business. Sometimes grievances can carry on after a dispute. This could result in poor motivation and communication.
- Industrial disputes divert managers' attention away from planning. If a business is concerned with solving a dispute that exists now, it may neglect plans for the future.
- Loss of output and delays in production or deliveries caused by action can harm the firm's reputation. This may lead to lost business in future.

Employees' problems

- A work to rule, go slow or strike can lead to a reduction or a loss of earnings.

- Prolonged industrial action may, in some cases, lead to the closure of the business. Employees would then be made redundant.
- Action is likely to place stress on the workforce. It can also cause friction between levels of the hierarchy. For example, managers on the other 'side' in a dispute are unlikely to find their employees motivated.
- If action is unsuccessful, the employees' position may be weaker in future. Members may also leave a union if they feel that it is unable to support their interests.
- Public support may suffer if the action affects people's everyday lives.
- Strike action must conform to current legislation or unions may be liable for damages and employees may be disciplined or dismissed.

Benefits of industrial action

Industrial action is often used as a 'final' measure by unions and employers because of the disruption it causes. There are, however, some benefits for both groups.

- It 'clears the air'. Employers and employees may have grievances. Industrial action can bring these out into the open and, once the dispute is solved, this could improve the 'atmosphere' in the business.
- Introducing new rules. How groups operate in businesses is influenced by rules, such as rates of pay or what is meant by unfair dismissal. Conflict is often about disagreement over these rules. When industrial action has been resolved, this often leads to new rules which each group agrees upon.
- Changing management goals. Management often change their goals and the ways they are achieved after industrial action. For example, a business may have attempted to introduce new working practices without consulting unions, which led to industrial action. In future it may consult with unions before changing work practices.
- Understanding the position of each group. Industrial action often makes the position of employers and employees very clear. It allows each group to hear the grievances of the other, consider them and decide to what extent they agree.

In July 2003 the firefighters dispute finally came to an end, having begun in November 2002. The Fire Brigades Union (FBU) voted three to one to accept the offer of a 16 per cent cumulative pay rise. All references to job losses and other unacceptable elements were cut and future pay rises were not to be traded for job losses.

There was now to be a stronger emphasis on negotiated change. Under new integrated risk management plans the fire authority would decide on how many personnel would be on duty at any time 'having consulted with appropriate parties'. Any proposed changes in the existing duty system had to be discussed with unions and a proper disputes procedure was put in place. Arguments over duty systems could be referred to an independently chaired technical advisory panel.

The dispute had been long running and sometimes acrimonious. The government used troops with antiquated 'green goddess' trucks to answer 999 calls. Some people died as a result of fires during the dispute, although it was argued that this was not directly as a result of the dispute. It was even suggested that emergency powers under legislation not used since the Second World War might be used to take control of the fire service. Some tube stations in London said that they might close if the firefighters went on strike on safety grounds.

One firefighter in Liverpool, although in favour of a pay increase, feared the union could not win the dispute. 'This is all degrading and detrimental to morale' he said.

Source: adapted from *Labour Research*, July 2003, Guardian Unlimited website.

(a) Examine the possible benefits and problems that might have resulted from the firefighters dispute.

Knowledge

1. Why might the number of days lost through stoppages in the UK have fallen over the last decade?
2. Explain 4 types of industrial action that employers can take.
3. State 6 types of employee action.
4. Why might employees be reluctant to use strike action?
5. Explain the difference between a sit-in and a go slow.
6. What factors might influence the success of employees' industrial action?
7. State 3 problems of industrial action for:
   (a) employees;
   (b) employers.
8. How might industrial action benefit a business?

key terms

Go slow - the reduction of output by workers whilst still carrying on tasks in their contract of employment.
Lock-out - action by employers which prevents employees entering the factory to work.
Sit-in/Work-in - the illegal occupation of premises by workers, which allows workers to gain control of the factory.
Work to rule - when employees do not carry out duties which are not in their employment contract.

Case study Industrial action by council staff and civil service workers

In July 2002 over a million council staff were ready to strike. The action could cripple services such as elderly care, meals on wheels, street cleaning and pest control. The national officer at Unison said 'Our members have voted for industrial action because they are sick of being treated as the poor relations of the public sector. Their case for a realistic pay rise is indisputable'. Union leaders said the action would continue until they got a better pay offer. The T&G and GMB unions said two-thirds of their members had voted in favour of a strike, while the largest town hall union, Unison, had an 80 per cent vote.

Unions wanted a 6 per cent rise. This was rejected as unrealistic by council leaders, who said they did not have the money to increase their 3 per cent offer. A spokesperson for the local government Employers' Organisation said 'The strike action won't achieve anything. You can put a mark on a ballot paper but it can't conjure up more money.'

The services affected would vary from council to council because staff working in privatised services negotiate pay directly with their private employers, rather than joining the national bargaining process which covers most publicly employed council officers. Strikes by Unison in Scotland two years ago saw tonnes of rubbish piling up on the streets, empty offices in Edinburgh and museums and leisure centres closed.

Source: adapted from *The Guardian*, 5.7.2002.

In 2004 up to 90,000 members of the Public and Commercial Services Union (PCS) began a two day strike sparked by workers' anger over pay. This followed the collapse of pay talks, with the threat of further industrial action to come. The strike forced hundreds of job centres and social security offices to close. Up to 5,000 driving tests were also expected to be cancelled as driving examiners joined the picket line. The PCS claimed the strike was the result of the government's refusal to resolve 'appalling' levels of pay and an unacceptable performance appraisal system in the Department for Work and Pensions (DWP).

The union's general secretary claimed that low pay was endemic in the civil service and called on government ministers to intervene in the dispute. He said that civil servants were sick of a lack of recognition. Workers' anger was worsened by reports that a government inquiry into the civil service was to recommend 80,000 job cuts. The PCS general secretary said the union would oppose any moves to cut jobs because vital services such as the New Deal, immigration and customs were carried out by frontline as well as back-office civil servants.

The DWP described the strike as 'indefensible' and said contingency plans were in place to minimise disruption.

Source: adapted from *The Guardian*,16.2.2004.

(a) Describe the industrial action taken by (i) employees and (ii) employers in the two cases. (6 marks)

(b) Examine the reasons for the industrial action. (10 marks)

(c) Explain the possible benefits and problems of industrial action for both sides. (10 marks)

(d) Assess the factors that might affect the relative strengths and weaknesses in the two disputes. (12 marks)

(e) Evaluate the likelihood of success of the industrial action in each case. (12 marks)

24 Managing Human Resources

The importance of human resources

The role of the personnel department is to plan human resources. Many businesses have shown a renewed interest in the management of human resources in recent years. They have come to realise the importance of employees and their knowledge and skills as an asset of the business. For example, in 1999 every one of Shell's 105,000 employees around the world were asked for their opinions, which were to be used as an 'agenda for change' in the company. Companies such as ICL have come to recognise the importance of retaining and using workers' knowledge. Siemens, the electronics company, has developed its pension department's team building skills in freezing Arctic Circle conditions. It has also used personality tests to evaluate staff. Companies such as Jaguar and Peugeot have made use of psychological testing of managers.

Businesses also seem to be placing greater emphasis on motivation, customer care and training. In the late 1990s BT's 'for a better life' programme encouraged staff to make their own decisions to benefit the customer. In the early twenty first century there was a growing number of employer and union partnerships and works councils in business aimed at improving industrial relations (☞ units 21 and 22). Many businesses were also moving towards a **flexible workforce**. This is discussed later in this unit.

Human resources management

One of the most important tasks that involves the personnel department in a business is HUMAN RESOURCE MANAGEMENT (HRM). A business is only likely to achieve its objectives if its employees are used effectively. Planning how best to use human resources will help a business to do this. Human resources management has **strategic** implications. It must be integrated into the strategic and corporate planning of the business (☞ units 6 and 7). It means constantly looking for better ways of using employees to benefit the organisation.

What is involved in the management of human resources? It is often said that it has a 'soft' side and a 'hard' side. This is shown in Figure 24.1.

The soft side of human resources management

This is mainly concerned with the way in which people are managed. It may include:

- how to motivate and satisfy workers;
- how to develop an organisational culture (☞ unit 5) or approach in employees, for example good relations with customers, flexibility, or quality at all stages of production;
- how to support and develop employees, for example by training or by improving health and safety;
- the most suitable relationships between employer and the employees or their representatives;
- evaluating alternative policies and their likely costs.

Figure 24.1 *Elements of human resources management*

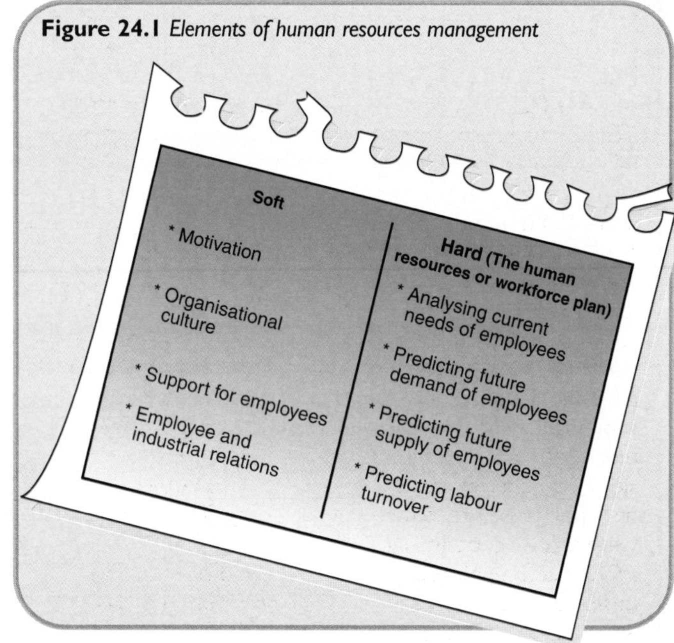

Soft
* Motivation
* Organisational culture
* Support for employees
* Employee and industrial relations
Hard (The human resources or workforce plan)
* Analysing current needs of employees
* Predicting future demand of employees
* Predicting future supply of employees
* Predicting labour turnover

There are various methods that a business could use when managing human resources. Take the example of a hotel with a variety of staff working in different jobs.

Changing business aims into employee goals The hotel may have decided that its main aim was to provide an excellent service to customers. To achieve this aim, goals would have to be set for the behaviour of employees of the hotel, such as always being polite to the customer. It is likely that staff training in customer care would be used to help employees.

Examining the environment There are factors 'outside' a business that could affect human resources management. The hotel would aim to gather as much information as possible to predict the effects of changes in these factors. For example, if health and safety regulations changed that affected the working of the kitchen, staff would need to be aware of these changes and may need training or support to carry them out. Information about external factors can be found from many sources, ranging from industrial journals to competitors' annual reports.

Analysing the current situation It is important for the hotel to be aware of current staff needs. It could do this by using:

- questionnaires to staff and customers;
- interviews with staff;
- discussions with managers;

Despite the uncertain future of the business in 2003, Safeway, the supermarket chain, was able to keep labour turnover steady. At the time, a number of supermarket rivals, including Morrisons, the eventual winner in 2004, was looking to take over the business. The challenge was to keep 'business as usual' faced with changing conditions and retain the commitment, morale and enthusiasm of staff.

The human resources strategy devised by the business had two main objectives - to retain as many good people as possible whilst they were still needed and to improve morale and motivation during the changes taking place. The company also recognised the need to retain vital knowledge. Although some analysts predicted that in mid-June 2003 the business would be falling apart, it managed to keep staff turnover constant and, in some cases, it even fell. Part of the programme involved improved redundancy packages for workers who would be most vulnerable to redundancy after the takeover. Another part involved a motivation programme designed to improve leadership skills for managers, teaching them how to cope with uncertainty and resilience during change. The outcomes were linked to bonus incentives.

Clear communication was also seen to be vital. The business set up an area on the company intranet called 'Our Future', to keep people informed of new developments. There was also a meeting for 'everyone' every four weeks.

Source: adapted from *People Management*, 28.8.2003 and 18.12.2003.

(a) Explain the different aspects of the (a) soft side and (b) hard side of human resource management at Safeway.
(b) Explain why the management of human resources was so important to the business at the time.

Question 1

- performance data;
- recruitment or promotion information.

A questionnaire given to staff and customers at a hotel, for example, might find that customer service is not as good as it could be at the checkout desk because staff are too concerned about getting the paperwork right. A solution might be to simplify the checkout system or use extra staff at busy times. This would help to motivate employees and improve the chances of meeting the goal of improved customer service.

The hard side of human resources management

The hard side of human resources management is concerned with quantifying the number and type of employees that a business will need, deciding whether they are available and planning how to get them. It is often known as the **human resources** or **workforce plan**. The human resources plan will:

- anticipate the likely future demand for workers;
- analyse current employees and their skills;
- anticipate future supply of workers from inside the business or outside. It will take into account factors such as promotion and labour turnover - the extent to which people leave the business;
- plan how to make up any shortfall of workers or reduce an excess of workers.

The quality of the human resources plan depends on the data on which it is based. A business must have accurate and relevant details for the human resources plan to be effective. For example, details about anticipated future business and the volume of production and sales may be needed. It will then be possible to predict the likely numbers and types of employees that are needed. The human resources plan must also make allowance for changes, such as improvements in technology or new products which might increase or reduce the number of employees needed. The information a business would require to develop an effective human resources plan might include:

- the implications for human resources of changes in corporate strategy, eg a possible reduction in the workforce as a result of removing layers of the organisation or deciding to concentrate on core activities of the business;
- the assumptions on which decisions about the workforce have been made, eg that there is likely to be growing competition in future;
- all other relevant data that may affect human resources plans, eg planned spending on new plant or machinery;
- the timing of changes, eg when new products might be introduced;
- anticipated issues in future, eg renegotiation of conditions at work;
- a detailed analysis of the current workforce.

Factors affecting human resources management

There are many factors that could affect the management of human resources in a business.

Changing goals of a business If a chemical company, for example, decided that the most effective way to increase profits or turnover was to become more **market orientated**, this is likely to change the personnel the business needs. There would be a need perhaps for employees with market research skills or training in how to promote products. This is an example of how changing goals can affect the demand for labour.

Changes in the market Changes in purchasing patterns of consumers may mean that the demand for labour or labour skills have to change. One example might be the redundancies in the coal industry as a result of demand for cheaper forms of power. Another might be the need to develop good customer relations in fast food retail outlets or financial services as competition has increased.

Changes in the economy can also affect human resource planning. In a recession, a business is likely to reduce its workforce as demand for its products falls.

Technology The introduction of new technology may lead to retraining or a need to recruit workers with specialist skills. For example, many former typists have become computer operators with the introduction of computer systems for storage, retrieval and presentation of information. The business may also have to consider the effect that new technology could have on the motivation of its employees and how to deal with this.

Competition Competition by other firms for workers may affect the supply of labour available to a business. If competitors offer high wages to workers with specialist skills then a business may have to raise its wage levels to recruit the staff it needs.

Competition for customers may also affect a human resources plan. Many firms are now aiming to meet the ISO 9000 quality standard, as customers refuse to use their services without this. An example might be in the electronics industry, where if one firm does not have approval it may lose business to another supplier. A business that obtains the quality standard must employ workers with specialist skills to check the standard is maintained. This can be costly for some small firms.

Population As well as the total population size, the distribution of population in a country can affect the supply of workers available. It is argued that Britain, after the year 2000, faces a number of changes in population distribution that are likely to affect the management of human resources in many businesses.

- Activity rates. These are the percentage of any population in the labour force. There has been a growing number of women seeking employment. The activity rates of women of working age is predicted to rise to 2011 but for men over 25 it is predicted to fall slightly. A growing number of women seeking employment is likely to affect many aspects of human resources management, including how a business recruits workers, work conditions and employee relations.
- An ageing of the population (☞ unit 95). This means that older people are predicted to be a larger percentage of the population. There are also likely to be relatively fewer school leavers and younger workers. A greater proportion of older workers means that more employees may be looking to retire. Older employees may also be less flexible than younger workers and motivated by factors other than money.

  An older population may affect the demand for certain goods. Businesses might switch their products to appeal to a more mature consumer. Examples include the revival of 1960s and 1970s music on compact disc and the growth in residential care homes. Fewer school leavers mean that employers will have less choice of younger people. Businesses may have to set up apprenticeships to train school leavers as they become relatively scarce. They may also look to fill jobs by recruiting from older workers that may not have previously been considered. B&Q is an example of a business that has a policy of recruiting older workers.

Corporate culture and structure The corporate culture of the organisation (☞ unit 5) is likely to influence human resources management. If a business sees its employees as an asset that need to be trained, developed and motivated then it is likely to regard the management of human resources as important. It would be prepared to spend money and time on developing workers for the benefit of the business. Changes in the hierarchy of a business may affect human resource planning. A removal of a layer of management may mean that fewer employees at this level are required.

Trade unions The relationship between a business and trade unions is likely to affect the management of human resources. In the 1980s unions were unlikely to have been involved greatly in planning. In some businesses unions were derecognised and businesses often negotiated with individuals on terms and conditions of work. The growth of business and union partnerships, union consultation and union recognition in the early twenty first century is likely to have resulted in greater flexibility in human resource management.

Government legislation Government legislation will affect human resource management. Changes to the conditions of part time workers, the maximum number of hours that can be worked in a week and the minimum wage are all likely to influence the number and type of workers that businesses hire and the way in which labour is used. Government legislation on equal opportunities or a minimum wage has affected the wage costs of businesses and their recruitment and selection procedures. Businesses may also operate a policy where they guarantee disabled workers or ethnic minorities a proportion of jobs.

Finance The finance available to employ, reward or train workers will depend on many factors, such as the overall performance of the business, cash flow and the liquidity of the company. A small business that is building a new factory is unlikely to have funds available to hire new employees, pay large bonuses or carry out extensive training.

The implications of a strategic approach to human resources management

Businesses are increasingly regarding their human resources as an important asset. Developing a human resources management policy is likely to have an number of effects on a business.

- A strategic approach is needed. This means that a business must integrate human resources considerations into its overall corporate planning and strategy (☞ units 6 and 7). For example, a business that decides to merge with another company must take into account how the workforce needs to change, whether staff need training and assess how motivation may be affected. Alternatively, the hierarchy of the business could be redesigned to suit the needs of employees.
- The business must develop an organisational culture (☞ unit 15) that sees employees as an important part of the company. Managers who are unprepared to listen to employees' views on improvements will prevent the policy from working effectively.
- Motivation, training and support must be given to staff. Staff must be encouraged in the workplace. Businesses may make use of incentives such as bonuses or non-monetary benefits such as job redesign. Training and support must also be given. Marks & Spencer, for example, has employed counsellors to give advice to single parents on coping with children and work.
- Group involvement and participation. Employees must be made to feel part of the business and be committed to its objectives. They must also be prepared to contribute to improvements in quality and productivity.
- Coordination with other functions. The management of human resources must be built into all parts of the business, including production, marketing and the finance department, and at all levels in the hierarchy.
- Flexible practices and thinking must be encouraged. Workers must be prepared to change jobs, accept new working methods and conditions. This is dealt with in the next section.
- Recruitment, redundancy and redeployment. Businesses must be able to reduce staff if necessary. Cuts in staff may be achieved in a number of ways. Staff may be allowed to leave without being replaced, known as **natural wastage**. A business may ask for **voluntary redundancies**, where workers agree to leave in return for redundancy payments. The company may also offer **early retirement** to workers close to the compulsory retirement age. If there is no longer enough work, workers may be made redundant. It may also be possible to **redeploy** staff within a business. Training should help workers adapt to working in a different job in a business. Moving to another part of the country may be more difficult.

Advantages of human resources management

There are certain advantages to a business in taking a strategic approach to managing human resources.

- It may allow a business to gain a competitive advantage over rivals. A business which has a well trained, motivated and planned workforce and a human resources policy may be more efficient than competitors.
- It can solve human resources problems that occur in the business such as high rates of turnover and absenteeism.
- Effective human resources management will make the most efficient use of workers and reduce the potential costs of the business.
- A business will be able to anticipate changes to its workforce requirements and plan for these. It will also be able to manage change more effectively (☞ unit 25).
- Industrial relations problems may be prevented if employers and employees are working towards the same goals.
- Human resources management aims to provide long term benefits for the business. Employing part time workers in a crisis may solve a short term problem. But a planned, flexible workforce will give benefits to the business over a longer period.

In 1999 B&Q opened its first store in China. By 2003 it had 8 stores and aimed to have 58 by 2005. It was not the policy of the business to saturate overseas businesses with too many expats. Rather their role was to transfer skills, to train and coach local successors, and then move on. These individuals maintain links with the UK through B&Q's central international HR team.

B&Q does not simply transfer UK HR policy to other countries such as China. Instead HR management focusses on meeting local requirements. Human resources in China tends to be a policing and administrative function, so finding people with the right experience proved difficult. The company designed an application form asking candidates about their skills and aspirations. Many ignored the form and simply attached a letter with interesting but irrelevant information. So whilst attracting a large number of candidates it was often difficult to assess them. Despite being warned that the process would not work in China, B&Q has successfully introduced performance appraisal. The company also sends between 12 and 15 people to the UK each year for a two week period so they can learn about the business.

Source: adapted from *People Management*, 17.4.2003.

(a) Explain the possible benefits of B&Q's human resource approach in China.
(b) Examine the problems B&Q may have faced with managing human resources in the country.

Question 2

The problems of human resources management

There is a number of problems a business will face when managing its employees.

- Problems with predicting the behaviour of people. A business may have filled a position, but after being appointed the individual may decide he does not want the job. This could mean another costly and time consuming series of interviews for the firm.

- Problems with predicting external events. Sometimes it is difficult to predict exactly how many employees are required. We have seen that many factors can affect human resource planning. For example, the opening up of markets in the Far East, such as China, or the expansion of the EU into eastern Europe in 2004 could have meant changing plans for businesses aiming to break into these markets. It is likely that employees with knowledge of the business and language of these countries would have been in demand.
- Planning has to be constantly monitored. It is unwise for a business to plan its human resource needs and not alter them in the light of changing events. Planning has to be checked, revised and updated as other factors change.
- Human resources management must be well thought out or it is likely to lead to industrial relations problems. Cuts in the workforce or wage reductions that are not negotiated could affect workers' motivation and may even lead to industrial action (☞ unit 23).

Measurement of personnel effectiveness

A business might evaluate the effectiveness of human resources management by considering some of the following. Similar methods can be used to evaluate the management of change (☞ unit 25).

Labour turnover One of the most important tasks in the management of employees is to make sure that labour turnover is minimised and that all vacancies that exist are filled. Labour turnover is a measure of the number of people that **leave** a business in a given period of time as a percentage of the average number of people employed during that period. If labour turnover is high, how will this affect a business? There are likely to be costs as a result. These include:

- the cost of advertising, interviewing and training a new employee;
- a loss of production while the place is filled;
- low morale amongst other employees;
- reorganisation before the place is filled and perhaps after a new worker is hired.

The business will need to identify groups that are likely to leave and be ready to fill any vacancies that occur. Employees may leave because they are ill, retiring or having children. In some cases, they may be dismissed.

These are all unavoidable. However, some workers leave voluntarily because they are not satisfied with the job. It is these workers that a business should be most concerned about. Evidence suggests that those workers who leave voluntarily tend to be younger employees, who are often new recruits. They may be looking for promotion and better pay. To prevent dissatisfaction, a firm may:

- set up an internal promotion system;
- develop a staff training programme;
- make sure there is good communication between management and workers to avoid grievances and ensure that employees' views are taken into account;
- increase levels of pay.

Absenteeism High levels of staff absence may lead to a number of problems for a business. The output and productivity of the business may fall. The business will still have the costs of paying workers who are absent even though they are not working. Constant staff absence may also affect the motivation of other workers in the business. The reputation of the business may suffer if staff absence leads to unfulfilled orders or late deliveries.

A reduction in the number of days that employees are absent may be an indication that human resources management is effective. The motivation of staff may be better. Improved work conditions may have reduced stress and other factors which may lead to absence. Staff may feel more committed to the organisation and more likely to work, when they may have taken time off.

Labour productivity and turnover per employee The management of human resources may improve **labour productivity**. Labour productivity is a measure of the output per employee over a period of time. For example, if 20 workers in an engineering company produce 1,000 components in a period of time, their productivity is 50 components (1,000 ÷ 20). If work schedules were changed to create more flexibility and motivation improved so that output increased to 1,200, labour productivity would rise to 60 components (1,200 ÷ 20).

If a large multinational company employs 26,000 staff and has a turnover of £2,000 million a year, the **turnover per head** is nearly £77,000 (£2,000 million ÷ 26,000). However, if changes to the workforce meant that the company had the same profit next year with only 22,000 workers, turnover per head would be nearly £91,000 (£2,000 million ÷ 22,000).

Industrial relations The management of human resources may also improve industrial relations (☞ unit 21). A business may consider that a reduction in the number of:

- industrial disputes;
- days lost through industrial action;
- grievances against the business by employees;

might indicate effective management. Improvements in staff motivation indicated in appraisal questionnaires, attitude surveys or in meetings may also be an indication of the success of the business's policy.

Relations with stakeholders Stakeholders are all the people with an interest in the business. They include employees of the business, such as workers and managers, and shareholders who may or may not work for the business. They also include people who are affected by the activities of the business, such as clients, customers, suppliers and the general public. An indication of the success of HRM might be found in improved relations with suppliers. It may also be indicated in the views of customers about how the workforce is treated.

Profitability The main aim of most private sector businesses is to make profit. Modern approaches to HRM suggest that the management of human resources should be geared towards improving productivity of workers, reducing costs, raising revenue and increasing profit. It is a vital part of the overall strategy of the company rather than a series of processes, such as recruitment, selection and training. Increasing profit may be a result of improvements in HRM.

Table 24.1 *Evaluation of human resources management*

- Commitment - employees' loyalty and motivation, assessed by surveys, labour turnover and absenteeism.
- Competence - employees' skills and training - assessed through appraisal systems and skills inventories.
- Congruence - employees and managers sharing the same values, assessed by absence of grievances and conflict.
- Cost effectiveness - employees' efficiency, assessed by cost, output and profit figures

One model that has been suggested to evaluate the human resources management is the '4Cs model' of the Harvard Business School. This suggests that HRM should be evaluated under four headings as shown in Table 24.1.

Health and safety Improvements in the health and safety of employees might be an indication that the personnel department is managing human resources more effectively. This might be shown by a reduction in absenteeism due to illness, as explained earlier. It could also be indicated in a fall in the number of accidents at work. Staff surveys might also indicate that the number of workers who feel that they work in a more 'protected' environment has increased.

The flexible workforce

Employers have always wanted workers to be as flexible as possible. In the past this has meant paying overtime for extra hours worked, or higher rates for 'shift' work. Faced with competition, businesses attempted to use their existing employees more effectively. Sometimes this could benefit the employee. A single woman with a child may be able to work between the hours of 9am to 3pm each day while her child is at school. Working flexible hours could mean an employee may take time off for personal reasons and still work their required number of hours a week.

Training may also be given to workers so they become

Tesco is the UK's largest food retailer. It underwent considerable change in order to improve customer service, lower prices, and increase turnover and market share. It attempted to evolve into a customer focussed business in a market where prices were often very similar but service could make the difference. To achieve the change in culture Tesco developed a 'balanced scorecard' in the form of a steering wheel with four quadrants - people, finance, customers and operations. Every store's performance was measured against this. The people quadrant covered issues such as recruitment, retention, employee development and morale.

Section managers who were responsible for recruitment and training showed high levels of commitment to the business. Around 90 per cent said that they worked very hard and felt that theirjob was challenging. One said 'I believe in the organisation. It looks after staff well, although it expects a great deal and stretches people'.

A survey of staff at four Tesco stores found significant differences with employee's with the HR policies of the business, as shown in Figure 24.2. One explanation for the difference was the extent to which managers put into action the instructions from head office. One of the regional directors of the business said 'One of the biggest challenges we have is getting the right managers into the right stores'.

Source: adapted from *People Management*, 15.5.2003.

(a) Explain how the effectiveness of personnel and human resource management was measured at Tesco.
(b) Evaluate how effective the management of human resources has been.

Figure 24.2 *Survey of employees' commitment and satisfaction with HR policies and line managers' behaviour at four Tesco stores*

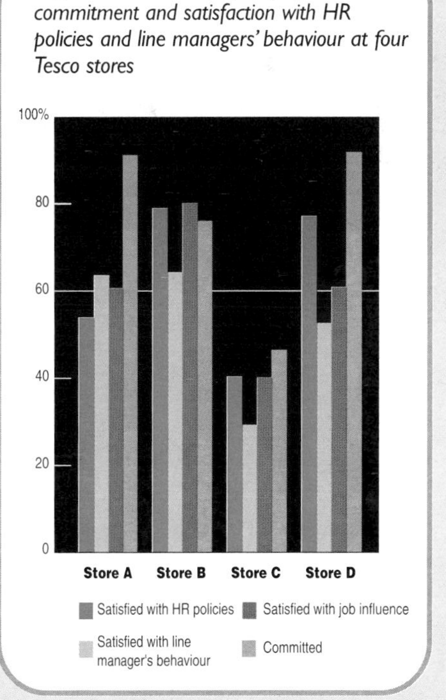

multi-skilled - able to switch from one job to another if needed. This example of job rotation may perhaps lead to the employee being more motivated. From a firm's point of view, an employee that can change jobs may prevent the need to have temporary workers to cover for illness etc. and so reduce labour costs. An example of this is the 'workstyle' initiative at Birds Eye/Wall's, where team working has been introduced so the workers can change from one process to another and do the work of others in the team if necessary.

In 1985 John Atkinson and The Institute of Manpower Studies developed the idea of the **flexible firm**. They suggested that businesses have a 'core' and a 'periphery', as in Figure 24.3. As a result of increasing competition, firms have attempted to make the workforce as flexible as possible, to increase productivity, reduce costs and react more quickly to change. The business would try to motivate core workers, giving them job security, and employ periphery workers only when needed.

Increasingly employers looked to make plans that allow a business to respond to changes. For example, if a large unexpected order arrives, a business will need workers that can 'get it out on time'. Using a FLEXIBLE WORKFORCE enables a business to react effectively to changes that take place outside the business. Examples of workers that are used by a business might include:

- part time employees, such as cleaners, who only work a few hours a day;
- temporary employees to deal with increases in demand, such as agricultural workers;
- workers on **zero hours contracts** who are employed by the business but only work and are paid when both the business and the employee agree;
- workers who work to annualised hours contracts, where they work a certain number of hours over a year rather than in a week;
- workers who 'bank time', by not working when demand is slack but being asked to work that time at a later date.
- office temporary workers to cover for illness or sickness;
- self-employed workers, such as management consultants, for specialist tasks;
- job sharing, where two workers are employed to do a full time job that may in the past have been carried out by one person.
- outworkers and teleworkers.

It has been argued that there are both benefits and disadvantages for these types of employee. On the one hand, a single parent may be able to find work at a convenient time, and job sharing could mean employment for two people, instead of unemployment for one of them. However, the position of flexible staff has often been a source of industrial relations problems for businesses and has led to conflict with trade unions.

In the 1990s individual bargaining increasingly took place. Conditions were negotiated without union involvement and based on the contract of employment. Union recognition and union partnerships with business after the year 2000 may

Figure 24.3 *Organisation of a flexible workforce*

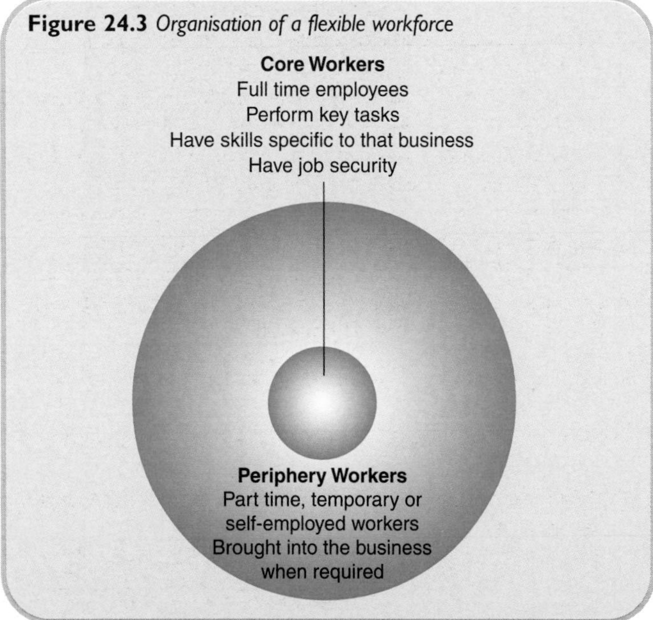
Core Workers
Full time employees
Perform key tasks
Have skills specific to that business
Have job security
Periphery Workers
Part time, temporary or
self-employed workers
Brought into the business
when required

Many supermarkets brace themselves for the rush at Christmas. Sainsbury's employed an extra 10,000 staff at Christmas in 2003. Tesco hired an extra 12,000.

Eli-Lilly, the pharmaceuticals firm, has a family friendly culture. It encourages term time working, reduced hours and career breaks. This was particularly helpful to single parents. However, certain departments operated the policies differently. It was suggested by Randall Tobias, the chief executive, that 'This is a matter of changing the culture, not only the policy. There are still barriers for women trying to convince management of their commitment and career goals.'

The North East Wales Institute of Higher Education (NEWI) employed a pool of workers on zero hours contracts to combat problems of a lack of commitment amongst agency temps. Workers were not guaranteed work, but they have to be available at times that suit the business and the individual. Workers had a right to refuse work and look for another job. NEWI argued that this approach was important as it expected pool members to be flexible, so it was only fair that it was also flexible.

Source: adapted from *People Management*, various.

(a) Comment on the extent to which the practices of the businesses in the cases have (i) increased flexibility and (ii) benefited the businesses.

Question 4

have changed industrial relations, although some argue that flexibility will still be encouraged by both sides.

There has been a number of criticisms of both Atkinson's model and the approach used by business towards human resources, for example, it may be argued that part time workers, contract work and the self employed can not be placed into a single category called 'peripheral work'. Part time workers, for example, may have secure contracts of employment and could be part of the 'core'. It has also been suggested that growth of a flexible workforce has been exaggerated and much has been due to the expansion of the service sector where such employment is common. It has also been suggested that most of the benefits are in favour of the business at the expense of employees. Employees see it as a means of getting them to work harder for less. Although workers have more involvement, management makes all the important decisions. Workers as individuals are ignored as a corporate culture develops and employees feel that they are being manipulated. It is also argued that human resources management takes a lower priority when a business is in difficulty.

Relocation and outsourcing

In the early twentieth century businesses in the UK attempted to reduce costs and improve the flexibility of employees. Faced with growing competition, but also aided by the development of global markets, the Internet and computer technology, businesses attempted to manage their human resources in more efficient ways.

One method favoured by some companies was to relocate businesses in low cost countries, whilst keeping their head offices in the UK (☞ unit 28). A whole operation might be moved to a country where average earnings were lower than in the UK, employees would be hired in those countries and workers would be made redundant in the UK. This was particularly suitable for operations such as call centres where skills were easily transferrable and there was no need for direct contact with consumers. One of the problems faced with such a reorganisation was control from a distance, although it could be argued that this is no different from the challenges facing a multinational business operating in many countries.

Increasingly businesses have also outsourced operations (☞ unit 30). In some cases this might be to teleworkers working from home, using computers to communicate with employers. Operating from home might reduce costs for the business, although this type of work might only be suitable for certain operations. If these employees were part time or employed on flexible contracts, as explained earlier, this might improve efficiency and reduce costs even further. In some cases businesses have even outsourced entire operations to other businesses which might be able to produce goods or provide services more effectively.

Knowledge management

Many businesses today see knowledge management (☞ unit 25) as important to their operation. It involves:

- identifying the knowledge of a business, such as the knowledge of employees;
- assessing how the knowledge can be used and planning how to use it effectively;
- ensuring that knowledge is shared by all people in the organisation.

The management of knowledge can have a number of benefits for a business. The speed at which a business gains knowledge and puts it to good use is one way in which it can gain an advantage over its rivals. For example, Sky was the

When Shell in Brazil needed help retrieving broken tools from a borehole, it asked its international colleagues. 24 hours later ideas flooded in from a global knowledge network devoted to wells. Shell was able to save $7 million as a result. The wells network is one of eleven global knowledge communities set up by Shell International Exploration and Production (SIEP). 'This is a very knowledge intensive business because there are so many variables but so many commonalities' says Arjun van Unnik, founder of Shell's New Ways of Working Department. 'Six years ago we had the idea that if we encountered a problem in ... Nigeria, it could be that something similar had happened in the North Sea' and that someone there had the solution. Engineers working in the communities have a culture of sharing knowledge. 'It's all factual stuff' says van Unnik. 'You either extract oil or you don't.'

Initially the communities had 'yellow pages' lists of members. But now they are web-based and online. Some of the communities have up to 4,000 members each. Each has a moderator and a co-ordinator. The co-ordinator has to search for answers to questions. Every few days all the answers will be pulled together and sent by e-mail. As larger communities have developed they have amassed a hugh bank of material. People have started using them as libraries and, using a search engine, can get detailed and precise answers from people who they can contact

Although sharing knowledge is a worthy aim in itself, the real driving force behind the money being spent is 'the bottom line'. Shell has already saved over £134 million and this only takes into account savings which can be quantified. 'There are many other cases where we cannot add precise value to a solution' says van Unnik. For example, a Shell sales company in Singapore beat rivals to a contract after using the network to research Shell's history with the client and those of competitors.

Source: adapted from *People Management*, 27.6.2002.

(a) Explain why knowledge management might be suited to Shell.
(b) Examine how the use of knowledge management might affect Shell.

Question 5

first company to launch digital television in the UK. It could be argued that this will give it an advantage in future as many customers will have 'signed up' and be unwilling to change to another supplier.

It may also prevent a duplication of services. For example, ICL found that several of its businesses were bidding for the same project at the same time without each knowing about the others' activities. It also found 23 different uncoordinated information services for employees, often providing the same information. Knowledge management could have prevented this waste of resources.

Sometimes people leave a business and take years of knowledge and experience with them. It often exists 'in the head' of the employee, who has found the best way to carry out a task or the most suitable skills to use. Making sure that this knowledge is collected and passed on may prevent problems for new employees to the job. It will also reduce time and costs for the business.

Unit 25 examines how knowledge management is important in the management of change.

key terms

Flexible workforce - a workforce that can respond (in quantity and type) to changes in demand a business may face.

Human resources management - an integrated approach which ensures the efficient management of human resources. It is part of the overall business plan.

Knowledge

1. Explain the difference between the soft and hard side of human resources management.
2. Briefly describe 5 factors that might affect the managing of human resources by a business.
3. 'A business that does not manage its human resources effectively may face industrial relations problems.' Explain this statement.
4. State:
   (a) 5 implications of taking a strategic approach to HRM;
   (b) 4 advantages of human resources management;
   (c) 4 problems of human resources management;
   for a business.
5. Briefly explain how a business may evaluate its management of human resources.
6. Suggest 3 ways in which a business might reduce labour turnover.
7. State 3 examples of:
   (a) flexible work practices;
   (b) flexible workers.
8. Suggest 3 advantages of:
   (a) a flexible workforce;
   (b) knowledge management.

Case study A five star strategy

Claridges is one of London's most luxurious hotels. It has changed little in 50 years, retaining the feel of glittering chandeliers and society afternoon tea. But behind the opulent surface there appeared to be human resources issues to be dealt with.

Sara Edwards took over as HR Director in 1998. Claridges was battling to maintain its place in the market. Other hotels offered luxury service. Cheaper hotels were shooting up all the time. Visits were down. Occupancy rates were falling at the hotel, complaints were high and staff turnover was running at 73 per cent. She argued that people weren't enjoying the experience at the hotel and staff weren't enjoying working there. A staff satisfaction survey revealed the extent of the problems. Only 47 per cent of staff bothered to respond. Of those that did, only 67 per cent said they felt proud to work for the business. Most felt a mistrust of management. As a result, the executive team came up with a new vision for the business, based on seven values. Edwards argued 'If you don't get it right for the employees, you won't get it right with the guests'.

By the end of 2002 staff turnover had fallen to 27 per cent. Pride at working in the hotel had risen to 99 per cent and every member of staff responded to the survey.

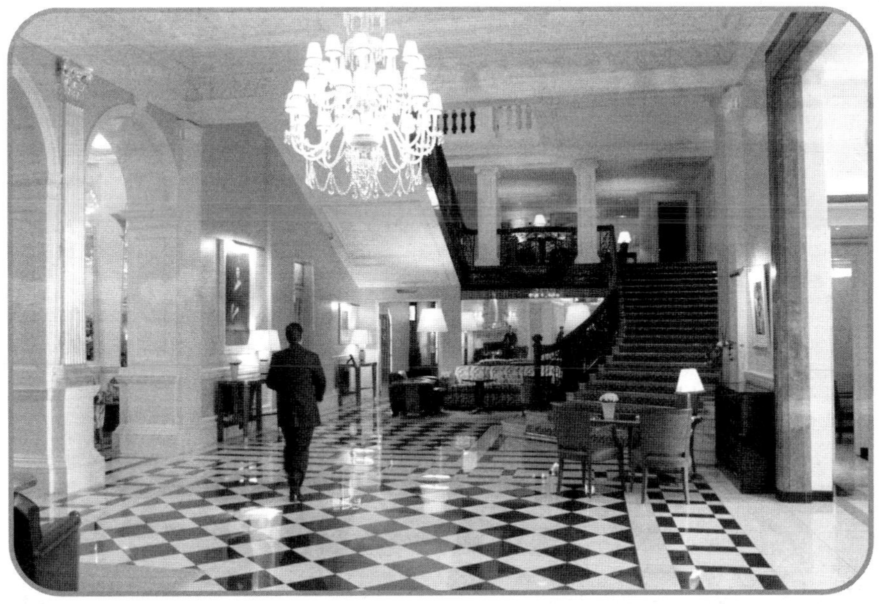

What was the secret behind such a change in employees' views? The seven core values of:

- commitment;
- passion;
- team spirit;
- interpersonal relations;
- service perfection;
- maximising resources;
- responsibility of actions;

were at the heart of the matter. They were depicted as a rainbow and this image helped to reinforce the idea that staff should have fun as well as doing their job. This was a novel idea for a hotel that had traditionally been seen as 'straight-laced'.

To train staff in the new philosophy, managers were taken off site on an away day. Each was asked to give a five minute performance to demonstrate one of the values. Edwards argued that the business had to do something very significant to show that things were going to be different, but fun as well. A new reward scheme 'Going for Gold' builds on the idea of the 'rainbow values'. Staff demonstrating special value for the business are given a gold card and take a lucky dip. Prizes range from a limo home to a night in a penthouse which would normally cost £3,850.

The 450 employees in the business are now encouraged to look to the future. Internal recruitment used to be rare, but now anyone taken on is viewed as someone who could eventually do a more skilled job. Staff are also encouraged to move across departments to develop their skills. New jobs are advertised in a newsletter. People who do not get the job are given training, as they have shown aspirations to improve.

People who visit the hotel say that they recognise the same faces. This seems to imply that people are staying longer in their jobs. This helps to maintain standards in the business. Another scheme is designed to improve staff pride. Employees are invited to experience staying as guests at the hotel for a night. One employee who stayed felt that it brought home why Claridges was unique and reminded the employee why they worked at the hotel.

Such reminders were important after the September 11 terrorist attacks in New York. Many hotels experienced falls in trade. Claridges called a meeting and a plan of action was drawn up. Employees were kept informed at all times and redundancies were kept to a minimum.

Source: adapted from *People Management*, 8.4.2004.

(a) Identify examples of the hard and soft side of human resource management at the hotel. (6 marks)

(b) Explain how the flexibility of staff might be improved at the hotel. (10 marks)

(c) Explain the factors which may have influenced the change in approach to human resources management. (10 marks)

(d) Examine how the changes in the management of human resources may have affected the business. (10 marks)

(e) Evaluate the effectiveness of personnel and human resources management at the hotel using appropriate methods. (14 marks)

25 The Management of Change

What causes change in business?

Businesses today have to operate in rapidly changing markets and conditions. They can no longer rely on a constant stream of customers, the same production process or the same product over a long period of time. They must constantly be aware of, and be prepared to respond to, changes in a number of areas.

Developments in technology The introduction of new technology can affect a business in many ways. There have, for example, been rapid changes in communications technology, production techniques and electronic components in recent years.

Market changes Businesses must respond to changes in the markets in which they sell. There may be competition from new businesses. This has been the case in the energy supply market. Former public sector owned gas and electricity suppliers were privatised and markets opened up to competition. New markets have opened up, such as the mobile phone market for companies such as BT. Competition may also come from new businesses entering a market, such as the offering of financial services by supermarkets. Other factors such as the Single European Market, globalisation, the opening up of markets in eastern Europe and China, the introduction of the euro and the expansion of the EU in 2004 were all likely to change how businesses operate.

Consumer tastes Businesses must also be prepared for changes in the tastes of consumers. Examples might be the purchase of environmentally friendly products, the desire for greater knowledge about products or the need for more efficient methods of shopping, such as purchasing via the Internet.

Legislation Government legislation can force changes in business activity. Taxation of pollution (☞ unit 41) would affect the production methods of many firms. Safety standards, such as EU regulations for VDU users, are also likely to affect how employees operate. Government aid or subsidies may affect the possible location of a business (☞ unit 28). Legislation on the number of hours employees can work may change work practices.

Changes in the workforce Population changes will affect the age and make-up of the workforce. The ageing of the population in the UK in the early part of the twenty first century was likely to result in changing recruitment policies for businesses. A falling population is also likely to change how a business plans its human resources.

Changes in the economy It is argued that economies go through periods of boom and slump, recession and recovery. This is known as the business cycle. Income, spending, saving, investment and economic variables such as unemployment and inflation are all likely to be different at different stages in the cycle.

The effects of change

The changes illustrated in the last section can have a number of effects on business.

- Product life cycles could become shorter. This means that businesses must constantly be looking to develop new and profitable products or services.
- The role of marketing research is likely to increase. A business must not be 'surprised' by sudden changes in the market. Research and forecasting techniques should help a firm to predict more accurately the situation in future.
- Research and development (☞ unit 27) will be essential in industries where rapid change is taking place. As well as anticipating market changes, a business must be prepared to respond to the needs of the market with new products, which can compete with those of competitors.
- Retraining of managers and 'shop floor' workers might be necessary. This may be to learn skills associated with new technology or to develop skills to meet changing consumer tastes. Examples may be the education of office staff in communications technology, such as e-mail or videoconferencing or the learning of foreign languages by UK business people wishing to enter foreign markets.
- Businesses must take account of changes in their human resource planning (☞ unit 24). This could mean employing a more flexible workforce that could be changed quickly to meet the needs of the business, for example employing part time workers, or the use of job sharing. It might also mean employing workers in low cost countries, such as in call centres abroad.
- A business must develop a culture and organisation which is prepared to respond to change (☞ unit 5).
- Businesses must be aware of competitors' actions and be prepared to react to them. Businesses now benchmark their activities against those of rivals or other companies. Business must also be able to respond to new and emerging markets. These might be new markets abroad or markets for new products within a country.
- Quality is likely to become more important as consumer awareness develops and competition increases. Firms must consider the quality of their products and also their after sales service and customer relations. For example, many businesses have tried to achieve the international IS0 9000 quality standard.
- Changes in equipment. Rapid change often makes equipment redundant. Businesses may find problems

from the inability to read computer disks because software has been updated to the need for new systems to cope with just in time requests. These changes could involve a large amount of spending if businesses do not wish to become outdated.

- Changes in production methods. Rapid changes can sometimes lead to increasing costs. Some businesses have reacted by outsourcing their production to low cost countries. Others have changed the technology they use to reduce costs.

Why manage change?

The management of change in business has grown in importance in recent years. Under pressure from competitors, higher costs and economic conditions, many firms in the UK developed company-wide change programmes. Companies such as BT, BA and ICI have 'turned around' their organisations through managed change.

There are some examples of firms that have made only minor changes to their business operations and remained successful. The Morgan Car Company still retains many of the original production methods and design features that have been part of its operation since the 1930s. It argues that it is exactly these 'original' features that attract consumers. However, many firms have refused to change or did not respond and went out of business, such as the British motorcycle industry and certain holiday firms. In the face of rapid change and competition, it is likely that firms must respond or go out of business.

Eversholt Ltd manufactures metal sheets used in the production of a wide range of products. It has recently found that it has been producing increasing amounts of waste metal in its manufacturing processes. As a result charges at landfill sites have risen considerably over the last two years.

Jemma and Niall Kilburn, two of the directors, have come back from a fact finding mission to other countries to see how to make use of recycled waste. In the USA they found a number of businesses which, with the right machinery, were able to move into associated production areas. There was a strong and growing interest in recycled products in the US. Consumers were often prepared to pay a little more knowing their money was helping to preserve the environment. This had led to a growth in a number of new businesses manufacturing recycled metal products.

Jemma and Niall drew up a business plan and presented it to the other directors. They felt that some of them would require a great deal of convincing before the business could make such as great change in direction. The reorganisation also had some wide ranging implications. The recycling machinery would require a large initial investment and would need to have the latest specification to conform to operating standards. Some of the workers at the business would need to be retrained to operate the machines. It was also likely that if the business took off, the operation would need to expand, with everything that would involve.

(a) Identify the factors which might have led to change at the business.

(b) Examine the implications for the business of any change in its operations

The role of the personnel department

Traditionally, personnel managers in personnel departments enforced rules and procedures and were less concerned with change. It has been suggested that if they became human resources managers, and more concerned with the following, then change would take place more effectively in business.

- A move away from job evaluation and fixed grades towards appraisal and performance related pay.
- Pay and conditions negotiated with individuals rather than collectively.
- An emphasis on team work rather than individual job design.
- A flexible workforce trained in a variety of skills.
- Encouraging employees that are **empowered** and self-motivating rather than needing to be 'controlled'.

Resistance to change

Businesses are likely to face some resistance to change from parts of the workforce for a number of reasons.

- Workers and certain levels of management sometimes fear the unknown. They feel safe with work practices, conditions and relationships that they have been used to for a period of time.
- Employees and managers may fear that they will be unable to carry out new tasks, may become unemployed or may face a fall in earnings.
- Individual workers might be concerned that they will no longer work with 'friends', or may be moved to a job which they dislike.

If change is to be carried out effectively, the business must make certain that these fears are taken into account. Only if employees feel they can cope with change, will the business be operating to its potential.

Owners of businesses may also be resistant to change for similar reasons. They might fear operating in unknown markets and conditions. They might not want the cost of any changes. They may also fear that they might not be able to adjust to new situations and be forced out of business.

Resistance may also be found in the culture of the organisation (see next section). Custom and practice are embedded in systems which reflect the norms, values and beliefs of the organisation. While this may give stability, it presents problems of rigidity when a business needs to change.

In order to deal with resistance to change, many theorists have suggested the need for a multi-step approach. Psychologist Kurt Lewin emphasised a three step process.

- Introducing an innovation with information aimed to satisfy a need.
- Overcoming resistance by group discussion and decision-making.
- Establishing a new practice.

Removing resistance to change

There are certain ways in which resistance to change might be prevented and barriers to change removed.

- Employees should be kept informed about all changes. This might be face to face discussions, the use of company newsletters or the use of technology, such as e-mails or a business website on the Internet.
- People who are affected by change might be involved in discussions about the changes that are taking place. This will give them the feeling that they are involved in shaping change and have a stake in its outcome.
- The business should attempt to prevent misinformation and rumours. It may be possible to organise formal meetings where employees are informed about decisions taking place.
- Businesses that have European works councils, where employers and employees are involved to a greater extent in decisions, might be able to discuss and remove resistance to change more easily.
- Legislation, such as EU regulations regarding information given to employees about decisions, might help to remove resistance. Also, businesses that abide by regulations regarding work time might find less resistance to change from employees.
- Training might be introduced so that employees are able to cope with the new demands of operations which have changed.
- The business should try to ensure that its organisational culture fits in with its new operations and organisation. This is discussed in the next section.

Developing an organisational culture for change

An **organisational culture** (☞ unit 5) includes the beliefs, norms and values of a business. It is a generally held view about how people should behave, the nature of working relationships and attitudes. Many companies, especially Japanese firms such as Honda, Toyota and Sony, place great emphasis on all employees understanding the company's 'culture'.

It has been suggested that a business which creates a culture of change is likely to manage it far more effectively. Management at the top must have a clear idea of how they expect the business to change. Structures, methods of training, management styles etc. must then alter to reflect this. Finally a culture must be established where all employed are aware of the new relationship and methods of working.

One model that has been used to implement change is total quality management (TQM). A feature of TQM is that everyone in the business is responsible for maintaining and improving quality, including the quality of the product, production methods and the supply to the customer. TQM's motto is 'getting it right the first time' and this is applied to external customers and what are known as 'internal customers' - the people employees work with. This approach helps develop a culture where all employees, managers etc. are trying to achieve the same goal, which should motivate, develop teamwork and improve communication, accountability and rewards.

There are those, however, who suggest that organisational culture is not something that can be easily manipulated. They argue that culture depends on human interaction and is continuously being recreated. Hence, to believe that a senior management team can unilaterally change an existing culture

---

In the early twenty first century Ashank Desai, chairman of global e-consultancy business Mastek, said that British business must embrace e-commerce more strongly or run the risk of being left behind other leading industrial nations. He said 'A certain complacency and resistance to change in IT advancement have been visible in the attitudes of many of the chief executives in the UK'.

Mr Desai claimed that the corporate culture in Britain was not conducive to IT. Technological advancement, he said, is restricted partly because IT managers do not sit on the board of directors of British companies. That meant firms failed to spot the potential of 'e-opportunities'. He also argued that at the time there was an 'alarming dearth of skills in Britain'.

He suggested further that businesses which did not change would experience massive problems. 'Whole industries such as financial services and the travel industry are going to change completely the way they do business' he argued. The warning came as countries in the west were increasingly trying to recruit computer programmers from around the globe, especially India.

Source: adapted from *The Guardian*, 19.9.2000.

(a) Suggest reasons why (i) employers, (ii) managers and (iii) employees in the UK might be resistant to the introduction of e-commerce.
(b) Examine the problems that might face financial service organisations which do not adapt to change.

---

according to some blueprint is mistaken. Organisational culture, according to this view does change, but often slowly and in unpredictable ways. There is also a danger of thinking of organisational culture as a single over-arching idea to which all members of the business subscribe. Organisations, however, may have sub-cultures linked to particular groups. There may be conflict between these subcultures. In addition, even if new culture is established, there is no evidence that simply having a new culture improves performance.

Different approaches to managing change

Research by John Storey has suggested that the way businesses manage change can be classified into four different approaches.

A total imposed package One approach to managing change is for people at the 'top' of the business to plan out major restructuring programmes without consultation with workers or worker representatives. The main advantage of this method is that a company can have a 'vision' of where it is going. It can compare where it is 'now' with where it was 'then'. It is possible, using this approach, to prepare departmental action plans, set timetables and measure how far change has been achieved. The business can also make changes without having to take into account the wishes of other groups. The disadvantage of planning change from the top is that middle managers, supervisors and employees may not feel involved.

Imposed piecemeal initiatives A different approach is to have unplanned or piecemeal initiatives designed to bring about change. Initiatives might be introduced by employers to solve particular problems or only at times when they are needed in the business. Examples of initiatives that might take place are:
- the introduction of team meetings or quality circles;
- improvements in technology or channels of communication;
- improvements in incentive payments or rewards;
- improvements in the flexibility of work practices;
- changes in the workforce, such as teleworkers or subcontracting;
- the introduction of performance appraisal.

A problem with piecemeal initiatives is that they sometimes have different objectives. One might be trying to improve management leadership. The other might to trying to encourage greater participation. Another difficulty is that piecemeal initiatives tend to be short lived. In difficult times businesses may decide to drop costly changes.

Negotiated piecemeal initiatives Productivity agreements are often used to help change take place. Unions agree to changes in work practices, usually in exchange for extra payments or improved conditions for workers. These negotiated changes tend to be ad-hoc, without any coordinated policy by the business.

Negotiated total packages This is where a 'total package' for change is put together. It is negotiated by employers and union representatives. It may be in the form of a 'national deal', which involves changes in work practices for all employees in every plant or office in exchange for increased rewards or improved conditions. In practice this method of managing change was rarely used in Britain before the 1990s. However, the changing roles of trade unions and the likelihood of partnerships between business and unions after the year 2000 may have seen this type of negotiation taking place more often.

Remploy is the UK's largest employer of people with disabilities. It manufactures products as diverse as car headrests, furniture and shower units. It has bucked falling industry trends by achieving a five per cent increase in profits largely by embracing changes in those who make a difference - the workforce.

Two years ago the company decided it wanted to increase staff from 12,000 to 25,000 and triple output over a five year period. The personnel director and resource director were asked to work closely to start a major change programme. The idea was that roving internal consultants focus on Remploy sites that had more work than they could cope with. They investigate the 'weakest link' in the production process, then move on to find the next 'weakest link'.

The crux of the change programme was to make sure that every person had a say in how the day to day processes were to be run. This meant that even simple ideas could be shared. For example, one employee suggested sticking coloured tape on the machinists' tables during sewing to improve accuracy and to speed up the process. Staff also wanted to remove a huge overhanging machine so that they could see each other and help to communicate when a constraint in the flow of work had built up.

Assessment is now based on the end product, so that staff have a feeling of ownership and team spirit. Staff morale improved greatly as changes were made with all the factory involved and not just management. The business argues that there were short term benefits but also a long term change in culture. One of the machinists at the company said 'Change is frightening but, because we all have a say, we feel more confident in making those changes'.

Source: adapted from *People Management*, 29.5.2003.

(a) Identify the approach to managing change at Remploy using examples from the article.
(b) Examine the benefits to (i) employees and (ii) the business of such an approach.

Evaluating the management of change

Managers will have a clear idea of the improvements to performance that they want from change in business. They may want productivity gains as a result of the use of multi-skilled teams or improved response times to customer demands due to new communication technologies. These are sometimes referred to as **performance indicators**. Performance indicators can be used to evaluate the management of change. Any evaluation strategy will have quantitative and qualitative methods of analysing changes in working practices.

- A rise in output from 10,000 to 15,000 as a result of change or an improvement in average delivery time from two days to 24 hours would be measurable, quantitative improvements.
- Employees' responses to a questionnaire, stating that change had improved their motivation, could be a qualitative method of evaluating the management of change.

Learning organisations and change

In recent years there has been a growing interest in learning organisations. A LEARNING ORGANISATION (☞ unit 24) is a business which absorbs knowledge, acquires skills and changes its attitudes. Solutions that are found to problems become the 'knowledge' of the business. They then become part of the firm's 'memory' and are used when reacting to future events. For example, a business may find that setting up a graduate training programme is more effective than trying to headhunt managers from other organisations. It may use this approach when setting up a branch of the business overseas.

There is a number of implications for a business that wants to be a learning organisation.

- Human resource development strategy must be central to business policy.
- A business must constantly change its decision making in the light of new events.
- Employees must be regularly retrained in new working methods. Managers must develop coaching skills.
- Current practices must be questioned and workers must experiment with new solutions.
- Rewards must be geared to finding new solutions and workers must be allowed to manage themselves in work groups.
- There must be communication between all areas of the business.

There are certain advantages of this approach. Such businesses are more likely to grow and develop naturally to meet new demands because learning is integral to the way they operate. The business will not be using outdated plans and procedures to solve problems. Decision making may therefore be more effective. A business may also be better able to cope with change because it can take into account unpredictable events. Because businesses are constantly adapting their approaches to problems there should be less resistance to change from employees. However, an organisation can quickly go back to 'old ways of doing things' unless it constantly makes use of new knowledge. There may also be resistance from some

The National Blood Service (NBS) is the body in the UK responsible for ensuring there are sufficient blood reserves to meet the needs of the NHS. In the past it operated 15 autonomous centres, but this was changed to three 'zones' because it was thought to bring greater efficiency and economy. Many NHS workers interpreted this as an attack on the NHS's fundamental values. Now it has been restructured again to remove difficultes.

The three zone system, had been a major problem for people. Management teams had to take on a 'zonal' rather than local responsibility. Some didn't want to adopt the new working practices and 'fifteen into three does not go' it was argued. Leaders did not want to move sideways or downwards and so some left. Back-up from the human resources team was also fragmented across the zones.

People felt threatened by the latest restructuring only three years after the last one. It has helped that the reorganisation has not been as far reaching this time and clearly wasn't done for cost savings.

When the organisation began the restructuring process it started a staff survey. The results at first were as many feared. Directors were not thought to be interested in staff well being or views, workplace stress was not dealt with effectively and workloads were excessive. The survey also highlighted that terms and conditions were not applied equally. Fortunately much of the scepticism was misplaced. The top ten problems were identified and 300 staff were asked to join focus groups. They then drew up a mission statement and a set of values. This helped the organisation to see staff as a key resource. Now the lines of communication have improved and the culture is starting to change. 'We are getting away from the blame culture and taking best practice from other parts of the service' says a team leader.

Not everyone agrees with this, however. The regional officer of UNISON says that problems in negotiating terms and conditions still hinder the organisation. He says 'It's a bad, old-fashioned industrial relations attitude. There's a complete detachment between the senior management and what happens at ground level'.

Source: adapted from *People Management*, 20.3.2003.

(a) Explain how managing change might be assessed in the organisation.
(b) Discuss to what extent change has been managed well.

managers, who see their control diluted, or workers who do not want to or are not able to learn.

The management of change and enterprise

Research by Salaman (2002) has suggested that all change programmes can be analysed by focusing on one particular theme - **enterprise**. The idea is that a business should strive to become more enterprising in the way that it is organised and in the way it works. In order to achieve this a business needs to train employees to become more enterprise focused. For example, employees might go 'one step further', by trying to resolve a customer's problem even if it is not their responsibility. Over time individual employees will begin to police their own actions and will be critical of themselves if they don't achieve particular goals that they have set. Previously, employees may have undertaken tasks because of rules and regulations and because of performance or appraisal measures. Now they are more likely to become the guardians of their own performance because training, support and new working styles within the business have developed an enterprising approach in employees.

key terms

Learning organisation - a business in a changing environment that constantly revises its working methods.

1. State 5 factors that may cause change in a business.
2. How might change affect:
   (a) market research
   (b) research and development;
   in a business?
3. Why is it important for businesses to manage change?
4. Explain 4 ways in which the personnel department can plan human resources to deal with change.
5. What is meant by 'developing an organisational culture for change'?
6. Briefly explain 4 approaches to change.

Case study Ringing the changes at BT

BT has a huge property portfolio. It includes a massive infrastructure of wires, cables, junction boxes, buildings and phone boxes. It is managed by people who know that they do an essential job, unglamorous as it might seem. Faced with a debt mountain of £2.38 billion, BT felt the only way to reduce this was to outsource its property operation.

Staff were shocked. The average length of service was 21 years. Most had never worked anywhere else. They had excellent terms and conditions of work, a final salary pension scheme and the ability to work flexibly. In fact, 90 of the employees in the area were homeworkers. How would they all be affected?

BT decided its outsource partner would be Telereal, a company set up between LS Trillium and the Pears Group to bid for BT's property arm. It aimed to set high standards in the way that workers who transferred from BT would be treated. Part of LS Trillium's corporate culture was that 'we couldn't attract the people we needed solely on the strength of pay, so we emphasised the opportunity they would have to shape the business' according to HR director Robbie Wheeler. Wheeler and her team at

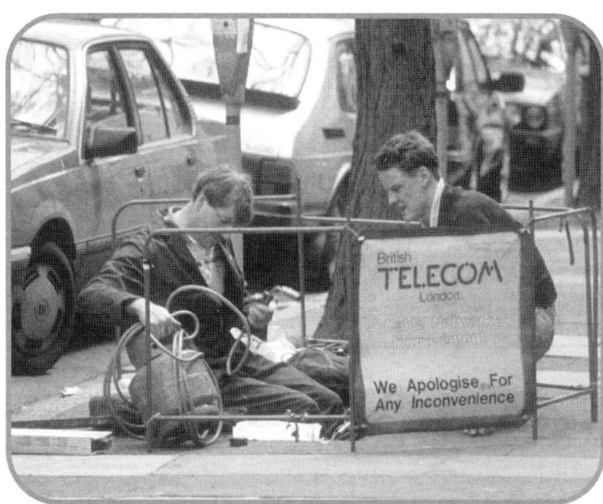

Telereal know that timing is crucial, stating 'When you tell staff something, you have to be sure you can deliver'. The business was used to a corporate emphasis on loyalty.

Telereal started communicating with staff who were transferring from BT about the changes as early as possible. It began by opening a dialogue with BT's HR professionals and the two trade unions involved, CWU and Connect. In the months before the transfer a dedicated helpline was set up, a Internet site was run and a roadshow was taken around the country at which Telereal's MD answered staff questions. This was followed by a further roadshow and audio conferences set up to handle the important question of future pensions.

A key decision made early on by Telereal was to retain the final salary pension scheme. Staff would also transfer initially not to Telereal, which was an unknown name, but to LS Trillium, which had a good property track record and reputation as an employer. Staff who transferred were doing the same work in the same clothes, but for a different business.

So far the results were positive. A survey showed that 80 per cent of staff said they were proud to work for Telereal. Only 2.3 per cent have left. Commitment is high and financial results had exceeded expectations. Having been on the margins at BT, some of the staff who transferred were now an integral part of the new company and experiencing new opportunities.

Source: adapted from *People Management*, 6.11.2003.

(a) Identify the possible sources of resistance to change mentioned in the article. (4 marks)

(b) Explain how the corporate culture of LS Trillium and Telereal might have helped to manage change. (6 marks)

(c) What approach to managing change did Telereal use? Explain your answer using examples from the passage. (6 marks)

(d) Examine the factors that helped to remove the resistance to change at BT. (12 marks)

(d) Assess the extent to which the approach taken by the business might be of benefit in future. (12 marks)

26 Resources and Waste

What are resources?

Businesses use resources in production. These are the factors of production in business activity - land, labour, capital and enterprise. This unit deals with land and the materials and resources used by businesses. There are many different materials used in business products. Some are manufactured into other materials or components, which are then used to make different products.

- Silk, a natural resource, is used in the textile industry. Silk fibres are made by caterpillars and are used to make a silk yarn. The yarn is then woven into a fabric. This fabric can be dyed or printed on and used in the manufacture of scarves or shirts, for example.
- Lycra is a SYNTHETIC fibre made from chemicals. It is usually combined with other materials such as wool, nylon, cotton or silk to produce clothes, for example. It allows clothing to stretch and recover its shape.
- Sugar is made by a variety of processes from the natural materials sugar cane or beet. It can be added as a sweetener to products such as jam. When sugar is processed it produces BY-PRODUCTS. These are materials which are created as a 'side effect' of the process. For example, raw sugar is separated from syrup, called molasses, in sugar production. This molasses is used in the food industry and as animal feed.
- Pine is a natural wood used in the production of many items, including tables and chairs, beds, toilet roll holders, children's toys and CD racks.
- Medium density fibreboard (MDF) is produced from waste wood, such as pine or spruce, left over after wooden products are made. Cuttings are combined with water, wax and resin to produce MDF boards. The boards are then used to make products such as furniture, shelving, toys, display stands and flooring.
- Plastics are manufactured from chemicals. Pigments can be added to change their colour and plasticisers make them more bendy. Plastics include polythene (made into bottles, crates and carrier bags), ABS (kettles and telephone bodies), polystyrene (packaging and model kits) and acrylic (as a glass substitute in baths, spectacles and street signs).
- Metals may be natural materials found in rocks, such as iron, copper or tin. Carrying out processes can change metal. Heating iron while blowing oxygen on it produces steel. Joining metals into alloys gives the new metal the combined advantages of the original metals. Brass is an alloy of copper, which conducts electricity, and zinc, which is hard but brittle. An alloy of aluminium and copper resists corrosion and is used for outdoor window frames and motor car parts, as it is lightweight and can be shaped.

Waste

In the production of many goods or services some materials are wasted. WASTE also results from production processes. Waste is any material which is no longer useful in a particular production process and has to be disposed of. The **Special Waste Regulations, 1996** classifies different types of waste.

Unilever is a large international supplier of food, personal care and home care products. A summary of its products is shown below.

- Savoury and dressings. Some of the company's best selling brands in this category include Knorr soups and noodles, Bertolli's pasta sauces and Hellmann's salad dressings.
- Spreads and cooking products. This sector is responsible for producing brands such as Blueband, Flora, Brunch Boursin and Crème Bonjour.
- Ice cream and frozen foods. Unilever produces Cornettos, Magnums and Soleros for the ice cream market. It also owns the Findus and Bird's Eye range of frozen ready meal solutions.
- Health & wellness beverages. Two popular brands in this category are Slim.Fast and Lipton's drinks which include Lipton Ice Tea, Lipton Brisk and a range of leaf teas.
- Home care and professional cleaning. Unilever is a world leader in this sector which includes hygiene and cleaning products such as Snuggle, Comfort, Omo, Persil, Surf, Skip, Domestos, Cif and many others.
- Personal care. This sector accounts for around 25 per cent of Unilever's turnover. It includes brands such as Dove, Sunsilk, Pond's, Lux, Axe, Rexona and Signal toothpaste.

Figure 26.1 shows the contribution to turnover made by each of these sectors.

Figure 26.1 *Turnover by category - Unilever 2002*

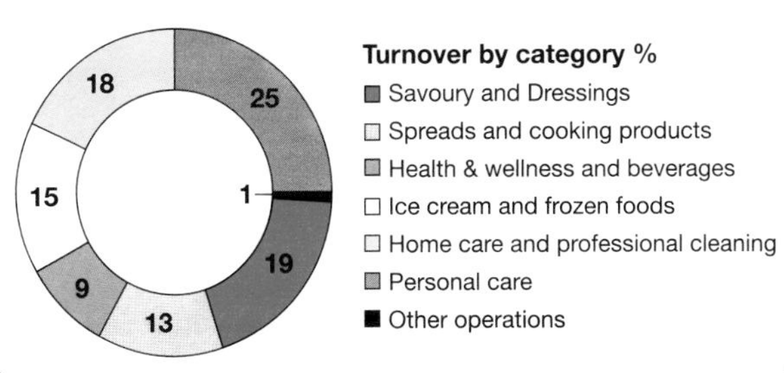

Source: adapted from Unilever, *Annual Report and Accounts, 2002.*

(a) State six examples of natural resources that Unilever might use in production.
(b) To what extent do Unilever make use of plastics in its operations?

Inert waste This includes materials which will not cause environmental pollution and will not have physical, chemical or biological reactions. Examples include stone, brick, most mining waste or subsoil from road widening schemes.

Biodegradable waste Biodegradable waste, such as wood, waste food and garden waste, rots away by the action of living micro-organisms. It can lead to unpleasant smells. Biological reaction may also take place. This can result in landfill gases containing methane and carbon dioxide. Landfill gases are thought to be a major factor affecting global warming (☞ unit 41).

Hazardous waste Hazardous waste can damage health. **Clinical waste** is materials from hospitals and vets, which may be contaminated with blood. It must be disposed of by being burned. **Special wastes** are wastes that appear on an EU list of hazardous wastes and include:
- toxic (poisonous) materials such as lead, rat poison and cyanide;
- materials which cause health risks if inhaled, swallowed or absorbed by the skin, such as asbestos;
- corrosive materials, such as acid, which can burn the skin, eyes and lungs;
- flammable wastes, such as gas cylinders which may ignite.

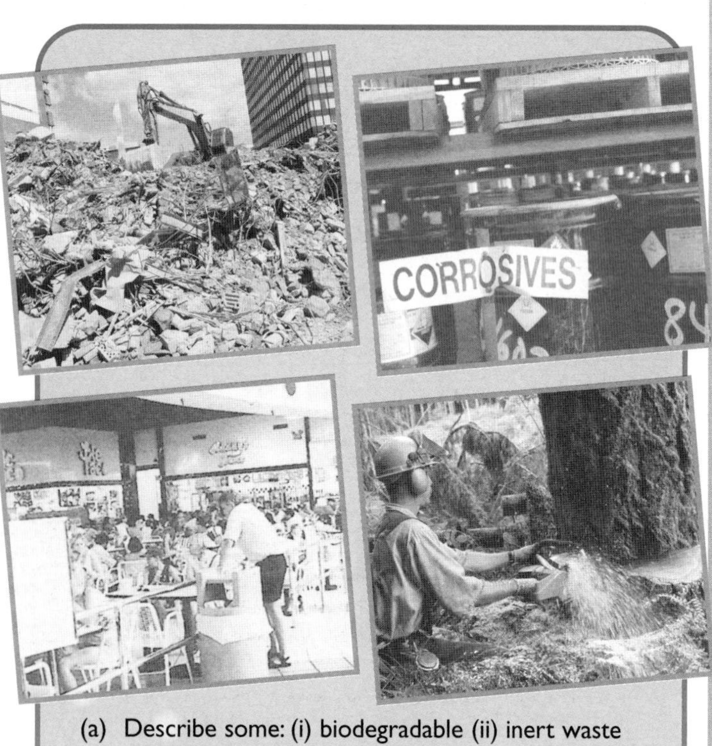

(a) Describe some: (i) biodegradable (ii) inert waste (iii) hazardous waste which the businesses in the photographs might generate.
(b) Comment on the difficulty of disposing of waste for each business.

Question 2

Businesses must treat some special wastes, such as acids, engine oils and industrial materials, in treatment plants before disposal. Special wastes such as solvents must be disposed of in high temperature incinerators.

Waste management

WASTE MANAGEMENT describes how businesses deal with waste material. In a small hotel or bookshop, it may just involve making sure that waste material is collected regularly by the local authority. In a chemical processing plant toxic waste may be produced, which must be treated and then disposed of safely. This task might use up a great deal of resources and need continuous monitoring.

Why is waste a problem for a business and for society? For a business, unnecessary waste is expensive. It will raise costs and reduce profit. A firm may try to raise its prices to pay for these extra costs, which might deter customers. For society, some waste is hazardous. If not treated properly it can harm people or the environment. Radioactive waste may kill people if not disposed of carefully. Some resources that are wasted may be non-renewable, such as oil. If waste is reduced, this will mean that such resources will last longer.

Methods of dealing with waste

Waste minimisation Perhaps the best way to reduce business waste is to avoid producing it in the first place. Government measures, such as a landfill tax, to make sure businesses meet the cost of waste disposal and environmental effects have encouraged firms to minimise waste. The government has also helped by setting up special schemes to reduce industrial waste. The Environmental Technology Best Practice Programme (ETBPP), set up in 1994, aimed to encourage practices that would reduce costs by £320 million per annum by the year 2015. Savings could be as a result of businesses:
- using information from benchmarking publications and case studies and guides on good practice;
- asking advice from an environmental helpline;
- establishing regional waste minimisation projects to reduce costs.

Re-use One way of minimising waste is to re-use materials and products which would otherwise be disposed of. Milk bottles, for example, are collected daily and reused. Plastic containers can be reused for different liquids. Pallets are used again and again by businesses when transporting goods. Charity shops sell second hand clothing. Voluntary groups such as Waste Watch and Going for Green have helped to promote this practice.

Recycling Recycling involves the collection of a waste material such as paper, plastic, glass, aluminium or steel, and producing a new raw material from that waste. For example, Plysu makes containers to hold liquids such as detergents from recycled plastic. It is possible to collect material for recycling in a number of ways.

- Bring systems, where people take materials to collection points, such as bottle banks or clothes banks.
- Collect systems, where households separate certain materials and put them outside the house for collection by voluntary groups, the council and organisations such as the Scout movement. These groups sell the waste collected to businesses for processing.
- Central processing is carried out by or on behalf of local councils. It involves sorting mixed waste at a central processing plant where household refuse is collected. Such plants not only recycle materials but also generate energy.

Incineration This involves burning waste materials at very high temperatures. It reduces the volume of waste by turning about 70 per cent of it into carbon dioxide gas, other gases and water vapour. The ash that results from burning the waste is often used in the construction industry or taken to landfill sites. Some gases are poisonous and must be prevented from entering the atmosphere by special pollution control equipment. Although new incinerators are expensive, interest in them is gaining because of the rising costs of other methods of disposal.

Landfill Around 90 per cent of all solid waste in Britain is LANDFILLED. This is a fairly safe way of disposing of waste which involves burying it in the ground. This is not without problems. In the past gas has escaped leading to explosions. Today landfill sites contain 'liners', such as clay or polythene to prevent escape. Pipes and pumps are used to release them. In some cases landfill gas is cleaned and used to provide energy for nearby factories or to generate electricity. When a site is full, a top is constructed, which is covered in clay and layers of soil so rain water can drain off. It is then planted with crops or plants.

Composting Composting involves collecting organic waste such as potato peelings, kitchen scraps, grass cuttings and other garden waste and allowing it to decompose. It can then be returned to the soil, where it will act as a natural fertiliser. Composting tends to be carried out in people's gardens rather than as a business activity because compost can vary in standard and there is a problem finding markets for it.

Design Increasingly businesses are considering the impact of waste when designing products and processes. Design teams are developing products and processes which minimise waste in a number of ways.

- Production processes can reduce waste. For example, JIT and kaizen methods have helped to reduce waste in production.
- Firms are using less packaging. For example, single portion yogurt pots now use 5 grams of plastic instead of 12 grams.
- Manufacturers are designing cars which use less fuel. Cars are now more aerodynamic. Components are made from plastic rather than metal or aluminium rather than steel, which makes them lighter.
- The development of concentrated products. For example, in the detergent industry producers sell concentrated fabric conditioner in pouches rather than plastic bottles. A 1 litre bottle of conditioner weighs 70 grams. However, a 12 gram plastic pouch holds 1 litre of conditioner concentrate.
- In the electronics industry designers are continually trying to reduce the size of many products such as computers, mobile phones, hi-fi systems and TVs. Smaller versions use fewer resources.

Increasing efforts have been made in the UK to encourage recycling. Many local councils have set up collection schemes and awareness has been raised, to an extent, through the use of publicity campaigns. Businesses have become more aware of the savings that can be made from recycling and are beginning to look more diligently for ways of recycling their waste. Table 26.1 shows recycling and recovery data for a sample of European countries between 1998 and 2000.

Table 26.1 *Recycling and recovery data for a sample of European countries, 1998-2000*

Country	Recycling 1998 (%)	Recycling 2000 (%)	Recovery 1998 (%)	Recovery 2000 (%)
Austria	64.9	68.1	69.7	72.9
Denmark	50.1	55.7	88.6	91.2
Finland	44.6	49.5	55.5	60.0
France	41.5	42.2	56.0	57.0
Germany	81.4	78.1	83.6	80.7
Italy	31.6	38.4	35.1	42.5
Netherlands	56.9	58.8	56.9	58.8
Spain	34.1	38.9	37.9	44.1
Sweden	74.9	57.8	81.8	65.6
UK	**31.4**	**36.7**	**36.3**	**42.1**

(a) Comment on the performance of the UK with regard to the recycling and recovery of waste.
(b) How might businesses benefit from recycling programmes?

Question 3

Benefits and problems of waste management

Businesses which carry out waste management measures may enjoy certain benefits

- Waste management can help businesses reduce their costs. For example, by minimising waste a business may use fewer resources. In addition, if less waste is generated the cost of disposal will be lower.
- If businesses reduce waste they may be able to offer products at lower prices to consumers. This may give the business a competitive edge.
- By spending money on research and development in waste management businesses may be able to find ways of using their waste productively. For example, they may produce a material from waste which they might be able to sell.
- If a business has a well developed waste management policy, designed to protect employees and the environment from hazardous waste, its image may be improved.
- By reducing certain wastes businesses might be able to reduce the amount of tax they pay. Businesses that use landfill sites to dispose of waste must pay landfill tax.
- An effective waste management policy should help a business to avoid breaking the law regarding waste disposal, and thus avoid paying fines.

There are also some disadvantages of waste management.

- Some aspects of waste management are very expensive and contribute to higher business costs. The proper disposal of hazardous waste, such as nuclear waste, can be very expensive.
- Higher business costs resulting from waste management activities may raise the prices of products to customers. This may be a problem if a business is trying to sell goods in overseas markets where foreign laws regarding waste disposal are less restrictive.
- Small businesses might be at a disadvantage. They may not have the resources to spend on waste management which larger companies have.

Factors affecting waste management

Needs of stakeholders Waste management decisions may be complicated. Different business stakeholders can have needs which may conflict. For example, shareholders are keen to maximise returns. They may want a business to maximise profits, which may mean spending less on waste management. However, the local community may want a business to devote more resources to waste management in order to improve the environment. But this could reduce profits. Employees will also be concerned about waste management for health and safety reasons.

There may even be conflict within groups. Some consumers might prefer businesses to keep waste management costs to the minimum, so that prices are kept low. Others may prefer businesses to spend on waste management activities, even if it means paying higher prices, because of the impact on the environment.

Legislation There is a growing body of UK and EU legislation regarding the disposal and treatment of waste. Complying with the various Acts of Parliament will affect the

Biffa Waste handles around 10 per cent of the UK's waste, in 2002-2003 Biffa's turnover increased by 3.3 per cent to £510.9 million. Biffa offers waste services to industry, commerce, retail customers and the health and public sectors. These services include the following.

- **Dry waste collection**. Most types of heavy or bulky waste can be collected and disposed of. Biffa's services include regular scheduled collection, rapid response call out for collection, guaranteed safe transportation and full documentation which complies with all relevant legislation.
- **Special waste services.** A wide range of services are offered here, such as the collection and disposal of clinical and hazardous waste, the treatment and disposal of waste water and the packaging and transportation of sensitive waste materials.
- **Cleaning/industrial services**. These include water jetting and air conveyancing, sewer surveying services, drainage system support services, environmental maintenance services and forecourt services.
- **Biffa environmental technology**. Services such as landfill gas control and utilisation, site investigation and monitoring service, technology maintenance services and drilling.
- **Landfill operations**. Help with landfill profiles and landfill introduction, contaminated land, special and difficult waste, reclaimed resources and construction and demolition.
- **Recycling**. Biffa can offer help and advice recycling a huge range of wastes including glass, polymers, metals, wood, mobile phones, textiles, batteries, office paper, packaging, toner cartridges, electronic equipment, tyres, fluorescent lamps, furniture, compost and paint.
- **Biffpack**. This is the leading waste management industry-based Compliance Scheme. The Producer Responsibility Obligations (Packaging Waste Regulations) 1997 set targets for British industry for the recovery and recycling of packaging waste. Under the regulations, companies above thresholds for both turnover and the amount of packaging handled have the option of following the individual route and attempting to meet these targets themselves or of passing their obligations over to a Compliance Scheme.

Source: adapted from Biffa Waste website.

(a) Explain, using examples, how Biffa's services may benefit (i) businesses; (ii) consumers; (iii) the environment.

way businesses handle waste. For example, the government raised the standard rate of landfill tax from 7 to 13 per cent over the period 1996-2002. As a result, some businesses may have decided to find other methods of disposal or tried to reduce the amount of waste they generated.

Costs As already shown, the disposal and treatment of waste is becoming a highly commercialised activity. Businesses need to consider the costs of different methods of waste management and charges made by different businesses in the industry.

Ethical stance As the importance of image and social responsibility (☞ unit 40) grows, businesses are likely to pay more consideration to waste management. Firms must operate within the law when managing waste. But they may go further. For example, a business might incur extra costs by using recycled materials in production or ensure that the liquid waste discharged into rivers was actually cleaner than the minimum legal standard. This type of ethical behaviour might help to improve their image.

Local initiatives In some regions support groups have been established which encourage businesses in their area to reduce waste. For example, the West Midlands Waste Minimisation Club provides support and advice on waste minimisation in the West Midlands area. The existence of such groups is likely to encourage firms to adopt waste minimisation programmes.

key terms

By-products - materials which are produced as a result of a process designed to produce a different material.
Synthetic materials - materials which are produced artificially, for example by chemical process, rather than naturally.
Landfill - a way of disposing of waste which involves burying it in the ground
Waste - any material which is no longer of use to the system that produced it and which has to be disposed of.
Waste management - the way in which businesses deal with the problem of waste materials.

Knowledge

1. State 3 materials used in:
   (a) the clothing industry;
   (b) the construction industry;
   (c) the car industry;
   (d) the food industry.
2. Give 2 examples of: (a) inert waste; (b) biodegradable waste; (c) hazardous waste.
3. Why is waste a problem for: (a) a business; (b) society?
4. Why might waste minimisation be the best way to reduce the impact of waste?
5. What is the difference between re-use and recycling?
6. Why is design important in waste management?
7. Suggest 4 advantages and 4 disadvantages of waste management.
8. Explain how the needs of stakeholders can affect waste management decisions.
9. State 4 measures taken by the government to reduce waste.

Case study BOC

The BOC Group serves over two million customers in over 50 countries. It is one of the largest suppliers of gases in the world. The business employs around 43,000 people and generated a turnover of £4,017.9 million in 2002. For over 100 years, BOC's gases have been supplied to a variety of industries, such as steel-making, refining, chemical processing, environmental protection, waste water treatment, welding and cutting, food processing and health care. However, two other businesses have grown in parallel with the supply of gases. One is BOC Edwards, which supplies ultra-high purity gases and associated equipment to the semi-conductor industry and is also world-famous for its vacuum pumps. The other is Gist, a specialist logistics company serving a number of major customers such as Marks & Spencer.

Although classified in the 'chemicals' sector, BOC does not have the conventional environmental issues that other chemical producers have to deal with. The nature of BOC's activities and chemicals are quite different. However, like all other businesses, it produces waste and is obliged to deal with it according to environmental legislation. BOC's performance with regard to waste management and other environmental issues is overseen by the SHEQ (social, health, environment and quality) Department. BOC reported the following in 2002.

- A special global environmental working party was set up to develop the group's environmental and waste management practices. Its aim was to develop the best environmental operating practices in the world.
- Many BOC businesses have ISO 14001 environmental certification.
- A fuel efficiency programme was implemented to reduce fuel consumption costs and carbon dioxide emissions. In the UK alone, BOC operates over 2,000 large delivery vehicles. The programme has resulted in an annual saving of more than £340,000.
- BOC incurred no fines or prosecutions for breach of any environmental regulation. It was also compliant with external standards. However, it was unable to comply with all internal codes or practices.
- BOC patented systems to recover carbon dioxide from other company's productive processes and put it to constructive use. For example, carbon dioxide is infused in drip-irrigation water or used to enrich atmospheres to enhance growth.
- The development of technology that is more energy efficient is a priority at BOC. This helps to support customers meet their carbon dioxide emission reduction targets.
- The UK-based BOC Foundation for the Environment, which was set up in 1990, has so far supported more than 110 projects focusing on waste management, water quality and pollution control.

BOC has had some criticism. The US Environmental Protection Agency named BOC as a potentially responsible party for clean-up costs at a number of hazardous waste sites. Liability for the restoration of the sites may be legally imposed without regard to the quantity of waste contributed. However, the cost was expected to be insignificant.

(a) Identify five types of waste that BOC generates. (5 marks)

(b) Define the terms (i) waste management; (ii) hazardous waste. (6 marks)

(c) How might BOC benefit from having ISO 14001 environmental certification? (6 marks)

(d) Explain three ways in which BOC disposes of its waste. (9 marks)

(e) What evidence is there in the case to suggest that BOC takes waste management seriously? (12 marks)

(f) Discuss how different stakeholders might benefit from BOC's approach to waste management. (12 marks)

Figure 26.2 *Waste record, BOC*

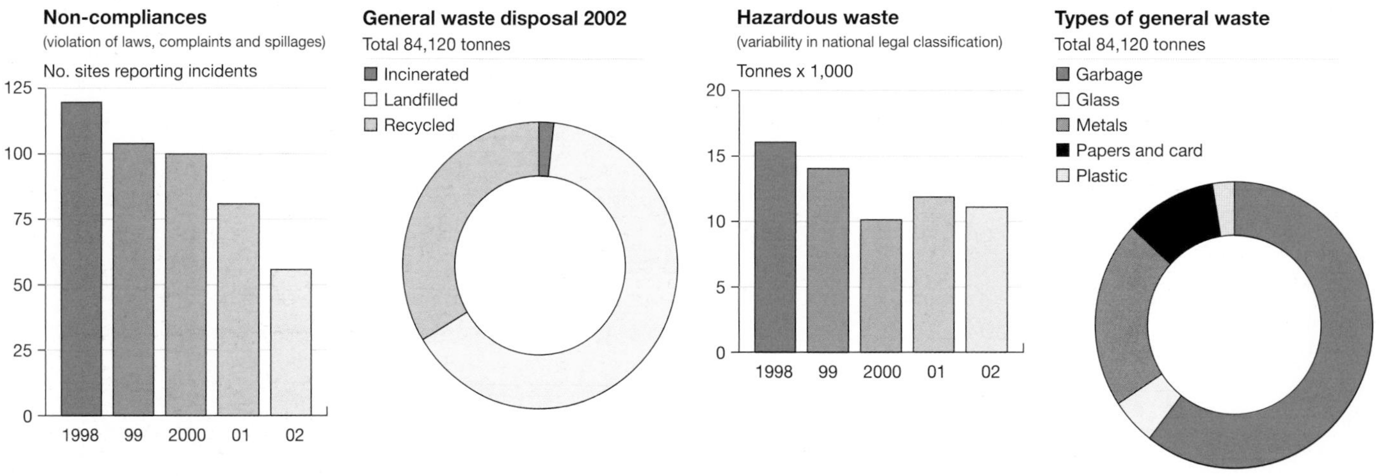

Source: adapted from BOC, *Annual Report and Accounts, 2002*

27 Product Design and Research & Development

Product choice

New businesses have to decide what product to manufacture or what service to provide. Once a business is established, it is unlikely to supply exactly the same product or service indefinitely. Over time businesses modify products, withdraw declining products and introduce new ones. They tend to extend product lines and may even diversify into completely different product areas. Decisions to launch new products or adapt existing ones are often complex and can be uncertain. Most businesses will carry out marketing research before making these decisions. This will help to evaluate the likely success of a new product before production begins.

What influences the products a firm chooses to produce?

The approach of the business Some businesses may be **product orientated**. The nature of the product itself (what it could do and its quality) would be enough to make sure that it sold. For example, when cars were first produced they were unique and a novelty and so the product sold itself. Many firms recognise the need to design products that meet consumers' wishes. These are **market orientated firms**. Increasingly businesses are becoming **asset-led**. They are launching products based on the strengths of the business. For example, a company with a strong brand name for a product may develop other related products.

Competitors' behaviour In order to survive in a competitive market, businesses must supply products which customers prefer at the expense of those supplied by competitors. This may mean developing products which are not available, or copying rivals' ideas and improving them.

Technology New inventions and innovations often result in new products. For example research has resulted in mobile telephones, satellite television, with pay per view options, and digital television, with improved picture quality and interactive options. New materials have been created which have led to improved products. Kevlar is a fibre which is used in the manufacture of bullet proof vests because of its resistance to impact. Carbon fibre racing cycles have been created which are lighter and faster than traditional cycles. Totally new products may be created. DVD players play films stored on discs similar to CDs. However, they contain far more information.

Management The choice of product is often made by senior management. It is a crucial decision because it may decide the fate of a company.

Financial viability Do the benefits of new or adapted goods or services outweigh the costs? The benefit to the firm might be the revenue it gains from selling the product. Accountants often act as a **constraint** on production decisions. They are unlikely to approve funds for products which will make long term losses.

Approaches to product development

Businesses may prefer to develop a new product which is unique. In practice this is difficult. New product development is expensive and highly risky. As a result most 'new' products tend to be adapted from those which already exist. Product ideas can come from a number of sources.

Ideas from customers The most successful firms will be those which provide products which match the wants of customers. Thus it makes sense to listen to the views of customers when forming ideas for new products. The marketing department is likely to play an important role. Questionnaires and interviews can be used to gather data from customers. However, it is often argued that less structured methods are more appropriate for collecting new ideas. The use of **focus groups**, where 7 to 10 participants sit to discuss and share ideas about new products, is one approach. Another is to

(a) What factors might have influenced the development of the products above?

Question 1

analyse all customer communications, such as complaints and suggestions. It is important for all staff who are in contact with customers to pass on such comments.

Ideas from competitors Companies sometimes rely on copying the products of competitors. This is to avoid the cost and risk of new product development. It is also difficult to be original. A firm will gain a competitive advantage if it can develop a brand new product and be the first in the market. However, a large number of firms wait for competitors to launch new products and then bring out their own versions. Supermarkets often copy famous brand names when launching their own-label brands of goods. In some cases the copying extends to closely imitating packaging as well as the product. TV companies are quick to bring out their own versions of new quiz games, cookery programmes and other popular TV shows which rival broadcasters launch. Some companies undertake REVERSE ENGINEERING. This process involves taking apart a product to understand how a competitor has made it. A business will closely analyse the product's design and how it has been produced, and identify those key features which are worth copying.

Ideas from staff Businesses may rely on the ideas of their staff for new products. Some staff will work closely with customers and might pass on suggestions for new products as a result of their conversations. Suggestion schemes, where staff might be rewarded for offering new product ideas, are often used.

Ideas from research and development (R&D) Many organisations have research and development facilities. Money is allocated specifically for the invention, experimentation and exploration of new product ideas. This is probably the most expensive source of new ideas. However, the money invested can generate huge returns if a unique product is developed. R&D is discussed in more detail later in this unit.

Ideas from other products Businesses may adapt their own products into new goods or services. They tend to concentrate on best selling brands. Examples might be the development of 'bite sized' versions of well known chocolate bars or diet and low fat versions of drinks or meals.

Product design

In practice, once a business has identified a need for a product, a **design brief** can be written. This will contain features about a product which the designers can use. For example, a firm aiming to produce a new travel iron may write a design brief such as 'a new travel iron is needed which is compact and possesses all the features of a full-sized model'. Designers can work from this design brief. When designing the new travel iron they may take into account:
- the shape and appearance of the iron;
- whether it fits the intended need;
- how easily and cost effectively it can be produced from the design;
- the dimensions and preferred materials to be used;
- the image it gives when displayed;
- whether the design should create a 'corporate identity', saying something about the image of the company.

The design process

The design process has a number of stages which take the design from an initial idea to a final product. These stages are shown in Figure 27.1.

The design process usually begins when a need is found for a new, adapted or redesigned product. Needs may be identified by the marketing department in a **design brief** for the design team, like the one described for the travel iron above.

The next stage is to produce a **design specification** and **analysis**. One way of achieving this is for the design team, market researchers and the client to meet and discuss their ideas. The design specification and analysis will give a clear description of the purpose of the product, state any functions the product must have and mention constraints, such as cost, size or quality.

Several techniques can be used to produce specifications. One way is to note down all the essential features of a product and be less interested in those which are only desirable. A pair of walking boots might have essential features such as durability, being waterproof, made of leather and comfortable, and desirable features such as attractiveness, lightness and economy in manufacture. Another technique involves listing all possible alternatives or solutions, even those which initially might be considered unlikely.

Next it is necessary to find some practical **solutions** to the design brief. Solutions which the design team have suggested should be assessed. Sketches and working examples will help the evaluation. Finally, the team must decide which model or prototype is the most suitable solution to the problem.

The firm can then **realise** the design solution by making the product. The first production run is likely to be very small because the total design process is not yet complete.

Figure 27.1 *Steps in the design process*

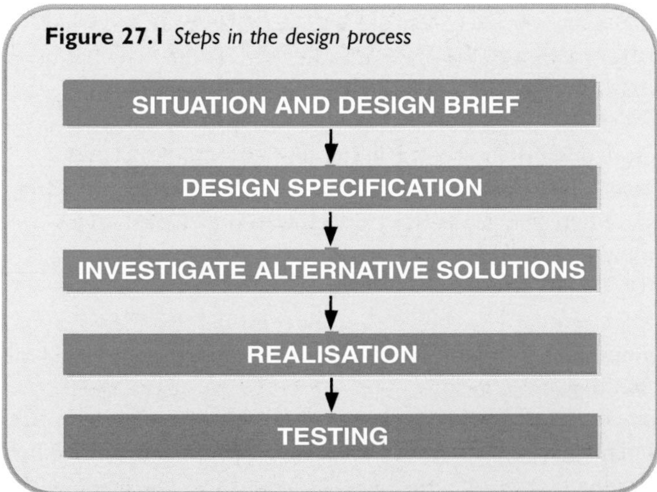

The final stage in the design process is **testing.** Most designs are tested to check that they satisfy the customer. It is often necessary to refine or modify the product. Sometimes new ideas might be generated once the design solution is in a working situation.

Design features

When designing any product a number of features have to be considered by the designer or design team.

Commercial viability Businesses must be able to produce and sell a product at a profit. Thought must be given to the choice of materials and the production techniques that are used so that production costs can be kept down. If the costs are likely to be too high, the design may well be dropped.

Reliability Designers must ensure their designs satisfy customers' expectations about the reliability of the product. Unreliable products may harm the company's image in the eyes of the consumer. The business will also incur costs if products are frequently returned.

Safety Designers must ensure that their design solutions are safe. Safety is particularly important if products are used by children, the elderly, pregnant women and people with injuries. Safety issues which might be important could include:

- ensuring that products do not contain poisons or dangerous materials such as toxic paint;
- designing products which do not have sharp edges or spikes or providing adequate protection if such features are necessary;
- ensuring that products are finished properly so that edges and faces are smooth and clean;
- incorporating safety features such as child proof caps on bottles;
- ensuring that products are durable because a product which breaks could be dangerous.

Maintenance Technical and mechanical products often need maintenance. Products should be designed so that this can be easily carried out. It is particularly important in the design of machinery.

Environment In recent years consumers have begun to question the effect certain products have on the environment. Designers now have to take this into account. One example is the use of 'roll on' deodorants instead of sprays which cause CFCs to be emitted.

Convenience and efficiency Products should be designed so that they are convenient and practical to use. For example, some tin openers are 'hand held' whilst others are electrically operated. Consumers are increasingly prepared to pay for products which are easier to use. Businesses also look for machinery and equipment that will lead to a more efficient workforce. Products which are well designed ERGONOMICALLY should increase efficiency and operator safety and also involve less effort for the user.

Manufacture Designers must ensure that their designs are not expensive or technically difficult to make. For example, they may suggest a cheaper material for lining the inside of a suitcase.

Toyota hopes to reflect the interests of today's teenagers in its latest concept car unveiled at the Geneva Motor Show in February 2004. According to Toyota sport, fashion and video games were the guiding themes for its Motor Triathlon racer, aimed at car buyers of the future. The tandem seat racer is designed for three different types of circuit:

- a smooth and high-grip racetrack;
- a narrow city race circuit;
- an off-road course.

The Triathlon, built at Toyota's European design studio, has an electric motor driving each wheel, powered by a fuel cell.

In contrast, Volvo is more interested in meeting the demands of women customers. The YCC (Your Concept Car) has been designed by an all-women team, on the basis that 'if you can meet the expectations of women, you can exceed the expectations of men'. The YCC features:

- 'Autopark' technology;
- gull-wing doors for better access;
- easily personalised interiors;
- easy-clean paint;
- a self-diagnostic system that is capable of automatically booking services.

Source: adapted from *The Engineer*, 5.3.2004.

(a) Explain the design features that may have been important when the two cars above were designed.

Market The designer must consider the marketing mix when designing products. Products are very difficult to market if they are unattractive, clumsy to store and display, expensive to distribute and overpriced.

Aesthetics Designers must consider the colour, size, appearance, shape, smell and taste of products. Many consumers would not wish to be seen wearing poorly designed clothes, for example.

Legal The product should be designed so that it is legally 'fit for purpose'. For example, if a manufacturer claims that a new type of paint is designed to dry within two hours after application, then legally, it must.

Computer aided design

Computer aided design (CAD) is an interactive computer system which is capable of generating, storing and using geometric and computer graphics. It helps design engineers to solve design problems. CAD is used in many industries today. What benefits does CAD offer to a designer?

- CAD has meant huge cuts in **lead time**, ie the length of time between the initial design and actual production. Long lead times result in lower profits as firms lose out to competitors in the race to launch new products.
- A wide range of designs can be shown on the computer screen. Two and three dimensional engineering drawings, wire-framed models, electronic circuit board designs and architectural drawings are examples.
- CAD systems handle repetitive work, allowing the designer more time to concentrate on 'creating' the design. The need for specialists is also reduced, which helps keep down costs.
- Modifications and changes are easily made. The size or shape of a design can be changed in seconds, for example.
- Problems are often more quickly identified. This sometimes prevents the need for expensive reworking later on. Also, the final design, once manufactured, is more likely to be right.

Increasing use is being made of CAD by businesses. In America, customers entering the Digitoe shoe store in Seattle sit in a seat which has a scanner attached to a computer. The equipment takes detailed pictures of their feet. It sends them to a factory where a shoe mould is made and a pair of custom made leather shoes are produced. The first pair are ready in two weeks, but the moulds can be reused and further pairs can be produced within hours of a new order. This sort of individualised production line, called **mass customisation**, is a direct result of improvements in CAD and manufacturing software.

Value analysis and value engineering

The aim of VALUE ENGINEERING is to reduce costs and avoid unnecessary costs before production begins. This technique is used by most manufacturers in Japan. It aims to eliminate any costs which do not add value to, or improve the performance of, products and services. VALUE ANALYSIS is a similar process, but is concerned with cost reduction after a product has been introduced.

Value engineering helps businesses to design products at the lowest cost. It is usually carried out by cross departmental teams. Team members might include designers, operations managers, purchasing specialists and cost accountants. The process involves carefully checking components of a product to find ways to reduce their costs. The team will analyse the function and cost of each element and investigate ways to reduce the number of separate components, using cheaper materials and simplifying processes.

The success of value engineering will often depend on how departments work together. Value engineering cannot be undertaken by an individual. Costs can only be reduced if departments take into account each other's needs. For example, in an effort to cut costs, the quality of a product may suffer to such an extent that the marketing department may find it impossible to sell it. The advantages of value engineering include:

- lower costs, resulting in lower prices for consumers;
- more straightforward methods of manufacture;
- fewer components in products, resulting in lower maintenance and repair costs;
- improved co-operation and communication across departments;
- possible 'spin-offs' for other products.

In the late 1990s value engineering was used by Unilever in its capital investment projects. These included plants making products from ice cream to washing powders and speciality chemicals. This helped to reduce the amount of capital needed for a project.

Value analysis has been used by the government to help improve efficiency in some of its departments. For example, the Edinburgh Healthcare NHS trust set up value analysis groups to look at catering services, portering services and laundry. As a result around £400,000 of savings were made on a budget of £5 million. In addition, the quality of services was also improved in some cases.

The nature of research and development

There is a constant need for invention and innovation in business. Businesses must be able to develop new products and improve existing ones in order to grow and to survive. Today, the pace of technological change, coupled with the rising wants and spending power of consumers, has forced firms to respond by investing in research and development (R&D).

- RESEARCH is the inquiry and discovery of new ideas in order to solve a problem or create an opportunity. Methods used to generate new ideas include laboratory research, product evaluation of a business' own and its competitors' products and and discussion groups designed to think up new ideas.

- DEVELOPMENT involves changing ideas into commercial products. Quite often a business will identify a number of possible ideas which have scope for development. The first stage is to select the idea which shows the most promise. One of the problems with development is the time scale involved. Some projects take many years to complete and success cannot be guaranteed.

The benefits of research and development

Not all businesses can afford to invest in R&D. Those that do may enjoy a number of benefits.

New products R&D leads to the development of new products. Firms which are able to develop new products ahead of their rivals will enjoy a **competitive advantage** in the market. If they can obtain a **patent**, they will be able to sell the product without competition from other business for a period. During this time they may be able to raise price and make higher profits. Examples of businesses benefiting from new products include Dyson, the bagless vacuum cleaner manufacturer, and Microsoft, the creators of the world's main operating system for computers.

New materials Some R&D projects develop new materials. Synthetic materials have helped to reduce the use of natural resources. New materials often have features and characteristics which make them better than natural ones. They might be more durable, heat resistant or malleable, cheaper or lighter. DuPont, for example, created Tactel, a lightweight fabric with great strength. Two years after its invention it had captured 50 per cent of the skiwear market. In addition, the development of new materials often results in the creation of new products.

New production techniques In some industries, such as mechanical and electrical engineering, research projects are designed to develop new types of machines. Computer controlled machines, for example, have been introduced into many component and textile manufacturers and assembly plants. New technology is capable of cutting costs and raising productivity. In addition, new machinery is often safer, cleaner and more ergonomically designed. This helps to make the working environment better for employees.

Image It is often argued that expenditure on R&D helps to enhance a firm's image. Consumers may be impressed by businesses which are committed to R&D. This is because consumers themselves appreciate the benefits of R&D and often recognise that such expenditure is risky. Also, breakthroughs in R&D can be highly prestigious. For example, a pharmaceuticals company developing an effective vaccination to combat Aids would receive a huge amount of positive publicity and recognition.

Motivation Investment in R&D creates opportunities for creativity and invention. Many employment positions in the R&D department will help staff to satisfy their higher order needs, such as esteem and self-actualisation. A successful R&D department might also generate a mood of optimism and anticipation in the organisation. This is likely to have a positive effect on the motivation of staff.

Consumer benefits Consumers enjoy an increasing variety of goods and services as new products come on to the market. They are likely to pay lower prices for products because new technology lowers costs. They may also enjoy better quality products resulting from higher grade materials and more effective production methods. New medicines and drugs will improve health.

The research and development budget

The amount of money allocated to R&D by different businesses varies greatly. The size of the R&D budget may depend on a number of factors.

- It is common for firms to vary their investment according to the funds available in any year. If profits fall for a period of time, R&D spending might fall. Also a business might be criticised by shareholders if too much profit is allocated to R&D at the expense of dividends.
- Certain industries, such as pharmaceuticals, chemicals, motor cars, computers and defence, tend to have high levels of spending on R&D. This is due to the nature of the industry. For example, new drugs are constantly needed to prevent or cure new or existing illnesses.
- Larger public limited companies tend to be more committed to R&D. They are better able to meet the cost and bear the risk involved than smaller businesses.
- Some businesses are committed to high levels of R&D spending because it is part of their corporate objectives and culture (☞ unit 5).
- In some industries businesses are forced to invest in R&D to compete. Failure to keep pace with the investment of rivals may mean that a business struggles to survive in the market.
- Businesses are more likely to invest in R&D when the economy is booming. During a recession R&D funding might be cut or frozen.

Setting a budget for R&D expenditure can be difficult. R&D departments often spend more than they are allocated. Businesses may have to raise funds externally to finance R&D projects. In recent years a number of pharmaceuticals companies have had to use rights issues to raise extra finance to fund research in medicines and drugs. There are several reasons why setting an R&D budget might be difficult.

- The cost of a scientific research project may be difficult to estimate accurately. This is because researchers will not know when a breakthrough is going to occur. Some

research, such as cancer and aids cures, has been ongoing for many years.
- During an R&D project, there may be unforeseen spending. For example, a business might have to unexpectedly recruit staff with specialist knowledge and experience to further the programme.
- Some R&D programmes run for many years. Therefore their costs tend to rise with inflation. There is a tendency to underestimate inflation and businesses then have to obtain further funding to meet rising costs.

R&D expenditure

Figure 27.2 shows total global R&D investment by region. The Americas make a huge contribution to global R&D, spending around £90 billion. Nearly half of this spending is in the electronics and IT sector. In comparison, Europe spent around £70 billion on R&D during 2003, with the UK making a very large contribution in the pharmaceuticals and health sector. Europe also spent a bigger proportion of its total R&D on engineering than the Americas. The rest of the world spent around £50 billion with significantly less on pharmaceuticals and health than the Americas and Europe.

Figure 27.2 *Total R&D investment by region*

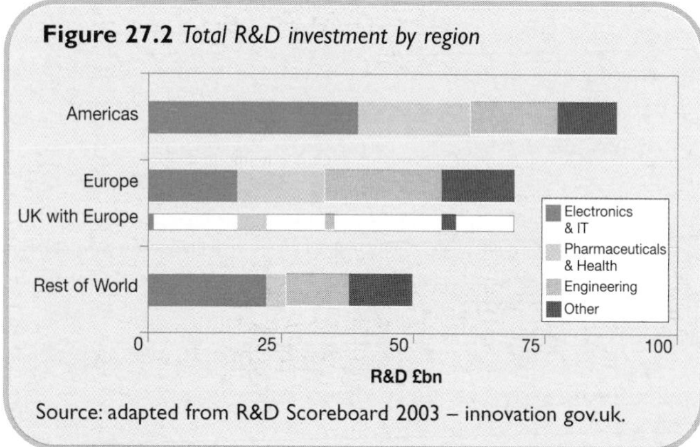

Source: adapted from R&D Scoreboard 2003 – innovation gov.uk.

Patents

A patent aims to protect the inventor of a new product or manufacturing process. It allows a business to design, produce and sell a new invention and attempts to prevent competitors from copying it. New inventions are protected for fifteen years. The developer must make details of the invention available to the Patent Office.

Obtaining a patent can be a lengthy process. To qualify for a patent the invention must be brand new. Checks are then made to ensure it is authentic. The patent is published eighteen months after its application and signed and sealed some time after this. The developer must pay annual fees to the Patent Office which become more expensive after the first four years. This is to encourage production of the new idea.

Both the inventor and the consumer can benefit from patents. Some benefits to businesses of patents are:
- a higher level of sales;
- reduced competition;
- legal protection that encourages continued research;
- higher profits which can be ploughed back into further research and development;
- the industry benefits from the technical information as a result of the patent;
- high risk research and development is encouraged.

Consumers also benefit. New products mean more variety and perhaps a better standard of living. New, more efficient, productive techniques mean lower costs and lower prices.

There is a number of criticisms of the patent system. The granting of sole production and distribution rights to one firm creates a legal monopoly. If this monopoly power is abused then consumers may be exploited. Table 27.1 shows the number of applications made for patents and the number of patents granted in 2001 and 2002. The Patent Office granted more patents in 2002 than 2001 when the number of applications actually fell slightly.

Table 27.1 *The number of applications made for patents and the number of patents granted in 2001 and 2002*

	Applications made	Patents granted
2001	30,577	7,555
2002	29,911	8,690

Source: adapted from the Patent Office website.

key terms

Development - the changing of new ideas into commercial propositions.
Ergonomics - the study of people in their working environment and the adaptation of machines and conditions to improve efficiency.
Research - an investigation involving the process of enquiry and discovery used to generate new business ideas.
Reverse engineering - a method of analysing a product's design by taking apart the product.
Value analysis - a procedure to evaluate a product after manufacture to see how costs may be reduced
Value engineering - a procedure designed to reduce and avoid unnecessary costs before production begins.

In April 2000, the UK government introduced a tax incentive for companies undertaking research and development. It was designed to encourage greater innovation and would be particularly attractive for members of Tech Track 100 (the 100 fastest growing unquoted technology companies). The government recognised that a strong link existed between R&D, productivity and economic growth. Other countries, such as America and Australia, have similar tax incentives. Depending on how much is spent on R&D, companies may be entitled to a reduction in tax or a cash repayment from the Inland Revenue. What may be surprising is the number of firms in the Tech Track 100 that have not claimed the tax credit, especially as it was introduced more than three years ago. Some of the reasons for this include:

- lack of awareness;
- some companies do not understand the rules;
- some thought they were ineligible;
- some found the system too complicated.

Examples of companies that have claimed the tax credit include Celoxia, a microchip software developer, that has claimed an amount equivalent to 25 per cent of its spending on R&D. Another is Cambridge Silicon Radio which has claimed £1.5 million in the last two years.

Figure 27.3 *R&D tax credit claims*

Never heard of them 12%
More than £100,000 received 10%
Less than £100,000 received 12%
Unspecified amount received 16%
Claimed but not yet received 13%
Thinking about it 16%
Not claiming 19%

Source: adapted from *The Sunday Times*, 28.9.2003.

(a) (i) What percentage of the Tech Track 100 have not received any of the R&D tax credits?
(ii) What measures might the Inland Revenue take to help companies investing in R&D to claim the tax credit?

(b) What might be the benefits to (i) businesses and (ii) consumers of the tax credits for R&D?

1. How can the behaviour of competitors and the state of technology affect the product a firm chooses to produce?
2. How might a business find out if there is a need for a product?
3. What is meant by a design brief?
4. Describe the stages in the design process.
5. What is meant by a design feature?
6. State 6 design features that a firm might consider important when designing a product.
7. How does CAD improve business efficiency?
8. How will value analysis benefit consumers?
9. What is the difference between value analysis and value engineering?
10. State 3 benefits of R&D to businesses.
11. State 2 industries where R&D expenditure tends to be high.
12. What are the benefits of patents to a business.

Case study FireAngel

In 1998, Nick Rutterand Sam Tate submitted a patent specification to the Patent Office. This included drawings and a technical description of their new smoke alarm. Nick and Sam developed the alarm after setting up a company and identifying problems with conventionally designed smoke alarms.

- Conventional smoke detectors are positioned on ceilings because smoke and heat rise. However, this makes them inaccessible, particularly for the elderly.
- Smoke alarms are normally powered by battery and research shows that about 20 per cent of fires go undetected because the batteries are flat or missing.
- Many detectors are unreliable and go off accidentally.
- Many models are unattractive.

Nick and Sam designed a smoke alarm with the following features.

- The alarm fits into a light socket on the ceiling, so installation is as simple as changing a light bulb.
- If the alarm goes off accidentally, it can be silenced by switching the light on and off.
- It is designed aesthetically and can be hidden by a lampshade.
- When the batteries run low, the alarm will sound and by turning on the light the battery will be charged automatically.

During the design process, Nick and Sam had to overcome some problems with the early prototypes. For example, the heat from the light bulb caused difficulties. Also, they had to develop a rechargeable power source which was capable of charging quickly and lasting for ten years under variable temperature conditions. The size of this power source was an issue, it had to fit into a small space in the alarm system.

Once the final prototype was ready, Nick and Sam completed a graduate training programme at their old university. The programme could provide them with some initial funding if they could present their product idea and business plan to a panel of judges successfully. They were able to do this, and thus, submitted details of their innovation to the Patent Office. The pair also came up with a name for their product – FireAngel – which then became their trademark.

To bring the product to the market, Nick and Sam had two options.

- License their invention and sell the manufacturing rights to a large company. They could negotiate a one-off fee for selling the design or royalties on future sales. This would generate a short-term profit without having to invest time and money in development and setting up production facilities.
- Develop and launch the product themselves. This would involve raising more finance, researching into manufacturing processes, acquiring all the production resources and marketing the product. However, if successful, the financial rewards would be considerably greater.

Nick and Sam decided to go it alone. They received £55,000 from the EU but this soon went. Eventually, they persuaded a group of Business Angels to invest £250,000. By concentrating on product development and marketing, within 12 months their product was independently tested to the relevant British Standards and was launched in the UK. They won a contract with B&Q for an exclusive sale period of three months and eventually the FireAngel PS-101 Plug-in Smoke Alarm was available in over 3,000 outlets in the UK.

Within four years the FireAngel had won a number of awards including the Real Business/CBI New Product of the Year. In 2001, Sprue Aegis, the company they set up to market the product, became a plc with a turnover of £515,000 (for the quarter ended June 2003). Nick and Sam have obtained a further 18 patents internationally, plus protection for a range of trade marks. A new name, AngelEye, has been registered specifically for the American market. The company is committed to investment in new product development. They believe that future success depends on their ability to continue innovating and securing further patents.

Source: adapted from the Patent Office website.

(a) What are the key design features in the FireAngel? (6 marks)

(b) Explain the advantages to Nick and Sam of applying for a patent. (8 marks)

(c) Explain the design process that Nick and Sam may have used. (10 marks)

(d) Do you think that Nick and Sam made the right decision to launch the product themselves? (12 marks)

(e) Discuss whether research and development will be important to Sprue Aegis in the future. (14 marks)

28 Where to Locate the Business

Location decisions

The decision about where to locate is crucial to many businesses. It can affect their sales, costs, profitability and perhaps even their survival.

Why might a company need to make a decision about where to locate?

- New businesses will need to carefully consider where to locate their initial premises.
- Existing businesses may need to expand, but may be unable to do so on their present sites.
- The modernisation of a business may involve moving to more up-to-date premises.
- A business aiming to cut its costs might achieve this by re-locating.
- A multinational company aiming to set up a new plant in another country for the first time may evaluate a variety of possible locations worldwide.

There are many factors which will influence a business's decision about where to locate. It is likely that any location decision will be influenced by a few or many of these factors. When deciding where to locate its premises a business usually weighs up all potential costs and benefits of setting up in a particular area. This may be carried out with the use of **cost-benefit analysis** (☞ unit 31).

Power and raw materials

Primary industry needs to be located near to raw materials. In the UK, agricultural production has been, and still is, found in areas such as the South, East Anglia, Wales and Scotland. The location of mining and extraction is determined by deposits of raw materials like coal, oil and iron ore. In the UK such deposits in the past have been found in the North. This is also true of offshore oil findings.

After the Industrial Revolution, secondary manufacturing industry largely located close to raw materials and sources of power. This is true of most western industrialised countries. In the UK industry moved to the North and Midlands, in Germany to the Ruhr region and in the USA to areas such as the Mid-West. One of the reasons for this was that coal was the main source of power for these industries. Also, transport systems were poor by today's standards and raw materials were costly to carry.

It could be argued that these 'traditional factors' are no longer as important as they were. Gas and electricity systems mean that being close to a power source is no longer a constraint for most firms. Also, transport systems now carry goods relatively cheaply and efficiently to manufacturers. Businesses which are still located close to raw materials tend to be ones which have extremely bulky raw materials, which are then reduced to easier-to-transport final products. For example, timber yards and saw mills might be located close to forests and food canning plants may be located close to agricultural areas.

Markets

For some businesses, being close to their market is often the single most important factor in choosing a location. A variety of businesses may be influenced by this factor.

- Businesses that produce products which are more bulky than the raw materials that go into them, such as North Sea oil platforms, are likely to locate close to their market. The components and materials used to assemble North Sea oil platforms are far less bulky than the end product – the platform itself. Therefore, the production of such platforms takes place in locations close to where they will eventually be used – the North Sea coast – in cities such as Aberdeen. If production was located elsewhere transport costs may be very high. There may also be problems transporting the product to its final destination.
- Suppliers of components and intermediate goods may set up close to their main customers. For example, a number of firms emerged in the Liverpool area supplying shipping companies with packing cases for transportation. After the dock industry declined in Liverpool, some of these companies still existed. The introduction of Just-In-Time (JIT) manufacturing has encouraged component manufacturers to locate nearer to their business customers. The JIT system requires suppliers to provide reliable and immediate delivery. It is likely to be easier to deliver reliably if customers are located less than a mile away, for example.
- Many financial service businesses locate their premises in London. Some would argue that London is the 'financial centre' of the world.
- The growth of the tertiary sector and the decline in 'heavy' industry has resulted in many FOOTLOOSE secondary and tertiary industries. Businesses in these industries are able to locate premises where they wish. Given this freedom many have chosen to locate by their markets. The South East of the UK developed a service economy as a result, made up of retailing, financial services, leisure industries and a small amount of 'light' manufacturing.
- Most service industries tend to be located near to markets. Businesses providing the general public with services like dentistry, dry cleaning and car maintenance must locate their premises in areas which are accessible to people.

Closeness to the market can also be a SITE FACTOR affecting the location of a business. Site factors affect the choice of one plot of land or one premises rather than another after the business has decided to locate in a particular area. For example, WH Smith originally located its outlets in railway stations because its main market was railway passengers buying newspapers and magazines. When it moved out of railway stations, it located its outlets in the nearest available premises. Small retailers supply the needs of local communities. The 'corner shop', for example, relies mainly on customers from a very small local catchment area.

Transport links

The ease of transport can be important in a firm's location decision. Access to motorways, rail networks, ports and airports may all be important. By reducing travel time, motorways may encourage firms to locate premises in areas which might have been regarded as remote from markets or costly in terms of transport. The building of the M4 between London and South Wales has encouraged location along the 'M4 corridor'.

The accessibility of ports and airports might also be important. This is often true of firms which export their goods. For firms which produce light, low bulk, but high value products, air transport might be the best means of reaching both overseas and domestic markets. More bulky and heavy goods might be transported by sea. Businesses which use a great deal of imported raw materials might also locate close to a port.

The building of the Channel Tunnel improved trade links to the Continent when it was opened. It allowed UK businesses to distribute goods easily and effectively to Europe. It also encouraged firms to locate in the South East if they have markets in Europe. The Channel Tunnel became even more important when trading restrictions with Europe were lifted in 1992. Other regions in the UK have benefited from increased trade with Europe via rail links. However, with increasing congestion on all motorways, firms with European interests could have favoured the South East.

Good transport links can also be a factor influencing the choice of site. For example, a business locating in Leeds may choose to build a factory close to the M62/M1 junction rather than north west of the city. In many towns and cities, industrial estates tend to be located close to motorways or railway stations.

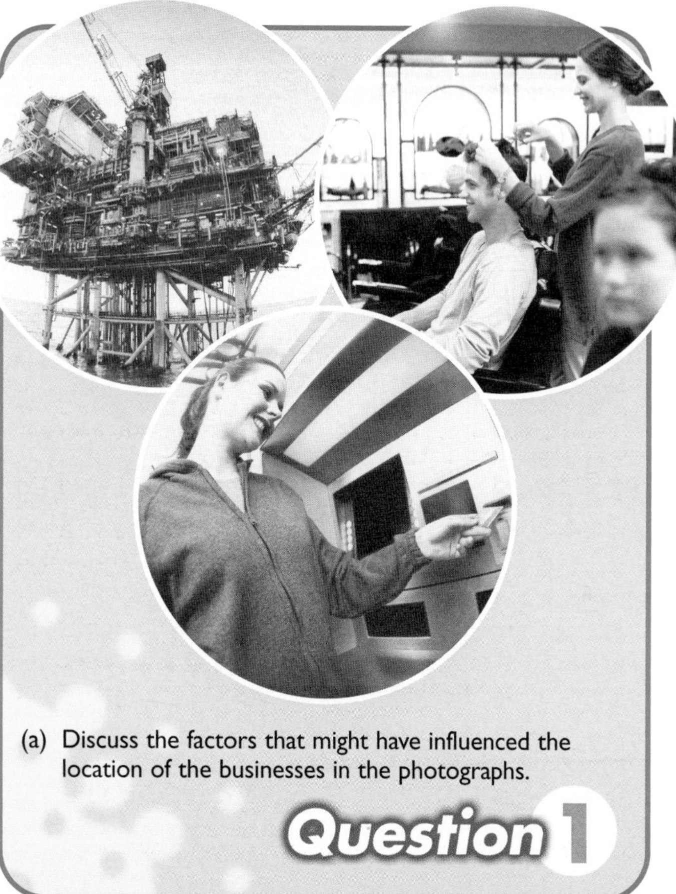

(a) Discuss the factors that might have influenced the location of the businesses in the photographs.

Question 1

Land

When choosing where to locate or re-locate premises, firms need to select the 'right' piece of land. This might be a newly completed factory unit, a derelict inner city site, an old factory in need of modernisation or a piece of land never previously used for a business development. When choosing an appropriate piece of land, firms are likely to take into account some combination of the following site factors.

- The cost relative to other potential sites. A firm must compare purchase prices of alternative sites, consider whether or not renting would be more cost effective and compare the level of business rates in each location.
- Certain businesses may need to locate near to rivers or in coastal areas to dispose of waste. Examples might be chemical plants or coal fired power stations.
- The amount of space available for current needs. Some businesses require large areas of land. For example, car manufacturers need sites of several hundred acres.
- Potential for expansion. It is important that firms look into the future when locating premises. When Kellogg's acquired a new cornflake manufacturing plant in Northern Italy, one of the reasons why it favoured Brescia was because of the large amount of adjacent land which they hoped to use in the future for expansion.
- The availability of planning permission. This is particularly important if a firm is going to change the use of some land or premises, or construct new buildings. Local authorities will not always grant planning permission allowing land development, for example in GREEN BELT areas.
- Geological suitability. Some businesses require particular geological features. A nuclear power station must be sited on a geologically stable site.
- Good infrastructure. Facilities such as good road links, appropriate waste disposal facilities and other public utilities are often an important influence.
- Environmental considerations. Today, firms may face pressure from public opinion when locating premises. There can be opposition from pressure groups if they attempt to locate in environmentally sensitive areas.

Some firms in recent years have opted to move their premises out of traditional industrial areas to GREENFIELD sites. These are, literally, rural locations generally found on the outskirts of towns and cities. Here the land tends to be cheaper and more plentiful. However, there may be opposition from environmentalists and greenfield sites can only be developed if there is adequate access. These sites are becoming more popular and are particularly suitable for hi-tech industries. An example was the new location for the Lancashire Evening Post. It moved from the centre of Preston to a greenfield site adjacent to junction 32 on the M6 on the outskirts of the town. Brand new premises costing £28 million were built on a plot of land which was previously used for non-commercial purposes.

The use of BROWNFIELD sites for business location is also increasing. According to the government, a brownfield site is an area of land which was previously used for urban development. Some brownfield sites in the UK have been derelict for many years. One such site is the Greenwich peninsular in London. The site used to house a huge gasworks, but became a rubbish dump and scrapyard for much of southeast London. In the late 1990s it was chosen as the location for the Millennium Dome and a number of businesses competed for contracts to build on the land.

Labour

Firms re-locating from one part of the country to another will aim to take most of their staff with them. This should cut down on disruption and avoid the need to recruit and train large numbers of new staff. Sometimes, businesses try not to move very far so that staff can travel from their existing homes. For example, the Woolwich Building Society, when re-locating from North London, chose Bexley Heath in North Kent – already the home of a large number of its employees.

However, if re-location is a long way from the original position, persuading existing staff to move can be difficult. Selling existing homes, buying new homes, disrupting childrens' education and removal costs can be real obstacles. When choosing a site, firms need to find out whether existing employees can be persuaded to move and whether other sources of labour with the right skills can be recruited locally. Factors that existing staff may feel are important may be the cost of housing, the quality of the local environment, the quality of local schools and perhaps the number of traffic jams in the area.

Labour skills are not evenly distributed throughout the country. If a firm needs a particular type of skilled labour there may be regions which are especially suitable. For example, a firm which is contemplating a new venture in carpet manufacturing might choose Kidderminster as a possible location. Kidderminster is famous for carpet manufacturing and could offer a firm new to the industry a ready supply of appropriately skilled and semi-skilled workers. Other examples of these regional advantages include car workers in the West Midlands, pottery workers in Stoke-on-Trent and steel workers in Sheffield. Where an industry is concentrated in a particular region, advantages, such as expertise in local schools and colleges, research facilities in nearby universities and sympathetic and supportive local government agencies often exist. These are known as **external economies of scale.**

3S is a software engineering firm based in Balham, London. It develops software solutions for signalling systems on rail networks. In recent years the company has looked further afield for its customers. This has proved a succesful strategy and has led to ezpansion of the business.

In 2004, the company outgrew its small office in Balham and decided to relocate. 3S employs 14 software engineers and 6 administrative staff. Regular meetings are often held with clients to discuss their needs, update the technology and deal with health and safety issues. Perhaps most importantly, technicians need to be available within a few hours as technical breakdowns can cause a complete shutdown in production.

One option that 3S is considering for relocation is rural France. The majority of the staff are in favour of such a move. However, a recent survey showed that the cost of IT training in France is higher than in the UK. And a further factor which might affect labour supply could be the rural location of the factory. Figure 28.1 shows turnover by geographical area in 1999 and 2003.

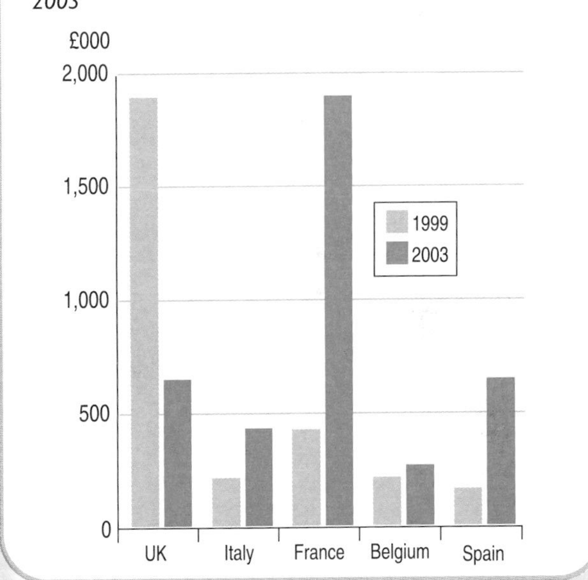

Figure 28.1 *3S turnover by geographical area in 1999 and 2003*

(a) What evidence is there to suggest that relocation in France might be a good move for 3S?
(b) What obstacles might make the move difficult for 3S?

Question 2

Information and communication technology

An increasingly important factor in location is access to

telecommunications links. Modern telecommunication networks have the capacity to send and receive voices, data and pictures at great speed. The information technology revolution has meant that firms can link separate branches or sections of their operations by computer. Large firms with a Head Office in London, for example, are able to place personnel in locations hundreds of miles from the Capital. Businesses no longer need to concentrate their office staff or production in one location because of communication problems. They can also employ people working at home and contact them via e-mail or fax machine.

Company intranets now allow large numbers of employees to have easy access to the same information. For example, information collected by a member of the marketing department on customers' characteristics will be available to other members of other areas of the business such as R&D. The use of ICT can also affect international location. This is dealt with later in this unit.

Government influence

The UK government has influenced the location of business for many decades, probably since the 1920s. There has been a need to revitalise certain areas where key industries have declined. For example, the North East was hit when the shipbuilding industry declined. The North West region suffered when the textile industry collapsed. The main reasons for government intervention in business location are to:

- control development where there is 'business congestion' and adequate employment;
- encourage firms to locate their operations in regions where unemployment is high and business activity is lacking;
- attract foreign businesses to the UK.

The government has attempted to help areas with particular problems in the UK through REGIONAL POLICY (☞ unit 34). This has involved the use of incentives to attract businesses to regions in need of revitalisation. Incentives have included investment grants, tax breaks, employment subsidies and rent-free factory space.

In the early twenty first century a number of initiatives were used in the UK to encourage businesses to locate in certain areas.

Regional selective assistance This involves discretionary government grants given by the DTI for investment projects that would create or safeguard jobs in ASSISTED AREAS. Assisted areas in the UK are 'locations of considerable development potential. They all have an available workforce, competitive labour costs and high labour flexibility. They share the benefits which Britain as a whole has for the investor in terms of market proximity, good communications, low taxes, the language of business, a deregulated business environment and a government attitude which welcomes investment and enterprise'.

Assisted areas are divided into **development areas** and **intermediate areas**. Development areas are those which are most severe in terms of decline and need, such as the Glasgow area or Tyneside. Between 1999 and 2002, £299 million was spent on this scheme, protecting 91,000 jobs.

EU structural funds The EU allocates funds to areas within member countries which are classed as Objective 1 areas (with income per head less than 75 per cent of the EU average) and Objective 2 areas (with severe structural problems). The funds are used 'to support the economic and social conversion of areas facing structural difficulties'. Objective 1 areas in the UK include Merseyside, Cornwall and South Yorkshire. A variety of grants are available including the European Regional Development Fund (ERDF) and the European Social Fund (ESF).

Regional development agencies Regional Development Agencies (RDAs) are government funded bodies which promote economic development in the regions. In 2003 they had a total budget of £1.7 billion. All regions have one agency, but more funding is given to areas such as the North West and the North East.

Enterprise zones ENTERPRISE ZONES are small geographical areas, perhaps just a few hundred acres of land, located in urban areas. They are designed to encourage private sector businesses to create jobs and bring derelict land back into use. Areas are given enterprise zone status for 10 years. Location in these areas can be attractive. Businesses may be exempt from tax and statutory and administrative controls may be relaxed or speeded up.

Learning and skills councils The Learning and Skills Council (LSC) is responsible for funding and planning education and training for over 16 year olds in England. There is a national head office in Coventry and 47 regional councils. In 2003 it had a budget of £8 billion. Part of this would have been used to fund work-based training and education business links.

European Investment Bank (EIB) The EIB grants loans to SMEs anywhere in the UK for investment projects in most industrial sectors. Loans are available from a range of financial institutions. The EIB also provides large loans for capital investment projects in industry or infrastructure. Examples of sectors eligible for EIB loans include advanced technology, environmental protection, transport, telecommunications and energy.

Public sector operations Government might be able to locate offices in areas with difficulties to directly influence employment and spending. Employment might be encouraged from the local area. For example, the introduction of Welsh, Scottish and London regional assemblies might create jobs in these areas. If regions voted for local assemblies in areas such as the North West, this would also tend to create jobs in regions.

In 2003 the UK government put forward a new approach to regional policy. It aimed to improve gross value added per head of the population in regions. This is a measure of the productivity of workers in the areas. It is not just about the poorest areas, but about improving productivity in all areas.

EU influence

The EU provides a range of funds for businesses which locate in assisted areas. Most are structural funds. Structural funds include the following.

- The European Social Fund (ESF) provides money for the development of human resources. The money can be used to fund training schemes and is designed to solve labour market problems. For example, a Horizon project in Bristol designed to train childcare workers was funded from this source.
- The European Regional Development Fund (ERDF) provides money in the most disadvantaged regions for the development of infrastructure. Examples might be the building of roads and improvements in telecommunications.
- The Agricultural Guidance and Guarantee Fund provides money for the creation and protection of jobs in rural areas.
- The Financial Instrument for Fisheries Guidance helps the development of the fisheries industry.

The East Durham Enterprise Zone is located in the heart of the thriving North East of England. It is home to some of the region's major industrial estates. Parts of East Durham, around the Peterlee and Seaham areas, have been designated an enterprise zone. Companies locating in this area can benefit from the following.

- Freedom from business rates for 10 years.
- 100 per cent tax allowances on the costs of industrial and commercial buildings.
- A streamlined planning process.
- Possible rent free periods from developers.
- Regional Selective Assistance for most manufacturing and some service type businesses. Applicants must be expanding their business, creating jobs and spending over £0.5 million on equipment, plant and machinery and associated building costs. Typically grants are negotiated at around 15 per cent of eligible expenditure.
- SME Enterprise Grants for SMEs involved in similar activities to those described above. Projects of under £0.5 million can be granted aided to a maximum of 15 per cent of eligible expenditure where job creation exists.
- A Property Development Grant for manufacturing businesses and those providing a service to business on at least a regional scale, which are building new premises. Grants are given towards the cost of various areas of site preparation in the form of £10 per square metre of floorspace constructed to a maximum grant value of £25,000.

One example of a business located in the East Durham Enterprise Zone is Prima Windows. It moved into a 15,000 sq. ft. factory in Seaham Grange in 2002. A total investment of £0.75 million has bought the business a new factory, offices and state of the art CNC machinery for its UPVC profile manufacturing business. The company will increase staff from 25 to 40 and double sales within two years. Director Paul Hewitt said Seaham Grange is a quality estate and the Enterprise Zone benefits made this a massive investment for the company.

Source: adapted from the East Durham Enterprise Zone website.

(a) Using examples from this case, explain what is meant by an enterprise zone.
(b) Explain three possible reasons why Prima Windows located in Seaham Grange.

Industrial inertia

When businesses in the same industry locate in an area with similar businesses this is referred to as INDUSTRIAL INERTIA. Even when the original advantages cease to exist, new firms might still be attracted to the area. An example might be the textile industry in the North West. The original attractions such as coal and water which influenced business to locate in the region have ceased to be important. Newer power sources have been developed and the natural humidity of the area can be recreated by technology. In addition, natural fibres have been replaced by synthetic materials. However, businesses continue to locate in the area for other reasons, including skilled workers, support services aimed at the textile industry and perhaps the reputation. Similar reasons might account for ceramics and pottery still existing in the area around Stoke.

Industrial inertia does have some disadvantages. When a region relies heavily on one industry it will suffer if that industry declines. For example, in the 1990s many UK coal mines were closed down in areas where the local pit was the main employer.

International location

Increasingly businesses are looking to locate parts of their operations in different countries around the world. In the 1990s, for example, Asian companies such as Honda, Nissan, Daewoo and QPL located production in Europe. Businesses will aim to locate their operations where costs are minimised and customers can be best served.

A number of factors may influence international location. Some of the factors influencing the location of businesses in other countries may be the same as those affecting location in a different region of a particular country.

- Protectionism. When a business **exports** to another country, the country receiving the product may raise its price by placing a tariff or tax on the good. It might also restrict the number of goods entering the country by quotas. One way to avoid these restrictions is to produce and sell products in the country which imposes the restriction. These goods are then classified as domestic output and avoid tariffs or quotas. Many Japanese companies have located in the EU because it imposes tariffs on products entering the EU from foreign countries. In recent years it could be argued that protectionism has declined. Countries such as India, Japan, China and Russia have allowed foreign products to enter their countries.

- Legislation and bureaucracy. Businesses want to avoid countries which impose restrictive laws and time consuming bureaucracy when locating operations. They are more likely to locate in countries where there is a liberal approach to issues like health and safety, the environment and employment legislation.
- The growth of ICT has also affected international location. It is now possible for a UK company with its main market in the UK to have its head office in the UK, its orders department in a low cost country in Asia and its production in the far east or eastern Europe. The immediate communication through e-mail or other media makes it possible to run such an organisation efficiently.
- Political stability. Businesses will tend to reduce risk by avoiding the location of plants in countries where the political system is unstable or there is the possibility of military action.
- The labour force. The cost of labour in different countries may affect the location decision of a business. Multinationals have set up production operations in Asia, where wages are comparatively low. The quality of the workforce is also a key factor. Companies will locate plants in countries where the workforce is flexible, cooperative, highly motivated, well trained and talented.
- Market opportunities and transport costs. Some businesses locate plants in countries where they see selling opportunities. When trying to enter a new market, it may be more cost effective to supply the market from within. In particular, if the products are bulky like motor cars, shipping costs from one side of the world to markets on the other side can reduce profit margins. For example, the growth of the Chinese economy in the period 2000-04 created market opportunities for businesses that did not exist previously when the government operated a closed economic system. Opportunities were also likely to take place with the expansion of the EU in 2004 (☞ unit 36).
- Financial incentives. Businesses may be attracted to a particular country or area if cash or other financial incentives are offered if they locate there. Some of the regional aid available in parts of Europe may have influenced the location of Asian multinationals in the 1990s.
- Globalisation. It has been suggested that businesses are facing globalised markets (☞ unit 38). Selling into a global market, rather than a single country or area, is likely to be more effective if a business produces and sells in many different countries. For example, it may be able to take into account regional characteristics in its products or establish a corporate brand image.
- Corporate image. Some multinationals (☞ unit 38) set up parts of their business in other countries, but keep their

A number of businesses have shifted their service jobs to India because labour costs are roughly one-third of what they would be in the UK. Large corporations such as BT, Lloyds, TSB, Abbey, British Airways and HSBC are all taking advantage of the low-cost services in India. Officials in Delhi expect IT-enabled services, which include call centres, to grow by 65 per cent a year. This is not surprising when you consider that staff in a typical call centre, located in one of the Software Technology Parks in India (STPIs), gets paid 10,000 rupees (£132) a month. Staff are also well qualified, many with university degrees.

STPIs play an important role in attracting foreign businesses. They are responsible for granting licenses to Indian companies that want to export IT services. STPIs have also pushed hard to develop the infrastructure. They have set up broadband networks right across India. STPI-licensed companies do not have to pay corporation tax in India. This has encouraged entry into the industry and helped to supply IT services to the growing band of foreign companies looking for cheap locations.

Bangalore is one of the cities to have benefited most of all from the boom in IT exporting. The invasion of foreign customers began in 1984 when Texas Instruments, the US IT company, arrived. It was attracted by Bangalore's concentration of high-quality graduates, specialising in software design, and low salaries. Since then Bangalore has developed into the self-styled IT capital of India. Today, Bangalore has some excellent colleges and produces 40,000 engineering graduates each year. However, this success has brought with it some problems. Water and power shortages are common and the traffic is horrendous.

Figure 28.2 *IT export growth in India*

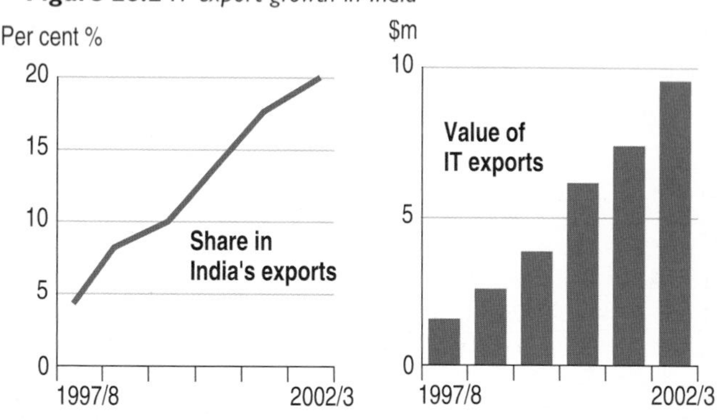

Source: adapted from *The Sunday Times*, 9.11.2003.

(a) Describe the location factors that have attracted foreign businesses to India.
(b) Examine the possible benefits of foreign companies being attracted to India for cities such as Bangalore.

head offices and take back profits to the home country. Others have head offices and operations in many different countries. They use labour from the country in which they operate. They reinvest profits in that country and develop infrastructure. This approach could allow a business to improve its corporate image (☞ unit 5), as it is seen as providing benefits to the countries in which it operates.
- The introduction of the single European currency (☞ unit 36) may have influenced business location after the year 2000. Multinational companies may have located inside Europe to gain the benefits of simplified accounting, pricing and marketing.

Inward investment

INWARD INVESTMENT is the flow of foreign funds into a country for the purposes of setting up business operations. In the 1990s the UK attracted billions of pounds of inward investment from foreign companies setting up production plants in the country. The success of the UK in attracting this investment was largely the work of national, regional and local agencies. Examples included English Partnerships, the Commission for the New Towns, the Mersey Partnership and the West Midlands Development Agency. These played vital roles in attracting overseas investment in new factories and decisions by foreign firms to invest in existing operations. For example, English Partnerships played a key role in attracting Samsung Electronics, the Korean firm, to invest in a £450 million multi-product complex in Teeside.

Inward investment can have a number of benefits to UK industry.
- Foreign businesses which locate in the UK will need supplies, perhaps from UK suppliers of components and specialist commercial services.
- Businesses will recruit workers. Retailers, cinemas, restaurants and other local businesses will gain from the extra spending.
- Some UK businesses may already supply the overseas business. If production is switched to the UK then transport costs may fall and profits rise.
- UK businesses may learn about new production methods and working practices.
- If UK businesses make a good impression with overseas investors, this might generate publicity which could lead to further investment in the UK.

key terms

Assisted areas – areas that are designated as having problems by the UK or EU and are eligible for support in a variety of forms.
Brownfield site – areas of land which were once used for urban development.
Enterprise zones – small inner city areas designated by the government which qualify for financial assistance.
Footloose industries – those industries which are neither influenced by their market or the source of raw materials when deciding where to locate.
Green belt – areas designated by government, usually in agricultural areas, where the development of business is prohibited.
Greenfield sites – areas of land, usually on the outskirts of towns and cities, where businesses develop for the first time.
Industrial inertia – the tendency for firms in the same industry to locate in the same region even when the original locational advantages have disappeared.
Inward investment – the setting up of business, or investment in business, by a company from another country.
Regional policy – measures used by central and local government to attract businesses to 'depressed' areas.
Site factors - factors affecting the choice of a plot or premises rather than an area.

Knowledge

1. Under what circumstances will transport costs be particularly influential in business location?
2. State 3 types of business that will benefit from locating close to the market.
3. Give 4 methods of communication that may influence a location decision.
4. For what type of business activity is land an important factor in influencing location?
5. Why might it be important to transfer existing employees when relocating?
6. Give 3 problems that a business might have in transferring its existing labour force to a new location.
7. How might the geographical distribution of labour affect location?
8. Identify the help which the UK government and the EU gives to businesses when locating in the UK.
9. Describe 6 factors which might be important when locating a business operation overseas.
10. State 3 examples of inward investment.

Case study Business location in Cumbria

To some, Cumbria might be an unlikely location to set up a new business or develop an existing one. Sparsely populated, slightly isolated in the far North west and apparently offering little in the way of modern urban infrastructure, there appears to be little to attract business activity. However, there is plenty of evidence to suggest that businesses are impressed with the area.

- Cumbria is England's second largest county, covering 6,810 square kilometres (2,629 miles).
- Situated in the north-west of England, the county represents 48 per cent of the region's land mass.
- Around half the county is designated as National Park or Areas of Outstanding Natural Beauty.
- The total population of Cumbria is 490,000 with 63 per cent of the inhabitants of working age.
- There are 204,000 households in Cumbria.

Cumbria is well represented in all business sectors. Around 23 per cent of the total workforce is employed in manufacturing, with this figure rising to 38 per cent in some parts of Cumbria. Table 28.1 lists the main national and international companies with operations in Cumbria.

The Research, Development and Advanced Technologies sector has seen significant growth and offers huge potential to investors as advances in telecommunications and IT, give companies the freedom to locate in a high quality environment. Expanding fields in Cumbria include small and medium sized enterprises and research centres in specialist areas such as bio-technologies, genetics and health care treatments, marine technologies, terrestrial ecology, paper and film technologies and waste management control.

As in most other regions, the service sector is the biggest. In Cumbria it accounts for two thirds of the working population, creating a high level of office-based, computer and IT skills. Customer Service Centres are a growing industry with operations at the Barrow BT Call Centre and mail order centres at Lakeland Limited, Hawkshead Countrywear and Historical Collections.

Around 15 per cent of the Cumbrian workforce is employed in tourist related industries and Cumbria receives nearly 15 million visitors a year with over £400 million being generated in direct tourist related spending.

Table 28.1

COMPANY	SECTOR
BAE Systems	*marine engineering*
British Nuclear Fuels Ltd	*nuclear fuels*
Breed UK	*car safety restraints*
Carnaud MetalBox	*cans/containers*
Carrs Milling Plc	*food manufacture*
Corus	*rail track and steel manufacture*
James Cropper Plc	*paper manufacture*
Eastman Chemicals	*chemicals*
Eddie Stobart Ltd	*transport and distribution*
Enesco European	*giftware*
Farley Health Products	*baby foods*
Glaxo SmithKline	*pharmaceuticals*
Iggesund Board	*paper and board manufacture*
Kangol	*clothing*
Kimberley Clark	*paper manufacture*
K Shoes	*footwear manufacture*
Lawson Mardon Packaging	*flexible packaging*
Nestlé	*food manufacture*
New Balance Athletic Shoes	*footwear manufacture*
Pirelli	*tyre manufacture*
Robert McBride	*detergent manufacturer*
Sealy United Kingdom	*bed manufacture*
UCB Films	*films for labels, securities and packaging*
United Biscuits	*food manufacture*
James Walker	*fluid sealing technology*

Examples of three businesses located in the region are shown over the page.

Eddie Stobart A private company with headquarters in Carlisle, Eddie Stobart Ltd is the UK's largest transport and logistics organisation. Chairman and Chief Executive, Edward Stobart, believes the Cumbrian location has played a vital role in the company's success. The Group's strategic position is adjacent to the M6, linking Scotland with the rest of the UK motorway network. From 100 vehicles in 1991 to a fleet that numbers 700 today, 20 depots nationally and 3 million square feet of warehousing, Eddie Stobart Ltd is constantly expanding. New opportunities include property and development, mail order and retail, and there are even plans for a new rail service and roadside restaurants. This growth has led to more jobs, where the emphasis is on training to achieve maximum efficiencies. This is proof that Cumbria provides the place and the people to transport a business forward.

Farley's Farley's is part of the largest baby food manufacturers in Britain and owned by H.J. Heinz. To produce the highest quality baby foods, the highest quality environment is essential. The clean air, clean water and committed workforce have all contributed to Farley's continued success. The company is market leader in the UK and has worldwide exports. In 1998, Heinz demonstrated its commitment to the plant with a £3.5 million investment programme. Farley's is surrounded by Lakeland fells, close to the market town of Kendal and dual carriageway creating a fast link with the M6 motorway. So the healthy Cumbrian environment is not just good for people, it's good for business.

Kimberly Clark Kimberly-Clark is the global number one in facial tissues, bathroom tissues, hand towels and wipes. Mill Manager, Peter Taylor, credits the adaptability of the highly skilled workforce and the low operating costs in Cumbria which maintains his company's competitiveness, as key factors for success. The Barrow-based paper mill is expanding rapidly as a result of this success. To help meet increasing demand, the company invested £15 million in 1997/98 for a new mill and machinery.

Source: adapted from Cumbrian Inward Investment Agency website.

(a) British Nuclear Fuel has a power station at Sellafield in Cumbria. Why might this have been chosen as a site? (6 marks)

(b) What are likely to be important location factors for a logistics company like Eddie Stobart? Explain your answer. (8 marks)

(c) Explain the advantages to a footloose business of locating in Cumbria. (8 marks)

(d) Analyse the advantages and disadvantages of locating a small hotel, catering for hill walkers, in Whitehaven which is situated on the Cumbrian coast. (10 marks)

(e) Do you think Cumbria is likely to qualify for any regional aid? Explain your answer. (8 marks)

(f) Discuss whether or not a blue chip company would consider moving its head office from London to Cumbria. (10 marks)

29 Mergers and Takeovers

Reasons for mergers and takeovers

Mergers and takeovers take place when firms join together and operate as one organisation. Why do some businesses act in this way?

- It is a quick and easy way to expand the business (☞ unit 4). For example, if a supermarket chain wanted to open another twenty stores in the UK, it could find sites and build new premises. A quicker way could be to buy a company that already owns some stores and convert them.
- Buying a business is often cheaper than growing internally. A business may calculate that the cost of internal growth is £80 million. However, it might be possible to buy another company for £55 million on the stock market. The process of buying the company might inflate its price, but it could still work out much cheaper.
- Some businesses have cash available which they want to use. Buying another business is one way of doing this.
- Mergers have taken place for defensive reasons. A business might buy another to consolidate its position in the market. Also, if a firm can increase its size through merging, it may avoid being the victim of a takeover itself.
- In response to economic changes. For example, some businesses may have merged before the introduction of the euro in 1999 in certain European countries or before the expansion of the EU in 2004.
- Merging with a business in a different country is one way in which a business can gain entry into foreign markets. It may also avoid restrictions that prevent it from locating in a country or avoid paying tariffs on goods sold in that country.
- The globalisation of markets (☞ unit 38) has encouraged mergers between foreign businesses. This could allow a company to operate and sell worldwide, rather than in particular countries or regions.
- A business may want to gain economies of scale. Firms can often lower their costs by joining with another firm. This is dealt with later in this unit.
- Some firms are asset strippers. They buy a company, sell off profitable parts, close down unprofitable sections and perhaps integrate other activities into the existing business.
- Management may want to increase the size of the company. This is because the growth of the business is their main objective.

Merger activity

In the late 1990s and early twenty first century both the number and value of mergers reached record levels. What might have been the reasons for this 'merger boom'?

- There was growth in the UK economy and a buoyant stock market. Higher profits attracted companies to buy shares in or take over other businesses. Companies were also prepared to pay higher prices, which raised the value of mergers and takeovers.
- Faced with greater competition in providing services, there was a number of mergers between financial institutions. Examples of mergers in the financial sector include Lloyds Bank and the TSB and The Royal and Sun Alliance insurance companies.
- Deregulation and liberalisation freed markets. For example, deregulation of the communications industry in the USA allowed an 'alliance' between AT&T and BT. Deregulation of electricity in the UK led to the creation of 14 electricity companies in 1990. By 1998, 12 had either merged together or been bought by outside businesses, mainly because the merged companies would be better able to compete.
- Improvements in information and communication technology meant that it was far easier for businesses to deal with each other. Before, companies in different parts of the country, or in different countries, may have been reluctant to merge because of problems with passing information. Private company **intranets** greatly reduced this problem.
- A growing number of large businesses merged. For example, BP's takeover of Amoco in 1998 was the UK's largest industrial takeover. It was suggested that the merger would lead to cost savings of 6 per cent.
- Many firms adopted a company strategy of 'going global'. They wanted operations in many countries and many markets.
- Companies were 'bargain hunting' by taking over companies in Asia. Economic problems in that part of the world meant that companies could be bought relatively cheaply.

It appears that the merger boom peaked in 2000 in the UK. Figure 29.1 shows the merger and acquisition activity between 1995 and 2003. Activity was greatest in 2000. However, both

Figure 29.1 *Quarterly volume of merger and acquisition activity, UK*

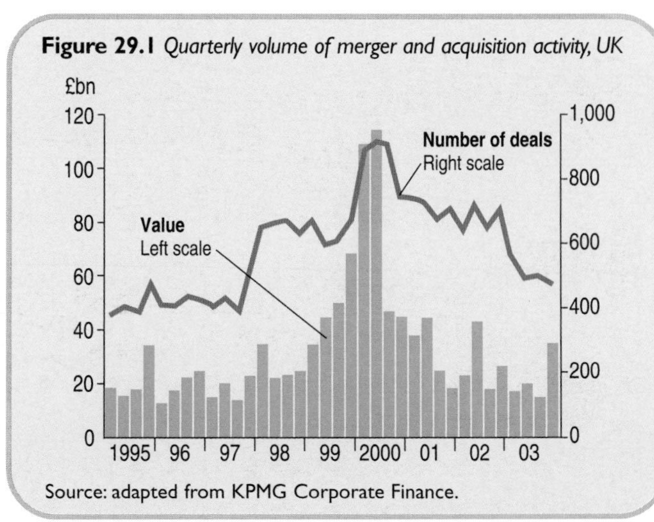

Source: adapted from KPMG Corporate Finance.

the number of deals and their value fell after that. By 2004 many investment bankers thought that activity would begin to rise again, with America leading the way. For example, in February 2004 Comcast, the US cable giant, made a £28.6 billion hostile bid for Disney.

Types of merger or integration

As Figure 29.2 shows, mergers can be classed in a number of ways. Not all mergers fit neatly into these categories, however. HORIZONTAL INTEGRATION occurs when two firms which are in exactly the same line of business and the same stage of production join together. The merger between BP and Amoco, the two oil companies is an example of a horizontal merger. The benefits of mergers between firms at the same stage of operation include:

- a 'common' knowledge of the markets in which they operate;
- less likelihood of failure by moving into a totally new area;
- similar skills of employees;
- less disruption.

VERTICAL INTEGRATION can be FORWARD VERTICAL INTEGRATION or BACKWARD VERTICAL INTEGRATION. Consider a firm which manufactures and assembles mountain bikes. If it were to acquire a firm which was a supplier of tyres for the bikes, this would be an example of backward vertical integration. The two firms are at different stages of production. The main motives for such a merger are to guarantee and control the supply of components and raw materials and to remove the profit margin the supplier would demand. Forward vertical integration involves merging with a firm which is in the next stage of production rather than the previous stage. For example, the mountain bike manufacturer may merge with a retail outlet selling bikes. Again this eliminates the profit margin expected by the firm in the next stage of production. It also gives the manufacturer confidence when planning production, knowing that there are retail outlets in which to sell. Vertical mergers tend to be rare in the UK.

LATERAL INTEGRATION involves the merging of two firms with related goods which do not compete directly with each other. Production techniques or the distribution channels may be similar. Cadbury-Schweppes is perhaps an example. The two companies used similar raw materials and had similar markets, but did not compete with each other directly.

There are some motives for firms in completely different lines of business to join together. This type of merger is called a CONGLOMERATE or DIVERSIFYING MERGER. A firm might fear a loss of market share due to greater competition. As a result it may try to explore new and different opportunities.

Figure 29.2 *A summary of the methods of integration*

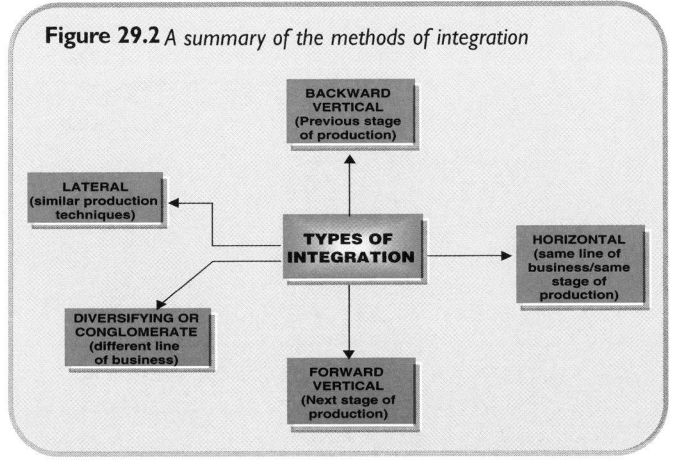

One of the most high profile mergers to take place in 2003 was between the two ITV broadcasting companies, Granada and Carlton. The £4.6 billion merger took a long time before it was finalised. It was subject to lengthy investigation by the Competition Commission. The Commission found that the proposed merger would be expected to operate against the public interest in two areas.

- Its impact on Channel TV, SMG and Ulster TV in relation to networking arrangements and the sale of their advertising airtime.
- The sale of Carlton's and Granada's advertising airtime and, in particular, the share of discount deals struck with advertisers and media buyers.

After wide consultation and an unusually large number of hearings with interested parties, the Commission concluded that the expected adverse effects of the merger could be remedied if Carlton and Granada agreed to a package of safeguards and conditions.

Carlton and Granada believe that the merged group will be in a better position to compete with the BBC and BSkyB in the future. The following benefits were expected.

- Viewers will benefit from better programmes with improved quality and choice, more premieres, more event entertainment and more dramas.
- Advertisers will benefit from the greater ability of the merged group to improve audience share and commercial impacts, particularly to the key demographic groups. This will allow advertisers to increase the size and efficiency of their reach.
- Shareholders will benefit from a simpler and clearer structure, greater efficiency and lower costs. Shareholders will also benefit from significant synergies together with the increased scale and cash flow of the merged group.

Source: adapted from Competition Commission press release, 7.10.2003 and *The Guardian*.

(a) What type of merger is taking place in the example? Explain your answer.
(b) Who is likely to benefit most from the merger?

Takeovers

Takeovers amongst public limited companies can occur because their shares are traded openly and anyone can buy them. One business can acquire another by buying 51 per cent of the shares. Some of these can be bought on the stock market and others might be bought directly from existing shareholders. When a takeover is complete, the company that has been 'bought' loses its identity and becomes part of the **predator** company. Private limited companies, however, cannot be taken over unless the majority shareholders 'invite' others to buy their shares.

In practice, a firm can take control of another company by buying less than 51 per cent of the shares. This may happen when share ownership is widely spread and little communication takes place between shareholders. In some cases a predator can take control of a company by purchasing as little as 15 per cent of the total share issue. Once a company has bought 3 per cent of another company it must make a declaration to the stock market. This is a legal requirement designed to ensure that the existing shareholders are aware of the situation.

Takeovers or mergers can result in situations which may be against consumers' interests. As a result the Department of Trade and Industry might instruct the Competition Commission to investigate the merger. This may result in the government allowing the merger to take place provided certain conditions are met. In extreme cases a merger may be completely blocked. For example, in 2003-04, there was a battle between Tesco, Asda, Sainsbury's and Morrisons to take over supermarket rival Safeway. But the Competition Commission concluded that a Safeway takeover by one of its big rivals would lead to too much concentration in the sector, to the detriment of consumers. It blocked bids by Tesco, Asda and Sainsbury's which led the way clear for Morrisons to buy the company, subject to certain conditions.

Takeovers of public limited companies often result in sudden increases in their share price. This is due to the volume of buying by the predator and also speculation by investors. Once it is known that a takeover is likely, investors scramble to buy shares, anticipating a quick, sharp price rise. Sometimes more than one firm might attempt to take over a company. This can result in very sharp increases in the share price as the two buyers bid up the price. During 2003-04, for example, rumours were circulating that Manchester United Football Club would be subject to a takeover bid. As a result, in one month between September and October 2003, the share price rose by 30 per cent.

Hostile and friendly takeovers

Takeovers can be **hostile** or **friendly**. A hostile takeover means that the victim tries to resist the bid. Resistance is usually co-ordinated by the board of directors. They attempt to persuade the shareholders that their interests would be best protected if the company remains under the control of the existing board of directors. Shareholders then have to weigh up the advantages and disadvantages of a new 'owner'.

A takeover may be invited. A firm might be struggling because it has cash flow problems, for example. It might want the current business activity to continue, but under the control of another, stronger company. The new company would inject some cash in exchange for control. Such a company is sometimes referred to as a 'white knight'.

The mergers and takeovers described above all refer to public limited companies. It is possible for private limited companies to be taken over. However, an unwanted takeover cannot take place since the shares in private limited companies are not widely available.

Asset stripping

Some takeovers in recent years have resulted in ASSET STRIPPING. The asset stripper aims to buy another company at a market price which is lower than the value of the firm's total assets. It then sells off the profitable parts of the business and closes down those which are unprofitable. Such activity has often been criticised since it leads to unemployment in those sections which are closed down and generates a degree of uncertainty. In 2002, it was alleged that AMP, the

Oxford GlycoScience, the cash-rich biotechnology firm, surrendered to a £102 million takeover bid in April 2003. Celltech, the predator, planned to close the business. OGS had initially dismissed Celltech's offer as 'opportunistic, and a bid to acquire OGS on the cheap'. Chief executive, David Ebsworth, conceded he would be unable to deliver a higher breaking-up price. He also insisted that Celltech's price did 'not reflect the intrinsic value of the business and cash in OGS'. OGS's cash reserves last year stood at £135 million. The loss-making Oxford firm said all other interest from potential merger partners and rival asset-stripping predators had been exhausted. The day before, biotech investors Sir Chris Evans and Alan Goodman abandoned plans for a rival £111 million hostile bid. They claimed that the firm's head office would saddle any asset-stripping bid with an unforeseen leasehold liability of more than £10 million - though some analysts questioned this figure and claimed the liability was well known. A source close to Sir Chris Evans said a two-week intensive examination of OGS's books by the two entrepreneurs pointed to 'a fair break-up value of about £90 million'.

Source: adapted from *The Guardian*, 12.4.2003.

(a) What evidence is there in the case to suggest that the takeover of OGS was hostile?
(b) What is likely to be the effect of the takeover on OGS (i) employees and (ii) shareholders?

Australian insurance company, asset-stripped Pearl, the UK life assurance company. AMP paid £1.2 billion for Pearl in 1989, regarded as a knockdown price. A few years later AMP won permission from the DTI to unlock Pearl's 'orphan assets', built up from the surplus on millions of policies sold between 1929 and 1965. AMP shareholders gained £918 million from Pearl. In effect, it was suggested that AMP used Pearl's own money to pay for the acquisition of the company.

Reverse takeovers

REVERSE TAKEOVERS usually occur when a smaller company takes over a larger company. They tend to be friendly takeovers because a small company is unlikely to have sufficient financial resources to take over a much larger company against its will. The larger company may allow the takeover because it feels that the smaller company has a lot to offer in the way of expertise or future potential. Alternatively the larger company may be part of a larger organisation and is up for sale. One example of a reverse takeover in 2003, was the acquisition by Content Film, the American production house, of Winchester Entertainment, the London-based film finance and distribution company. It would be come the UK's biggest listed film company.

Another motive for a reverse takeover is to obtain a stock market listing. A large unquoted company might allow a smaller quoted company to 'reverse into it' so that the new company can trade as a plc. For example, Bolton Wanderers Football Club allowed a reverse takeover by Mosaic Investments, the bar and catering products company, in 1997. After the takeover a new company, Burnden Leisure, was formed. However, Bolton Wanderers shareholders retained control of 67 per cent of the new company.

Mergers and economies of scale

One of the motives for merging is that costs will be lower if two firms join together. This is because when firms increase their size they gain **economies of scale**. It is possible that horizontal mergers may benefit most from economies of scale. For example, two banks with similar operations may each have a branch in a high street. If they merge together, costs may be reduced by closing one of the branches.

In 1980 Professor Dennis Mueller studied the effects on efficiency of 800 mergers in seven countries. He found that they were unlikely to lead to economies of scale. He also suggested that small firms would be the main gainers from mergers. A study by Professor Keith Cowling in 1980 supported this view. He investigated the performance over 7 years of companies involved in horizontal mergers. The results showed that efficiency gains were no greater than in non-merged businesses, and in some cases were worse. This may have been because of a fall in turnover as the merged company 'rationalised' its factory and cut output. Also profits of the combined company may have been lower than what they would have been without the merger.

Many of the businesses involved in mergers and takeovers, however, suggest that cost savings are the main reason for joining together. Some even produce figures to indicate the cost savings they would make. Examples of the economies of scale to be gained were:

- the elimination of duplicated resources. For example, cost savings from the merger between BP and Amoco in 1998 were to be gained from not duplicating oil exploration. The takeover of Amersham in the UK by Nycomed, a Norwegian biotechnical firm, resulted in savings of £9 million one year later;
- the reduction of risk. A small company may be reluctant to operate in a politically unstable country. The BP-Amoco merger may be willing to do so, because it will have other projects which may be profitable if it has problems in certain countries;
- the spreading of the fixed costs of promotion. For example, the design of an advert or promotion is a fixed cost. An advert may cost £200,000 to make. If it reaches 1 million in the UK, the average cost is 20p (£200,000 ÷ 1,000,000). If it is shown to 10 million in the US the average cost falls to 2p;
- the ability to sell a wider range of products because of a wider sales network. This is known as ONE STOP SHOPPING or **cross selling**. Selling more products from the same distribution network will again reduce the average fixed cost of the sales network;
- that merged companies which become global operators may find that their suppliers also set up in the many countries in which they operate;
- that larger businesses are in a stronger position to negotiate with suppliers and can negotiate to reduce prices;
- that merged businesses may have COMPLEMENTARY ASSETS. John Kay (1996) suggested that businesses may only be able to operate in certain markets if they have certain assets. For example, a business may advertise nationally to create a brand name. This is unlikely to be successful if it only has shops in Newcastle. It needs a complementary asset such as a chain of national shops.

Joint ventures and alliances

A JOINT VENTURE is where two or more companies share the cost, responsibility and profits of a business venture. The financial arrangements between the companies involved will tend to differ, although many joint ventures between two firms involve a 50:50 share of costs and profits. There are many examples of joint ventures. In March 2004, US computer giant Microsoft joined forces with mobile operator Vodafone, handset manufacturer Nokia and six other technology companies to form a joint venture to drive Internet usage on mobile phones. The new venture aimed to kick-start the development of websites designed specifically to be accessed by mobile phones ahead of the launch of new high speed third generation networks later that year. In another joint venture, Jarvis, the construction and maintenance company, and Interhealth Canada, formed Interhealth Care Services (UK). This new venture won a contract from the government in January 2004 to build and run orthopaedic units for patients waiting for hip or knee replacements.

There is a number of advantages of joint ventures.

- They allow companies to enjoy some of the advantages of mergers, such as growth of turnover, without having to lose their identity.
- Businesses can specialise in a particular aspect of the venture in which they have experience.
- Takeovers are expensive. Heavy legal and administrative costs are often incurred. Also, the amount of money required to take over another company is sometimes unknown.
- Mergers and takeovers are often unfriendly. Most joint ventures are friendly. The companies commit their funds and share responsibility. Such an attitude may help to improve the success of the venture.
- Competition may be eliminated. If companies co-operate in a joint venture they are less likely to compete with each other. However, the venture must not restrict competition to such an extent that consumers' interests are harmed.

There are some disadvantages to joint ventures:

- Some joint ventures fail to achieve the desired results. They are often compromises when an all-out takeover would be better. There may be control struggles. For example, who should have the final say in a 50:50 joint venture?
- It is possible for disagreements to occur about the management of the joint venture. As with any partnership, sometimes there are different views on which course of action to take.
- The profit from the venture is obviously split between the investors. A company might regret this if it became evident at a later date that a particular venture could have been set up by itself.

Alliances may take looser forms than joint ventures. They are usually for three reasons.

- Marketing. For example, McDonald's and Disney have promoted each other's products.
- R&D (☞ unit 27), where businesses work together in developing a new product. Each business will be able to contribute its individual expertise.
- Information. Supermarkets gather information on customers' buying habits which they share with food manufacturers. This is perhaps a form of **forward vertical integration.**

Demerging

A DEMERGER is where a company sells off a significant part of its existing operations. A company might choose to break up to:

- raise cash to invest in remaining sections;
- concentrate its efforts on a narrower range of activities;
- avoid rising costs and inefficiency through being too large:
- take advantage of the fact that the company has a higher share valuation when split into two components than it does when operating as one.

In the spring of 2004, Six Continents, the largest hotel group in the world, planned to split off its pubs, bars and restaurants business. The split would see the creation of two separate listed companies - InterContinental Hotels, which will include the InterContinental and Holiday Inn operations, alongside the group's Britvic soft drinks operation, and retail,

In August 2003, Slough Estates, the UK's biggest quoted property group, was considering the demerger of its American biotech park portfolio into a separate listed company. This was considered to be a radical proposal, but the new chief executive, Ian Coull, wanted to revitalise the company by unlocking some of its capital. Coull planned to convert Slough Estates into a development company rather than a pure property investment group. He felt that returns on capital employed could be increased by changing business emphasis. After visiting the group's $1 billion assets in America, demerger was one of three possible options to raise capital to develop the company.

Slough identified some areas in the US around Boston, Washington, Baltimore and Philadelphia with an unfulfilled requirement. It was considering the provision of specialist developments such as laboratories, specialised cooling rooms and ionisation systems. The company was keen to increase its US investor base and put some life into the shares which at the time were trading at a discount to the asset value of the company.

Source: adapted from *The Sunday Times*, 10.8.2003.

Figure 29.3 *Slough Estates' share price*

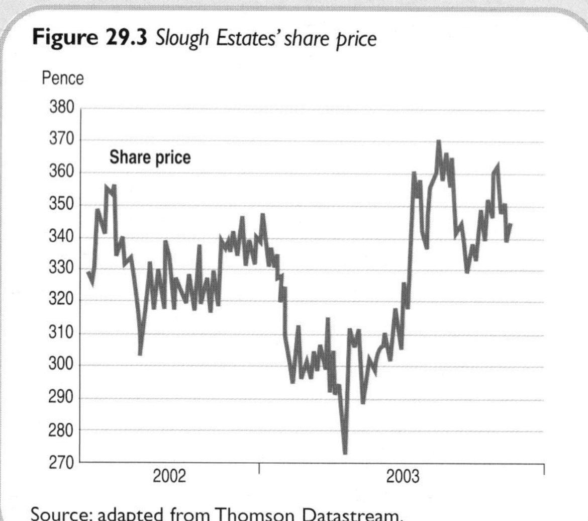

Source: adapted from Thomson Datastream.

(a) Using this case as an example, explain what is meant by a demerger.

(b) Explain Slough's motive for the demerger.

which spans brands such as Harvester, Hollywood Bowl and All Bar One and which will take the name Mitchells & Butlers. It was believed that growth would be much faster if the group was split in two.

Management buy-outs

A MANAGEMENT BUY-OUT is where the ownership of a business is transferred to the current management team. The team is likely to buy shares from the existing owners. Funds for the buy-out might be provided by members of the management team itself or financial institutions, such as banks or venture capitalists. Venture capitalists, such as CinVen, 3i and Schroder Ventures, are specialists who are prepared to take the risk of investing directly in a business. The capital they provide is sometimes called risk capital. Some buy-outs involve these venture capitalists taking complete control. This is known as a **leveraged buy-out**.

What might account for the popularity of management buy-outs?

- Many buy-outs occur when large companies restructure their operations. They sell off parts of the business which do not fit into their future plans. For example, in 2003, Teco Information Systems Europe was bought out by a management team from its Taiwanese parent for £17 million. Teco, one of the top 20 conglomerates in Taiwan, sold the business because it was withdrawing from non-core activities.
- As part of the privatisation programme the UK government sold businesses to management buy-out teams. For example, in 1996 two rail leasing companies, Porterbrook and Eversholt, were sold to management buy-out teams. So was the British Rail heavy maintenance depot at Eastleigh in Hampshire, for around £10 million.
- It is an alternative to full or part closure of a family business or its subsidiary. In the early 1990s, BSM, the driving school business, was sold to a management team.
- To resurrect all or part of a company that has been struggling or has gone into receivership. In 1997 Country Casuals sold the loss-making Elvi, the large sized women's wear retailer, and Lerose, a clothes manufacturer, for small sums to management teams.
- To allow founders to retain an interest. For example, it was announced that Lexis Public Relations, whose clients include NTL, Guinness, Powergen, Piat d'Or, Barclaycard and Southern Comfort, was bought by its management in 2002 for £5 million. It was founded by Bill Jones and Tim Adams. The MBO team will own the majority of shares between them. The founders would retain a preference share, convertible into stock and take consultancy roles, Mr Jones as part time chairman of the operating board and Mr Adams as a part time consultant.

What might be the advantages of a management buy-out? From the sellers' point of view it lets them raise finance for a possibly ailing firm or subsidiary, which might otherwise have closed down. From the managers' and employees' point of view it would enable them to keep their jobs in the same occupation and area as they had before. It is also argued that the efficiency of the business would be improved by a buy-out. This is perhaps because there is an increased incentive for managers to perform well. Following a buy-out the management team will benefit financially from any profit made by the company, so there is an incentive to keep costs down and motivate the workforce, for example. In addition, the potential for conflict between the owners and the managers is reduced because after a buy-out the owners are the managers.

Generally, it seems that buy-outs are successful as they keep the business going. A study by the Warwick Business School reported that management buy-outs outperformed their industry average for the first three years. However, after that, they tended to underperform. Other, longer term, studies have suggested that performance after the first three years continued to be better than the industry average.

Management buy-ins

MANAGEMENT BUY-INS are where an outside management team takes over a business. Deals of this type are becoming more complex.

- Investor buy-outs (IBOs) are where the seller negotiates more closely with the fund provider rather than the management team.
- Buy-in management buy-outs (bimbos) are when an external management team, combined with the existing management team, buy the business from its owner.

For example, in September 2003, Northern Foods sold Foxes Glacier Mints to a management buy-in team. The team paid £7 million plus £2.4 million in debt for a business which also owns brands such as Paynes Poppets, Just Brazils and XXX Mints. The new team raised most of the money from family and friends. It argued 'It will be a business run by industrialists with financial backers rather than one run by financiers with industrial managers'. Northern Foods decided to sell the business because it was too small.

In June 2002, Whitbread, the leisure conglomerate, sold its Pelican chain of 153 restaurants, including the Café Rouge and Bella Pasta brands, to an outside management team backed by private equity firm ECI Group. Tragus Holdings, the management team, paid £25 million in cash for the

Table 29.1 *Larger UK buy-ins and buy-outs by value (£m)*

£m	1996	1997	1998	1999	2000	2001
10-25	870	990	1,070	870	1,010	690
25-50	1,010	920	1,280	1,040	750	890
50-100	1,060	1,900	2,420	1,860	1,690	1,070
100-250	1,020	1,770	1,980	3,580	3,320	2,960
250+	1,970	2,810	6,130	7,030	13,840	13,330
Total	**5,930**	**8,390**	**12,880**	**14,380**	**20,610**	**18,940**

restaurant business which had been underperforming. A spokesperson for Whitbread said that in recent years it had transformed itself from a brewer to a leisure group through a number of acquisitions and divestments.

Table 29.1 shows that the value of management buy-ins and buy-outs has increased since the mid-1990s. In 1996 the total value of buy-ins and buy-outs was £5,357 million. By 2001 this had risen to £18,940 million, although there had been a fall since 2000. There was an increasing tendency for larger buy-ins and buy-outs to take place.

1. Why might firms choose to join together?
2. Why might external growth be quicker than internal growth?
3. Give 2 examples of:
   (a) horizontal integration;
   (b) vertical integration;
   (c) lateral integration.
4. Why might a firm diversify?
5. Briefly explain how an acquisition is carried out.
6. Why is asset stripping often criticised?
7. What might be a motive for a reverse takeover?
8. Explain why mergers might not result in an improvement in efficiency.
9. What is the difference between a joint venture and a merger?
10. What might be the advantages of demergers?
11. Explain the difference between a management buy-out and a management buy-in.

Crabtree is a globally respected name in a niche market. It produces printing presses. It is based in Gateshead and was established in 1849. However, like many other manufacturers in recent years, it has experienced difficulties. In 1990, Crabtree won a Queens Award for Export and by the mid-1990s it had a market capitalisation of £70 million, employing around 400 staff. By 2003 it employed just 120 staff and was owned by a heavily indebted German company who acquired Crabtree for just £10 million.

In March 2003, Crabtree was bought from the German company by a management team. The team were confident that the company could flourish. It has a customer base of more than 500 companies worldwide and more than 2,500 machines in operation in 68 different countries. Raising funds for the MBO was not easy. After being turned down by all the big banks in the UK the team approached Northern Venture Managers (NVM), a venture capital company. It put £1.8 million towards the £2.2 million buy-out. Tim Levitt, investment director of NVM said 'It's time somebody stood up and said that investing in manufacturing can still make money in the UK'.

Crabtree exports more than 90 per cent of its output and now that it is independent again it can push harder for sales. 'Now we have our own sales team we feel we have our own destiny' said a spokesperson for the team.

Source: adapted from *The Financial Times*, 27.5.2003.

(a) Why do you think the German company sold Crabtree?
(b) What role did NVM play in the management buy-out?
(c) What might be the benefits to the business now that it is owned by the managers?

Question 4

key terms

Asset stripping - the selling off of profitable sections and closing down of loss making sections of a business following an acquisition.
Backward vertical integration - merging with a firm involved with the previous stage of production.
Complememtary assets - assets that a business requires together to be successful.
Conglomerate or diversifying merger - the merging of firms involved in completely different business activities.
Demerger - where a business splits into two or more separate organisations.
Forward vertical integration - merging with a firm involved with the next stage of production.
Horizontal integration - the merging of firms which are in exactly the same line of business.
Joint venture - two firms sharing the cost, responsibility and profits of a business venture.
Lateral integration - the merging of firms involved in the production of similar goods, but not in competition with each other.
Management buy-in - the sale of a business to an outside management team.
Management buy-out - the sale of a business to the existing management team.
Reverse takeover - where a company takes over a larger company than itself.
Vertical integration - the merging of two firms at different stages of production.

Case study Virgin and BMI

In May 2003, Virgin Atlantic, Sir Richard Branson's long haul airline, and BMI British Midland, the short haul carrier controlled by Sir Michael Bishop, met to discuss the possibility of closer co-operation. Some analysts in the industry suggested that a merger would make a great deal of sense. However, according to an adviser close to the talks, this was not an option that was being discussed. It was suggested that the talks were being held to explore issues like selling seats on each others' flights, synchronising networks, more efficient use of BMI slots at Heathrow Airport and sharing facilities to cut costs.

If a merger were to materialise, there would be a significant restructuring of European aviation and the forces of the sector's two most successful entrepreneurs would be combined. It would also create a powerful second force to compete with the dominant British Airways (BA) at Heathrow, which currently has 40 per cent of the slots. Another issue is that both companies control low cost airlines, BMIbaby in the UK and Virgin Express based in Brussels. Both need to expand their limited geographical presence.

Virgin Atlantic has been keen for some time to do a deal with BMI because it has the second largest pool of take-off and landing slots at Heathrow – 13 per cent compared with Virgin's 3 per cent. Virgin's shortage of Heathrow slots has severely restricted its growth. The airline has also suffered from the lack of better access to the feeder traffic arriving at Heathrow from the rest of Europe. BMI would benefit from an alliance if it could break into the lucrative transatlantic market. In the past BMI has been blocked by the severely restrictive bilateral air services treaty between the UK and the US. BMI has started limited services from Manchester but the operation is currently making a loss.

The two groups have got together before in the past 15 years. However, it seems that each time egos, ambitions and strategic directions have kept them apart. One difference this time though is the current trading environment for airlines. Since the September 11 incident in America, the airline industry has been struggling. Passenger traffic has fallen and could fall further as fear of terrorist attacks continues to escalate. Survival in this competitive market might be easier for the two groups if they can both benefit from some form of co-operation.

Source: adapted from *The Financial Times*, 23.5.2003.

(a) What might be the motives for possible co-operation between Virgin and BMI? (6 marks)

(b) Using this case as an example, explain the difference between an alliance and a merger. (8 marks)

(c) What economies of scale might be enjoyed if the two airlines did merge? (12 marks)

(d) Analyse the benefits to both airlines of some form of co-operation. (12 marks)

(e) Discuss whether further consolidation in the airline industry is likely. (12 marks)

Table 29.4 *Virgin Atlantic and BMI British Midland financial and other information*

Virgin Atlantic		BMI British Midland	
Sales	£1.4bn	Sales	£724m
Pretax profit/loss	£10m	Pretax profit/loss	-£19.6m
Share of slots at Heathrow airport	3%	Share of slots at Heathrow airport	13%
Passengers	4m	Passengers	7.5m
Number of destinations	22	Number of destinations	51
Fleet size	26	Fleet size	54
Workforce	6,800	Workforce	5,100
Ownership	51% - Richard Branson 49% - Singapore Airlines	Ownership	50% plus 1 share - BBW partnership controlled by Sir Michael Bishop 30% minus 1 share - Lufthansa 20% - SAS Scandinavian Airlines

30 Efficiency and Strategy

Efficiency and business

A business may use various methods to measure and improve efficiency. A food manufacturer producing large numbers of pizzas may find that the average cost of each pizza could have fallen over a year. This might **indicate** an improvement in efficiency. The reasons for the fall in costs may be because workers are producing more products. It may also be because operations have been changed so that machines can run for longer periods.

Increasingly businesses are adopting company-wide or corporate strategies (☞ units 6 and 7) that they believe will lead to improvements in productivity. This will involve the whole organisation. It will only be successful if the business has a corporate culture (☞ unit 5) which supports its attempts to improve efficiency.

Tom Peters - 'In search of Excellence'

Tom Peters and R.Waterman in their book *In Search of Excellence* identified eight key characteristics of good performing companies from financial statistics and interviews with managers, as shown in Table 30.1.

Table 30.1 *Characteristics of good performing companies*

- Large firms were too slow when making decisions, particularly launching new products. They spent too much time analysing data. A better approach was to launch new products quickly, correct problems after and then market the improved version. Cutting lead times was also emphasised by certain managers.
- Successful companies were those which listened to consumers. Customers tended to know what they would buy and firms should supply products which customers want.
- The generation of new ideas was a key factor for success. All employees should be encouraged to try out new ideas even if they did not always work. Mistakes were not criticised in organisations where ideas were encouraged, but viewed as 'good tries'. Employees should operate as though they were running their own small business.
- Top companies recognised the qualities and potential of their workforce. Given the opportunity, workers would act creatively and solve their own problems. If workers generated ideas which management took into account, improvements in productivity would occur.
- Successful businesses stressed values such as continuous innovation, good customer service and dependable quality. Leading by example was also considered important for managers.
- Diversification could weaken a company. Expanding through the development of strengths would be more profitable than trying to do something completely different.
- Organisation charts in leading companies tended to be flatter. Flat structures and a simple chain of command are more effective than matrix structures.
- Successful businesses tended to be decentralised.

Peters later revised his ideas to take into account changes in the business environment.

- Businesses should revolutionise their approach when adapting to external influences on the business environment.
- Businesses should aim to develop new 'stars' in their product portfolio. Stars are products with a high market share and a high growth potential.
- Businesses, because they cannot control market events, should try to anticipate changes and continually move forward.

Downsizing

A large number of firms have attempted to improve their efficiency by DOWNSIZING. This term, coined by US management theorist Stephen Roach, has been used to describe the process of reducing capacity, ie laying off workers and closing unprofitable divisions. The advantages of this for businesses may be:

- cost savings and increased profit;
- a leaner, more competitive operation;
- only having efficient, profitable business, with no 'dead horses' to flog;

Twenty thousand civil service posts could be moved away from London and the south east and a further 7,000 lost altogether in a drive to improve efficiency in the civil service. This was according to the *Lyons Review*, a report on relocating government work, published in March 2004. The proposals, which were expected to be endorsed by the Chancellor of the Exchequer, would involve more than 6,500 redundancies, 6,300 relocations and the recruitment of 11,700 staff locally. Sir Michael Lyons, author of the report, said 'This is just the first stage'. Potentially between 40,000 and 60,000 jobs could be moved over a 15 year period if regulators and policy workers were relocated away from the south east. There was also a huge scope for cutting the size of departments' headquarters and moving their agencies out of London.

Implementing the recommendations will require firm action from the government, led by a minister at cabinet level, with potential up-front costs of around £942 million over seven years. This includes average redundancy costs of £65,000 and relocation packages averaging £32,000.

Source: adapted from *The Financial Times*, 16.3.2004.

(a) Explain how the Lyons Review involves downsizing.
(b) Examine the possible relationship between downsizing and delayering.
(c) Explain how downsizing might improve efficiency in the civil service.

Question 1

- profitable businesses not subsidising unprofitable ones.

Downsizing became popular amongst companies in the late 1990s and early twenty first century. Many businesses cut the number of employees, even in developing areas. For example, LogicaCMG, the computer services group, cut 1,400 jobs when it was formed from the merger of UK and Dutch companies in 2002. In 2003 it announced a further 800 job cuts as it aimed to improve cost savings from £60 million to £80 million a year.

Despite this enthusiasm, there is some evidence to suggest it is not always the most effective strategy. For example, a report by the Employers Forum on Age (EFA) based on 80 of its members suggested there were few real gains from downsizing. In addition, businesses lost the skills, experience and knowledge of employees. Some companies even hired back redundant staff as consultants.

Delayering

DELAYERING also involves a business reducing its staff. The cuts are directed at particular levels of a business, such as managerial posts. Many traditional organisational charts are hierarchical, with many layers of management. Delayering involves removing some of these layers. This gives a flatter structure. In the late 1980s, the average number of layers in a typical organisational structure was 7, although some were as high as 14. By 2000 this was reduced to less than 5. The main advantage of delayering is the savings made from laying off expensive managers. It may also lead to better communication and a better motivated staff if they are **empowered** and allowed to make their own decisions.

However, remaining managers may become demoralised after delayering. Also staff may become overburdened as they have to do more work. Fewer layers may also mean less chance of promotion.

Reengineering

REENGINEERING was defined by Michael Hammer and James Champy (1993) in their book *Reengineering the Corporation* as: 'the fundamental rethinking and radical redesign of business processes to achieve dramatic improvements in critical contemporary measures of performance such as cost, quality, service and speed'.

Features Reengineering has a number of features as shown in Table 30.2

Table 30.2 *Reengineering*

- Businesses should organise their work around processes. Examples of processes that might be redesigned include assembly or purchasing of stocks.
- Traditional methods of improving efficiency involve small changes to existing practices. Reengineering involves radically changing processes or introducing new ones. A business should discard old practices and 'start from scratch'.
- Reengineered processes operate without assembly lines. This allows several jobs to be combined. For example, jobs such as quality checker, paint sprayer and stock orderer may be combined.
- Workers make decisions and are empowered. This should reduce delays in decision making and shorten processes.
- In traditional production, tasks are completed one after the other in a strict sequence. Reengineered processes allow tasks to be completed in a 'natural order', which could be out of sequence.
- Traditional processes produce standardised products, which limits choice. Reengineering allows multiple designs or products, without the loss of scale economies.
- Most large businesses are divided into departments, which have a function. Reengineered processes cross boundaries. For example, the production department might market its own products.
- In traditional processes there is too much checking. Sometimes controls and checks cost more than the money they save. Reengineered processes only employ cost-effective controls and checks.
- Reengineered cuts down on the external contact points. For example, a supplier chasing payment will only have one point of contact. This prevents different people in the business giving out different information.
- Reengineered processes are able to gain the advantages of centralisation and decentralisation.

What processes are redesigned? These might be processes which are no longer working, for example, a quality assurance system that results in high levels of faulty products, processes which affect customers, such as lead times, and processes which are relatively easy and cheap to redesign.

How might reengineering of processes affect a business?

- Process teams, such as an assembly team, will take the place of functional departments, such as the production department.
- Jobs change from simple tasks to multi-dimensional work. Repetitious assembly line work disappears. It is replaced by individuals working in process teams, responsible for results.
- Workers will be empowered and no longer follow a set of rules laid down by management. They have to think, interact, use judgment and make decisions. Reengineered processes require workers to have an understanding of their jobs.
- Employees will not be promoted because they have a good performance record, but because they have the ability to do another job. Good performance is rewarded by bonuses.
- Employees must believe that they are working for customers and not their bosses.
- Managers no longer issue instructions and monitor the work of subordinates. They assist, guide and help staff to develop.
- Organisational hierarchies become flatter. Staff make decisions for themselves so there is less need for managers. Flatter organisations bring executives closer to customers and workers. Success depends on the attitudes and efforts of empowered workers rather than the actions of task

Pressman Associates is a property development company. It was born out of a construction company called Pressman Construction in 2001. Carl Pressman, the owner of both companies, decided to focus on property development when he realised that a lot of his construction company's time was being wasted on doing things that other companies could do for him - more effectively and efficiently. He sold off all the physical assets of Pressman Construction and opened an office in Newcastle.

Working from his quayside location, he searches for suitable sites, draws up plans for properties, builds large detached houses and sells them at lucrative prices. Carl is able to do this almost without leaving his office. Building plots are found by a specialist estate agent, plans are drawn up by architects, legal issues such as planning and contracts are dealt with by a solicitor, the dwellings are constructed by builders and fitted by a number of subcontractors. The properties are finally marketed and sold by another firm of estate agents. Carl co-ordinates all of these activities from his office. However, he employs a project manager to oversee construction. Working in this way Carl can undertake a number of developments all at the same time.

(a) What evidence is there in the case to suggest that Pressman Associates is a virtual company?
(b) Explain the benefits to Pressman Associates of operating in this way.

Question 2

orientated managers. Executives must be leaders who can influence and reinforce employees' values and beliefs.

Agile manufacturing

Some have suggested that businesses need an approach to cope with turbulent markets, competition, changing tastes, fast growth in technology and increasing consumer expectations. Today, customers want to buy products which are custom made and tailored to individual needs. All these trends have led to the development of AGILE MANUFACTURING.

The main aim of agile manufacturing is for a business to be able to perform effectively in a changing market. It will allow customised products to be made with short lead times and without rising costs. Agile manufacturers will be able to adopt new technologies more quickly and have a high degree of flexibility. This will allow large and rapid changes in output, product mixes and delivery dates.

How will a business be able to do this? An agile manufacturer will need flexible people, a reduction in rigid structural hierarchies, broader-based training, flexible production technologies and computer-integrated manufacturing. Radical changes in organisation will also be needed. Figure 30.1 shows the differences in approach of three production methods. Agile manufacturers need short term relationships with suppliers. This will allow supply

Figure 30.1 *The organisation of three production methods*

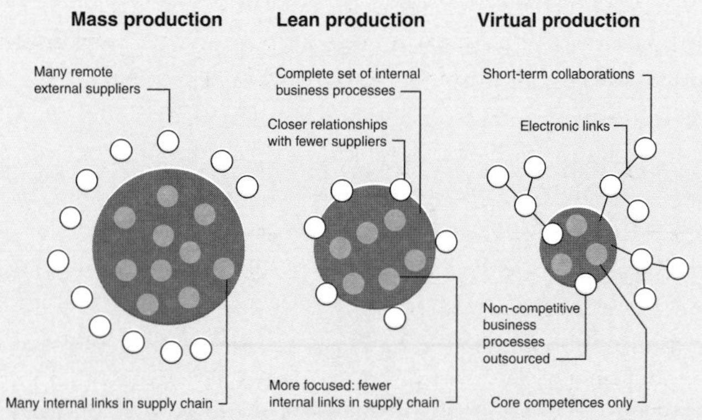

contracts to be set up and ended quickly to cope with changes in technology and demand. There is evidence of this happening already, with a growing number of joint ventures across industries. They will also make greater use of OUTSOURCING. This involves finding a contractor to supply components or to carry out processes that a business may have undertaken. Car manufacturers often outsource production. Brakes, brakepads, electronics, mirrors, windows and seats are all produced by outside suppliers. It leaves the business able to concentrate on its 'core' areas. This growth in outsourcing will require quick and effective communication

In 2002 GlaxoSmithKline (GSK), the pharmaceuticals group, was considering outsourcing its entire information technology operation. The company was negotiating with a number of IT suppliers, including IBM, EDS and CSC, asking them to come up with cost-saving plans. The suppliers were told to consider all options, including moving some of the IT work offshore, which could mean substantial job losses.

The IT operation at the company is huge. It involves 66,000 desktop computers which are used for tasks including payroll operations and scientists' research work. A GSK spokesperson said 'It is not just about costs. It is to do with improving services and increasing quality and efficiency'. Outsourcing IT functions is becoming increasingly popular. The Inland Revenue has a 10 year, £2.8 billion deal with EDS and the Royal Mail announced in October it planned to outsource its IT services to CSC in a £1.5 billion contract.

One fear was that the changes could affect staff morale within GSK. In recent months the company had been hit by the departure of three of its six most senior scientists.

Source: adapted from *The Guardian*, 5.9.2002.

(a) Examine the possible effects of outsourcing on the stakeholders of:
(i) GlaxoSmithKline;
(ii) IT companies.

with suppliers and workers. Improved communications technology will allow this.

These ideas have led to term the VIRTUAL COMPANY. It refers to a group of closely linked separate 'entities' which can quickly disband and reform to cope with a turbulent environment.

The learning organisation

In his book *The Fifth Disciple*, Peter Senge put forward the idea of the learning organisation. According to a definition in the IRS Management Review, a learning organisation is one 'that facilitates the learning of all its members and thus continually transforms itself'. It has been argued that to compete in the uncertain and changing conditions of the global market place, a business needs to be able to learn.

There are two types of learning. **Learning how** involves processes designed to transfer and improve skills that will improve performance. **Learning why** involves looking at how things are happening using diagnostic skills.

An example of its operation took place in 1998 when Reed Elsevier, the publishing group, began to prepare for the 'age of the Internet'. The Reed Elsevier Technology Group (RETG) was set up to educate other parts of the group about new technologies. The aim was to ensure that Reed Elsevier's different business units acquired technological expertise themselves. When part of the company acquired some new technological knowledge RETG passed it around the whole organisation. This ensured that something was only learnt once and time was not wasted.

Knowledge management

The aim of knowledge management (☞ unit 25) is to unlock the information held by individual members of the workforce and share it throughout the company. If this can be done, efficiency should improve. For example, the marketing department may find that customers are unhappy with the stitching on a shirt. If this knowledge was passed to the production department, it may help to reduce returns. Information and communication technology has a vital role to play in the storage, manipulation and presentation of information to all staff in the organisation.

Kaizen

Kaizen means continuous improvement. It is a company wide strategy designed to eliminate waste in business and lead to continual improvement in all aspects of a firm's operations. All staff in the organisation are trained to be on the lookout, all of the time, for ways of making improvements. If small improvements are made continually, their impact over long periods of time will be great. In addition, the company will always be moving forward. Kaizen includes a wide range of different production techniques and working practices, such as quality circles, suggestion schemes, automation, discipline in the workplace, just-in-time manufacturing and zero defects. Businesses which have adopted Kaizen in the UK have enjoyed enormous efficiency gains. For example, GSM Graphic Arts of Thirsk, which makes metal and plastic labels for the motor and electronics industries, operates Kaizen in its factory. In 10 years, GSM improved many aspects of its operations, attracted high profile customers, such as Nissan, GM and Ford, and saw employment grow from 17 to 200.

BP, the oil company, and Bovis Lend Lease, a project management and construction company, established Global Alliance in 1996. Its aim was to improve capital productivity in BP's retail site development process. The Alliance has run a successful 'Lessons Learnt' initiative for several years and its knowledge sharing system (called 'konnect') gives all its staff access to lessons learned and expertise worldwide. Knowledge management is not a separate business activity. It is the result of numerous daily acts of searching for better ways of doing things. In 2002, the new challenge for the Alliance was to cut the total cost of the standard service station by more than 25 per cent and reduce construction time by 2 weeks.

The Alliance met the challenge by using Foresight Review and standard value management techniques such as focus on function not on product,' and involvement of experienced staff to get the benefit of their individual and collective knowledge.

Foresight Review

This three-phase approach to identifying possible sources of cost savings and efficiency improvements was undertaken by a multidisciplinary team of eight. It included representatives from design and innovation, project management, commercial, procurement and external suppliers and contractors. Further knowledge and experience was brought in on an ad-hoc basis from Bovis Lend Lease. The team met for four half-day sessions and worked through the following phases.

- Understanding the challenge and identifying the focus areas.
- Brainstorming ideas and alternatives, including experience from previous projects.
- An analysis and evaluation of proposed solutions.

By following this process, sharing knowledge, learning from past successes and developing ideas creatively, a new approach was developed which cut the cost of building service stations by 29-33 per cent, substantially beating the 25 per cent target.

Source: adapted from LfE case study, 2003.

(a) Using this case as an example, explain what is meant by knowledge management.
(b) Explain how the approach used by BP to share knowledge in its organisation might affect the business.

Question 4

Michael Porter - competitive advantage

Michael Porter suggested that businesses could achieve a competitive advantage over rivals by following one of three generic strategies. One of these strategies is cost leadership. A cost leader will be the firm with the lowest unit costs. Low costs may be achieved through the mass production of a fairly standardised product, exploiting economies of scale, automating and reducing overheads.

The flexible labour force

In the past many UK businesses felt that their workforces were too inflexible. Labour productivity in many industries was significantly lower than in other countries. Workforces were uncooperative, resistant to change and lacking in motivation. In order to compete with overseas competition firms needed to improve the flexibility of the workforce (☞ unit 24). Methods of improving flexibility included:

- training workers in a number of tasks so that they can be switched around at short notice;
- allowing staff to choose their hours of work between certain limits;
- using temporary staff to cope with seasonal demand;
- using part time staff or workers on or zero hours contracts to cope with fluctuations in demand;
- encouraging staff to solve their own work problems;
- allowing staff to plan their own work schedules;
- encouraging staff to share information, help each other and check each other's work;
- the use of annualised hours schemes.

It was argued that a business with a flexible workforce would be more efficient in a number of ways. They could operate more freely if workers can be switched from one task to another. Fluctuations in demand could be dealt with more comfortably. The use of overtime payments could almost be eliminated. Stores, offices and other premises could also stay open for longer hours.

Criticisms

There are certain criticisms of modern production and management theories.

- After implementing strategies such as downsizing, delayering, reengineering and outsourcing, a number of businesses have found problems. For example, two thirds of the companies identified by Tom Peters as standard-bearers of excellence in 1982 were in trouble five years later. Michael Hammer admitted that 70 per cent of the firms that claimed to have 'reengineered' themselves failed to improve their market position.
- Michael Hammer admitted that a flaw existed in his own theory. In an article published in *The Wall Street Journal* in November 1996, he reported to have told a business conference that he had forgotten about one factor - people. He said: 'I was reflecting my engineering background and was insufficiently appreciative of the human dimension. I've learned that is critical'.
- Reengineering in many businesses has simply meant downsizing. Businesses have tried to cut jobs without appreciating the long term effect of their actions. Job cuts have led to a stressed out, insecure and demotivated workforce.
- Peter Drucker and other management theorists emphasise the role of people as a firm's main asset and the corporation as a social as well as a commercial institution. Approaches which seek to remove employees with important business knowledge may have an adverse effect on the business. This is perhaps why knowledge management was said to be important for businesses in the early twenty first century.
- Many new management theories have been described as 'fads' or 'bandwagons'. They have failed to deliver improvements in profit or positive change. Business may simply use whatever theory happens to be in fashion at the time.

key terms

Agile manufacturing - a strategy which allows a business to react to rapidly changing conditions.
Delayering - the removal of managerial layers in the hierarchical structure.
Downsizing - the process of reducing capacity, usually by laying off staff.
Outsourcing - the contracting out of work to other businesses that might otherwise have been performed within the organisation.
Reengineering - redesigning business processes, such as product design, to improve efficiency in the organisation.
Virtual company - a company which has outsourced every business activity.

1. What is meant by a company-wide strategy to improve efficiency?
2. Describe four of Tom Peters' characteristics of good performing companies.
3. State 4 benefits of downsizing.
4. State (i) 2 advantages and (ii) 2 disadvantages: of delayering.
5. State 4 possible effects on businesses of reengineering.
6. Suggest 2 ways in which a business may become more agile in manufacturing.
7. Give 4 examples of labour flexibility.
8. What is the aim of Kaizen?
9. What is the difference between knowledge management and the learning organisation?
10. Suggest 2 criticisms of modern management theories to improve efficiency.

Case study Gregsons

Gregsons is a large mail order company, selling a wide variety of electrical goods such as kettles, irons, food blenders, microwave ovens, TVs, music systems and computers. Its products are advertised heavily in daily newspapers, magazines and on TV. The business sells on price, by offering well known brand names at prices that are typically 20 per cent below those of other outlets. The company operates from a site in Staffordshire where it owns a warehouse and an office block. It is organised into five departments.

- Finance and HR.
- Marketing.
- Goods inward.
- Order-picking and dispatch.
- Logistics.

In 2000 Gregsons attempted to diversify into furniture by mail order. However, this was unsuccessful and it withdrew from the operation after two years at a cost of £5.6 million. In 2002 the directors decided to embark on a new strategy. They decided to improve efficiency across the whole organisation and increase sales by going online. A number of strategic initiatives were implemented.

Reengineering. The entire ordering process was reengineered. Before, orders were received by post or over the telephone and dealt with manually. A new system was introduced which could cope simultaneously with telephone orders and online orders and process them automatically. A voice recognition system is now used for telephone orders. Mail orders are still accepted, but order forms were redesigned to be read by computer. The IT system installed to run the process also allows customers to track their order status on the Internet. Staffing in the department was cut from 120 to 32. However, many of the staff were retrained to work in a new customer services function. The purpose of this function was to deal swiftly and sympathetically with customer complaints and to try to sell more products by developing relationships with customers once an order had been dispatched successfully.

Flexibility. More flexible working practices were introduced. Staff would be able to choose 80 per cent of their hours of work in return for being on call at certain times. One problem that Gregsons experienced was a surge in demand immediately after a TV advert.

Table 30.3 *Key performance indicators 2001 and 2004*

	2001	2004
Lead time	10 days	3 days
Order-picking errors	7,350	2,100
Absenteeism	8.70%	5.60%
Customer complaints	1,290	320
Sales revenue	£231m	£275m
Wage bill	£34m	£28m

This often meant that staff were overworked for a period and mistakes were made with order picking and dispatch. Vehicle drivers were also included in this arrangement. Staff would also be trained in more tasks and encouraged to solve their own problems.

Delayering. A delayering process was undertaken. Three management and supervisory layers were 'stripped out'. The purpose of this was to cut costs, improve communications, empower staff and speed up the decision making process. It was also felt that delayering was necessary to help introduce the flexible working practices described above. It was expected that delayering would cut the wage bill by several million pounds per year once voluntary redundancy and early retirement payments had been met.

In 2004, by monitoring a number of key performance indicators, Gregsons was able to conclude that its new strategy was beginning to generate some very encouraging results. Table 30.3 shows some performance data.

(a) Identify two benefits to Gregsons of delayering. (6 marks)

(b) Using this case as an example, explain what is meant by reengineering. (8 marks)

(c) Identify elements of Tom Peters' 8 key characteristics of good performing companies in the Gregsons case. (10 marks)

(d) Analyse the possible advantages and disadvantages to Gregsons of the flexible working practices introduced. (12 marks)

(e) To what extent might the increase in sales revenue be attributed to the new efficiency strategy? (14 marks)

31 Operations Management Techniques 1

Operational research

Businesses constantly make decisions. The production department may have to find the cheapest way to carry out a task. The marketing department may have to choose between two advertising campaigns. Unit 1 explained the steps involved in decision making. Businesses can use a number of **quantitative techniques** to help them make decisions and to solve problems that arise. These OPERATIONAL RESEARCH (OR) methods were developed by American scientists in the 1960s. They were based on problem solving methods used in Second World War operations, such as the most effective way to destroy submarines. OR methods use models (or simplified real world situations) to investigate solutions to the problems businesses may face. However, such models are only aids to decision making - the decision itself will still need to be taken and might involve other quantitative and qualitative data which is not included in the model. The types of decision where such models might be used include the following.

- Where should a new plant be sited?
- In what order should a new product be assembled?
- Which method of distribution has the cheapest transport costs?
- How should resources be allocated in production?
- How should the launch of a new product be organised?
- How can customer waiting time be reduced in busy retail outlets?
- How can a building project be timetabled?

This unit deals with network and cost-benefit analysis, and simulation, while the next looks at linear programming, transportation and the economic order quantity.

Critical path analysis

CRITICAL PATH ANALYSIS or NETWORK ANALYSIS is a technique which allows a business to:

- estimate the minimum time that could be taken to complete a possibly complex operation;
- identify whether resources are being used efficiently;
- anticipate any tasks that may or may not cause delays in the operation.

Critical path analysis is used in many industries, particularly manufacturing and construction. For example, a builder may consider the use of network analysis when planning the sequence of tasks to build a new house. In such industries the time and resources used are vital to the project.

Take a simple operation, such as painting a window frame, that a builder might carry out. This could involve many different tasks, for example:

- preparing the woodwork;
- applying the undercoat;
- waiting for the undercoat to dry;
- applying the gloss.

Figure 31.1 *A network diagram showing the sequence of activities in painting a window frame*

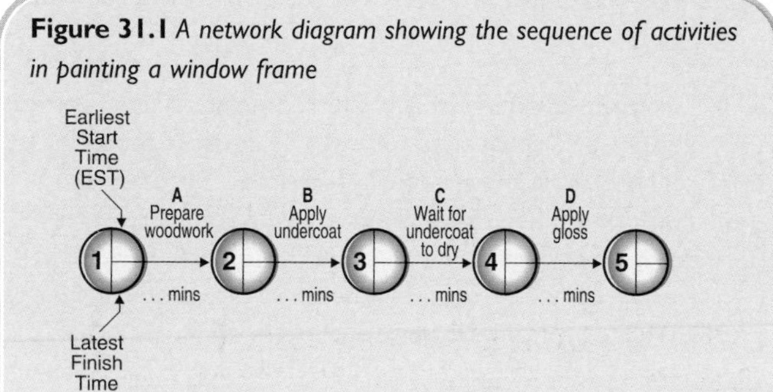

This is shown in Figure 31.1 as a network diagram.

There are certain features in Figure 31.1 that are important when constructing any network.

- The circles are called **nodes.** They show the start or finish of a task. The arrows show the tasks involved in painting the window. They use up resources as they are carried out. For example, even waiting for paint to dry uses up resources, such as time. The activities are **dependent** on each other. So the undercoat cannot be applied until the woodwork has been prepared.
- Nodes contain information. Figure 31.1 shows that nodes are divided into three sections. In the left hand semi-circle the **node number** is written. This makes it possible to follow tasks more easily through the network. The number in the top right is the **earliest starting time** (EST). This shows the earliest time that the next task can begin. The number in the bottom right is the **latest finishing time** (LFT). This shows the latest time that the previous task can finish without delaying the next task.
- Arrows show the **order** in which the tasks take place. They often have letters next to them to show what the order is. The length of time each task takes is placed below the arrow.

Constructing a network

Figure 31.1 is a rather simple example of a network. In practice operations in business may be more complex with many different tasks, some of which can be carried out at the same time as others. For example, the tasks involved in producing an advertising campaign for a company could be:

- A - plan the advertising campaign;
- B - make a TV video;
- C - make a poster;
- D - test market the TV video;
- E - test suitability of poster;
- F - present campaign to the board of directors;
- G - communicate the campaign to all company personnel.

The estimated length of time for each task and the order, ie the tasks that **depend** upon others being completed, are shown in Table 31.1. The total estimated time is 49 hours, but

Table 31.1 *The order and times of tasks when producing an advertising campaign*

Tasks	Order/dependency	Estimated time (hours)
A	Must be done first	4
B	Can only start when A is complete	6
C	Can only start when A is complete	7
D	Can only start when B is complete	8
E	Can only start when C is complete	10
F	Can only start when D and E are complete	9
G	Must wait for D, E and F to be completed	5

this is not important because activities B and C, and D and E can be done at the same time by different employees.

Figure 31.2 shows the network for the marketing campaign summarised in Table 31.1. The tasks, node numbers and time durations are all included.

Once the network has been constructed it is possible to 'fill-in' the earliest start times and latest finishing times, and then show the critical path. This will tell the business how long it will take to launch the advertising campaign, and indicate where delays could take place.

Figure 31.2 *The network for the marketing campaign*

Earliest start time Assuming that the **earliest time** task A can be started is hour 0 then tasks B and C cannot start for 4 hours (0 + 4), ie until task A has been completed. These are shown in the top right of nodes 1 and 2.

Task D cannot start until A and B have been completed, this takes 10 hours (0+4+6) which is shown in node 3. Task E cannot start for 11 hours (0+4+7) and is shown in node 4. Task F cannot start until E and D are complete. The EST for task F is 21 (0 + 4 + 7 + 10). It is important to choose the longest route when calculating the ESTs. The route A,B,D is

Figure 31.3 *The ESTs for the tasks in the marketing campaign*

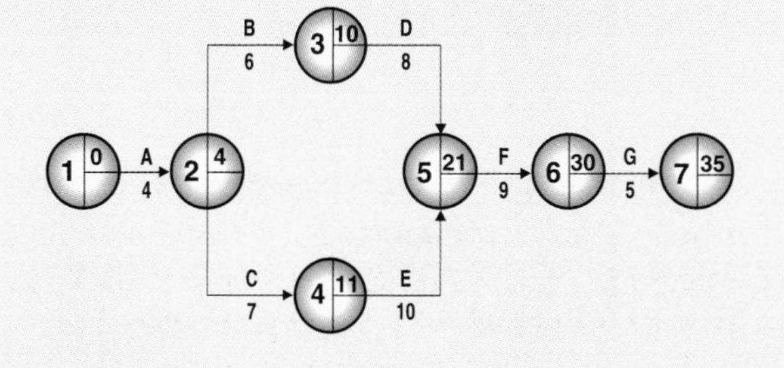

only 18 (0 + 4 + 6 + 8). The EST of the longer route (21) is shown in node 5. The EST in the final node also shows the time it takes to complete the whole marketing campaign. It is 35 hours (0 + 4 + 7 + 10 + 9 + 5) and is shown in node 7. All this information is shown in Figure 31.3.

Latest finish time The next step is to identify the **latest finish time** (LFT) of each task without extending the project duration. We must start at node 7 and work back. Task G must be completed by the 35th hour. This LFT is shown in the bottom right of node 7. To calculate the LFT for task F, we subtract the time it takes to perform task F from the previous LFT, ie 30 (35 - 5). This LFT is shown in node 6. The LFTs for tasks D and E are 21 (30 - 9), as shown in node 5. For task B the LFT is 13 (21 - 8) and for task C 11 (21 - 10). The LFT for task A is 4, following the route that will give the earliest time, ie C (11-7=4) rather than B which would give (13-6=7). The LFTs for all tasks are shown in Figure 31.4.

Figure 31.4 *The ESTs, the LFTs and the critical path for the marketing campaign*

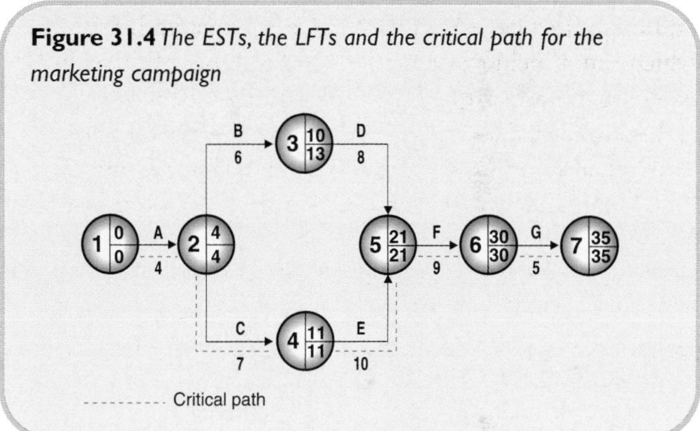

The critical path Once all the LFTs have been identified it is possible to outline the CRITICAL PATH. This can be drawn through the nodes where the ESTs and the LFTs are the **same.** This means that there can be no delays between completing the preceding tasks and starting the next ones on this path without prolonging the total time of the marketing campaign. The critical path for the campaign, A, C, E, F, G, is shown by a dotted line in Figure 31.4. It is critical because any task on this path which is delayed will delay the whole campaign beyond the 35 hours identified earlier as the minimum time.

The float What about tasks which do not lie on the critical path, ie B and D? B and D together could be delayed up to 3 hours without prolonging the campaign's completion time. This is called the **float.** We have already seen that the critical path is the longest route through the network. Activities C and E take longer than B and D by 3 hours, so speeding up activities B and D will not help the business to finish earlier.

- The **total float** is found by subtracting the EST and the duration from the LFT. So for task B it would be:

  13-6-4=3.

  This is the total float up to that activity (B).
- The **free float** is found by subtracting the EST at the start

Table 31.2 *The duration, EST, LFT and floats for each task in the marketing campaign*

(Hours)

Task	Duration	EST	LFT	Total Float	Free Float
A	4	0	4	0*	0
B	6	4	13	3	0
C	7	4	11	0*	0
D	8	10	21	3	3
E	10	11	21	0*	0
F	9	21	30	0*	0
G	5	30	35	0*	0

of the task and the duration from the EST at the end. So for task B this would be:

10-6-4=0.

This is the free float for that task. It shows that task B can be delayed, but this will interfere with other tasks, ie D. Table 31.2 shows the total float after each task in the marketing campaign. The tasks without a float (shown by a *) are 'critical' - any delay in these and the whole campaign will be prolonged. Only non-critical tasks have a float.

It is important for a business to know how much float there is. If tasks in the operations could be delayed without delaying the whole job, then resources in these tasks, (such as labour, machinery etc.), could be used more productively elsewhere or shared between tasks. It is also important when tasks may take days or weeks. If an operation is delayed, a business will not be too worried if there is some float, only if the float disappears.

Figure 31.5 shows a network for the installation of a new piece of machinery. The times shown are for the number of days taken.

Figure 31.5

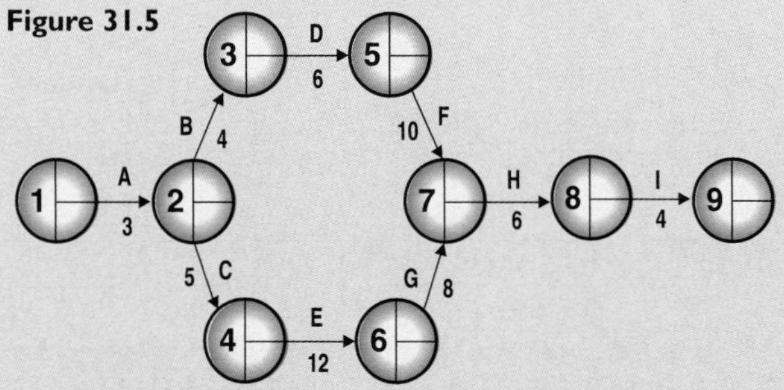

(a) Calculate the earliest start time for each task.
(b) Calculate the latest finish time for each task and the minimum time for the whole project.
(c) Determine the critical path.
(d) Identify the amount of total float and free float in a table.
(e) Determine the critical path if task D took 12 days.

A more complex network

Sometimes it is necessary to include a **dummy activity** or task in a network diagram. Take an example made up of four tasks A, B, C and D. Assume that task C cannot start until tasks A and B have been completed. Task D can only start when B has been completed. The network in Figure 31.6 appears to represent this sequence of tasks. However, the diagram also shows that task D cannot start until A and B have been completed, yet this is not a requirement in our example. In order to show a **dependency** the network can be redrawn using a dummy activity as shown in Figure 31.7.
The dummy task is shown by a dotted line and now the diagram shows that task D is only dependent upon the completion of task B. Dummy activities do not use up any time - they always have a time duration of zero.

Let's look at a network which involves a variety of tasks and a dummy activity. Table 31.3 and Figure 31.8 show tasks involved in the assembly of a vehicle engine. The earliest start times and latest finish times have been calculated using the

Figure 31.6 *A network diagram representing four tasks A, B, C and D*

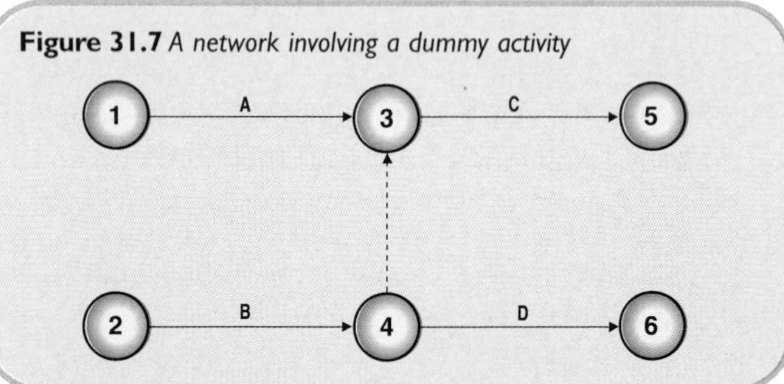

Figure 31.7 *A network involving a dummy activity*

Task	Order/dependency	Estimated time (hours)
A	Can start at the same time as B	2
B	Can start at the same time as A	2
C	Must follow A	6
D	Must follow A	3
E	Must follow B	1
F	Must follow B	8
G	Must follow C	2
H	Must follow D,E	1
J	Cannot start until C,H have finished	3
K	Cannot start until C,H have finished	3
L	Must follow G,J	4

The operation is complete when F, K and L have finished.

Figure 31.8 *A network involving a dummy activity*

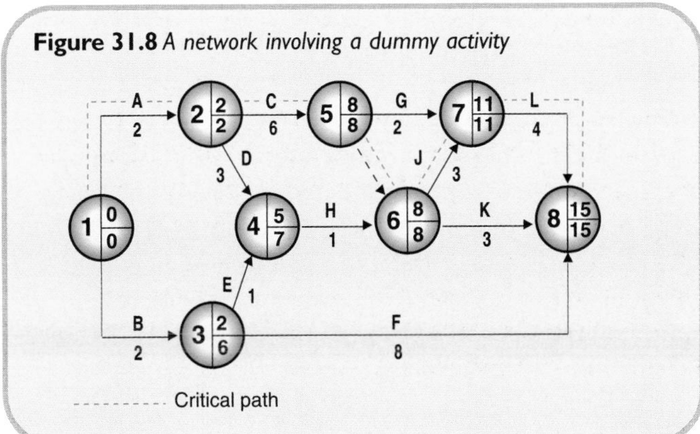

Table 31.4

Task	Duration	EST	LFT	Total Float	Free Float
A	2	0	2	0*	0
B	2	0	6	4	0
C	6	2	8	0*	0
D	3	2	7	2	0
E	1	2	7	4	2
F	8	2	15	5	5
G	2	8	11	1	1
H	1	5	8	2	2
J	3	8	11	0*	0
K	3	8	15	4	4
L	4	11	15	0*	0

method in Figures 31.3 and 31.4 earlier. There are certain features about this network.

- A dummy activity or task links J and K to the completion of C. This is because whilst J and K are dependent upon C finishing, they are also dependent upon H finishing. It would be impossible to illustrate these dependencies in the network without the use of a dummy line, which shows a logical connection, but does not show any time passing.
- The critical path through the network is shown by a broken (blue) line, linking activities A,C,J and L. Notice that these are the nodes where the ESTs and LFTs are equal. It is also the route with the longest ESTs, as explained earlier in this unit.
- The minimum time to complete the assembly of the engine would be 15 hours.
- The float in the network is shown in Table 31.4.

Advantages of critical path analysis

The major advantage of critical path analysis is that it provides decision makers with a picture of a problem which may be easier to interpret. It can be used to suit a range of circumstances and help solve a variety of business problems.

- Reduce the time lost between tasks, ensuring that projects run smoothly.
- Encourage forward planning. The process ensures that all the tasks in a particular operation have been identified and timed from start to finish. The construction of the network forces decision makers to consider all aspects of a project.
- Improve efficiency in production. The level of working capital can be minimised by ordering and receiving materials and components 'just-in-time'. By identifying float and critical activities, resources such as labour and capital can be used more effectively.
- Control cash flow. This is achieved by not ordering supplies too early and only making purchases when they are required.

Ashington Ltd uses batch production to make a range of ready meals for supermarkets and other retailers. It has recently introduced lean production methods to speed up changeover times between batches. The aim of the company in the first year of the new system was to get changeover times below 15 minutes. The tasks needed to re-set one machine, when switching from one product to another, are shown in Figure 91.9. The times shown are for the number of minutes taken.

Figure 31.9

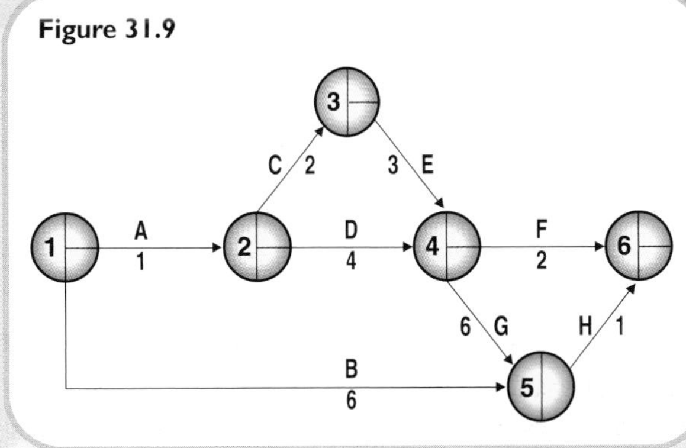

(a) Calculate the earliest start times and latest finishing times for each task.
(b) Identify the critical path.
(c) Does Ashington achieve its aim when switching production on this machine?

Disadvantages of critical path analysis

Despite the advantages of critical path analysis, there are drawbacks.

- The construction of a network alone will not guarantee the smooth completion of a project. The co-operation and commitment of the entire team of staff is needed to ensure that each task is completed according to the estimated duration. Staff should also be consulted when management decides how long tasks will take.
- Some projects are immense. Network diagrams may become complex and unmanageable. Computers may be used to manage information more effectively.

- Network analysis will only be helpful if the data used to construct diagrams is reliable. If the task durations are inaccurate or the order of tasks is wrong, then the ESTs, LFTs and the critical path will all be misleading.

A toy manufacturer has designed a new wooden toy. The construction of the toy involves 9 activities A to J. The order and the duration of tasks are shown in the network diagram illustrated in Figure 31.10. The time durations shown are in minutes.

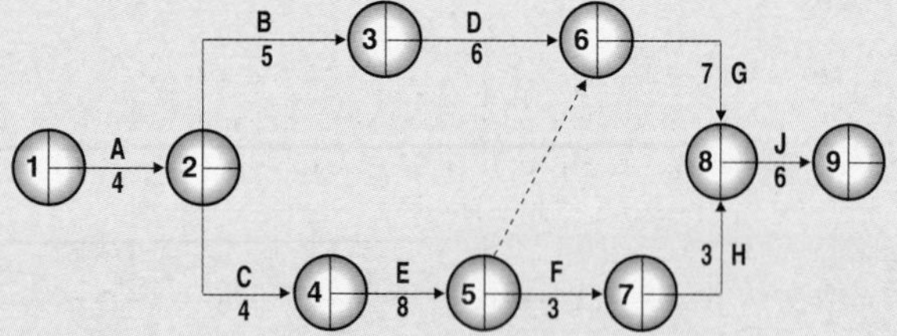

Figure 31.10 *Network diagram for the construction of a new wooden toy*

(a) What is the minimum construction time for the new toy?
(b) What is the critical path?
(c) If task D and task H were each delayed by one minute what would be the effect on:
 (i) the minimum construction time;
 (ii) the critical path?
(d) Explain how critical path analysis might benefit the toy manufacturer.

Queueing and simulation

SIMULATIONS are models which try to reproduce in a dynamic way what is going on in reality. Business simulations, such as business games, have become common tools in management training and Business Studies teaching. But simulations can also be used to look at a very specific problem, such as queueing. People who are kept waiting in queues may look for a different place to buy goods and services. Queues also waste resources, such as time spent dealing with customer complaints.

Such problems often result when customers arrive at random. Examples may be people using a cashpoint or a public telephone, patients arriving at casualty or cars arriving at a toll booth. It is the random element which causes the problem. If people used these items regularly it would be easy to decide on the number of staff required to deal with customers without causing delay. This assumes, however, that the service time is constant. This is not always the case. Where the service time is variable, such as at a supermarket checkout, a problem will exist.

Take an example of how a simulation can be used to reduce queuing at checkouts in a supermarket. A number of variables need to be considered:

- The number of customers arriving at the checkouts.
- The number of checkouts in operation.
- The frequency of arrival at checkouts.
- The length of time each customer takes at the checkout.

A simulation will allow a business to work out the number of checkouts it must operate at different times of the day to keep queues at a minimum.

The first stage is to collect information about how the system operates at present. The supermarket collected information about 100 customers who 'checked out' between 5.00pm and 5.30pm. Table 31.5 shows this information.

Table 31.5 *Information relating to customers arriving at a supermarket checkout*

Time between arrivals at checkout (mins)	Frequency (per cent)	Cumulative frequency	Time at check out (mins)	Frequency (per cent)	Cumulative frequency
0	8	8	1	7	7
1	20	28	2	25	32
2	32	60	3	32	64
3	21	81	4	16	80
4	9	90	5	12	92
5	10	100	6	8	100

Table 31.5 also shows the **cumulative frequency** (☞ unit 3) of people at the checkout. The information forms the basis of a model which will try to simulate the arrival of customers at checkouts. Random numbers are used to indicate the time between arrivals and the length of time spent at the checkout. Random numbers are obtained from computers and have no pattern provided they are used in a random way. For example a random series of 50 numbers may be:

20 84 27 38 66 19 60 10 51 20
35 16 74 58 72 79 98 09 47 07
98 82 69 63 23 70 80 88 86 23
94 67 94 34 03 77 89 30 49 51
04 54 32 55 94 82 08 19 20 73

Table 31.6 *Cumulative frequencies and allocated random numbers*

Time between arrivals (mins)	Cumulative frequency	Random numbers	Time at check out (mins)	Cumulative frequency	Random numbers
0	8	01 - 08	1	7	01 - 07
1	28	09 - 28	2	32	08 - 32
2	60	29 - 60	3	64	35 - 64
3	81	61 - 81	4	80	65 - 80
4	90	82 - 90	5	92	81 - 92
5	100	91 -100	6	100	93 -100

The random numbers are allocated to the 'Time between arrivals' and the 'Time spent at the checkout', according to the cumulative frequencies as shown in Table 31.6. The simulation can now begin, using the random numbers in the order they are shown above:

Random number 20 - customer 1 arrives after 1 minute
Random number 84 - customer 1 takes 5 minutes to be served
Random number 27 - customer 2 arrives 1 minute after customer 1
Random number 38 - customer 2 takes 3 minutes to be served

Random number 66 - customer 3 arrives 3 minutes after customer 2
Random number 19 - customer 3 takes 2 minutes to be served

The simulation can be recorded as shown in Table 31.7. It is assumed that there is just one checkout in operation to start with.

Table 31.7 *The results of the simulation showing the arrival times, waiting times, service times, and the leaving times of customers*

Customer	Random number Arrival	Random number Service time	Simulated times Between arrival (mins)	Simulated times Service time (mins)	Arrived at	Served at	Leaves at	Cust wait (mins)	Checkout wait (mins)
1	20	84	1	5	5.01	5.01	5.06	0	1
2	27	38	1	3	5.02	5.06	5.09	4	0
3	66	19	3	2	5.05	5.09	5.11	4	0
4	60	10	2	2	5.07	5.11	5.13	4	0
5	51	20	2	2	5.09	5.13	5.15	4	0
6	35	16	2	2	5.11	5.15	5.17	4	0
7	74	58	3	3	5.14	5.17	5.20	3	0
8	72	79	3	4	5.17	5.20	5.24	3	0
9	98	09	5	2	5.22	5.24	5.26	2	0
10	47	07	2	1	5.24	5.26	5.27	2	0

With just one checkout in operation, the average customer waiting time is about three minutes - this might be considered acceptable. Also, the checkout has been working constantly. Let us now run the simulation with two checkouts in operation. The results are shown in Table 31.8.

Table 31.8 *Results from simulation with two checkouts employed (the random numbers are excluded)*

Customer	Simulated times Between arrival (mins)	Simulated times Service time (mins)	Arrived at	Checkout number	Served at	Leaves at	Cust. wait (mins)	Checkout wait (mins)
1	1	5	5.01	1	5.01	5.06	0	1
2	1	3	5.02	2	5.02	5.05	0	2
3	3	2	5.05	2	5.05	5.07	0	0
4	2	2	5.07	1	5.07	5.09	0	1
5	2	2	5.09	1	5.09	5.11	0	0
6	2	2	5.11	2	5.11	5.13	0	4
7	3	3	5.14	1	5.14	5.17	0	3
8	3	4	5.17	2	5.17	5.21	0	4
9	5	2	5.22	1	5.22	5.24	0	5
10	2	1	5.24	2	5.24	5.25	0	3

With two checkouts in operation, customers are never kept waiting. However, both checkouts are waiting for customers on many occasions. The results from this simulation can help the supermarket decide whether it wants to operate one or two checkouts. The final decision will also depend on its policy towards customer queueing and staff productivity. For example, if its policy is to keep staff fully employed then it will use just one checkout. Simulations like this may appear cumbersome, but the use of a computer will help speed up the process. They are used quite commonly in business. Other OR techniques are too complex to deal with problems like queueing and congestion. However, simulations are only as good as the data upon which they are based. Inaccurate data could lead to incorrect conclusions being drawn. Also, the data may be expensive to collect in the first place.

A warehouse receives lorry loads of corn from local farmers. It currently operates one tipping facility. Table 31.9 shows the arrival intervals of successive lorries and the times taken to tip their loads.

Table 31.9 *Information regarding the arrival of lorries at a warehouse and the time it takes to tip their loads*

Time between arrivals (mins)	Frequency (per cent)	Cumulative frequency	Tipping time (mins)	Frequency (per cent)	Cumulative Frequency
3	5	5	10	12	12
4	10	15	11	20	32
7	45	60	12	30	62
10	30	90	13	28	90
13	10	100	14	10	100

(a) Use a simulation to show the (i) arrival time and (ii) waiting time of 10 lorries which begin arriving at 9.00am. Use the random numbers in the text on the previous page.
(b) Using another simulation, show the effect of operating two tipping facilities.
(c) Do you think a second tipping facility would be a worthwhile investment? Explain your answer.
(d) Explain one possible disadvantage of using simulation in this case.

Question 4

Cost-benefit analysis

Many decisions in business are 'financial' decisions. When considering different courses of action decision makers often weigh up the financial costs against the financial benefits. Normally, a business will choose the course of action which generates the greatest net financial benefit. Recently, some firms have begun to consider the costs and benefits of their decisions to the rest of society. Take an example of a chemical company. It is likely to face the 'private' costs of machinery etc., but may also generate pollution into the atmosphere. Pollution is one example of negative externalities (☞ unit 41) or external costs. Similarly, the business will aim to sell its product to earn revenue (a private benefit), but may build a factory and a new road which eases traffic congestion in the area (an external benefit). We can say:

Social costs = private/financial costs + external costs.
Social benefit = private/financial benefit + external benefit.

COST-BENEFIT ANALYSIS is a method used to take into account social costs and benefits when making decisions. A business must place a monetary value on any social costs and benefits which a particular course of action might lead to. For example, consider a business calculating the cost of locating a new factory in a rural area. Part of the external cost might be the potential loss of wildlife. The business must find a way of evaluating this cost in monetary terms. Quite obviously this would be difficult and this is one of the problems with cost-benefit analysis.

Cost-benefit analysis is more commonly used in the public sector. Government investment projects have often been the subject of cost-benefit analysis. For example, the decision whether or not to build a bypass would look at external costs, such as the loss of custom to local businesses when the traffic is diverted. These would be compared with the possible external benefits, such as less congestion and fewer accidents on the local roads. The overall decision would depend on both the external costs and benefits, and the financial costs of constructing the bypass. The abandoning of a Thames crossing at Oxleas Wood because of the impact it would have had on the environment is an example of a project that took social costs and benefits into account.

Knowledge

1. What is meant by a network?
2. What does the critical path show a firm?
3. What is meant by a float in a network and what does it tell a business?
4. Briefly explain 3 uses of critical path analysis to a firm.
5. State 3 problems of critical path analysis
6. State 3 situations where a simulation might be used.
7. Explain what is meant by:
   (a) private costs and private benefits;
   (b) external costs and external benefits.
8. 'The private costs of building a new motorway through a rural area are not the only costs that must be taken into consideration.' Briefly explain this statement.

key terms

Cost-benefit analysis - a technique which involves taking into account all social costs and benefits, when deciding on a course of action.
Critical path - in an operation which consists of a sequence of activities, this is the one sequence which cannot afford any delays without prolonging the operation.
Critical path analysis or network analysis - a technique used to find the cheapest or fastest way to complete an operation.
Operational research - a logical and scientific approach to decision making which uses calculations.
Simulation - a technique which imitates what might happen in reality by using random numbers.

Case study Newport Holdings

Newport Holdings manufactures electronic components for domestic appliances. The company has received some large orders recently after a successful sales drive. However, to increase capacity and improve productivity it must replace the entire assembly line with up to date technology. The directors are keen to go ahead with the investment, but are worried about the disruption that will be caused. During the construction of the new assembly line production will be zero. The company can hold up to 30 days of stocks so the new line must be up and running within one month. If the new line isn't ready, Newport Holdings will lose approximately £200,000 per day. This will be unacceptable to the directors.

Table 31.10 *The tasks, task order and task times required to construct the new assembly line*

Task	Description	Order/dependency	Duration
A	Dismantle old line	Must be done first	3 days
B	Retrain staff	Must follow A	15 days
C	Position lifting gear	Must follow A	2 days
D	Remove roof panels	Must follow A	2 days
E	Lower in new plant	Must follow D	2 days
F	Replace roof panels	Must follow C and E	3 days
G	Install new plant	Must follow F	11 days
H	Test run	Must follow B and G	3 days
I	Safety checks	Must follow H	2 days

Figure 31.11 *Network diagram for the installation of new technology at Newport Holdings*

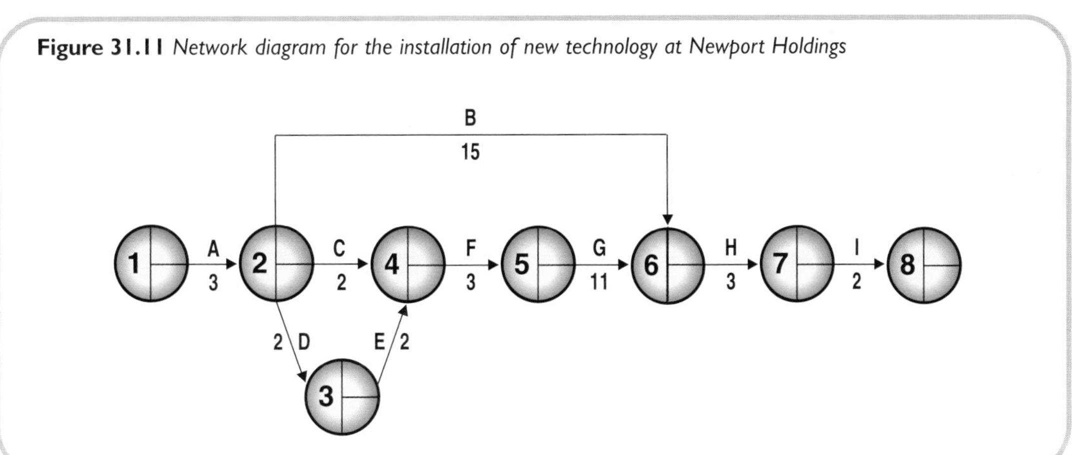

(a) State two objectives of critical path analysis. (4 marks)

(b) For the activities required to install the new technology, calculate the (i) earliest start times (ESTs) and (ii) the latest finish times (LFTs). (12 marks)

(c) Identify the critical path on the network diagram. (4 marks)

(d) Will the construction be completed in time? Explain your answer. (4 marks)

(e) How will the construction time be affected if task B is delayed by 4 days? (6 marks)

(f) Evaluate the advantages and disadvantages to Newport Holdings of using critical path analysis. (10 marks)

Blending

BLENDING is a technique which shows a firm how 'best' to allocate its resources, given a number of constraints. Firms usually aim to allocate resources in a profitable and cost effective way. Blending is one example of LINEAR PROGRAMMING. This method sets out a business problem as a series of linear or mathematical expressions. A linear expression is an equation which links two variables such that their behaviour, if plotted on a graph, would be represented by a straight line. These expressions are then used to find the **optimal** or best solution. How can firms use blending? It may be used when they are making decisions about production. Take, for example, a firm producing two products, denim jeans and denim jackets with a number of constraints:

- the same resources are used for each product;
- the three main operations in their manufacture are cutting, sewing and studding;
- the time taken for each operation is shown in Table 32.1;
- in a working day there are 900 minutes of cutting time, 800 minutes of sewing time and 700 minutes of studding time;
- the denim used in jeans costs £5 and in jackets £8;
- jeans sell at £7 per pair and jackets at £11 each.

The firm has to decide what combination of jackets and jeans should be produced to maximise profits, given these constraints.

Table 32.1

Minutes

	Cutting	Sewing	Studding
Jeans (jn)	3	2	1
Jackets (jk)	1	2	2

The cutting constraint The first step when using this technique is to show the information on constraints as a set of **inequalities** where ≤ means less than or equal to and ≥ means greater than or equal to. The firm knows that the amount of cutting time needed for jeans is three minutes and for jackets one minute. So the total cutting time is:

$$3jn + 1jk$$

There is also a constraint. The amount of cutting time must be no more than 900 minutes. So:

$$3jn + 1jk \leq 900$$

We can show this on a graph. If the firm used **all** its time for cutting to make jeans (and no jackets were made), it could make:

$$\frac{900 \text{ minutes}}{3 \text{ minutes}} = 300 \text{ jeans}$$

If all the time was used to make jackets (and no jeans were made), it could produce:

$$\frac{900 \text{ minutes}}{1 \text{ minute}} = 900 \text{ jackets}$$

The cutting constraint is shown in Figure 32.1. The line shows combinations of jeans and jackets that could be cut if all available cutting time is used. So, for example, the firm could make 300 jackets and 200 pairs of jeans. The area inside the line is called the **feasible region**. It shows all combinations of jackets and jeans that could be cut in the time available, ie when 3jn + 1jk ≤ 900.

Figure 32.1 *The cutting constraint*

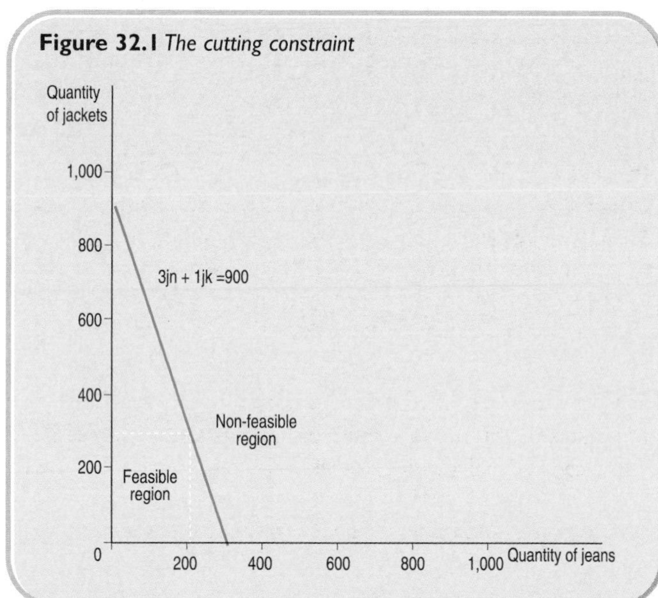

Sewing and studding constraints The time available for sewing is 800 minutes. Sewing jeans and jackets takes 2 minutes each. So:

$$2jn + 2jk \leq 800$$

Similarly, the constraint for studding is 700 minutes. Studding jeans takes 1 minute and jackets 2 minutes. So:

$$1jn + 2jk \leq 700$$

Again we can illustrate these lines on a graph. If all sewing time available was used on jeans **or** on jackets, the firm could make 400 jeans **or** 400 jackets. If all the time available for studding was used on jeans **or** jackets the firm could make

Figure 32.2 *All constraints and the feasible region*

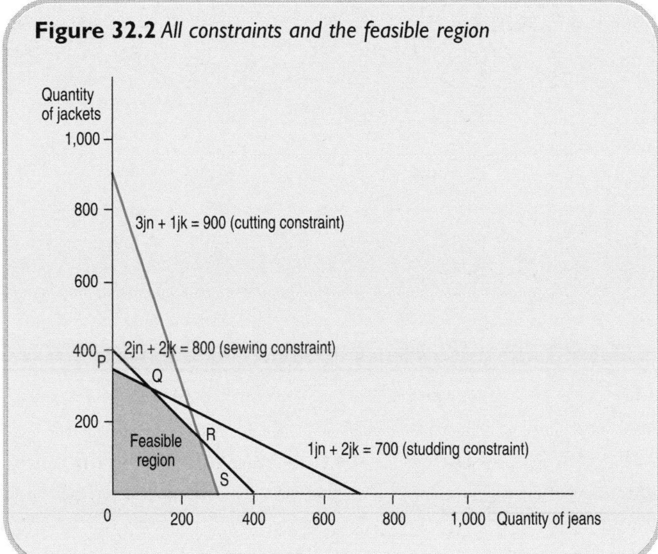

Figure 32.3 *The optimal or best solution*

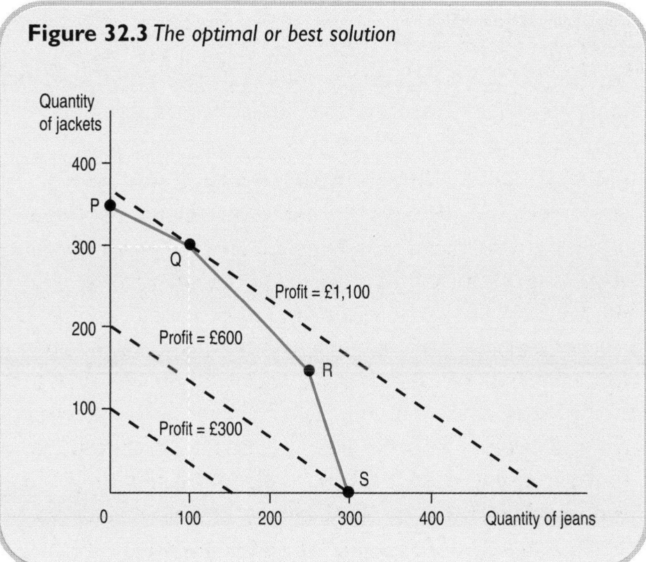

700 jeans **or** 350 jackets. These two lines are added to the other constraint and are shown in Figure 32.2. All constraints are now illustrated on the graph. The shaded area represents the feasible region taking all these constraints into account. This shows all the combinations of jeans and jackets that **could** be made.

Deciding on a solution How will a firm allocate its resources to maximise profits? This depends on the profit level a firm chooses. The firm knows that the profit made from the sale of a pair of jeans is £7 - £5 = £2. From the sale of a jacket it is £11 - £8 = £3. So the total profit from both is:

$$2jn + 3jk$$

This line can be plotted on the graph. Say that the firm wants to make a profit of £300. This could be gained if the firm produced 150 pairs of jeans and no jackets:

$$£300 = (150 \times 2) + (0 \times 3)$$

or no jeans and 100 jackets:

$$£300 = (0 \times 2) + (100 \times 3)$$

This profit line is shown in Figure 32.3 (which shows the feasible region PQRS of Figure 32.2). A higher level of profit can be shown by moving the line parallel and to the right, eg £600. The optimal or best solution for the firm is at Q. If the profit line is moved away from the origin, this is the last point in the feasible region that the profit line would touch. The firm would produce 300 jackets and 100 pairs of jeans. The profit would be £1,100 (300 x £3 + 100 x £2). There is no other combination of jackets and jeans in the feasible region that will earn more profit. Profit will always be maximised on the edge of the feasible region.

Blending can be very useful when firms are deciding how to make best use of their resources. Businesses might use this method to allocate factors of production between different products so that profits are maximised or costs minimised. However, it does have problems. It is a production technique which does not take the demand for products into account. The example used here only uses two products. In practice, firms produce many different products. The **Simplex Method** is used to cope with this, but requires detailed calculations and the use of computers by business.

Stonewold Brewery produces two types of ale, best bitter (BB) and strong ale (SA). Three brewing processes are required; malting, mashing and fermenting. The amount of time each process takes and the capacity available is summarised in Table 32.2. The profit made on a barrel of best bitter and strong ale is £24 and £30 respectively.

Table 32.2 *Time constraints for the three brewing processes*

		Malting	Mashing	Fermenting
Hours needed to	(BB)	4	8	2
produce 1,000 barrels	(SA)	6	4	3
Capacity, total hours available		240	240	150

(a) Write out the problem as three equations showing the constraints.
(b) Draw the constraints on a graph.
(c) On the graph, plot a point that shows the allocation of resources that will maximise profit.
(d) Calculate the profit that will be earned at this point.

Transportation

TRANSPORTATION is another linear programming method. It is useful when firms have the problem of transporting items from a number of different origins to various destinations. For example, distribution companies have to decide the most cost effective way to distribute goods from their warehouses to a number of customers. Take an example, where two factories, F1 and F2, supply three warehouses, W1, W2, and W3.

- The output of each factory is constant at 14 and 23 loads per day respectively.
- The warehouses need 16, 18 and 3 loads every day respectively.
- The transport costs per load are shown in Table 32.3.

Table 32.3 *Transport costs from factories to warehouses*

£00s per load

Factory	W1	Warehouses W2	W3
F1	3	4	2
F2	1	1	5

The firm must now decide on the most cost effective way of transporting the loads. The first step is to build a model which can be used to help decision making. The information is organised into a matrix as shown in Table 32.4. This shows that any factory can deliver to any warehouse. The small numbers at the top of each box show the transport cost per load in hundreds of pounds. Notice that the total output of both factories, 37 loads (14 + 23), is the same as the warehouses' demand (16 + 18 + 3).

Table 32.4 *A matrix showing transport costs, factory output and warehousing capacities*

	W1	W2	W3	Output
F1	[3]	[4]	[2]	14
F2	[1]	[1]	[5]	23
Demand	16	18	3	37

The firm must now decide which factories will supply which warehouses. One way of doing this is to start in the top left hand corner. Say that 14 loads are transported from F_1 to W_1. This is shown in the top left hand corner in Table 32.5. This represents the whole of F1's output. If W_1, W_2 and W_3 need supplying, they must be supplied from F_2.

Table 32.5 *The start of the solution*

	W1	W2	W3	Output
F1	[3] 14	[4]	[2]	14
F2	[1]	[1]	[5]	23
Demand	16	18	3	37

Now assume that F_2 sends 2 loads to W_1, 18 loads to W_2 and 3 loads to W_3. All output has been delivered to the warehouses. Also, the warehouses' demand for goods has been satisfied. This is known as a **feasible solution** and is shown in Table 32.6.

Table 32.6 *A feasible solution*

	W1	W2	W3	Output
F1	[3] 14	[4]	[2]	14
F2	[1] 2	[1] 18	[5] 3	23
Demand	16	18	3	37

It is now possible to work out the cost of this solution. The total cost will be:

(14 x £300) + (2 x £100) + (18 x £100) + (3 x £500) = £7,700

It is unlikely that this arbitrary method of deciding on deliveries will give the **least cost solution**. The solution for the firm is shown in Table 32.7.

Table 32.7 *The least cost solution*

	W1	W2	W3	Output
F1	[3] 11	[4]	[2] 3	14
F2	[1] 5	[1] 18	[5]	23
Demand	16	18	3	37

The cost of this solution would be:

(11 x £300) + (3 x £200) + (5 x £100) + (18 x £100) = £6,200

An alternative method used to find this optimal solution involves the use of **shadow costs** and **opportunity costs**. However, if the figures are simple it may be easier to use trial and error - keep manipulating the data until any further attempt to move the loads around would either increase the total cost or leave it unchanged. In business, a computer

Two warehouses W1 and W2 supply three retailers R1, R2 and R3. The supply capacity of the warehouses is 20 and 40 loads per week respectively. The demands of the retailers are 14, 20 and 26 loads per week respectively. The transport costs between the warehouses and retailers are summarised in Table 32.8.

Table 32.8

(£00s)

Warehouse	Retailers R1	R2	R3
W1	1	3	6
W2	4	10	3

(a) Set up a transportation model by constructing a suitable matrix showing, costs, demands, and supply capacities.
(b) Determine the least cost solution for the distribution of loads from warehouses to retailers using your answer to (a) and calculate the cost. (Use trial and error.)

Question 2

would be used to look at all possible combinations and choose the least cost solution.

The economic order quantity (EOQ)

Businesses use a number of quantitative techniques to make decisions about their purchases and stock levels. It is possible, for example, for a business to calculate the **order size** of its stocks, materials or components which minimises total costs. This is called the ECONOMIC ORDER QUANTITY. Total costs are made up of the costs of acquiring stock and the costs of holding stock. Acquisition costs include costs involved with the choice of vendor, negotiation, administration and the inspection of incoming goods.

Acquisition costs, holding costs and total costs are shown in Figure 32.4. Holding costs rise as order sizes get larger. Holding costs are zero when there are no orders. The larger the order size, the greater the costs of holding it in stock. Acquisition costs fall as order sizes get larger. For example, there is likely to be lower costs in negotiating a few large orders than constantly negotiating many small orders. The order size which minimises total costs will always be at the point where the acquisition cost and the holding cost curves cross each other. This is shown at point EOQ on the diagram.

Figure 32.4 *The economic order quantity*

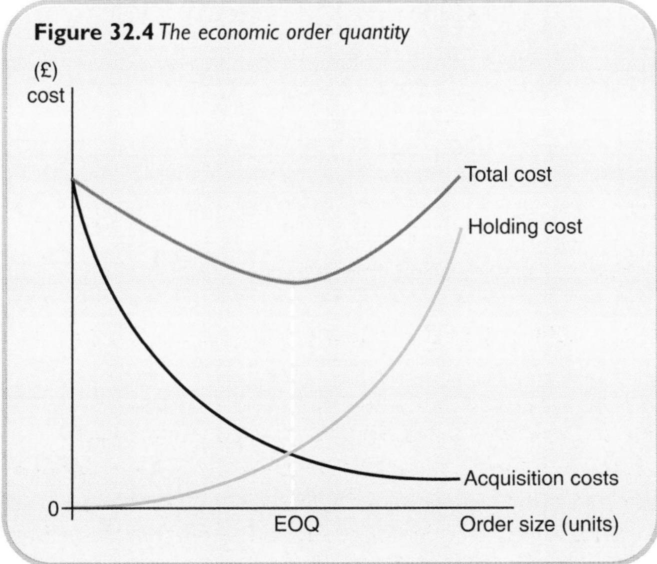

Calculation Say that a builder wants to know what order size of bags of cement will minimise its costs. How can it calculate this? One method used to calculate the EOQ makes the following assumptions.

- Demand for stocks is uniform and does not vary a great deal.
- Store capacity is unlimited.
- Acquisition costs and stock holding costs are not related to the order quantity.
- Material prices are stable.
- Order and delivery quantities are equal.
- Stocks do not fall in value due to deterioration or obsolescence.

The economic order quantity (Q) can be found using the formula:

$$Q = \sqrt{\frac{2CA}{HP}}$$

where C is the acquisition cost per order, A is the total number of units used each year, H is the holding costs as a percentage of the average stock value and P is the price of each unit.

The building contractor uses 5,000 bags of cement each year which cost £10 each. The holding cost of the cement is 5 per cent of average stock value and acquisition costs are £8. The economic order quantity for cement purchases will be:

$$Q = \sqrt{\frac{2 \times £8 \times 5{,}000}{0.05 \times £10}}$$

$$Q = \sqrt{\frac{80{,}000}{0.5}}$$

$$Q = \sqrt{160{,}000}$$

$$Q = 400 \text{ bags}$$

Thus, the builder will be minimising the total cost of ordering and holding cement if 400 bags are bought each time. In addition, it is possible to calculate the optimum number of orders (A÷Q) by transposing the above formula:

$$\frac{A}{Q} = \sqrt{\frac{HPA}{2C}}$$

$$= \sqrt{\frac{0.05 \times £10 \times 5{,}000}{2 \times £8}}$$

$$= 12.5 \text{ orders per year}$$

Limitations The assumptions on which the economic order quantity formula is based may be unrealistic in practice. The price of many materials, particularly commodities like oil, copper, coffee and cotton, tends to fluctuate with changing market conditions. Businesses are unlikely to have unlimited storage space. Materials, such as perishable goods, may deteriorate if left for a period of time. Changes in these assumptions may lead to different costs for a business, which might affect the EOQ. On the other hand, it could be argued that assumptions are not important, as long as a business realises the limitations and finds the predictions of the model useful.

Moss Peters Ltd assembles domestic drying machines. It buys components from all over Europe and is keen to minimise storage costs. One component, the drum, is bought from Northern Spain. Moss Peters has just acquired a new warehouse where it hopes to hold larger quantities of certain key components. The drum is one of these components and the purchasing manager has been asked to review the economic order quantity now that there is almost unlimited space for its storage. The drums cost £40 to buy and Moss Peters uses 40,000 of them each year. The acquisition costs are £50 and the holding cost is 8 per cent of the average stock value.

(a) Calculate the economic order quantity for the drums.
(b) Calculate the total cost of holding and acquiring the drums for one year (do not include the cost of the actual drums).
(c) What would happen to the economic order quantity if the price of the drums rose to £45?

Question 3

key terms

Blending - a graphical approach to linear programming which deals with resource allocation subject to constraints.
Economic order quantity (EOQ) - the level of stock order which minimises ordering and stock holding costs.
Linear programming - a technique which shows practical problems as a series of mathematical equations which can then be manipulated to find the optimum or best solution.
Transportation - a method designed to solve problems where there are a number of different points of supply and demand, such as a number of manufacturers distributing their products to a number of different wholesalers.

Knowledge

1. State 5 problems that operational research methods could be used to investigate.
2. Why are blending and transportation examples of linear programming?
3. Explain briefly two problems that businesses might have when using blending.
4. What does the use of blending show a business?
5. What types of problem does the transportation technique help to solve?
6. What does the use of transportation show a business?
7. Why might a business want to calculate its economic order quantity?
8. State 2 problems with calculating the economic order quantity.

Case study Westmoore Metal Products

Westmoore Metal Products (WMP) is a medium sized engineering company. It employs 45 staff and operates cell production in its factory. Each cell concentrates on a particular family of products. One such cell, the metal rod cell, makes two of the most popular products. These are high precision steel rods for an Austrian customer which makes machine tools. Their component codes are MK and MG.

The metal rod cell contains three machines and employs five staff. The staff organise their own work patterns, but must keep the cell operating for 15 hours per day, 6 days per week. The three machines include a CNC lathe, a CNC milling machine and a vertical profile projector (an inspection machine). To manufacture the MK and MG three key processes are required - turning, milling and inspection. The vertical profile projector is used by other cells for some of the week. The amount of time each process takes and the capacity available is summarised in Table 32.9. The profit made by each component is £100 for the MK and £80 for the MG.

Westmoore introduced cell production about 5 years ago. One of the problems it had in the factory was a lack of space. In the past the company tended to hold quite high levels of stocks. Westmoore imported most of its steel from northern Spain. Although it is some of the cheapest steel in the world, lead times are long and delivery very unreliable. Thus, the high stock holdings occupy a lot of factory space. At the moment WMP orders about 80 tonnes of steel at a time from its Spanish supplier.

In order to keep stock holding costs to a minimum at WMP, a newly recruited cost accountant has suggested using the economic order quantity (EOQ) to determine the amount of stock to purchase when placing a new order. This takes into account the acquisition cost per order (C), the total number of tonnes used each year (A), the holding cost as a percentage of the average stock value (H) and the price of each tonne (P).

(a) Write out the problem above as three equations showing the constraints. (3 marks)

(b) Draw the constraints on a graph. (6 marks)

(c) (i) On the graph identify the point which maximises profit. (2 marks)

(ii) State how many of each component should be produced to maximise profit. (1 mark)

(d) Calculate the weekly profit made from the two components at the profit maximising point. (4 marks)

(e) Assuming that C = £100, A = 500 tonnes, H = 20 per cent and P = £200, calculate (i) the EOQ and (ii) the number of orders to be placed during the year. (6 marks)

(f) Using the information in (e), evaluate whether WMP's current ordering policy is cost effective. (8 marks)

Table 32.9 *Time constraints for the three engineering processes*

		Turning	Milling	Inspection
Hours needed to produce one unit	MK	1.5	4	2
	MG	4.5	2	2
Total hours per week available		90	80	50

33 The Labour Market and Business

The market for labour

In the markets for goods and services the forces of demand and supply determine prices. It could be argued that the market for labour operates in a similar way. This is because it is concerned with the demand for labour, the supply of labour and the price of labour, the wage rate. An individual business might plan its workforce by looking at its current and future worker requirements (demand) and the availability of workers (supply).

The demand for labour

In order to produce goods and services businesses need labour. Therefore, the demand for labour comes from businesses. The demand curve for labour is determined by the combined behaviour of individual businesses and their approach to employing workers.

To examine the demand for labour it is necessary to consider how businesses reach decisions about taking on extra staff. Most businesses need to make sure that the costs of taking on extra staff are lower than the extra revenue generated by those staff. Take the example of a design business employing another designer at a cost of £2,200 per month. If the additional monthly revenue generated by this designer was more than £2,200 the design business may be satisfied. However, if the extra monthly revenue generated by the new designer was less than £2,200, the design business is unlikely to be satisfied with the decision to take on the new employee.

Table 33.1 illustrates this. It shows that, at a monthly cost of £2,200, Link Design might be prepared to employ five designers. This is because the first to the fifth designers are all adding more to revenue than they are costing Link Design to employ. However, the sixth designer is adding less to revenue than she is costing the business. Therefore, at a monthly cost per designer of £2,200 Link Design would employ five designers. At a monthly cost of £1,300 per designer it would employ six designers. If the cost per month of employing designers were to rise to £3,100, only four designers would be employed.

Table 33.1 *Employing extra designers at Link Design Ltd*

Number of designers employed	Total revenue monthly (£)	Additional revenue from each extra designer (£)
1	3,500	3,500
2	8,000	4,500
3	12,000	4,000
4	15,100	3,100
5	17,300	2,200
6	18,600	1,300

Figure 33.1 *The demand curve for labour*

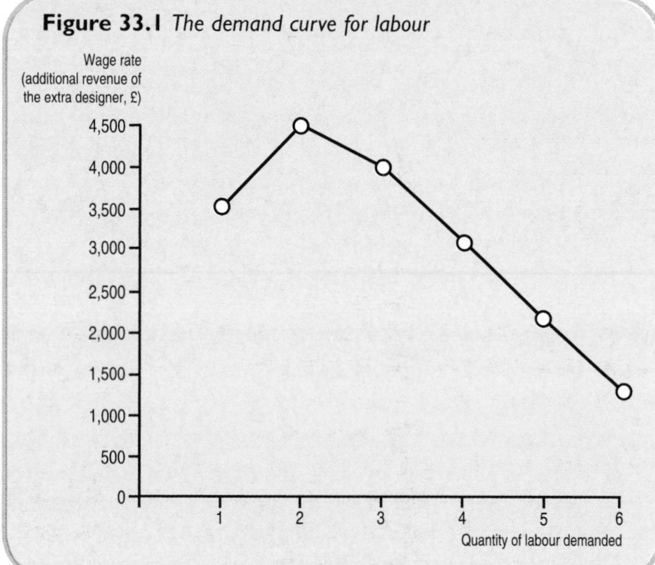

Fentons is a dry cleaning business. Table 33.2 shows information about employees at the business.

Table 33.2

Number employed	Total revenue annually (£)	Additional revenue from each employee (£)
20	350,000	-
21	390,000	-
22	425,000	-
23	450,000	-
24	470,000	-
25	480,000	-

(a) Complete the third column in the above table for the 21st to the 25th worker.
(b) How many workers would Fentons employ at a cost of: (i) £40,000; (ii) £25,000; (iii) £10,000?
(c) What is the most likely employment level in this business? Explain your answer.

In general, therefore, it could be argued that the higher the wages of employees, the fewer will be employed by businesses. Similarly, the lower the wages paid to employees the more likely businesses are to employ more workers. This is shown in Figure 33.1, which illustrates the demand curve for labour.

Increasing or decreasing demand for labour

Certain factors may increase or decrease the demand for labour.

Changes in labour productivity It is suggested that if workers are able to improve their productivity, the business might be more willing to hire extra workers. For example, Link Design employees may increase productivity so that the additional revenue generated by each employee doubled. This would mean that the sixth worker would now add £2,600 extra revenue (£1,300 x 2). If the wage rate was still £2,200 a month, it would be worth the business employing this worker. If workers in the design industry become more productive, then design businesses may be willing to employ more workers.

Demand for the product The demand for labour is said to be a DERIVED DEMAND for the products or services that businesses produce. For example, Link Design may receive a contract to design a national monthly magazine. It may employ more workers as a result. The design industry may need to employ more workers as a result of increased spending by businesses on design and promotion.

The effect of these changes can be shown by a shift to the right in the demand curve for workers from D to D_1, as shown in Figure 33.2. Businesses will increase the number of workers employed from Q to Q_1. Falls in productivity and reduced sales of products will move the curve to the left, reducing the demand for workers.

Figure 33.2 *Changes in the demand for labour*

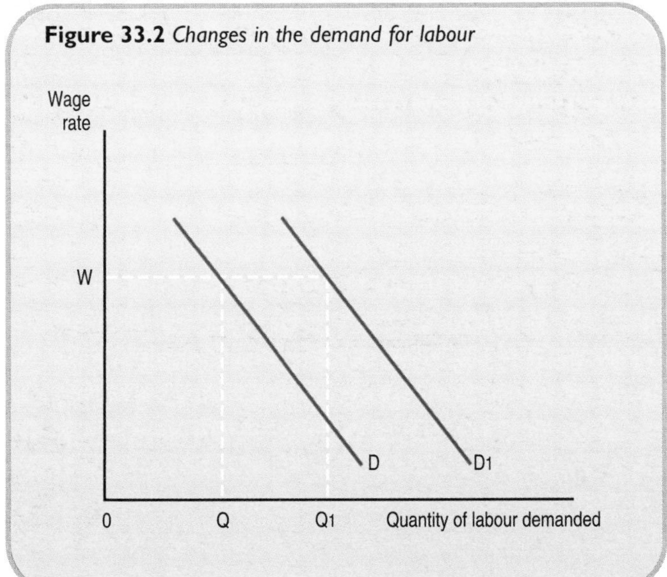

The supply of labour

The supply curve for labour shows the amount of labour which will be supplied to the market at a particular wage rate. It is possible to show how individual workers, workers in an industry and the total supply of workers will react to a particular wage rate.

Individual workers For an individual worker, the supply of labour is the number of hours that he or she is prepared to work. As the REAL WAGE RATE rises, a worker is likely to want to work longer hours. The real wage shows what the wage of the worker can actually buy because it takes into account changes in the prices of goods. This is shown in Figure 104.3. At a real wage rate of OW, OQ hours are worked. Above OW it has been suggested that an increase in the price of labour may lead to less labour being offered to the market. This is because a higher wage may allow individuals to earn the same amount as on a lower wage, but by working for less time. So, for example, someone working for 40 hours per week at £25 per hour would earn £25 x 40 = £1,000 per week. If the wage were to be increased to £30 per week, the same person could work for 35 hours per week (£30 x 35 = £1,050) and earn the same quantity. The effect of this tendency for individuals to work less creates the backward sloping individual supply curve for labour, shown in Figure 33.3.

BMW, the German car group, was considering plans to increase production of its Mini range at Oxford to about 200,000 a year to meet booming demand in November 2003. Helmut Panke, BMW's chief executive, said that Mini sales could top 165,000 in 2003 after the record of 144,000 in 2002. The company was planning to remove bottlenecks at the plant by a number of means. One option was to lengthen shifts from eight to nine or 10 hours.

Mr Panke told reporters in London that, with an annual productivity increase of 4 per cent, output at BMW car plants could grow by between 40,000 and 50,000 units a year - with minimum investment. Increased output and sales of the Mini, which aimed to launch a convertible model in 2004, were integral to BMW's plans to lift global sales from 1 million to 1.4 million by 2008, including 1,000 new Rolls-Royce Phantoms. The BMW chief hailed the Mini as 'a UK manufacturing success story', belying the myth that Britain's manufacturing sector was in terminal decline.

Source: adapted from *The Guardian*, 13.11 2003.

(a) Identify the factors which may influence the demand for labour at BMW.
(b) Examine how these factors might affect the demand curve for labour in future.

Question 2

Figure 33.3 *The backward sloping individual supply curve for labour*

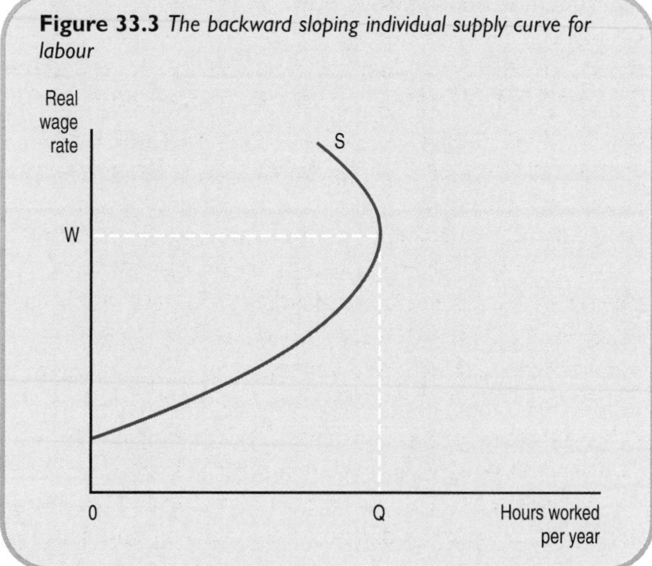

Supply to an industry It is argued that the supply curve for workers in an industry is generally upward sloping, from left to right. This is shown in Figure 33.4. More workers are prepared to offer their services to the labour market at higher real wage rates. As real wages rise from OW to OW_1, more workers are prepared to offer their services, OQ to OQ_1.

Figure 33.4 also shows shifts in the supply curve. A shift to the right indicates an increase in supply of workers, from OQ to OQ_2. What may lead to a change in the supply of workers to businesses?

- Improvements in geographical mobility. Businesses in Essex may be trying to recruit labour, but find labour shortages in the area. The success in recruiting new labour may depend upon the ability to attract employees from other parts of the country. If labour is GEOGRAPHICALLY MOBILE, willing and able to move from one part of the country to another, businesses may be more able to recruit new labour. Geographical mobility may be influenced by people's attitudes to certain areas of the country, family ties to certain areas and government help to change location (☞ unit 28).
- OCCUPATIONAL MOBILITY is the extent to which labour is able to move from one occupation to another. Occupational mobility is linked to the qualifications and skills of labour. Highly qualified and skilled employees tend to be able to change occupations more easily. The levels of skills and qualifications required for some occupations are very high. This means that it is not straightforward for those trained in other occupations to move into these jobs. For example, a shortage of forensic scientists could not be quickly solved by recruiting labour from other areas.
- The availability of training schemes may improve the supply of labour. These may be business or industry schemes or government funded schemes. They may retrain existing workers or to train unemployed people.

Total supply The total supply curve for labour is also said to be upward sloping. The total supply of labour for the whole population will depend upon a variety of factors, such as:

- birth and death rates;
- migration;
- the age distribution of the population;
- the number of people physically capable of work.

Wage and employment determination

In highly competitive labour markets the price of labour (the real wage rate) is likely to be determined by the interaction of the demand curve for and supply curve of labour. As in other markets, the equilibrium price is the point at which the demand and supply curves intersect. In competitive labour markets this will determine the rate that wage earners are paid by businesses. This is show in Figure 33.5. The diagram also shows the number of workers employed at this equilibrium real wage rate.

Figure 33.4 *The supply of labour in an industry*

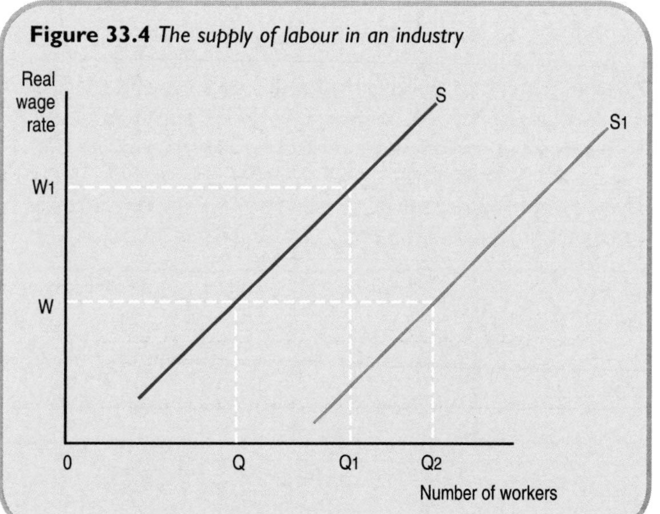

Figure 33.5 *Equilibrium real wage rate and employment in the labour market*

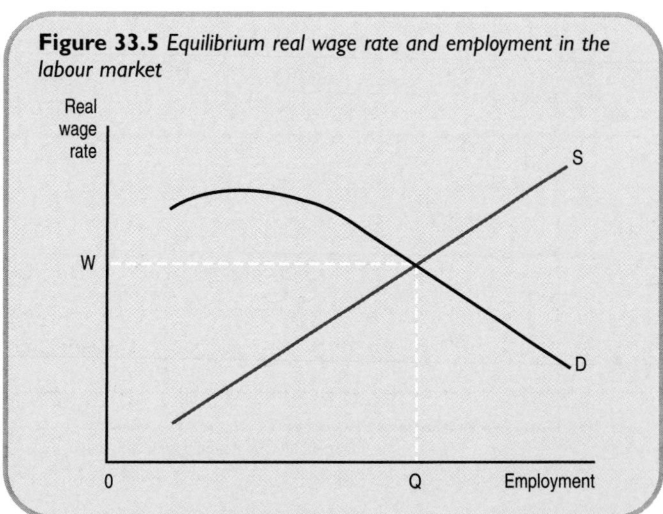

Labour market conditions and business

Different conditions in the labour market influence the demand and supply of labour by businesses. These conditions are influenced by factors that are often outside the control of businesses. They may lead to situations were there are changes in the demand for or supply of labour. They may also create situations of excess demand or excess supply.

Government intervention in the labour market

Governments usually intervene in labour markets in order to pursue 'social' aims, such as ensuring that all employees are paid at least a minimum amount or to prevent discrimination. For example, the **Equal Pay Act of 1970** aimed to prevent businesses paying women less than men for the same or similar work. Some businesses which had previously been paying women less than men, faced increased wage costs as a result. In certain circumstances, this led to a reduction in employment. This can be seen in Figure 33.6, which shows the demand and supply curves for labour in an industry. The equilibrium wage rate is OW and employment is OQ. The effect of equal pay legislation is to raise the wage rate to OW_1. As a result of the higher wages, workers are prepared to supply OQ_1 labour, but employers only want OQ_2 workers. Unemployment is therefore OQ_1-OQ_2. The OQ_2 workers still employed have higher wages, but OQ-OQ_2 workers have lost their jobs. The analysis will be similar if a **minimum wage** is set above the equilibrium wage rate.

Trade unions and professional groups These organisations seek to further the aims of their members (☞ unit 21). One of the ways in which they do this is by attempting to increase or maintain the pay levels of their members. The main way in which they attempt to do this is through collective bargaining (☞ unit 22). Trade unions and professional organisations which are successful may be able to push wage levels above the equilibrium level. The effect of this is similar to that shown in Figure 33.6.

Unions and professional organisations may also seek to restrict the supply of labour to a particular market. The solicitors' organisation known as the Law Society, for example, has testing examinations which all aspiring solicitors must pass. Many believe that one of the functions which these examinations serve is to restrict the supply of new solicitors. The effect of this is shown on Figure 33.7. It can be seen that a restriction in the supply of solicitors causes a shift to the left of the supply curve from S to S_1. The result in the fall in the supply of labour is a rise in the equilibrium wage rate from W to W_1. This is because labour is more scarce. The demand for labour by businesses will also fall because of the higher wage rate, from Q to Q_1.

The amount of unemployment At higher levels of unemployment businesses are able to recruit from a larger pool of labour. This means that suitable labour may be more readily available and the increased supply of labour may force down the equilibrium wage. Labour shortages at times of high employment, either in the economy as a whole or in particular sectors of the economy, are likely to have the opposite effect. This will mean that businesses have a smaller pool of available labour from which to recruit and upward pressure on the equilibrium wage.

Figure 33.6 *The effect of equal wage legislation*

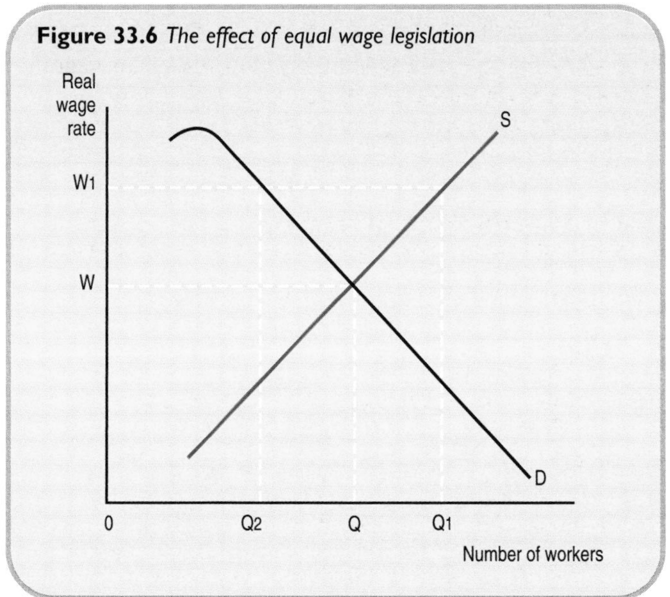

Figure 33.7 *The effect of a restriction in supply on the equilibrium wage rate of labour*

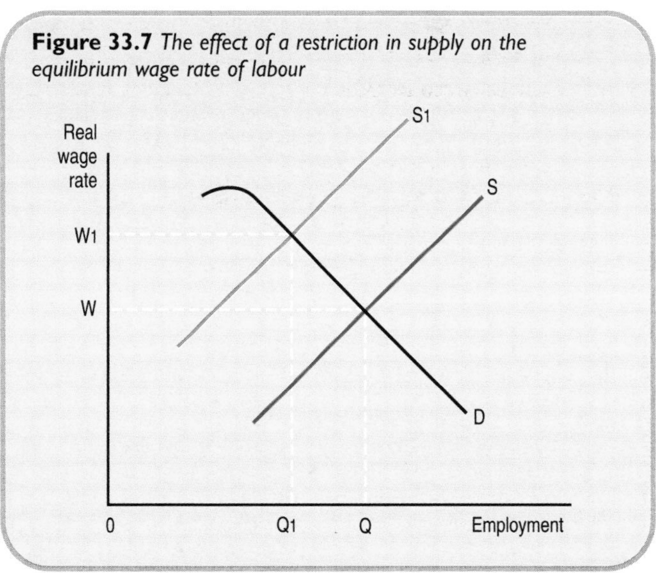

key terms

Derived demand for labour - when the demand for workers by business is the result of demand for the product or service produced by business.
Geographical mobility - the ease with which workers can move from one occupation to another in a different location.
Occupational mobility - the ease with which workers can switch from one type of job, with particular skills, to another requiring different skills.
Real wage rate - the value of the wage rate taking into account the effect of prices. It shows how much the value of the money wage rate can purchase.

The UK has a national minimum wage. This means that businesses cannot pay employees a wage rate below a certain level. From 1 October 2004, these minimum wage rates were:

- Main (adult) rate for workers aged 22 and over - £4.85 per hour;
- Development rate for workers aged 18-21 inclusive - £4.10 per hour.

In addition the government accepted the Low Pay Commission's recommendations for a new rate for 16 and 17 year olds (above compulsory school leaving age) of £3.00 per hour. However, 16 and 17 year old apprentices would be exempt from the new young workers rate.

Source: adapted from www.dti.gov.uk.

(a) Assume that the introduction of a minimum wage sets wage rates higher than the equilibrium wage rate paid in the food industry. Using a demand and supply diagram, explain how this might affect the demand for and supply of labour in the industry.
(b) A cafe pays all its kitchen staff, whatever their age, a wage rate of £7.50 an hour. Discuss the effects of the minimum wage rates in 2004 on this business.

Question 3

Knowledge...Knowledge...Knowledge...Knowledge...Knowledge

1. What is meant by the demand for labour?
2. What is likely to happen to the demand for labour by businesses if wage rates rise?
3. State 2 factors that can lead to an increase in the demand for labour by businesses.
4. What happens to the amount of hours individual workers may want to work at higher wages?
5. What happens to the supply of labour by workers as wage rates rise?
6. State 2 factors that may lead to an increase in the supply of labour by workers.
7. How might a fall in the supply of workers affect: (i) wage rates; (ii) demand by businesses?
8. How might wage legislation affect a business's demand for labour?
9. If unemployment is high, how might this affect recruitment by a business?

Case study Changes in the UK labour market

10 May 2004 saw the official launch of the largest national campaign ever aimed at employers by the Learning and Skills Council (LSC). Its aim was to redress the imbalance of supply and demand for labour in Modern Apprenticeships (MA). The level of young people wanting to supply their labour for MAs was three times the level of demand by employers. The campaign was designed to create thousands more high quality places for young people entering Modern Apprenticeships.

Modern Apprenticeships were introduced ten years earlier. In 2004 there were more than 160 MA frameworks offered in over 80 industry sectors in the UK. They allow young people to learn on the job, building their skills and gaining qualifications as they earn money.

Source: adapted from the Learning and Skills Council website, April 2004.

In 1999 the chairperson of the National Skills Task Force suggested that in future a compulsory levy might be placed on employers that would be used to pay for increased training for workers. It was argued that the UK was falling behind its competitors by not providing workforce training. A major skills deficiency in the UK was identified, which could damage productivity among UK craftspeople.

The major areas of skills and supply shortages in England are shown in Table 104.3. It shows, for example, that in skilled construction trades, 48 per cent of vacancies are due to skills shortages. In skilled metal trades 36 per cent are due to skills shortages. The average for all industries is 21 per cent.

Source: adapted from *Labour Market Trends*, March, 2004.

Table 33.3 *Number of vacancies and vacancies due to skills shortages, ranked by intensity of skill shortage vacancy, England, 2001*

Rank and occupation	Total vacancies	Vacancies due to skills shortages	
	Number	Number	Intensity (skill shortages divided by vacancies)
1 - Science & technology professionals	30,084	16,587	55%
2 - Science & technology associate professionals	24,502	12,352	50%
3 - Skilled construction building trades	**24,013**	**11,636**	**48%**
4 - Business and public sector professionals	20,957	9,708	46%
5 - Skilled metal and electrical trades	**32,345**	**11,517**	**36%**
6 - Leisure and other personal service occupations	24,615	6,134	25%
7 - Process plant and machine operatives	29,597	7,046	24%
8 - Corporate managers	28,349	6,570	23%
...			
21 - Secretarial related occupations	15,756	1,958	12%
...			
25 - Customer service occupations	13,512	753	6%
Average			**21%**

Source: adapted from Department for Education and Skills (DFES).

(a) What is meant by (i) 'an imbalance of demand and supply of labour' and (ii) 'skills and supply shortages'? (6 marks)

(b) Identify the factors that might affect (i) demand for and (ii) supply of labour mentioned in the articles. (4 marks)

(c) Why might the occupations in Table 33.3 have skills shortages? (6 marks)

(d) Assume the suggestions of the chairperson of the National Skills Task Force were implemented. Examine how this might affect (i) the demand for labour and (ii) the supply of labour. (8 marks)

(e) (i) Using a demand and supply diagram, examine the position of young workers wanting Modern Apprenticeships. (8 marks)

(ii) Discuss the effects of the LSC actions on the demand and supply of labour on the diagram. (8 marks)

34 Government Economic Policy and Business

Government policy

Governments use a variety of methods of intervention, including spending and taxation, to influence the economy. Part of the government's involvement in the economy is the use of policies to control economic variables such as inflation, unemployment and trade. The use of these different policies can affect businesses.

Fiscal policy

Fiscal policy aims to manage the level of total spending or aggregate demand in the economy. The government can use fiscal policy in a number of ways to achieve its objectives.

- It can boost total spending in the economy when there is unemployment.
- If there is inflation in the economy, linked to the level of demand, fiscal policy can be used to reduce demand in the economy as a whole.
- If there is a current balance deficit the government could raise taxes or cut spending on imports.
- It may try to redistribute income. It may spend money or reduce tax on low income groups to give them more disposable income.

Fiscal policy may involve governments making the following changes.

Changes in government spending If the economy needs a boost, government expenditure can be raised. For example, spending on building new hospitals can create jobs, income and increased spending by the people in those jobs. On the other hand, if the economy needs to be slowed down, government expenditure can be lowered. This may also be used to control inflation.

Changes in direct taxation **Direct taxes** are those which are levied directly on individuals or businesses. Income tax rates, as part of a fiscal policy, can be lowered in order to encourage consumers to buy more goods and services. This should raise the level of spending in the economy. Corporation tax, a tax on company profits, may be cut to encourage businesses to invest and increase output. Raising income tax is likely to have the opposite effect, ie to lower the level of aggregate demand. This could be used to cut disposable income and control inflation.

Changes in indirect taxation **Indirect taxes** are taxes on goods or services. The main indirect tax in the UK is VAT. Governments raise indirect taxes as part of fiscal policy in order to raise the price of goods and services and discourage spending. Indirect taxes are also used by governments as a means of raising revenue in order to finance spending plans. There is much debate as to whether it is individual businesses or consumers who have to pay for indirect taxes. Take the example of a 2 per cent increase in VAT. If this was passed on to consumers in the form of a 2 per cent price rise, then consumers would be paying for it. However, firms might be reluctant to pass on the price rise to consumers because of fears of falling demand for their product. In this case, they might only raise the price by 1 per cent and pay the other 1 per cent VAT increase themselves. This would lead to a 1 per cent increase in their costs.

If a government spends more than it receives in revenue from taxation and other sources, then it is said to have a **budget deficit**. This will mean it has to borrow money from a variety of sources, such as individual members of the public or banks. This is will increase the PUBLIC SECTOR NET CASH REQUIREMENT (PSNCR). Governments may have budget surpluses, ie higher revenue than spending. In this case the government is able to pay off past debts.

Monetary policy

Monetary policy is also used to manage the level of aggregate demand in the economy, with a particular emphasis upon controlling the money supply. Monetary policy can be used to:

- expand the economy by allowing more money to circulate

Nearly 1,000 cinemas in the western Indian state Maharashtra, including the entertainment capital Bombay which makes Bollywood films, called off a three-week strike in April 2004. Cinema owners said that the government had accepted their demand for a 10 per cent cut in tax on tickets. During the strike cinemas lost an estimated £130,000 per day - twice as much as the government.

The government had placed a 55 per cent entertainment tax on each ticket sold in Maharashtra, one of the highest in India. RV Vidhani, chairman of the cinema halls owners' association, said the government's acceptance of only one of its demands was 'like a drop in the ocean'. But they had to accept it in the face of stiff competition from multiplexes, which did not pay entertainment tax.

Source: adapted from news.bbc.co.uk.

(a) Identify the type of taxation mentioned in the article.
(b) Examine the possible effects of a reduction in taxation on:
(i) cinemas in Maharashtra;
(ii) cinema goers;
(iii) other businesses;
(iv) government revenue.

Question 1

and increase spending;
- control spending and restrict increases in money flowing around the economy which may lead to price rises;
- control spending on imports if there is a current balance deficit.

The government has used a variety of methods in the past to control the money supply.

Changing interest rates An increase in interest rates can reduce the money supply. If interest rates increase, the cost of borrowing rises. This could reduce the amount that businesses and consumers borrow from banks and building societies.

Restricting bank loans By restricting the ability of banks to give out loans, the size of the money supply can be regulated. The BANK OF ENGLAND could instruct banks to keep a higher proportion of their assets in reserve. This means that they are able to lend less. The government may also sell financial securities. This will reduce the size of the bank's assets and leave banks with less to lend out.

Credit or hire purchase restrictions The government can place controls on the amount of credit and hire purchase agreements which banks and other financial institutions are allowed to give to businesses and consumers. Over the last 25 years the UK government has encouraged competition in financial markets. This has led to an explosion in the amount of credit available and made restricting credit more difficult.

Independent central banks In certain countries, such as Germany, the central bank has responsibility for control of inflation and the money supply. Governments in the UK traditionally controlled interest rates directly. In 1997, control of interest rates passed to the Monetary Policy Committee of the Bank of England. It is argued that an independent bank is in a better position to control monetary policy. For example, it will not allow a government to increase the money supply before an election to finance spending in order to win votes.

The Bank of England's Monetary Policy Committee decided to keep interest rates at 4 per cent after twice raising the interest rate in the last six months. The Bank made clear its desire not to give a shock to consumers at a time when they were heavily in debt. Prior to the decision not to raise interest rates, union leaders warned about possible job losses arising from a further increase in interest rates. Roger Lyons of the union Amicus warned that higher rates would hurt businesses and debt burdened households. 'High rates will harm business first and then cast a shadow over millions of people who've borrowed money in the past couple of years and who aren't used to paying higher rates on their loans.'

Source: adapted from *The Guardian*, 4.3.2004.

(a) Why do you think the Bank of England decided not increase interest rates at the time the article was written?
(b) Explain how an increase in interest rates might affect a retail business.

Question 2

An increase in interest rates and restrictions of loans and credit are aimed at controlling the money supply and inflation. However, this will also affect spending and may reduce output, employment and imports.

Exchange rate policy

The exchange rate is the price of one currency in relation to another. The value of the pound, for instance, can be shown against a variety of other currencies, such as the dollar, the yen or the euro. Some governments take the view that the exchange rate should be left to find its own market value. Such governments do not try to intervene in foreign currency markets to influence the exchange rate.

Other governments seek directly to influence exchange rates. This involves the buying and selling of the currency on foreign exchange markets to influence its price. A government may want to:
- support the currency to prevent its value from falling. This might involve buying up currency to restrict its supply. A fall in the exchange rate may raise the price of imported products, possibly leading to **imported inflation**;
- allow the value of the currency to fall to improve the competitiveness of businesses in export markets. A fall in the value of a currency should make exports relatively cheaper;
- 'shadow' or follow another currency. For example, the British government has tried to shadow the value of the euro (☞ unit 36). This is so that UK businesses operating within the single European market do not experience variations in prices compared to those of European competitors.

There is a link between monetary policy, explained in the previous section, and exchange rate policy. Changes in interest rates have an effect on the value of a country's currency. An increase in US interest rates, for example, will tend to raise the value of the dollar. Higher interest rates attract short term investors who buy the currency. This increases the demand for the dollar. As a result its price rises. Lower US interest rates cause short term investors to move assets elsewhere. They will sell the dollar and buy other currencies with which to invest. This increases the supply of the dollar and lowers its price.

Protectionism

This involves the use of controls to restrict the amount of imports coming into a country. TARIFFS are a tax on imports. They raise the price of imports and, hopefully, discourage consumers from buying them. For example, there is a Common External Tariff (☞ unit 36) on goods entering the EU. QUOTAS are a limit on the number of goods that are allowed to enter a country. For example, a government may specify that only 1,000 Japanese television sets are allowed to enter the country each month.

A more subtle approach is to impose technical restrictions or 'waiting' periods on goods entering a country. For example, Japan has been known in the past to reject imports because they do not meet standards they have set for products being sold in domestic markets.

Why might a government impose tariffs?

- To protect INFANT INDUSTRIES or newly emerging industries which have yet to find their feet. This is often used by developing countries to protect their manufacturing industries.
- To protect strategic or declining industries which governments feel are important to the future of the country. Also industries whose decline may lead to a loss of jobs are sometimes protected.
- Anti-dumping. Dumping occurs when goods are sold in foreign markets at prices below their cost of production. This may occur because of excess capacity in an industry or as a deliberate attempt to quickly gain market share at the expense of domestic businesses. Because dumping is seen as unfair, many governments act to protect their own businesses from its effects.

There are some difficulties with protectionist policies.

- They may lead to retaliation by the exporting country. This may 'cancel out' the effect of protection. It will also harm the imposing country's exports to other countries.
- They can lead to inflation in the country imposing the tariff. This may be the case if, despite the tariff, the country still has to buy the goods. They might be essential raw materials, for example.
- International agreements, such as those controlled by the World Trade Organisation, prevent the use of tariffs by those countries that have signed the agreement.
- Faced with paying an import tariff, which may raise the price of goods, businesses might resort to illegal methods of trading.

In 2004, Vietnam had around 1.6 million mobile phone subscribers out of a population of 80 million. The number was predicted to reach 7 million by 2005. Nokia has 45 per cent of the market and Samsung 26 per cent. Other major brands like Motorola, Siemens and Sony Ericsson account for the rest.

In July 2003 the General Department of Taxation (GDT) announced a reduction in import tax on handsets from 15 to 10 per cent, but VAT would remain at 10 per cent. The previous month seven telecom associations had urged the government to bring down both tariffs to 5 per cent. Traders claimed that high tariffs encouraged smuggling. They were worried that the cuts were not deep enough to dissuade phone smugglers. The associations suggested that tax revenues would rise 20 per cent if the government was able to collect import tariffs on 90 per cent of handsets in the market, instead of the current 25 per cent.

Telecom experts argued that smuggled mobile phones, which usually enter the country through the air or across land borders, cost 10-15 per cent less than legally imported ones. They were said to account for a staggering 75 per cent of the market. The Vietnam Post and Telecommunications Corporation, VNPT, estimated that 740,000 mobile phones were sold in 2002, but the customs office reported a mere 190,294 imported through legal channels.

The tax authorities, however, argued that import taxes were not the major reason for smuggling. They pointed to many low tariff commodities also being smuggled into the country.

Source: adapted from vietnamnews.vnagency.com.vn.

(a) Why might the government have placed import tariffs on mobile phones?
(b) Examine the effects of a reduction in tariffs.

Supply side policies

SUPPLY SIDE POLICIES are policies that:

- encourage the workings of the free market;
- encourage competition;
- attempt to change the aggregate demand or AGGREGATE SUPPLY in the economy;
- give incentives to businesses and individuals.

Supply side policies can be viewed in two main ways.

Policies which allow the labour market to function efficiently Unemployment can result from real wages being too high. Supply side policies seek to reduce the impact of those factors which are believed to distort the free workings of the labour market. Such policies might include the following.

- Reducing the power of trade unions and professional organisations. This would result in them being less able to force wage levels up.
- Cuts in taxation will give lower paid workers a greater incentive to take jobs. This is because such workers will be left with more income.
- Improving the mobility of labour (☞ unit 33). Workers may be encouraged to move to parts of the country where work is available. Such policies might include making the buying and selling of houses more straightforward.
- Greater availability of information about jobs.
- 'Job clubs' where people seeking work can find advice and facilities, such as telephones and word processors, to help them apply for jobs.
- Encouraging young workers to find paid work and to provide occupational advice.

Policies to improve the efficiency of businesses and industries Such policies focus upon the competitiveness of business and the markets within which they operate. They also involve the education, skills and training of employees. Policies in this area are based upon the view that competition forces individual businesses and the economy as a whole to operate more efficiently. Such policies include the following.

- Privatisation of industries and the removal of the government from directly controlling businesses.
- Deregulation of industries which results in industries being opened up to competition. This allows businesses the opportunity to enter markets from which they were previously excluded.
- Reducing income and corporation tax to encourage businesses and employees to be more efficient by allowing them to keep more of their income or company profits.
- Competition policies designed to prevent monopolies and restrictive trade practices. Both the EU and the British government monitor business takeovers and mergers to ensure that competition within markets remains. They also regulate and monitor the activities and pricing of water, electricity and communications businesses, for example.
- Supporting businesses that provide training in order to create a more efficient and productive labour force.
- Reduction of the amount of 'red tape', such as form filling and returns required of business.
- Removal of restrictions to employment such fixed hours of work.
- Reduction of employers' National Insurance contributions to reduce the cost of employing workers.

Supply side policies are seen by their supporters as anti-inflationary for two reasons.

- They try to remove the ability of trade unions and professional associations to increase wage levels above market rates. This removes one of the main pressures on business costs.
- Policies such as privatisation and deregulation create competition. This should force businesses to lower their prices to compete with rivals.

Incomes policy

Incomes policy is a method used to control inflation by imposing limits upon pay or price increases. In the past, in the UK it was widely used in the battle against inflation. Low inflation rates in the 1990s and early twenty first century and changing attitudes to human resources may have led to a reduction in its use.

The effects of government policies on business

The policies outlined above are used to help governments achieve their objectives. The effects of these policies upon businesses depends mainly upon the objectives the government is trying to achieve.

Anti-inflationary monetary policy There are two main effects depending upon the type of monetary policy used. First, if interest rates are raised by the Bank of England this will make borrowing by businesses more expensive and might lead to the cancellation of investment projects. Higher interest rates will also hit the pockets of many consumers. They will find it more expensive to borrow money on credit and their mortgage repayments will increase. This is likely to lead to fewer sales, particularly for those firms manufacturing and selling consumer goods.

Second, if bank lending or credit is restricted, loan capital will be harder to come by, particularly for small firms. Again this may result in less investment and a lower level of demand from consumers as they find money harder to come by.

Anti-inflationary fiscal policy This can be in the form of tax (usually direct) increases or public expenditure cuts. Tax increases will mean that consumers have less money in their pockets and they are therefore likely to spend less. This will affect the sales of many firms. Public expenditure cuts will mean less money spent on, for example, schools, colleges, hospitals, road building, and local leisure services. This will hit a wide range of firms, especially those who work for local authorities and central government. The construction industry, for example, is always adversely affected by cutbacks in public expenditure.

Anti-inflationary exchange rate policy Such a policy will try to ensure that the exchange rate does not fall too greatly, as explained earlier in this unit. However, a high exchange rate causes the price of UK products in export markets to be relatively high. This makes it difficult to sell products in foreign markets. It also causes the price of imported goods to be relatively cheap, making it difficult for UK firms to compete 'at home'. Maintaining exchange rates at a particular level often requires a high interest rate. This will also lead to major problems for businesses.

Anti-inflationary supply side policies The effects of anti-inflationary supply side policies on businesses will depend upon the circumstances of those businesses. Businesses in monopoly positions in their markets may be forced, by deregulation, for example, to compete with other businesses. This is likely to have the effect of lowering their profits, at least in the short term. For other businesses, these policies have the potential to create opportunities for entering markets which never previously existed. The bus company Stagecoach, for example, has grown as a result of the deregulation of the coach and bus industries.

Policies to increase demand, output and employment Firms can both benefit and suffer from government policy to increase demand in the economy. Fiscal policy involving increases in the amount of government spending on new capital projects, such as hospitals and colleges, can lead to an increase in the demand for many firms' products. Cuts in income tax may also increase demand. Similarly, monetary policy that reduces interest rates can make the cost of borrowing cheaper for firms, allowing them to invest in new plant and machinery. Lower interest rates also make it cheaper for consumers to borrow. This can increase the demand for a variety of goods, particularly those, such as consumer durables, bought on credit.

However, the government may have to finance its spending by borrowing or taxation. The former may involve a rise in interest rates, which makes loans to firms more expensive. Increased corporation tax or income tax will take away a firm's profits or income. Increasing the money supply or government spending may lead to inflation, which can also be harmful to businesses.

Supply side policies, output and employment Supply side policies can affect the output and employment of businesses in a number of ways.

- Policies which aim to cut wages reduce the cost of employing labour for firms.
- A more mobile and flexible workforce could make recruitment easier for businesses. It may also improve the efficiency of businesses (☞ unit 30).
- A better trained workforce could improve labour productivity and output.
- Greater competition may force businesses to be more efficient.
- Incentives aimed at improving training may lead to increased employment.

A criticism of supply side policies is that they can lead to the creation of significant numbers of low paid jobs. Not only may this reduce the morale and motivation of low paid workers, but it may also lead to a lower level of demand in the economy.

There is also concern that supply side policies, giving greater freedom to businesses, could result in damage to the environment. This is because businesses, left to themselves, often fail to take account of the true social costs of their activities (☞ unit 41).

Trade and exchange rate policy Trade policy by the UK government may affect businesses in a number of ways.

- Quotas can help a domestic businesses by restricting competition from imports. However, they may also restrict the supply of components or raw materials available to a business and could result in retaliation from another country which may affect the exports of UK businesses.
- Tariffs tend to raise the price of imports, making them more expensive to UK customers. UK businesses may sell more products as they are relatively cheaper. Tariffs, however, may raise the price of imported materials and may lead to retaliation.
- Allowing the value of the currency to fall should make exports relatively cheaper and businesses should sell more products abroad. The price of imported materials for business may rise, however.

In 2003 there was trade friction between the US and China. China's fixed exchange rate policy was blamed for undervaluing the yuan, leading to a surge of cheap exports to the USA, as shown in Figure 34.1. Exports grew by 75 per cent between 2000 and 2002. US critics say that this has claimed 2.7 million US manufacturing jobs since 2000.

China's economy has not dipped below 7 per cent growth for many years, in painful contrast to the US. China is also the world's top destination for foreign investment. Western firms have moved there to take advantage of its mix of cheap skilled and semi-skilled labour, which have been encouraged by government policies. Wages are roughly one fortieth of US levels.

Source: adapted from news.bbc.co.uk.

Figure 34.1 *China's exports to US*

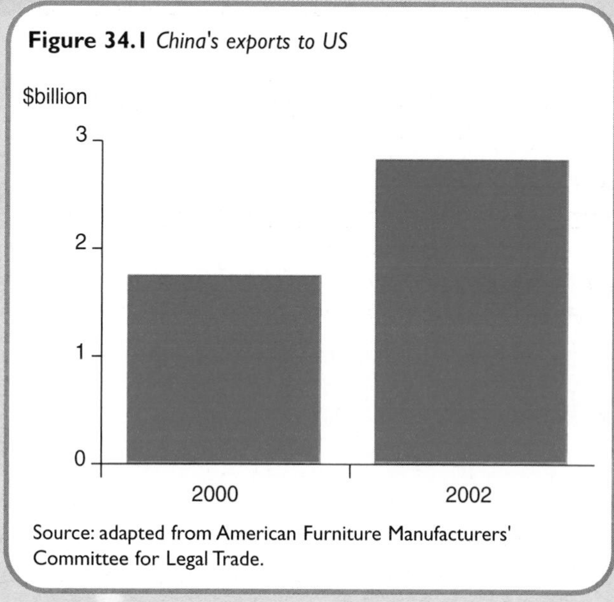

Source: adapted from American Furniture Manufacturers' Committee for Legal Trade.

(a) Examine how government policy in China has affected:
  (i) businesses in China;
  (ii) business in the USA;
  (iii) businesses in other countries.

key terms

Aggregate supply - the level of output in the economy as a whole.
Bank of England - the central bank of the UK which controls the supply of money.
Infant industries - newly set up industries that are unable to compete with established foreign competition.
Public sector net cash requirement - the amount of money the government has to raise when spending is greater than receipts.
Quota - a limit placed upon the number of particular categories of goods allowed to enter the country.
Supply side policies - policies designed to make markets operate more efficiently.
Tariff - a tax upon imports.

Knowledge

1. Give 3 examples of:
   (a) fiscal policy;
   (b) monetary policy.
2. Explain the difference between direct and indirect taxation.
3. What are the methods of controlling the money supply?
4. Briefly explain 2 policies used to tackle a balance of payments deficit.
5. State 6 examples of supply side policies.
6. How might supply side policies control inflation?
7. What is an incomes policy?
8. In what ways might businesses be affected by anti-inflationary policies?
9. What effect would cutting income tax have on:
   (a) businesses;
   (b) consumers?
10. State 3 policies to:
    (a) increase demand;
    (b) increase supply.
11. How might government policy to solve unemployment benefit a firm?
12. Give 2 reasons why government spending to solve unemployment may be a problem.
13. Briefly explain the benefits of supply side policies to firms.

Case study UK government economic policy

The Bank of England's Monetary Policy Committee cut interest rates by 0.5 per cent in August 2001 to create a new interest rate of 5 per cent. Interest rates were cut in response to signs of worsening economic conditions. Companies around the world have been announcing plans to axe thousands of workers with depressing regularity. The Trades Union Congress had predicted that at least 100,000 manufacturing jobs would go by the end of the year as the UK heads towards a recession. Economic growth dropped to its lowest level for a number of years and there were concerns that the effects of a weakening US economy were beginning to bite in the UK. In addition, the Monetary Policy Committee's inflation target of 2.5 per cent had been undershot.

Prior to the interest changes NTL, Britain's largest cable communications company, said that it had plans to cut up to 5,000 jobs over the next two years. Britain's manufacturing sector, already under pressure from a strong pound, was reeling from a world economic slowdown.

Source: adapted from *The Guardian*, 2.8.2001.

Table 34.1 *UK Interest changes, 2000-2004*

Date	Base rate
05 Feb 2004	4.00
06 Nov 2003	3.75
10 Jul 2003	3.50
06 Feb 2003	3.75
08 Nov 2001	4.00
04 Oct 2001	4.50
18 Sep 2001	4.75
02 Aug 2001	5.00
10 May 2001	5.25
5 April 2001	5.50
12 Feb 2001	5.75
10 Feb 2000	6.00
13 Jan 2000	5.75

Source: adapted from www.moneyworld.co.uk.

Christina and David Romer, economists at the University of California, examined the link between changes in interest rate and changes in the output of businesses and inflation. Economists have always seen interest rate setting as being a little like a game of pin the tail on the donkey. This is because of the volatility of economic conditions and the unreliability of the statistics upon which interest rate decisions are made.

However, the findings by the two economists at the University of California were that interest rate changes lead to rapid changes in the output of businesses. The effects of interest rate changes on inflation, they found, took longer but were still very marked.

Source: adapted from *The Guardian*, 13.10.2003.

The British Chambers of Commerce (BCC) called on the government to encourage electronic business by introducing tax credits for technology training and resisting further regulation. It argued that the government must resist the urge to regulate unnecessarily. 'Already we see emerging a rush to regulate and legislate for these new technologies, with the result that much of the regulation and codes of practice are leading to duplication and confusion.' The BCC called for the government to:

- make a serious commitment on training and skills. It said there was a strong case for a tax credit linked to training or investment in information and communications technology;
- permanently increase the 100 per cent capital allowance for small and medium-sized companies for hard and software';
- ensure government departments were e-competent enough to support business effectively;
- scrap the IR35 legislation and work with business to define who is and who is not allowed to call themselves self-employed;
- resist the temptation to over-regulate a fledgling industry and stop the introduction of overlapping regulations.

'Over the last year more and more small businesses across the country have realised the benefits of getting online' said Jenny Searle, director of the government's advisory service UK Online for Business. 'The challenge now is to encourage these firms to move beyond a more basic website towards true online trading, dealing directly with their suppliers and customers through e-commerce.'

Source: adapted from news.bbc.co.uk.

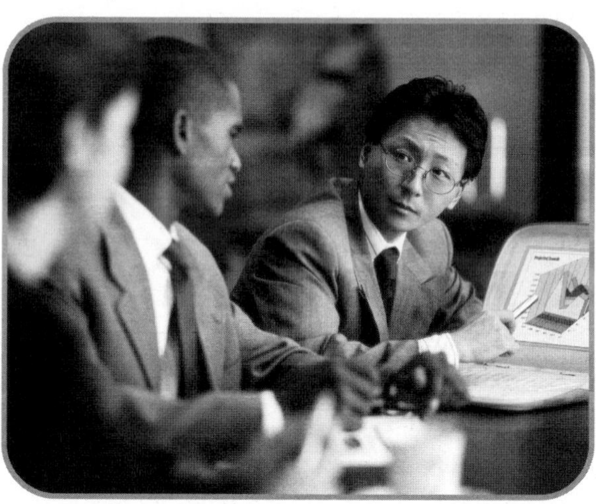

(a) Why should signs of worsening economic conditions cause the Bank of England to cut interest rates? (8 marks)

(b) Explain how a strong pound might cause pressure for Britain's manufacturing businesses. (8 marks)

(c) Examine how fiscal policy might help in responding to the economic conditions which led to the fall in interest rates. (10 marks)

(d) (i) Why might government policies be necessary in ICT related businesses? (4 marks)

(ii) Examine how these proposals might affect businesses and their employees. (10 marks)

(e) To what extent do you think that NTL's plans to shed jobs would be affected by the 0.5 per cent change in interest rates? (10 marks)

35 Business Strategy, Government Policy and the Economy

Government economic policy and business

A government has a range of **economic policies** at its disposal in order to achieve its **objectives** of low inflation, high economic growth, high employment levels and control of the balance of payments situation). These policies include fiscal policy, monetary policy, exchange rate policy and supply side policies. Policies can affect businesses in many ways as explained in unit 34. It is therefore important for businesses:

- to understand why a government is using a particular policy;
- to be able to respond to policy changes and their effects with appropriate strategies when they occur.

Policy changes and disagreements

There is often disagreement about the **extent** to which changes in economic policies may affect variables, such as inflation and unemployment, and also businesses. At the root of policy disagreements are the different approaches which economists have to solving economic problems.

One approach favours the free operation of markets. Supporters of this believe that the role of government should be limited to providing the right environment for businesses to flourish. Another approach to policy favours using government intervention in the economy.

The operation of markets The free market approach suggests that markets will achieve equilibrium providing they are free to operate. Take the market for labour. Say that in a depressed area there are more workers wanting jobs than are available. This would put pressure on wages to fall. Employers would offer lower wages to workers and some workers would, as a result, not offer their labour to employers at this wage rate. This would occur until the labour market returned to equilibrium, ie to the point where the demand for labour was equal to the supply of labour at a given wage. This approach would argue for the removal of all restrictions to markets and the free movement of wages and prices.

Interventionists argue that the operation of a market economy results in a variety of problems, such as:

- high levels of unemployment;
- inadequate merit goods, such as housing, health care and education;
- a lack of provision of some public goods, such as defence;
- inequalities in income.

Wages and unemployment Market supporters suggest that if real wage rates (that take into account inflation) are free to move up and down, the economy would always achieve full employment. Workers must be flexible in their demands and prepared to react to changes in the market. If there is any unemployment, it is likely to be voluntary. Some people may not want to work by choice at a given wage rate.

Interventionists argue that in a depression (and perhaps even in recession) wage rates fall, or are held down, but unemployment is still high. They dispute whether real wage rates will actually operate to allow markets to achieve equilibrium at full employment. In modern economies this is because:

- labour may be reluctant to move from one area to another;
- trade unions and some legislation protect real wage rates;
- businesses may not reduce wages because of the dissatisfaction it may lead to.

Instead they argue that unemployment is caused by a lack of aggregate demand in the economy. It is the government's role in such circumstances to use policies which will lead to an increase in consumption, investment, government spending and exports.

Inflation Providing markets operate freely, the economy will achieve full employment, according to market economists. At this point an increase in output would only be possible if the state of technology changed. Increases in aggregate demand by government would simply lead to inflation. Businesses could not take on more workers or produce more output even if they wished. Price increases would be the only result of government spending. Some economists, sometimes called monetarists, argue that increases in the money supply over and above increases in output lead to inflation.

Interventionists argue that money supply increases merely reflect the state of the economy and do not cause inflation. Instead, they believe that inflation is caused by an excess of consumer demand in the economy as a whole or a rise in firms' costs.

Government policy Market economists argue that obstacles to the operation of markets should be removed by government. These occur on the **supply side** of the economy. For example, workers may not be able to move to other jobs because they do not have the skills needed. This will prevent the labour market from working. Incentives to businesses to retrain workers may help solve this. The aim of supply side policies is to increase the level of output in the economy as a whole. This is known as **aggregate supply**. Supply side economists believe that this can be increased by using the supply side policies (☞ unit 34).

Interventionists argue that government should attempt to solve problems of the market. They argue that government policy should include:

- fiscal and regional policy to increase employment, generate economic growth, help ailing industry and

encourage firms to invest in new plant and machinery;
- protection for UK firms against foreign competition;
- the use of prices and incomes policy to prevent wage costs rising as a result of increases in aggregate demand;
- government ownership or close involvement in particular sectors of the economy.

One of the more significant shifts in policy comes about through the election of a new government. A new government is likely to introduce new economic policies. In the past, in the UK, Labour governments had been associated with interventionist policies and Conservative governments with a more free market approach. Increasingly, political parties in the UK and other countries have placed the operation of markets at the centre of their economic policy approach.

In 2003/04 the industrial sector in India was booming. Economic growth was expected to be over 7 per cent. Car sales in November were 41 per cent higher than the previous year. Record share prices sparked a trading frenzy on the stock market. But there were debates about India's position. Some argued that if it wanted a sustained growth of over 8 per cent and the benefits to reach all of society, the government must do more. This might include investing more on infrastructure and social improvement, including investment in people, improving efficiency and making it easier for new private firms to start up business. It was argued that 'a sustained growth rate of over 8 per cent would not be possible unless the investment rate rose to 30 per cent. That, in turn, required the government to put its fiscal house in order'.

Comments on the economy included:
- '... India is on the threshold of becoming an economic super power. For this to materialise, India has to ... cut subsidies, reduce fiscal deficit, increase investment, eliminate red tape, ramp up efficiency and, above all, develop human capital';
- 'India, has been doing it the right way. It would be foolish for the country to allow full privatisation of foreign businesses in India. The Indian companies are learning from their partnerships and producing a better product. Who wants India to start looking like your local American neighbourhood suburban mall?'
- Although the economic situation has definitely improved judging from the lifestyle of acquisition of cars, tvs, computers, foreign cable connections and advanced education in every field especially technology, all these remain in the hands of very few compared to the vast majority who are still ... trying to eke out a living from their meagre resources. India will only be a prosperous society when every level of society enjoys a taste of its economic wealth.'

Source: adapted from www.news.bbc.co.uk.

(a) Identify examples of government intervention and free market policies in the articles.
(c) Discuss the arguments for and against these approaches for (i) Indian businesses and (ii) Indian consumers.

Policy conflicts and business strategy

In practice governments may find it difficult to achieve all of their objectives at the same time. This is because of the way in which individual economic policies have varied effects upon employment, growth, inflation and the balance of payments. Businesses need to plan for and respond to policies as they change over time to meet different economic conditions.

Inflation and employment conflicts In order to achieve a targeted level of inflation the Bank of England may make the decision that it is important to maintain interest rates at a higher level. Higher interest rates tend to control inflation. Businesses and people tend to borrow less and spend less. Higher interest rates may also cause the value of sterling to be high relative to other currencies, which should help to keep the price of imported goods low.

However, there can be problems with higher interest rates. They discourage consumer spending, leading to lower levels of output by businesses and possibly job losses. They may discourage investment by businesses in projects such as new factories and offices. Again, this may have the effect of reducing employment or preventing the creation of new jobs.

They can also lead to a higher exchange rates and a rising value of the pound relative to other currencies, leading to higher prices in export markets for UK businesses. This may reduce the competitiveness of UK businesses in export markets and lead to a loss of jobs.

A business may react to higher interest rates by:
- finding alternative methods of borrowing to raise funds;
- finding cheaper suppliers of finance;
- lengthening its periods of repayment;
- passing on its charges to suppliers or consumers.

It may react to a high value of the pound by:
- attempting to improve its competitiveness in foreign markets in other ways, such as improving the quality of its products or changing its marketing mix;
- not raising the price of its products in foreign markets and accepting a reduction in profits;
- buying low cost imports as a result of the higher value of the pound;
- concentrating on sales in the home market.

Some economists would argue that conflicts between inflation and unemployment are only likely to be short term. This is because the competitiveness of UK businesses in both domestic and export markets is likely to depend upon lower inflation rates.

Economic growth and inflation / trade deficit conflicts Governments may find it difficult to achieve higher rates of economic growth and control inflation at the same time. One of the reasons for this is because economic growth is associated with higher levels of aggregate demand, which can lead to inflation. At times of higher economic growth many consumers find their incomes rising and use this income to spend more on goods and services. This can lead to increased inflationary pressures in the economy. This increased consumer spending, as a consequence of high economic growth, can also contribute to a deficit on the balance of payments. If the increased spending of consumers is on domestic products, there would be no problem in terms of the balance of payments. However, UK consumers have tended to buy imported goods in growth periods. This higher economic growth has tended to be associated with a increased balance of payments deficit in the UK.

In periods of higher inflation a business may:

- attempt to reduce its costs by cutting wages, rationalising its organisation (☞ unit 30) or finding cheaper suppliers of materials or components;
- pass on some of the increase in cost to consumers;
- hedge against possible future price rises by agreeing to pay before prices increase;
- sign long term, fixed payment contracts.

Economic growth and the environment Governments are becoming increasingly aware of the need to consider the impact of their policies on the environment. Many commentators are concerned that the higher levels of business activity associated with economic growth can have a negative effect upon the environment. For example, the amount of traffic on the roads generally increases in line with increases in business activity. This can lead to air pollution and congestion. Increased business activity also leads to increased usage of non-renewable resources, such as oil and gas, and to the pollution associated with their use.

Growth and business strategy

Economies move through booms and slumps in the business cycle. In a boom there are likely to be increased earnings, spending, production and employment. These conditions are associated with growth periods.

What strategies might a business adopt during periods of growth or when high growth is anticipated in future?

- Analyse the extent to which the incomes of existing customers will be affected by economic growth. Although economic growth leads to increased average incomes across the country, not all groups of consumers will experience an increase in their incomes.
- Assess the income elasticity of demand of the business's products. The demand for some products, such as basic foodstuffs, is largely unaffected by increases in consumer incomes. For other products, such as new cars and restaurant services, demand is strongly linked to consumer incomes.
- Consider market opportunities which may arise in either existing markets where people have more money or new markets that have developed. For example, in a period of growth people may be more prepared to spend on leisure activities or holidays. It may be safer to expand into foreign markets in growth periods.
- Take the opportunity to diversify into new areas which are potentially risky. There might be less of a risk in a period

Figure 35.1 *Interest rates, 2000-01*

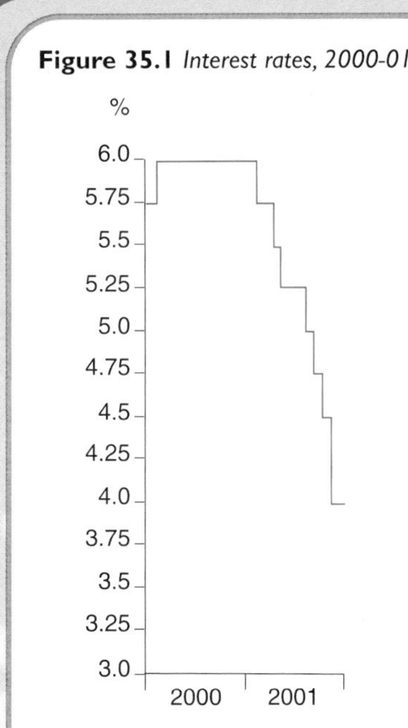

Source: adapted from *Economic Trends Annual Supplement*, 2003.

Figure 35.2 *Inflation (% annual change), 2000-01*

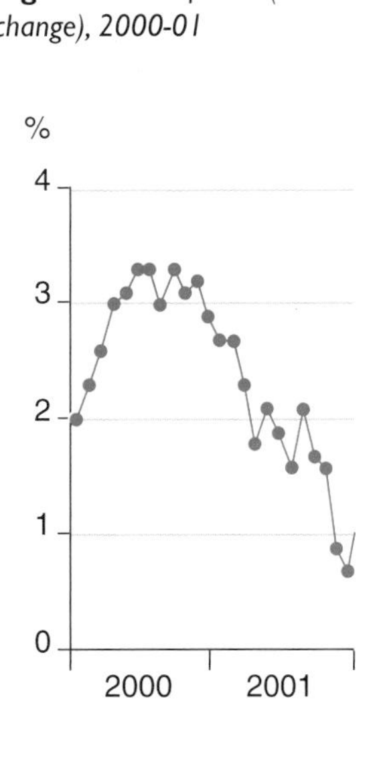

Source: adapted from www.statistics.gov.uk.

Realworks is a manufacturer of children's toys. Faced with the challenges of the new century, in 2000 it decided to expand into new markets. The business knew that it would have to borrow to finance the expansion. It was concerned about the relationship between inflation and interest rates, as they would both affect the business. However, the company thought that it would be able to pay back any borrowing fairly quickly and decided to go ahead with the expansion.

(a) Explain how interest rates and inflation might have affected the business.
(b) Discuss the decision of the business to expand given the information above.

of growth if spending is higher.

- Analyse the likely impact of economic growth on competitor products. For example, in a growth period small producers or service providers may develop which would not survive in a slower growth period.
- Consider the ability of the business's organisational structure to cope with and positively respond to a growing business environment. This might mean employing more specialists or taking the opportunity to use more updated technology.
- Evaluate capacity to provide goods and services in sufficient quantities to meet demand. There may be a need to purchase new equipment to cope with larger quantities being produced.
- Assess the ability of the business to raise finance from either internal or external sources to fund expansion where this is required.

Recession and business strategy

Periods of recession are usually accompanied by falling incomes and spending, and business failure.

It is useful for businesses to find strategies which they can use to weather a recession or increase their chances of doing so. Possible strategies may include some of the following.

- Focusing upon parts of the market where a business has an advantage. A business, for example, may produce a number of product lines. It may close down certain plants or lines and concentrate only on those that are profitable.
- Accurate and up to date financial information. Businesses need to identify quickly where losses are being made and act decisively with the use of this information.
- Credit control. Small firms, in particular, are often forced to close down due to the failure of a major customer to pay their bills. A tight credit control policy which involves promptly chasing up slow payers and taking out credit insurance can be useful.
- Realistic planning. Too many firms set their plans (☞ unit 6) on the assumption that nothing will go wrong. In a recession it is vital that firms build room into their plans for setbacks.
- Identify niche markets. A business may try to find markets which are largely unaffected by recession.
- A business may concentrate on safer home markets or those in countries which are less prone to recession.
- Analyse the extent to which the incomes of existing customers will be affected by recession. Although recession can lead to reduced average incomes across the country not all groups of consumers will experience a reduction in their incomes. Many groups of high earners have, in the past, been largely untouched by recession in terms of their earnings.
- Assess the income elasticity of demand of the business's products. The demand for some products, such as basic foodstuffs, is largely unaffected by decreases in consumer incomes. For other products demand is linked to consumer incomes.

Business failure

A number of terms are used to explain business failure. Businesses ultimately fail because they are **insolvent.** This means that they are unable to pay their debts. The **Insolvency Act, 1986** set out certain regulations for terminating businesses that become insolvent. The **Enterprise Act, 2002** allows businesses 12 months to deal with their insolvency. The aim is to ensure fewer good businesses go under.

Sole traders and **partnerships** can be declared BANKRUPT. The process of a person being declared bankrupt begins when one or more creditors of a business present a petition to a court. Petitions can only be presented by creditors who are

Within a few hours of the liquidator arriving at Ms Jennifer Bond's Leicestershire leather-processing business a £65,000 order arrived. The order, for the tanning and dyeing of about 50,000 feet of leather, would have kept the factory busy for more than a month. But underfunding had already brought about the demise of the five year old business, and a meeting of creditors expected to put it into voluntary liquidation. Ms Bond said, 'The recession has passed but we can't finance the orders we are getting.'

Ironically the Leicestershire company's fate was sealed by its efforts to expand the business. It increased turnover by switching from the cheaper leathers and varied colours used in women's shoes to better quality leather for men's shoes, most of which are dyed black. The improvement in business increased the company's need for working capital and put further pressure on its already overstretched finances. 'We were very successful in opening up new markets but we didn't have the money to go on', said Ms Bond. 'We couldn't afford to buy in the chemicals or the other raw materials.'

The problem of how to finance growth is one which faces many businesses in a recession. Ms Bond's company had barely established itself when the recession began to bite and it lost money. The company was unable to return to profit and finally Ms Bond decided to call in the liquidator.

If the creditors approve, the liquidator will sell off the plant and equipment, the remains of the lease on the factory and any other assets he can find. Ms Bond, in spite of her disappointment at the loss of the business and concern at the personal liability she may still face when the business is liquidated, is relieved that it is all over. 'I feel better', she said, after her first meeting with the liquidator. 'It has been two years of ifs and buts.'

Source: adapted from the *Financial Times*.

(a) What factors contributed to the collapse of Ms Bond's business?
(b) Discuss possible strategies that Ms Bond might have used to survive the recession.

owed a certain amount by a business. If this is successful, then a receiving order will be made out against the debtor. An OFFICIAL RECEIVER is then appointed who has legal rights over all of the owner's property. Nothing can happen to this property without the permission of the Official Receiver. If the Official Receiver believes that the business is still a going concern, a manager will be appointed to run the business on the Receiver's behalf. Within a fixed period of time from the bankruptcy being declared, a meeting of creditors will be called. At this meeting the debtor has the opportunity to present proposals to meet debts. If this is unsuccessful, the debtor will return to court and, if the court is satisfied, the debtor will be declared bankrupt.

Private or **public limited companies** face LIQUIDATION. Liquidation can be either compulsory or voluntary, depending upon the circumstances. It involves the appointment of an Official Receiver as a **Liquidator.** This person is responsible for the winding-up of a company, taking control of a company's affairs and gathering assets with a view to finding a buyer. The liquidator is also responsible for paying off any debts the company may have. The law states the order of priority in the payment of debts. For example, payment of taxes comes before payments to firms. Some creditors may receive nothing if the company was heavily in debt.

Figure 35.3 *Insolvencies in England and Wales*

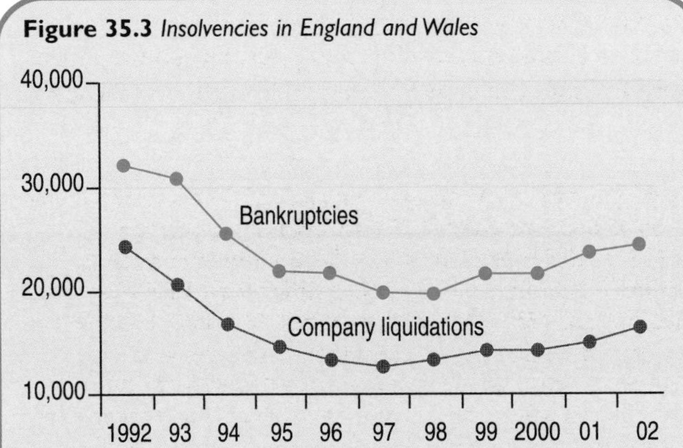

Source: adapted from *Annual Abstract of Statistics*, Office for National Statistics.

Figure 35.4 *Company insolvencies in England and Wales in agriculture*

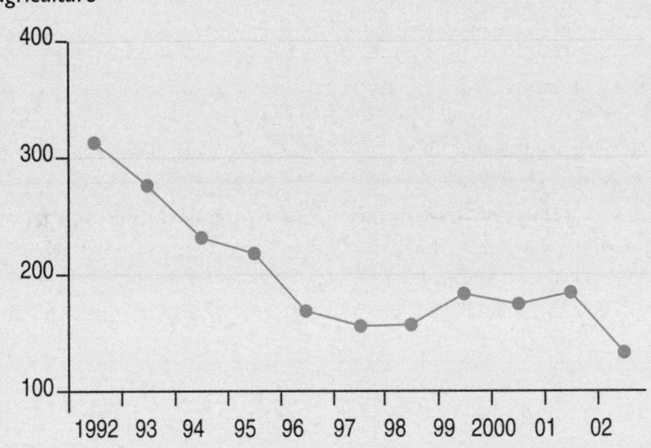

Source: adapted from *Annual Abstract of Statistics*, Office for National Statistics.

(a) Identify the trends taking place in Figure 35.3.
(b) Comment on the likely changes in conditions over the period.
(c) Discuss possible strategies that a business in agriculture might have considered in 1997.

key terms

Bankruptcy - declared by a court when a sole trader or partnership cannot meet its debts.
Liquidation - declared by a court when a company is unable to meet its debts.
Official Receiver - the person called in to handle the affairs of a business facing bankruptcy or liquidation.

1. Briefly explain the free market approach to:
   (a) the operation of markets;
   (b) reducing unemployment .
2. Briefly explain the interventionist approach to:
   (a) the operation of markets;
   (b) reducing unemployment.
3. Identify 3 examples of government policy conflicts.
4. State 3 strategies a business might use when interest rates are high.
5. State 3 strategies a business may use when exchange rates are high.
6. State 3 strategies a business might use in periods of high inflation.
7. State 5 ways in which a business might react during a growth period.
8. Why are small firms especially vulnerable to recession?
9. What is the difference between bankruptcy and liquidation?
10. What strategies might a business pursue in order to survive a recession?

Case study Recession and UK manufacturing

In 2002 the UK's manufacturing sector had stagnated, while manufacturing in the euro zone countries showed signs of improvement, according to two surveys. Figures from the Chartered Institute of Purchasing and Supply (CIPS) showed manufacturers suffering their weakest month since July. Companies cut costs to cope with weak markets, which led to a fall in production growth. The CIPS director said that manufacturing activity was likely to stay at current levels for some time. Ciaran Barr of Deutsche Bank said 'It was a little bit of a surprise that it fell. Output is where the damage was done. It shows manufacturers are still facing a tough time and that things don't seem to be improving anytime soon.'

However, Audrey Child-Freeman at CIBC World Markets argued that the news might be more positive. She suggested that the figures confirmed 'for the time being, UK manufacturing is struggling. But a rise in new orders, the most forward looking of the indicators, offered some hope that there were better times ahead'.

Manufacturing in the euro zone exceeded analyst expectations. Strong export demand fuelled the rise in new orders. Robert Lind at ABN Amro in London said the numbers meant the worst of the downturn was over for European industry.

Source: adapted from *The Guardian*, 2.12.2002.

Figure 35.5 *UK interest rates, 2002-03*

Figure 35.6 *UK inflation (% change), 2002-03*

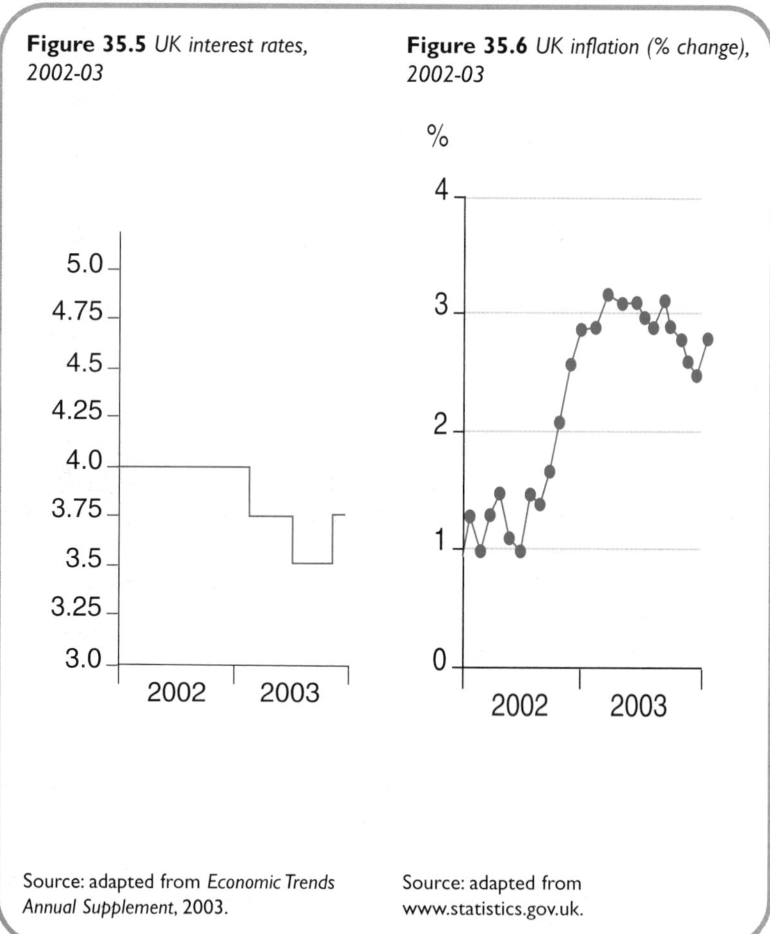

Source: adapted from *Economic Trends Annual Supplement*, 2003.

Source: adapted from www.statistics.gov.uk.

Figure 35.7 *UK pound against the euro, 2002-03*

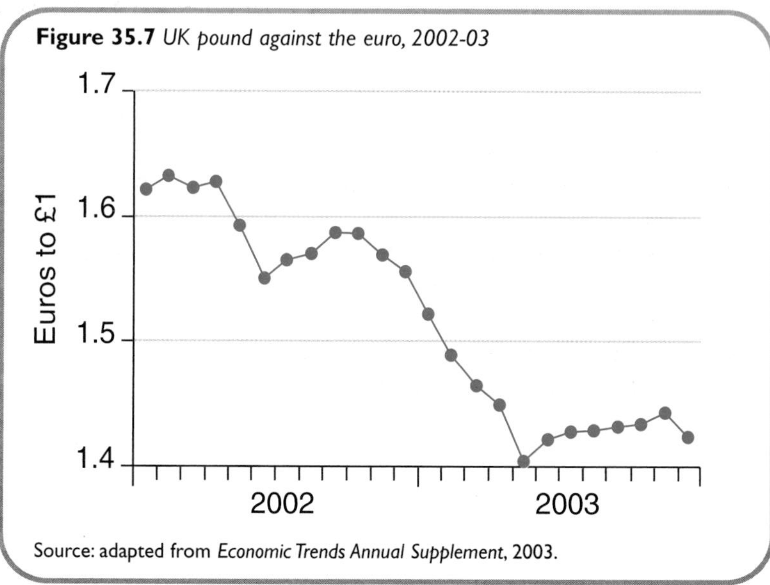

Source: adapted from *Economic Trends Annual Supplement*, 2003.

The Confederation of British Industry (CBI) argued that Britain's manufacturers had lost hope of getting out of recession in late 2002. Profit margins had been squeezed, prices were falling and orders were declining at their fastest pace for three years. The CBI said shrinking order books and a renewed decline in output had dashed the 'pattern of unfounded optimism' from earlier in the year. 'Manufacturers had hopes that life was going to get easier but instead it has become tougher' said Doug Godden, the CBI's head of economic analysis.

The confidence of UK manufacturers fell as total orders declined at their fastest rate since July 1999, with demand weakening at home and abroad. As a result, firms said they would cut spending on plant and machinery for the eighteenth consecutive quarter. Manufacturers also expected to make job cuts. The number of people employed in manufacturing fell by more than 150,000 in the year to June. The CBI projected that a further 33,000 could be laid off in the last three months of 2002.

The CBI was not, at the time, calling for a reduction in interest rates. But it did expect the Bank of England to cut them by half a per cent if the economic climate deteriorated further. The fall in optimism was especially sharp in the aerospace and engineering sectors, although chemicals and metal manufacturers were more confident. Firms making consumer goods managed to record an increase in output, shielded by resilient demand in the household sector.

Source: adapted from *The Guardian*, 24.10.2002.

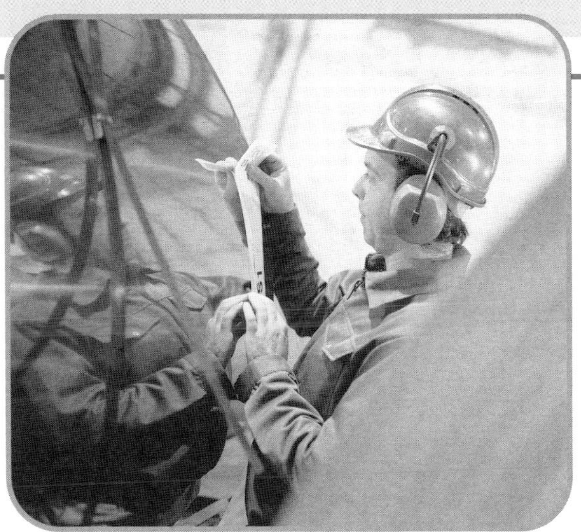

(a) Describe the situation of UK manufacturing in 2002 using examples from the articles. (6 marks)

(b) Suggest factors which may have led to the situation facing UK manufacturers in 2002. (8 marks)

(c) Explain how UK businesses might have reacted to this situation. (12 marks)

(d) Examine reasons why businesses in the eurozone might have been affected differently to UK businesses. (10 marks)

(e) Assess how businesses in the UK might be affected by changes in 2003. (14 marks)

36 The European Union and Business

The European Union

The European Union, then known as the European Economic Community, was set up in 1958. The six member countries (West Germany, France, Italy, Belgium, the Netherlands and Luxembourg) committed themselves, in the Treaty of Rome, to establishing a **Common Market**.

By the late 1990s the EU consisted of 15 countries. They included the original six plus countries such as the UK, Spain, Eire, Greece and Sweden. At that time other countries such as Slovenia, Hungary and Bulgaria were hoping to join in future. On May 1st 2004 ten new countries joined the EU. These countries were Hungary, Poland, the Czech Republic, Slovakia, Slovenia, Estonia, Latvia, Lithuania, Malta and Cyprus.

A COMMON MARKET exists when a group of countries forms a CUSTOMS UNION, with free trade between member countries, and establish a common external tariff on imports of goods and services from outside. Free trade should take place in goods and services, as well as factors of production such as land, labour and capital. For example, it should be possible for a worker from Denmark to work in Newcastle on the same terms as in her home country. Also, a German company should be able to buy land in London to develop offices. In practice, the free movement of factors of production has proved a lot more difficult than mobility of goods and services.

A common external tariff is placed on all imports into a customs union. If tariffs were different for different EU countries, this might lead to problems. Say Germany had a 10 per cent tariff and France a 20 per cent tariff. An American firm exporting to France could bring products in through Germany, paying the lower tariff, and then import them into France paying no extra tax. To avoid this, a common external tariff harmonises all tariffs on imports. This means the tariff is the same for imported products into all member countries.

There are some advantages to businesses operating in countries belonging to a customs union or common market.

- Firms operating within customs unions have free access to markets which would otherwise be protected by tariffs or quotas. In this way British firms, for example, have access to all other EU markets.
  For many firms this provides them with the opportunity to operate in EU markets in much the same way that they would at home. A Blackburn based firm would operate in Berlin or Bilbao in much the same way as it would in Brighton or Birmingham.
- Firms will have access to the most appropriate factors of production. A British firm might purchase cheap land in Southern Portugal for a new factory location, skilled designers from Italy or capital equipment from France.
- Customs unions provide firms with large markets to sell to. The bigger the market a firm is selling to, the greater the economies of scale it is able to benefit from.
- Businesses operating within a common market will be protected from competition from outside this area by an external business. Such protection allows businesses to be sheltered from the potentially damaging effects of competition such as price wars.
- Increased competition from European firms may act as an incentive for British firms to increase efficiency and standards.

There are, however, disadvantages for businesses operating within a customs union or common market.

- Before Britain joined the EU, British firms could buy goods and services from the lowest cost producers around the world. Foodstuffs were imported in huge quantities from New Zealand and the USA in this way. Since joining the EU, however, British firms have had to pay far more for foodstuffs from New Zealand and Australia because of the common external tariff.
- Whilst a British based firm will have free access to other EU markets, businesses based in these markets will also have access to the UK market. Such competition may reduce the market share which domestic businesses have established.
- Protection from external tariffs is not always beneficial to firms operating from within a common market. This is because being sheltered from external competition may result in less incentive for a firm to become more efficient. In the long run, this may lead to a deterioration in the firm's performance.

P Clark Ltd, a Stafford based firm specialising in the manufacture of hi-tech exercise machines, had enjoyed enormous success in the US market with its rowing machines and running tracks. However, it could not have failed to notice a fall in its share of the UK market as a result of competition from Italian and French firms.

It had been poised to enter the European market for over a year, but had been held up by recurrent production difficulties which meant that it could barely satisfy the demand for its products in the UK and US markets. With free access to EU markets, and unlike in the US no tariff barriers to overcome, it had begun planning for the launch of its products in Europe. Its initial plan was to increase production by 50 per cent. If successful, its long term plan was to open a new manufacturing and distribution plant in a suitable EU location.

(a) In what ways will P Clark be able to benefit from operating within a common market?
(b) What problems has operating from within a common market brought it?

- Firms may have to adapt their marketing strategies to suit the needs of consumers in each country within the customs union. For example, surveys have found that of the thousands of products commonly sold in European supermarkets, only a small proportion are widely on sale in identical format in at least the four largest countries.

EU policies and business

The European Union has economic policies which are designed to help businesses within member countries. These policies vary from employee protection and consumer protection to transport and energy policies. Here we will concentrate on three policies and their effects on business.

The Common Agricultural Policy (CAP) This policy operates in all EU countries and accounted for approximately half of the EU's £60 billion budget in 2003. Article 39 of the Treaty of Rome states 5 objectives of agricultural policy:

- to increase the productivity of agriculture;
- to ensure a fair standard of living for farmers;
- to stabilise markets;
- to guarantee supplies;
- to ensure fair prices.

The CAP aims to achieve this. Farmers are guaranteed a fixed minimum price by the EU for their produce. The EU will buy up any amount that farmers produce at this price. Farmers could, of course, always sell on world markets if the market price was higher. If the market price drops below the minimum, however, CAP maintains the price to farmers, thus guaranteeing their income.

For farmers the CAP guarantees them a price for their produce so that they are not at the mercy of fluctuations in price. This means that fewer farmers will go out of business during difficult years and, to some extent, their incomes will be guaranteed.

The CAP has a number of problems associated with it.

- Overproduction. The setting of high, guaranteed prices has often caused excess supplies of a variety of agricultural products. Any excess supply is purchased by EU authorities. They prevent it from being sold on markets by storing it, resulting in butter mountains, wine lakes etc.
- High prices. The minimum price set by the EU for agricultural products as part of CAP is very often higher than the price which would have resulted without their intervention. It is consumers and businesses such as food retailers who suffer as a result of these high prices.
- Purchasing excess supplies of agricultural products is expensive for the EU. It is possible that the money spent on this could be better diverted to projects such as providing grants to firms engaged in producing new high technology products.
- The EU cannot use all its agricultural products, so it sells them cheaply to developing countries. This undercuts farmers in developing countries who are unable to compete with heavily subsidised imports.
- 70 per cent of CAP's funds go to only 20 per cent of Europe's farms. Small farmers are the main losers in this. The biggest beneficiaries have been larger farmers. For example, in the UK in 2002 five farms received more than £1 million per year in subsidies.

Attempts have been made to reform the CAP. In order to prevent over production farmers are now paid to 'set aside' land and to leave it fallow. In addition, reforms have made to encourage farmers to produce what the market requires rather than paying them to produce crops that are already overproduced.

The Regional Fund This provides funds to member states to help reduce unemployment in depressed parts of the EU. It also aims to encourage development in areas on the edge of the EU, such as Southern Italy and Northern Ireland. For example, construction firms may win contracts to build new roads, or industrial units could be financed through the Regional Fund. Similarly, firms may receive investment grants if they locate in particular parts of the EU. This is dealt with in more detail in unit 88

The Social Chapter The **Maastricht Treaty** was signed by all EU member states in December 1992. One section of this treaty is the Social Chapter. The aim of the Social Chapter is to standardise working conditions throughout the EU so that all workers within the community are guaranteed basic rights. These include the following.

- A minimum wage to be paid to all workers.
- A maximum working week.
- A minimum paid holiday per year.
- The freedom to join a union.

In the recent round of Common Agricultural Policy negotiations there were two main pressures on EU ministers. First, there was the issue of the enlargement of the EU to include agricultural economies such as Poland and Slovakia. Hardly anyone believed that the 10 new states could join on the same terms as existing members. Second, the EU was coming under fire during international trade talks for its lavish farm subsidies. These were causing difficulties for farmers in developing countries. During the October 2002 summit to discuss CAP reforms there was a high profile fall out between Tony Blair and the French President Jacques Chirac. Mr Blair reportedly told Mr Chirac that the French concern for Africa would sound hollow if it blocked further CAP reform.

Source: adapted from *The Guardian*, 26.6.2003.

(a) Why might the enlargement of the EU create pressures to reform the CAP?

(b) Explain how farmers in developing countries might be affected by the CAP.

- Access to appropriate training.
- The right to be consulted and informed about company plans.
- The protection of young workers.

The UK initially opted out of the Social Chapter, when all other EU nations signed it. However, the UK signed up to the Social Chapter after the election of a Labour government in 1997. What might be the implications of the Social Chapter for businesses?

- Workers may be better motivated. This should make them more effective and productive employees, able to raise the efficiency of the firm for which they work.
- Industrial relations may improve as employees are involved in making company decisions and consulted about the work which they carry out.
- It may raise the labour costs of those firms currently employing workers at wages below the minimum level set out in the Chapter. Those firms expecting their employees to work longer than maximum may also find their costs rise as they are required to employ more people.
- Higher labour costs may make it more difficult for EU based firms to compete with businesses in low wage countries, such as China or South Korea.

The Single European Market

A major event in the EU's move towards free trade was the signing of the Single European Act in 1986, which established a SINGLE EUROPEAN MARKET which came into being on 31 December 1992. Despite the existence of a customs union for over 30 years, there were still many non-tariff barriers to trade in the EU. This Act aimed to remove those barriers between EU member countries. The effects of this should be to encourage the freer movement of people, goods, services and capital. Three categories of barriers were removed.

- Barriers which prevented entry into markets. For example, differing technical standards were required of products by different member states. This made it difficult for firms to enter certain markets. Also, the practice of public sector contracts being given only to domestic firms prevented free trade.
- Barriers which caused firms' costs to rise. Often complex documents were needed in order to move goods from one country to another. Also, there were long delays waiting to get exports through customs posts.
- Barriers which lead to the market being distorted. Such barriers are said to prevent firms from competing on equal terms. They included differing rates of VAT in EU countries and subsidies given by EU governments to domestic industries.

Not all firms have been affected to the same degree by the Single Market. In some industries, very few barriers to trade existed between EU countries before December 1992. Firms operating in such industries have seen little or no changes to their situation. However, in other industries, where trade barriers were high, the Single Market has resulted in major changes for those firms operating within them. What effects has the Single Market had on firms in member countries?

- Product standards. Firms have, for example, had to alter their products so that they meet new product standards. Many firms have had to improve the safety aspects of their products in order to meet new EU regulations.
- Harmonisation of tariffs and taxes. There have been attempts to harmonise VAT rates throughout the EU. For businesses this may mean that the selling prices of their products rise or fall in line with VAT rate changes. In the UK, a number of products such as childrens' clothes and books, which had previously not attracted any VAT, were faced with the prospect of this tax if the UK was to fall into line with other EU countries. Attempts have also been made to harmonise EXCISE DUTIES on products such as petrol, tobacco and spirits. This has affected the price at which these products are sold and, therefore, the businesses marketing them.
- Ease of trading. The reduction in the number of customs posts, and the amount of paperwork which is required for goods traded between EU countries, should save businesses time and reduce costs.

The European Union yesterday condemned Microsoft for an abuse of its near monopoly. It ordered it to change its business practices and pay a record fine of nearly £333 million. After a five year investigation, Mario Monti, the EU Competition Commissioner, said the world's second largest company must now offer its Windows operating system without its digital media player to PC manufacturers. The Windows operating system is found in 90 per cent of PCs worldwide. 'Today's decision restores conditions for fair competition and establishes clear principles', Mr Monti said. 'Dominant companies have a special responsibility to ensure that the way they do business doesn't prevent competition on merit and does not harm consumers and innovation'.

Microsoft's rivals welcomed the decision. Lee Patch, vice president of legal affairs at Sun Microsystems, said the decision would lead to increased competition in the server market. 'We want to be able to have products competing on their merits rather than on the basis of whether they can effectively communicate with Microsoft's desktops,' he said. Microsoft legal counsel Brad Smith said that the company would appeal and the issue is therefore likely to be bogged down in the courts for five years.

Source: adapted from *The Guardian*, 25.3.2004.

(a) Explain why the EU Competition Commissioner might have argued that Microsoft's practice with regard to its media player was an abuse of its dominant position.
(b) Why might the EU wish to promote more competitive practices?

Question 3

The single European currency

EUROPEAN MONETARY UNION (EMU) became a reality in January, 1999 when a single European currency was introduced. At the time, some of the member states of the EU signed up to the single European currency, known as the euro. The UK was not one of them, preferring to leave a decision about whether to join to a later date.

Participating countries fixed their exchange rates so that they could not move against each other and against the euro. On 1st January 2002 actual euro notes and coins were introduced in 12 of the EU's 15 member states at the time. The UK, Denmark and Sweden continued with their own currencies. In the participating countries, known as 'euroland' or the 'euro zone', the old national currencies were withdrawn during the first three months of 2002.

In order to manage the single currency a European Central Bank (ECB), based in Frankfurt, was established. Amongst other things the European Central Bank is responsible for setting interest rates throughout the participating countries.

It has been argued that European Monetary Union will have a number of benefits for businesses within the euro zone.

A reduction in transactions costs It is expensive for a business to change currencies when trading abroad. There are administration expenses in exchanging the currencies and possible charges. The costs of exchanging one currency for another are eliminated if all trading between countries is done in euros. For example, a French business exporting telecommunications equipment to Italy will no longer have to convert Italian lira into French francs. It has been estimated that the savings made from the introduction of the single European currency would be between 0.25 to 0.5 percent of national income for a member country.

A reduction in uncertainty The uncertainties of trading are reduced for those businesses within the euro zone. It has been argued that greater stability within the euro zone would lead to greater confidence amongst businesses, thus leading to more trade between member countries.

One reason for stability is because there is no possibility of exchange rate fluctuations. Fluctuations in exchange rates can make it difficult for importers and exporters to know what price they will receive or have to pay for future transactions. For example, a Spanish business that received the value of 500,000 lire instead of 600,000 for a sale as a result of a fall in the value of the pound will find that its profit margins are cut. Some businesses try to hedge against rising prices by stockpiling stocks of components, which can be expensive.

It is also argued that the control of monetary policy by the ECB is less likely to lead to sudden, large changes in interest rates, for example. The control of interest rates to restrict inflation should also lead to more stable conditions in which businesses may operate. Businesses may also have a greater choice of finance if the euro encourages more investors in stock exchanges.

Transparent prices Pricing all products and services in one currency makes price differentials for products in different countries more obvious. This may show that a company is offering good value for money in the products it is selling. Companies that charge different prices in different countries may decide to reduce their prices to be more competitive, or to round up prices, which may increase profits. Companies will also be able to see the prices of competitors more easily.

Merger activity The introduction of a single currency will make cross-border mergers between businesses in member countries easier. They will each have the same pricing and accounting system, which should help the coordination of the business.

There is, however, a number of potential problems with the single currency for businesses in member countries.

Costs The initial conversion which all businesses needed to make was costly. It affected businesses in a number of ways. Accounting systems changed to take into account the new currency. New pricing led to redesigned packaging, advertising and display material. Staff needed to be trained to use the new currency. In addition, there was a general 'levelling up' of prices as businesses converted their prices from the old national currencies into the euro. Businesses must constantly review prices due to price transparency.

The impact of the ECB The European Central Bank's central role in setting interest rates and controlling monetary policy for all nations within the euro zone could have a damaging effect upon some businesses. This is because the interest rates and monetary policy pursued by the ECB will reflect the needs of the member countries as a whole. If there are inflationary pressures in the euro zone the ECB is likely to pursue tight monetary polices, such as the raising of interest rates. However, there may be particular countries within the euro zone which do not have inflationary pressures, but which are seeking to avoid recession. Such countries would also be subject to tight monetary policies, but for them it would be inappropriate. These policies could help drive these countries into recession with damaging effects for business.

Effects of the euro on non-member countries

Businesses in countries which remained outside the euro zone in the early twenty first century, such as the UK, were far less likely to enjoy the benefits or incur the costs of operating within the zone. There was great debate about whether and under what conditions the UK might join the euro zone in future at the time.

For businesses outside the euro zone, the introduction of the euro has had a number of effects.

- Businesses trading with the member states now have to quote their prices in euros and be able to make transactions in this currency.
- The uncertainties of dealing with a number of different EU nations, all with their own separate currencies, have been reduced.
- There have been some reduction in transactions costs, although not as great as for members' businesses.
- UK businesses selling into the euro zone may be at a competitive disadvantage against competitors that share the same currency.
- The competitiveness of businesses may depend on the value of their country's currency against the euro. For example, if the value of the Swedish krone against the euro fell, this may make Swedish exports to countries in the euro zone more attractive.

It is suggested that the UK businesses most affected by the euro zone are:

- exporters and importers who would need to quote in euros;
- UK multinationals (☞ unit 38) who adopted the euro as their trading currency. This had an effect upon businesses supplying them. It meant that even businesses trading entirely in the UK were asked to price, invoice and accept payment in euros;
- banks who are asked to provide euros, make payments in euros and open euro accounts;
- some retailers, perhaps in tourist areas, who need to quote prices in euros;
- subsidiaries of multinationals in the euro zone who are asked to deal in euros.

The expansion of the EU

On May 1st 2004 the EU expanded to include ten new countries. These were Hungary, Poland, the Czech Republic, Slovakia, Slovenia, Estonia, Latvia, Lithuania, Malta and Cyprus. Figure 36.1 shows details of all members of the EU in 2004.

There is a number of implications of EU expansion.

- All of the new nations seeking membership of the EU are poorer than existing members. This will inevitably place a strain on the EU's budget. Cyprus, for example, the wealthiest of the new member countries, has a national income per head that is a fifth below the EU average. In countries such as Lithuania and Estonia, the differential is significantly greater. The poorer countries may not be in a position to contribute greatly to EU funds, whilst requiring large amounts in payments to help their development. This could affect businesses operating in existing EU countries.
- By including countries such as Poland, Slovakia and Malta in the EU there may need to be significant changes to policies. Many of the new member countries have economies that are more agriculturally based than those of existing members. The CAP may need to change to prevent large sums being paid to economies that are more agriculturally based.
- Enlargement will increase the size of the EU market from

Figure 36.1 *EU members and countries joining in 2004 (including GDP per capita*)*

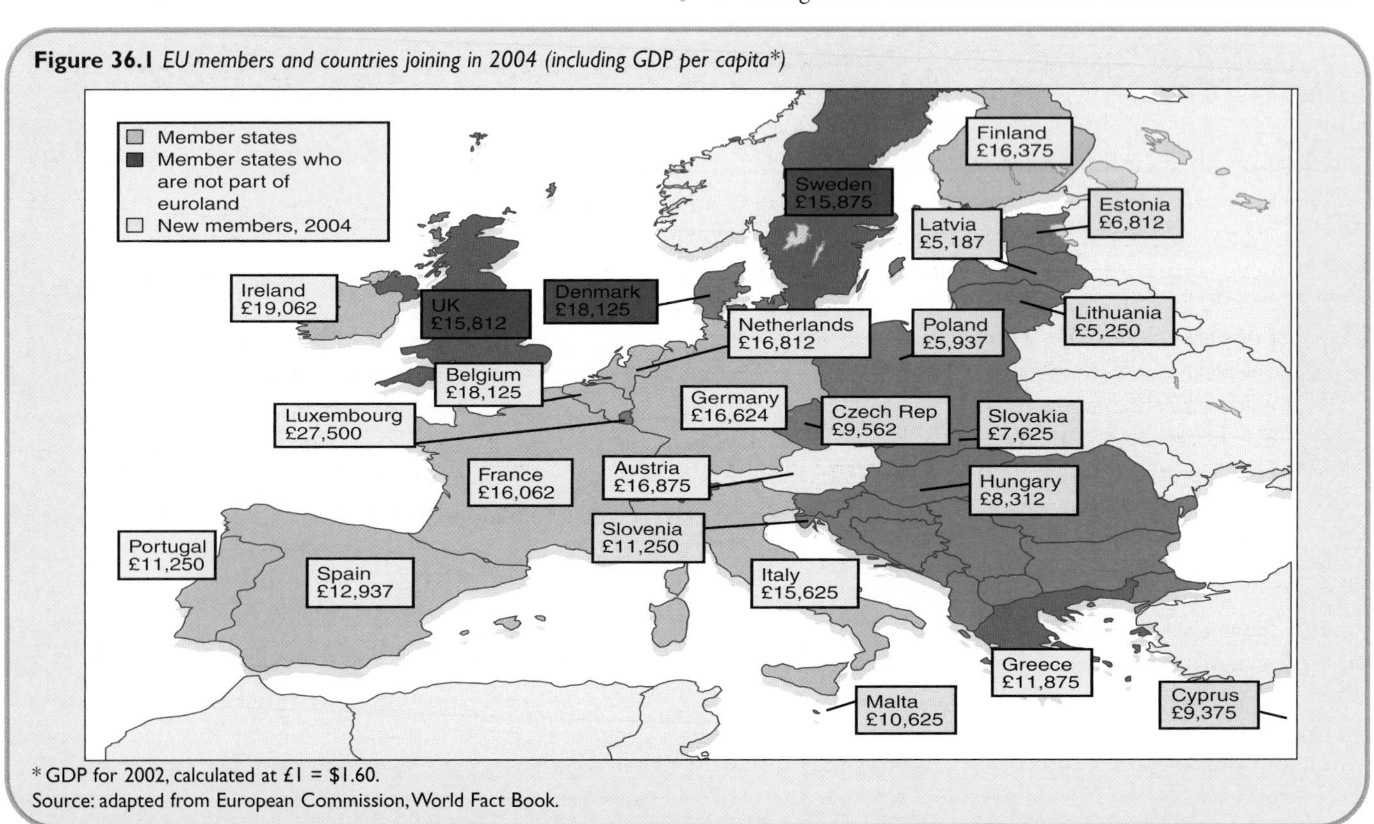

*GDP for 2002, calculated at £1 = $1.60.
Source: adapted from European Commission, World Fact Book.

370 million to 450 million. This will provide a huge increase in the potential number of customers for many EU businesses and offer further opportunities for them to enjoy economies of scale.

- Including eastern European countries within the EU should generate greater economic and political stability within them. This will provide improved investment opportunities within these countries for existing EU businesses.
- The eventual adoption of the euro by these countries could lead to major benefits. The area would also operate as a strong trading bloc with the rest of the world.
- Many more countries will now be involved in the decision making process involving EU regulations and legislation. Such legislation affecting employees and employers will now need to take into account the concerns of many. This might affect the type and style of regulation. The decision making process is likely to become more involved, which may lead to delays.

key terms

CAP - the Common Agricultural Policy of the European Community. It is designed to stabilise EC agricultural markets by fixing minimum prices for agricultural products.

Customs union/Common market - a group of countries with free trade between them and a common external tariff.

European Monetary Union - the adoption of a single currency by members of the EU.

Excise duties - taxes levied on fuel, alcohol, tobacco and betting.

Single European Market - an agreement by EU countries to remove all barriers to trade.

Knowledge...Knowledge...Knowledge

1. Why is the EU said to be a customs union?
2. What is the Common Agricultural Policy?
3. What changes have occurred as a result of the Single Market?
4. State 5 implications of the Single Market for British businesses.
5. State 3 benefits of a single currency for businesses in member countries.
6. State 2 problems of a single currency for businesses in member countries.
7. Explain 3 effects that the single European currency might have on businesses in non-member countries.
8. What effects might EU enlargement have on businesses in existing member countries?

Case study EU enlargement and UK businesses

Countries joining the EU in 2004 have been identified as targets for businesses in the East Midlands. In a report on new business opportunities, the regional development agency, Emda, highlighted Poland, Estonia, Latvia and Lithuania, and future candidates such as Romania. The main industries recommended for targeting were environmental technologies and food processing. The report urges quick action in new countries where opportunities exist. Emda's EU enlargement projects manager, Helen Whitehead, said 'There will be greater potential to export to the accession states, but because forging relationships with local partners is often fundamental to winning business, there's real mileage in developing a presence there sooner rather than later'.

Source: adapted from news.bbc.co.uk, 23.4.2004.

In 2003 it was announced that Stansted would get two new runways as part of the government's 30 year plan for air travel in the UK. Expansion was to cope with the increasing amount of air traffic expected to come through the UK. A sixth terminal at Heathrow was also being considered, although a series of environmental conditions would have to be met to keep within EU limits on pollution.

Source: adapted from news.bbc.co.uk, 16.12.2003.

It has been estimated that the UK could gain as many as 80,000 nurses under EU expansion. Up to 20 per cent of nursing staff from countries joining the EU could decide to come to the UK for better pay. The increase in the UK's nursing workforce could stop the rising cost of agency staff, used to fill vacant posts in hospitals. However, nursing leaders in Europe argue that the transfer of staff could lead to major difficulties in the new EU member states, many of which could have staffing shortages of their own.

Source: adapted from *The Guardian*, 20.4.2004.

The Lovebytes digital arts festival in Sheffield is the longest-running event of its kind in Britain. It has grown from an afternoon of presentations in a converted garage, to a six-week-long internationally renowned event of digital art and culture. The festival largely continues because of EU funding. But with EU expansion, the worry is that the financial support the festival receives will move to Eastern Europe.

Source: adapted from *The Guardian*, 13.3.2003.

According to one study, the gain of EU expansion to the existing EU countries will be about £6 billion and approximately £15 billion to the newcomers of EU enlargement. The Home Office, however, believed that 5,000-13,000 people a year would enter the UK from new member states. There was criticism by some that large numbers of workers from new member states would flood into the UK, claiming benefits. The government acted by introducing restrictions. For example, migrants from the new member states will have to get a work registration certificate from their employers, rather than applying for work permits before they arrive in Britain. It was suggested that this would allow the government to monitor whether the numbers were getting too big and will pave the way for identity cards, which would be issued to all EU nationals living in the UK.

Source: adapted from *The Guardian*, 23.2.2004 and www.bbc.co.uk, 23.2.2004.

The new member states were bracing themselves for the impact of UK travellers in 2004. Previously UK airlines wanting to fly into these European countries had to complete mountains of bureaucracy to obtain a licence. 'This is all swept away come 1 May,' explained a spokesperson for the Civil Aviation Authority. An expanded free trade zone would create cut throat competition and low prices to attract the punters. In April, EasyJet planned to launch flights from Britain to Budapest in Hungary and Ljubljana in Slovenia, with prices starting from as little as £6.99 one way.

Source: adapted from *The Guardian*, 29.2.2004.

In September 2003 Sweden rejected the euro by 56 - 44 per cent. The rejection in Sweden also makes it less likely that Britain and Denmark will scrap their own currencies. It opens up the prospect of a two-speed, or even multi-speed, Europe, in which some share a currency, others defence policies, and others border controls or perhaps environmental standards.

Source: adapted from *The Guardian*, 2.9.2003.

(a) How might the decision by Sweden affect businesses in that country? (6 marks)

(b) Explain how being a member of the EU affects UK businesses using examples from the articles. (12 marks)

(c) Examine how EU enlargement might affect:

(i) businesses in the UK; (10 marks)

(ii) businesses in the new member countries. (10 marks)

(d) Discuss to what extent further enlargement of the EU might be in the interests of UK businesses. (12 marks)

37 International Competitiveness and Business

Business competitiveness in international markets

Unit 36 explained how the European Union might affect businesses in member and non-member countries. This unit examines the effects of international trading in other areas around the world and the effects of trading conditions on businesses. There is a number of factors that might influence the competitiveness of businesses trading in international markets.

The existence of trade barriers Some countries and groups of countries, known as TRADING BLOCS, such as the EU (☞ unit 36), erect trade barriers. These are designed to prevent businesses based outside the trading areas from competing with those who are members of the trading area.

Tariffs, a tax on imports, are one form of restriction. The effect of a tariff on products exported to countries which impose them is to increase the price charged by businesses or to lower their profit margins.

Quotas may also be used, which restrict the amount of a product that can be exported to a particular country or trading bloc. For individual businesses, quotas can mean that they can only export small quantities of their products, or indeed none at all, to countries which impose them. It is easier for businesses exporting abroad to compete with local businesses when they do not have to pay a tariff or have quotas imposed upon them.

The costs of production For some businesses their ability to compete in international markets depends upon their ability to have the same or lower costs of production than their international competitors. Lower costs of production allow businesses to have lower prices and therefore undercut their competitors. Because of the importance of labour costs these have traditionally been taken to indicate the competitiveness of a country and the businesses operating within it.

The behaviour of businesses Keeping production costs low and matching or beating competitors' prices are important in many markets. However, it is increasingly the view of business commentators such as Michael Porter that competitiveness in international markets depends upon how businesses behave. Competitiveness may depend on the extent to which businesses innovate and produce new products desired by consumers. Those businesses which produce quality goods and services, which meet the needs of consumers and stand out from those offered by competitors, are likely to be successful in international markets. The ability of businesses to produce innovative products and make good use of new technology will depend on their ability to recruit and train suitable employees.

Trading agreements In certain international markets, trade agreements regulate competition. For example, countries may belong to The World Trade Organisation, which is committed to increasing free trade. This is discussed in the next section. Another example is Mercosur, a free trade area agreed between Brazil, Paraguay, Argentina and Uruguay.

Ten South-East Asian countries signed an accord to turn their very different states into an integrated, tariff free trading and economic community by 2020. It will resemble the European Union in its earlier years.

At a summit, on the Indonesian resort island of Bali, the Association of South-East Asian Nations (ASEAN) agreed to eliminate tariff and non tariff barriers, standardise customs procedures, gradually reduce capital controls and abolish visas in a region that is home to 500 million people. The member states of ASEAN are Brunei, Indonesia, Thailand, the Philippines, Malaysia, Singapore, Cambodia, Burma and Vietnam.

In a further development at the summit the ASEAN agreed to complete deals with China, India and Japan by 2012. The pact with China would create by far the world's largest free trade zone.

Source: adapted from *The Guardian*, 8.10.2003.

(a) Identify the changes taking place in the article which might affect international competitiveness.
(b) Explain how these changes might affect businesses in ASEAN nations.

Developed economies

Western Europe and, in particular, the EU (☞ unit 36) is an important market for British firms. However, there are many other parts of the world which are significant trading partners for the UK. Particularly important are the US, Japan and Canada. They provide large export markets and have rival firms operating in the UK market. The way these countries trade with the UK and the EU is largely determined by two organisations - the G7/G8 countries and the World Trade Organisation.

G7/G8 countries The G7 (Group of seven) nations are the seven leading industrial countries - Germany, Japan, US, UK, France, Italy and Canada. Between them they are responsible for over two-thirds of the world's total output, and a similar proportion of its expenditure. Their main aim is to promote growth in the world economy. In 2002 Russia became a full member, and the group is now referred to as the G8 countries.

The success of G8 nations in reaching agreements has implications for firms trading in all parts of the world. For example, the break-up of G8 nations into rival trading groups centred around Europe, North America and the Pacific Rim could lead to a reduction in the quantity of goods and services traded. This may result in a reduction in business opportunities for firms. The failure of G8 nations to reach agreement on promoting economic growth could have similar effects.

Trading agreements between non-EU G8 nations can also affect EU-based firms. For example, the US, Canada and Mexico formed the North American Free Trade Agreement (NAFTA). This is a regional trading bloc similar to the EU. Such regional trade blocs place barriers in the way of external firms seeking to export into them. Trade barriers of this kind can be damaging to firms wishing to enter such markets.

The World Trade Organisation (WTO) The WORLD TRADE ORGANISATION (WTO) was set up in 1995. Its aim is to promote free trade and to prevent protectionist measures by member countries. The WTO is made up of 147 countries (in 2004) that account for around 90 per cent of world trade. It has a number of roles, including being responsible for policing the world trade system. For example, it has annual reviews and also oversees individual members' trade policies.

All countries that join the WTO must agree to abide by its decisions. At the heart of the WTO system (known as the multilateral trading system) are agreements which are negotiated and signed by the majority of the world's trading nations. These agreements are the legal rules for international commerce. They are like contracts which guarantee member countries important trade rights. They also force governments to keep their trade policies within agreed limits.

Major conferences held by the WTO can last for years. At these conferences negotiations take place and agreements are made on major policies to promote trade. For example:

- the Uruguay Round, signed in 1995, agreed to phase out the 'multi-fibre agreement' which had previously protected the textiles industries of certain countries, removed voluntary export restraint and introduced rules on intellectual property rights, such as copyright and patents, to prevent them being copied;
- the DOHA Agenda in Qatar, which was due to end by January 2005, discussed anti-dumping rules to prevent cheap goods flooding developing countries, trade issues relating to e-commerce and tariff cutting for example.

The reason the WTO is important is because of its potential for increasing the amount of trade in the world. Such an increase in trade, many believe, can lead to greater prosperity. Indeed, the increase in the wealth of many nations has, perhaps, been due to the success of the WTO in lowering trade barriers. There are concerns that, without the WTO, the world could divide up into trading blocs resulting in a reduction in trade and possibly a worldwide depression. For individual firms, the WTO makes it more likely that they can operate in export markets on equal terms with locally based companies.

Japan and the USA Many of the world's largest and most famous businesses, such as Exxon Mobil, Toyota and Microsoft, are based in Japan and the USA. In addition to these famous large businesses there are many small and medium sized businesses producing innovative and highly sought after products. Despite a severe economic problems in the late 1990s and early twentieth century, the growth of the Japanese economy in the post war years was arguably the most dramatic economic miracle of the twentieth century. The USA has the largest economy in the world. For UK businesses this means that non-EU developed economies represent both opportunities and threats.

- Opportunities. These arise because the income levels in these countries and the size of their markets provide numerous openings for UK businesses.
- Threats. These arise because many businesses based in non-EU developed nations are renowned for their innovation, use of new technology and general ability to gain a competitive advantage over rivals. Consequently, businesses originating in these countries are able to challenge UK businesses both in domestic and international markets.

Eastern Europe

The fall of the communist governments of eastern Europe and the countries' attempts to move to market economies in the 1990s and early twentieth century presented many opportunities for UK and EU businesses.

Countries such as the Czech Republic, Russia, Poland and Hungary have introduced the operation of markets into their economies. In 1992, East Germany united with West Germany to form one country. This meant that businesses in the former East Germany were faced with the prospect of competing in a market economy with domestic and foreign businesses.

Prior to the dramatic economic changes of the 1990s, most products in this part of the world were provided by state-owned monopolies. These were protected from overseas competition by trade barriers. Today, most of these state-owned monopolies have been privatised and investment from foreign firms is positively encouraged.

A number of eastern European countries joined the EU in 2004 (☞ unit 36). Those countries which were new members of the EU, such as Poland and Latvia, may grow and develop in ways which are different to the eastern European countries such as Russia, Bulgaria, Romania and Hungary that remained outside the EU.

For British firms, the changes in eastern Europe have presented a number of opportunities. Many UK firms see these economies as largely untapped export markets for their products.

- The opening up of these markets has provided western-based firms with access to a huge number of consumers. They can be used as a manufacturing base for western firms, taking advantage of workforces and land prices which are relatively cheaper than those in western Europe.

Russian companies in the market for 'juice' were expecting an increasing threat from foreign multinationals in 2004. Attracted by the potential for growth and recovery from the financial crisis of the late 1990s, they were slowly returning to eastern Europe.

Multinationals have the financial 'clout' that local businesses cannot compete with. But they must have the right strategy. In Russia, for example, multinationals tend to sell to the 'super premium sector'. This has more limited demand, restricted to higher income consumers in major cities. Examples of businesses setting up included the following.

- Coca-Cola started local production of Minute Maid in 2002 in Ukraine, reducing its production costs and making it a more price-competitive option. It was in direct competition to Wimm Bill Dann (WBD), the Russian market leader. In Russia, the company added more flavours to its locally produced Minute Maid range in order to attract a wider range of consumers.
- In Hungary, PepsiCo launched its Toma fruit juice brand in 2001.
- In 2002, the Russian company Nidan-Ekofruct became the official distributor of Capri-Sonne juice drinks, bottled under the license from German company Wild.
- In 2002, Danone took a 4 per cent shareholding of WBD when it floated in New York.

It was estimated that the growing health trend and the impact of multinationals would raise juice sales by around 58 per cent between 2003-2008. The joining of the EU by countries such as Poland and Czech Republic was expected to raise levels of disposable income and living standards in the region. As a result it was predicted that consumers would buy better quality juices.

Source: adapted from www.euromonitor.com.

(a) Examine how changes in eastern Europe might affect:
(i) eastern European businesses;
(ii) multinationals from countries such as the UK.

Question 2

- There are opportunities for joint ventures (☞ unit 29) with former state-owned firms. This allows British and other western firms to combine their international business skills with local knowledge of markets and trading conditions.
- Businesses and individual entrepreneurs have the opportunity to sell their expertise and skills to Eastern European businesses.

Although there are many opportunities for UK businesses in eastern Europe, some businesses based in these countries also represent an increasing threat. Countries such as the Czech Republic adapted more effectively to the demands of a market economy than other countries. Consequently, the businesses based in more successful former communist countries are beginning to rival their western counterparts. This is a trend which is likely to continue in future years.

There is also a number of problems with trading in eastern Europe.

Bureaucracy Many of the institutions and regulations under the old planned system are still in existence. These can present a number of obstacles. For example, there are huge delays in receiving permits and licences for western businesses wishing to set up and trade in some of these countries. With membership of the EU, many of the former bureaucratic obstacles may no longer exist for the new EU member countries.

Political instability Since their transition to market economies, there has been political instability in a number of these countries. This ranges from full scale war, as in Bosnia and Kosovo, to weak and fragile governments. Such instability may be off-putting for potential business investors. They may argue that their businesses are unlikely to flourish in the 'turmoil' which results from such instability. Many believe that membership of the EU will create greater stability in the new eastern European member states (☞ unit 36).

Low incomes Although eastern Europe represent a huge potential market for western-based businesses, opportunities are likely to be limited whilst average incomes remain low. The bulk of the population of these countries is unlikely to be able to afford many of the products manufactured by western-based firms. This could, however, be less of a problem over time if businesses in these countries develop and earnings increase.

Infrastructure The INFRASTRUCTURE of a country includes roads, railways, schools, airports, hospitals and office accommodation. In many ways the infrastructure of the eastern European nations is of a high standard. For example, the hospitals and public transport in some of these countries are better than those found in some western countries. However, there are also problems. Poor telecommunication systems, banking services and law enforcement are all problems which may affect the prospects of western firms.

Developing economies

These economies are almost always found in the southern hemisphere. They are often known as 'the South', Third World Countries, developing countries or low and middle income countries.

Their main features are that they have poorly developed infrastructures and low average incomes per head of population. However, it is difficult to place countries in the South into one single group. This is because some have developed a wide range of industries which can compete with those in the West. Such countries are sometimes known as the Newly Industrialised Countries (NICs). Others are hardly developing at all. They continue to struggle with a range of economic and social problems on a scale almost unimaginable in the west.

The Newly Industrialised Countries (NICs) Many of these countries are found in South East Asia and include Singapore, South Korea and Malaysia. Others are in South and Central America, including Mexico and Brazil. Such countries have been developing home-grown businesses with products which are increasingly able to compete in the domestic markets in the west. Examples include Proton cars from Malaysia, Daewoo from South Korea and Creative Technology from Singapore. In addition, multinational companies (☞ unit 38) that locate their production facilities in NICs can take advantage of their relatively cheap wage costs. Businesses in NICs, therefore, present competition to Western companies on two fronts.

- Undercutting the costs of western producers.
- Companies based in SE Asia are expanding via takeovers or via inward investment into western countries where their imports have reduced the strength of the competition.

These countries have also experienced a rise in overall income levels. As a result, they now provide significant export markets for western produced consumer goods.

Low income countries Most of these countries are to be found in Africa and some parts of Asia and Central America as shown in Figure 37.1. For western businesses, such countries can either provide a base for manufacturing products or act as potential export markets. The infrastructure of such countries, however, is often poor. It can be difficult for multinational companies to establish manufacturing facilities. For example, the road system may be limited. Income levels may be low. Export opportunities for most western firms might be limited to providing goods to very small sections of the population who enjoy western incomes and lifestyles.

Many of these poorer countries are crippled by debt arising from balance of payment deficits and loans which they had been given by western banks and governments. This means that they are required to make large, regular payments to western banks. As a result, despite the aid which is given by those in the richer North, there is a net outflow of money.

Despite these problems, many western-based businesses continue to operate in these countries. They represent an enormous market. The majority of the world's population lives in these countries and they can provide low cost facilities. Unfortunately, such business activities have often attracted bad publicity.

- Some western businesses have provided aid for military goods or inappropriate projects, such as enormous hydro-electric schemes, which are unlikely to meet the needs of the majority of the population.
- Some companies have been accused of acting unethically by persuading poor consumers to purchase goods which can be harmful, such as drugs banned in the West.
- Large multinationals (☞ unit 38) are said to exploit cheap labour and raw materials and provide little in return.

China

In the period between 2000 and 2004 the Chinese economy experienced rapid growth. China for many years was a centrally planned economy. In the early twenty first century there were still elements of a command economy and government control and involvement in the economic system, including The People's Central Bank, a fixed/managed

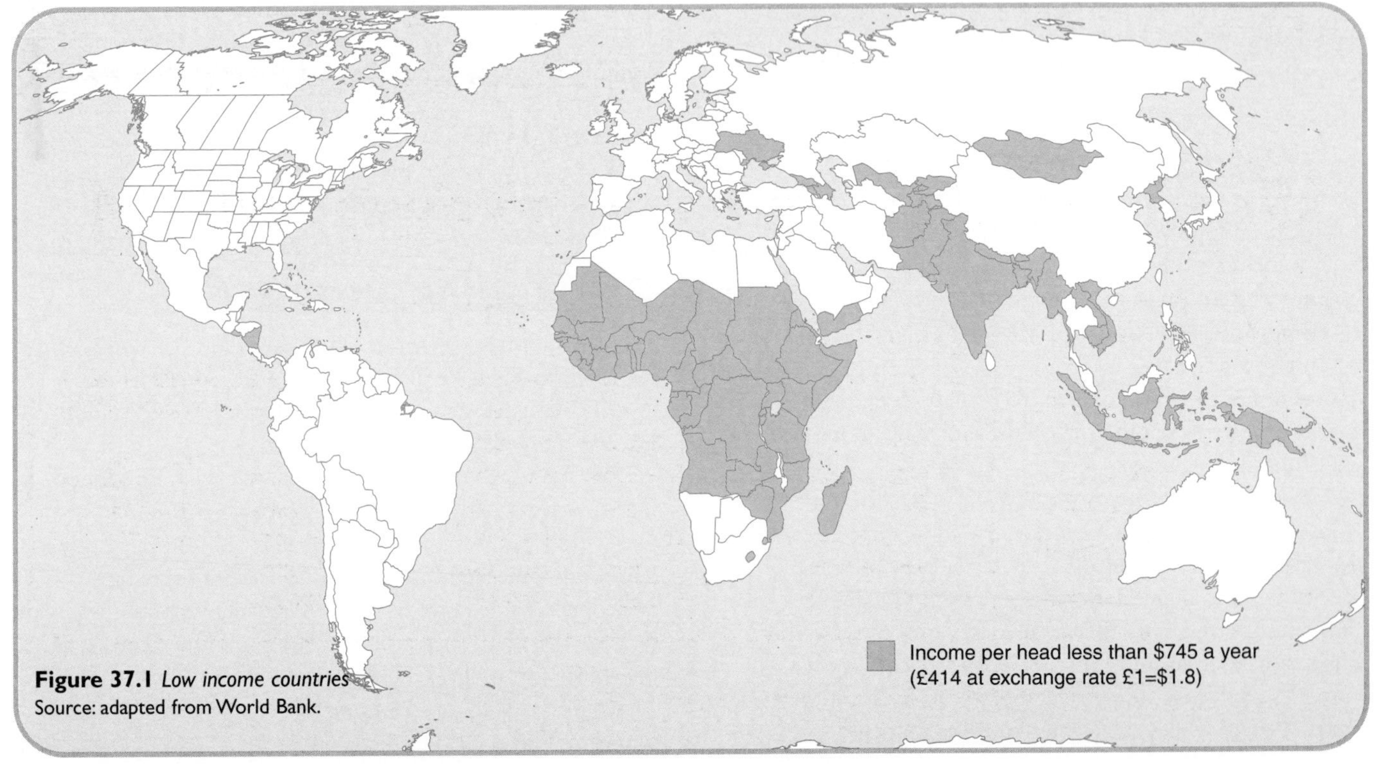

Figure 37.1 *Low income countries*
Source: adapted from World Bank.

floating exchange rate, high levels of government expenditure and control by the Communist Party. However, the economy has been opened up to competition, foreign businesses have been allowed to invest in the country and private property was being debated. This has led to growing exports, internal investment from overseas and rapid economic growth. In 2004 it was estimated that exports were growing by 20 per cent a year and economic growth was around 9 per cent.

Some of the challenges facing the country at the time were:

- to maintain the rapid growth without overheating the economy;
- to balance the growth, which had led to a widening distribution of income and problems for poorer sectors such as agriculture;
- to ensure minimum standards of health and education;
- to decide if the currency would be allowed to float freely in future.

1. Why is the EU said to be a trading bloc?
2. Explain 4 facts that may affect the competitiveness of business in international markets.
3. What is the aim of the G8 group of countries?
4. How might the work of the WTO affect trade between businesses?
5. What opportunities have the changes in Eastern Europe presented for British firms?
6. What problems exist in poorer countries which can make it difficult for Western firms to operate within them?

Question 3

Farmers in the EU and US are given production subsidies and income support for producing their agricultural products. One consequence of this is the overproduction in these countries of a range of goods such as wheat, rice, sugar, cotton and dairy products. These overproduced goods are then dumped in developing countries at a price lower than their cost of production. This has the effect of undercutting local farmers and has led to the destitution of millions of farms in developing countries. At a meeting of the World Trade Organisation in Cancun, Mexico, 17 influential developing countries including Brazil, India and China called for an end to the dumping of goods at below cost price.

Source: adapted from *The Guardian*, 7.9.2003.

(a) Explain why farmers in developing countries might struggle to compete with farmers in the EU and the USA.

key terms

Infrastructure - those aspects of a country which support its economy. These include schools, roads, airports, telecommunication systems, hospitals etc .

NICs - Newly Industrialised Countries. These are countries such as Singapore, Malaysia and Mexico which have recently gone through the process of industrialisation.

Trading blocs - countries that join together to restrict trade from countries outside the bloc.

World Trade Organisation - an organisation which seeks to promote free trade between nations and monitors world trade.

Case study Business in Asia in 2003/04

Table 37.1 *China's exports*

1982:	$22.32bn
1992:	$84.92bn
1998:	$207.24bn
2001:	$266.15bn
2002:	$325.56bn

Source: adapted from World Bank.

Table 37.2 *Top foreign investors (2002)*

Hong Kong*	$373bn	Germany	$14.3bn
USA	$76bn	Macao*	$10.8bn
Taiwan*	$61.5bn	Canada	$10bn
Virgin Islands	$49.3bn	Cayman Islands	$9.5bn
Japan	$49bn	Netherlands	$9bn
Singapore	$40.1bn	France	$7.2bn
S.Korea	$27.5bn	Malaysia	$6bn
UK	$19.6bn	Others	$6.3bn

* Officially part of Republic of China.

Source: adapted from Chinese Ministry of Commerce.

The world is transfixed by China. In a few days in 2004:

- Korea's INI Steel Company launched a $500 million steel project in the Dalian development zone;
- France's Saint Gobain invested another $70 million in one of its existing glass production lines;
- Germany's Siemens opened its fortieth office in China, to develop software applications in Nanjing, and warned that it could shift thousands of jobs from Europe and America to China;
- Finnish paper giant Stora Enso invested $1.6 billion in a pulp-paper project in South China.

In the past businesses had struggled to make profit in China, but not now. For example, microprocessors made previously were the wrong type and sales were poor as a result. In 2004 Infineon, the giant German producer, makes plenty of profit. As a result China will get 30 per cent of the German firm's $1.2 billion investment total over the next three years.

What makes China special? Size is one thing - it has 1.3 billion people and a $1.23 trillion economy. Its middle class is growing and consumption is booming. There is also low inflation, cheap and plentiful labour, urbanisation driving demand, and a savings rate of 30 per cent providing easy capital. It is said that 'China is a manufacturer's dream'.

Source: adapted from news.bbc.co.uk, 19.2.2004.

A US report in 2004 said that China had made great strides since joining the WTO in 2001. But deregulation had stopped and in many sectors import barriers made it difficult for foreign businesses to operate in China. Tariffs had been reduced but officials were accused of tweaking technical standards on issues such as safety or packaging to the detriment of foreign firms. Counterfeiting and piracy also took place as intellectual property rights were still inadequate.

Source: adapted from news.bbc.co.uk, 1.4.2004.

In 2003 the Sars virus terrified millions in Asia and threatened the economies of several nations in the region. Although the disease originated in China, consumers in Japan and other Asian nations were taking no chances as it was suggested that Sars may be airborne. The UN revised its growth forecast for Asia down from 5.4 to 5 per cent, partly because of a fall in tourism caused by Sars. Morgan Stanley estimated that the virus will shave more than $15 billion off the output of Asia's economies. Singapore estimated that Sars could knock one per cent off the island's GDP (worth $875 million). The government in Singapore announced a series of measures for the hardest hit industries. 'It's having a negative impact but people need to put it in perspective' said Gerard Lyons of Standard Chartered Bank. 'In the short term it dents sentiment and it dents spending, but if Sars is contained, the impact could be short term.'

The impact of Sars was felt by airlines that would normally be carrying people to and from China, Hong Kong and Singapore. Potential travellers were staying at home and this was affecting business. For example, Hong Kong carrier Cathay Pacific was forced to cut more than 40 per cent of its flights. The airline business said it was losing $3 million a day while the outbreak persisted.

Hotels were also suffering from the Sars outbreak. Bookings were down and staff at hotels in Hong Kong were being encouraged to take annual leave. In the tourist resort of Phuket in Thailand, hotels faced a 30 per cent fall in demand. In Vietnam, restaurants were asking staff to take early holidays because customers were so reluctant to eat out.

Tourists to Japan used to laugh at the sight of people wearing face masks in the street. But this Japanese custom was increasingly being adopted as a prudent measure elsewhere in Asia as fears of Sars grew around the world. Hakujuji, the face mask business in Japan found its products flying off the shelves. Yoshi Izumi of the company said 'people are buying five or six masks at the same time. Most are families travelling overseas, others work in airports and some have relatives in China where good masks are harder to get hold of.' Profits were being made from the Sars outbreak in other ways. In China, sales of traditional medicines were rising. In Thailand home delivery pizza businesses and shopping websites were getting more business as people did not want to mingle with crowds.

Source: adapted from *The Guardian*, 22.4.2003.

(a) Suggest factors that might have affected businesses in the region in 2002/04. (8 marks)

(b) Analyse how these factors might have affected the international competitiveness of businesses based in:

(i) Asia; (10 marks)

(ii) the EU. (10 marks)

(c) Recommend possible strategies that businesses might take in these situations. (12 marks)

38 Globalisation and Business

What is globalisation?

GLOBALISATION is the term used to describe the growing **integration** of the world's economy. It is suggested that as globalisation takes place, national economies are becoming integrated into a single 'global economy' with similar characteristics. There are interrelationships throughout the world between related businesses, between competitors and between businesses and consumers. Decisions taken in one part of the world affect other parts. Businesses base decisions on what is happening in the 'world market' rather than national markets.

Evidence of the integration of the world's economy can perhaps be seen in businesses that design and market their products to a world market, such as Coca-Cola. This product is sold in many countries throughout the world. Consumers in different countries recognise the product easily and have similar tastes for the product. Coca-Cola is able to market its products worldwide. It has close relationships with businesses in other countries, some of which manufacture Coca-Cola products.

Three important aspects of globalisation might be identified.

The growing importance of international trade Businesses and consumers are increasingly relying on overseas markets and suppliers. Over a six year period between 1997 and 2003 world trade rose by 50 per cent. The value of air freight out of the UK doubled over a 10 year period to 2003.

The rise of the multinational business The operation of multinational companies (MNCS) can be seen in many countries around the world. Familiar products and brand names appear worldwide. Examples might be Microsoft, Nokia, Exxon Mobil, Coca-Cola, PepsiCo, McDonald's, General Motors, Ford, Intel, Sony, Nike and IBM. It has been suggested that multinationals are bigger than some nations. Figures sometimes quoted include 'Fifty one of the world's top 100 economies are corporations' and that 'MNCs make up twenty nine of the world's 100 largest economic entities'. However, there is great debate about the size and impact of multinationals. This is dealt with later in this unit.

The emergence of businesses which think globally about their strategy Such businesses base their strategic decisions (☞ unit 7) on the global market rather than national markets. For example, a business may make parts for a product in several different countries and assemble them in another because this is the most cost effective and efficient method to get the product to its consumers. They will tend to make use of their business's **competitive advantage** by locating production wherever it is most efficient. This means businesses with widely spread networks of research, component production, assembly and distribution. Asea Brown Boveri (ABB), the world's leading supplier of power and automation technology, is an example of a global business. It employed 115,00 people in 2004 and operated in 100 countries around the world.

Factors affecting globalisation

It could be argued that certain factors have contributed to the growth of globalisation.

- Technological change has played an important role in globalising the world's economy. More powerful computers and communications technology have allowed the easy transfer of data. The Internet has revolutionised the way in which consumers purchase products.
- The cost of transportation and communication has fallen. For example, an survey in Australia in 2002 found that over the period 1990-2002 air freight rates declined by 25 per cent. This may have reduced the cost of goods transported to and from the country. The costs of videoconferencing and Internet-related communications have also fallen.
- The deregulation of business. Throughout the 1980s, 1990s and early twenty first century many businesses were privatised in countries throughout the world. In the UK the privatisation of former state owned monopolies allowed competition. The removal of restrictions on foreign businesses operating in eastern European and Asian countries (☞ unit 37) also increased the ability of businesses to operate globally. New markets were opened up to foreign competition.
- The liberalisation of trade. Trade protection has been reduced due to the operation of organisations such as the World Trade Organisation (WTO) (☞ unit 37). For example, reduction of restrictions on trade in textiles is likely to have opened up markets in Asia and the West.
- Consumer tastes and their responses have changed. Consumers in many countries are more willing to buy foreign products. Examples might include cars from Korea and Malaysia which are now purchased in Europe. It could also be argued that consumers around the world increasingly have similar tastes. Some food products are sold in many countries with little difference to their ingredients.
- The growth of emerging markets and competition. New markets have opened up in countries that have seen a growth in their national income. Examples might include countries in South East Asia and the more successful countries in eastern Europe. As businesses in these countries have become more successful, they have been able to compete in western economies.

The Post Office has signed up to an international alliance to deliver business mail around the world. The new venture links the British postal operator with Holland's TPG and Singapore Post in an operation spanning 200 countries and with an initial annual turnover of one billion euros. The Dutch group will take 51 per cent of the venture, while the Post Office and Singapore Post will have 24.5 per cent each. 'This innovative venture heralds a new era in the global mail market by creating the world's largest business mailing partnership' said the Post Office chief John Robertson. The alliance is being put together ahead of the full liberalisation of the market for postal services within the EU in 2003.

Source: adapted from *The Guardian*, 10.3.2000

(a) Explain the likely factors behind the Post Office's decision to form the world's largest business mailing partnership.
(b) Discuss to what extent the market for business mail could be a globalised market.

Question 1

The effects of globalisation on business

Globalisation has had many effects upon businesses throughout the world. The impact of globalisation has not been evenly spread. Some businesses, for example those in telecommunications, have witnessed dramatic changes. Others, such as small businesses serving niche markets in localised areas, may have been little affected by globalisation.

There is a number of effects of globalisation upon businesses. Some provide opportunities whilst others present threats.

Competition The impact of globalisation on many larger businesses has been to dramatically increase the level of competition which they face. There is a number of reasons for this.
- Foreign competition has increasingly entered markets previously served mainly or exclusively by domestic businesses.
- Deregulation has meant that many businesses which previously had little or no competition are now opened up to the forces of global competition. For example, in 1980 British consumers were able to purchase telecommunications services from only one company, BT.
- Globalisation has provided opportunities for new, innovative businesses to enter markets and compete with all comers, including well established industry leaders. For example, Microsoft, Intel, Compaq and Dell, once relative newcomers to the computer industry in the past, were able to compete effectively against the market leader at the time, IBM.

HYPERCOMPETITION has been used to describe competition in the new global economy. This term refers to the disruption of existing markets by flexible, fast moving businesses.

Meeting consumer expectations and tastes Competition by businesses seeking to meet customer needs in increasingly effective ways has raised customer expectations in many markets. Businesses must now meet ever greater consumer demands about quality, service and price. They must also provide the greater choice of products expected by purchasers. The global market has made predicting consumer preferences more difficult. For example, few businesses predicted the huge rise in the popularity of mobile phones or the speed with which consumers would accept the internet.

Economies of scale Businesses able to build a global presence are likely to enjoy a larger scale of operations. This will enable them to spread their fixed costs over a larger volume of output and reduce unit output costs. A larger scale of operations also allows businesses to exercise power over suppliers and benefit from reduced costs. For example, global hotel chains such as Holiday Inn and Marriott are in a position to benefit from volume discounts from catering supply companies.

Choice of location Businesses with a global presence can choose the most advantageous location for each of its operations. When locating its operations, a business may consider:
- reduction of costs. For example, Nike's decision to locate its shoe manufacturing operations in countries such as China and Vietnam was perhaps based on cost reduction factors. Low cast labour has also resulted in some UK businesses locating call centres in India.
- enhancement of the business's performance. Production and service facilities are located in parts of the world which are likely to improve factors such as product or service quality. For example, Microsoft may have taken this into account when deciding to locate its research laboratories in Cambridge.

Mergers and joint ventures Businesses are increasingly merging or joining with others (☞ unit 29), often in other countries, in order to better provide their goods or services to a global market. Both manufactures and retailers are operating on a global basis. A manufacturer, for example, may merge with another in order to make products in the country in which they will be sold. A DIY retailer may merge with a supplier of toilet seats in another country in order to distribute its products more easily to customers in that country.

Multinationals

A MULTINATIONAL company is an organisation which owns or controls production or service facilities outside the country in which it is based. This means that they do not just

Coca-Cola boasts that it has 2,000 customers a second. Almost 120 years ago a chemist called John Pemberton invented Coca-Cola as a tonic which cured headaches, hysteria and melancholy. The company's corporate headquarters are in Atlanta, USA. After nearly 120 years of advertising it also boasts the advantages of being the world's best known brand name and the world's best known expression after 'okay'. The company's biggest selling product seems to have universal appeal. In spite of worries that Coca-Cola would not be accepted in societies with strong preferences for other drinks, it outsells the leading tea in Britain and the leading coffee in Brazil.

Yet Coca-Cola is diversifying. In less than ten years the company has launched more than 300 non-cola drinks in 200 different countries. In Britain the main brands are Fanta, Sprite, Lilt, Five Alive, Dr Pepper, Oasis fruit drinks, Minute Maid, Powerade, Malvern Water and for 10 days in March, 2004 Dansani bottled water. Dansani was withdrawn from the market after it was revealed that Dansani had been derived from tapwater in Sidcup. This was compared in some newspapers to the episode of Only Fools and Horses in which Del Boy bottled tap water and passed it off as 'Peckham Spring'.

Source: adapted from the *Observer Food Monthly*, April 2004 and the *Financial Times*.

(a) What evidence is there that Coca-Cola is a global business?
(b) Using data from the article describe the possible threats and opportunities for Coca-Cola arising out of globalisation.

Question 2

export their products abroad, but actually own production facilities in other countries.

These companies usually have interests in at least four countries, but there are many which operate in a huge range of countries throughout the world. Examples of multinationals include Ford, British American Tobacco, Volkswagen, Matsui (producers of electrical goods), Unilever, Mobil, Sony and Ciba-Geigy (producers of chemicals). The very largest of the multinationals such as Exxon Mobil, General Motors and Royal Dutch Shell are enormous organisations. They have turnovers that are in excess of the GNPs of all but the wealthiest countries.

There is a number of reasons why firms become multinationals.

- To avoid protectionist policies. By actually producing within a particular country, a firm can usually avoid any tariffs or quotas which that country may impose. This is why Japanese car firms, such as Nissan, Toyota and Honda, have established themselves within EU countries in recent years.
- The globalisation of markets. National boundaries, many believe, are becoming irrelevant for firms as instant communications and high speed travel make the world seem smaller. This is sometimes referred to as the 'global village'. Multinationals, which are global or international in outlook, are the ideal type of business organisation to take advantage of this situation.

A criticism of levelled against globalisation is that it leads to powerful multinationals which have a turnover greater than the national income of some countries in the world and that certain multinationals are too powerful. Two Belgian economists, Paul De Grauwe and Filip Camerman (2002) examined these arguments. They suggested that the GDP of countries and sales of multinationals are different measures of size and may not be useful as a comparison. They also argue that counting sales of multinationals in many countries is 'double counting' and leads to an overemphasis of the size of multinationals.

The influence of multinationals

There is great debate as to the actual effects of multinationals. Whilst there are clear benefits of multinationals operating in a particular country, there is also a number of problems associated with them.

The balance of payments and employment One benefit of multinationals is their ability to create jobs. This, along with the manufacturing capacity which they create, can increase the GNP of countries and add to the standard of living. As well as this, multinationals benefit the balance of payments of a country if their products are sold abroad. The setting-up of a car manufacturing plant by Toyota near Derby helps to illustrate this. Not only has this plant created jobs, but it has raised the GNP of the UK. The balance of payments has also been helped as a large proportion of the Derby plant's cars are shipped out to other EU nations.

However, whilst multinationals can create jobs, they are also capable of causing unemployment for two reasons. First, they create competition for domestic firms. This may be beneficial, causing local firms to improve their efficiency, but it can also be a problem if it results in these firms cutting their labour force or closing down plants. Second, multinationals often shift production facilities from one country to another in order to further their own ends. The effect of this is that jobs are lost and production is either reduced or completely stopped.

In addition, multinationals can have a negative impact upon the balance of payments. This is because many of them receive huge amounts of components from their branches abroad, thus adding to the total quantity of imports.

Technology and expertise Multinationals may introduce new technology, production processes and management styles and techniques. This has been one of the benefits to western countries of Japanese multinationals. Techniques such as just-in-time stock control and management methods such as

Unilever is an Anglo-Dutch business formed in 1930. It is one of the world's largest producers of consumer goods and is known for its branded food and drinks, detergents and personal products. Such brands include Birds Eye Wall's, Surf, Vaseline, Mentadent, Magnum, Flora and Brooke Bond. Unilever employs around 265,000 people worldwide.

Unilever is one of the world's leading suppliers of fast moving consumer goods in foods, homecare and personal care products. The company operates with two global divisions - Foods and Home and Personal Care. This structure allows improved focus on foods and home and personal care activities at both the regional and global levels.

Unilever attempts to 'meet the needs of people everywhere.' It states that 'Every day, all around the world, 150 million people choose to make our brands part of their lives'. Its world famous brands include Lipton's teas, Findus frozen products, Magnum ice cream and Surf washing powder.

Speaking the local language
We think globally when it comes to strategy, product innovation and creative ideas. But when regional and local marketing teams put these plans and ideas into action, they have the freedom to tailor their approach for local consumers and create joint promotional opportunities with, for example, local retailers. Across the world, the brand message is consistent, while its execution has a uncompromisingly local flavour.

Creating the world's best creative partnerships for growth
We are working closer than ever before with our brand agencies. Acting as strategic partners, they are fully involved in developing our brands and their rewards are increasingly linked to the major contribution they make to brand growth.

Source: adapted from www.unilever.com.

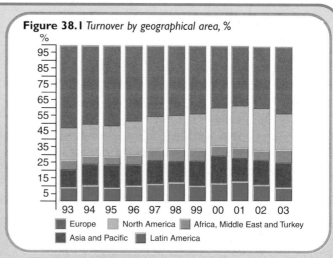

Figure 38.1 *Turnover by geographical area, %*

%
95 85 75 65 55 45 35 25 15 5
93 94 95 96 97 98 99 00 01 02 03
Europe, North America, Africa, Middle East and Turkey, Asia and Pacific, Latin America

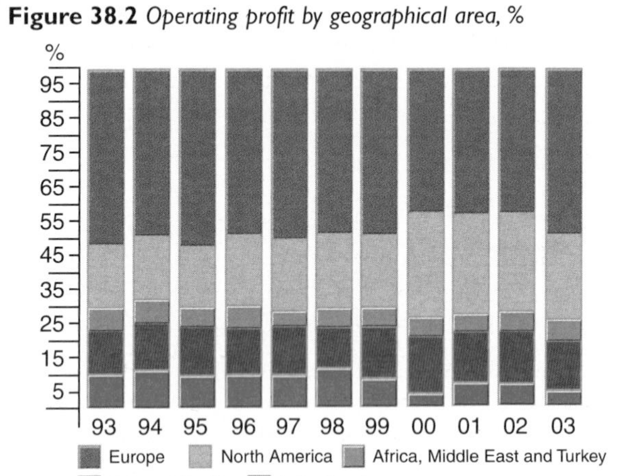

Figure 38.2 *Operating profit by geographical area, %*

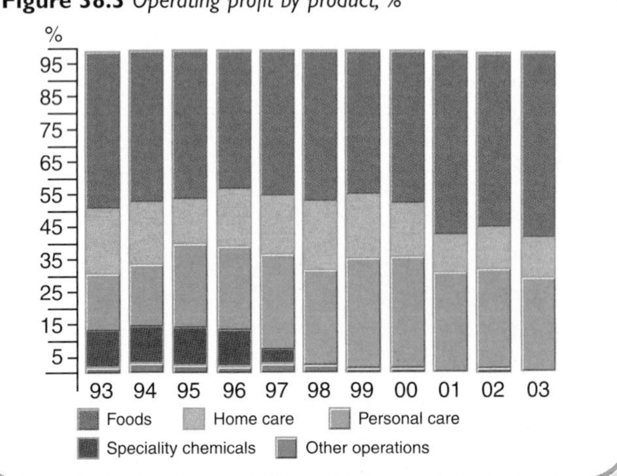

Figure 38.3 *Operating profit by product, %*

(a) Using examples from the data, explain why Unilever might be described as a multinational company.
(b) Using examples from the data, explain how the business might interact with the countries in which it operates.
(c) Suggest reasons why the business may operate as a multinational organisation.

Question 3

quality control circles have been successfully used by Japanese firms in foreign countries. Such techniques have also been adopted by home based firms. These raise the standards of local firms who become aware of these new developments. The process by which multinationals benefit countries in this respect is known as **technology transfer.**

Technology transfer can be especially important to developing countries, which may lack technical expertise and know-how. However, this is not always the case. Managers and supervisors are often brought in from the multinationals' home country, with little training being given to locally recruited staff. As a consequence locals may be employed in low skilled jobs.

Social responsibility Multinationals have often been criticised, especially in their dealings with low income economies. The Union Carbide disaster in Bhopal, India, when hundreds were killed by the release of poisonous gases into the atmosphere, raised serious doubts about the safety measures used by multinationals in low income economies.

They have also been accused of marketing harmful products. One example was the aggressive selling of milk powder to mothers with new born babies when medical research indicated that breast feeding is far more likely to benefit infant health. In addition, environmentalists are concerned about the impact of multinationals on tropical rainforests and other natural resources. On the other hand, large multinationals are in a better position to finance projects that protect the environment from their activities. They also tend to offer better pay than local firms in developing economies.

Government control Because of the size and financial power of many multinationals, there are concerns about the ability of governments to control them. For example, they may be able to avoid paying corporation tax in particular countries.

Taxation can be avoided by the use of TRANSFER PRICING. This involves declaring higher profits in those countries with lower taxation levels, thus reducing the overall tax bill. A company may charge subsidiary branches in low taxation countries low prices for components bought in from overseas branches of the same firm. This means that costs in the low tax country are kept low and high profits can be declared. Similarly, subsidiary branches in high tax countries are charged high prices for components bought in from overseas branches. This means little or no profit is recorded.

Globalisation - an alternative view

Few would dispute that globalisation is a reality in today's world. However, critics such as the Global Justice Movement and Globalise Resistance oppose the way in which globalisation is taking place and argue for a form of globalisation that is less damaging to society and the environment.

Opponents of the current form of globalisation argue that it is driven by the needs of the most powerful in the world, including rich nations and multinational businesses. They believe that organisations such as the IMF and WTO work mainly to further the interests of powerful countries and businesses. They also suggest that it will lead to further concentrations of power and wealth with multinational businesses that will make ever larger profits. This process will be at the cost of increased environmental damage and greater inequalities of income. The effects in the short term will be seen most clearly in poorer, developing nations. They point to statistics such as:

- 2.8 billion of the world's 6 billion people live on less than £1.40 per day;
- the gap between the richest 20 per cent and the poorest 20 per cent of the world's population has doubled since the 1960s;
- the assets of the world's top three wealthiest people exceeded the total GNP of the 48 poorest countries in the world (with a combined population of 600 million).

key terms

Globalisation - the integration of the world's economy.
Hypercompetition - the disruption of existing markets by flexible, fast moving businesses.
Multinational - a company which owns or controls production or service facilities outside the country in which it is based.
Transfer pricing - a system operated by multinationals. It is an attempt to avoid relatively high tax rates through the prices which one subsidiary charges another for components and finished products.

Knowledge

1. What is meant by a global market?
2. State 3 important aspects of globalisation.
3. Suggest 5 factors which have contributed to the growth of globalisation.
4. How might globalisation affect the location of a business?
5. Why might globalisation increase competition for businesses?
6. For what reasons do firms become multinationals?
7. What are the potential benefits of multinationals?
8. What problems might be created by multinationals?

Case study What price coffee?

Ten years ago Vietnam barely registered on the world coffee markets. Then in the 1990s came trade liberalisation. Encouraged by international organisations such as the International Monetary Fund and the World Bank, the Vietnamese government began a programme to encourage its farmers to move out of domestic production of rice and into growing cash crops for export, particularly coffee. With the heavy use of pesticides and fertilisers Vietnam turned itself into the second largest coffee producing country in the world.

In 2000 the country experienced economic growth of 7 per cent. Many people and businesses benefited as a result. One effect of Vietnam's entry into large scale coffee production was the collapse in world prices sinking in 2002 to a 20 year low.

Nestlé states that it does not favour low coffee prices. When the price drops, roast ground coffee becomes cheaper in relation to its instant coffees and makes the company less competitive.

The company argues that the fundamental problem is the overproduction of coffee beans. 'Any solution to the low coffee price must address this basic issue, in order to reverse the disturbing increase in poverty and suffering among many coffee farmers', a spokesperson said.

Coffee processing is dominated by five businesses - Kraft, Nestlé, Procter & Gamble, Sara Lee and Tchibo. The production of coffee beans takes place mainly in developing countries, such as Uganda, Guatemala, Vietnam and Columbia.

Nestlé has a 57 per cent global share of the soluble (instant) coffee business. An analyst's report from the Deutsche Bank explains 'Martin Luther used to wonder what people actually do in heaven. For most participants in the intensely competitive food manufacturing industry, contemplation of Nestlé's soluble coffee business must seem like the commercial equivalent of Luther's spiritual meditation. This is a market where profit margins are 26 per cent. Nothing else in food and beverages is remotely as good'.

John Kafuluzisik sits on a wooden box outside his hut surrounded by his family. Coffee bushes are planted around his land. His children are sick and need medicine, but he can't afford it. Someone explains to John that the price of a cup of coffee in London is 5,000 Ugandan shillings (about £2.50). John says 'I got only 200 shillings (10 pence) a kilo for my coffee this year'.

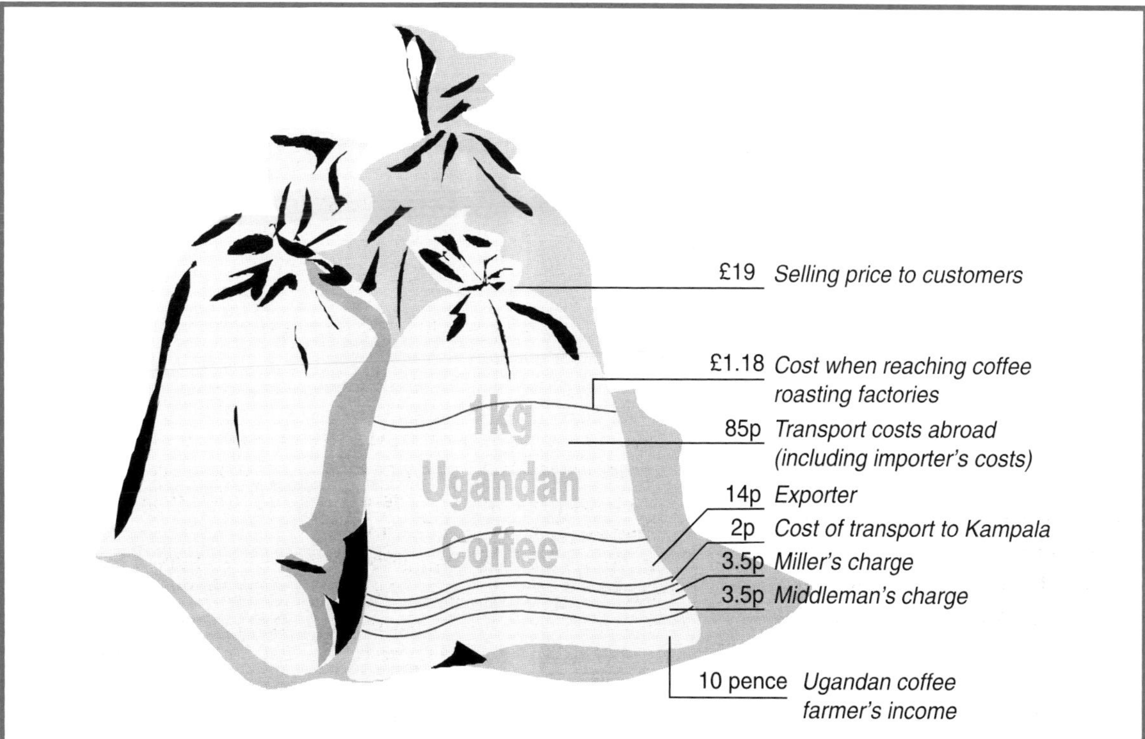

Figure 38.4 *How the price of 1 kg of Ugandan coffee selling in shops might be made up (not to scale)*
NB Calculations based on values of the dollar, Ugandan shilling and the pound in April 2004.

William Naggaga of the Ugandan Coffee Development Authority argues that 'The multinationals are taking too much out. They are so powerful they can determine the price. Just think of it - five men sitting in a room deciding the fate of 25 million coffee farmers around the world.' One way developing countries could increase their share of the final value of the coffee sold would be to process more of it themselves. But breaking into that market is almost impossible. 'Their brands are so powerful and they control the distribution chains. It is very difficult for anyone else to penetrate the part of the market where value is added. Globalisation taken too far is madness. A few men should not decide what millions eat and drink.'

Source: adapted from *The Guardian*, 17.5.2003.

(a) Why might coffee businesses be described as multinational companies? (4 marks)

(b) Explain reasons why multinational companies in the coffee business operate on a global basis. (8 marks)

(c) Examine the factors which have affected the globalisation of this market. (8 marks)

(c) Analyse the effects of globalisation on multinational coffee businesses. (10 marks)

(d) Evaluate the impact of the global coffee business on coffee farmers in developing countries. (10 marks)

39 Business Ethics

What are business ethics?

Ethics are a set of values and beliefs which influence how individuals, groups and society behave. BUSINESS ETHICS are concerned with how such values and beliefs operate in business. They help firms to decide what actions are right or wrong in certain circumstances. Ethics might influence the following business decisions.

- Should products which might damage the health of consumers be withdrawn from the market?
- What efforts, if any, should be made to ensure that business activities do not damage the environment?
- Should money be spent on wheelchair access to workplaces and retail outlets?
- Should a firm reject a bribe given to secure an overseas contract?
- Should part time staff be offered the same employment rights as full time staff?
- Should a workplace creche be provided for working mothers?
- Should a contribution be made to a local charity?

A business that says 'yes' to some or all of these questions might be described as ethical. A firm which is ethical with regard to society as a whole and the community within which it is based might also be described as 'socially responsible'. **Corporate responsibility** (☞ unit 40) is the term used to describe attempts by individual businesses to behave in an ethical manner.

Different individuals and groups have different viewpoints. It is these which can determine what they see as ethical business behaviour. For example, a firm polluting a river might only be able to take action against further pollution through savings made by job losses. What is ethical behaviour in this case - preventing the pollution or saving jobs?

To some extent the law attempts to ensure that businesses act ethically. However, obeying the 'letter' of the law does not necessarily mean that a firm is behaving in an ethical way. For example, some would regard water companies which pump untreated sewerage into the sea as unethical, even if the activity is legal. This is due to the possible pollution and health problems associated with such an activity.

There have been a number of businesses that could be described as acting unethically in the past. Examples which some believe fall into this category include BA for the 'dirty tricks' which it allegedly used against its competitor Virgin Airlines and Exxon for the safety standards on its oil tanker Exxon Valdez which sank in Alaskan waters. Other examples may include the large salary increases given to the chief executives of privatised companies, insider share dealing in the City of London, the trade of some businesses with countries that have oppressive regimes, or the trade in arms. Individuals within businesses also act 'unethically'. A well publicised example is the behaviour of Robert Maxwell, former owner of Maxwell Communications

YOU GET EXCELLENT COFFEE. YOU DON'T GET COCAINE.

The coffee growers of Latin America face a problem. Either they get paid a fair price for their coffee, or they face bankruptcy and may have to turn their land over to the illegal production of the coca plant for cocaine.

Cafédirect helps avoid this problem, because more of the money you pay for Cafédirect roast and ground coffee goes directly to the growers.

The result? They continue to produce high quality Arabica coffee for Cafédirect.

Cafédirect.
Fair trade. Excellent coffee.

(a) Would you describe the above as ethical behaviour? Explain your answer.
(b) Why might the (i) owners and (ii) customers of Cafédirect be concerned about Latin American coffee workers?

Question 1

Corporation. After his death, it was found that he had been supporting his business empire with money 'borrowed' from his employees' pension fund.

The ethical behaviour of businesses is, to some extent, controlled by laws and regulation. Increasingly, however, businesses and industries are placing greater emphasis on developing their own codes of conduct and practice. For example, the Chemical Industries Association has a Responsible Care programme which includes the requirement that individual chemical businesses must be open about giving relevant information to interested parties. They must also work closely with local communities in achieving required levels of performance. A number of businesses, including PepsiCo, Apple and Kodak, have stopped selling their products in Burma, a country with a record of human rights abuse.

The benefits of ethical behaviour

There are certain advantages for businesses in behaving in an ethical or socially responsible way.

Consumers' views Increasing numbers of consumers are taking into account a firm's 'behaviour' when buying products. As a result, ethical behaviour can be good for sales. Body Shop is a good example of this. A feature of the Body Shop's marketing is that its products are not tested on animals. The company has also lent support to groups helping firms in the world's poorest countries. This stance has perhaps helped the Body Shop become a successful business. There is a number of other firms which have responded in a similar way. The Co-operative Bank, for example, has conducted a wide ranging campaign. It refuses to invest money in or finance a variety of concerns. These range from countries with poor human rights records to companies using exploitative factory farming methods. This policy was introduced as a result of a survey carried out amongst the bank's customers, which found that they regarded a clear ethical policy as important for the bank.

Improvements in the recruitment and retention of staff Firms with an ethical approach believe that they will be more able to recruit well qualified and motivated staff. In addition,

Clerical Medical uses its Evergreen Investment Trust to invest in 'ethical' businesses. It uses the following guidelines to help make investment decisions.

Industry exposure

Investments considered appropriate will typically have interests in one or more of the following areas:

Air quality/emissions control	Pollution analysis
Drinking water purification	Recycling
Energy conservation	Site remediation
Environmental assessment	Waste reduction/disposal
Geothermal energy	Wastewater treatment
Natural gas	Wind power

Share Selection Criteria

The fund manager will seek to avoid companies which are involved in:

1 The production, sale or distribution of fur products.
2 The production, sale or distribution of cosmetics where animal testing may be involved.
3 The manufacture of ozone depleting chemicals (CFCs and halons).
4 The manufacture or distribution of harmful pesticides.
5 The supply of tropical hardwood.
6 The production, processing or sale of meat products.
Other types of company, which would normally be ineligible for an ethical portfolio, will also be avoided as they are inconsistent with Evergreen's objectives. These are companies which are involved in:
7 The manufacture or provision of armaments.
8 Companies involved in repressive regimes to a total extent of no more than 10% of group turnover. Fot this purpose "repressive regimes" are those listed by the Ethical Investment Research Service (EIRIS).
9 The provision of gambling services.
10 The production of tobacco products.
11 The production or distribution of pornography.

Source: Clerical Medical, Evergreen Trust Investment information.

Anita Roddick the founder of the Body Shop believes that 'it is a basic responsibility of business to be open and honest about its environmental and social impacts'. Alongside Greenpeace, the Body Shop has backed a global campaign encouraging organisations to use clean, renewable energy and so fight global warming. Employees of the Body Shop are encouraged to participate in campaigns designed to have a positive impact upon communities. Nicky Amos, the company's head of corporate responsibility says 'The Body Shop's integrity is based on what we do, rather than what we say. We ask ourselves what we can do that's different, and we will demonstrate our campaigns to our employees and customers. Employees must have the opportunity to get directly involved in a campaign. We provide a half day each month for people to participate in a project of their choice.'

Source: adapted from *People Management*, 10.7.2003.

(a) Why might these companies be said to be acting in an ethical manner?
(b) Using information above discuss the benefits to these businesses of an ethical stance.

ethical firms argue that they are able to retain their staff better if they adopt a more caring approach to employees. Polaroid in the US, for example, has subsidised child-care expenses for their lower paid workers. Marks and Spencer provide their staff with a range of benefits, over and above those usually provided in the retail sector. They have benefited by achieving one of the lowest rates of staff turnover in the UK. This has cut their recruitment and retraining costs.

Improvements in employee motivation Firms which behave in an ethical manner believe that their employees are more committed to their success as a result. They may be prepared to work harder to allow the business to achieve its aims.

Effects of ethical behaviour

What effect will acting in an ethical way have on a business?

Increasing costs Ethical behaviour can result in an increase in costs for a firm. An ethical firm may, for example, be forced to turn down cheaper supplies from a firm which tests its products on animals. Similarly, costs may be raised by pollution reducing filters put on coal-fired power stations.

Loss of profit Firms may be forced to turn down profitable business due to their ethical stance. A business, for example, may reject a profitable investment opportunity in a company which produces animal fur, as this is against its ethical policy. However, the ethical firm would hope that the gains it makes from its policy, by attracting increased numbers of customers, would outweigh these costs.

Conflict When a firm's overall profitability comes into conflict with its ethical policy, problems may result. In such cases the shareholders of a firm may object to the ethical policy as the return on their investment is harmed.

Business practice A firm seeking to act more ethically may need to alter the way in which it approaches a huge range of business matters. Such a firm might, for example, need to consider the impact of its activities on the environment (☞ unit 41), whether or not its recruitment policy was providing equal opportunities for all applicants regardless of age, sex, ethnic background or disability, the extent to which its advertisements are offensive or in poor taste, and the protection given to consumers buying their products.

Relations with suppliers Some suppliers will only supply products to businesses that meet ethical criteria. This might include agreeing not to trade with certain countries or businesses that deal in arms, that exploit workers or that abuse human rights.

Should businesses be expected to act ethically?

There is considerable debate about how businesses should actually behave.

Some argue that businesses have a responsibility to act ethically. Those who hold this view stress the fact that firms do not operate in isolation. They are a part of society and have an impact upon the lives of those communities in which they operate. As such they should act in a responsible manner and consider the possible effects of any decisions they make. This means that profit making should not be the only criterion used when making decisions. Other factors which firms might consider include the effect of their decisions upon the environment, jobs, the local community, consumers, competitors, suppliers and employees.

Others argue that businesses should not be expected to act ethically. There are two main views in support of this argument. The first is from supporters of free market economics. They argue that the primary responsibility of businesses is to produce goods and services in the most efficient way, and make profit for shareholders. Firms should attempt to do this in any way they can, providing it is legal.

Question 3

Mobile phone firm O_2 is taking measures to ensure that all the mobile phone manufacturers it deals with are complying with its own social and corporate responsibility polices. O_2 does not make phones itself. But it does provide the network on which they operate and it sells their handsets through its retail outlets. David Varney, the company's chairman, said the move was designed to protect the reputation of the company. Varney argued that there is 'a new risk for corporations - which is a risk to reputations'. He was particularly concerned about the damage to reputation caused by manufacturers which use illegally mined quantities of a substance called 'coltan' which is present in nearly all mobile phones. As the prices of coltan increased, some manufacturers had taken to using illegally mined coltan from the Democratic Republic of Congo. As a result, the habitat of endangered gorillas was being destroyed.

Varney warned that ordering manufacturers to produce 'coltan free' phones could be 'seriously compromising' to the business, but it was in discussions with manufacturers about how to address the problem.

Source: adapted from *People Management*, 15.5.2003.

(a) Explain why O_2 might be said to be acting ethically in this situation.
(b) Discuss the likely effects of the actions of the business on:
(i) the business itself;
(ii) its suppliers;
(iii) its competitors.

Only by doing this will the general good of everyone be served. If firms are expected to act 'ethically', then consumers may suffer because the ethical behaviour could lead to inefficiency, higher costs and higher prices.

A second argument is that in most cases it is naive to expect businesses to act ethically. Whenever there is a conflict between acting ethically and making greater profits, the vast majority of firms will choose the latter. Those firms which do act in an ethical manner only do so because it is profitable. This view is often held by those who favour government intervention to regulate business. They argue that it is necessary for the government to force firms to behave responsibly through a variety of laws which it must enforce.

Are businesses becoming more ethical?

It could be argued that businesses are increasingly taking a more 'caring' attitude. The growth of companies producing health care products which are not animal tested, the use of recyclable carrier bags and the sale of organically grown vegetables by many retailers could all be an indication of this. Some pension funds and a number of investment schemes are now termed 'green'. They will only invest savers' money in companies which promote the environment.

Others argue that ethical attitudes have failed to penetrate the boardrooms of the UK and that firms continue to act unethically in a variety of ways. An extensive survey undertaken by the University of Westminster found that junior executives and women took the moral 'high ground', with more concern about green issues, staff relations and trade with countries that had records of abusing human rights. This was in contrast to the greed driven motives of company directors, the majority of whom were old and male. One respondent summed up the climate. 'In general, business ethics does not come very high in the scale of human behaviour. Professional standards and levels of caring sometimes leave a lot to be desired.'

One explanation for the findings of the survey is that business culture (☞ unit 5) continues to be driven by short term profit. This suggests that the stakeholders such as shareholders and directors hold most influence in setting the objectives of the business. These groups tend to be most interested in the profit of the business.

Mr Richard Branson and his Virgin Atlantic airline won near record libel damages of £610,000 at the end of a two year 'dirty tricks' legal battle against British Airways. In charging BA with going 'beyond the limits of commercially acceptable practice', Mr Branson listed details of its rival's campaign to discredit Virgin. These included:

- the illegal use of Virgin Atlantic's computer information;
- the poaching of Virgin passengers by bogus Virgin representatives;
- the shredding of documents relating to Virgin activities;
- the spreading of hostile and discreditable stories to destabilise Virgin.

BA, which also had to meet several million pounds in legal costs, apologised 'unreservedly' to Mr Branson in court for alleging that Virgin Atlantic, in claiming BA was conducting a 'dirty tricks' campaign, was only seeking publicity.

Sir Colin Marshall, BA's chief executive and deputy chairman, said his airline was taking steps to ensure 'regrettable incidents' undertaken by BA employees did not occur again.

In a special message to BA staff intended to bolster morale, Sir Colin said the 'overwhelming majority' of the airline's workforce had no involvement whatsoever in the campaign against Virgin. He urged them not to be distracted by the publicity surrounding the affair.

Mr Branson also demanded BA directors give a full explanation of a separate covert activity targeted at Virgin which, he alleged, was carried out by private investigators.

Source: adapted from *The Financial Times*.

(a) What elements of BA's behaviour could be termed
(i) illegal;
(ii) unethical?
(b) Which view about the behaviour of the firms might BA's actions lend support to? Explain your answer.

Question 4

Business ethics - the influence of values and beliefs upon the conduct and operation of businesses.

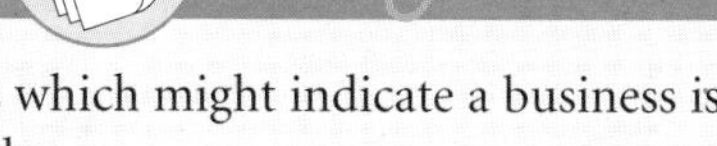

1. Give 5 examples which might indicate a business is behaving ethically.
2. Give 5 examples which might indicate a business is behaving unethically.
3. Why might firms draw up a code of ethics?
4. Briefly explain 5 effects that ethical behaviour may have on businesses.
5. 'Businesses should not be expected to act ethically.' Explain the 2 sides to this argument.

Case study Boots Group plc

Boots Group, the Nottingham based chemist and retail chain, was nominated for a Business in the Community award in 2003. It was amongst the first businesses to champion family friendly policies for its employees. In 2001, Boots was the first organisation to offer staff formal accreditation for their work in the community. The company started a 'Skills for Life' scheme that offered employees the chance to be involved in community activities during company time. In 2002, Boots' employees spent 50,000 hours on voluntary activities, which equates to £500,000.

The company also began a 'My Health' programme to support and develop initiatives and events delivering health promotion messages in the community. It has teamed up with primary care trusts, hospital NHS trusts and New College, Nottingham to execute its many projects. One scheme is the creation of a dedicated 'Look Good ... Feel Better' beauty room at Nottingham City Hospital. This provides free workshops for women with cancer. Its 'Time for a Treat' programme expands on that concept, providing health and beauty treatments aimed particularly at elderly patients, NHS staff and wider community groups, including those who are socially excluded or have mental health problems. Volunteers from Boots are trained to provide basic therapeutic massages for these groups.

Each volunteering opportunity is matched to the skills required by a specific job role, including leadership, relationship building and creativity. Employees work with their line managers to select the voluntary activities that will best complement any skills that need to be developed. This can take the form of managing someone on work experience, becoming a literacy volunteer, giving patients massaging or mentoring – all activities that will help to improve someone's professional competency.

Boots conducted a survey of its main site in Nottingham and found that 80 per cent of employees felt either 'positive' or 'very positive' about the company when told how much it gave back to the community. 'Surveys confirm that a reputation for responsible business practice help companies to recruit and retain the talent they need' says Mike Emmott, a specialist in the social responsibilities business.

Source: adapted from *People Management*, 10.7.2003.

(a) Describe examples of ethical behaviour mentioned in the article. (6 marks)

(b) Using evidence from the article, suggest reasons why managers at Boots might encourage team members to volunteer for the schemes. (8 marks)

(c) Analyse the possible effects on:
(i) the Boots Group; (8 marks)
(ii) other internal and external stakeholders in the business; (8 marks)
of participating in the local community programmes mentioned in the article.

(d) To what extent to you think that businesses have a responsibility to engage in the sort of community programmes described in the article? (10 marks)

40 Corporate Responsibility

Business responsibility

Unit 3 explained that the influence of stakeholders has led many businesses to take into account the effect of their activities on others. A business that accepts CORPORATE RESPONSIBILITY will be prepared to be responsible for and willing to justify its actions. It will also consider the impact of its actions on a variety of individuals and groups, both inside and outside the organisation.

For example, a mobile phone business will aim to provide as wide a coverage as possible for its customers. However, in order to do so it is likely to have to erect masts in the places that give the best reception. Masts tend to be fairly ugly and may disrupt the environment in which they are placed. If the business accepts this and is prepared to pay for innovative designs that blend in with the environment then it could be said to be accepting corporate responsibility. Orange, the mobile phone company, for example, has introduced tree shaped transmitters which blended in with the surrounding area and were also comfortable enough for squirrels to live in.

Methods of encouraging corporate responsibility

There is a number of ways in which businesses can be encouraged to accept corporate responsibility.

Government intervention Governments can intervene directly to ensure that a business accepts the consequences of its behaviour. One of the most common methods of achieving this is through the creation of legislation which businesses must adhere to. For example, in Germany all retailers and manufacturers are required to recycle 80 per cent of their packaging. Although legislation can control the behaviour of businesses and the creation of negative externalities (☞ unit 41), there are some problems with this method of control. First, businesses can obey the 'letter of the law' rather than the 'spirit of the law'. This might mean, for example, a business adopting practices which are legal, but which do not greatly reduce negative externalities. Second, legislation which only applies within national boundaries may not affect businesses in other countries. For example, legislation governing the behaviour of the UK or EU nuclear industry would have had no impact on the Chernobyl disaster in the former Soviet Union. This led to radioactive materials being deposited in the UK and other Western European countries.

Self-regulation Governments can work with particular industries and business sectors to encourage the creation of regulatory bodies which help to control the activities of business. These tend to be voluntary organisations which aim to monitor the behaviour of relevant firms. The Press Complaints Authority and The Advertising Standards Authority are examples of such organisations. The Press Complaints Authority aims to encourage newspapers and other media organisations to act in a responsible way. Governments can help such organisations to control businesses by threatening legislation if the self-regulatory bodies are not seen to be working.

Market pressures Some commentators believe that there is no need for governments to exert direct pressures on businesses to act responsibly. This is because the free market will act effectively to police less responsible businesses. The argument is that such businesses will be unpopular with consumers, who will be less likely to purchase their products. Thus consumer behaviour will force irresponsible businesses to act with greater accountability. Businesses which refuse to act responsibly will fail.This is only likely to be the case, however, if consumers have information about the behaviour of businesses. Without sufficient information, consumers may be unable to make judgments about the levels of corporate responsibility of companies. For this reason, some firms have tried to make more information about their activities available to the public. The EU has introduced an Eco-Label system which identifies products which have had the least negative impact upon the environment.

Pressure groups Pressure groups can sometimes affect businesses. In recent years, certain groups have had notable successes. For example, animal welfare pressure groups have encouraged cosmetics businesses not to test their products on animals. The campaign of some pressure groups for a complete ban on animal testing continues, however. Some pressure groups, frustrated in their attempts to change

The American drinks giant Coca-Cola came under fire in 2003 from courts in the Kerala region of India for excessive water consumption. A 40 acre bottling plant was closed and the factory's licence to operate revoked after the corporation was accused of using up to 1 million litres of water every day and contaminating ground water in the village. In India, as in many other developing countries, access to clean water is vital for the survival of communities. Coca-Cola denied the allegations and blamed natural forces for the depleted water reserves. The business recharged the water supply by the same amount it had used.

Source: adapted from *The Observer*, 21.3.2004.

(a) Identify factors which may have influenced the corporate responsibility of the business.

corporate behaviour, have called for greater democracy in the corporate decision making process. This would involve stakeholders being involved as a matter of routine in decisions that have a direct effect upon them.

Barriers to corporate responsibility

There is a number of incentives for businesses to behave in a responsible manner. They might attract more customers as a result of their stance or avoid penalties from legislation. However, there are certain reasons why businesses may fail to act in a responsible manner.

Costs and profit Responsible behaviour can raise the costs of businesses. Some businesses may consider that the costs of accepting corporate responsibility are too great. For example, a business which uses the cheapest overseas contractors, regardless of how it treated its workforce, may find that it is able to achieve lower production costs. This could enable the business to price its product more competitively than rival products and possibly make higher profits. Similarly, a local garage may find it cheaper to dispose of engine oil in a local stream than to pay for it to be disposed of in an environmentally friendly manner.

Values and beliefs The values and beliefs of the senior managers and employees of a business may not correspond with what the majority of others in a society regard as responsible. For example, a public house or bar which continued to serve alcoholic drinks to a drunken customer may be regarded as irresponsible. However, the manager or employee of the business may regard this as the concern of the customer and a matter in which he should not become involved. This view may lead him to continue serving alcoholic drinks to the customer. In this case the business is not accepting the responsibility of possible problems that the customer may have, nor the potential danger to others as a result.

Information available to consumers, governments and pressure groups In the absence of useful information about the behaviour of a business it is difficult for interested parties to monitor its activities. For example, the nuclear industry has been accused by pressure groups of being secretive about its activities. Nuclear industry representatives have argued that this is due to defence and national security reasons. However, this secrecy has made it difficult for consumers and pressure groups to make judgments about its behaviour. For other businesses it is the complexity and scope of their activities that makes it difficult to evaluate their actions. Multinationals, in particular, because of their global activities, can be very difficult to monitor. Other businesses are involved in such technically complex work that it can be difficult for consumers, governments and pressure groups to understand issues relevant to their behaviour. Businesses involved in genetic modification may fall into this category.

Implications of taking corporate responsibility

To some extent a business which takes greater corporate responsibility will face similar challenges to those which follow a more ethical approach (☞ unit 39). A business accepting greater corporate responsibility might have to change some of the following to take into account the effects of its actions.

- The aims and objectives of the business.
- Operating methods, which might lead to increasing costs.
- The relationship with employees. This might involve changing work practices.
- The relationship with other stakeholders, including suppliers and people in the local community.
- Changing the organisation of the business.
- Taking into account the needs of consumers when making marketing decisions.
- Providing help to bodies and organisations outside the business.

American Apparel is a Los Angeles based business that specialises in the manufacture of T-shirts. It is the largest company in the business in the US. American Apparel operates in an industry renowned for 'sweatshops'. These are manufacturing units where business methods in some countries include, the use of child labour, enforced prison labour, starvation wages and 16 hour working days. The President of American Apparel has always adopted an anti-sweatshop mentality. His workers receive much higher than average wages, English classes and health insurance.

Source: adapted from *Metro*, 9.10.2003.

Levi Strauss & Co. Global Sourcing and Operating Guidelines

'Our Global Sourcing and Operating Guidelines help us to select business partners who follow workplace standards and business practices that are consistent with our company's values. These requirements are applied to every contractor who manufactures or finishes products for Levi Strauss & Co. Trained inspectors closely audit and monitor compliance among approximately 600 cutting, sewing, and finishing contractors in more than 60 countries.'

Source: www.itglwf.org/doc/Levis.doc.

(a) Suggest why there might not be barriers to corporate responsibility in these businesses.
(b) Explain how taking a greater corporate responsibility has affected these businesses.

Social auditing

A business that produces its final accounts must have them **audited** by law. An audit is a check to make sure the financial performance of the business is accurately shown in its accounts.

Social auditing is the process by which a business organisation attempts to assess the impact of the entire range of its activities on stakeholders. It might try to produce a set of 'social accounts' to evaluate its performance against a set of non-financial criteria. This might include its effect on the environment and its attempts to meet social obligations to employees. Social auditing may involve:

- identifying the social objectives and ethical values of the organisation;
- defining the stakeholders of the business;
- establishing social performance indicators;
- measuring performance, keeping records and preparing social accounts;
- submitting the accounts to an independent audit and publishing the results.

The social audit might include details such as:

- the salary difference between the highest and lowest paid employee;
- health and safety information;
- the extent to which employees feel valued;
- the views of consumers about whether the business is living up to its ideals.

The benefits of social auditing

Increasingly businesses are carrying out their own social audit. Some publish the results in their Annual Report and Accounts. Businesses as wide ranging as The Co-operative Bank, Ben & Jerry's, the US ice cream manufacturer, and St Lukes, the ethical advertising agency, have carried out social audits. Why might they be seen as useful?

- They provide valuable information to pressure groups and consumers about the corporate responsibility of a business. Consumers can take account of this information, often issued through press reports, when making purchasing decisions. Pressure groups can use them as the basis for further enquiries.
- They allow the managers of a business to gain a complete picture of the impact of the business's activities. Especially in large businesses, managers may be unaware of some practices which they would regard as undesirable. This can allow the business to make better informed decisions about the impact of its activities upon stakeholders.
- A business can use a social audit as a means of preventing future criticism of its activities. By opening up its activities to scrutiny a business can deflect suspicions which some stakeholders may have about less than responsible behaviour. The use of an independent social audit is especially valuable. There can be a lack of credibility associated with social audits which are generated from within the business itself. It is also important that a business commits itself to full publication of an independent social audit. Edited versions are unlikely to persuade more critical stakeholders.
- A business will be able to identify the extent to which it is meeting some of its non-financial objectives. For example, a social audit may indicate a growing agreement with the corporate culture of the business (☞ unit 5).
- Shareholders can use social audits to raise questions about a business's activities at annual shareholder meetings.
- Governments can use social audits of a range of businesses in a particular industry as one means of assessing the need for legislation or regulation of businesses in the industry.

As businesses are subjected to increasing levels of scrutiny and as consumers and pressure groups have access to more information about business behaviour, it is likely that an increasing number of businesses will use social audits.

Corporate responsibility - an alternative view

Many businesses, especially larger multinational businesses, claim to be enthusiastic supporters of corporate responsibility. They publicise these claims, producing glossy brochures which refer to their good work in a range of areas. They produce **social** and **environmental** audits, detailing how their spending is benefiting society or improving the environment.

However, critics have suggested this is merely 'window dressing', offering a positive, but perhaps misleading picture of the overall business position. In practice, corporate responsibility may apply mainly to superficial and less important aspects of business activity. A corporate accountability specialist at Friends of the Earth argues that 'Glossy corporate social responsibility reports are filled with references to commitments, dialogue, transparency, partnerships and stakeholders. The company is there to do good, they suggest, and a smiling ethnic face on the front cover completes the picture. But read these reports and you realise their focus is nearly always on the superficial aspects of business; lots of detail on trees planted and light bulbs changed, but rarely anything about the social and environmental impacts of the core business of the company.'

It could be argued, therefore, that in some cases social audits and a stress on corporate responsibility may simply be used to deflect attention away from other aspects of business, such as unethical activities or business practices which harm the environment.

A further problem with social audits is that the businesses themselves select what to include and measure. This means that there is no standard or regulated method of assessing the impact of their activities. For example, what if a business shows that it has reduced pollution greatly in an audit, but continues to use a supplier which pays very low wages which is not disclosed? To what extent is it acting in a socially responsible way?

The Cooperative Bank is famed for its ethical stance. It uses a number of criteria against which to assess its performance. For example in 2001 it set a number of SMART indicators. It reported that 'Of the 65 targets set last year, the bank has fully achieved 43, made acceptable progress against 15 and has not yet achieved 7. Broadly speaking, the bank is satisfied with these latest results; particularly considering how far it has progressed since 1997. But, of course, there is always room for improvement, which is why in this section there are also details of the 62 new targets set for 2002.'

Examples of its performance against indictors included the following.

'Maintain the continued growth in profits and the reductions in the cost/income ratio as envisaged in the bank's Strategic Plan 2001-2003, whilst at the same time adhering to the culture and the principles of 'co-operation.' **TARGET ACHIEVED**

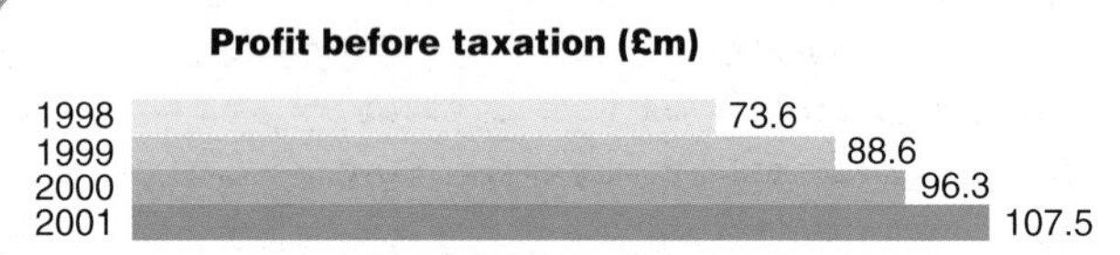

'Encourage and increase the level of support given to ethnic minority and disability groups as part of the community involvement policy.' **TARGET ACHIEVED**

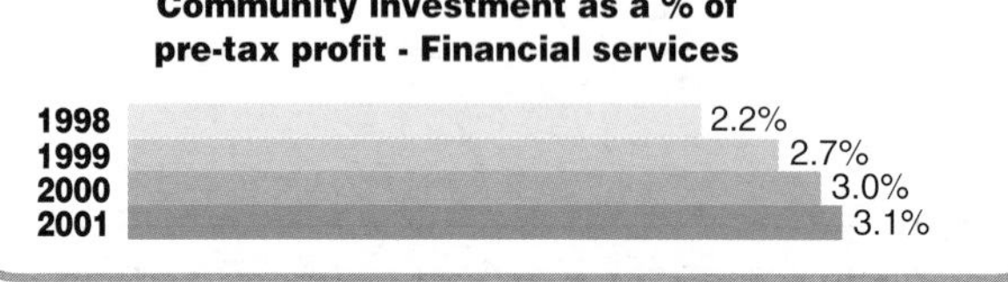

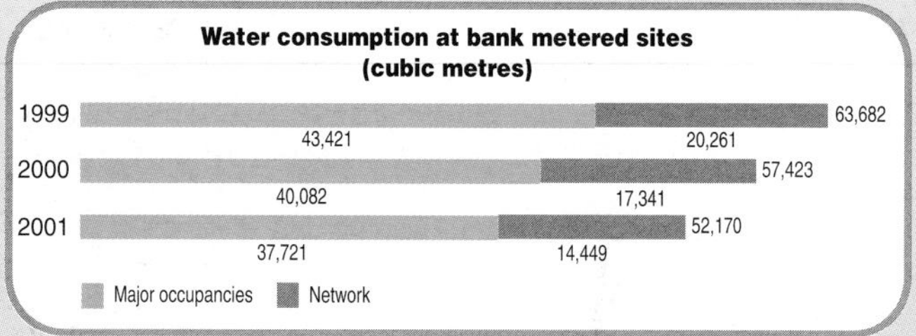

'In line with Building Research Establishment best practice, undertake to reduce water consumption across all major occupancies to 9m³ per employee by 2005.' **ACCEPTABLE PROGRESS**

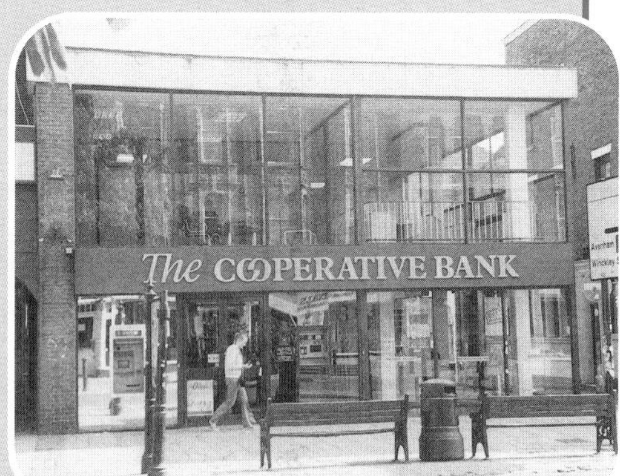

Source: adapted from www.co-operativebank.co.uk.

(a) Using examples from the data and other suggestions, explain what might be included in (i) an audit, (ii) a social audit, (iii) an environmental audit.
(b) Explain how producing a social audit might be useful to the Cooperative Bank in future.
(c) Discuss to what extent the Cooperative Bank might be operating in a socially responsible way.

Question 3

key terms

Corporate responsibility - the willingness of a business to accept responsibility for its actions and their impact on a range of stakeholders.

Knowledge

1. Give an example of a business acting with corporate responsibility.
2. State 4 ways in which corporate responsibility may be encouraged.
3. Why might legislation to control companies be a problem?
4. State 3 possible barriers to corporate responsibility.
5. What might be involved in social auditing for a business?
6. What details might be included in a social audit?
7. How might a business benefit from a social audit?
8. How might other stakeholders benefit from a social audit?

Case study Centrica

Do socially responsible companies win the war for talent? Certainly many of the businesses which stress corporate social responsibility (CSR) argued that they do. But firms often do little to measure the effect of their activities on their ability to recruit, retain and motivate employees.

It has been suggested that CSR is often an intuitive approach and could become 'an expensive exercise in compliance that has minimal impact' unless businesses are careful. One business that has risen to the challenge, however, is Centrica. Over three years it has participated in a research project which scrutinises how corporate community involvement and wider corporate citizenship can contribute to business success by enhancing employee morale, motivation, commitment and performance.

Centrica's Cardiff call centre has been involved with Business in the Community's 'Cares' volunteering project for three years. Employees have devoted a total of around 1,000 hours to helping a range of local charities and causes, including the Cystic Fibrosis Trust and Ty Hafan Children's Hospice. In one project, volunteers cleared 7.5 million tonnes of rubbish in an attempt to encourage the return of freshwater wildlife. In another, managers acted as consultants to local businesses in areas such as web design.

Improvements in employee retention, absenteeism levels, positive customer relations and job satisfaction were all found as a result of the 'Cares' project. The retention rate for employees participating in the project was 99.6 per cent, 19.6 per cent over target. Six employees were also chosen for an initiative to develop team leaders to achieve promotion. The project developed their skills, making them candidates for promotion in the company.

But has the programme proved cost effective? Certainly at Centrica. Previously the company had spent on team building exercises. Now these were replaced with 'Cares' at a fraction of the cost. Employee satisfaction ratings increased in four areas - customer focus went up four points, performance and development improved by one point, management impact increased by three and satisfaction about working life rose two.

Anne Minto, Centrica's group HR director says 'We look at corporate responsibility as a core part of our overall strategy. We can't expect to thrive as a business unless we involve ourselves in the communities we operate in and respond to the needs of people within them'.

Centrica is by no means the only business to take corporate responsibility seriously. Marks & Spencer recently developed its CSR activities to create employability amongst disadvantaged groups. The 'Ready to Work' programme offered 600 work experience placements to people affected by homelessness. Employees in the business acted as 'mentors' or buddies to help and give advice. The company had already piloted schemes for people with learning and physical difficulties. The company says 'Our focus on employability has delivered real, measurable benefits to the people who have taken part in our work placements - many of whom now have jobs with us or with other employers'. It also argues 'Our workers have benefited too. Those that had responsibility as a buddy have fed back to us that their personal and management skills have developed as a result'.

Source: adapted from *People Management*, 18.12.2003.

(a) What may have influenced corporate responsibility at Centrica? (6 marks)

(b) Using examples, explain why the businesses in the article might be said to be acting in a socially responsible manner. (10 marks)

(c) Explain how Centrica might make use of the information in the article to produce a social audit. (10 marks)

(d) Assess the impact which corporate responsibility at the businesses in the article might have had on;

(i) the businesses themselves;

(ii) the employees in the businesses;

(iii) other stakeholders. (12 marks)

(e) Discuss to what extent corporate responsibility might be 'an expensive exercise in compliance that has minimal impact' at Centrica. (12 marks)

41 Business and the Environment

The costs and benefits of business activity

When businesses produce and sell products or services it is relatively easy for them to see the costs involved and the benefits they will gain. These costs are known as PRIVATE COSTS. They might include such things as the wages paid to employees, the cost of an advertising campaign or the purchase of raw materials. The PRIVATE BENEFITS to the business and its owners include the total revenue earned from sales, any resulting profit and the dividends paid to shareholders.

A business may find, however, that it creates other costs. Take a factory producing cement which is located in a small 'scenic' town. The firm may dispose of some of its waste in a local river or discharge dust into the atmosphere. Lorries making deliveries to the factory may disturb the local residents. The factory may be sited close to a local beauty spot, ruining the view. These are all examples of spillover effects or EXTERNALITIES. So the costs to the whole of society, the SOCIAL COSTS, are made up of the private costs of the business plus **negative externalities** (the costs to the rest of society). Social and environmental audits (☞ unit 40) take into account the social costs of business activity.

There may also be **positive externalities** which result from the business. It may create other jobs in the area for companies producing components or design a factory that complements the landscape. The firm may create skills which can be used for other jobs in the area. We can say that SOCIAL BENEFITS to society are the private benefits to business plus positive externalities (the benefits to the rest of society).

There are obvious problems that result from negative externalities. Many externalities affect the environment. Furthermore, when firms set their prices these usually only reflect the private costs of production. Prices will not, therefore, reflect the cost of pollution, noise etc. As a result of this firms may not be concerned about negative externalities as they do not have to pay for them. For example, a chemical company may produce toxic waste from its production process. It might be faced with two choices - disposing of this waste in a nearby river without treating it, or treating it and removing any toxins. The first measure would cost next to nothing, but the second measure could be relatively expensive. The rational choice for the firm, assuming this is legal, is to dispose of the waste untreated in the river. However, for other users of the river, such as anglers and water sports enthusiasts, this decision would have serious effects.

In order to assess the impact of business activity, cost - benefit analysis is sometimes used, particularly for large projects (☞ unit 31).

In 1991 Shell, the owner of the Brent Spar oil platform, was looking for ways to dispose of the structure. With the approval of the UK government, it decided to sink it in a deep part of the Atlantic. Sinking it in its place of operation in the North Sea would have caused a hazard to shipping and would have caused further environmental damage to an already polluted area. In 1995 the platform was towed to the Atlantic for sinking. Pressure from groups such as Greenpeace led to Shell abandoning the plan to dump the platform. In 1998 Shell decided to dismantle the platform and use the parts to construct a ferry quay in Norway. Shell had already spent £20 million preparing the platform for sinking. It would cost £26 million for the recycling of the structure.

Using examples from the article, outline the possible:
(a) private costs;
(b) negative externalities;
(c) positive externalities;
of the proposed methods of disposal of the Brent Spar oil platform.

Question 1

Environmental costs

There are many different types of negative externality that may result from business activity. Some are dealt with in other units, eg consumer exploitation and employee exploitation. This section will focus on environmental costs.

Air pollution This is pollution from factories, machines or vehicles emitting poisonous gases into the atmosphere. We need only look into the sky above some factories to see evidence of this. Other forms of air pollution may be catastrophes such as at the Chernobyl nuclear plant in 1986, when massive quantities of radioactive materials were released into the atmosphere and surrounding countryside. The results were seen in many countries in Europe.

What are the main causes of air pollution?

- Acid rain. Thousands of acres of forests have been destroyed by acid rain, as a result of sulphur dioxide emissions into the atmosphere.
- Chlorofluorocarbons (CFCs). The use by some firms of CFCs in aerosols and refrigerators has contributed to the breakdown of the earth's ozone layer. The ozone layer acts as a filter for the sun's rays. Without it, exposure to sunlight can increase the risk of skin cancer.
- Carbon dioxide (CO2) and other gases. There has been a growing awareness that the release of CO2, and other gases such as methane and nitrous oxide, into the atmosphere is causing a 'greenhouse effect'. The build-up of these gases is associated with the rise in the use of cars and with the generation of electricity with fossil fuels such as coal.

Scientists argue that the 'greenhouse effect' could result in the earth's atmosphere warming up (**global warming**) to such an extent that the polar ice caps melt. This could lead to significant areas of land being submerged by rising sea levels. The 'greenhouse effect', many scientists believe, has also been responsible for the climatic extremes experienced in parts of the world.

Figure 41.1 shows the emissions of air pollutants in the UK. It suggests that concern over their effect on the environment has led to an effort to cut emissions.

Figure 41.1 *Air pollutants*

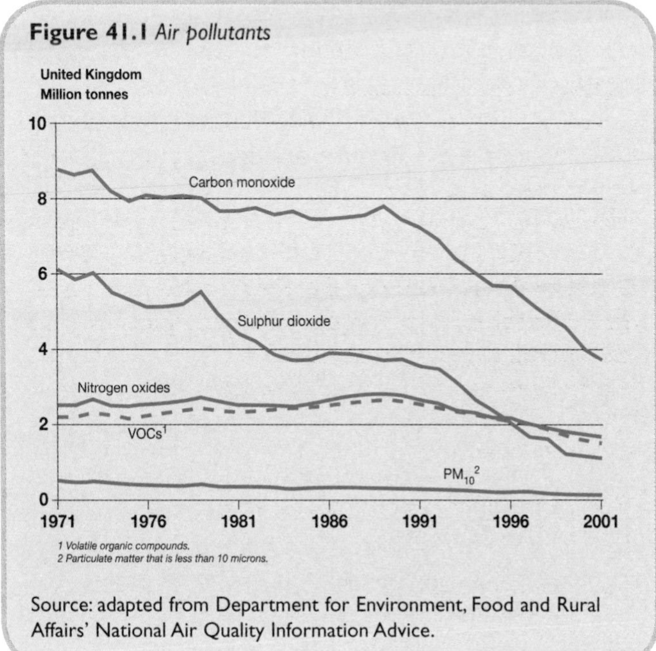

Source: adapted from Department for Environment, Food and Rural Affairs' National Air Quality Information Advice.

Water pollution Water pollution can occur in a number of ways. Many industries, such as brewing and chemical manufacturing, use water in production. Their plants are usually located by rivers and it is fairly easy, therefore, for them to dispose of waste into nearby water. It is also possible for our drinking water from reservoirs to be polluted by chemicals used in agricultural production. People are starting to drink bottled water or have water filters fitted to their water supply in the home as a result.

Table 41.1 *Water pollution indicators, England*

	1990	1995	2000	2002
Chemical quality of rivers and canals (percentage of total river length)				
Good	43	55	64	65
Fair	40	35	29	28
	1998	**2000**	**2002**	
Compliance with EU bathing water standards (percentages)				
	90	95	99	

Source: adapted from Department for Environment, Food and Rural Affairs and Environment Agency.

The sea has also been polluted over many years. Industries sited near to the coast have used the sea as a dump for their waste. The effluence and cargo of ships are also sometimes dropped into the sea. The North Sea, for example, is one of the most polluted seas in the world as a result of years of discharges from a variety of industries. These have included sewage and the by-products of chemical production. A number of beaches in the UK are unsafe for bathing, according to the European Union, which grades the quality of beaches. Table 41.1 shows that there has been some success in reducing water pollution in England in recent years.

Congestion and noise Business activity has resulted in more roads becoming congested with traffic. For example, many firms now transport their goods by rail rather than road. Recent estimates have put the cost of this congestion on British roads as high as £15 billion.

Some business activity can also result in noise pollution. For example, a decision by an airport to open a new runway would affect noise levels experienced by local residents.

Destruction of the environment One example of this is logging and associated industries, which have been responsible for the destruction of sections of the Amazonian rainforests. Another example might include the effects of new buildings in a rural area. A new housing estate in a village, for example, may deprive villagers and visitors of previously unspoilt countryside. It may also increase noise and congestion levels in the village.

In 1989 the oil tanker, the Exxon Valdez, crashed onto a reef in Prince William Sound in Southern Alaska, USA. The accident covered one of the world's cleanest and most beautiful stretches of coastline with 11 million gallons of crude oil. Exxon spent an initial $2 billion on the clean up and also paid $300 million in compensation to 11,000 individuals. Additionally, following legal action, $5 billion in damages was awarded by a court to the local fishing communities in 1994.

There is disagreement about the longer term effects of the Exxon Valdez disaster. An Exxon company statement said 'the environment in Prince William Sound is healthy, robust and thriving.' Environmentalists, however, point to respiratory illnesses, brain tumours and cancers amongst the local population linked to the oil spills and the clean up. They also point to the pollution remaining on the coast and the failure of fish stocks, including herrings, to return to the area.

Source: adapted from *The Independent*, 25.3.2004.

(a) Describe the costs associated with the Exxon Valdez crash.

Question 2

Waste disposal Many business operations result in waste products (☞ unit 26). This may be in the form of waste chemicals resulting from the manufacture of plastics or waste materials from the manufacture of wooden products. The packaging used in products can also be waste and needs to be disposed of.

It has been suggested that some water operators in the UK impose external costs. If a company does not maintain its pipes and leaks occur, this can result in hosepipe bans. It also means that it has to take more water from reservoirs and rivers because of the waste water it has created by leakages.

The impact on the environment of business is not always negative. In derelict urban areas, for example, businesses have converted rundown buildings into office space and have landscaped waste land around the site. Also, some of the buildings may be thought to have architectural merit.

Controlling environmental costs

Because of concern about the impact of business on the environment, attention has been focused on how pollution, congestion and other environmental costs can be controlled. There is a number of ways this can be done.

Government regulation Various pieces of legislation exist in the UK and Europe to prevent the pollution of the environment by business activity. For example, in the UK **The Environment Act, 1995** set up the Environment Agency to the monitor and control pollution. It also set up regulations concerning contaminated land, abandoned mines, national parks, air quality and waste. EU directives often become regulations in the UK. For example, the **Air Quality Limit Values Regulations, 2003** sets targets for reductions in levels of ozone in the air by 2010.

Some countries have government bodies designed to control pollution. For example, in the US the Environment Protection Agency attempts to ensure US businesses do not contravene legislation. There are also agreements between countries to control pollution. The Kyoto Protocol agreed to limit greenhouse gas emissions between 2008 and 2012 to 5.2 per cent of their 1990 levels. In certain cases voluntary agreements between governments and manufacturers also take place.

Taxation The aim of taxation in this context is to ensure that the social cost of any pollution caused by a firm is paid for. This means that the government must estimate the actual cost to society of different types of pollution. As a result prices would more accurately reflect the true cost of using environmental resources. So, for example, a firm which produced a £5 product with 'environmentally unfriendly' packaging might be taxed 50p for this packaging, raising the price to £5.50. There are two advantages to this. First, the tax revenue might be used to minimise the impact of this packaging on the environment. Second, it might act as an incentive for the firm to produce more environmentally sensitive packaging, so that the tax is either reduced or removed.

In this example the consumer pays for the environmentally unfriendly packaging in the form of a price rise. Some would argue that the firm itself should pay for such costs. In this way, the price would remain at £5.00, but the firm would be taxed 50 pence for externalities created by its packaging. The consumer would not directly suffer as a result of the taxation.

Increases in fuel prices in the UK have been justified by governments on the grounds that consumers should pay prices which accurately reflect the impact of car use on the environment. In the late 1990s the UK government introduced a **landfill tax**. This taxed businesses £15 per tonne in 2004 for dumping waste in a landfill site.

Compensation Firms could be forced by law to compensate those affected by externalities. For example, it is common for airports to provide grants to nearby residents. This allows them to purchase double glazing and other types of insulation, which provides protection from aircraft noise. Business may also be forced by court action to pay compensation to people affected by their actions.

Government subsidies This involves governments offering grants, tax allowances and other types of subsidy to businesses in order to encourage them to reduce externalities. Such subsidies can allow environmentally desirable projects, which otherwise might not be profitable, to go ahead. For example, a business may be given a grant so that it can build a recycling plant for plastics. This should encourage domestic and industrial users to recycle rather than dump plastic products.

Government subsidies could also be used to encourage more environmentally friendly habits amongst consumers. For example, many councils are attempting to encourage the use of bicycles through schemes such as setting up cycle lanes and giving grants to employees wishing to use bicycles for travelling to and from work.

Road pricing and charges Charging road users could be used to reduce pollution and congestion. There is a long history of charging for motorways in European countries such as France, Spain and Italy. In the UK the first toll motorway was opened in 2004, with travellers and business users paying to travel around Birmingham to reduce traffic on the M6. In 2003 a £5 charge was introduced on most vehicles entering the centre of London.

Park and ride schemes These are also designed to encourage a reduction in car use in city areas. They are often run by local authorities. Car users, for a fee, can park their cars outside the city areas and are taken by bus or rail into and out of the city. A single bus, if full, reduces traffic in the city area and also reduces the need for inner city car parking spaces.

Pollution permits In the USA pollution permits have been introduced. These allow businesses a certain amount of emissions. If the business reduces its pollution below a certain level, it can save the allowance for later or even sell it. Some have argued that Western economies should adopt the same approach to developing countries as they pollute the atmosphere across the world.

Working together It may be possible for business and/or government to work together to control the effect of business action on the environment. Examples might be:
- the sharing of best practice on environmental controls;
- producing environmental codes of practice;
- developing waste strategies.

Education Governments and other agencies, such as charities, could try to influence consumers and producers through educational and promotional campaigns.

Consumer pressure Consumers have forced a number of firms to consider the impact of their activities on the environment. There is evidence that a new breed of consumer is emerging, who considers factors other than price and quality when buying products. Such consumers take into account the effect on the environment and society of those products which they purchase. So, for example, such a consumer may not buy aerosols containing CFCs, furniture made from trees which have been chopped down in the Amazon rainforest or cosmetics which have been tested on animals.

Although this approach has influenced a wide range of firms, it does have one major problem. Consumers often do not have sufficient information with which to evaluate the impact of business activity upon the environment. Such information is often not disclosed to members of the public. Also, many firms have not been slow to realise that presenting themselves as being environmentally conscious can be very good for sales. However, the actual record of such firms with regard to the environment may well fall short of the claims which they make for themselves. For example, a battery producing company placed an environmentally friendly label on its products. However, this had to be removed when it was revealed that batteries use up more energy in their construction than they create in their use.

Environmental audits An environmental audit is one method by which consumers have a fairer chance of assessing the environmental impact of a firm. This could be much like the financial audits which all companies are at present required to have by law. An environmental audit can be one part of a wider social audit (☞ unit 40). This perhaps indicates the growing pressure put on firms to be concerned about their impact on the environment.

Business and environmemental policies

With public concern increasing about the dangers of damaging the environment, pressure is building on many firms to become more environmentally friendly. Adopting such environmental policies can affect businesses in a number of ways.
- They may need to change production techniques or the materials which they use. Such changes may range from

Electricity prices in the UK could rise as a result of plans to cut carbon dioxide emissions beyond EU targets. The UK energy minister, Stephen Timms, said 'Our suggestion is that industrial electricity prices will increase ... by something like 6 per cent, not just in the UK but in major European industrial economies. The comparable figure for domestic bills would be about 3 per cent ... '.

The government had plans to cut carbon dioxide emissions by a fifth by 2010 in preparation for a new EU scheme on emissions trading to start in 2005. The initiative introduces caps on the amount of carbon dioxide emitted by industry. The scheme would force EU companies to pay to pollute. It will be mandatory for around 12,000 factories, of which 2,000 are in the UK. Under the scheme, the government would set emission limits on industry and allow companies to trade the right to produce emissions. Carbon emission limits for power stations have been cut so that, by 2007, their allocations will be 2.75 million tonnes of carbon dioxide below the government's updated energy projections for the sector..

Britain only imports around 2 per cent of its electricity and exports much less than that. The government said the fact that UK producers do not face competition from generators not affected by the EU scheme means they are better placed to absorb the costs of reducing their emissions.

The overall number of allowances for UK industry have been set at level beyond the Kyoto Protocol commitment. Industry voiced its displeasure at this. 'Emissions trading is the right approach, but if we go too far and other countries don't make similar commitments, we are going to put our hard-pressed manufacturers in an extremely difficult position in global markets' said Digby Jones, the director general of the Confederation of British Industry. But Friends of the Earth pointed out that the UK will not be introducing the toughest limits in Europe. It said some countries, such as Spain and Ireland, will have to take tougher action simply to meet Kyoto targets. Germany was also expected to follow the UK in going further than its Kyoto target.

Source: adapted from *The Guardian*, 19.1.2004.

(a) Explain the types of control on environmental costs mentioned in the article.
(b) Discuss to what extent the competitiveness of UK industry would be affected by these controls.

Question 3

the simple, such as the use of recycled paper in offices, to the complex, such as the installation of new recycling plants.

- Businesses may have to change their operations. For example, they may have to seek different methods of waste disposal. They may have to reduce or alter the packaging used in products. They may consider reducing the size of company cars or encouraging transport on trains by representatives.
- Firms may find that their costs increase. For example, a firm previously dumping waste products into the sea would find it more expensive to process this waste. Similarly, a firm which encouraged its employees to use bicycles rather than cars on company business might find that this takes employees longer and is, therefore, more expensive. Such increases in costs may well be passed on to customers in the form of higher prices.
- Some activities which improve a firm's environmental practices may lead to lower rather than higher costs. For example, a firm which sought to improve its energy efficiency might insulate the workplace, turn down heating appliances and turn off unused lights. Such actions are likely to reduce fuel bills and thus reduce costs. Encouraging employees to re-use items, such as paper clips, envelopes and elastic bands, is likely to have a similar effect.
- Business might be forced to work together more closely to reduce their impact on the environment. For example, businesses might work with suppliers to avoid charges on pollution, congestion or waste disposal. Industry bodies may be set up by businesses in certain areas to monitor environmental effects and work to develop solutions.
- There may need to be a change in its ethical stance (☞ unit 39). This may have a knock-on effect on other aspects of a firm's activities and lead to a re-examination of a number of its business practices.
- There is growing evidence that consumers are attracted to firms with environmentally friendly policies. Adopting such policies may lead to an increase in sales and possibly in profit levels.
- Research and development expenditure may need to increase as a firm seeks to find new, more environmentally friendly, products and production processes. Such an increase in expenditure may go on testing and creating new packaging materials or materials to be used in production.

Conservation

All businesses depend, to a greater or lesser degree, on the use of non-renewable resources (☞ unit 26). These are resources which cannot be replaced and which might in some cases, with current usage, run out within the next 100 years. Such resources range from raw materials, like oil, iron, copper and aluminium, to living creatures.

Conservation ranges from banning the use of such resources altogether, to encouraging businesses to use them sparingly. There is a number of measures which seek to conserve non-renewable resources.

- Recycling schemes. Bottle banks set up to help the recycling of glass are now a common sight in supermarket car parks. Not only do glass recycling schemes help to conserve natural resources, but they can be profitable for those companies involved. Recycling

Congestion charging is a way of ensuring that those using valuable and congested road space make a financial contribution. It encourages the use of other modes of transport and is also intended to ensure that, for those who have to use the roads, journey times are quicker and more reliable.

The London scheme requires drivers to pay £5 per day if they wish to drive in central London during the scheme's hours of operation.

The following explains why the Mayor has decided to introduce congestion charging in central London.

- London suffers the worst traffic congestion in the UK and amongst the worst in Europe.
- Drivers in central London spend 50 per cent of their time in queues.
- Every weekday morning, the equivalent of 25 busy motorway lanes of traffic tries to enter central London.
- It has been estimated that London loses between £2 and 4 million every week in terms of lost time caused by congestion.

Not surprisingly, Londoners say congestion is one of the biggest issues facing the capital.

Surveys have shown that Londoners do not want to see congestion clogging up roads, threatening businesses and damaging London's status as a thriving world city.

Source: adapted from www.cclondon.com.

It was argued that the London congestion charge cut traffic so effectively that London faced a cash crisis because drivers were avoiding the charging zone. Figures suggested that so many cars kept out of central London after the charge was introduced in February 2003 that traffic levels fell by around 40 per cent. The lack of drivers paying £5 to enter the zone meant that Transport for London's budget for the scheme would be £65 million short by the end of the financial year, according to the mayor's estimates.

Source: adapted from *The Guardian*, 13.6.2003.

(a) Examine how the London congestion charge might affect:
(i) businesses;
(ii) individuals;
(iii) local government in London.

schemes also exist in the paper, plastics and aluminium industries.

- Multilateral agreements. These are agreements between a number of countries which seek to limit the use of natural resources. Agreements now exist which place limits on the amount of fishing and whaling which countries are allowed to carry out. In addition, some countries now have import bans on commodities such as ivory which come from endangered species.

Table 41.2 *Management of municipal waste by method, England*

Thousand tonnes

	1996/97	1998/99	2000/01	2001/02
Landfill	20,631	21,534	22,039	22,317
Incineration with energy from waste	1,446	2,117	2,391	2,459
Recycled/composted	1,750	2,525	3,446	3,907
Other	761	160	182	140
Total	24,588	26,337	28,057	28,823

Source: adapted from Department for Environment, Food and Rural Affairs.

Table 41.3 *Electricity generated from renewable sources, UK*

GWh

	1991	1996	2001	2002
Wind and wave	9	499	965	1,256
Solar photo-voltaics	-	-	2	3
Hydro	4,624	3,393	4,055	4,788
Landfill gas	208	708	2,507	2,679
Sewage sludge digestion	328	410	363	397
Municipal solid waste combustion	151	490	929	958
Other biofuels	1	197	777	870
Wastes	88	417	479	494
Total	5,409	6,102	10,077	11,444

Source: adapted from Department of Trade and Industry.

(a) Describe the methods used to improve conservation and protect the environment in the tables.
(b) Comment on the extent to which these methods have been successful.

Question 5

- Government subsidies. These have been used to encourage farmers to conserve the countryside through retaining features such as dry stone walls and hedgerows, for example.

Business opportunities

The growth in the importance of conservation and the management of waste (☞ unit 26) in recent years has led to a huge expansion in commercial opportunities in the provision of waste management services. Examples of businesses that have grown as a result of these trends include:

- chemical treatments such as metal precipitation, pH adjustment and acid/alkali neutralisation, cyanide treatment and ammonia stripping and recovery;
- special waste transfer stations where a wide range of waste material can be dealt with;
- domestic refuse collection on behalf of local authorities;
- clearing contaminated land;
- waste transportation from business sites to disposal or treatment points;
- clinical waste disposal on behalf of hospitals, dentists and veterinary surgeons;
- laboratory chemicals packing and disposal;
- dry waste disposal services;
- on-site treatment technologies;
- water jetting and air conveyancing;
- backtrack services to help businesses recycle and recover difficult and special wastes;
- drainage systems and support services;
- integrated waste management services;
- sewer surveying services.

key terms

Externalities - occur when private costs are different to social costs and private benefits are different to social benefits.
Private benefits - the benefit of an activity to an individual or a business.
Private costs - the cost of an activity to an individual or a business.
Social benefits - the benefit of an activity to society as well as to a business.
Social costs - the cost of an activity to society as well as to a business.

Knowledge...Knowledge...Knowledge...Knowledge...Knowledge

1. Give an example of:
   (a) a private cost;
   (b) a positive externality;
   (c) a private benefit.
2. State 5 examples of negative externalities that may be created by a business.
3. Briefly explain the effect that:
   (a) a tax on a business;
   (b) a subsidy from government to a business;
   might have on the creation of negative externalities.
4. Why might a business be concerned about the views consumers have about how it affects the environment?
5. Briefly explain 3 consequences of following an environmentally friendly policy for a business.
6. 'Conservation can be profitable for a business.' Explain this statement with an example.
7. State 5 examples of businesses that may develop as a result of the growth of concern over the effect of businesses on the environment.

Case study Air Traffic pollution

The number of people flying into and out of the UK is expected to increase from 180 million to 500 million by 2030, says the Department for Transport. This has led many environmentalists and others to raise concerns about the possible impact of this on the greenhouse effect leading to global warming - the process by which the earth's temperature rises above levels associated with natural cycles leading to floods, droughts and even, possibly, a new ice age. If the predictions are correct aviation, will be responsible for two thirds of all UK greenhouse gas emissions by 2050. Other environmental concerns relating to the increase in air traffic include asthma and noise.

Source: adapted from *The Guardian*, 2004.

Figure 41.2 *Terminal passengers to UK airports*

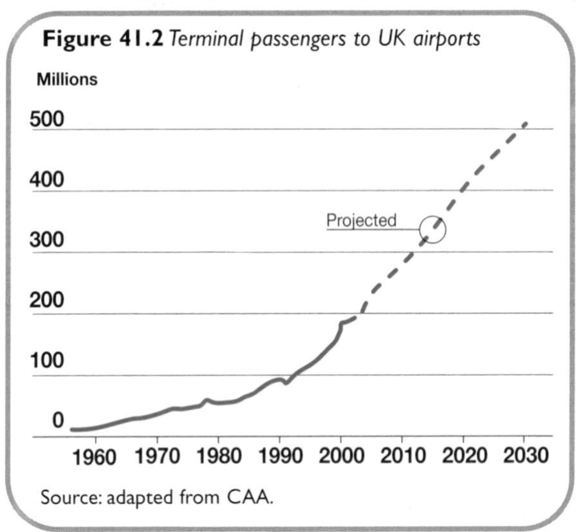

Source: adapted from CAA.

Figure 41.3 *Emissions caused by moving 1 tonne, 1 km*

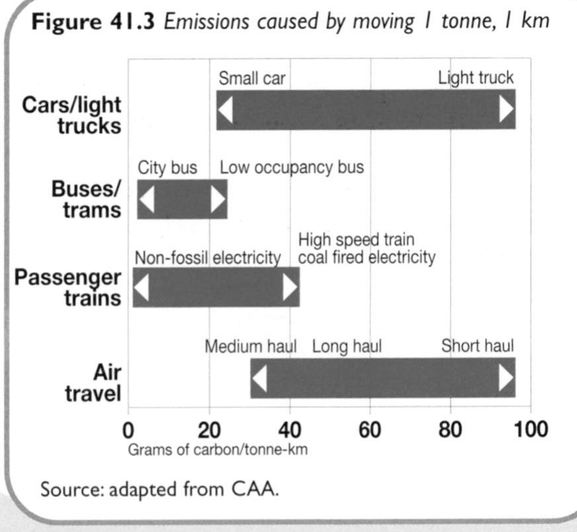

Source: adapted from CAA.

Figure 41.4 *Emissions of carbon dioxide by end user*

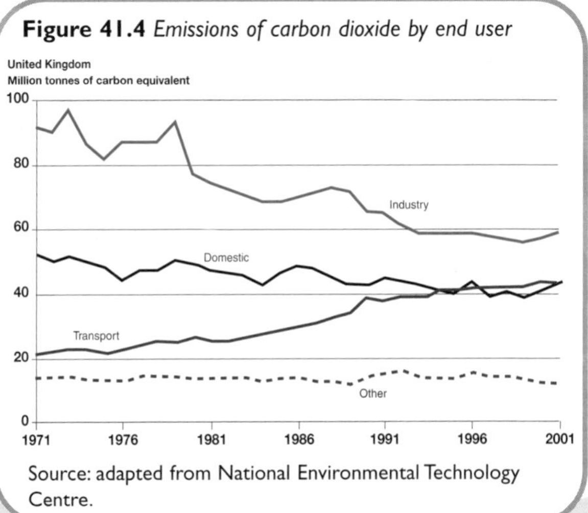

Source: adapted from National Environmental Technology Centre.

The village of Bamber Green close to Stansted airport is scheduled to disappear beneath concrete by 2011. Campaigners from the Stop Stansted Expansion group were dismayed by the announcement that a second runway was to be built at the airport. Peter Gowan the Deputy Chairman of the Group has a home that would be just yards away from the new runway. Maggie Sutton whose home in nearby Broxsted may disappear, was angry. She said. 'We can't keep covering the countryside with concrete.' Professor Jangu Banatvala, a retired doctor who lives in nearby Bishops Stortford, warned that permitted noise levels did not respect World Health organisation guidelines. Among likely casualties were two ancient monuments and 29 grade 11 listed houses. The 500 year old Three Horseshoes pub would also be bulldozed.

Source: adapted from *The Observer* 21.3.2004.

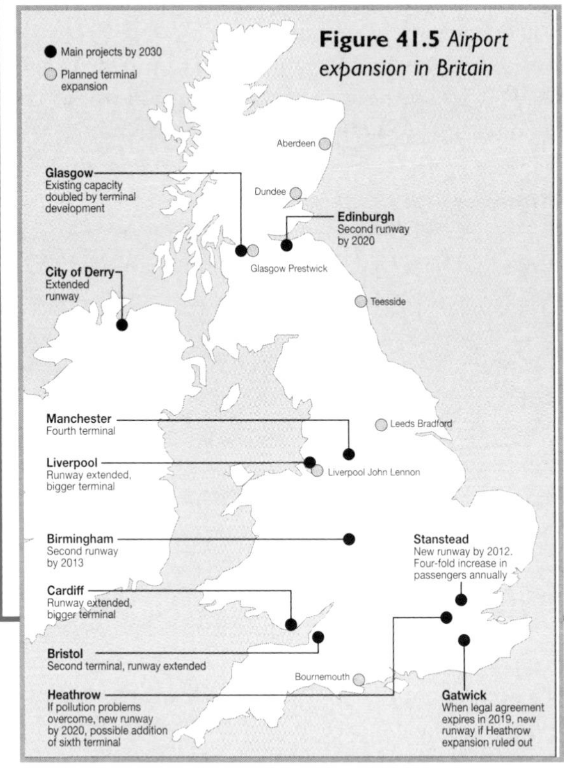

Figure 41.5 *Airport expansion in Britain*

Experts believe that the aviation industry could clean up its act. The latest planes are more efficient and less noisy and the following generation should be even better. With efficient use of fuels comes less noxious exhausts. Aero engine fuel efficiency improved by 70 per cent between 1960 and 2000. The passenger plane that taxis down the runway in 2050 could be 40-50 per cent more efficient than today's up to the minute designs.

Source: adapted from *The Guardian*, 21.8.2001.

(a) Describe the trends taking place in airline usage using examples from the articles. (6 marks)

(b) Suggest the environmental costs associated with an increased use of airlines in the UK. (10 marks)

(c) Explain how the environmental costs of increased aviation usage might be controlled. (10 marks)

(d) Examine ways in which businesses in the aviation industry might change their practices to minimise their environmental impact. (12 marks)

(e) Discuss whether the environmental costs associated with air travel are likely to increase in future. (12 marks)

42 Study Skills

Studying and assessment

Study skills are the skills that a student needs to plan, organise and carry out their work effectively. They also help a student to answer questions and carry out tasks which are designed to test their abilities. Units 42 and 43 are set out like a manual. They provide guidance and examples to help students when working in term time or when taking examinations. Examples are shown in italics. The units could be used:

- at the start of the course to get ideas on the best way to study;
- constantly throughout the course when studying;
- before examinations during revision preparation.

Action planning

Studying is more effective if there is a **plan** or **strategy**. An action plan can be formally written out, but it does not have to be. For any piece of work, it is important for a student to plan:

- how long it will take, bearing in mind any deadline;
- where the student will work;
- when the student will work;
- in what order tasks will be carried out;
- factors likely to affect the work, such as unforeseen occurrences.

A plan can be made for an individual piece of work, work over a term, coursework or project work, revision or an entire scheme of work. It is important for a student to develop a **routine** of work that is effective. It is also important for students to be **committed** to complete the plan. The table below shows a possible action plan that may be used for study, work or revision.

Title and nature of work	*What needs to be done? What is the focus? How will it be judged?*
Start and finish date	*What is the deadline? How long will it take?*
Collecting information	*Where from? How can it be obtained? What help is needed? How long will it take? How will it be used?*
Carry out the work	*Where? When? How long? Who with? What order? Continuous or broken down? Help needed? What factors might affect the work? Possible changes?*
Review	*Did the plan work? Was the outcome successful? How could it have been done better? Was everything covered?*

Time management

An important part of the action plan is planning how long to study or work. Certain factors must be considered when deciding how much time to take when studying.

When to start and when to finish There is a deadline for most pieces of work. This is the date by which it has to be completed. It is important to start early enough and to leave enough time to finish the work. Some people work faster than others. This will affect the time they allocate.

How long the work will take Some pieces of work will take longer than others. Short answer questions will perhaps take less time than an essay. A piece of coursework or project work may take months. So will revision. Some people work quicker than others, which may reduce the time taken.

How long to work The length of time spent on work can affect its quality.

- Spending a greater amount of time preparing and planning may improve a piece of work.
- The time spent writing may also improve work.
- Working for too long can be tiring and work may suffer. Sometimes it is better to take a short break.
- Some work, such as coursework and revision, can not be done all at once and must be broken up.
- It is useful to try to break up revision, by learning as you go along. There is likely to be too much to learn in one session at the end. Spreading the work also allows practice.

When to study This will depend on the time available. Some people have a free choice of time. They could work in free time in the day, at lunchtime, in the evening or at weekends. People with part time jobs or with great commitments may find it more difficult. They may have to work when they can. Sometimes there may be free time which could be usefully used, such as travelling to school or college on a bus or train. Students should also consider that it may not be useful to work:

- late at night because they are tired;
- after strenuous exercise because it may be difficult to concentrate;
- when they are doing lots of other things.

Where to study

It is important to consider where to work. Some students will work better in certain environments than others. Should you work at home or in a different place such as school, a library or another person's house? Issues to consider might be:

- the availability of materials. A library will have books you can use. It may also have a facility to find book titles,

newspapers and magazines, perhaps on CD Rom, and access to the Iinternet. If you keep all your materials at home, it may be better to work there;
- ease of access. Working at home allows easy access to drinks and food. Some people may also want to take a break to watch television or do something else;
- comfortable or not? Working in a familiar environment, such as home, can make work easier. Other people prefer to work in a more 'academic' atmosphere;
- alone or in a group? Some people prefer to work alone. Others like to work with someone else, even if they are doing their own work. Sometimes group activities demand that people work together;
- silent or not? Some people prefer to work in silence as they concentrate better. Working in a library would allow this. Others prefer things to be happening around them.

Other learning considerations

There are other factors that students may want to take into consideration when working.
- Some people prefer to sit on a hard chair. Some prefer to be more comfortable and sit on a soft or relaxing chair.
- Some people like to listen to music whilst they are working. Others prefer silence.
- Some people prefer bright lighting so that everything is clear. Others work better in dimmed lighting.
- Some people prefer to carry out several tasks or activities at once. Others prefer to do one task and then move on to another.
- Some people prefer to eat or chew while they are working as it helps them to concentrate. Others don't.
- Some people learn better by moving around from time to time and some by standing up.

Learning and memory strategies

Different people learn in different ways. Some people learn and remember more easily when they hear something. Others prefer to see it written down and to read it. Some prefer a diagram or picture. Each of these styles of learning may be useful in different circumstances. If a student finds learning something difficult in one way, he or she might try another.

Written methods In many cases students will have to read information and take notes. This is often the most common form of learning on a course at advanced level.

A possible technique used to read information is to:
- choose a section of written material that you will read and quickly scan through it to get the overall idea;
- read the material more slowly;
- put the written material aside and recite the key ideas or points that you have read;
- check that you have covered the main points;
- if you have missed anything, re-read the information.

Often in work or for revision students have to condense large amounts of information into shorter note form. This makes it easier to remember. Steps to note taking may involve the following:
- reading the information and making sure that you understand it first;
- dividing up the information into topic headings and subheadings;
- making suitable notes that are clear and easy to read, and are in a logical order;
- underlining or highlighting important words or key phrases that will trigger memory of the point;
- using page references to the written material;
- leaving space for additions;
- creating an index for your notes, either using a card system or a computer package and updating the order.

Once you have a set of notes you can use the reading technique above to make sure you understand them or for revision.

Example

In 1999 The European Commission was poised to open an investigation into BP Amoco's proposed $26bn merger with Atlantic Richfield (Arco). EU sources said the merger, which would further tighten the oligopolistic structure of the oil market, had to be examined in the context of other anti-trust investigations involving the sector - notably the Exxon-Mobil project. Competition authorities in Brussels and the US were worried that these and other deals would enhance the power of a small number of oil companies in the exploration and production of oil and gas worldwide. If the two mergers went through, the top three oil majors - including the Anglo Dutch group Shell - would account for close to 50 per cent of crude oil production by publicly quoted western companies, bankers estimated.

EU officials had serious doubts about the BP Amoco-Arco merger. One problem involved the high joint share BP Amoco-Arco would have in pipeline transportation of natural gas in the UK sector of the North Sea. The potential blocks to the approval of Exxon-Mobil were greater. As well as its doubts about the global structure of the industry, Brussels identified numerous problems affecting Europe as a whole, as well as the EU member states. One was that the deal could harm competition in the onshore production and distribution of low calorific gas in the Netherlands and Germany, where the two companies jointly had a high market share. The Commission said that it was determined not to let the merger damage the consumer benefits expected to flow from the liberalisation of the European gas market.

Oil mergers
- *Possible investigation by European Commission of BP Amoco -Arco and Exxon-Mobil mergers.*
- *Concern that the mergers would increase oligopolistic nature of oil market. If mergers went through, BP Amoco-Arco, Exxon- Mobil and Shell would have nearly 50 per cent of crude oil production.*

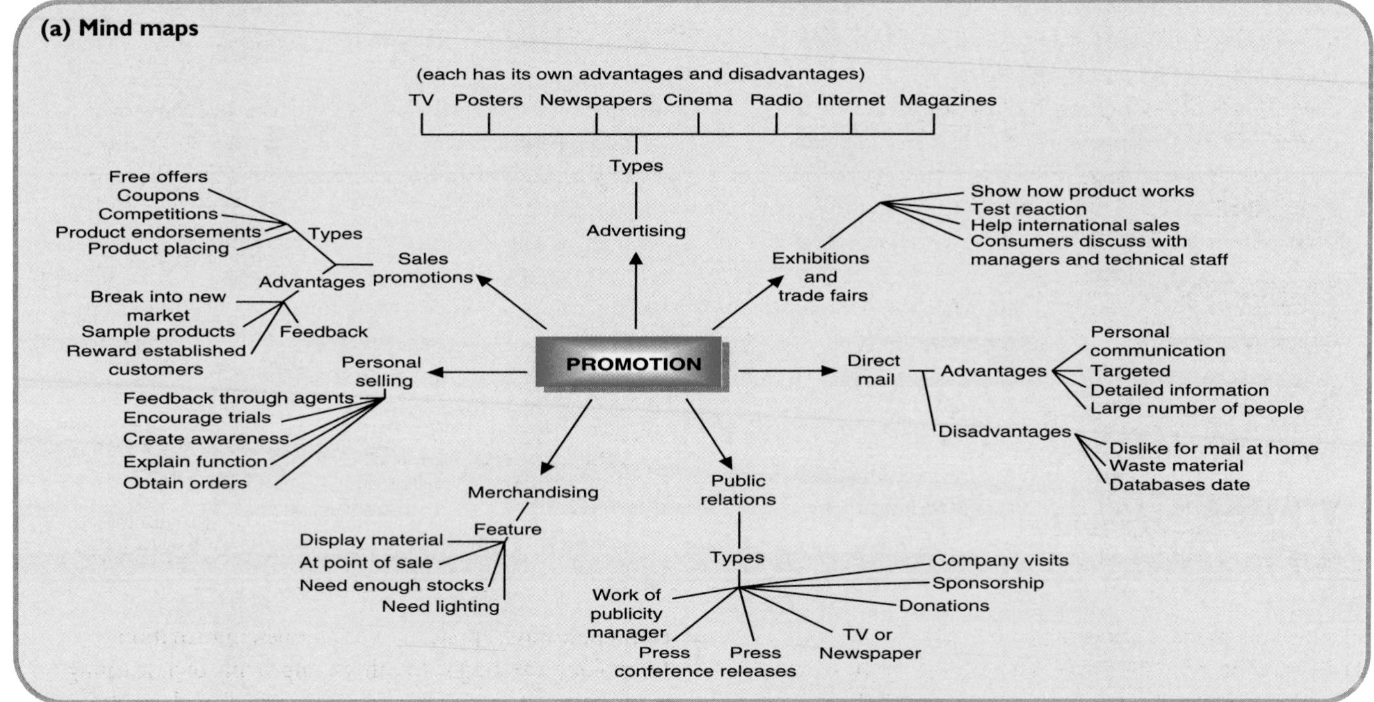

- *Problem of BP Amoco-Arco merger. Domination of natural gas pipelines.*
- *Problems of Exxon-Mobil merger. Harm to competition, transport of low calorific gas in Holland and Germany and possible benefits of market liberalisation (lower prices, better choice etc.)*

Oral methods It is sometimes easier to remember or understand something if you hear it. When you meet people do you remember their name? If so you may have a strong oral memory. Strategies for learning might include:

- answering questions asked by another person;
- making oral notes onto a tape recorder which are played back regularly;
- constantly repeating phrases or key words, perhaps in an order;
- make up a **mnemonic**, rhyme or phrase which can be repeated. For example, PEST analysis stands for the Political, Economic, Social and Technological factors that affect a business.

Pictorial/visual When you meet people do you remember their face? If so you may have a strong visual memory. Visual material can provide an instant 'picture' of information. Sometimes it is easier to see relationships by visual representation. Visual information may make use of some of the note taking techniques explained above. It may also make use of photographs. Examples of visual presentation include the following.

(a) Mind maps. *Promotion methods.*
(b) Family trees. *The sources of funds.*
(c) Flow diagrams. *The stages in the design process.*
(d) Horizontal family trees. *Herzberg's two-factor theory.*

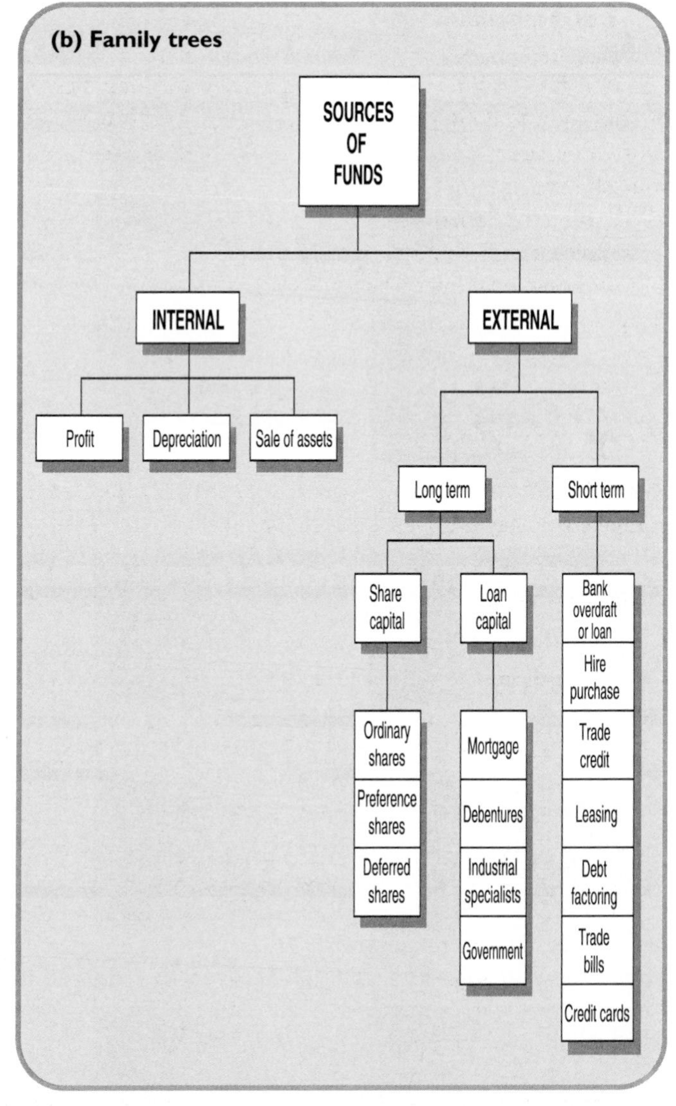

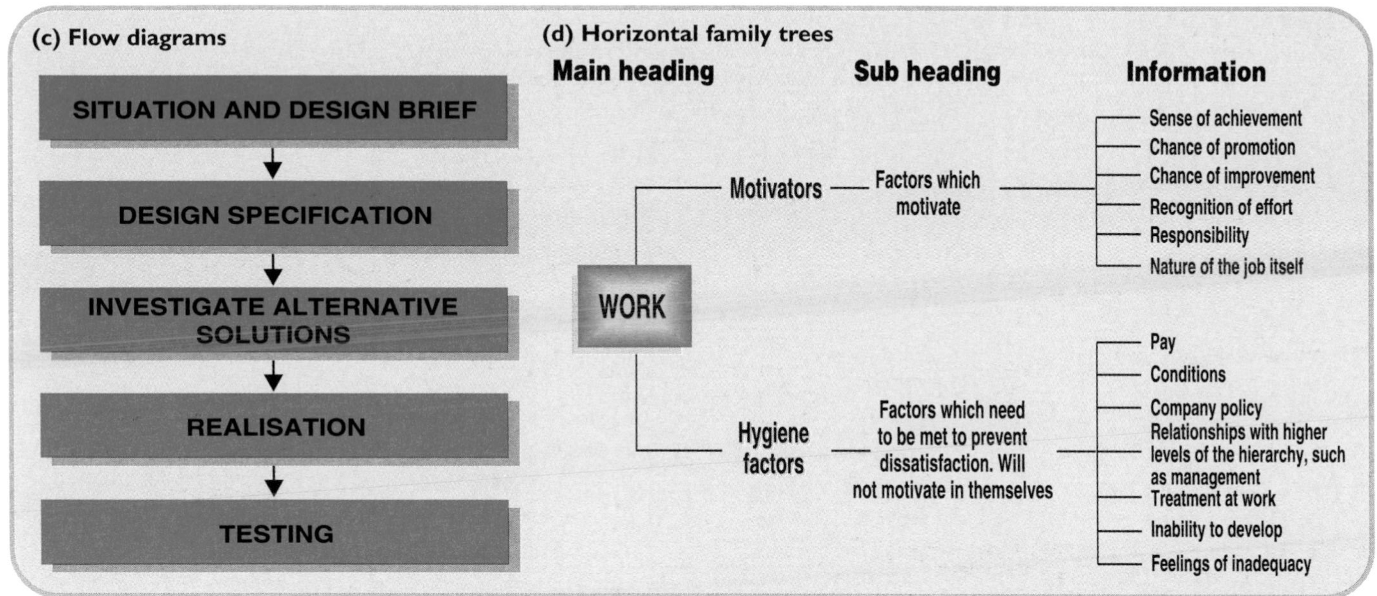

(e) Block diagrams. *Calculating profit and loss.*
(f) Method of loci. This involves taking a room you know and imagining certain key words in parts of the room. *Types of integration.*

Learning by doing You may think that you know something or know how to do it. But you might only find out if you test yourself by doing something. It may be possible to test yourself by using:

- classroom or homework activities you have already completed earlier in the course;
- activities in textbooks or workbooks;
- applying ideas in a project or a piece of coursework;
- past examination questions;
- your own activities.

Key skills

Key skills allow a student to learn, select and apply important competences. Key skills at advanced level include communication, application of number, information technology, working with others, improving own learning and performance, and problem solving. All of these skills can be developed by a student taking a course in Business Studies. Some examples of each key skill are shown below.

Communication

- Debates. *The extent to which business ethics should influence profit.*
- Role play. *An interview scenario or a meeting with a pressure group.*
- Group discussions. *How a business might promote a new product.*
- Interviews. *A one-to-one interview with a manager about a business problem.*
- Oral presentations. *The results of marketing research.*
- Passing information. *A memo to staff about reorganisation following the introduction of new technology.*
- Written analysis. *A report recommending action to solve*

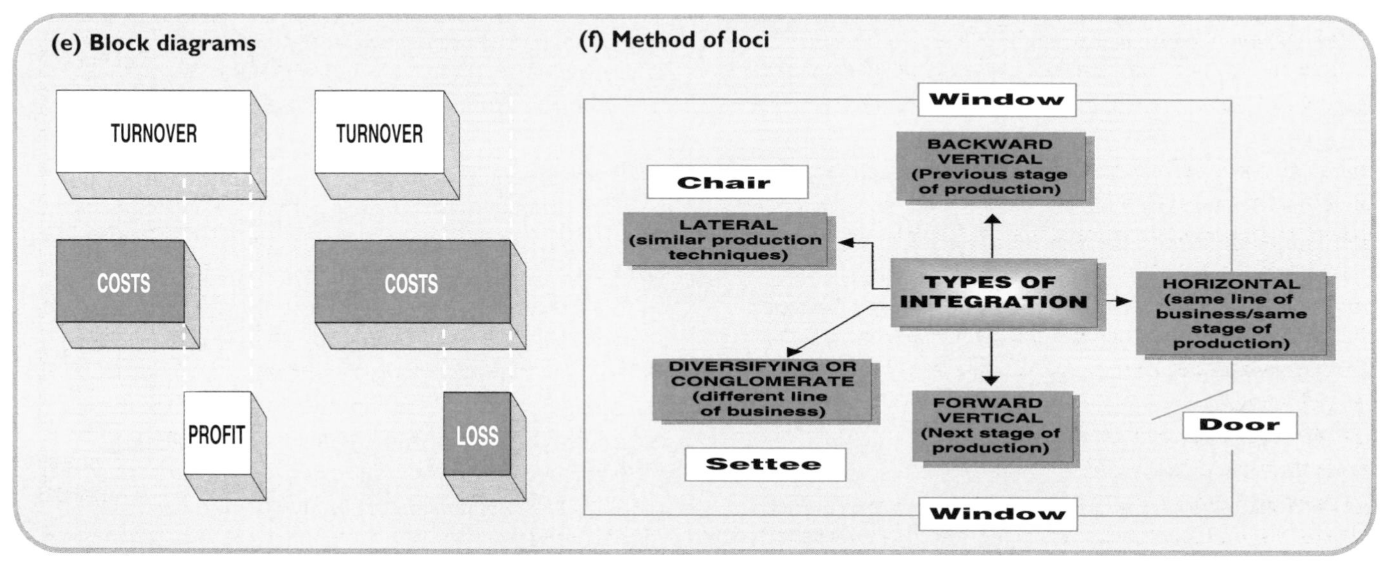

problems identified in the profit and loss account and a balance sheet or a strategy to deal with entry into foreign markets.

- Written and visual presentations. *Producing a business plan or charts showing the market share of businesses in an industry.*
- Summarising information. *Producing a business organisational chart or a summary of performance from financial ratio data.*
- Written responses. *A letter to a dissatisfied customer.*
- Communication using technology. *An e-mail to the manager showing sales figures on a spreadsheet.*

Application of number

- Numerical calculations. *Calculating the depreciation of assets using different methods or calculating labour turnover.*
- Planning information. *Preparing information for a sales revenue budget.*
- Interpreting results. *Identifying gearing problems from ratios.*
- Numerical analysis. *Investment appraisal using various methods.*
- Graphical analysis. *Identifying stock problems from a chart.*
- Construction of graphs. *Constructing a break-even chart.*
- Construction of tables. *Constructing a balance sheet.*
- Collection and presentation of data. *Sales figures used to produce product life cycle diagrams or market research information showing customers' responses.*
- Forecasting. *Estimating future sales figures from a trend.*

Information technology

- Searching for information. *Finding information on a CD Rom or an Internet website.*
- Reviewing and selecting information. *Selecting appropriate information from the Internet to show accidents at work.*
- Written presentation and manipulation of information. *Writing a report using appropriate software on the impact on the business of the euro.*
- Visual presentation of information. *Illustrating the number of full time, part time and outworkers in a business as percentages in a pie chart.*
- Calculation using data. *Calculating cash flow using a spreadsheet.*
- Collection of data. *Marketing research information on a database.*
- Manipulation and management of data. *Updating stock figures over time on a spreadsheet to show stock balances.*
- Transfer of data. *Storing cost information on disk so that it can be used for financial calculations by someone else.*
- Communication technology. *Sending an e-mail containing ideas for a new product.*

Working with others

- Discussions. *To discuss possible effect on a business of lean production methods.*
- Group debates. *Should multinational businesses take their profits back to the 'home' country or spend it in foreign countries in which they operate?*
- Searching for information. *When dealing with a great deal of information such as changes in government legislation over a period.*
- Collecting information. *When dealing with a great deal of information such as the effects of government policy on a business over a year.*
- Summarising. *When a great deal of information has to be summarised, each group member could take one aspect. For example, when looking at changes in a business, summaries of marketing, production and approaches to human resources could be made.*
- Question practice and cross checking. *Using another person to ask questions or to check your answers.*
- Brainstorming. *Developing possible promotional methods using brainstorming sessions.*
- Using outside sources of information. *Discussing the effects of pedestrianisation of a town on a local retailer.*

Improving own learning performance

- Identifying areas to improve. *Knowledge, memory, time management, work and resource management, such as where to find information and what resources to use, interpreting questions, answering questions, working with others, the work environment, motivation.*
- Evaluating work. *Own evaluation, others' opinions, evaluation against criteria, past experience of problems.*
- Identifying methods of improvement. *More practice, changing the method of learning, identifying strengths and applying to other areas, reorganisation of environment such as changing the place or time of work, changing attitudes, changing resources.*
- Identifying help. *Resources, other people, self-help.*

Problem solving

- Identifying problems. *Identify the need to change operations or strategy as a result of variance analysis.*
- Identifying the possible solutions to a problem. *Identifying the different strategies that a business might use to effectively manage change.*
- Choosing solutions from alternatives. *Choosing the most effective advertising campaign using decision trees or the most effective method of work using critical path analysis.*
- Evaluating solutions. *Evaluate the reorganisation of a business to improve productivity using mean and standard deviation calculations.*
- Using IT. *Using spreadsheet calculations to solve problems by identifying the most cost effective or profitable solution.*
- Problem solving in students' own work. *Identifying and solving problems involved in coursework, such as collection of data, storage of data, presentation of data.*

43 Assessment

Assessment criteria/objectives

It is possible to use a range of criteria when assessing the performance of students. This means that examiners or assessors want students to demonstrate a range of different skills. In order to be successful students must:

- understand the skills required by examiners or assessors;
- recognise the skill that is being assessed in a particular question;
- demonstrate all of the skills assessed by the examiner;
- practice skills before the examination.

The criteria used by examiners may fall into the following categories.

Knowledge Students have to demonstrate that they:

- understand business theories and concepts;
- recognise and understand business terms;
- interpret information given in a business context.

Students can recognise questions which test knowledge by looking at the command words in the question. Such words are explained in the section above. An example of a question assessing knowledge might be: *What is meant by best practice benchmarking?*

Application and understanding This assessment criterion requires students to apply theories and concepts in both familiar and unfamiliar situations. This might involve:

- using a business formula in appropriate circumstances, for example, calculating the current ratio for a business;
- using a theory to explain why a business has chosen a particular course of action, for example, using McGregor's Theory Y to explain why a business has introduced quality circles;
- using a business theory to suggest a suitable course of action for a business, for example, suggesting a chainstore uses loyalty cards to increase repeat sales.

Questions requiring application can again be recognised by looking at the command word. An example of a question requiring application might be: *Explain why the business has cut its research and development budget.*

Analysis Students have to demonstrate that they can break down information and understand the implications of what they have been presented with. Students will encounter both qualitative and quantitative information and will need to:

- identify causes and effects and interrelationships, for example, recognise from a graph that sales are falling and could be a result of new competition in the market;
- break down information to identify specific causes or problems, for example, realise that a business is suffering from inefficiency because according to the information staff motivation has fallen, equipment is worn and working practices are outdated;
- use appropriate techniques to analyse data, for example, use ratio analysis to assess the solvency of a business;
- use appropriate theories, business cases/practices to investigate the question, for example, use elasticity theory to show that raising price may be ineffective.

Questions requiring analysis can be recognised by looking at the command word. An example of a question requiring analysis might be: *Examine the factors which have influenced the firm's decision to close its Cardiff factory.*

Evaluation Evaluation involves making a judgment. Evaluation questions are often used to award the highest grades in examinations. Students might be expected to:

- show judgment in weighing up the relative importance of different points or sides of an argument, in order to reach a conclusion;
- comment on the reliability of information or evidence;
- distinguish between fact and opinion;
- distinguish between relevant and irrelevant information;
- draw conclusions from the evidence presented;
- show judgment on the wider issues and implications.

Questions requiring evaluation can be identified by looking at the command word. For example, *To what extent has the decision to delayer the business been successful?*

When evaluating it is often possible for a student to draw a number of different conclusions. Examiners may be less concerned with the particular conclusion drawn. Very often in business studies there is no 'right' answer. They are more interested in whether students have actually made a judgment and also the quality of their argument in support of the judgment.

Synthesis Opportunities to demonstrate this particular skill may be limited. Synthesis is required in long written answers such as essays, project work or report writing. It involves bringing together a wide range of information in a clear and meaningful way. In particular, students must:

- develop points and themes in a way which builds on previous material and ends with a rounded conclusion;
- produce an argument in a logical sequence;
- provide a clear summarised argument which draws on all the individual elements.

Examiners will tend to look for evidence of synthesis in essays and report writing questions. The sections below on essay writing and report writing will explain how students can demonstrate synthesis.

Quality of language Codes of Practice may require the assessment of candidates' quality of language wherever they

are required to write in continuous prose. In these circumstances students are required to:
- avoid errors in grammar, punctuation and spelling;
- provide well structured arguments which are consistently relevant;
- write in sentences and paragraphs which follow on from one another smoothly and logically;
- express complex ideas clearly and fluently.

Command, directive or key words

When presented with a task or question as part of internally assessed work or externally assessed examinations:
- how do you know what the question is asking?
- how do you know what the assessor or examiner wants you to do?

In many forms of assessment certain **command, directive or key words** in a question will tell the student what is expected of them. Sometimes two or more words appear together in a question. They must all be taken into account when giving the answer.

Information and knowledge Certain command words are designed to find out what a student knows about the subject.
- Define - to state the exact meaning of a term or a phrase. *Define what is meant by marketing research.*
- Describe - to give an account or a portrayal of something. *Describe the hierarchy and span of control of the business.*
- Give - to write down or say something. Sometimes followed by 'an example' or 'an account of'. *Give an example of a private limited company.* May also be followed by 'reasons for' which may involve greater analysis.
- How - to present an account of something. *How has the business raised funds to buy new machinery?*
- Identify - to pick from a variety of information. *Identify three reasons for the merger.*
- Illustrate - to show clearly, often with the use of an example. *Illustrate the main methods used to promote the product.*
- Outline - to give a short description of the main aspects or features. *Outline the view of workers by management.*
- State - to write down or say something. Sometimes followed by what that 'something' should be. *State 3 features of an effective leader.*
- Summarise - to provide a brief account covering the main points. *Summarise the approach to quality at the business.*
- What - to clarify something. *What is meant by a stakeholder?*
- Which - to select from certain options or to indicate a choice. *Which location did the business find most suitable?*

Application and explanation Certain command words are designed to allow the student to apply knowledge to a given situation, to work out why something has happened and to give reasons for something that has happened.
- Account for - to give reasons for. *Account for the growth in part time workers over the period.*
- Analyse - to examine in detail, showing relationships, the importance of certain things and criticisms if applicable. *Analyse the approach to lean production of the organisation.*
- Apply - to bring knowledge to bear on a situation. Note that sometimes the word does not appear in the question. For example, 'Using examples from the article, explain how the business might promote its product' requires an application of knowledge to a particular situation. *Apply the Boston Matrix to the product mix of the company.*
- Calculate - to work out mathematically, usually numerically, but sometimes from a graph for example. *Calculate the return on net assets for the business.*
- Compare and contrast - to show the similarities and differences between two or more things. *Compare and contrast the approaches to recruitment of the two companies.*
- Distinguish - to show the differences between two or more things. *Distinguish between job and batch production.*
- Examine - to investigate closely to find out the 'truth' of the situation as if carrying out an inquiry. *Examine the factors that may have led to cash flow problems.*
- Explain - to make clear a concept, idea or viewpoint. It may involve giving an illustration of the meaning or examples. Note that it is sometimes followed by the word 'why' (see below). *Explain the pricing strategies used by the business.*
- Explore - to investigate or examine in detail, as explained above. *Explore the ways in which a business is affected by changes in interest rates.*
- Investigate - to carry out a detailed examination. *Investigate the factors that may have led the business to go into liquidation.*
- Suggest or give reasons for - to explain why, giving a justification. *Suggest reasons why the business chose to reduce its workforce.*
- Why - to present reasons for something. *Explain why labour turnover has increased.*

Evaluation Certain command words are designed to allow students to make a judgment or to evaluate a judgment that has taken place.
- Assess - an invitation to measure or place a value on the importance of something. *Assess whether the change to just in time manufacturing is likely to be successful.*
- Comment on - to give an opinion about the extent to which something has occurred. *Comment on the environmental policy of the organisation.*
- Criticise or critically analyse - to pass judgment on a debatable area. *Critically analyse the growing globalisation of business.*
- Determine - to settle, decide, or find out the nature of. *Determine the most suitable new location for the business.*
- Do you think - to comment on or give an opinion on the basis of evidence. *Do you think the decision of the business to expand was a suitable strategy in the circumstances?*

- Discuss - to consider a contentious statement or to review an area which might have two or more views. *Discuss whether the business should have introduced group decision making.*
- Evaluate - to make an appraisal of something and to find out how important it is. *Evaluate the strategy used by the business over the period.*
- To what extent (does/do) - to make a judgment or to measure. *To what extent has the change in corporate culture been successful?*

Levels of response

Examiners and assessors may award marks according to the levels of response demonstrated by the student in the answer. The higher the level of response the more marks are awarded to students. An example of different levels that might be identified is shown below.

Level 4 This is the most sophisticated of responses and attracts the most marks. At this level students must provide good evidence of the appropriate skill. Responses must be accurate, extensive, balanced and logical. For example, in evaluation, judgments must be well made and supported by logical arguments. Students must draw original conclusions from the evidence and show awareness of underlying and related themes or issues.

Level 3 At this level student responses are classified as good but with some weaknesses. For example, with regard to knowledge of the subject, to attain level 3 a student must demonstrate that his or her knowledge is satisfactory or better. However, there may be some weaknesses or perhaps the focus is too narrow.

Level 2 If students show that they have clearly used a particular skill, but evidence is limited and there are obvious weaknesses, the response may be classified as level 2. For example, a level 2 response in evaluation would mean that a student has made judgments but they are not well supported by arguments. The evidence will be generally too limited and often below average.

Level 1 This is the most basic of student responses. Some marks will be awarded if a student can demonstrate that they have at least tried to provide some evidence of a particular skill. For example, in analysis a level 1 response would involve some attempt at analysis of data, but lacking in insight and depth.

Level 0 There are no relevant points made and no application, analysis or evaluation.

This approach may be used by examiners when assessing performance in all of the above criteria, even quality of language. However, examiners do not expect students to offer level 4 responses in all of their answers. It depends on the type of question being asked. For example, level 4 responses may only be required in essays, report writing questions and parts of structured questions in decision making case studies. Some examination questions may only require level 1 or level 2 responses. If this is the case, the answers required at level 1 and level 2 may be slightly different from the descriptions above. For example, a question which offers just 4 marks in an examination may require the responses described below.

- Level 2. Students must develop in detail at least one of the relevant factors identified and show some clarity in their explanation.
- Level 1. Students must identify at least one relevant factor and demonstrate some limited attempt at development.

The levels of response required are not normally shown on examination papers. However, students will understand that those questions which carry more marks will require higher levels of response.

Structured questions

The main features of structured questions are as follows.

- They contain several parts.
- The parts normally follow a sequence or pattern.
- Some of the parts may be linked in some way.
- They are generally accompanied by some data to provide students with a stimulus.
- The whole question may require students to demonstrate all skills covered by the assessment criteria, but only one part may be testing a particular skill.
- The parts of the question generally get more demanding as students work through it.
- Different parts may be assessed by different levels of response.

Structured questions are broken down into 'parts'.

First part The first part of the structured question is usually the easiest. This may help students to 'settle' into a question and perhaps give them some confidence. The first part of a structured question:

- is usually designed to test knowledge of a business concept or business term;
- may require a student to perform a simple skill, eg a calculation;
- may require a student to give a straightforward explanation or definition;
- usually requires students to provide a basic level response.
- would carry only a few marks.

Examples

(a) Explain the term 'working capital'.

(a) Distinguish between job analysis and job evaluation.

Middle part The middle part of structured questions may vary. There is no set pattern and this gives examiners and assessors some flexibility when setting structured questions. However, the middle part of structured questions:

- may contain two or more parts;
- usually test knowledge, application, analysis and sometimes evaluation;
- may require students to perform simple or more difficult calculations;
- may require a mixture of straightforward explanation and more complex analysis;
- may carry more marks than the first part.

Examples

(b)(i) Calculate the gross profit margin and the net profit margin for the business.
(ii) Comment on your findings in (i).
(b)(i) Explain the meaning of the term price inelastic.
(ii) To what extent is the concept of price elasticity helpful to a business?
(c) Analyse the possible reasons why increasing numbers of companies are introducing flexible working practices.
(c) Examine the possible implications of the data for:
(i) employees;
(ii) a large manufacturer planning to export for the first time.

Final part This part of the question is usually the most demanding part. The final part of the structured question:

- will nearly always require a higher level response;
- will usually test knowledge, application, analysis and evaluation;
- will usually carry a higher mark allocation;
- may not be broken down into smaller parts.

Examples

(d) Assess the view that business advertising practices should be more heavily regulated.
(d) Evaluate the non-financial factors which might influence the firm's decision to relocate its operations.
(d) Discuss the factors that have influenced the business to change its marketing strategy.

Data response questions

Data response or case study questions are used to test student skills in unfamiliar circumstances. The key features of data response questions include:

- the provision of qualitative or quantitative data, or both, to provide a stimulus for students;
- hypothetical or real case study data;
- the use of structured questions;
- opportunities for students to demonstrate knowledge, application, analysis and evaluation.

Hints

- Always read the data at least twice.
- Use a felt pen to highlight important words, sentences or key numerical information.
- Read the structured questions very carefully, perhaps highlighting command words and other key terms.
- Some of your answers **must** be related to the data provided.
- Some of your answers **must** use ideas, concepts and theories not mentioned in the data.
- Answer the parts of the question in order.
- Allocate your time according to the number of marks offered for each part.
- Show all your working out when performing calculations.
- Always attempt all parts of the questions.
- **Do not** use bullet points when writing your answers.

Answering the first part The information below contains data from a case study question. The data is just a small extract from the question.

The directors are recommending a final dividend of 18p, making a full year dividend of 27p, an increase of 8 per cent over the previous year. The Directors will consider further limited reductions of dividend cover in the medium-term, allowing real dividend growth to be maintained.

(a) Explain the term 'dividend cover'.

- To begin with it is helpful to highlight the key words in the question and the key words in the data as shown above. This might help students to focus.
- To pick up all marks in this case it would be necessary to use a couple of sentences to explain the term and then give the formula which is used to calculate the dividend cover.
- The explanation needs to be crisp, clear and uncomplicated. Students need to demonstrate in their answer that they understand the term. The formula can be added at the end.
- A student could give a numerical illustration here. *For example, if a business made a total dividend payment of £300m and net profit for the year was £500m, dividend cover would be given by:*

$$\frac{\text{Net profit}}{\text{Dividends}} = \frac{£500m}{£300m} = 1.67 \text{ times}$$

Answering the middle part The data below is from another case study.

One of the things troubling Renton's is the accumulation of stock. Both stocks of raw materials and stocks of finished goods have been building up over recent years. The build up of finished goods is linked to poor sales performance.

However, there seems no real reason why stocks of raw materials should have grown. The suggestion made by the production manager to introduce Just-in-Time methods may be worth considering.

Renton's current assets and current liabilities 2000 - 2003

	2000	2001	2002	2003 (£)
Raw materials	21,000	22,900	26,600	34,200
Finished goods	31,300	36,800	42,300	49,600
Other current assets	42,300	41,200	44,900	43,800
Current liabilities	109,900	113,500	119,400	138,600

(b) (i) Use ratio analysis to show how the build up of stocks is causing liquidity problems for Renton's.
(ii) Analyse the advantages and disadvantages to Renton's of introducing just-in-time methods.

- Again the first step is to highlight the key words in the question as shown above.
- The question **cannot** be answered without reference to the data. The first part of the question requires students to analyse the data using a quantitative technique (ratio analysis)
- Students need to calculate the current ratio and/or the acid test ratio to comment on Renton's liquidity position.
- To earn all the marks in this question the student would need to perform the calculations correctly, interpret the results appropriately and draw a meaningful conclusion.
- In this case both the current ratios and the acid test ratios are below the 'ideal' range of 1.5:2 and 1:1 respectively. The acid test ratio is particularly low. This suggests that Renton's has liquidity problems.

The second part of this question requires more analysis.

- Again, begin by highlighting the key words in the question and data as above.
- Before writing the answer it is helpful to jot down a few key points for analysis, such as two advantages and two disadvantages of JIT. Advantages could be less money tied up in stock, more space for other activities or less waste stock. Disadvantages might be vulnerability to a break in supply, loss of flexibility in production or increased ordering and administration costs. These points are not likely to be in the case material. Students will have to bring in outside knowledge. There is nothing to be gained from identifying lots of advantages and disadvantages. The quality of application and analysis will generate marks for this question.
- Marks will be awarded for knowledge, application and analysis. Evaluation marks might also be awarded at this stage.

Answering the final part It is important that students leave enough time to answer this part properly as it usually carries high marks. The data below contains an extract from another case study.

It has been suggested that the economy will grow at around 3 per cent next year. Currently interest rates are relatively low and consumer confidence is buoyant. The use of credit cards to borrow money to finance spending is also likely to remain high.

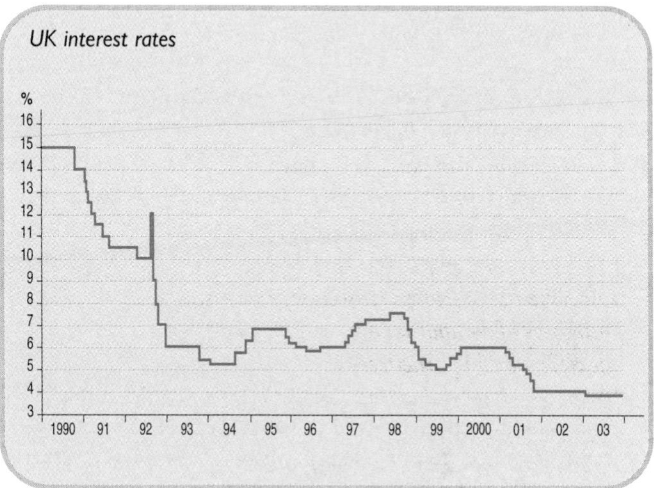

(d) To what extent do external factors, such as those mentioned in the case, influence the performance of a business?

- Students will need to introduce a lot of their own material into their answer.
- Before writing, students should jot down a plan. A plan for this question might appear as follows.
  1. *Explain how external factors, eg interest rates, affect businesses.*
  2. *Identify 2 other factors which might affect businesses, eg consumer confidence, borrowing.*
  3. *Analyse the 2 factors.*
  4. *Evaluate, for example, by saying that external factors have a great influence because they are beyond the control of businesses. However, a good business will include their effect in its forecasting.*
- If the above plan is executed effectively the student will demonstrate all the skills required.
- Students should remember that it is not necessary to identify and list lots of factors. Listing is a low order skill and more marks are awarded for application, analysis and evaluation.

Decision making and problem solving case studies (unseen)

These are often in the form of extended case studies. They can be demanding and require a slightly different approach to answering than shorter data response questions.

- The case material tends to be hypothetical but usually based on a real life situation.
- The case material tends to focus on a single business.
- The volume of material given is much greater.
- There tends to be some financial information in the case material.
- The case often emphasises analysis and evaluation skills.
- Many of the case questions require an integrated approach when answering. This means that students will need to embrace the full range of the specification in their answers. A single answer may need to address issues such as marketing, production, human resources, finance and external factors all at the same time.
- Questions set usually require students to make decisions or solve problems. For example, a question may require students to suggest a suitable future strategy for a business.
- One question will often require students to use a quantitative technique when answering.
- Examiners often want students to be critical.

Hints

- Skim read the case material to get a feel for the business, its people, its circumstances and its objectives (see section below on things to think about).
- Read again thoroughly highlighting key information.
- Look at the numerical information and analyse it briefly, without performing any calculations.
- Make brief notes on the key objectives and key themes.
- Read the questions highlighting command words and other key terms.
- Identify some business theories you might consider discussing in your answers. Questions will probably not request specific theories. The onus is on students to introduce relevant theories.
- Reread hints on answering data response questions above.

Issues to think about when planning answers

- People. Business is about people and your answers need to reflect this. Consider the age, family circumstances, the attitudes and personal interests of the people involved in the case material. What motivates them? What is their background? What are their objectives? What are their strengths and weaknesses? These are some of the people issues which students need to consider when shaping their answers.
- Situation. It is important to think about the context in which the business is set. Examples of issues to consider include the type of business organisation (Ltd, plc or sole trader), the prevailing culture, the type of industry, the nature of competition, the size, its financial position, its age, history and potential. It is often helpful to liken the case material to a business which actually exists in a similar context. However, this may not always be possible.
- Objectives. Answers to questions are bound to be linked to what the business is trying to achieve in its given context. A business may be trying to survive following a recession, it may be trying to break into new markets, it may be trying to raise finance for a big investment project, it may be trying to change its culture or take over another business. It is often useful to consider, and distinguish between, short term and long term objectives.
- Theories. Students should introduce business theories into their answers. There may be little or no guidance as to what theories are required. Students need to be on the lookout for opportunities to introduce some business theory in every answer they write. For example, if a business is considering a price change, price elasticity theory could be introduced. If a business is merging with another, economies of scale may be discussed. If a business is downsizing the effect on staff might be discussed, in which case motivational theories such as Herzberg or Maslow might be applied.
- Be critical. Be prepared to challenge statements or claims made in a case study if relevant and applicable. Students with an enquiring and critical approach will be rewarded.

Example 1

Most of the structured questions in decision making/problem solving case studies usually require lengthy answers with analysis and evaluation. Therefore it is important to plan before writing an answer. Below is an extract from part of an extended case study. The case study is about Henshaws Ltd, a components manufacturer for the computer industry. It has faced difficulties in recent years due to escalating costs. It is considering ways of improving efficiency and reducing costs.

One option currently being considered by Henshaws Ltd is to outsource its marketing activities. The directors of the company have not been impressed with the performance of this department. Their expenditure has consistently exceeded their budget and they seem to get new business and then lose it. In addition, communications between the department and others in the organisation have not been good. Two of the four company directors have long claimed that the company's strength is manufacturing high quality components, although the other two directors argue that the company must avoid clinging to 'past glories' and move forward with the times. A number of marketing agencies have given presentations to the board of directors and a decision whether to outsource marketing is imminent.

(b) Assess the likely advantages and disadvantages to Henshaws Ltd of outsourcing its marketing function.

- To answer this question it is necessary to identify and

analyse 2 or 3 advantages, identify and analyse 2 or 3 disadvantages and then evaluate by making a judgment about whether Henshaws should outsource marketing or not.

- Although the question does not specifically ask for a judgment examiners are probably expecting one. This is because the mark allocation may be quite high.
- A plan should be drafted which might look like this:

Adv. 1. Costs fall
2. More focus on manufacturing
3. More effective marketing by specialists

Disadv. 1. Redundancies
2. Loss of control of a vital function
3. Long term marketing costs might rise.

Eval. Yes - outsource because current marketing is expensive, ineffective and is causing problems. Henshaws will then be more focused and able to exploit its strengths.

- In the answer it is necessary to analyse the above advantages and disadvantages in detail explaining their relevance.
- In the evaluation some students may suggest that Henshaws should not outsource its marketing function. This does not matter. Examiners just want students to make a judgment and support it with a coherent and plausible argument. Remember that these case studies are decision making case studies and therefore a decision must be made!

Example 2

Some quantitative analysis is usually required in extended case studies. It may be quite complex and students often make the mistake of spending too long on this section.The data below contains an extract from an extended case study about a business which is considering a new investment. Arpan Shrinath & Co manufactures training shoes and Arpan is deciding which investment project to go ahead with.

Project 1. *Arpan has considered buying a large delivery van and undertaking his own distribution. At the moment he pays a local company to distribute training shoes to his customers. This has proved expensive and often ineffective.*

Project 2. *A new moulding machine has just been launched on the market by a German machine manufacturer. It is computer numerically controlled and would help to improve the quality of Arpan's products. It would also be more productive than his existing machine.*

Project 3. *Arpan is becoming increasingly concerned that his office staff are working in conditions which are too cramped. Staff frequently complain and he is aware of inefficiencies due to a lack of space. He is considering the construction of a purpose built annex to the factory where office staff can work more effectively.*

The table below shows the costs and expected returns for each of these projects over a 6 year period.

Expected returns

	Cost	Year 1	Year 2	Year 3	Year 4	Year 5	Year 6	Total
Project 1	£15,000	£4,000	£4,000	£4,000	£4,000	£4,000	£4,000	£24,000
Project 2	£40,000	£12,000	£10,000	£10,000	£9,000	£9,000	£9,000	£59,000
Project 3	£30,000	£7,000	£7,000	£7,000	£7,000	£7,000	£7,000	£42,000

(c) Calculate the (i)payback; (ii)average rate of return for the 3 investment projects and decide which project is the most attractive. Take into account your results from the calculations and any other information you feel is appropriate.

- This question requires knowledge and understanding of investment appraisal techniques. Provided students have revised the quantitative techniques required they just need to apply the appropriate formulae.
- It is often helpful to produce calculations (or the results of calculations) in tables. One way in which the answers to the above question might be presented is:

	Project 1	Project 2	Project 3
Cost	£15,000	£40,000	£30,000
Total return	£24,000	£59,000	£42,000
Total profit	£9,000	£19,000	£12,000
Profit p.a.	£1,500	£3,167	£2,000
ARR	10%	7.9%	6.6%
Payback	3.75 years	3.88 years	4.29 years

- According to the calculations above project 1 appears the most attractive. It has the highest ARR and also the shortest payback period.
- There is likely to be other information in the case which will influence the decision here. For example, if customers are complaining about the quality of products, Arpan might decide to buy the new machine to improve quality, even though the projected financial returns are slightly lower.
- This question is likely to offer a high mark allocation. The calculations alone would not generate all the marks. Students must bring in other information from the case, use their own ideas and also evaluate.
- Some thought must be given to the setting out of numerical answers. Good presentation is important. Avoid deletions and sprawling calculations. Space answers generously and underline final answers.

Example 3

The final question in an extended case study often requires students to suggest a strategy or give an overall view. The question might also carry higher marks. A possible question might be:

(d) *Taking the whole case into account, do you consider that the board of directors should discontinue production at the Newport factory?*

- Again, planning is very important here. A lengthy answer is required with relevant points being identified, thorough analysis and evaluation. Students need to bring together a range of relevant points and make a decision.
- Timing is also crucial. Students must ensure that they leave sufficient time to plan and write the answer to this final, and important, question properly.
- Students may use some of the material generated in other answers in the case. But obviously repetition must be avoided.
- Again, it probably does not matter in this question whether students suggest that production is discontinued or not. Examiners want to see a well structured, logical argument with a meaningful conclusion drawn.
- Remember to consider the people, the situation, the objectives and to introduce theories.

Pre-seen case studies

A pre-seen case study is a method of assessment which involves giving students case study material before the day of the examination. This allows students to prepare more thoroughly for the examination by analysing the information and forming ideas in advance.

- Case study material may be issued a number of weeks before the day of the examination.
- The structured questions relating to the case study will not be known until the day of the examination.
- Additional information regarding the case may also be supplied within the question structure.
- The nature of the material provided in the case is likely to be the same as any other case study, but perhaps in more detail. Students should read the previous sections on data response and decision making questions.

Hints

- The general approach to pre-seen case studies is little different from those which are not pre-seen. The only important difference is that students have a great deal of time to study the data. Again, the hints in previous sections on answering data questions should be read.
- There is much more time to read the material so more time can be spent highlighting key words and terms. Students could also note theories, issues or themes which are relevant.
- Any words, terms or theories which are unfamiliar or forgotten can be looked up in the text book. For example, if the case contains an extract from a balance sheet, it might be helpful to consult the balance sheet unit to reinforce understanding of balance sheet terms and structure.
- It is helpful to try and predict possible questions which the examiner might set. This will allow students to prepare answers.
- Try to identify trends, patterns and links in the data and account for them.
- Get help from friends and parents.
- When answering the questions in the examination it is very important to answer the ones set. Students should not try to reproduce their own 'model answers'.

Essay writing

An essay is an assessment method used to find out how students can respond in depth to an open question. It involves writing in continuous prose and provides an opportunity to explain something in detail.

- The quality of grammar, vocabulary, sentence construction and spelling is particularly important.
- A strong emphasis is usually placed on analysis, evaluation and synthesis.
- Essay questions may be integrated and synoptic. This means that students must consider the full range of the specification areas when writing answers. Essays based on one section of a specification or syllabus, such as marketing, may draw on all areas within it.
- The length will vary depending on the time allocated.
- They require a great deal of thought and planning before writing begins.
- The use of real world examples to illustrate points is essential.
- The use of diagrams, such as the Boston Matrix, is encouraged.
- There is rarely a 'right' answer. It is possible for two students to put forward opposing arguments and both be awarded high marks. It is the quality of the argument which is important, not the nature of it.

Planning

- Read the question very carefully.
- Highlight the command words and other key words to help provide focus.
- Planning could be in two stages. Stage one might involve a 2 or 3 minute session where students jot down an explosion of points and issues they think might be relevant.
- Stage two would then involve sorting points into an appropriate order and planning out a structure which will accommodate an argument.

Introduction

- It is common to begin with a short introduction where key

terms are defined and the question is put into context. Some general information may also be given. An introduction should be no more than a third of a side long, for example.

The main body

- When writing the main body of an answer it is important to follow the plan and write in detail, ensuring that evidence of analysis and evaluation is provided.
- It is vital to answer the question. It is better to write one side of relevant material than five sides of 'waffle'.
- Never use bullet points in essays.
- Never use subheadings in essays.
- Never write lists in essays. Extra marks are not awarded for identifying a large number of relevant points.
- Remember to include real world examples where appropriate.
- It is inadvisable to switch emphasis during the essay. It is best to stick to the plan.
- Diagrams, graphs and other illustrative material may be used but make sure it is clearly labelled and explained in the text.

Conclusion

- It is important to write a conclusion. It may be a statement which answers the question 'in a nutshell', drawing on the points analysed in the main body.
- Conclusions should not repeat material used elsewhere.
- The best conclusions are those which demonstrate evaluation and synthesis.
- Students are often required to make a judgment or give an opinion. Do not 'sit on the fence'.

Example

It has been argued that the productivity of UK businesses falls well behind that of its overseas rivals. Suggest possible reasons why this might be the case and examine the measures which might be taken by UK businesses to improve productivity?

- Essay questions can carry a relatively high number of marks.
- The words highlighted in the title are productivity, UK businesses, overseas rivals, suggest possible reasons, examine, measures and improve productivity.
- The following ideas may be suggested for the essay.
  Define productivity, labour, capital, Rover productivity poor, Nissan good, lack of investment, lack of funds, lack of R & D, dividends too high, too short termist. Standardisation, reengineering, kaizen, JIT, outsourcing, virtual companies, TQM, benchmarking, work study, culture, trade unions, weak management, quality circles, technology, training, labour flexibility, delayering, downsizing.
- The ideas generated may not be in any particular order. The focus in the above responses appears to be on production and ways of improving efficiency.
- Another 2 or 3 minutes spent planning might deliver the following essay structure.

Introduction

- *Define productivity - output in relation to inputs.*
- *An example of evidence which might support the statement is the low productivity of Rover compared with, say, Japanese car makers.*
- *Suggest that there is a number of approaches to improving productivity, some specific and some strategic.*

Main body

- *Analyse 3 possible reasons why productivity is lower in UK.*
- *Low investment, therefore inadequate and dated technology.*
- *Lack of R & D because the City wants higher dividends NOW.*
- *Trade unions may have resisted changes which might improve productivity.*
- *Explain that measures designed to improve efficiency might be specific or strategic.*
- *Analyse 3 specific measures - JIT, benchmarking and new technology.*
- *Analyse 3 strategic measures - kaizen, re-engineering and TQM.*

Conclusion

- *Argue that the statement is probably right for the reasons given. Evaluate by saying that one particular reason may be more important eg lack of investment.*
- *Argue that the methods employed to improve efficiency depend on the individual firms and their needs.*
- *Evaluate by suggesting that particular methods may be more suitable, if, for example, a business has dated machinery new technology may have a very significant impact on productivity.*
- *Argue that all measures will require cooperation of staff if they are to be successful.*

- When the essay is finished it is important to read through it and check for errors such as spelling, grammar and punctuation. However, avoid frantic crossing out at the last minute because this tends to have a negative effect on presentation.

Report writing

A business report is a formal method of communication. It is a written document designed to convey information in a concise but detailed way. A report is written in a structured way so that information is broken down into manageable parts. The end section of the report is very important. It will contain recommendations for action that a business should take.

- A report begins with a formal section showing who the report is for, who has written it, the date it was written and the title.
- A report is broken into a series of sections. Each section

might address a particular issue.

- Each new section should begin with a clear heading and each section could be numbered.
- Each section can be broken down into sub-sections, which again can be numbered. Each sub-section may be a single paragraph.
- Information should be written in sentences and not in note form. Sections will require application, analysis and evaluation.
- Numerical information such as tables, graphs and charts should be shown in an appendix. Similarly, calculations should be shown in an appendix.
- The conclusion is very important and should aim at bringing together points raised and analysed in previous sections. No new material should be introduced at this stage. A conclusion is often an action plan or a series of recommendations.

Features Sometimes examiners require a report in a data response question. Students may be required to write reports based on a wide range of numerical data presented to them in tables or charts. It is this latter style which is the focus of attention here. It is sometimes called the numerical report. In a numerical report:

- information is presented in a number of tables or charts, perhaps 5 or 6 distinct pieces of data;
- the data will relate to a particular business and its market, there may also be some general economic data;
- students are required to interpret and analyse the data;
- some data may not be very helpful and should therefore be ignored, examiners deliberately give more information than is required to force students to be selective;
- the report question will normally be very specific and require students to make a decision, ie make recommendations;
- students are often allocated a role when writing the report;
- the structure of the report will often be indicated in the question.

Hints

- Read the introduction and become familiar with the type of business, its market and circumstances.
- Read the tables of data and begin to form views about what they show.
- Make brief notes and comments adjacent to tables and graphs relating to trends and patterns shown by the data.
- Decide whether any data is irrelevant.
- Try to spot links between the different tables of data.
- Start to plan the report structure by identifying some appropriate section headings, **but do not use a heading for each piece of data**. Identify 4 or 5 key issues.
- Identify the points to be raised in each section.
- Decide what your conclusions and recommendations will be. Remember that there is not likely to be a right or wrong answer, but you must make a judgment.
- Write the report using the structure outlined above and remembering that the student is playing a role.
- Remember to analyse and evaluate throughout, and also, that the conclusion requires synthesis.

Example

Moa Kuk Ltd is a family business which imports a wide range of oriental soft furnishings and household artifacts. The business has two large stores in London. The second store was opened two years ago and has very quickly returned a profit. Moa Kuk, the managing director, believes that the company could grow very quickly and become a successful franchising operation.

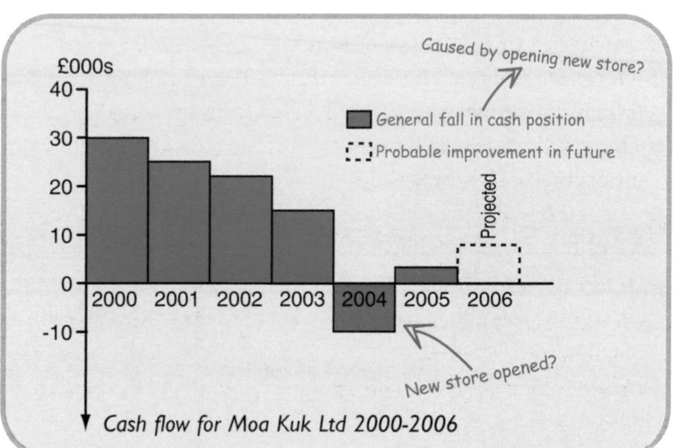

Big increase in borrowing - more highly geared

No new capital from owners

Extracts from Moa Kuk's balance sheet 2000-2005

	2000	2001	2002	2003	2004	2005
Share capital	£25,000	£25,000	£25,000	£25,000	£25,000	£25,000
Long term borrowing	£10,000	£12,000	£13,500	£15,000	£24,500	£27,000
Current assets	£17,500	£18,900	£21,400	£21,000	£36,700	£39,900

Not relevant. Increase due to more stock?

You are employed by a firm of business consultants. You have been asked to write a report to assess whether or not Moa Kuk should set up a franchising operation or grow independently.

- The question is likely to carry a relatively high number of marks.
- Begin to think of suitable section headings for the report structure. We only have an extract from a question here, but the limited information does provide some guidance for appropriate headings. For example:
  - ➤ *The financial position of Moa Kuk Ltd*
  - ➤ *The advantages of franchising*
  - ➤ *The disadvantages of franchising*
  - ➤ *Recommendations*

- Write brief notes by each data box. These are shown in the graph and the table.
- A plan can be drawn up for the first section.
  - *Cash flow has deteriorated over the period particularly in the last two years when the new store was opened.*
  - *The owners have not contributed any more capital to the business over the period.*
  - *The development of the business has been funded by increased borrowing.*
  - *Borrowing has increased steadily over the period making the company more highly geared.*
- A plan should be drawn up for the other sections in the answer. For example, the information may lead to a conclusion that: *Moa Kuk Ltd is not really in a financial position to fund independent growth. Therefore setting up a franchising operation may well be an effective strategy.*
- There will obviously be other points to consider based on other data which is not provided here.

Project/Coursework

A project or piece of coursework usually involves:

- extended research carried out over a period of time within a real business setting;
- the investigation of a problem or decision that the business is facing;
- the use of both qualitative and quantitative data and analysis in researching and analysing the problem or decision;
- the application of a range of business knowledge, skills and methods to the problem or decision;
- the identification of a number of feasible strategies that the business might pursue;
- evaluation of these strategies and making recommendations about which strategy should be pursued and why;
- the production of an extended report which presents the research and findings and use of a range of methods of presentation to enhance the quality of the report.

Unlike other elements of Business Studies examinations, this work is carried out over a period of time during the course. There will be a deadline by which time the project has to be completed, but it is largely the student's responsibility to set up and carry out the investigation and to produce the report by that deadline. The required length of the report is laid down by the awarding body.

Assessment The teacher is the first assessor for project work. He or she will mark the project as a whole and award marks based upon the assessment criteria set by the awarding body. This will vary between different examinations, but typically covers the following skills:

- the way the problem or decision has been explained and objectives for the project set;
- the use made of relevant business knowledge, ideas and concepts in tackling the problem;
- applying appropriate research methods;
- carrying out relevant analysis using both qualitative and quantitative information;
- evaluating evidence to draw conclusions and make recommendations;
- presentation of evidence in a structured way that shows a logical development of ideas;
- employing a good quality of language including spelling, punctuation and grammar.

There may then be some internal moderation of your teacher's marking by another teacher or lecturer in the school or college to check that all the teachers are marking in a consistent way. Finally a sample of projects will be sent to an external moderator, employed by the awarding body, who will check that the marking has been carried out to the criteria set by the examining body.

Hints

- Choose an organisation for your project with which you have contact, perhaps through family or friends and which will allow you access to the information you require. Your teacher may also have established initial contact with a number of organisations which will provide appropriate projects.
- Don't be too ambitious with your choice of problem. *How might Marks & Spencer improve its profitability?* would be too much of a challenge, whereas *How might Marks & Spencer's Wilmslow branch increase its sales of microwave meals?* might be a more realistic title.
- Produce a project/coursework action plan before you start your research - *what are your objectives? what information do you want to collect? what will be the sources of information? who do you want to talk to? when will you collect the information? what analysis will you carry out? when does the report have to be completed?*
- When carrying out your research within an organisation you will need to collect background information about the organisation as well as information specific to your project.
- Listen carefully and give yourself time each day to write up your notes - you will find that you will collect much more data than you will need, but you won't know which is relevant until you write up the project.
- When you analyse of the data, use the concepts and techniques that you have been learning in your lessons and explain in the project why you are using a particular technique as a means of analysis.
- Try to use both quantitative as well as qualitative analysis if the project lends itself to both.
- There are always alternative strategies for solving a problem - one alternative is always for an organisation to do nothing. You must present alternatives and evaluate

their strengths and weaknesses.
- Make your recommendations and relate these back to your project objectives. It does not matter if the organisation would not necessarily follow your advice; but your recommendation should be firmly backed by evidence from your analysis.
- There will always be more that you could have done, but keep to the time deadline and keep to the word limit.

Example
What is the feasibility of extending a 9-hole golf course to 18 holes?

This is an example of a project title that a student has negotiated with the local golf club where she plays as a junior member.

Objectives For this particular project the student, in discussion with the organisation, might set the following objectives:
- to identify the potential demand for an 18-hole course;
- to explore the local competition for the golf club;
- to examine the financial feasibility of building an 18-hole extension;
- to identify possible sources of finance for the extension to 18 holes;
- to make recommendations to the club on whether they should go ahead.

This is a piece of coursework that provides a reasonable problem for the student to tackle; it has scope for both qualitative and quantitative research and analysis and allows the student to make a clear choice at the end. By negotiating the objectives with the club, the student can hope to receive good access to the necessary people to talk to and the club's financial information. Access to accurate financial data is often the major constraint the students face when carrying out project research.

The scope of the project does not require the student to explore the legal background to expanding the golf course. This is a reasonable limitation that makes the project more manageable and the student would not be penalised for this provided the objectives and limitations of the project are made clear at the start.

Collecting information The student might plan to collect a range of data from primary and secondary sources. **Primary research** might include:
- a survey of existing members to establish their demand for an 18-hole course;
- a survey of potential members who might use the course if it had 18 holes;
- interviews with club officials who would be responsible for carrying out the extension;
- identifying the costs of building an extension;
- identifying the costs and availability of different sources of finance;

Secondary research might include:
- identification of the demand for golf through national statistics;
- identification of the location, size and facilities of other golf courses in the area;
- looking at the club's existing financial position through its published income and expenditure statements;
- looking at economic trends that might affect the future costs and revenue for a golf club;
- making use of any previous data that the club had collected if this problem had been considered previously.

Analysis Once the above research has taken place, the student would be in a position to carry out the following analyses of the information collected:
- a forecast of likely demand for the 18-hole course and thereby of the revenue that the club might generate;
- a forecast of the likely flow of expenditures on the project in order to set up and maintain the extended course;
- a cash flow for the project over the next 5/10 years;
- using the pay-back method or discounted cash flow method, an analysis of the financial benefits of the project when compared to other possible investments;
- a comparison of the costs and benefits of different sources of funding for the extension of the course.

Evaluation Before making his/her final recommendation, the student would need to consider the following questions, making use of evidence drawn from the information and analyses presented in the report.
- Does the decision to expand the course fit into the overall strategy of the club?
- On purely financial grounds, is the expansion a viable option? Are there better financial options for the club, eg leaving the money in a high interest bearing account?
- Can the club raise the necessary finance for the expansion? Would the costs of increased borrowing outweigh the benefits?
- How reliable are the forecasts of the demand and revenue figures and the cost and expenditure figures? How accurate is the research on demand? What might change to increase the cost estimates?
- What other external and internal factors would the club need to take into account before making a final decision?

This evaluation would help to provide the basis upon which the student is making their final recommendation as well as pointing forward to other areas that might be considered in a longer report. It should not be seen as a sign of weakness that the report writer asks such questions of their own work. It shows that he or she understands both the strengths and weaknesses of their final decision. It is important to remember that there is no correct answer in report or coursework writing.

Index

A

B

C

D

E

F

G

H

I

J

K

L

M

N

O

S

T

U

V

W